GAMING LAW

CASES AND MATERIALS

ROBERT M. JARVIS
Professor of Law
Nova Southeastern University

SHANNON L. BYBEE, JR.
Associate Professor of Law and Hotel Management
and Executive Director, International Gaming Institute
University of Nevada Las Vegas

J. WESLEY COCHRAN
Professor of Law
Texas Tech University

I. NELSON ROSE
Professor of Law
Whittier Law School

RONALD J. RYCHLAK
MDLA Professor of Law
and Associate Dean for Academic Affairs
University of Mississippi

LexisNexis™

ISBN#: 0-8205-4906-1

Editorial Offices
744 Broad Street, Newark, NJ 07102 (973) 820-2000
201 Mission St., San Francisco, CA 94105-1831 (415) 908-3200
701 East Water Street, Charlottesville, VA 22902-7587 (804) 972-7600
www.lexis.com

To Judith, Norma, Glenda, Patricia,
and Claire
for betting on us

Preface

Despite its long history and prominent place in modern society, gaming has not until now been a subject of serious study in American law schools. The recent expansion of casino gaming, however, coupled with the spectacular growth of riverboat gaming and the advent of Indian and internet gaming, makes this an auspicious moment to bring out the first law school casebook devoted to the subject.

The materials collected herein are current through January 2003. Because they have been edited for ease of readability, omissions in the original text generally have not been noted.

We welcome your comments and suggestions, and ask that they be forwarded to Professor Robert M. Jarvis, Nova Southeastern University Law Center, 3305 College Avenue, Fort Lauderdale, FL 33314-7721, telephone (954) 262-6172, telefax (954) 262-3835, jarvisb@nsu.law.nova.edu.

Lastly, we wish to acknowledge both our respective institutions and the many individuals who assisted us in this endeavor, particularly our editor Alexandra VonHockman and our research assistants Amy Hu, David Leamon, Joanna Maurer, Jennifer E. Meehan, Michael Montrief, and John B. Noone, Jr. We also wish to thank Frank J. Fahrenkopf, Jr., Theresa A. Gabaldon, and Mike Roberts, as well as their publishers, the American Law Institute-American Bar Association, *Journal of Coporation Law*, and *Whittier Law Review*, for allowing us to reprint their works in Chapter 1.

TABLE OF CONTENTS

There are two great pleasures in gambling: that of winning and that of losing.

—French proverb

I am now eased in my finances and replenished in my wardrobe.

—Andrew Jackson, after winning a horse race

The gambling known as business looks with austere disfavor upon the business known as gambling.

—Ambrose Bierce, author of *The Devil's Dictionary* (1911)

Judged by the dollars spent, gambling is now more popular in America than baseball, the movies, and Disneyland—combined.

—Timothy L. O'Brien, *Bad Bet: The Inside Story of the Glamour, Glitz, and Danger of America's Gambling Industry* (1998)

A dollar won is twice as sweet as a dollar earned.

—Paul Newman, *The Color of Money* (1986)

Chapter 1

INTRODUCTION

A. OVERVIEW

If you have had an opportunity to review this book's table of contents, you already know that each of the remaining chapters examines a distinct form of gaming. In this first chapter, however, our focus is on issues that cut across the entire field.

B. HISTORY

THE NATIONAL GAMBLING DEBATE:
TWO DEFINING ISSUES
Mike Roberts
18 Whittier L. Rev. 579 (1997)

Before further discussion, a linguistic conundrum must be explored. That conundrum is the distinction between the words "gaming" and "gambling." Common usage gives these terms the same meaning. The public, and certainly gamblers, are not particularly discriminating in the choice of terms. By precise definition, however, there may be some distinction between the use of the words in the formal versus informal context. Generally, the preferred word is "gaming." However, when used in advertizing and entertainment, the preferred usage is "gambling." These differences may be no more than historical semantical usage driven by current financial commerce.

The history of gaming fills tomes. Much ink has been put to paper. Wonderful stories and anecdotes fill the historical texts. Any reader can explore mysterious links between gaming and witchcraft, idolatry, sacrifice, ritual, mysticism and imagery. These are but a few fascinating subjects that primitive travelers and nomads, as well as city dwellers, wove into the fabric of various games of risk and chance.

Gaming existed as far back in time as the recorded mind can recollect. Our English word for "gaming" or "gambling" was probably derived from the ancient Middle English word "gamen," which meant "to amuse oneself." Interestingly, certain words in our exceedingly modern language are derived from the Old English words descriptive of gambling transactions. For example, the word "rook" has been consistently applied to describe a small piece upon a chess board. "Rook" can also describe a transaction in which at least one of the parties concludes that he has been taken advantage of by the other. The origin of the word comes from the ancient English description of calculating thieves and scoundrels who hung about the taverns and inns of rural England. These people took advantage of the less well-schooled or traveled, the naive. These rooks were skilled in crooked games of chance, such as borrowing without the intent to repay their debts, cut edge cards (which would tell the fingertips what the face of the card showed), table gaming, and assorted mischief. The targets of the rooks were well-dressed, younger, and presumably less experienced men drinking at the pub or staying at the inn who could be induced to enter into a game of chance represented as a game of skill. Rooks were known as gamblers and cheats who moved among the tables looking for the naive to exploit. Interestingly, the "rook" in chess games, upon which some have been known to gamble intensely, has always been known as a low, small figurine with a round button head signifying the lowly state of poverty and ignorance in the hierarchy of chess pieces.

Games of chance certainly existed long before the time of Christ. The ancient Egyptians, Chinese, Japanese, Greeks, Romans, and Germanic tribes all engaged in games of skill and chance for amusement. Dice, estimated to be some two thousand years old, were discovered during excavations in London, England. Other estimations of the advent of dice games date back to 2300 years B.C., which was the time between the poets Homer and Aristophanes. This estimation is based upon the observation that Homer never wrote of dice or similar games while the latter poet did. Even earlier descriptions of dice play can be divined from discussions of the tossing of animal bones. This usually involved tossing the carved and numbered knuckle bones of sheep or goats into the air with the bones falling in patterns on the earth with the lowest numbers obtained taking the prize. This is similar to winning a poker game as a result of having four aces.

English history is replete with prose, poetry, and song of the doings in drawings of chance. In 1732, a stage play, "The Lottery," was a resounding success at the Drury Lane theater in London. The English lottery was the precursor to the lotteries in the Colonies, particularly in Virginia in 1612, when the King of England sponsored a lottery there. In 1776, the Continental Congress authorized a lottery to finance the insurrection against the British Crown. Then General George Washington purchased the first ticket and signed the first "American government" lottery documents. A portion of the funds were used to renovate the New York City assembly hall which was used for the First Continental Congress.

Organized governmental regulation of gambling, as opposed to taxation by force of private army or the like, is recorded as early as 321 B.C., in India. In America, the first gaming craze began in colonial times and lasted until the beginning of the [19th century]. The founding fathers of the colonies themselves ran lotteries, and notable academic institutions received funding from gambling. Once a state granted a charter for a lottery, the operation was self-sustaining and probably immune from state revocation of its charter.

The second wave of gambling evolved from Civil War destruction. Devastated by war, many Southern states adopted the lottery as a means of raising operating funds. Louisiana can be accredited with the explosion of gaming after the Louisiana Purchase and until the close of the Civil War and Reconstruction Period. Events in Louisiana, however, signaled the end of the second wave.

The Louisiana post-Civil War lottery became known as "the Serpent" and developed as a nationwide monopoly run by alleged organized crime figures.

Interestingly, this lottery was started by a New York gaming corporation doing business in Louisiana. The Serpent began operations in August 1869, and overwhelmed the popularity of the Havana, Cuba Lottery which sold tickets at any street corner and announced the winners by carrier pigeons flying from Cuba monthly with the list of winners. Tickets were sold throughout the United States, and ninety-three percent of the gross revenue of the Serpent came from outside of Louisiana. The Serpent replaced the original Louisiana Lottery started in 1865 and adopted by the Louisiana Legislature in 1868.

Beginning in 1878, yearly legislation was introduced in Congress to curb or eliminate lotteries. The lottery became the controlling political issue in the Louisiana gubernatorial campaign of 1892. The company running the Serpent offered the State of Louisiana more than $1.25 million as an annual fee to continue the Serpent and for the renewal of its charter. The electorate voted down all lotteries in 1893 and the Louisiana legislature prohibited sales of tickets in 1893. The United States Congress banned lottery tickets from the mail (in 1890) and from interstate commerce (in 1895).

It is interesting to note the relationship between early gambling and the great rivers of America, and then consider the present proliferation of river boat gaming on the Mississippi, Ohio and Arkansas Rivers. The cradle of gaming during this period was New Orleans. After the ban on lottery tickets, punch boards, prize cards, and other gaming devices from the mail and interstate commerce, the tide of public opinion slowly began to turn against gaming. The earliest anti-gambling crusades were logically aimed at eradicating those colorful practices, lifestyles, and individuals who brought gambling to the Mississippi river boats. Throughout this time, New Orleans licensed gaming houses, as well as places to drink, dine, and pursue other vices commonly housed in dwellings.

This phase of regulating or legislating against gambling began during the Great Depression. However, in 1931, Nevada again legalized casino gambling, and by the 1930s, twenty states had legalized parimutuel betting at horse tracks. The drive for legalization of casino gaming was again underway.

The third wave of gambling involved a unique partnership between what traditionally might be considered evil and immorality, in the form of Messrs. Bugsy Siegel and Meyer Lansky, and the State of Nevada. Lansky financed the construction, and Siegel oversaw the building, of the first gambling casino in Nevada, the Flamingo. Las Vegas and the Flamingo will always carry the moniker of a place where reality is suspended. For example, traditionally no clocks are found in casinos, and it has been rumored for years that pure oxygen is piped into the gaming areas to create a more competitive and aggressive commercial environment. The casinos operate twenty-four hours a day, providing sumptuous accommodations, particularly relative to a middle-income budget. In addition, they have extravagant, nationally-prominent entertainment available at relatively modest fees.

The next major expansion of gaming during the third wave occurred when New Jersey enacted gaming, subject to strict zoning, rationalized as a method of urban redevelopment. New Jersey had previously been one of the leading lottery states, having lotteries as early as 1727. It is well known that

Alexander Hamilton was an early supporter of gaming and the promoter of a New Jersey lottery as early as 1793.

From 1900 to the early 1960s, legalized gambling was strictly limited to a few locations. When New Hampshire enacted its state lottery in 1964, the dice were cast for a radical change in the social perception of gaming and in the political articulation of that perception. State legislatures became the active promoters of gaming as a means of financing the state, and to some extent, local government. Once this shift took place in the public conscience, the state legislators could not dare to run too far behind.

For example, when the Mississippi Attorney General concluded dockside river boat gambling—including video poker and other accoutrements of casino gaming—was acceptable to the State of Mississippi, Mississippi launched, with an economic splash, into the dockside gaming business. This led to the promotion of gaming as a direct revenue source for the state.

The third wave of gambling was also promoted by charity gambling. This involved gambling for the benefit of and at the venue of recognized charities, such as religious congregations. Once the charities developed sophisticated gambling and fund-raising methods, the sovereign American Indian tribes followed that lead. With the rise of gaming directly promoted by state governments, the states began to compete with the American Indian tribes. Indian gaming has long flourished in various forms on the sovereign Indian reservations. It is the public policy of the United States to promote gaming on American Indian lands. The 1988 Indian Gaming Regulatory Act evidences a congressional intent to allow four kinds of gaming on Indian lands: traditional social or religious Indian gaming; bingo and technological games, such as video poker and casino gaming; off-track betting; and the lottery. Indian gaming has thus come into direct competition with the sovereign states' promotion of gambling.

In addition to the Indian Gaming Regulatory Act, there are many other federal gaming regulations. These regulations include: preventing radio and television advertizing of the lottery, regulating interstate off-track betting, prohibiting bribery of amateur or professional athletes participating in athletic contests, prohibiting use of the mails or interstate commerce to run or participate in a lottery, prohibiting racketeering activity in interstate commerce, taxing of gambling winnings, mandating a withholding tax on gambling winnings, taxing of gambling businesses, authorizing the Federal Bureau of Investigation to obtain wiretaps for suspicion of illegal gaming activity, and authorizing the Postal Service to seize gambling materials from the mails.

Much of the legislative history of gaming regulation can be explained by the apparent emphasis on preventing the rise and establishment of organized criminal operations. Responding to a congressional investigation into the then activities of organized crime, Congress in 1951 passed the Johnson Act, prohibiting the use of the mails, federal wire and wireless communications frequencies, or interstate commerce for the transportation of gaming equipment devices or carrying on gaming activities. The legislative intent was to support the states in their respective regulation of gambling activity. This legislation specifically allowed the sovereign states to seek exemption from the Act, thereby delegating the regulation of gaming to the states.

Any analysis of the question of possible organized crime control of gaming must start with a look at what is at stake: lots of money. Gross legal wagering in 1993 totaled $394.3 billion while operators of legal gaming generated $34.7 billion of gross revenue, including $12.8 billion going directly to state run lotteries. A study by the United States Department of Justice in 1974 estimated that gambling, both legal and illegal, took in gross proceeds of $17.3 billion. This would mean that legal gaming grew at a significant rate in the period from 1974 to 1993. Studies by the Bureau of Alcohol, Tobacco and Firearms of the Department of the Treasury estimated that $67 billion was wagered in 1974. A study by the President's Commission on Law Enforcement and the Administration of Justice estimated that $20 billion was wagered in 1967.

In point of fact, there is no accurate estimate of the amount of money wagered on legal gambling, much less illegal gaming. One interesting estimate, based on better record-keeping systems and the requirement that records be accurate, is the lottery business, mostly run by state governments. United States lottery sales were approximately $25.3 billion in 1993. The United States led the list and far exceeded the next five largest lottery countries: Germany, Japan, Spain, France, and Canada.

Even conceding there are millions of dollars available to be stolen or skimmed, as the industry watchdogs would say, does not establish that the legalized gaming industry is in the clutches of organized crime. In point of fact, the presumption must be that large hotels, publicly traded corporations, and their associates and employees require routine investigation.

Furthermore, commentators acknowledge a growing respectability and honesty with the entry into the gaming business of well capitalized corporations and publicly traded companies. There is evidence of rigorous controls designed by states, like Nevada and New Jersey, to prevent the incursion of organized crime into the gaming industry network. Further, the following factors make criminal infiltration and ownership of publicly traded gaming corporations nearly impossible: the participation of public investors with their accompanying brokerage house's due diligence; the required periodic reporting to the Securities and Exchange Commission; the requirement of audited financial statements; and an auditor-approved discussion of the description of corporate operations, management, and financial results.

In addition to these public reporting and auditing requirements, the states have passed legislation to criminalize ownership of gambling interests by individuals who do not comply with state licensing requirements. The New Jersey Casino Control Act legalized gaming in Atlantic City, but required licensing of gaming emporium employees. Despite these various state based regulatory approaches, valid arguments can be made that organized crime has encroached upon the legitimate gaming industry. The classic example is the encroachment of corrupt labor unions into the service and food preparation departments of gambling casinos and hotels.

With the legalization of various kinds of gambling in numerous states, questions arise about the effect of gambling upon the economy and the effect on individuals. The litany of social ills produced, at least in part, by individuals who gamble to excess, which results in extreme personal financial difficulty and subsequent harm to business and the economic community, is well documented by scholars. As the various forms of gaming (lotteries, dog racing, horse racing, river boat gambling, and legalized casinos) proliferate, individuals and the economy are exposed to potentially disastrous financial results from incurring gaming losses. While such losses do not occur to every gambler, they are often unexpected and cannot be sustained, resulting in bankruptcy.

Considering the differences of opinion regarding the percentages of the population who can be defined as either probable or potential compulsive gamblers, as low as 3.10% or as high as 4.27%, it can be argued that compulsive gambling does not seem to be a statistically serious problem in society, although the disease or condition may be especially serious for the individual. Further, it is necessary to note these figures on compulsive and problem gambling fail to differentiate very important temporal limitations. Not every compulsive or problem gambler is currently and continuously gambling. While the incidence of pathological gaming per one hundred citizens may exceed 4.27%, this does not mean these persons are continuously gambling since many are in recovery programs for addicted gamblers, lack funds to play, or are controlling their problem gaming behavior. Thus, the incidence of current, timely problem and pathological gambling will be lower than the rates disclosed by field research.

Given the relatively small number of gamblers who are problem or potentially problem gamblers and may be classified as pathological gamblers, it is difficult to understand the attacks upon legal, volitional gaming as made by the critics. This difficulty is compounded by the critics' failure to keep their focus on the effect of illegal gaming on the legal economy. In point of fact, the illegal gambling "industry" cannot be entirely quantified. Nevertheless, studies show that for every one dollar bet with the legal sports booking industry an additional thirty-four dollars is bet with illegal bookies. The illegal gambling market for sports betting and every other form of illegal gaming employs few people, operates clandestinely, engages in extortion and loan sharking, and creates no need for collateral goods and services like jobs in the hotel and service industries. The illegal gambling "industry" dwarfs legalized gaming. Law enforcement estimates illegal gambling provides organized crime, defined in the broadest sense and excluding the organized drug business, with its largest single source of cash flow. Critics of legal gambling may want to consider refocusing their attack to make illegal gaming their target.

For the voting majority, gambling is no longer immoral or sinful conduct, nor is it considered inherently evil. Public acceptance of gaming has been growing since the end of World War II. Legalized gambling, quantified on a consolidated basis, for the sake of analysis, presents the picture of a powerful and successful business enterprise. Consolidating all legal American gaming operations which publicly report their gross handle—including the gross amount bet by players with the house, and their profits, sometimes referred to as the "hold" or net profits—would make legal gaming the twelfth largest corporation on the Forbes Sales 500.

Another interesting comparison illustrative of the acceptance legalized gambling has found in the general population is the fact that Las Vegas trumps Disney World as a tourist attraction. Until 1992, Orlando, Florida had more hotel rooms than Las Vegas, Nevada. Since 1992, gambling may be holding the ace. In hotel rooms, occupancy of rooms, visitor count, airport traffic, and other indicia, Las Vegas out-draws Orlando.

JOHN LAW, WITH A TULIP, IN THE SOUTH SEAS: GAMBLING AND THE REGULATION OF EUPHORIC MARKET TRANSACTIONS
Theresa A. Gabaldon
26 J. Corp. L. 225 (2001)

Attitudes toward gambling have varied by culture and by time period; discussion here will be modestly limited to the last thousand years or so of Anglo-American tradition. This tradition initially provided, as a matter of common law, that gambling was legal and that gambling debts were enforceable. Courts could, however, regulate public nuisances, and therefore could close down activities posing a risk to peace or public morals.

The first English statute directly affecting gambling was passed in 1388. This statute, passed primarily to preserve the strength of the nation in preparation for war, prohibited laborers and serving men from playing (among other things) "tennis, football, coits, dice, casting of stone kaileg, and other such importune games." Later laws, inspired by the Protestant work ethic, were intended to prevent laborers from missing work and to avert poverty. King Henry VIII is credited with consolidating gambling regulation in 1541, and with making illegal the maintenance of a house or place of dicing, table or carding, or other gambling. This rule became a fixture of Anglo-American common law. Exempted throughout these developments was the game of horse racing, which was viewed both as a pursuit of the upper class and as a tool for improving the bloodlines of horses.

In 1710, the Statute of Anne was enacted to enforce the existing anti-gambling statutes (which by that time included several in addition to those referred to above). It provided, among other things, that anyone losing money at gambling could sue for its return, if he or she acted within three months. It also provided that notes, mortgages, and the like, won at gaming or betting would be void. It is thought that the purpose of the Statute was to prevent the transfer of land out of the hands of the gentry.

This country inherited the English legal tradition, and each of the foregoing developments found its way into American common law. The common law has been supplemented by a patchwork of state statutes and state constitutional provisions providing variously for the legalization of some forms of gambling, the criminalization of other forms, and for other types of regulation. For instance, Nevada has permitted casino gaming for decades (somewhat surprisingly leaving until the mid-1980s the common rule that gambling debts are unenforceable). California originally prohibited by constitution all lotteries; the constitution was later amended to permit a state lottery.

Despite a great deal of variety, it is easy to identify major trends in approaches toward the regulation of gambling throughout America's history.

For instance, there were numerous statutes adopted during the eighteenth and nineteenth centuries which prohibited most types of gambling (even horse racing), but permitted the operation of public lotteries (which were seen, in many cases, as a voluntary form of taxation). By the 1830s most of the "civic" lotteries "were outlawed due to massive fraud and a perception that they eroded the moral fabric of society." A brief revival occurred in response to the needs of post-Civil War Reconstruction. Public lotteries once again fell into disfavor during the "Populist Revolt" of the late nineteenth century. "By 1878, all states except Louisiana prohibited lotteries by constitution or statute." A wave of legalization (in many cases starting with charitable bingo) occurred during the Great Depression. Lotteries reemerged in the 1960s and 1970s, and are now sponsored by no less than thirty-seven states and the District of Columbia. Casino gaming on Indian reservations and other locations has increased dramatically in the last decades of the twentieth century.

Outlawing gambling is a way of regulating it, and some forms of gambling are still illegal in most, if not all, places. In recent decades, however, regulation has taken many other forms. These include the following: restricting and licensing providers, restricting the time and place in which the activity can occur, restricting the clientele, monitoring the practices of providers, taxing the proceeds, and regulating advertising.

Where, for instance, casino gaming is legal, the number and character of casino operators are strictly limited. Those applying for licenses typically must undergo stringent background checks for criminal connections, financial responsibility, sources of financing, and business competence. Where lotteries are permitted, it is quite usual for the state to be the only lawful provider.

Casinos, race courses, and other gambling venues may have limited hours of operation—although round-the-clock casino operation is sometimes the order of the day. More importantly, the places where gambling can take place are frequently quite restricted. Thus, for instance, a number of local jurisdictions have chosen to restrict legalized casino-type gambling to riverboats anchored or navigated off shore. Even in Nevada, there are rules about the location of games and gaming devices.

Not too surprisingly, patronage of legalized gambling is restricted to adults. Some jurisdictions have also attempted to limit patronage to non-residents. In addition, several jurisdictions have restricted the access of known criminals.

Casinos may be closely monitored for evidence of skimming and theft, and may be required to operate games offering set odds. They may also be prohibited from serving alcohol, or, at any rate, from providing it for free. They also are frequently limited with respect to the extension of credit to patrons.

Gambling is often subject to special "sin" taxes. These taxes may or may not be a way of discouraging the practice. More likely, they simply constitute a not-too-resented method of raising government revenue. They also may be justified as a way to extract licensing and monitoring costs from the industry and its patrons.

The placement of advertisements for gambling establishments may be monitored. There may also be regulation of their content. Truthfulness of claims with respect to pay-outs is a particularly logical object of regulatory attention.

THE STATUS OF GAMING IN THE UNITED STATES
Frank J. Fahrenkopf, Jr.
SF89 ALI-ABA 1 (Mar. 29, 2001)

As many of you know, my organization, the American Gaming Association (AGA) (www.americangaming.org), is the trade organization representing the commercial casino industry. While commercial casino gaming is legal in 11 states—Nevada, New Jersey, Mississippi, Louisiana, Indiana, Missouri, Illinois, Iowa, Colorado, Michigan, and South Dakota—the AGA's role is national in scope. We represent casino operators, along with equipment manufacturers, suppliers and vendors, financial services companies, and others that work with the gaming industry, on federal legislative and regulatory issues that affect our business.

But we have another important mission: to serve as an information clearinghouse—a truth squad of sorts—to correct the many misperceptions about our industry. We're all familiar with the colorful history of this business. Some people still believe this is the way we operate. But it is precisely because of this past that the gaming industry now operates in a legal and regulatory environment unlike any other industry. Every aspect of our business—from the hours we operate to the people we employ—is monitored and enforced.

Despite these safeguards, which make our industry one of the most scrutinized in the country, those opposed to gaming like to perpetuate misinformation in an effort to turn back the clock. During the time I have here today, I would like to share a little about this environment—the environment that will face anyone involved in the business of gaming.

Let me start by giving you a snapshot of the social issues that have swirled around this industry for years, as well as an overview of the latest research on this topic. Fortunately, a lot of good, independent research has been done recently that disprove nearly everything opponents of our industry have ever said about our business. The most comprehensive study in the past 20 years on the subject of legalized gambling was completed in 1999 after a two-year federal commission appointed by Congress conducted a comprehensive legal and factual study of the social and economic impacts of gambling on federal, state, local, and Native American tribal governments, and on communities and social institutions. The final report of the National Gambling Impact Study Commission (NGISC) addresses many of the issues the industry faces, and I would urge you to get a copy and familiarize yourself with it.

For years, anti-gaming advocates had been selling the American people, media and decision makers a defective bill of goods based on so-called economic theories with no basis in fact. That bill of goods faced intense public scrutiny for the first time ever during the commission's deliberations. Today, I'd like to give you an overview of what the commission heard to refute that and add what the latest independent research reveals.

Let's start with the morality argument. The United States is a wonderful country where a divergence of opinion is not only tolerated but encouraged.

The United States and Canada share a common ancestral heritage with England. But as you are probably aware, the first settlers in our country were the Puritans—religious extremists of their era. In some ways, this cultural heritage still manifests itself today. And so there are many who find what we do immoral. So be it. Nothing we can say or do will change their minds. While we respect their right to maintain their moral views, the fact is they are not shared by the vast majority of Americans. The latest polling data says that more than 80 percent of Americans believe that casino gambling is acceptable for themselves or others. And U.S. households visited casinos more than 162 million times last year.

Even the most religious Americans believe in the public's right to choose whether or not to gamble. According to a national survey we did in 1998, three of four Americans who attend religious services regularly (at least once a week) consider casino gaming an acceptable form of entertainment. What is interesting in this survey is that the overwhelming majority of regular churchgoers not only share that attitude, but also are pretty much like the rest of America when it comes to their attitudes and actions about gaming.

Some people, however, make exceptions about acceptability for one segment of the population: senior citizens. And so last year we surveyed seniors and found that they are even more likely than other customers to always set a budget when gambling (69 percent vs. 62 percent), overwhelmingly believe in personal freedom and in making their own choices about how they spend their time and money (over 90 percent) and cite fun and entertainment as the primary reason they visit casinos, not just the gambling.

Moral questions, of course, cannot be proven or disproved with numbers, research or testimony. But I venture to say that with this widespread acceptability our opponents have a difficult case to make.

Anti-gaming advocates more often rely on the faulty argument that the social costs from gaming exceed the benefits. They will argue that people go to casinos, lose their money, lose their jobs, end up on welfare or commit crimes, go into bankruptcy and then the public has to pay the price. That reasoning is just not very sound, and is contrary to the facts.

The NGISC made a number of remarkable findings about the positive impact of commercial casinos. The commission makes clear that gambling in the United States is not monolithic and that there are seven very distinct types or classes of gambling with different impacts and benefits on society: 1) commercial casinos; 2) tribal casinos; 3) lotteries; 4) pari-mutuels; 5) charitable gaming; 6) Internet gambling; and 7) illegal gambling.

The commission clearly and unequivocally found that "destination type resorts," such as casinos, offer major economic advantages over what they called "convenience-type gaming," such as non-casino electronic devices or Internet gambling, because they offer quality jobs, economic development and capital investment in their communities. As the report states: "Research conducted on behalf of the commission confirms the testimony of . . . casino workers and government officials that casino gaming creates jobs and reduces the level of unemployment and government assistance in communities that have legalized it."

The report also found that: ". . . Without exception [the elected officials who testified before the commission] expressed support for gambling and recited instances of increased revenues for their cities. They also discussed community improvements made possible since the advent of gambling in their communities and reviewed the general betterment of life for the citizenry in their cities and towns."

The research conducted for the commission backed up those statements. The National Research Council of the National Academy of Sciences (NRC) found that "[g]ambling appears to have net economic benefits for economically depressed communities." Additional research for the commission found that ". . . a new casino of even limited attractiveness, placed in a market that is not already saturated, will yield positive economic benefits on net to its host economy." And the National Opinion Research Center at the University of Chicago (NORC) determined that "[t]hose communities closest to casinos experienced a 12% to 17% drop in welfare payments, unemployment rates and unemployment insurance."

But of course you will not hear about these benefits from industry opponents. You will hear about the so-called social costs, in spite of the facts that came out of the commission report—facts that our opponents like to forget.

Despite documentation to the contrary, opponents continue to recite their "ABCs of gambling"—addiction, bankruptcy and crime. But let me tell you what the commission found on these issues.

Starting with the A's. On addiction, the commission concluded that "[t]he vast majority of Americans either gamble recreationally and experience no measurable side effects related to their gambling, or they choose not to gamble at all. Regrettably, some of them gamble in ways that harm themselves, their families, and their communities." The NORC study conducted for the commission found that the prevalence of problem gambling is approximately 0.1 percent of the U.S. adult population. The NRC study estimated the number at 0.9 percent. A 1997 industry-funded study by Harvard Medical School's Division on Addictions estimated the number at about 1.29 percent. Based on this research, there is a general agreement that approximately 1 percent, or about 2 million people, can be classified as pathological gamblers. That's a far cry from the numbers alleged by opponents of gambling, which we see now had no basis in fact.

But the commission also found that the problem is significant enough to warrant further research. And we agree. When the American Gaming Association was founded in 1995, it was with the commitment that this industry would not repeat the mistakes made by the tobacco industry, by denying the existence of a problem. The vast majority of our customers enjoy gambling as entertainment. The research confirms that. But a small percentage doesn't gamble responsibly. These people deserve our attention and our help, regardless of their numbers.

That's why our segment of the industry, the commercial casino industry, has devoted significant resources to raise awareness of this issue among our employees and customers. We've committed approximately $7 million since 1996 to fund peer-reviewed research on pathological gambling, establishing an independent organization called the National Center for Responsible Gaming. The National Center's organizational structure and decision-making procedures were modeled after the National Institutes of Health to ensure that the highest standards are used to evaluate research grant proposals. The National Center already has awarded more than $3 million in grants to leading researchers at some of the preeminent universities and medical research facilities in the United States and Canada to conduct research in the fields of neuroscience, behavioral social science, with an emphasis on prevention and youth gambling.

The work funded by the National Center has earned the respect of top researchers and scholars. In recognition of that, the grant-making arm of the National Center will now be housed at Harvard Medical School's Division on Addictions, where the newly renamed Institute for Pathological Gambling & Related Disorders will continue to drive the pioneering research we began just four years ago in hopes of furthering our understanding of this disorder and minimizing its impact.

Still on the subject of addictions, opponents will argue that increased availability of gambling, access to funds and expanded hours of operation has led to an increase in pathological gambling. While this might seem like a logical assumption to some, it is not valid. The first federal gambling commission during the 1970s found that the number of "probable compulsive gamblers" was 0.77 percent of the U.S. adult population, virtually identical to the findings of the more recent federal commission, despite the growth of gambling opportunities during that time. In addition, research conducted for the 1999 federal commission stated, "The availability of casinos within driving distance does not appear to affect prevalence rates." Similar government-sponsored research in Minnesota, South Dakota and Texas all showed statistically stable rates of pathological gambling in those states, despite increases in the availability of gaming.

Another accusation opponents will make about the industry is that the more people gamble, the more likely they are to become pathological gamblers. Again, all you need to do is look at the commission's research. The NORC report found that while many more people have gambled at least once in their lifetimes (68 percent in 1975, compared to 86 percent in 1999), the number of people who have gambled in the past year has remained relatively unchanged (61 percent in 1975, versus 63 percent in 1999). As Lance deHaven-Smith, executive director of the Public Sector Gaming Study Commission, pointed out in his analysis of the National Gambling Impact Study Commission's final report: "[T]hese findings mean that Americans have become much more likely to have experimented with gambling, but this experimentation has not turned them into people who gamble regularly or routinely."

Gambling opponents also will assert that half of our revenues come from problem and pathological gamblers. In contrast, the NORC report's survey data suggested that between 5 percent and 15 percent of gaming revenues come from problem and pathological gamblers. Despite this lower percentage, it's important to point out that the industry does not want those with gambling disorders as customers.

Now on to the B's. There is absolutely no credible evidence establishing a link between bankruptcy and gambling, although that is one of the industry's opponents' favorite stories. To counter them, you need only look to two independent government studies that failed to find any connection between bankruptcy and gambling. NORC's analysis for the federal commission found that "the casino effect is not statistically significant for . . . bankruptcy . . . ." On top of that, the U.S. Treasury Department investigated this issue and released a report, also in 1999, finding "no connection between state bankruptcy rates and either the extent of or introduction of casino gambling." In preparing its analysis, the Treasury Department examined existing literature on gambling and bankruptcy and conducted new empirical research. According to the study: "Much of the earlier increase in the national bankruptcy rate has been attributed to the changes in the bankruptcy law of 1978. Other economic and social factors cited by researchers as contributing to more recent increases include higher levels of debt relative to income, increasing availability of consumer credit through general purpose credit cards and the reduced social stigma of declaring bankruptcy." This particular study was requested by a leading opponent of gaming in the U.S. Congress after he discovered that the commission's findings were not what he had hoped, costing taxpayers an additional $250,000.

Opponents contend that the economic losses incurred by gambling cause people to commit suicide. As has been demonstrated through recent research by the NRC and Harvard Medical School, individuals who are pathological gamblers often suffer from other disorders; a simplistic approach linking gambling with suicide cannot explain away a decision this complex. While opponents of gambling use anecdotal evidence to attempt to prove a link, recent studies contradict their assumptions. A 1997 report from the Centers for Disease Control (CDC) found that suicide rates are a regional phenomenon and do not mirror the availability of legalized gambling. The CDC study pointed out that suicide levels in the West are 70 percent higher than in the Northeast. A study written for the AGA by a team of researchers from the University of California-Irvine compared actual suicide rates and found that gaming communities have "no higher risk" of suicide than non-gaming communities.

And finally, the C's: opponents' attempts to associate gambling with crime and corruption. Let's start with their contentions about crime. The federal commission found no link between the two, stating in its research, ". . . the casino effect is not statistically significant for any of the . . . crime outcome measures . . . ." The federal commission's final report also cited a study in which a comprehensive review of publicly available information on gaming and crime found no documentation of a causal relationship between the two.

On the other "C" claim, again, there is no credible evidence other than innuendo suggesting any link between corruption and gambling. But the federal commission did make two very important findings related to this. First, they put to rest any notion that there is continued organized crime involvement in the modern casino industry. According to the final report, "All of the evidence presented to the commission indicate that effective state regulation, coupled with the corporate takeover of much of the industry, has eliminated organized crime from the ownership and operation of casinos." The commission also found that "[c]asino gambling, in fact, is the most highly regulated component of the industry." In fact, our industry is one of the most highly regulated in the entire country. Because most of our companies are publicly traded, they come under the stringent scrutiny of the Securities and Exchange Commission (SEC). More than 1,500 regulators and control board members oversee the industry at a total cost of more than $135 million, helping to ensure that only legitimate interests are involved in casino entertainment.

It is amidst this contentious social debate over gambling that we battle a litany of legislative and regulatory issues that face our industry. As we look ahead to this year's challenges, the saying "the more things change, the more they remain the same" is right on target. While there is a new president in the White House, a new administration in executive agencies, and new players in key positions on Capitol Hill, the issues next year will largely be the same as those we battled last year.

There is no doubt that the question of whether Nevada will continue to be able to offer legal wagering on college sports will be the most difficult issue we face. While we face an uphill battle, we must continue to fight hard—and prevail—to protect state decision-making on gaming, the tourist and economic benefits of legal sports wagering to our state, and to make sure that something positive and effective is actually done to address the serious problem of illegal sports gambling among college students.

All of those associated with Nevada's gaming industry and regulatory system, led by the congressional delegation, worked together to block the NCAA's attempt to repeal the federal grandfather that allows Nevada to operate legal sports books for college games.

AGA coordinated an extensive research, public relations and lobbying campaign to assist the Nevada delegation and other congressional allies in arguing against the NCAA's draconian proposal. These efforts included preparing for two major congressional hearings on the issue.

While the NCAA's legislation was adopted by the Senate Commerce Committee with only two dissenting votes, the delegation and industry effort paid off in the House Judiciary Committee, which belatedly passed the NCAA bill late in the session by a narrower margin. The congressional leadership played an important role in this strategy. Repeated efforts by the bill's Senate sponsors to bring it to a Senate vote were blocked by Nevada's senators.

Efforts are under way to consult with congressional allies and others to fashion a new strategy for the 2001-2002 session that takes into account the fact that the NCAA will have a full two-year congressional cycle to push its agenda.

While the NCAA issue will likely dominate our lobbying efforts, there are other issues, chief among them Internet gambling, on this year's agenda as well. Since 1995, U.S. Sen. Jon Kyl, later joined by House members, has tried to amend the Wire Communications Act of 1961 to make it clear that federal law prohibits all forms of Internet gambling, whether sports or casino games, and whether over the wires (as prohibited by current law) or through use of newer, wireless technology.

While it appeared for much of the last Congress that this effort would be successful, it ultimately fell short. The Senate unanimously passed a bill in November 1999 and while a majority of the House did so in July of this year, the bill needed two-thirds of the House to support it without taking up amendments. The two-thirds mark was missed by only a handful of votes. Strenuous efforts to bring it back to life ultimately failed.

It remains to be seen whether the congressional sponsors will have as much vigor in the new Congress. However, during the course of the debate over the past five years, there have been both technological and marketplace developments that bear watching. It is important to stress that what we and others oppose is Internet gambling, or any other gambling for that matter, that is not subject to the same strict regulatory standards as commercial casinos, including taxation, money laundering, problem gambling and access by minors.

We have emphasized that any federal legislation that seeks to block unregulated, foreign-based sites should not interfere with the traditional right of each State to prohibit or, in the alternative authorize and regulate, gaming transactions. This also holds true for the use of technology by state-licensed operators.

The ranking Democrat on the House Banking Committee, John LaFalce of New York, is expected to reintroduce his legislation to impose federal regulation of ATMs on casinos, including restrictions on where they can be located. His bill would place them away from the immediate area where gaming takes place, but not ban them from gaming complexes entirely. This issue has also come up in several states, where we have worked with the banking industry to defeat these ill-advised proposals.

While Rep. LaFalce introduced similar legislation two years ago, the House took no further action on the legislation. AGA successfully opposed his efforts to attach the bill to legislation that would have prohibited the use of credit cards to facilitate Internet gambling.

Two new committee chairmen in the House are expected to play significant roles in legislation affecting our industry. On the House Judiciary Committee, which handles the NCAA betting ban issue and Internet gambling legislation, Rep. Jim Sensenbrenner of Wisconsin has taken over from Rep. Henry Hyde as a result of term limit rules on chairmen. Rep. Mike Oxley is chairman of the newly named House Financial Services Committee, the panel that considers bills on the location of ATMs in casinos and credit card use in Internet gambling.

As these issues are debated on Capitol Hill and in state legislatures and communities across the country, it will be up to the industry and its representatives to bring the facts about these issues to policy-makers and the public. Working with the gaming industry requires an understanding of the unique circumstances surrounding this business. If you are knowledgeable about these issues, you can provide the value-added service that your clients in this industry demand.

Notes

1. An extensive literature exists describing the history of gaming. Among the more important works are: John Ashton, *The History of Gambling in England* (1969); Henry Chafetz, *Play the Devil: A History of Gambling in the United States from 1492 to 1955* (1960); Ann Vincent Fabian, *Card Sharps, Dream Books, and Bucket Shops: Gambling in 19th-Century America* (1990); John M. Findlay, *People of Chance: Gambling in American Society from Jamestown to Las Vegas* (1986); Alice Mulcahey Fleming, *Something for Nothing: A History of Gambling* (1978); Philip Jones, *Gambling Yesterday and Today* (1973); Roger Munting, *An Economic and Social History of Gambling in Britain and the U.S.A.* (1996); Gerda Reith, *The Age of Chance: Gambling in Western Culture* (2000); William N. Thompson, *Gambling in America: An Encyclopedia of History, Issues, and Society* (2001).

2. As Professor Roberts points out, gaming has its own language, and one speaks of holds, handles, rooks, and skims, for example, rather than net profits, gross revenue, swindlers, and theft. For additional betting expressions, *see, e.g.*, Thomas L. Clark, *The Dictionary of Gambling and Gaming* (1987); George G. Fenich & Kathryn Hashimoto, *Casino Gaming Dictionary: Terms and Language for Managers* (1995); Donald D. Spencer, *Looking at Casino Chips and Tokens: A Guide to Technical Terms* (1994). *See also* www.800gambler.org/lingo.htm; www.allgam.com/gambling_glossary.php; www.allrank.com/gloss.shtml; www.casino-info.com/gambling_tips/glossary_a_b.html; www.netcasinoplay.com/glossary.asp.

3. Besides studying gaming's language, you may find it useful to spend a little time learning the basics of betting. There are many handbooks available in print and on-line, including, of course, Richard D. Harroch et al., *Gambling for Dummies* (2001), and Stanford Wong & Susan Spector, *The Complete Idiot's Guide to Gambling Like a Pro* (2d ed. 1999).

4. There are eight distinct types of gaming in the United States, and each is the subject of a separate chapter in this book. However, it may be helpful here to briefly describe them.

Lotteries (chapter 2) are conducted by numerous state governments, with the proceeds usually pledged to the support of education and other social services. Similarly, many charities (chapter 3) hold "bingo nights" and sponsor raffles to raise money for their causes.

Pari-mutuel wagering (chapter 4), which originated in France and normally involves betting on greyhounds or horses, takes place at some 150 tracks located throughout the country. It is distinctive because all the money bet (less deductions for overhead and taxes) is divided among the winners. Thus, going against the crowd (i.e., placing a wager on a "long shot") greatly increases one's payout. This type of gaming also includes jai-alai, a type of Spanish handball, that is played in arenas called "frontons."

Sports betting (chapter 5) is legal only in Nevada; nevertheless, many people engage in such betting where they work by entering "office pools." These types of wagers are particularly popular during the NFL's Super Bowl (held in January) and the NCAA's basketball tournament, better known as "March Madness."

Casinos (chapter 6) typically feature games involving cards or dice, such as baccarat, blackjack, craps, and high-stakes poker, as well as big six, roulette, and slot machines (which provide the bulk of any casino's revenues and often are referred to as "one-armed bandits" by losing patrons). Casinos can be found in certain cities (with Atlantic City and Las Vegas being the best known), on various types of ships (chapter 7), and on Indian reservations (chapter 8) (which, depending on state law, may or may not offer a full set of games).

The newest type of betting is internet gaming (chapter 9). Such web sites normally operate from overseas locations (to avoid United States law) and require players to provide a credit card. As Mr. Fahrenkopf's speech points out, there is a great deal of opposition to this type of gaming because of the regulation and taxation challenges it poses.

Although figures vary (due to a lack of uniform reporting requirements), it is estimated that Americans bet $1 trillion-a-year. This amount is distributed as follows: traditional casinos $488 billion, sports books $370 billion (almost all of it wagered illegally), Indian casinos $99 billion, lotteries $49 billion, pari-mutuels $18 billion, charities $7 billion, shipboard casinos $7 billion, and internet sites $3 billion.

5. A distinction is sometimes drawn between "games of chance" and "games of skill." *See* I. Nelson Rose, *Gambling and the Law* 80-81 (1986) (identifying seven characteristics of games of skill, including the ability of players to improve their odds of winning through practice and study). *See also* Joshua McCrory, *Video Poker and the Skill Versus Chance Debate*, 6 Gaming L. Rev. 223 (2002). Of course, all games involve some amount of luck, and even the most skillful participant cannot control every variable affecting the outcome of a particular contest. Nevertheless, many courts and legislatures find the two categories useful. *See Opinion of the Justices*, 795 So. 2d 630 (Ala. 2001) (collecting cases). *See also People v. Hunt*, 616 N.Y.S.2d 168 (N.Y.C. Crim. Ct. 1994), in which the judge rather naively held that "three-card monte," a notorious con game, is not a game of chance because when "[p]layed fairly, skill rather than chance is [its] material component." For a brief history of three-card monte, *see* Luc Sante, *Knowing a Con When You See It*, N.Y. Times, Apr. 15, 2001, § 4, at 2.

6. As Professor Gabaldon explains, gaming regulation is of ancient origin. Today, it runs the gamut from outright prohibition (as in Hawaii and Utah) to unabashed promotion (as in Nevada and New Jersey). Although we will have more to say about the subject in subsequent chapters, you may find it useful to peruse some of the studies mentioned by Mr. Fahrenkopf. The oft-criticized final report of the National Gambling Impact Study Commission (the nine member review board set up by Congress in 1996), is available at govinfo.library.unt.edu/ngisc/, while the National Opinion Research Center's final report to the Commission can be found at www.norc.uchicago.edu/new/gambling.htm. Other useful resources include: John Lyman Mason & Michael Nelson, *Governing Gambling* (2001); I. Nelson Rose & Robert A. Loeb, *Blackjack and the Law* (1998) (as well as www.gamblingandthelaw.com, a web site created by Professor Rose that provides a state-by-state listing of gaming laws); *International Casino Law* (Anthony N. Cabot et al. eds., 3d ed. 1999);

Cory Aronovitz, *The Regulation of Commercial Gaming*, 5 Chap. L. Rev. 181 (2002); and the web site of the International Association of Gaming Regulators (www.iagr.org).

7. While organized crime no longer controls Las Vegas, it still profits handsomely from illegal betting and such related activities as loan sharking, money laundering, and credit card fraud:

Since the 1940s, gambling has been important for Cosa Nostra, because of its profitability and because, relative to other illicit activities, gambling enjoys a greater degree of social acceptability. Gambling replaced prostitution as Cosa Nostra's moneymaker. Explanations for Mafia abandonment of prostitution emphasize that it simply did not pay as well as gambling.

Bookmaking for races and sporting events, placing and laying off bets for numbers, pools, and lotteries have proven lucrative for Cosa Nostra ([with] sports betting as the biggest revenue source). Some of the mid-century titans of organized crime, including Arnold Rothstein, and later Meyer Lansky and Bugsy Siegel (both of whom were closely allied with Cosa Nostra), were bosses of huge gambling operations. Frank Costello became a millionaire many times over through his gambling interests, especially slot machines. Indeed, his gambling machine partnership with Louisiana political boss Huey Long is one of the best examples of the alliance between organized crime figures and politicians.

The development of Las Vegas is a critical chapter in Cosa Nostra gambling history. With financial backing from Meyer Lansky, Frank Costello, and other Cosa Nostra figures, Bugsy Siegel projected organized crime into Las Vegas. Through control of the wire service in Las Vegas, he directed Las Vegas's bookmaking operations.

With mob financing, Siegel also built the Flamingo, the first of the huge Las Vegas gambling hotels. Over time, Cosa Nostra bosses obtained interests in many of the largest casinos in Las Vegas. At one point, approximately a quarter of a billion dollars of the Teamsters central states pension funds were invested in the mortgages of those casinos. In effect, this huge Teamsters fund functioned as a bank for the mob. In addition, Cosa Nostra bosses enjoyed huge returns on their Las Vegas investments by skimming money from casino profits.

Because the 1968 President's Commission's Task Force on Organized Crime ("PCOC") theorized that gambling was the main money maker for Cosa Nostra, the FBI's first real anti-organized crime thrust in the early 1970s focused on gambling. While the gambling program ultimately was regarded as unsuccessful, it did generate dozens of prosecutions and, more important, extensive intelligence information on organized crime.

In the 1980s, the PCOC directed much of its attention to Cosa Nostra gambling operations. According to the 1985 PCOC estimate, in the tristate New York area alone, $1.5 billion is spent each year on numbers games, sports bookmakers, and other forms of illegal wagering controlled by organized crime. FBI agent Frank Storey, Jr. told the PCOC that, by a conservative estimate, more than one-half of Cosa Nostra revenues came from gambling[.]

The PCOC articulated the special problems of gambling regulation, including the distinction between gambling, which is not popularly viewed as harmful, and drug trafficking, which is "universally condemned." Michael DeFeo, U.S. Department of Justice Deputy Chief of the Organized Crime and Racketeering Section, Criminal Division, explained to the PCOC that these perceptions ultimately influenced the allocation of law enforcement efforts. During the early 1970s, over 50 percent of federal organized crime law enforcement efforts were directed at gambling, but three-quarters of those convicted were sentenced to mere probation. Because "the game was not worth the candle," by 1986 only 10 percent of law enforcement investigations were directed at gambling (maybe 25 percent if the number includes cases where gambling is one of many predicate racketeering acts). This phenomenon, according to the PCOC, makes "illegal gambling the 'highest profit-lowest risk' business in which organized crime groups can involve themselves . . . ."

James B. Jacobs & Lauryn P. Gouldin, *Cosa Nostra: The Final Chapter?*, 25 Crime & Just. 129, 148-52 (1999) (citations omitted). For recent examples of gambling prosecutions involving organized crime, *see United States v. Bellomo*, 176 F.3d 580 (2d Cir.), *cert. denied sub nom. Ida v. United States*, 528 U.S. 987 (1999); *United States v. Riddle*, 249 F.3d 529 (6th Cir.), *cert. denied*, 534 U.S. 930 (2001); *United States v. Sapoznik*, 161 F.3d 1117 (7th Cir. 1998). For a further discussion, *see* Jeremy Margolis, *Casinos and Crime: An Analysis of the Evidence*, 2 Gaming L. Rev. 497 (1998).

8. Compulsive gambling has been called a "hidden illness" because, unlike alcohol and drug abuse, it leaves no visible marks on its victims. Indeed, television writers routinely surprise audiences by revealing that characters they thought they knew well are, in fact, recovering gamblers. *See, e.g., All in the Family* (Archie Bunker, during the show's fourth season, in the episode "Archie the Gambler"), *Seinfeld* (Cosmo Kramer, sixth season, "The Diplomat's Club"), *The Simpsons* (Marge Simpson, fifth season, "$pringfield (Or, How I Learned to Stop Worrying and Love Legalized Gambling")), and *Taxi* (Alex Reiger, fifth season, "Alex Goes Off the Wagon").

Since 1980, compulsive gambling has been recognized by the American Psychiatric Association as a serious medical disorder (the Americans with Disabilities Act of 1990, however, specifically excludes the condition from its coverage in 42 U.S.C. § 12211(b)(2)). Although recent studies have come to different conclusions, it appears that as many as five million Americans suffer from the condition and another 15 million are at risk. *See further* Darren Gowen, *Pathological Gambling: An Obscurity in Community Corrections?*, 60 Fed. Probation 3 (June 1996); James H. Juliussen, *Compulsive Gambling and Mitigation of Work Place Discipline: A Step Too Far?*, 27 Willamette L. Rev. 711 (1991); Lawrence S. Lustberg, *Sentencing the Sick: Compulsive Gambling as the Basis for a Downward Departure Under the Federal Sentencing*

Guidelines, 2 Seton Hall J. Sport L. 51 (1992); John O'Neil, *Sexes Take Their Chances Differently*, N.Y. Times, Sept. 11, 2001, at D6 (reporting on distinctions in the behavior patterns of male and female compulsive gamblers). The web site of Gamblers Anonymous (www.gamblersanonymous.org), the national self-help group founded in Los Angeles in September 1957, also provides useful information about the disease and its treatment.

9. Compulsive gambling is a particular problem among teenagers (due to immaturity) and senior citizens (because of loneliness), and special efforts are being made to reach and treat both groups. *See further* David Crary, *Gambling Poses Special Risks for the Elderly*, Bergen County (N.J.) Record, Apr. 2, 2001, at L5; Guy Gugliotta, *Young Gamblers Flock to the Internet*, Wash. Post, Jan. 28, 2001, at A2; Margo E. Schreiber, *Gambling Becoming 'Silent Addiction' for Seniors in the United States*, Chi. Daily Herald, Sept. 9, 2001, at 5; Michael Stet, *Betting on Their Future: Gambling's Allure Increasingly Being Peddled to Children*, S.D. Union-Trib., Feb. 2, 2002, at A1.

10. The recent rise of the gaming industry has increased dramatically the need for lawyers and lobbyists who, to paraphrase Mr. Fahrenkopf, are familiar with its issues and can provide "value-added service." *See generally* Tatiana Boncompagni, *Doubling Down*, Am. Law., Oct. 2001, at 39. This demand has led to the creation of the International Association of Gaming Attorneys (www.theiaga.org), establishment of a bi-monthly journal known as the *Gaming Law Review* (www.liebertpub.com/glr), and an array of CLE seminars (a list of upcoming programs can be found at gaming.unlv.edu/research/gaming_conferences.html). In addition, many general bar associations now have their own gaming law committees, including the International Bar Association (www.ibanet.org), American Bar Association (www.abanet.org), and Association of Trial Lawyers of America (www.atla.org).

If you are considering a career in gaming law, it is important to become conversant with the industry. One easy way to do so is to regularly scan a web site like *Rolling Good Times* (www.rgtonline.com), which contains extensive information about both domestic and foreign gaming and includes breaking news, articles, special reports, a bookstore, a chat room, and numerous links. You also may want to flip through such primers as *The Business of Gaming: Economic and Management Issues* (William R. Eadington & Judy A. Cornelius eds., 1999), and *The Gaming Industry: Introduction and Perspectives* (Vincent H. Eade & David J. Christianson eds., 1996).

11. As gaming has grown, it has become an ever-larger part of pop culture. Indeed, gaming has worked its way deep into the American psyche, and its influence now is felt in everything from architecture to fashion to product styling. *See further* Justin Henderson, *Casino Design: Resorts, Hotels, and Themed Entertainment Spaces* (1999); Stephen Kinzer, *Vegas Museums Play to Type: Where Elvis, Gamblers and Neon are Celebrated as Cultural Treasures*, N.Y. Times, Sept. 5, 2001, at B1; Matt Richtel, *Miss America Gets Her Own Slot Machine in Atlantic City*, N.Y. Times, Sept. 9, 2002, at C4. *See also* Mark G. Tratos, *Betting on the House: Gambling with Great Ideas: Intellectual Property Considerations for the Hotel / Casino / Resort Industry*, 2 Gaming L. Rev. 11 (1998).

At the same time, gaming has been featured in numerous novels (such as Jackie Collins' *Lucky* (1985) and Carl Hiaasen's *Lucky You* (1997)) and television shows (such as ABC's *Vega$*, which ran from 1978-81 and starred Robert Urich, and *Push, Nevada*, a 2002 interactive mystery series that invited viewers to play along at home for the chance to win $1 million). It also has inspired numerous painters and sculptors, as is vividly illustrated in Arthur Flowers & Anthony Curtis, *The Art of Gambling: Through the Ages* (2000).

Film makers have been particularly intrigued by the subject, as witnessed by the abundance of gaming-themed movies: *29th Street* (1991) (starring Danny Aiello and Anthony LaPaglia); *Atlantic City* (1980) (Burt Lancaster and Susan Sarandon); *Bleacher Bums* (2002) (Brad Garrett and Wayne Knight); *Bugsy* (1991) (Warren Beatty and Annette Bening); *California Split* (1974) (Elliott Gould and George Segal); *Casino* (1995) (Robert De Niro and Sharon Stone); *The Cincinnati Kid* (1965) (Ann-Margret and Steve McQueen); *The Color of Money* (1986) (Tom Cruise and Paul Newman, in a sequel to 1961's *The Hustler*, which paired Newman with Jackie Gleason); *Croupier* (1998) (Alex Kingston and Clive Owen); *The Gambler* (1974) (James Caan and Paul Sorvino); *Guys and Dolls* (1955) (Marlon Brando and Frank Sinatra); *Honeymoon in Vegas* (1992) (Nicolas Cage and Sarah Jessica Parker); *Indecent Proposal* (1993) (Demi Moore and Robert Redford); *It Could Happen to You* (1994) (Nicolas Cage and Bridget Fonda); *Leaving Las Vegas* (1995) (Nicolas Cage and Elisabeth Shue); *Let It Ride* (1989) (Richard Dreyfus and Teri Garr); *Lost in America* (1985) (Albert Brooks and Julie Hagerty); *Lucky Numbers* (2000) (Lisa Kudrow and John Travolta); *The Mississippi Gambler* (1953) (Piper Laurie and Tyrone Power); *Ocean's Eleven* (2001) (George Clooney and Brad Pitt, in a remake of the 1960 original that featured the Rat Pack); *Rain Man* (1988) (Tom Cruise and Dustin Hoffman); *Show Boat* (1951) (Ava Gardner and Howard Keel); *Snake Eyes* (1998) (Nicolas Cage and Gary Sinise); *The Sting* (1973) (Paul Newman and Robert Redford); *Vegas Vacation* (1997) (Chevy Chase and Beverly D'Angelo); *Waking Ned Devine* (1998) (Ian Bannen and David Kelly); and *Wise Guys* (1986) (Danny DeVito and Joe Piscopo). They have even managed to combine gambling and law school, as in *Rounders* (1998), which cast Matt Damon as Mike McDermott, a law student who loses his tuition money in a high stakes poker game, and Martin Landau as Abe Petrovsky, his law school dean. For a further look at gaming movies, *see* Jeffrey W. Dement, *Going for Broke: The Depiction of Compulsive Gambling in Film* (1999).

12. Lastly, a word should be said about the connection between gaming and superstition. Most people are familiar with "Lady Luck," but few know that her origins have been traced to the Greek goddess Aphrodite, who, besides being responsible for love and beauty, was felt to decide the fates of gamblers. Indeed, in ancient times the highest role of the dice was called an "epaphroditus" because it was said that Aphrodite directed the hand that threw it.

More recently, St. Camillus de Lellis, who lost his fortune through compulsive gambling and then became a penitent working in hospitals serving incurables, and St. Cayetano (also spelled Cajetan), a 15th century Italian priest, have come to be viewed as the patron saints of gamblers. In addition, various objects—such as a rabbit's foot, horse shoe, and four-leaf clover—are thought to bring good luck. For a further discussion, *see* John Curran, *Some Gamblers' Favorite Partner is Superstition*, New Orleans Times-Picayune, Jan. 15, 1995, at A2. *See also* www.ladylucks.net.

Problem 1

Except for a lottery used to fund public works and limited charitable gaming, a state prohibits all forms of gambling. As a result, a private school that teaches individuals how to run casinos and serve as croupiers was denied an operating license. If it appeals, how should the court rule? *See Michigan Gaming Institute, Inc. v. State Board of Education*, 536 N.W.2d 289 (Mich. Ct. App. 1995), *rev'd mem.*, 547 N.W.2d 882 (Mich. 1996).

C. ETHICS

UNITED STATES v. EDWARDS
303 F.3d 606 (5th Cir. 2002),
cert. denied, 123 S. Ct. 1272 (2003)

BENAVIDES, Circuit Judge.

After a long, complex trial, the former governor of Louisiana, his son, and several of his associates were convicted for their roles in various schemes to make money from Louisiana's riverboat gambling license process by exploiting the former governor's apparent ability to influence that process. The defendants appeal their convictions for, inter alia, extortion, mail and wire fraud, money laundering, making false statements, and RICO violations. Finding no reversible error, we affirm.

I.

Edwin Edwards was a prominent figure in Louisiana politics for more than two decades. After serving in the Navy during World War II and later obtaining his law degree, he spent several years in private practice and local politics. He served as a member of the United States House of Representatives from 1965 until 1972, when he was elected to the first of two consecutive terms as Governor.

In 1980, he left the governor's office and served briefly on the Louisiana Supreme Court. He then returned to private practice until 1984, when he was elected to a third term as Governor. After two federal corruption trials in 1985 and 1986, resulting in a hung jury and an acquittal, respectively, he lost his bid for re-election in 1987. In 1992, however, the voters sent him back to the Governor's office for an unprecedented fourth term. When that term ended in 1996, he once again returned to private practice. In private practice, he worked closely with his son, Stephen Edwards, who is also a lawyer.

Stephen and Edwin Edwards were convicted with several of the Governor's associates. Cecil Brown ("Brown"), an auctioneer and businessman, held the title of "Special Assistant to the Governor." Andrew Martin ("Martin") was a businessman who worked in the commercial fishing and marine towing industries, along with serving as a public official on state commissions. From 1992 to 1995, Martin held the title of Executive Assistant to the Governor. Bobby Johnson ("Johnson"), a self-made cement magnate, was a close friend of Edwin Edwards. In addition to these convicted defendants, two of Edwin Edwards' associates were acquitted: Gregory Tarver ("Tarver"), a Louisiana State Senator and Ecotry Fuller ("Fuller"), a former member of the Louisiana Gaming Control Board ("the Board").

Originally, these seven men were indicted en masse. The government alleged that each was a member of a conspiracy to violate the Racketeer Influenced and Corrupt Organizations Act ("RICO"). The indictment broke the conspiracy into five separate schemes. Pursuant to each scheme, the conspirators were alleged to have extorted money from various individuals who sought approval of riverboat casino projects. The conspirators promised to help these individuals obtain licenses in exchange for money and threatened to make obtaining the licenses impossible if they did not pay. It was further alleged that the conspirators attempted to launder the money obtained through the schemes.

In 1992 the Louisiana Riverboat Gaming Commission was created to evaluate applicants for fifteen riverboat gaming licenses available in Louisiana. The Commission was made up of seven panel members, each of whom was appointed by Edwin Edwards. By 1993, it had awarded all fifteen certificates of preliminary approval. The Commission did not have authority to issue the licenses, as it only determined whether the applicant was acceptable. Nevertheless, fourteen of the fifteen applicants awarded preliminary approval were granted licenses by the Louisiana State Police, Riverboat Gaming Division. In 1996, the Commission was replaced by the Louisiana Gaming Control Board, made up of six members appointed by Governor Mike Foster. The Board awarded the final certificate of preliminary approval. The appellants' extortion demands were based on their actual or apparent ability to manipulate the votes of these two entities.

Brown was the major player in the LRGC/NORC Scheme. Brown, ostensibly representing Edwin Edwards (who was acquitted of all acts relating to this scheme), defrauded and extorted the Louisiana Riverboat Gaming Corporation ("LRGC") and the New Orleans Riverboat Corporation ("NORC") (controlled by the same principals) by promising each a riverboat license if they paid exorbitant consulting fees despite the fact that he knew that LRGC and NORC would not receive licenses. Brown spoke with LRGC/NORC principals between the Fall of 1991 and the Summer of 1993, when the key licensing vote occurred. During that period, Brown was paid approximately $350,000.

Brown and Johnson carried out the Jazz Scheme. Claiming to represent Edwin Edwards, they extorted Jazz Enterprises, Inc. ("Jazz"), one of three applicants for two available Baton Rouge riverboat licenses. Brown and Johnson spoke with the Jazz principals between February 1994 and August 1994. Jazz did not agree to the extortion demand, but it received a license anyway in July 1994. Edwin Edwards was ultimately acquitted on all counts relating to this scheme.

Stephen Edwards, his friend Richard Shetler ("Shetler") and Edwin Edwards were the major players in the Players Scheme. Stephen Edwards, representing his father, extorted Players Casino ("Players"), demanding that it retain him as a lawyer and hire his merchandising firm and Shetler as consultants to obtain a license and receive other benefits. Stephen Edwards spoke with Players between May 1993 and approximately February 1995. During this time, Players paid Shetler and Stephen Edwards more than a million dollars.

The primary participants in the Treasure Chest Scheme included Martin, Edwin Edwards, and Stephen Edwards. Martin, representing the Governor, extorted Robert Guidry ("Guidry"), who was a principal of the Treasure Chest Casino. Martin was in contact with Guidry between April 1994 and April 1997. Over these years, Guidry paid Stephen Edwards, Edwin Edwards, and Martin more than a million dollars.

The 15th Riverboat License Scheme, so named because it was the final license to be awarded by the Board, was a father-son operation. Stephen Edwards and Edwin Edwards extorted Eddie DeBartolo, Jr. ("DeBartolo") and his business partner, Ed Muransky. DeBartolo, the then-owner of the San Francisco 49ers professional football team, was seeking a riverboat license pursuant to a joint venture between his company, DeBartolo Entertainment Corporation, and Hollywood Casino. Edwin Edwards and Stephen Edwards were in contact with DeBartolo between September 1996 and April 1997. DeBartolo made a one-time $400,000 payment to Edwin Edwards and Stephen Edwards in March 1997.

On August 4, 1999, a grand jury returned a 34-count superseding indictment, charging appellants Edwin Edwards, Stephen Edwards, Martin, Johnson and Brown with a violation of RICO [18 U.S.C. § 1961 et seq.], conspiracy to violate RICO [18 U.S.C. § 1962(d)], mail and wire fraud [18 U.S.C. § 1341 et seq.], extortion [18 U.S.C. § 1951], money laundering [18 U.S.C. § 1956], interstate travel and communication in aid of racketeering [18 U.S.C. § 1952] and false statements [18 U.S.C. § 1001].

The case was tried to a jury, and the appellants were convicted as follows: Edwin Edwards [Counts 1-2 (RICO), 12-15 (Players extortion), 17-19 (Treasure Chest extortion), 20-22 (15th Riverboat License fraud), 25-27 (15th Riverboat License fraud), 31 (15th Riverboat License extortion) and 34 (money laundering)]; Stephen Edwards [1-2, 12-15, 16 (Interstate Travel in Aid of Racketeering) 17-19, 20-22, 25-27, 31 and 34]; Martin [1-2, 17-19 and 34]; Brown [1-2 and 3-4 (Jazz extortion)]; and Johnson [3-4, 5 (Interstate Communication in Aid of Racketeering), 6 (fraud), and 7-11 (false statements)]. Subsequent to the verdict, the Supreme Court decided Cleveland v. United States, 531 U.S. 12, 121 S.Ct. 365, 148 L.Ed.2d 221 (2000), holding that mail and wire fraud convictions cannot be based on the theory that the government was defrauded of its intangible right to issue licenses (hereinafter, "license as property theory"). In light of Cleveland, the district court granted new trials as follows: Edwin Edwards [Counts 20-22 and 25-27]; Stephen Edwards [20-22 and 25-27]; and Johnson [6].

In the process of trying this case, the district court made a number of rulings that are now challenged. Specifically, the appellants contend that: (1) the district court erred by empaneling an anonymous jury; (2) the district court erred when it admitted evidence obtained via unauthorized wiretaps; (3) the district court erred when it admitted hearsay evidence pursuant to Fed.R.Evid. 801(d)(2)(E); (4) the district court erred when it ordered Johnson tried in absentia; (5) the district court erred when it dismissed Juror # 68 during deliberations; (6) the evidence at trial was insufficient to support all Brown and Johnson's convictions as well as Stephen Edwards's extortion conviction relating to the 15th Riverboat License Scheme; (7) the spillover effect from the counts based on the Cleveland-repudiated "license as property" theory requires reversal of appellants' convictions on some or all of the other counts; (8) Stephen Edwards' sentence should be vacated because the calculation of the extortion payments was overstated; (9) Johnson's sentence should be vacated because the calculation of the extortion payments was overstated and because the evidence did not support an adjustment for obstruction of justice; (10) the restitution award against Martin should be set aside because it was not supported by the jury verdict; and (11) various aspects of their trial violated their due process rights. We address each contention in turn.

II.

Aware of the intense media, political, and emotional atmosphere surrounding this case, the district court withheld certain identifying information about potential jury members. This omitted information included their names and places of employment. Regarding the potential jurors' residential information, the district court released their zip codes and parishes, but withheld the exact addresses. Despite the lack of access to this information, the parties were able to view a large amount of other information about the venirepersons, including a twenty-eight page questionnaire consisting of 116 questions, some with subparts. Moreover, they were allowed to propose questions for potential jury members and ask follow-up questions. The defendants contend that by withholding some juror information, the district court violated their right to a fair trial before an impartial jury. Additionally, they argue that this injury was exacerbated by the district court's decision to close the proceedings it held to determine whether to withhold juror information. The closure of these proceedings, the defendants contend, violated their Sixth Amendment right to a public trial.

A.

We have previously recognized the seriousness of the decision to withhold juror information, holding that it should be a last resort in a court's efforts to protect the jurors from intimidating or prejudicial influences. See United States v. Krout, 66 F.3d 1420, 1427 (5th Cir.1995).

In United States v. Branch, 91 F.3d 699 (5th Cir.1996), we affirmed the district court's decision to withhold certain identifying juror information in the trial of former members of the Branch Davidian sect. Cautioning that "[n]ot all celebrated trials merit an anonymous jury," we nevertheless relied on the intense press coverage and the passions that the trial incited, even though there was no indication that any of the defendants would interfere with the jurors. Branch, 91 F.3d at 723-24. In this respect, the present case closely resembles Branch. The overriding concern, and the most important factor in the district court's analysis, was the intense media interest and highly charged emotional and political fervor that surrounded the trial. Edwin Edwards was a four-term governor who, partly because of his previous legal entanglements, was a polarizing figure in Louisiana politics. His son, Stephen Edwards, had attracted intense media coverage. Tarver was a Louisiana state senator. In addition to these high profile defendants, several well known witnesses would testify at trial, including DeBartolo, the owner of the Super Bowl Champion San Francisco 49ers, and Cleo Fields, a state senator and former United States Congressman. .

Moreover, the district court did not base its decision on publicity alone. There were several allegations and examples of attempts to interfere with the judicial process and witnesses. The indictment charged Edwin Edwards and Stephen Edwards with the illegal wiretapping and countersurveillance of an FBI agent. In a related trial, Edwin Edwards was accused of witness tampering, and the government filed an affidavit accusing Edwin Edwards of using a state trooper to run records searches on certain persons during his previous criminal trials. Furthermore, the present case involved his efforts to corrupt the state's process for licensing riverboat gambling.

In addition to these indications of the defendants' disregard for proper administrative and judicial processes, the defendants all faced long periods of incarceration and significant prison sentences if convicted on all charges. Edwin Edwards alone faced a maximum of 375 years in prison and a fine of over $7,500,000. Furthermore, the district court was concerned with the possibility that persons not directly involved with the case would engage in juror intimidation or harassment. Intrepid members of the media, for example, published the identity of a juror when it was discovered. They also attempted to identify jurors by determining where they were parked and obtaining their license plate information. Moreover, Edwin Edwards had numerous close political operatives and allies who also might have attempted to influence the jurors. The prospect of such interference from the media and politically interested third parties militates in favor of withholding juror information.

In assessing the reasonableness of the balance that the district court struck between the defendants' rights and the protection of the jurors, we also note that the information withheld from the parties was limited. In referring to such juries as "anonymous," we have previously cautioned against "painting with too broad a brush." Branch, 91 F.3d at 723. As in Branch, the jury here was "anonymous" only "in the most literal sense." Id. The parties had access to the jurors' zip codes, parishes, and the extensive information contained in the long questionnaire. With this information, the defendants are hard-pressed in demonstrating that they were prejudiced in any way during voir dire.

Finally, we do not overlook the fact that the district court minimized the possibility of any prejudice to the defendants by giving an explanatory jury instruction, which was similar to the instruction upheld in Branch. This instruction referred to the intense media publicity as the reason for anonymity and gave no indication that the jurors should fear for their safety from the defendants. It reiterated that the defendants were presumed innocent until proven guilty and that the district court was using these procedures to protect juror privacy and ensure a fair trial for both sides. The district court then questioned the jurors to determine whether they had any bias toward either party as a result of the decision to withhold their names. All jurors assured the district court that they did not harbor any such bias. Accordingly, in light of the weighty reasons for concealing juror information, the limited scope of the concealment, and the district court's careful efforts to avoid prejudicing the defendants, we find no abuse of discretion.

B.

The defendants also contend that the district court's decision to close the hearing on whether to empanel an anonymous jury violated their Sixth Amendment right to a public trial. Their opposition to the closure represented a reversal of strategy. Initially, they had argued that the proceedings should not be public. Once damaging information appeared in the media, however, they began to worry about public speculation that Edwin Edwards had ties to organized crime. As a result of this concern, they changed their minds and unsuccessfully attempted to open the proceedings.

At the outset, we note that we have already approved the closure of voir dire proceedings in a related case, in which Edwin Edwards was also a defendant. See United States v. Brown, 250 F.3d 907, 922 (5th Cir.2001). Although Brown involved a First Amendment challenge to the closure of the voir dire proceedings, this distinction does not change our analysis. The caselaw applying the Sixth Amendment guarantee of a public trial was originally developed in cases involving the right of the public and press to attend trials, which is implicit in the First Amendment.

The defendants argue that the district court was not motivated by [an] interest in a fair trial for them, but rather closed the proceedings to protect the government. The record does not support this contention. The district court did worry about the association of "inaccurate motives with the government's motion," but its concern was clearly with the fairness of the impending trial and, in particular, the prejudicial effect of such public speculation on the defendants. Moreover, in case any doubt surrounded the district court's motives, it summed up its core concern: "The overall effect of conducting a public hearing on the motion would be just the harm the Fifth Circuit warns against: an unfair trial for the defendants." We therefore conclude that a substantial interest supported the district court's decision to hold nonpublic proceedings on the motion for an anonymous jury.

We also conclude that the district court's action was no broader than necessary, as the defendants have proposed no viable alternatives to closure. They propose that the district court should not have worried about the possible taint of the jury pool because any tainted potential jurors could have been removed during voir dire. Acknowledging the potential prejudicial effect of accusations about the defendants' alleged threat to juror integrity, however, we decline to require district courts to wait until voir dire to remedy any taint. Rather, we preserve the district court's ability, when necessary, to act prophylactically to avoid the problem. Accordingly, we hold that the closure of the proceedings surrounding the anonymous jury did not violate the Sixth Amendment guarantee of a public trial.

III.

At trial, the government relied in part on evidence obtained from the electronic surveillance of Cecil Brown's phones and Stephen Edwards' office. This surveillance began after the government was approached by an informant, Pat Graham ("Graham"). Based on information provided by Graham, the government filed an application to wiretap Brown's home and office phones. The information it learned from this surveillance led to the wiretap of Edwin Edwards' home. Eventually, the government also placed bugs, video cameras, and wiretaps in the offices of Edwin Edwards and Stephen Edwards. The defendants now challenge this surveillance. Their primary argument is that the original authorization for the Brown wiretap was improper because the FBI affidavit in support of the application was based on misleading information. This argument has already been considered and rejected by another panel of this Court in United States v. Cecil Brown, 298 F.3d 392 (5th Cir.2002). Upon our own review, we also find no merit in the defendants' arguments on this issue. In addition, Brown contends that the district court erroneously admitted intercepted communications between him and his civil attorneys in violation of the attorney-client privilege. Finally, Stephen Edwards argues that the government was not authorized to monitor his conversations with listening devices placed in his office.

A.

Brown contends that the district court erred in admitting wiretap intercepted conversations in violation of the attorney-client privilege. The conversations in question included several discussions, which at times involved Brown, his attorneys, Kenneth Pitre ("Pitre") and Robert J. Lenze ("Lenze"), and Edwin Edwards. They relate to lawsuits brought by principals of LRGC/NORC for the return of money extorted by Brown. In an October 21, 1996 conversation, Brown, Edwin Edwards, and Pitre discussed the possible characterization of the extortion money paid to Brown as a loan rather than income because "we are not ever going to admit that this is a payment to him because then we'd owe income taxes on it." They then discussed the failure of LRGC/NORC to obtain a license, with Edwin Edwards stating that "Cecil can take the position that he did what was asked," and Brown responding "I carried the water to the right places." Edwin Edwards then opined that they needed someone to testify that LRGC/NORC was not awarded a license because "they were not strong enough financially." This explanation covered up the true reason for LRGC/NORC's lack of success, as articulated by Brown: "the Governor has too many friends." In a separate conversation, Brown told his attorney that the handling of the LRGC/NORC payments could not be exposed "openly in court" because with that money he had to "take care" of a "guy on the [Gaming] Board; and because we were throwing money around like crazy."

The attorney-client privilege, the oldest and most venerated of the common law privileges of confidential communications, serves important interests in our judicial system. See Upjohn Co. v. United States, 449 U.S. 383, 389, 101 S.Ct. 677, 66 L.Ed.2d 584 (1981). Nevertheless, despite its venerated position, the privilege is not absolute and is subject to several exceptions. Under the crime-fraud exception to the attorney-client privilege, the privilege can be overcome "where communication or work product is intended 'to further continuing or future criminal or fraudulent activity.'" In re Grand Jury Subpoena, 220 F.3d 406, 410 (5th Cir.2000) (quoting United States v. Dyer, 722 F.2d 174, 177 (5th Cir.1983)). The government, as the proponent of the otherwise privileged evidence, "has the burden of establishing a prima facie case that the attorney-client relationship was intended to further criminal or fraudulent activity." Id. at 410. The district court agreed that the crime-fraud exception applied to these attorney-client communications, as Brown was using his lawyer's services to cover up crimes related to his extortion of LRGC/ NORC. Because the application of the attorney-client privilege is a fact question to be determined in light of the purpose of the privilege and guided by judicial precedents, we review the district court's finding for clear error only. United States v. Aucoin, 964 F.2d 1492, 1498 (5th Cir.1992).

In determining whether the crime-fraud exception applies, we focus on the client's purpose in seeking legal advice. In re Grand Jury Proceedings, 43 F.3d 966, 972 (5th Cir.1994) (per curiam). Brown relies heavily on the fact that the lawsuits that he hired Pitre and Lenze to defend did not allege any fraud or other crimes. He further contends that the communications are privileged because they relate only to a defense against allegations of past wrongs, not continuing or future crimes. The district court agreed with the findings of Judge John V. Parker of the Middle District of Louisiana, who determined that (1) the payments at issue in the lawsuits were made to Brown in exchange for his guarantee of obtaining riverboat licenses for LRGC/NORC through means of bribery and fraud and (2) Brown subsequently sought legal services to conceal and cover up the crimes committed with respect to the payments. We cannot conclude that these findings were clearly erroneous. Rather than merely defending himself against civil actions alleging past wrongdoing, Brown was actively continuing the cover-up of his extortion and perpetuating his tax fraud. Cf. Dyer, 722 F.2d at 177-78 (holding that a defendant's use of a civil attorney to obtain a false exculpatory letter was not privileged under the crime-fraud exception). Accordingly, we find no abuse of discretion in the admission of the communications between Brown and his attorney.

B.

The information it learned from consensual recordings and covert surveillance of Brown and others led the government to seek permission to increase its monitoring of Edwin Edwards and his associates. On December 6, 1996, the government obtained an authorization order to intercept oral communications "at the premises known as the law office of Edward [sic] W. Edwards located at 4621 Jamestown Avenue." The named interceptees included Edwin Edwards, Brown, Richard L. Stalder, Pitre, Marion D. Edwards, and Wanda Edwards. Pursuant to this authorization order, the government placed listening devices in the personal office of Stephen Edwards and intercepted at least two of his conversations. The defendants contend that these actions exceeded the scope of the December 6 order in two ways. First, the government was not allowed to place monitoring devices in the office of Stephen Edwards. Second, even assuming arguendo that the order permitted the placement of devices in Stephen Edwards' office, it did not provide for the interception of his conversations because he was not a named interceptee. The district court rejected these arguments. We review its interpretation of the December 6 order de novo. See United States v. Smith, 273 F.3d 629, 632 (5th Cir.2001) (legal conclusions on motion to suppress reviewed de novo); United States v. Reyna, 218 F.3d 1108, 1110 (9th Cir.2000) (wiretap suppression reviewed de novo).

Certainly, the defendants are correct in noting that the December 6 order does not explicitly refer to Stephen Edwards' personal office. This omission, however, does not end the inquiry, as we must still determine whether the placement of devices in Stephen Edwards' office was justified under the order's reference to "the premises known as the law office" of Edwin Edwards. Central to the resolution of this issue is the definition of "the premises known as the law office," specifically, whether it referred to the entire group of legal offices at 4621 Jamestown Avenue or merely to Edwin Edwards' personal office within the suite. Because it is not clear from the face of the order how expansive that term was intended to be, it is helpful to consult the affidavit and application upon which the order was based. A reading of the detailed, sixty-seven page affidavit submitted by FBI Special Agent Geoffrey C. Santini supports an expansive interpretation of "the premises known as the law office." The affidavit states, in part:

> On December 3, 1996, a separate cooperating witness (CW-3) advised that if an individual entered the front door of the law office and turned right at the reception desk, the first office on the right as one proceeded down the hall is the personal office of Stephen R. Edwards. The next office on the right down the hall is the personal office of Edwin W. Edwards. (Affiant asserts that Edwin W. Edwards' office is located in the front corner of the law office). CW-3 advised that Edwin W. Edwards currently conducts business in his personal office and on occasion in the office of Stephen R. Edwards.

As this passage suggests, there is a difference in usage between the terms "law office" and "personal office." This distinction is further supported by an attachment to the affidavit, which diagrams the layout of the entire office. The attachment indicates that although Edwin Edwards and Stephen Edwards had separate personal offices, the entire group of offices comprised a single, cohesive office area. There was a common reception desk, library, conference room, clerical/secretary area, and coffee area. Finally, the affidavit stated that, according to a cooperating witness, Edwin Edwards "would in effect use the entire office for meetings and on many occasions the CW would meet and observe [Edwin] Edwards in Stephen R. Edwards [sic] office." Our review of the affidavit, therefore, clarifies that the December 6 order's reference to the law office of Edwin Edwards includes the entire group of legal offices at 4621 Jamestown Avenue, not merely the personal office of Edwin Edwards. Accordingly, we agree with the district court that the order permitted the government to place listening devices in the personal office of Stephen Edwards.

The defendants further contend that even if the listening devices were properly placed in Stephen Edwards' office, the government was not permitted to listen to his conversations because he was not a named interceptee. In particular, two conversations are at issue. The first conversation, which took place on December 19, 1996, involved Edwin Edwards and Stephen Edwards discussing how to write checks so that they could disguise the criminal proceeds. The next day, the government intercepted a second conversation featuring Stephen Edwards talking with Wanda Edwards, Marion Edwards, and Cecil Brown, all three of whom were named interceptees. Again, it is beyond dispute that Stephen Edwards is not among the named interceptees in the December 6 order, and that he was not added to that list until January 15, 1997, when the first thirty-day extension was granted. The order, however, does not limit its scope to named interceptees only. Instead, it provides that interception may take place only when

> one of the named interceptees are [sic] within the target premises and are engaged in conversation or activity with any named or known coconspirator or any other individual that was caused to go to the target premises by a named interceptee or named or known coconspirator as related to the criminal offenses as set forth in paragraph A.

The government contends, and the district court agreed, that the interception of Stephen Edwards' conversations was appropriate because he was a coconspirator, as evidenced by the December 19 and 20 conversations. It further relied on the fact that the government kept the issuing court fully abreast of the monitoring through a December 27, 1996 status report. Therefore, it argues, the interception of these conversations was fully authorized.

We do not reach the same conclusion. As the government concedes, because Stephen Edwards was not a named interceptee, the interception could be legal only if he was a "named or known coconspirator." Contrary to the government's suggestion, however, our focus in determining whether Stephen Edwards was a coconspirator must be on December 6, not on the dates of the intercepted conversations. Relying on the content of the actual conversations to justify post hoc otherwise illegal interception would constitute impermissible bootstrapping. If the interception was not legal when the conversation began, it does not become legal simply because of what the participants discussed. We must therefore look instead for evidence that the government knew that Stephen Edwards was a coconspirator on December 6. Not only does the government fail to identify any such evidence, the clear terms of its December 6 application and affidavit suggest that none exists. As of December 6, the government was aware that Stephen Edwards maintained an office at the target premises and that Edwin Edwards often used that office to conduct business. Nevertheless, there is no indication in the affidavit that the government thought that Stephen Edwards was involved in the alleged extortion schemes. By contrast, other members of the Edwards family who had offices at the target premises, such as Wanda Edwards and Marion Edwards, were suspected of illegalities and therefore were listed as named interceptees. In other words, our reading of the December 6 order, application, and affidavit leads us to the conclusion that Stephen Edwards was not listed as a named interceptee precisely because the government did not think he was a coconspirator. Accordingly, because we conclude that Stephen Edwards was not a "named or known coconspirator" under the terms of the December

6 order, we hold that the December 19 and 20 conversations were illegally recorded and should have been suppressed. See 18 U.S.C. § 2518(10)(a) (providing for suppression remedy).

Having determined that the district court's admission of the December 19 and 20 conversations involving Stephen Edwards was erroneous, we now must decide whether that error was harmless. To the extent that the error implicates Stephen Edwards' Fourth Amendment rights, we ask whether it appears "beyond a reasonable doubt that the error complained of did not contribute to the verdict obtained." Neder v. United States, 527 U.S. 1, 15, 119 S.Ct. 1827, 144 L.Ed.2d 35 (1999) (quoting Chapman v. Cal., 386 U.S. 18, 24, 87 S.Ct. 824, 17 L.Ed.2d 705 (1967)). There is no dispute that the suppression of the December 19 and 20 conversations alone would not have made a difference in the verdict, as the evidence of the defendants' guilt was overwhelming. Rather, the defendants suggest that the evidence obtained from the December 19 and 20 conversations provided the basis for the inclusion of Stephen Edwards as one of the named interceptees on the January 15, 1997 wiretap application. Moreover, they contend that the conversations also led to the April 1997 search of Stephen Edwards' home. These arguments overstate the importance of the illegal interception. In its affidavit in support of its application for the January 15, 1997 wiretap authorization, the government detailed a January 9, 1997 conversation between Edwin Edwards and Martin. The two men discussed Stephen Edwards' role in the Treasure Chest Scheme, including a payment from Guidry to Stephen Edwards. Based on this evidence of Stephen Edwards' involvement in the extortion scheme, there was a solid basis for adding Stephen Edwards as a named interceptee on January 15, even without the December 19 and 20 conversations. After receiving the January 15 wiretap authorization, the government amassed extensive evidence of Stephen Edwards' criminal activities to support its subsequent April 1997 application for a search warrant. In light of this evidence, which was wholly independent of the December 19 and 20 conversations, we hold that the admission of the illegal interceptions was harmless beyond a reasonable doubt.

[The remainder of the court's opinion is omitted.]

In re MENNA
905 P.2d 944 (Cal. 1995)

PER CURIAM.

Joseph Menna (hereafter applicant) is permanently disbarred from the practice of law in New Jersey as a result of his felony convictions for theft of client funds, failure to file a state income tax return, and manufacture of methamphetamine.

Subsequent to his disbarment, he moved to California, passed the bar examination, and sought admission to the State Bar. After a preliminary investigation, the Committee of Bar Examiners (hereafter referred to occasionally as Committee) declined to recommend him for admission and referred the matter for a formal hearing before the State Bar Court. Following an evidentiary hearing, the Hearing Department of the State Bar Court determined he possessed the requisite good moral character to be certified to this court for admission. The Review Department of the State Bar Court affirmed. Pursuant to California Rules of Court, rule 952.6, the Committee of Bar Examiners petitioned this court. We granted review and now reverse on the grounds that determination is not supported by the weight of the evidence; nor is it appropriate in light of the record as a whole. (Cal.Rules of Court, rule 954(a).)

FACTS

1. Misconduct leading to disbarment

As summarized by the hearing department, applicant has "a significant background of compulsive gambling and excessive use of alcohol" and "an extensive history of professional misconduct, which led to his permanent disbarment in New Jersey in 1984" as well as four felony convictions.

Applicant's troubles began soon after his admission to the State Bar of New Jersey in December 1976. Following a short stint with the Camden County Prosecutor's Office, he joined the law office of Joseph Maressa, handling personal injury litigation before leaving in 1980 to begin a solo practice, which lasted until August 1982.

Through a client of the Maressa firm that held its organizational meetings in Atlantic City, applicant was introduced to the various casinos there and soon began to gamble compulsively. He also started to drink heavily while gambling and experimented with cocaine to remain alert. At the same time, applicant experienced marital difficulties exacerbated by his frequent forays to the casinos.

Beginning in 1980, applicant began to use funds from his client trust account to pay gambling debts. Over a two-year period, he cashed nineteen separate client settlement checks totaling over $98,000 for his own purposes. In addition, in 1979 he borrowed $70,000 from a former client, Mrs. Cruice, ostensibly to start up a practice but in reality to pay gambling losses. He made payments on the loan until 1982. That year, he also persuaded Mrs. Cruice to cosign a bank note to himself in the amount of $50,000. When the note came due in the summer of 1982, applicant defaulted. As a result, Mrs. Cruice filed an ethics complaint with the New Jersey bar. This complaint led to an investigation of applicant and his temporary suspension for irregularities in the handling of his trust account. (Mrs. Cruice eventually received a $25,000 settlement from the Maressa firm for negligent supervision of applicant.)

During this period of suspension, applicant devised a scheme to pay off his gambling debts by manufacturing illegal drugs. He acquired the necessary precursors to produce methamphetamine, but a former client, who was supposed to buy the finished product, informed the police of the plan. Applicant was arrested, indicted, and ultimately pled guilty to one count of manufacturing methamphetamine. He also admitted to one count of wilful failure to file a 1981 New Jersey state income tax return and two counts of theft by failure to make disposition of property received, which related to two separate instances of misappropriation of client trust funds totaling nearly $75,000.

In November 1984, applicant was sentenced to four years' imprisonment. He remained incarcerated in a minimum security correctional facility until

April 1985, and thereafter stayed at a halfway house until September 1985. He successfully completed parole in the spring of 1987. In May 1985, with New Jersey State Bar disciplinary proceedings pending, he consented to permanent disbarment, which applicant acknowledges precludes ever seeking reinstatement there.

In February 1989, applicant moved to Southern California for the purpose of eventually obtaining admission to practice law in this state. In July 1990, he passed the California Bar Examination. After a preliminary examination, the Committee of Bar Examiners notified applicant it had determined not to recommend his admission to this court and had referred his application to the Office of Chief Trial Counsel for a formal hearing before the State Bar Court. (Rules Regulating Admission to Practice Law, rule X (Deering's Cal. Rules of Court (State Bar) (1988 ed., 1995 cum. supp.) pp. 144-148).) As noted earlier, the Hearing Department of the State Bar Court, after several days of hearings in August 1992, issued a written decision holding that applicant possessed the requisite good moral character for admission to the bar. The Office of Chief Trial Counsel, acting on behalf of the Committee of Bar Examiners, requested review. The Review Department of the State Bar Court issued a written opinion affirming the decision of the hearing department as well as a supplemental opinion denying the Committee's motion for reconsideration.

2. Evidence of rehabilitation

In May 1983, while the aforementioned criminal and disciplinary charges against applicant were pending, he entered the Carrier Foundation Hospital, a psychiatric hospital in Princeton, New Jersey, specializing in compulsive behavior. While there, he was exposed to Gamblers Anonymous, an organization similar in structure and philosophy to Alcoholics Anonymous. Applicant has continuously attended at least one Gamblers Anonymous meeting weekly since leaving the Carrier clinic in 1983. While incarcerated, he organized and led a weekly meeting at the correctional facility. He has served as secretary of his Gamblers Anonymous room in Solano Beach, California, and has participated in seminars and workshops throughout California and New Jersey on compulsive gambling. Applicant has not gambled since 1982.

Two psychologists appeared on applicant's behalf. Dr. Durand F. Jacobs, an authority on addictive behaviors, had counseled applicant during the year prior to the hearing. Dr. Jacobs testified applicant had completely overcome the problems that led to his compulsive gambling and is no more at risk of repeating his earlier misconduct than any other practicing attorney. Dr. Clifford S. Marks was applicant's current therapist. In his opinion, applicant had fully recovered from his gambling addiction and would not regress. Dr. Marks believed applicant now possesses a high ability to handle stress and is of good moral character.

Applicant also presented 29 character reference letters attesting to his good moral character and unblemished record since release from prison. Knowing of the facts leading to applicant's conviction and disbarment, they nevertheless uniformly recommended his admission to the bar. These letters included five from California attorneys with whom he had worked as a paralegal. Each attested to applicant's skill and professionalism and recommended his admission without reservation. One of the attorneys, Michael Bruno, stated he had known applicant for two and one-half years and had employed him for part of that time as a legal assistant. They had worked particularly closely on one litigation matter in Northern California for over three months, during which time applicant had provided invaluable assistance and "demonstrated exemplary ethical standards." In addition, letters were received from an engineer who had worked for a small construction company formed by applicant following his release from prison, a Pennsylvania attorney who had known him for 7 years, a New Jersey certified public accountant and ordained deacon in the Roman Catholic Church who had known him for 12 years, a friend of 29 years, and applicant's sister. Each attested to applicant's complete rehabilitation and supported his admission to the bar.

Applicant called a number of additional witnesses to appear on his behalf, including four California attorneys for whom he had worked as a legal assistant. (One of the witnesses, Attorney Michael Bruno, also submitted the character reference letter referred to above.) Although fully aware of applicant's prior misconduct, convictions and disbarment, these attorneys attested to his professionalism and honesty and recommended his admission without reservation. Attorney McKenzie stated applicant was "very guilt-ridden" about his past and his financial debts to his former clients "weigh [] very heavily on him." Attorney Mills indicated applicant had expressed remorse for his misconduct and an interest in working for the poor "to pay something back to society." Two fellow members of Gamblers Anonymous also testified, and some fifteen additional members submitted letters describing applicant's extensive participation in Gamblers Anonymous and his efforts to help others confront and overcome their compulsive gambling and related problems.

Applicant testified in his own behalf. He provided background about his family, formative years, and education in Pennsylvania; his legal experience after graduating from law school; and the events leading to his criminal convictions and disbarment. He described his life since his release from prison: In 1985 he founded and operated a construction company until it went out of business in 1988. In September 1989, he moved to California with the intent to sit for the State Bar examination and apply for admission to practice. Since that time, he has worked as a legal assistant for several attorneys in Southern California. Applicant detailed his extensive involvement in Gamblers Anonymous both as a member and an officer of his local branch. He expressed "extreme sorrow" for the people he harmed in New Jersey and the injury he caused the bar of that state. He believed himself fully rehabilitated from his gambling addiction and hoped to obtain a second chance to be a "productive member of society" by providing assistance to those who "need help in the legal system."

Applicant's efforts to reimburse the clients he defrauded have been minimal. After his release from prison, applicant made some initial efforts to contact Mrs. Cruice and the Maressa law firm, and made several installment payments to the bank that had reimbursed the New Jersey Client Security Fund for his misappropriation of client funds. These ceased when he left the state. The hearing department found applicant had "failed to make a sufficient showing of an inability to make at least partial restitution, or an objectively verifiable effort to make restitution reasonably related to his ability to pay." Applicant stipulated that at the time of the hearing he still owed $121,750 to the Midatlantic Bank, $25,000 to the Maressa law firm, and $95,000 to his former client, Mrs. Cruice. All these debts were discharged by applicant's Chapter 7 bankruptcy petition in 1984, although he affirmed his "intention to make restitution on these debts." It was further stipulated that as of July 1992, applicant still owed the Internal Revenue Service about $535,000 in tax liabilities and penalties.

DISCUSSION

1. Standards on review

"This court may admit to the practice of law any applicant whose qualifications have been certified to it by the Committee of Bar Examiners." (Kwasnik v. State Bar (1990) 50 Cal.3d 1061, 1067, 269 Cal.Rptr. 749, 791 P.2d 319; see Bus. & Prof.Code, § 6064 ["Upon certification by the examining committee that the applicant has fulfilled the requirements for admission to practice law, the Supreme Court may admit such applicant as an attorney at law in all the courts of this State and may direct an order to be entered upon its records to that effect."].) To qualify, an applicant must, among other things, demonstrate he or she is possessed of "good moral character." (Rules Regulating the Admission to Practice Law, rule X, § 1; Bus. & Prof.Code, § 6060, subd. (b); Lubetzky v. State Bar (1991) 54 Cal.3d 308, 312, 285 Cal.Rptr. 268, 815 P.2d 341; Kwasnik v. State Bar, supra, 50 Cal.3d at p. 1067, 269 Cal.Rptr. 749, 791 P.2d 319.)

"Good moral character" has traditionally been defined as the absence of conduct imbued with elements of "moral turpitude." (Hallinan v. Committee of Bar Examiners (1966) 65 Cal.2d 447, 452, 55 Cal.Rptr. 228, 421 P.2d 76; Hightower v. State Bar (1983) 34 Cal.3d 150, 157, 193 Cal.Rptr. 153, 666 P.2d 10.) It includes "qualities of honesty, fairness, candor, trustworthiness, observance of fiduciary responsibility, respect for and obedience to the laws of the state and the nation and respect for the rights of others and for the judicial process." (Rules Regulating the Admission to Practice Law, rule X, § 1; Kwasnik v. State Bar, supra, 50 Cal.3d at p. 1067, 269 Cal.Rptr. 749, 791 P.2d 319; Pacheco v. State Bar (1987) 43 Cal.3d 1041, 1046, 239 Cal.Rptr. 897, 741 P.2d 1138.)

In a moral character proceeding, the applicant must first establish a prima facie case that he or she possesses good moral character; the State Bar may then rebut that showing with evidence of bad moral character. If it does so, the burden then shifts back to the applicant to demonstrate his or her rehabilitation. (Lubetzky v. State Bar, supra, 54 Cal.3d at p. 312, 285 Cal.Rptr. 268, 815 P.2d 341; Hallinan v. Committee of Bar Examiners, supra, 65 Cal.2d at pp. 449-451, fn. 1, 55 Cal.Rptr. 228, 421 P.2d 76.) Although we give "great weight" to the findings of the hearing panel on review, they are not binding on this court. "We examine the evidence and make our own determination as to its sufficiency . . . ." (Hightower v. State Bar, supra, 34 Cal.3d at pp. 155-156, 193 Cal.Rptr. 153, 666 P.2d 10; see also Lubetzky v. State Bar, supra, 54 Cal.3d at p. 312, 285 Cal.Rptr. 268, 815 P.2d 341.)

2. The evidence does not warrant admission

It is generally undisputed applicant established through extensive testimony and numerous written testimonials—including a number of California attorneys—a prima facie case he currently possesses good moral character. (See Lubetzky v. State Bar, supra, 54 Cal.3d at p. 315, fn. 3, 285 Cal.Rptr. 268, 815 P.2d 341 ["Our decisions in admission cases accord 'significant weight' in making a prima facie case to testimonials from attorneys on an applicant's behalf."].) It is also undisputed the Committee effectively rebutted applicant's showing through uncontested proof of his previous professional misconduct, criminal convictions, and permanent disbarment from the practice of law in New Jersey. The issue thus resolves to the sufficiency of his showing of rehabilitation.

As Chief Justice Lucas has observed, "The amount of evidence of rehabilitation required to justify admission varies according to the seriousness of the misconduct at issue." (Kwasnik v. State Bar, supra, 50 Cal.3d 1061, 1086, 269 Cal.Rptr. 749, 791 P.2d 319 (dis. opn. of Lucas, C.J.).) Indeed, in light of the seriousness of applicant's prior misconduct, the review department here noted that he "had a very high hill to climb in proving his rehabilitation." Specifically, it observed "[applicant's] heavy indebtedness was due to prior, extremely serious, criminal misconduct in the practice of law, injuring his clients and others because of his gambling addiction. Also, . . . it was not the result of an isolated incident, but [of] repeated criminal acts over a period in excess of three years." As summarized previously, applicant engaged in a protracted course of wilful misconduct during which time he misappropriated the trust funds of 19 separate clients, abused his fiduciary trust in obtaining a large loan from an elderly client, attempted to manufacture methamphetamine to offset his mounting indebtedness, and wilfully failed to file a New Jersey state income tax return. He pled guilty to four felony counts, served time in prison and a halfway house, and was disbarred from the practice of law there. By his own admission he is permanently barred from applying for readmission in New Jersey. In addition, applicant still owes $25,000 to his former law firm, $95,000 to Mrs. Cruice, over $120,000 to the bank that reimbursed the New Jersey Client Security Fund, and more than $535,000 to the Internal Revenue Service in tax liabilities and penalties.

As evidence of his rehabilitation, applicant submitted substantial evidence his previous misconduct resulted from a gambling addiction he has successfully overcome. The undisputed evidence that applicant has not gambled since 1982 and has participated regularly as a member and officer of Gamblers Anonymous since 1983, the laudatory testimonials from numerous friends and fellow members of Gamblers Anonymous attesting to his full recovery, and the expert testimony of two of his treating psychologists amply support the conclusion applicant has recovered from his compulsive gambling. As we have observed, "An alcoholic's rehabilitation is almost universally predicated on a choice to confront his or her problem, followed by abstinence sustained through ongoing participation in a supportive program, such as Alcoholics Anonymous." (In re Billings (1990) 50 Cal.3d 358, 368, 267 Cal.Rptr. 319, 787 P.2d 617.)

We have also long recognized that testimonials from acquaintances, friends and employers with reference to their observation of the daily conduct of an attorney who has been disbarred are entitled to "great weight." (Hippard v. State Bar, supra, 49 Cal.3d at p. 1095, 264 Cal.Rptr. 684, 782 P.2d 1140; see also Petition of Gaffney (1946) 28 Cal.2d 761, 764, 171 P.2d 873.) We give particular credence to such statements by attorneys, based on the notion that such persons "possess a [keen] sense of responsibility for the integrity of the legal profession." (Warbasse v. The State Bar (1933) 219 Cal. 566, 571, 28 P.2d 19; see also Pacheco v. State Bar, supra, 43 Cal.3d at p. 1053, 239 Cal.Rptr. 897, 741 P.2d 1138; Lubetzky v. State Bar, supra, 54 Cal.3d at p. 315, fn. 3, 285 Cal.Rptr. 268, 815 P.2d 341; Kwasnik v. State Bar, supra, 50 Cal.3d at p. 1068, 269 Cal.Rptr. 749, 791 P.2d 319.) Applicant presented over 25 letters from attorneys, friends, and fellow employees, as well as the testimony of 4 California attorneys. Despite knowing of his previous misdeeds, all attested to his good moral character, honesty, and responsibility and recommended his admission to the bar.

Although the evidence of applicant's recovery from compulsive gambling is substantial and the testimonials on his behalf are impressive, we are nevertheless not persuaded he has demonstrated his overall rehabilitation by clear and convincing evidence. While undoubtedly relevant, "character testimony, however laudatory" does not alone establish the "requisite rehabilitation." (In re Petty (1981) 29 Cal.3d 356, 362, 173 Cal.Rptr. 461, 627 P.2d 191; see also Seide v. Committee of Bar Examiners, supra, 49 Cal.3d at p. 939, 264 Cal.Rptr. 361, 782 P.2d 602.) Nor, when weighed against the enormity of his previous misconduct, does applicant's apparent recovery from a gambling addiction necessarily justify his admission.

We have long held in reinstatement cases that " 'the evidence of present character must be considered in the light of the moral shortcomings which resulted in the imposition of discipline.' " (Tardiff v. State Bar (1980) 27 Cal.3d 395, 403, 165 Cal.Rptr. 829, 612 P.2d 919, quoting Roth v. State Bar (1953) 40 Cal.2d 307, 313, 253 P.2d 969; see also Kwasnik v. State Bar, supra, 50 Cal.3d 1061, 1086, 269 Cal.Rptr. 749, 791 P.2d 319 (dis. opn. of Lucas, C.J.).) Applicant's repeated thefts of client funds over several years represent "a continuing course of serious professional misconduct." (Tomlinson v. State Bar (1975) 13 Cal.3d 567, 576, 119 Cal.Rptr. 335, 531 P.2d 1119.) He violated " 'the fundamental rule of [legal] ethics—that of common honesty—without which the profession is worse than valueless in the place it holds in the administration of justice . . . .' " (Rhodes v. State Bar (1989) 49 Cal.3d 50, 60, 260 Cal.Rptr. 266, 775 P.2d 1035.) His conviction for manufacturing methamphetamine involved an act of moral turpitude, which alone has been held to be sufficient to deny admission to the bar (Seide v. Committee of Bar Examiners, supra, 49 Cal.3d 933, 264 Cal.Rptr. 361, 782 P.2d 602); and his wilful failure to file an income tax return evinces a disrespect for law that further refutes his fitness to practice. (In re Rohan (1978) 21 Cal.3d 195, 203-204, 145 Cal.Rptr. 855, 578 P.2d 102.)

Applicant's previous misconduct was sufficiently egregious to warrant the ultimate sanction of his permanent disbarment in New Jersey. It is not unreasonable, therefore, to require a truly compelling demonstration of moral rehabilitation as a condition of his admission to the bar of this state, i.e., " 'overwhelming [] proof of reform . . . which we could with confidence lay before the world in justification of a judgment again installing him in the profession . . . .'" (Feinstein v. State Bar (1952) 39 Cal.2d 541, 547, 248 P.2d 3, quoting In re Morganstern (1927) 85 Cal.App. 113, 117, 259 P. 90.) The record evidence does not satisfy this standard.

In our judgment, such "overwhelming" proof must include at a minimum a lengthy period of not only unblemished, but exemplary conduct. The State Bar Court credited applicant with nine years of good conduct, measured from his last act of misconduct in 1983 to the time of his hearing in 1992. However, he was in prison and a halfway house for a portion of that time and did not successfully complete his parole until the spring of 1987. Good conduct is normally demanded of a prisoner and a parolee. (See Seide v. Committee of Bar Examiners, supra, 49 Cal.3d at p. 939, 264 Cal.Rptr. 361, 782 P.2d 602 ["It is not enough that petitioner kept out of trouble while being watched on probation; he must affirmatively demonstrate over a prolonged period his sincere regret and rehabilitation."]; In re Giddens (1981) 30 Cal.3d 110, 116, 177 Cal.Rptr. 673, 635 P.2d 166 [requiring further proof of rehabilitation "during a period when petitioner is neither on parole . . . nor under supervision of the bar."].) Considering that applicant's compulsive gambling began in 1978, shortly after his admission to the New Jersey bar, and that he engaged in a continuous course of professional and criminal misconduct for a period of five years ending only with his arrest in 1983, his five and one-half years of unsupervised good conduct is not a sufficient period of time to demonstrate genuine reform. (See Seide v. Committee of Bar Examiners, supra, 49 Cal.3d at p. 939, 264 Cal.Rptr. 361, 782 P.2d 602.)

Nor, in our view, does the record show applicant has engaged in truly exemplary conduct in the sense of returning something to the community he betrayed. Applicant's participation in Gamblers Anonymous and his efforts to help others deal with their addiction is commendable, even if somewhat mitigated by the personal benefit of helping to maintain his own recovery. More significantly, he has made almost no "effort to aid those upon whom he specifically preyed" (Seide v. Committee of Bar Examiners, supra, 49 Cal.3d at p. 941, fn. 6, 264 Cal.Rptr. 361, 782 P.2d 602), namely, the individuals and institutions whose monies (totaling over $270,000) he stole and whose trust he violated. He contacted Mrs. Cruice and the Maressa law firm after his release from prison, but never arranged for repayment. He made a number of installment payments to the Midatlantic Bank of New Jersey (in an unknown amount); however, these ceased when his construction company went out of business in 1988. Based on the record, the hearing department concluded applicant had "failed to make a sufficient factual showing of an inability to make at least partial restitution, or an objectively verifiable effort to make restitution reasonably related to his ability to pay."

While restitution "is not necessarily determinative of whether rehabilitation has been proven," it is a legitimate and substantial factor to be considered "in the overall factual showing made by the individual seeking reinstatement." (Hippard v. State Bar, supra, 49 Cal.3d at p. 1093, 264 Cal.Rptr. 684, 782 P.2d 1140 [denying application for reinstatement based in part upon petitioner's failure to demonstrate a meaningful attempt to make restitution or an inability to do so].) Notwithstanding the discharge in bankruptcy of applicant's debts resulting from his misappropriation of client funds, we may properly consider the relative absence of any serious effort to make even partial restitution "as an indicator of rehabilitation." (Id. at p. 1094, 264 Cal.Rptr. 684, 782 P.2d 1140; Kwasnik v. State Bar, supra, 50 Cal.3d at p. 1072, 269 Cal.Rptr. 749, 791 P.2d 319.) Furthermore, applicant stipulated that although they were discharged in bankruptcy, "it is his intention to make restitution on these debts." Actions speak louder than words. Sustained exemplary conduct must include proof applicant is making amends to the victims and the community he harmed.

Finally, applicant presented substantial evidence of his genuine remorse for the harm he caused his former clients and law firm and the disrepute he brought on the legal community in which he practiced. Applicant testified he hoped to become a "productive member of society" again and provide assistance to those who "need help in the legal system." The hearing department found he testified in this regard "with notable credibility and sincerity." We do not question the hearing department's finding or the genuineness of applicant's sincerity. However, "[r]emorse does not demonstrate rehabilitation . . . . In our view, a truer indication of rehabilitation will be presented if petitioner can demonstrate by his sustained conduct over an extended period of time that he is once again fit to practice law . . . ." (In re Conflenti (1981) 29 Cal.3d 120, 124-125, 172 Cal.Rptr. 203, 624 P.2d 253; accord, In re Schwartz (1982) 31 Cal.3d 395, 401, 182 Cal.Rptr. 640, 644 P.2d 833.) If applicant is committed to assisting those who "need help in the legal system," opportunities are available such as providing pro bono or volunteer work as well as other nonlegal means of contributing as a "productive member of society."

CONCLUSION

In seeking admission to practice law in this state, applicant assumes a most substantial burden on the question of his moral fitness. Although we do not disregard his recovery from compulsive gambling and the absence of further criminal conduct, the fact remains he has paid very little, monetary or otherwise, on his debt to his victims and to society for the acts of moral turpitude committed while a member of the New Jersey bar. In light of the extremely serious nature of his prior misconduct and discipline as well as his failure to make meaningful restitution to his many victims, we cannot conclude he has established the requisite good moral character.

We therefore reject the recommendation of the State Bar Court and decline to admit applicant to the practice of law.

Notes

1. For a further discussion of the events leading up to the trial and conviction of Edwin and Stephen Edwards, *see* Tyler Bridges, *Bad Bet on the Bayou: The Rise of Gambling in Louisiana and the Fall of Governor Edwin Edwards* (2001). The orders of the Louisiana Supreme Court suspending the pair's law licenses can be found at *In re Edwin W. Edwards*, 765 So. 2d 326 (La. 2000), and *In re Stephen R. Edwards*, 765 So. 327 (La. 2000).

2. If you had been on the California Supreme Court, would you have voted to admit Joseph Menna? Why or why not? For other cases involving lawyers with gambling disorders, *see, e.g.*, *In re Dovolis*, 572 N.W.2d 734 (Minn. 1998); *In re Goldberg*, 536 A.2d 224 (N.J. 1988); *In re Lobbe*, 660 A.2d 410 (D.C. 1995); *Matter of Nitti*, 541 A.2d 217 (N.J. 1988); *In re Olsen*, 487 N.W. 871 (Minn. 1992); *In re Kadish*, 746 N.Y.S.2d 503 (App. Div. 2002); *In re Petilla*, 4 Cal. St. B. Ct. Rptr. 231 (2001). *See also* William Leary, *Gambling: The Hidden Illness of the 1990s*, 47 R.I. B.J. 19 (Apr. 1999) (reporting on the increasing number of calls from gambling-addicted attorneys being fielded by Lawyers Assistance Programs).

3. The intersection between gaming and legal ethics is analyzed further in Stephanie A. Martz, Note, *Legalized Gambling and Public Corruption: Remove the Incentive to Act Corruptly, or, Teaching an Old Dog New Tricks*, 13 J.L. & Pol. 453 (1997), and Richard Morgan & Bob Faiss, Legal Ethics and the Gaming Lawyer (paper presented at the University of Nevada Las Vegas's Gaming Law Masters Forum on April 5, 2001).

Problem 2

When a court ruled their stock offering violated federal securities laws, the promoters of a planned Indian casino were forced to refund millions of dollars. To recoup their losses, they filed a malpractice action against the attorneys that advised them. At trial, should the law firm be held to the standard of care applicable to general practitioners or specialists? *See Day v. Dorsey & Whitney*, 21 Fed. App. 530 (8th Cir. 2001).

Chapter 2

STATE-SPONSORED GAMING

A. OVERVIEW

At one time, public and private lotteries flourished in the United States. But after the Civil War, they fell into disfavor, and by 1878 had been outlawed in every jurisdiction except Louisiana. When Congress subsequently banned the interstate transportation of lottery materials, America's experiment with lotteries was at an end.

In 1964, however, New Hampshire reintroduced its lottery (originally called a "sweepstakes" to get around federal mailing prohibitions). New York (1967) and New Jersey (1970) quickly followed with their own games, and by 1974 11 lotteries were in operation. Today, 39 states and the District of Columbia have lotteries, and annual ticket sales are estimated at $39 billion. It is thought that 72% of Americans play at least once a year, with 28% doing so regularly. In contrast, privately-run lotteries generally remain illegal.

B. ELEMENTS

GLICK v. MTV NETWORKS, A DIVISION OF VIACOM INTERNATIONAL INC.
796 F. Supp. 743 (S.D.N.Y. 1992)

DUFFY, District Judge.

Plaintiff Barry Glick commenced this civil action against defendant MTV Networks ("MTVN") in the Superior Court of New Jersey on May 7, 1990. On June 4, 1990, the matter was removed on the basis of diversity jurisdiction to the United States District Court for the District of New Jersey. MTVN moved to dismiss the complaint pursuant to Fed.R.Civ.P. 12(b)(6), or, in the alternative, to transfer the action to the Southern District of New York, pursuant to 28 U.S.C. 1404(a). Glick cross-moved for partial summary judgment and opposed the transfer. By opinion filed February 25, 1991, the action was transferred to the Southern District of New York.

The facts are not in dispute. MTVN is a division of Viacom International Inc., a corporation engaged in various entertainment and communications businesses. MTVN offers several different programming networks, or channels. From August 12 through October 11, 1989, one of those channels, known as VH-1, sponsored a national promotional event in order to increase viewership. That event, a sweepstakes called the "VH-1 Corvette Collection" (the "Sweepstakes"), is the subject of this litigation.

The Sweepstakes was publicized over MTVN channels, through the media and through publicity events conducted nationwide. Over 20,000 prizes, including inexpensive watches, T-shirts, hats and key chains, were awarded daily during the Sweepstakes. The grand prize was a choice of either a collection of 36 Corvette automobiles, one from each model year from 1953 to 1989, or a 1989 Corvette plus $200,000 in cash. There were three different ways of entering the Sweepstakes. Participants could: (1) call a "900" number, for which there was a $2.00 charge; (2) request a toll-free "800" number by mail; or, (3) complete and mail in an official entry blank.

Whichever way they entered, participants could enter as often as they wished, were eligible for daily prizes, and had an equal chance of winning. Over one million people entered the Sweepstakes: 136,506 by way of the mail-in entry blank, 30,094 by dialing the "800" number, and 1,065,624 by calling the "900" number. Bonus prizes were awarded daily by random selection throughout the Sweepstakes. On October 14, 1989, the grand prize winner was selected at random by an independent organization. The winner opted for the collection of 36 Corvettes.

DISCUSSION

Glick argues that the Sweepstakes was a lottery in violation of New Jersey law. The code defines "lottery" to mean:

> an unlawful gambling scheme in which (a) the players pay or agree to pay something of value for chances, represented and differentiated by numbers or by combinations of numbers or by some other media, one or more of which chances are to be designated the winning ones; and (b) the winning chances are to be determined by a drawing or by some other method based upon the element of chance; and (c) the holders of the winning chances are to receive something of value.

N.J.S.A. 2C:37-1(h).

The current statutory definition "lottery" requires that "something of value" be risked. The criminal code defines the term "something of value" to mean:

> any money or property, any token, object or article exchangeable for money or property, or any form of credit or promise directly or indirectly contemplating transfer of money or property or of any interest therein, or involving extension of a service, entertainment or a privilege of playing at a game or scheme without charge.

N.J.S.A. 2C:37-1(d).

For purposes of its motion, MTVN concedes that its Sweepstakes was a game of chance in which the winners were entitled to prizes. It maintains, however, that because the participants in the Sweepstakes were not required to give "something of value" (i.e., price) to enter, the Sweepstakes was not a lottery.

The Sweepstakes' official rules did not require that participants risk "something of value" because alternative cost-free means of entry were reasonably available. One or both of the cost-free methods of entry were publicized in the promotional spots aired several times a day over MTVN channels, in the advertisements MTVN took out in national magazines, through coverage of the Sweepstakes in newspapers and magazines, and on the free entry blanks distributed through stores and at promotional events. Further, the official rules explicitly stated that no purchase was necessary to enter and that all those who entered had an equal chance of winning. Finally, as many as 166,600 people entered the contest through the "800" number or by entry blank.

Glick argues that while MTVN may technically have provided alternative means of entering the Sweepstakes, it carefully crafted its promotion so that most entries would come through the "900" number. That approximately 87 per cent of the participants utilized the "900" number, Glick maintains, evidences the success of MTVN's promotional slant. Glick further states that, in late September, 1989, he mailed separate requests for a copy of the rules and for the toll-free "800" number. His request for the toll free number was never honored, and he received a copy of the rules only after the contest was over. Affidavit of Barry Glick dated 1/14/91. From these facts, Glick concludes that the "alternate means of entry, while facially supporting an argument that the contest was 'free' did, in fact, either require a participant to give something of value or subjected the participant utilizing the alternate means with a disadvantaged opportunity to win." Plaintiff's Brief at 18.

The record does not support Glick's contentions. Participants had two months in which to enter the Sweepstakes. Thus, the only people conceivably disadvantaged by utilizing either the "800" number or the mail-in entry forms were those who, having heard about the Sweepstakes in its last days, were not able to meet the October 3 deadline for requesting the "800" number or not able to mail in their entry blank by October 11. In an extensively publicized sweepstakes lasting two months, such a class of people simply are statistically insignificant. More importantly, as all those who entered had an equal chance of winning, there was no risk that certain entrants would secure a more favorable position than others.

In sum, Glick has failed to establish the "something of value," or price, element necessary to his claim. While certainly not determinative, that the State chose not to prosecute Viacom or MTVN supports this belief.

For the foregoing reasons, MTVN's motion for summary judgment dismissing the complaint is granted, and Glick's cross-motion for partial summary judgment is denied.

VALENTIN v. EL DIARIO LA PRENSA
427 N.Y.S.2d 185 (N.Y.C. Civ. Ct. 1980)

BLATT, Judge.

The defendant newspaper herein sponsored a voting contest late in 1979 to determine which of many entrants would be voted the "King of the Infants" or "Rey Infantil." The newspaper is published in the Spanish language and primarily services the Hispanic community of New York City.

Purchasers of the paper at a newsstand cost of twenty-five (25 cents) cents receive a coupon in each edition which entitles them to vote for the infant of their preference, and to cast twenty-five votes for each coupon they obtain from the paper. They may vote as many coupons as they purchase. In addition, individuals may go to the offices of the newspaper on Hudson Street in Manhattan and purchase individual pages of the newspaper containing the coupon at a cost of seventeen (17 cents) cents. This admittedly was for the purpose of allowing those who did not want to purchase the newspaper in its entirety and whose motivation was merely to obtain extra ballots to vote for their favorite infant. Oral testimony at the trial indicated that large numbers of people came in to purchase quantities of single pages containing the voting coupon.

It is clear that this was a most successful promotion. Defendant displayed a thick sheaf of invoices indicating those who had come in to purchase quantities of single pages containing the coupon with which to cast large quantities of votes for their favorite entrant.

Claimant came into defendant's offices on Hudson Street during business hours on December 11, 1979 and paid One Thousand ($1,000.00) Dollars for single newspaper sheets containing voting coupons. She then subsequently proceeded to vote them all for her son. On that same evening the contest closed.

The following day, claimant came back to the offices of the newspaper and demanded her money back. This was refused and she commenced this action to recoup her One Thousand ($1,000.00) Dollars. Subsequently, her son won a runner up prize of Five Hundred ($500.00) Dollars, which is allegedly being held by the newspaper.

The complaint alleges a refusal to return the money after cancellation. The Court asked for a memorandum of law on defendant's position and on the question of public policy. Defendant's Memorandum of Law contends that the contest as described herein is not a lottery and therefore not against the public policy of the State of New York. It is described as a "voting contest" with no element of chance, and only a mathematical calculation utilized to determine the winner. Cases are cited primarily from sister states, none of which are on all fours with the matter at hand.

Defendant also contends that the prize herein was to go to a contestant, not to a voter and that therefore it cannot be a lottery. They additionally claim that the infant winners furnish no consideration for the prize and that since one of the elements of a lottery is consideration paid by the winner for a "chance", that this cannot therefore be a lottery. Commonwealth v. Jenkins, 159 Ky. 80, 166 S.W. 794 (1914).

The definition of a lottery in New York State is set forth in a number of cases including People v. Miller, 271 N.Y. 44, 2 N.E.2d 38 (1936). It indicates that there are three elements necessary to constitute a lottery: 1) consideration; 2) chance; and 3) a prize.

Defendants basically contend that the two elements of consideration and chance were not present, and that therefore, the "voting contest" herein could not be constituted as a lottery.

It is not always crystal clear as to whether or not the element of chance is present. It has been held in our courts that "a business promotion scheme is not a lottery because of the motive for the scheme." On the other hand, if prizes are awarded, and chance determines the winner, a business promotion scheme will be held to be a lottery where, regardless of the subtlety of the device employed, it can be shown as a matter of fact that the scheme in actual operation results in payment, in the great majority of cases of something of value for the opportunity to participate. People v. Psallis, 12 N.Y.S.2d 796.

For another example, see People ex rel Ellison v. Lavin, 179 N.Y. 164, 71 N.E. 753. In that case it was held that "a contest to guess the number of cigars on which the United States would collect taxes during the month of November, 1903, was a lottery, where entrants were required to submit cigar bands to qualify, because chance rather than judgment was the dominating factor in the award of prizes."

There is something clearly analogous in the matter at hand. The critical factor herein is the ability of the public to purchase individual newspaper sheets with the coupon thereon for the price of seventeen (17 cents) cents and thereupon "vote" their choice. Logic forces us to conclude that this opportunity to buy single voting coupons in demonstrated large quantities was not in order to vote for "King of the Infants" in an objective sense, but rather in a race prior to deadline to see who could buy the greatest number of votes for their loved one regardless of the contestant's "regal" attributes.

The Court feels that the language in part of the last cited case applies: "chance rather than judgment was the dominating factor in the award of prizes." The chance was in purchasing and voting more coupons than others. The single sheets provided the opportunity.

Although the complaint asked for cancellation of the contract and did not plead illegality, this does not divest the court of that right when the agreement is antagonistic to the interests of the public. Klein v. D. R. Comenzo Co., 207 N.Y.S.2d 739.

Defendant had raised the factor of consideration in that they contend that the real winner was the infant who was not a financial participant in the event, and that he did not vote, but did receive the financial award.

Certainly the infant herein does not have the legal capacity to handle the funds. The parents or parent will have custody of the funds. The infant cannot indorse a check or understand the meaning of money. Therefore, the argument that the element of consideration is lacking is a specious one at best. Consideration for the chance was clearly present in the purchase of the coupons.

The winners are not chosen on their personal qualities, but rather on whether or not their loved ones can get together enough money to beat the competition in buying sufficient seventeen (17 cents) cent coupons. Here also chance rather than judgment was the dominating factor. People ex rel Ellison v. Lavin (supra).

Upon all of the above, the Court finds that the sale of voting coupons as described herein is void as against public policy.

Judgment in the amount of $1,000.00 is awarded to the claimant. Since the alleged contest herein has been declared void as against public policy, the award of a prize is nullified.

McKEE v. FOSTER
347 P.2d 585 (Or. 1959)

ROSSMAN, Justice.

This is an appeal by the state from a decree entered by the circuit court in a cause which the plaintiff, Marshall McKee, instituted against the District Attorney of Polk County, Mr. Walter Foster, and the Attorney General of this state, Mr. Robert Y. Thornton, for the purpose of securing a declaratory decree determining whether or not free play pinball machines are gambling devices.

ORS 167.535 apparently does not prohibit pinball machines which give free plays if no coin or token is dispensed by the machine. [It] outlaws only coin operated machines from which "there may be received" some tangible object which "May be deposited in such machine" for a replay. Although "credit or other representative of value or evidence of winning" are among the prohibited class of objects which "May be deposited" in the machine for a replay, we must conclude, if we construe words in their normal sense, that these things must be of a tactile, tangible character; that is, they must be of a sufficiently corporal nature so that they may be physically "deposited" in the machine.

Notwithstanding the fact that the single assignment of error is based exclusively upon ORS 167.535, the appellants make the following request in their brief:

> If the court should determine that ORS 167.535 does not prohibit free-play pinball machines, then it should enter judgment that such machines are prohibited by ORS 167.405 or 167.505.

Even though the parties "agreed that the applicable statute to be interpreted is 167.535," as the findings of fact state, we will go on and determine whether or not any of the other sections of our laws which the defendants cite, apart from ORS 167.535, outlaw the plaintiff's machines. The sections which the defendants cite are Article XV, section 4, Constitution of Oregon; ORS 161.310, 167.405 and 167.505.

Article XV, section 4 of the state's constitution, follows:

> Lotteries, and the sale of Lottery tickets, for any purpose whatever, are prohibited, and the Legislative Assembly shall prevent the same by penal laws.

The defendants render it clear that in their belief ORS 167.535 and none of the other enactments is applicable to pinball games. Their brief, referring to the specially concurring opinion which Mr. Justice Bailey filed in State v. Coats, 158 Or. 122, 74 P.2d 1102, 1119, says:

> Justice Bailey's reasoning, we believe, is clear. Because it represents the view we urge here, we will have occasion to comment more fully on Justice Bailey's view later.

In his specially concurring opinion Justice Bailey stated:

> If we are to pursue the intention of the Legislature in the instant case, we must conclude that it was intended that any one guilty of the crime with which the defendant is charged must be prosecuted

under the provisions of section 14-746, supra. It surely was not the intention of the Legislature that the defendant could be prosecuted under both the lottery act and the nickel-in-the-slot machine statute, or that of numerous offenders guilty of similar acts some might be prosecuted under a statute making the violation thereof a felony, while others could be charged with the violation of some other statute making the crime charged a misdemeanor.

Section 14-746, Oregon Code 1930, cited in the language just quoted, as subsequently amended, is now ORS 167.535. There are two cases which are entitled State v. Coats, 158 Or. 102, 74 P.2d 1120, and State v. Coats, 158 Or. 122, 74 P.2d 1102. According to 158 Or. 102, at page 103, 74 P.2d 1120, the facts in that case "are identical with those in the pinball machine case (State v. Coats) this day held to constitute a lottery." Those words and a re-examination of the record in our clerk's office seem to indicate that both charges were based upon a single machine possessed by Coats, but it may be that he had more than one machine and we will so assume. The patron of Coats' machine or machines, upon inserting a nickel in the device and pulling a lever, set the machine in operation. If chance favored him he could win as much as ten nickels which the machine paid out to him automatically. We see from those facts that the device which was the subject matter of the Coats decision was a pay-off machine. It granted no replays. In the first of the two cases (158 Or. 102, 74 P.2d 1120) the information filed against the accused mentioned no section of our laws, but the opinion stated:

> we assume from the briefs that the charge was brought under section 14-746, Oregon Code 1930, prohibiting the operation of nickel-in-the-slot machines.

In the other Coats case (158 Or. 122, 74 P.2d 1102, 1103) the information, referring to the defendant, stated that he "wrongfully, unlawfully and feloniously promote[d] and set up a certain lottery for money" by operating the machine. Each information was challenged by demurrer which the circuit court sustained. In each of the two decisions the majority opinion of this court, written by Mr. Justice Belt, held that the circuit court erred when it sustained the demurrer. The majority opinion ruled that each information charged the defendant with the operation of a lottery.

The decisions in the two cases of State v. Coats recognized that the term "lottery" has no technical or established legal meaning. They held that the essential elements of a lottery are prize, chance and consideration. Neither of the prevailing opinions undertook to define the word "prize." As we have said, Coats' machine issued to the winner as a prize as much as ten nickels. Section 14-801, Oregon Code, which was in effect when the Coats decisions were written, stated:

> If any person shall promote or set up any lottery for money or other valuable thing, or shall dispose of any property of value, real or personal, by way or means of lottery * * * or suffer the setting up, management, or drawing of any such lottery, or the sale of any lottery tickets, share of a ticket, or any writing, token, or other device purporting or intended to entitle the holder or bearer thereof * * * to

any prize * * * such person, upon conviction thereof shall be punished
* * *.

Section 14-802, Oregon Code, stated:

> If any person shall sell * * * a ticket or share of a ticket in any such
> lottery, or any writing, token, or other device as is mentioned in section
> 14-801, such person, upon conviction thereof, shall be punished * *
> *.

Section 14-803, Oregon Code, repeated much of the phraseology of which
we have just taken note. Those sections, apart from minor alterations in
language, are now ORS 167.405, 167.410 and 167.415.

Although the opinions written by Mr. Justice Belt in the Coats cases did
not define the word "prize" Mr. Justice Bailey, in his specially concurring
opinion of which we have already taken note, set forth a number of definitions
of lottery which indicated that the prize must be greater in value than the
amount hazarded. The majority opinion expressed no disagreement with that
view. It remained silent upon the subject. The machine in the Coats cases
paid to the winner, as we have said, ten times the sum which he deposited
in it when he placed it in operation. In view of that fact the majority may
have felt that since the winner received something of a tangible nature and
of measured worth the situation did not call for a definition of the word "prize."
A free play, on the other hand, is intangible and, in a sense, of immeasurable
value. The manufacturer of the plaintiff's machine assigned the arbitrary
value of a nickel to the replay, but in the market place the replay has no such
value. The replay cannot be sold. It cannot be carried away. It is intangible
in nature and after the mechanics of the replay have been undergone the
replay has disappeared for all time. It may appeal to the gambling instincts
of some and perhaps is the kind of prize which is a "representative of value
or evidence of winning" within the prohibition of ORS 167.535(2)(b). But there
is no reason to believe that State v. Coats contemplates "prize" as including
a free game within its interpretation of the lottery statute.

The lottery statute appears to exclude free games from its coverage. We have
in mind the language of the lottery statute which prohibits promoting or
setting up lotteries for "money or other valuable thing" and then reiterates
that same idea by prohibiting the disposal by lottery of any property of value,
real or personal. It seems clear that it is tangible property which is contemplated by those provisions. They cannot be construed reasonably in any other
way. The words of the lottery statute of which we have just taken notice are
very different from those which we find in ORS 167.535(2), that is "credit or
other representative of value or evidence of winning." Since "lottery" has no
fixed legal definition it was within the province of the legislature, acting under
the constitutional mandate, to provide a reasonable definition of the "prize"
element of a lottery. We believe that the prize must be tangible in nature and
have a value in the market place.

The challenged decree is affirmed.

Notes

1. In *Glick*, the court found that MTV was not operating a lottery because
players could enter for free. But to do so, a person had to request in writing

the 800 number or obtain a blank entry form and mail it in. Because these acts require both time and energy, has consideration been given?

Initially, courts felt that if a person had to do anything to participate—such as visit a store, fill out a coupon, present the winning ticket by a certain deadline, or go to a specific location to claim the prize—consideration existed. *See, e.g., Knox Industries Corporation v. State ex rel. Scanland*, 258 P.2d 910 (Okla. 1953) (to participate in free car drawing, players had to visit defendant's store and winners had to claim their prize at the company's headquarters), and *State v. Dorau*, 198 A. 573 (Conn. 1938) ("Bank Night" run by movie theater required players to sign registration book and winners had to come forward in timely manner). Today, however, courts typically find that such de minimis acts do not constitute consideration. *See, e.g., Pepsi Cola Bottling Company of Luverne, Inc. v. Coca-Cola Bottling Company, Andalusia*, 534 So. 2d 295 (Ala. 1988) (instant cash game not a lottery because no purchase required), and *Albertson's, Inc. v. Hansen*, 600 P.2d 982 (Utah 1979) (fact that customer had to visit defendant's store not sufficient consideration).

2. Businesses that conduct "free" sweepstakes often hint that players who buy something will increase their chances of winning. This tactic became a favorite of magazine subscription promoters, particularly American Family Publishers (best known for spokesman Ed McMahon's letter advising "you may already be a winner") and Publisher's Clearing House (whose Super Bowl Sunday commercials showed its "Prize Patrol" handing a check to a surprised winner). Eventually, the companies were sued by various state attorneys general, Congress passed the Deceptive Mail Prevention and Enforcement Act of 1999, 39 U.S.C. §§ 3001 et seq., and American Family Publishers was forced to file for bankruptcy. *See further Vollmer v. Publishers Clearing House*, 248 F.3d 698 (7th Cir. 2001); *In re American Family Enterprises*, 256 B.R. 377 (D.N.J. 2000); Julie S. James, Comment, *Regulating the Sweepstakes Industry: Are Consumers Close to Winning?*, 41 Santa Clara L. Rev. 581 (2001).

3. In *Valentin*, there was no way to play for free—one either had to buy a newspaper for 25 cents or go to the publisher's office and pay 17 cents for a coupon sheet. Given this fact, the defendant was forced to argue that its game was a "voting contest" that did not involve chance. Of course, the court rejected this contention.

Games can involve chance, skill, or a combination of the two. If a player can increase the odds of winning by becoming more proficient (such as through hours of practice), the game is probably one of skill rather than chance. Of course, even the most accomplished player cannot control every detail, and a certain amount of luck enters into any contest. Indeed, there would be very little incentive to play (or watch others play) a game where the outcome was predetermined.

In distinguishing between games of chance and skill, courts have formulated two different tests. Under the "English rule," a game is one of chance only if chance entirely controls the outcome. The "American rule," in contrast, considers a game one of chance if the outcome is predominantly determined by chance. *See further Johnson v. Collins Entertainment Company*, 508 S.E.2d 575 (S.C. 1998) (collecting cases).

4. In *McKee*, the court concluded that free plays did not constitute prizes because they had no "market value" and could not be "carried away" by the winner. Are you persuaded by these arguments? Of course, the game's manufacturer thought free plays were worth a nickel.

The court also found that because the machine cost five cents, a free play meant a winner merely got back his or her original wager. Given that people typically hope to do better than "break even," the court felt there was no prize. Yet if a person deposits a nickel and wins a free play, he or she gets two plays for the price of one. As a result, the cost of each game is reduced from five cents to 2.5 cents. Looked at in this way, has the player merely broken even?

Of course, some individuals will decline the free play (due to boredom, the need to leave, or by failing to realize they have won). Is the value of the free play affected by such possibilities? Alternatively, what if a person gives the free play to a friend (or perhaps a total stranger)? Aren't both now enriched— the player who suddenly has something to give and the recipient who gets something for nothing? For a further discussion, *see Trinkle v. Stroh*, 70 Cal. Rptr. 2d 661 (Ct. App. 1997) (upholding statute that specifically defined "anything of value" as including free play).

5. Is the stock market a lottery? Suppose an investor decides to buy 100 shares of stock. Even if she has carefully studied the market, isn't the outcome determined in large part by chance? As such, aren't all the elements necessary for a lottery in place: consideration (the price paid for the stock), chance (the stock may go up or down), and prize (if the stock goes up, the investor wins)? *See Rohrer v. Traina*, 342 N.E.2d 390 (Ill. App. Ct. 1976) (futures contract with no intent to deliver but merely speculate on the price is an illegal gaming contract), and *McDaniel v. Tullis, Craig & Company*, 11 S.W.2d 203 (Tex. Civ. App. 1928) (same). For a further discussion, *see* Lynn A. Stout, *Are Stock Markets Costly Casinos? Disagreement, Market Failure, and Securities Regulation*, 81 Va. L. Rev. 611 (1995).

6. Since 1985, the National Basketball Association has conducted a lottery to award the top picks in its college draft:

> This process was implemented to prevent teams with a chance to finish with the worst record from dumping games to insure the first pick in the draft. The lottery system had assigned ping pong balls to the seven worst teams, with the worst team getting the most balls. The balls were then placed in a blowdrum and the order that they "popped out" of the blowdrum became the drafting order. Today, with expansion and heightened fan interest in the game, the process has become more complex. Now fourteen balls, numbered 1 through 14, are placed in a blowdrum. By randomly pulling out four balls at a time, there are 1,001 possible combinations. Each team in the draft lottery is allotted a certain number of those combinations, based on their regular season finish. Four balls are drawn to see who gets the No. 1 pick by having the correct four-ball combination. All 14 balls are then returned to the blowdrum and the process is repeated twice, thus determining which teams will have the first three picks in the draft. The remaining teams simply are assigned picks 4-13, in reverse order of regular-season finish.

John C. Graves, *Controlling Athletes with the Draft and the Salary Cap: Are Both Necessary?*, 5 Sports Law. J. 185, 187-88 (1998). In 1995, the National Hockey League also began holding a draft lottery. Are the NBA and NHL acting illegally?

7. Not all lotteries carry a desirable prize. In her celebrated short story "The Lottery," which first appeared in *The New Yorker* on June 28, 1948, Shirley Jackson described a mythical New England town that held a lottery in the village square each June. The "winner" is stoned to death by the rest of the citizens in a rite designed to purify the community and ensure a good harvest. Of course, it is not until the end of the story that the lottery's true purpose is revealed to the reader.

In real life, there have been a number of lotteries in which winning actually has meant losing. In the famous English case of *Regina v. Dudley and Stephens*, 14 Q.B.D. 273 (1884), three sailors stranded in a lifeboat far out at sea, with little hope of rescue and their food gone, picked lots to decide who would be sacrificed (according to some versions, however, the men did not choose lots but simply killed the weakest crew member). Likewise, the United States often has conducted a lottery to determine who will be forced to fight. During the Viet Nam war, this practice led to an interesting lawsuit:

> In November 1969, a national lottery was held to determine the order in which young men would be drafted into the Armed Forces. Clyde Fitch received number 309, which should have guaranteed that he not be drafted. An error at Local Board 69 in Inez, Kentucky resulted in transcription of his number as 132. Eligible men with this number were inducted. Clyde Fitch received his induction notice and, after losing an appeal based on his wife's pregnancy and financial hardship, he reported for active duty on July 13, 1970. While stationed in Viet Nam, on July 9, 1971, Fitch was informed by an Army sergeant that his induction had been a mistake because of the erroneous assignment of his lottery number. Three months later he was discharged from active duty.

> The District Court held that the erroneous assignment of Fitch's lottery number established the United States' liability under the Federal Tort Claims Act, 28 U.S.C. § 2674. It assessed $11,661 in damages representing lost wages. It also held that Appellees had established "a right to punitive damages and such damages are assessed at $20,000."

> We agree with the District Court that just as citizen owes Government an obligation to aid in its defense, so Government owes citizen the duty of fair, equitable, and just treatment. While we sympathize with Appellees' plight and cannot condone the negligence which caused Clyde Fitch's induction, we must reverse the award because the District Court acted beyond the authority Congress has given it.

Fitch v. United States, 513 F.2d 1013, 1015 (6th Cir.), *cert. denied*, 423 U.S. 866 (1975).

Problem 3

A company sells three minute phone cards with an attached "scratch and win" game piece for $2.00, making the retail price of its minutes $.66. Other providers typically charge $.45 per minute. Free game pieces can be obtained by sending a self-addressed stamped envelope together with a 3" x 5" card bearing the words "Phone Card 25." Is the company operating a lottery? *See Mississippi Gaming Commission v. Treasured Arts, Inc.*, 699 So. 2d 936 (Miss. 1997).

C. CONSTITUTIONAL BARRIERS

CARROLL v. FIRESTONE
497 So. 2d 1204 (Fla. 1986)

PER CURIAM.

Appellants Todd and People Against Legalized Lotteries, Inc., seek review of a summary judgment that Proposition Five, a proposed initiative amendment to article X of the Florida Constitution, embraces only one subject and matter directly connected therewith and that the ballot summary accompanying the proposed amendment does not contravene section 101.161, Florida Statutes (1985). The First District Court of Appeal certified the judgment as being of great public importance requiring immediate resolution by this Court. We have jurisdiction. Art. V, § 3(b)(5), Fla. Const.

Petitioners Carroll, Little and Mann seek a writ of mandamus directing Respondent Firestone, Secretary of the State of Florida, to remove the proposed amendment from the November 1986 ballot. We have jurisdiction. Art. V, § 3(b)(8), Fla. Const.; Fine v. Firestone, 448 So.2d 984 (Fla.1984).

The proposed amendment was initiated by appellee/respondent Excellence Campaign: An Education Lottery, Inc. (E.X.C.E.L.). There is no question but that the procedural requirements of Florida law were followed and that the requisite number of elector signatures were obtained pursuant to article XI, section 3. Thus, appellee/respondent Firestone is not the real party in interest. The issues raised are of substance for which E.X.C.E.L. is the real party in interest.

Appellants/petitioners urge four grounds in support of their position that the proposed amendment should be removed from the ballot: that it violates the single subject requirement of article XI, section 3; that the ballot summary violates the requirements of section 101.161 and case law; that there was fraud in inducing voters to sign the petition forms; and that the schedule clause of the purposed amendment violates article XI, section 1 of the Florida Constitution. We find no merit in any of these arguments, affirm the judgment below, and deny the petition for writ of mandamus.

The proposed amendment reads as follows:

(a) Lotteries may be operated by the State.

(b) If any subsections of the Amendment of the Florida Constitution are held unconstitutional for containing more than one subject, this Amendment shall be limited to subsection (a) above.

> (c) This Amendment shall be implemented as follows:

> (1) On the effective date of this Amendment, the lotteries shall be known as the Florida Education Lotteries. Net proceeds derived from the lotteries shall be deposited to a state trust fund, to be designated The State Education Lotteries Trust Fund, to be appropriated by the Legislature. The schedule may be amended by general law.

In pertinent part, article XI, section 3 reads:

> The power to propose the revision or amendment of any portion or portions of this constitution by initiative is reserved to the people, provided that, any such revision or amendment shall embrace but one subject and matter directly connected therewith.

The relationship between the three subsections of the proposed amendment determines whether the amendment contains one subject and matter directly connected therewith. Subsection (b) is directly connected with subsections (a) and (c) in that it states, in effect, if subsection (c) is held to contain a different subject than subsection (a), that (c) will be stricken and (a) will stand alone. Petitioners Carroll, et al., suggest that subsection (b) impinges on this Court's constitutional authority to interpret the Constitution and thus amends article V of the Constitution. We think not. Subsection (b) has no force unless we determine that subsections (a) and (c) contain more than one subject. Moreover, while we are charged with the ultimate responsibility for interpreting the Constitution, the intent of the drafters or adopters of a constitutional provision is a highly relevant factor. We see no constitutional infirmity, but much to commend, in a drafter attempting to make clear the intent of a constitutional provision.

The controlling question then becomes whether subsections (a) and (c) contain only one subject and matter directly connected therewith. Subsection (a) identifies a potential revenue source and subsection (c) prescribes a tentative recipient of the revenue. We see no essential distinction between the amendment here and the one we approved in Floridians Against Casino Takeover v. Let's Help Florida, 363 So.2d 337 (Fla.1978). We recognize that in Floridians the taxes on casinos, assuming casinos were authorized and taxed, were committed to a specific purpose while here the revenues if any, are only tentatively committed to a specific fund. We do not consider this distinction significant and hold that subsection (c) contains matter directly connected to the authorization for lotteries, subsection (a).

The ballot summary reads as follows:

> The Amendment authorizes the state to operate lotteries. It provides a severance clause to retain the above provision should any subsections be held unconstitutional because of more than one subject. The schedule provides, unless changed by law, for the lotteries to be known as the Florida Education Lotteries and for the net proceeds derived to be deposited in a state trust fund, designated State Education Lotteries Trust Fund, for the appropriation by the Legislature.

Appellants/petitioners argue that this summary does not adequately inform the voter of the substance of the amendment as required by section 101.161.

We disagree. It is not necessary to explain every ramification of a proposed amendment, only the chief purpose. Miami Dolphins v. Metropolitan Dade County, 394 So.2d 981 (Fla.1981). The summary makes clear that the amendment authorizes state lotteries and that the revenues from such lotteries, subject to legislative override, will go to the State Education Lotteries Trust Fund. That is the chief purpose of the amendment and is all that the statute requires. It is true, as appellants/petitioners urge, that the legislature may choose not to authorize lotteries, not appropriate the proceeds to educational uses, and even to divert the proceeds to other uses. However, those questions go to the wisdom of adopting the amendment and it is for the proponents and opponents to make the case for adopting or rejecting the amendment in the public forum.

Appellants Todd, et al., also argue that the sponsors of the amendment committed fraud in inducing voters to sign the initiative petition by promising that a lottery could produce over $300 million annually for Florida. We express no opinion on the accuracy of this promise but note that the petition form signed by the electors is prominently identified as a paid political advertisement. We decline to embroil this Court in the accuracy or inaccuracy of political advertisements clearly identified as such.

Finally, subsection (c) of the proposed amendment provides that the schedule of implementation may be amended by general law. Petitioners Carroll, et al., argue that this permits the legislature to amend a portion of the Constitution by simple majority vote in violation of article XI, section 1. We see no merit in this argument. The clause, if adopted, reflects a decision by the voters to leave the ultimate disposition of the proceeds received from lotteries, if established, to the discretion of the legislature. Such delegations of authority to the legislative, executive, or judicial branches of government is not unusual or constitutionally infirm. Our Constitution consists in large part of a delegation of discretionary authority to the three branches of government and numerous provisions of the Constitution are contingent on general law. See, for example, article I, sections 15(b) and 22; article II, section 8; article III, section 14; article IV, section 4; article V, section 1; article X, section 13; and others too numerous to list.

We affirm the judgment below and deny the petition for writ of mandamus. No petition for rehearing will be entertained.

[The concurring opinions of Justices Boyd and McDonald are omitted.]

VAN WESTRUM v. SMITH
834 P.2d 261 (Colo. 1992)

ERICKSON, Justice.

Anthony van Westrum, registered elector (petitioner), pursuant to section 1-40-102(3)(a), 1B C.R.S. (1991 Supp.), seeks review of the validity of the title, submission clause, and summary set by the Initiative Title Setting Board (Board) for a proposed statutory amendment to modify the distribution of proceeds from the state-supervised lottery. The petitioner asserted that the title, submission clause, and summary set by the Board do not reflect the true intent and meaning of the proposed Initiative and, therefore, sought a

rehearing. The Board denied the petitioner's motion for a rehearing and retained the language originally set by the Board. We affirm.

I

The Board conducted the public meeting required by section 1-40-101(2) and set the title, submission clause, and summary for an initiated statutory amendment (Initiative) to section 24-35-210, 10A C.R.S. (1988 & 1991 Supp.). The Initiative would amend section 24-35-210 of the Colorado Revised Statutes to provide revenues from the state-supervised lottery as an alternative source of revenue for school financing. Beginning in fiscal year 1992-93, the Initiative proposes a reduction in the amount of lottery proceeds that are currently distributed from the lottery fund to the Conservation Trust Fund and to the Division of Parks and Outdoor Recreation. The Initiative also proposes a reduction in the amount of lottery proceeds that may be appropriated for state capital construction in fiscal year 1998-99 and places a limit on the amount of lease-purchase obligations that may be made after January 15, 1993. Beginning in fiscal year 1992-93, the Initiative proposes that all lottery proceeds not otherwise transferred or distributed be appropriated for financing public schools as an offset to property taxes levied for that purpose. The petitioner contested the validity of the title, submission clause, and summary fixed by the Board and filed a motion for rehearing under section 1-40-102(3)(a), 1B C.R.S. (1991 Supp.). On June 5, 1992, the Board denied the petitioner's motion for rehearing and voted to retain the language of the title, submission clause, and summary set by the Board. Pursuant to section 1-40-102(3)(a), review is sought in this court.

II

The question is whether the language set by the Board for the title, submission clause, and summary fairly and correctly expresses the true intent and meaning of the Initiative and adequately informs signers of petitions and voters of its effects. We answer in the affirmative.

The title, submission clause, and summary at issue provide:

Title

AN ACT TO MODIFY THE DISTRIBUTION OF LOTTERY PROCEEDS TO LIMIT THE AMOUNT OF LOTTERY PROCEEDS DISTRIBUTED FOR LOCAL AND STATE PARKS AND RECREATION AREAS; TO LIMIT STATE CAPITAL CONSTRUCTION PROJECTS AND THE TOTAL AMOUNT OF OBLIGATIONS WHICH MAY BE MADE IN FUTURE YEARS FOR CAPITAL CONSTRUCTION; AND TO PROVIDE THAT ALL REMAINING LOTTERY PROCEEDS BE APPROPRIATED FOR FINANCING PUBLIC SCHOOLS TO OFFSET LOCAL PROPERTY TAXES LEVIED FOR SUCH PURPOSE.

Submission Clause

SHALL THERE BE AN ACT TO MODIFY THE DISTRIBUTION OF LOTTERY PROCEEDS TO LIMIT THE AMOUNT OF LOTTERY PROCEEDS DISTRIBUTED FOR LOCAL AND STATE PARKS AND

RECREATION AREAS; TO LIMIT STATE CAPITAL CONSTRUC-
TION PROJECTS AND THE TOTAL AMOUNT OF OBLIGATIONS
WHICH MAY BE MADE IN FUTURE YEARS FOR CAPITAL CON-
STRUCTION; AND TO PROVIDE THAT ALL REMAINING LOT-
TERY PROCEEDS BE APPROPRIATED FOR FINANCING PUBLIC
SCHOOLS TO OFFSET LOCAL PROPERTY TAXES LEVIED FOR
SUCH PURPOSE?

Summary

This measure amends existing law to provide revenues from the
state-supervised lottery as an alternative source of revenue for school
financing. The amount of lottery proceeds which are currently distributed from the Lottery Fund to the Conservation Trust Fund and to
the Division of Parks and Outdoor Recreation in the Department of
Natural Resources is modified by reducing the total amount of lottery
proceeds which may be so transferred or appropriated in fiscal year
1992-93 and thereafter.

This measure modifies the amount of lottery proceeds which are
currently appropriated from the Lottery Fund for state capital construction, the current recipient of approximately two thirds of all state
lottery fund net revenues, by reducing the total amount of lottery
proceeds which may be so appropriated in fiscal year 1998-99 or at
an earlier date if existing lease-purchase obligations have been discharged. A limitation is established on the total amount of obligations
which may be made after January 15, 1993, for capital construction.

This measure requires, commencing in fiscal year 1992-93, the
appropriation of all lottery proceeds not otherwise transferred or
appropriated for financing public schools as an offset to property taxes
levied for said purpose.

This measure would limit the maximum amount of lottery proceeds
distributed to the Conservation Trust Fund to $7.5 million for each
fiscal year and to the Division of Parks and Outdoor Recreation in the
Department of Natural Resources to $7.5 million each fiscal year. The
annual amount of lottery proceeds for state capital construction would
be reduced; for example, by approximately $24 million in fiscal year
1992-93 and $44 million in fiscal year 1993-94. The remaining lottery
proceeds to be used for financing public schools would reduce property
taxes for schools; for example, by approximately 2.1% in fiscal year
1992-93 and 3.9% in fiscal year 1993-94.

III

The people's constitutional right to initiate legislation and constitutional
amendments is granted by article V, section 1(2) of the Colorado Constitution.
The statutory scheme for initiated legislation or a constitutional amendment
requires the Board to designate and fix a title, submission clause, and a
summary for initiative petitions before they are signed by electors. See § 1-40-
101(1), (2), 1B C.R.S. (1991 Supp.). "The purpose of the title setting process
is to ensure that both persons reviewing an initiative petition and the voters
are fairly and succinctly advised of the import of the proposed law." In re

Proposed Initiative on Education Tax Refund, 823 P.2d 1353, 1355 (Colo.1991) (hereinafter Education Tax Refund Initiative); Dye v. Baker, 143 Colo. 458, 460, 354 P.2d 498, 500 (1960).

In performing its statutory duty, the Board is not required to describe every feature of a proposed measure. In re Proposed Initiated Constitutional Amendment Concerning Limited Gaming in Manitou Springs, Fairplay and in Airports, 826 P.2d 1241, 1244 (Colo.1992) (hereinafter In re Limited Gaming in Manitou Springs); Education Tax Refund Initiative, 823 P.2d at 1355; In re Proposed Initiative Concerning "State Personnel System," 691 P.2d 1121, 1124 (Colo.1984) (hereinafter "State Personnel System" Initiative). Nevertheless, the Board must consider "the public confusion that might be caused by misleading titles." § 1-40-101(2), 1B C.R.S. (1991 Supp.). The title must correctly and fairly express the true meaning of the proposed measure, and the submission clause set by the Board should be brief and should "unambiguously state the principle of the provision sought to be added, amended, or repealed." Id. Similarly, the designated summary should be impartial and not an argument likely to create prejudice, either for or against the measure. Id.

In reviewing the Board's title setting process we: (1) should not address the merit of the proposed Initiative and should not interpret the meaning of proposed language or suggest how it will be applied if adopted by the electorate; (2) should resolve all legitimate presumptions in favor of the Board; and (3) will not interfere with the Board's choice of language if the language is not clearly misleading. Education Tax Refund Initiative, 823 P.2d at 1355; In re Proposed Initiative on Parental Notification of Abortions for Minors, 794 P.2d 238, 240 (Colo.1990). "Our duty is to ensure that the title, submission clause and summary fairly reflect the proposed Initiative . . . ." Education Tax Refund Initiative, 823 P.2d at 1355. Petition signers and voters should not be misled into support "for or against a proposition by reason of the words employed." Dye v. Baker, 143 Colo. at 460, 354 P.2d at 500.

IV

The petitioner claims that the title, submission clause, and summary are misleading because they suggest that the purpose of the Initiative is to fund school financing. He argues that the true purpose of the Initiative is to grant property tax relief and that voters will be unable to discern whether school funding has increased, decreased or remained unchanged. The petitioner also contends that the language is misleading because no new funds will be made available for financing public schools. We find no merit in the petitioner's claims.

Nothing in the text of the Initiative suggests that its purpose is to increase or decrease revenues for school funding. The title and the submission clause state that the statutory amendment would modify and limit the existing distribution of lottery proceeds and that the remaining funds would be appropriated for financing public schools to "offset local property taxes levied for such purpose." The summary provides that the amendment would provide revenues from the state-supervised lottery as an alternative source of revenue for school financing. The language set by the Board all but duplicates the language contained in the text of the Initiative. In setting the title, submission clause, and summary, the Board properly discharged its duty under the statute. See § 1-40-101(2), 1B C.R.S. (1991 Supp.).

The petitioner also contends that the summary is materially incomplete because it fails to state that an immediate reduction in the flow of lottery funds will probably lead to the insolvency of the state fund and require either a tax increase or budget cut to pay the cost of capital construction. This contention, however, is based on an erroneous view of the function of the Board and of the title-setting process. The designated summary of a proposed initiative should be impartial and not an argument that may create prejudice for or against the measure. Id. It is not the function of the Board or this court to educate the voters on all aspects of the proposal, In re Limited Gaming in Manitou Springs, 826 P.2d at 1244-45, or to consider the practical effects of a proposed initiative. In re Proposed Initiative on Surface Mining, 797 P.2d 1275, 1281 (Colo.1990). It is sufficient that the summary accurately reflects the purpose of the Initiative. See § 1-40-101(2); Education Tax Refund Initiative, 823 P.2d at 1355. Here, the title, submission clause, and summary correctly and fairly reflect the true meaning of the proposed Initiative.

Accordingly, we affirm the ruling of the Board.

ECUMENICAL MINISTRIES OF OREGON v. OREGON STATE LOTTERY COMMISSION
871 P.2d 106 (Or. 1994)

GRABER, Justice.

In this case, we are called on to decide the constitutionality of three statutes relating to the operation of the State Lottery—ORS 461.215, 461.217, and 461.546—under the present version of Article XV, section 4, of the Oregon Constitution. As originally adopted in 1857, Article XV, section 4, provided:

> Lotteries, and the sale of Lottery tickets, for any purpose whatever, are prohibited, and the Legislative Assembly shall prevent the same by penal laws.

In 1976, the voters adopted an amendment, which had been submitted to them by the Legislative Assembly, excepting charitable, fraternal, and religious organizations from the prohibition against lotteries in Article XV, section 4.

In 1984, Article XV, section 4, was amended through the initiative process. As pertinent here, Article XV, section 4, now provides:

> (3) There is hereby created the State Lottery Commission which shall establish and operate a State Lottery. All proceeds from the State Lottery, including interest, but excluding costs of administration and payment of prizes, shall be used for the purpose of creating jobs and furthering economic development in Oregon.

> (4)(a) The State Lottery Commission shall be comprised of five members appointed by the Governor and confirmed by the Senate * * *. * * * The Commission is empowered to promulgate rules related

to the procedures of the Commission and the operation of the State Lottery. * * * *

(d) The Director [of the State Lottery] shall implement and operate a State Lottery pursuant to the rules, and under the guidance, of the Commission. * * * The State Lottery may operate any game procedure authorized by the Commission, except parimutuel racing, social games, and the games commonly known in Oregon as bingo or lotto, whereby prizes are distributed using any existing or future methods among adult persons who have paid for tickets or shares in that game; provided that, in lottery games utilizing computer terminals or other devices, no coins or currency shall ever be dispensed directly to players from such computer terminals or devices.

(e) There is hereby created within the General Fund the Oregon State Lottery Fund which is continuously appropriated for the purpose of administering and operating the Commission and the State Lottery. * * * [T]he State Lottery shall operate as a self-supporting revenue-raising agency of state government * * *. The State Lottery shall pay all prizes and all of its expenses out of the revenues it receives from the sale of tickets or shares to the public and turn over the net proceeds therefrom to a fund to be established by the Legislative Assembly from which the Legislative Assembly shall make appropriations for the benefit of the public purpose of creating jobs and furthering economic development in Oregon. At least 84% of the total annual revenues from the sale of all lottery tickets or shares shall be returned to the public in the form of prizes and net revenues benefitting the public purpose. * * * *

(7) The Legislative Assembly has no power to authorize, and shall prohibit, casinos from operation in the State of Oregon.

In 1991, plaintiffs, Ecumenical Ministries of Oregon and various individuals, brought an action for declaratory judgment and injunctive relief against the Oregon State Lottery Commission and the Lottery Director, alleging that ORS 461.215 and 461.217 (providing for the initiation by the Lottery Commission of video lottery games) and 461.546 (providing for the distribution of some of the revenues generated by those games) violate certain provisions of Article XV, section 4. In particular, plaintiffs alleged that, when implemented, ORS 461.215 and 461.217 will result in the creation of "state-sponsored video poker" that will "have the effect of creating casino gambling in the State of Oregon," in violation of Article XV, section 4(7), of the state constitution. Plaintiffs further alleged that ORS 461.546(1) "mandat[es] the use of net revenues of the Oregon Lottery for purposes other than the constitutionally-mandated purpose of creating jobs and furthering economic development in Oregon" and "authoriz[es] that more than 16% of lottery revenues be expended on costs of administration, including gaming law enforcement," in violation of Article XV, sections 4(3) and 4(4)(e), of the Oregon Constitution.

The Oregon Restaurant Association and Video Lottery Consultants, Inc., intervened in the action. Defendants and intervenors moved for judgment on the pleadings pursuant to ORCP 21 B. Concluding that the case presented "only legal issues to be resolved by the court," that a "motion for judgment on the pleadings is the appropriate procedural device for disposition of the case" and that the statutes do not violate the relevant provisions of the Oregon Constitution, the trial court granted defendants' and intervenors' motion. Plaintiffs appealed.

The Court of Appeals, sitting in banc, reversed the decision of the trial court and remanded the case for further proceedings. Ecumenical Ministries v. Oregon State Lottery Comm., 118 Or.App. 735, 849 P.2d 532 (1993). The Court of Appeals held that the terms "casino" and "video poker" are ambiguous and that plaintiffs "are entitled to present evidence" to demonstrate the meaning of those terms and the manner in which "video poker" may violate the constitutional prohibition against "casinos." Id. at 740-42, 849 P.2d 532. The court also held that plaintiffs "are entitled to present evidence to support their claim that the allocations [mandated] in ORS 461.546 are not for the purpose of creating jobs and furthering economic development in Oregon." Id. at 742-43, 849 P.2d 532.

Rossman, J., joined by Edmonds, J., dissented. Judge Rossman reasoned that "video poker" is authorized by ORS 461.215 and 461.217 and that it is unconstitutional "casino gambling"; he also reasoned that the allocation of funds mandated by ORS 461.546(1) does not promote economic development. Ecumenical Ministries v. Oregon State Lottery Comm., 118 Or.App. 735, 849 P.2d 532 (1993) (Rossman, J., dissenting). Judge Rossman stated that, "in this straightforward, facial challenge to the statutes," plaintiffs were entitled to judgment on the pleadings. 118 Or.App. at 747, 849 P.2d 532.

Intervenors moved for reconsideration, arguing that the case presented questions of law requiring no evidentiary amplification. The Court of Appeals allowed reconsideration and adhered to its former opinion. Ecumenical Ministries v. Oregon State Lottery Comm., 121 Or.App. 389, 854 P.2d 952 (1993).

Plaintiffs sought review in this court on the issue of the constitutionality of ORS 461.546(1). Defendants and intervenors sought review on that issue and on the issue of the constitutionality of ORS 461.215 and 461.217. We allowed review in order to answer those questions of law. We now reverse the decision of the Court of Appeals and affirm in part and reverse in part the judgment of the circuit court.

"CASINOS"

A. Meaning of Article XV, Section 4(7)

We first consider the meaning of Article XV, section 4(7), of the Oregon Constitution, which is the subject of plaintiffs' first claim for relief. In particular, we consider the meaning of the term "casinos," as used in that section. The text of Article XV, section 4(7), does not define the term "casino" or otherwise disclose to us the intent of the voters in prohibiting the operation of casinos in this state. Neither does any other provision of the constitution define "casinos."

The ordinary meaning of the noun "casino" is a "building or room used for social meetings and public amusements * * * specif: a building or room for gambling." Webster's Third New International Dictionary 347 (1976). The noun "gambling" is defined as "the act or practice of betting: the act of playing a game and consciously risking money or other stakes on its outcome." Webster's Third New International Dictionary 932 (1976). Those definitions suggest only that a "casino" is a physical structure "for gambling." It seems doubtful that voters intended so literal and sweeping a meaning, however. If the meaning were that broad, a place such as a citizen's game room where friends play poker for pennies would be prohibited from operating, even though it had not been prohibited under the earlier versions of Article XV, section 4, since statehood.

We turn for further assistance to the context of Article XV, section 4(7). Other provisions of Article XV that were adopted at the same time as section 4(7) are part of that context. Sections 4(3), 4(4), 4(5), and 4(6) of Article XV provide in some detail for the establishment and operation of a state lottery, including the operation of "any game procedure authorized by the Commission," with certain exceptions not relevant here, and the operation of "lottery games utilizing computer terminals." Or. Const., Art. XV, § 4(4)(d).

Section 4(4)(d) also provides in part that, in lottery games utilizing computer terminals or other devices, "no coins or currency shall ever be dispensed directly to players from such computer terminals or devices." That directive suggests that the voters were not opposed to games using computer terminals, but had a more limited intent to prevent the use of lottery devices having the cash-or currency-dispensing features of so-called "slot machines."

By comparison, section 4(7) provides that the Legislative Assembly shall not authorize, and shall prohibit, "casinos" from operating in Oregon. The context described above suggests that the voters intended to distinguish between the authorized State Lottery and particular types of game procedures (expressly including game procedures utilizing computer terminals), on the one hand, and the general category of gambling establishments known as "casinos," on the other. That is, when the voters voted to prohibit "casinos," they did not intend to prohibit the State Lottery from operating game procedures using computer terminals.

The 1984 amendments to Article XV, section 4, were presented to the voters at the general election in that year as Ballot Measure 4. 1984 Ballot Measure 5 was the companion measure to Measure 4 and was adopted by the voters at the same election as was the latter. Measure 5 therefore also constitutes part of the context of Measure 4. We turn to an examination of Measure 5.

Measure 5 contained statutory provisions for the regulation of a state lottery, should one be authorized by the passage of Measure 4. The text of that measure neither defined nor referred to "casinos." Some portions of the text nevertheless assist us in determining the meaning of that term.

Section 4(2)(d) of Measure 5 repeated the following injunction from Measure 4:

> In games utilizing computer terminals or other devices, no coins or currency shall be dispensed directly to players from such computer terminals or devices.

Section 5(2) of Measure 5 provided in part:

> No person shall be a Lottery Game Retailer who is engaged exclusively in the business of selling Lottery tickets or shares.

The quoted provisions of Measure 5 suggest that the voters intended to prevent the use of lottery devices directly dispensing coins or currency and that they intended to prevent the establishment of enterprises "engaged exclusively" in lottery-related activities.

Considering all of the foregoing text and context, we conclude that, in adopting Article XV, section 4(7), prohibiting the operation of "casinos," the voters intended to prohibit the operation of establishments whose dominant use or dominant purpose, or both, is for gambling. The voters did not intend, in adopting Article XV, section 4(7), to prohibit the use of lottery games using computer terminals, with the exception of those that dispense coins or currency directly to players.

B. Constitutionality of ORS 461.215 and 461.217

Having thus interpreted Article XV, section 4(7), we next consider whether ORS 461.215 and 461.217 violate that constitutional provision. ORS 461.215 provides in part: "(1) The Oregon State Lottery Commission may initiate a game or games using video devices * * *."

ORS 461.217 provides in part:

> (1) A video lottery game terminal that offers a video lottery game authorized by the Director of the Oregon State Lottery shall be placed for operation only on the premises of an establishment that has a contract with the state lottery as a video lottery game retailer. The terminal must be within the control of an employee of the video lottery game retailer. It shall not be placed in any other business or location.
>
> (2) A video lottery game terminal shall be placed only on the premises of an establishment licensed by the Oregon Liquor Control Commission [OLCC] with a Class "A" dispenser, Class "B" dispenser, Retail Malt Beverage, Restaurant or Seasonal dispenser license. A video lottery game terminal shall be placed only in that part of the premises that is restricted to minors and that is used primarily for the consumption of alcoholic beverages.
>
> (3) No more than five video lottery machines shall be placed in or on premises described in subsection (2) of this section.

In order to understand what ORS 461.215 and 461.217 mean, we also examine the statutes governing the issuance by the OLCC of the licenses enumerated in 461.217. Class "A" and Class "B" dispenser licenses are governed by ORS 472.110(1), which provides:

> A dispenser's license may be issued to private clubs, fraternal organizations, veterans' organizations, railroad corporations operating interstate trains and commercial establishments where food is cooked and served, and shall be designated as Class 'A,' Class 'B,' and Class 'C.'

Retail malt beverage licenses are governed by ORS 471.265 and permit persons "operating a place of business where refreshments are served, to sell malt beverages * * *, hard cider * * * and wine." Such establishments also may allow dancing, singing, and "other proper forms of entertainment upon the licensed premises." Restaurant licenses are governed by ORS 471.250; restaurant licensees also may allow "any proper form of entertainment." Seasonal licenses are governed by ORS 472.205; such licenses are issued to establishments where food is cooked and served and permit the licensee to allow "dancing and other proper forms of entertainment upon the licensed premises."

We conclude that ORS 461.215 and 461.217, when considered in the context of limitations imposed by other applicable provisions of ORS chapters 461, 471, and 472, are consistent with the prohibition in Article XV, section 4(7), on "casinos," as we have interpreted that prohibition. The use of video lottery game terminals does not, per se, make a place a casino. Because ORS 461.215 and 461.217 prohibit the use of more than five video lottery game terminals in any one location and are subject to other provisions regarding the types of establishments in which such terminals may be located, those statutes are consistent with the constitutional prohibition against establishments whose dominant use or dominant purpose, or both, is for gambling.

It may be that some establishments in which video lottery game terminals are located are casinos within the meaning of Article XV, section 4(7), notwithstanding the limited number of terminals in each establishment and the requirement that the establishment be licensed to engage in a business other than the business of gambling. That kind of factual, as-applied inquiry is beyond the scope of or inquiry in this case, however. In response to this facial challenge, our task is only to determine whether ORS 461.215 and 461.217, on their face, are in harmony with Article XV, section 4(7). The presence of five video lottery game terminals in one place does not, in all circumstances, demonstrate that gambling is the dominant use or dominant purpose, or both, of the establishment.

We hold that ORS 461.215 and ORS 461.217, on their face, do not violate Article XV, section 4(7), of the Oregon Constitution.

"COSTS OF ADMINISTRATION"

ORS 461.546(1) provides:

An amount equal to six percent of the net revenue of video lottery games in the county shall be distributed to the county as administrative expenses to be expended as follows:

(a) Three percent for gaming law enforcement; and

(b) Three percent for community mental health programs to treat gambling addiction.

Plaintiffs argue that the expenditures provided for in that statute do not create jobs and promote economic development, as required by Article XV, sections 4(3) and 4(4)(e). Defendants counter that economic development is a broad term that encompasses the expenditures provided for in ORS 461.546(1).

It is unnecessary to reach those arguments. ORS 461.546(1) designates the expenditures as administrative expenses. Under Article XV, section 4(4)(e), administrative expenses (the nature of which we discuss below) may not exceed 16 percent of lottery revenues. The legislature has specified in ORS 461.546(1) that the expenditures are "distributed * * * as administrative expenses," that is, that they are to be taken from the administrative expense portion of lottery revenues, rather than from the portion (84 percent or more) devoted to paying prizes and to creating jobs and furthering economic development.

Intervenors pertinently argue in this court that the expenditures authorized by ORS 461.546(1) are permissible costs of administration. We turn to that argument.

A. Meaning of Article XV, Sections 4(3) and 4(4)(e)

The text of Article XV, sections 4(3) and 4(4)(e), does not define the terms "costs of administration" or "administering and operating." Neither does any other provision of Article XV define those terms.

Part of Article XV, section 4(4)(e), suggests, however, that the voters had in mind the costs associated with the internal procedures necessary to operate the State Lottery. Section 4(4)(e) requires the State Lottery to operate as a self-supporting and revenue-raising agency, which must pay "all of its expenses" out of the revenues that it receives.

The usual meaning of the words used in Article XV, section 4(3) and 4(4)(e) conveys a similar message. The ordinary meaning of the noun "administration" is "an act of administering." Webster's Third New International Dictionary 28 (1976). The verb "administer" is defined as "to manage the affairs of"; "to direct or superintend the execution, use, or conduct of." Id. at 27. Those definitions suggest that costs of administration are costs related to the management or implementation of the State Lottery.

In addition to considering the text of Ballot Measure 4, we examine its context, including its companion measure, 1984 Ballot Measure 5. Section 7 of Ballot Measure 5 stated in part:

> (1) All money payable to the Commission shall be deposited in an account within the General Fund known as the State Lottery Fund. * * * The State Lottery Fund is continuously appropriated for the purpose of administering and operating the Commission and the State Lottery.

> (2) Disbursements shall be made from the State Lottery Fund for any of the following purposes:

> (a) The payment of prizes * * *;

> (b) Expenses of the Commission and the State Lottery;

> (c) Repayment of any funds advanced from the temporary loan for initial start-up costs * * *;

> (d) Transfer of funds from the State Lottery Fund to the benefit of the public purpose described in Section 4, Article XV of the Constitution. * * * *

(4) Expenses of the State Lottery shall include all costs incurred in the operation and administration of the State Lottery and all costs resulting from any contracts entered into for the purchase or lease of goods or services required by the Commission, including but not limited to, the costs of supplies, materials, tickets, independent audit services, independent studies, data transmission, advertising, promotion, incentives, public relations, communications, compensation paid to Lottery Game Retailers, bonding for Lottery Game Retailers, printing, distribution of tickets and shares, reimbursing other governmental entities for services provided to the State Lottery, and for any other goods and services necessary for effectuating the purposes of this Act. No more than sixteen percent (16%) of the total annual revenues accruing from the sale of all Lottery tickets and shares from all Lottery Games shall be expended for the payment of the expenses of the State Lottery.

Because section 7(2) of Measure 5 does not include any category specifically denominated "costs of administration," that subsection informs us that the "costs of administration" of the lottery generally are categorized as "expenses" of the Commission and the State Lottery. Section 7(4) informs us that "expenses" are broadly and non-inclusively defined. However, we note that, although a broad range of goods and services apparently is permitted to be leased or purchased under section 7(4), those goods and services must be "required by the Commission" and must be "necessary for effectuating the purposes of this Act." That wording suggests that "expenses" relate to the internal implementation and management of the lottery.

Considering the foregoing text and context, we conclude that the term "costs of administration" and the phrase "administering and operating," as used in Article XV, sections 4(3) and 4(4)(e), relate to the "expenses" or "costs" of the internal implementation and management of the lottery.

B. ORS 461.546(1) and Administrative Expenses

Finally, we consider whether the expenditures authorized by ORS 461.546(1) are administrative expenses permitted by Article XV, section 4(3) and 4(4)(e). We begin by asking whether expenditures for "gaming law enforcement," as that term is used in ORS 461.546(1)(a), properly can be considered an administrative expense of the lottery.

ORS chapter 461 does not define "gaming law enforcement." The ordinary meaning of the noun "gaming" is "the act or practice of playing a game for stakes." Webster's Third New International Dictionary 933 (1976). The noun "game" is defined in part as "an amusement or pastime"; "a physical or mental competition conducted according to rules." Ibid. The noun "stake" is defined in part as a "sum of money or its equivalent risked"; "the prize set in any contest." Webster's Third New International Dictionary 2220 (1976). See also ORS 167.117(5) (defining "gambling" as the activity that occurs when "a person stakes or risks something of value upon the outcome of a contest of chance or a future contingent event not under the control or influence of the person, upon an agreement or understanding that the person or someone else will receive something of value in the event of a certain outcome"); ORS chapter 464 (providing for the regulation of bingo, lotto, and raffle "games" and establishing the Oregon Gaming Account). Those definitions suggest that the term "gaming" has broad applicability.

Giving the term "gaming" its ordinary meaning, we conclude that the term "gaming law enforcement" refers broadly and generally to enforcement of laws relating to the playing of games for stakes or prizes, including but not limited to games operated by the State Lottery. We turn to the question whether expenditures for "gaming law enforcement," as so understood, are administrative expenses of the State Lottery within the meaning of Article XV, sections 4(3) and 4(4)(e). We conclude that, even though "gaming laws" are laws that relate to the playing of games for stakes or prizes, including games operated by the State Lottery, expenditures for a county's enforcement of such laws are not an administrative expense of the lottery. That is because, although some gaming law enforcement complements the operation of the lottery, expenditures for gaming law enforcement are not expenses or costs of the internal implementation or management of the lottery.

It remains for us to decide whether the expenditures authorized in ORS 461.546(1)(b)—for "community mental health programs to treat gambling addiction"—are administrative expenses allowed by Article XV, sections 4(3) and 4(4)(e). Although the need for such programs may result in part from the operation of the lottery, expenditures for mental health programs to treat gambling addiction also are not expenses or costs of the internal implementation or management of the lottery. Accordingly, those expenditures are not administrative expenses of the State Lottery within the meaning of Article XV, sections 4(3) and 4(4)(e).

We hold that ORS 461.546(1), on its face, violates Article XV, sections 4(3) and 4(4)(e), of the Oregon Constitution.

CONCLUSION

In summary, ORS 461.215 and 461.217 do not, on their face, violate Article XV, section 4(7), of the Oregon Constitution. ORS 461.546(1), on its face, violates Article XV, sections 4(3) and 4(4)(e), of the Oregon Constitution.

The decision of the Court of Appeals is reversed. The judgment of the circuit court is affirmed in part and reversed in part, and the case is remanded to the circuit court for further proceedings.

[The concurring opinions of Justices Fadeley and Unis are omitted.]

TICHENOR v. MISSOURI STATE LOTTERY COMMISSION
742 S.W.2d 170 (Mo. 1988)

BLACKMAR, Judge.

The Missouri constitutions of 1865, 1875, and 1945 contained strict provisions against lotteries. These provisions have been gradually eroded in recent years, as the state has tried to fill its coffers from the pockets of willing gamblers in preference to further burdening reluctant taxpayers. At the 1984 general election the voters approved an amendment submitted by the legislature authorizing the general assembly to establish a "Missouri state lottery." Mo. Const. Art. III, Sec. 39(b).

The constitutional provision was not self enforcing, and the general assembly adopted enabling legislation at its next session, establishing the Missouri Lottery Commission and enjoining it to proceed so that "a lottery may be initiated at the earliest feasible and practicable time." L.1985, S.B. 44; Sec. 313.200-250, 220, RSMo 1986. The commission then approved and instituted various lottery games. Also in accord with the constitutional imperative, a maximum of 45% of the proceeds of ticket sales is distributed as prizes, a maximum of 10% is allocated for expenses, and a minimum of 45% is designated for the general revenue fund of the state treasury. Art. III, Sec. 39(b)(3), Mo. Const. The general assembly appropriated "start-up" money to get the enterprise in operation, but its power to do so was limited to the first year of operation and the advances must be repaid out of lottery proceeds within two years. Section 313.330, RSMo 1986. The lottery is now wholly dependent upon the yield from ticket sales, and no additional funds may now be appropriated. Section 313.321, RSMo 1986.

The lottery did not produce as hoped and the commissioners were vexed because Missourians have continued to venture large sums in lotteries with more attractive prize structures sponsored by neighboring states. They saw a solution in a proposed "Multi-State Lottery," in which a consortium of states would contribute to an attractive prize pool, to be awarded in a drawing for which all ticketholders in the participating states would be eligible. The commissioners sought statutory authority. The proposals cleared several legislative hurdles but fell short of enactment at the 1987 session of the general assembly. The commissioners then proceeded on their own initiative, entering into an agreement designed to bring Missouri into the multi-state lottery by February of 1988.

By the terms of this agreement the Missouri commission will receive all the proceeds from lottery tickets sold in this state, as in the past. Forty-five percent of the proceeds will be allocated to the state treasury and 10% will be retained for expenses. The balance will be transmitted to the managers of the multi-state enterprise, with its headquarters in Des Moines, Iowa, for inclusion in its pool. Holders of tickets purchased in Missouri may win prizes to which the other participating states have contributed, or the Missouri proceeds may benefit players in other states, depending on the luck of the draw. It is possible that prospects in other states will be lured by advertisements which would not be permissible by Missouri's strict standards, but there will be no advertising in Missouri which violates our constitutional or statutory provisions. No state funds will be appropriated to facilitate Missouri's participation in the multi-state lottery, but the commission has expended funds in its possession, presumably out of the 10% allocated for expenses, to "explore, join and participate in the multistate lottery," and no doubt will continue to do so. The commission estimates that as much as $300,000 may be so expended.

Even though a net gain from the multi-state lottery is expected and no money will be taken from the state treasury, we believe that the funds of the lottery commission are "state funds" in the broad sense, and that the plaintiff as a citizen and taxpayer of Missouri has standing to challenge the legality of these expenditures in court. *Berghorn v. Reorganized School District No.*

8, 364 Mo. 121, 260 S.W.2d 573, 581 (1953); Missourians for Separation of Church and State v. Robertson, 592 S.W.2d 825, 839 (Mo.App.1979). He alleges that Missouri's participation in a multi-state lottery is illegal by reason of several provisions of the state and federal constitutions and statutes.

The case was tried on stipulated facts. The trial court found that the plaintiff's points were not well taken and entered judgment denying the relief sought, without additional findings or opinion. The plaintiff appealed to this Court, suggesting that we have initial jurisdiction because the proposed action involves possible conflict with a provision of the constitution of this state (Article III, Sec. 39(b)), and because the construction of revenue laws of this state (Sec. 313.200 to 313.350, RSMo 1986) is required.

Although the jurisdictional grounds assigned are not pellucid, we conclude that the notice of appeal was filed in entire good faith and proceed to decide the case without further jurisdictional inquiry because of the importance of the questions presented. Mo. Const. Art. V, Secs. 3, 4; Sermchief v. Gonzales, 660 S.W.2d 683 (Mo. banc 1983). We are greatly helped by the excellent briefing and oral argument by counsel for both sides, on an expedited schedule. We find that the proposed entry into the multi-state lottery is not facially invalid for any of the reasons assigned, and affirm the judgment of the circuit court.

I.

It is first argued that the phrase "Missouri state lottery" as used in the constitution is a limitation on the authority of the legislature and of the commission, and that a lottery in which the proceeds of sales of Missouri tickets go into a pot which may be won by a person who has purchased a ticket in another state, and in which Missouri residents may win prizes to which ticket purchasers in other states contribute, cannot be brought within the compass of the constitutional designation. This point, if well taken, is dispositive of the case. Neither the legislature nor the commission may establish a lottery which is not within the constitutional authority.

The plaintiff-appellant argues that the constitutional authorization should be construed strictly because it represents an exception to the historic Missouri policy against lotteries and gambling enterprises of all kinds. The defendant officials contend, contrariwise, that the voters of the state showed that they wanted a lottery and that the constitutional authorization should be liberally construed to give effect to this authorization. We suggest that the words should be read in accordance with their plain meaning, so as to carry out the purpose manifested by the voters of the state in approving the amendment referred to them by the general assembly. By reason of the amendment, a lottery in which all the profits inure to the benefit of the state of Missouri accords with the public policy of the state, rather than contravening it. We should not construe the constitutional provision in such a way as to thwart the voters' purpose, and should impose only such restrictions as are clearly required by the statute.

The intent we look to, furthermore, is that of the voters. The legislature may only lay a proposed constitutional amendment before the electorate. Its intent is immaterial except to the extent that it may be found in the text of the proposal actually placed on the ballot. Thus the circumstance that an earlier legislative proposal contained language which might be more readily supportive of the authority to participate in a multi-state lottery enterprise is of little moment. Nor is it significant that the full text of the amendment does not appear on the ballot. The text is available to the voters, at the polling place and elsewhere. The text is our only authentic basis for ascertaining intent.

The plaintiff points out that, if the commission's proposal is upheld, the proceeds from Missouri tickets may be awarded as prizes to non-Missourians. This is not an important circumstance. The basic purpose of the Missouri state lottery is to lift money from the pockets of Missourians, not to reward them. The prizes are only a means to this end. Out-of-state residents are welcome to purchase tickets and to receive prizes in the present lottery operations, if they can handle the logistics.

The plaintiff points to constitutional and statutory provisions in other states which explicitly authorize multi-state lotteries. The fact that the framers of the amendment might have relieved us of the construction problem by doing a better job of drafting does not require us to indulge in a narrow reading of their composition. The manifest purpose was to permit the legislature to establish a lottery for the benefit of the state treasury. Restrictions deemed necessary in the public interest are clearly phrased. We should hesitate to imply restrictions which are not expressly stated.

We conclude that the phrase "Missouri state lottery" should not be read as a limitation on the authority of the State Lottery Commission to enter into a multi-state lottery venture otherwise complying with the details of the Missouri statute. The proposal accords with the clearly stated limitations on distribution of proceeds and advertising. The language, "Missouri state lottery," serves a substantial purpose in telling us that the general assembly may not authorize a lottery for the benefit of a political subdivision, or a charitable or private interest. The plaintiff's fears that a decision against his position would open the door to joint aleatory ventures with other entities within the state, therefore, are groundless. On considering the whole record, we are unable to say that the voters intended to restrict the legislature and the commission in the way the plaintiff suggests.

[The remainder of the court's opinion is omitted.]

WELLIVER, Judge, dissenting.

I respectfully dissent. I cannot join in the linguistic legal gymnastics which result in holding that the "plain meaning," 742 S.W.2d at 173, of the words "a Missouri state lottery" is "a Missouri state lottery and/or a multi-state lottery."

The principal opinion reaches this result by ignoring the only word used by the people to give meaning to the words "Missouri state lottery," that is the word "a". Mo. Const. art. III, § 39(b) states that there is excepted from the general prohibition against lotteries authority for the legislature to establish "a Missouri state lottery." Instead of saying "a Missouri state lottery," they could have said "lotteries," or "Missouri State lotteries," or any number of other words having a broader meaning.

I do not believe that the drafters of the lottery amendment chose the words which they used in a vacuum. I believe they were aware that some states authorized multi-state lotteries while some did not. True, the words used by other states do not bind us, but the prior existence of such words should be given some consideration in determining the meaning of the words selected to be used by the drafters of our amendment.

It is true that the unpassed attempted legislative enactments of 1987 have no binding effect on us, but where this constitutional amendment specifically authorized the legislature to establish "a Missouri state lottery" the actions of the legislature on the subject, both positive and negative, are matters to be given some degree of consideration by the court.

I am unable to perceive the wisdom of refusing to follow the long accepted rule of construction that exceptions to general prohibitions must be strictly construed. Tichenor, 742 S.W.2d 173. "[E]xceptions to general constitution provisions must be narrowly and strictly construed." 16 C.J.S. Constitutional Law § 18 (1984) (footnote omitted); accord Antieau, Adjudicating Constitutional Issues 52 (1985).

"State" is defined in Webster's Third New International Dictionary 2228 (1976) as "a body of people permanently occupying a definite territory and politically organized under a sovereign government almost entirely free from external control and possessing coercive power to maintain order within the community." "Lottery" is defined as "a scheme for the distribution of prizes by lot or chance; esp: a scheme by which prizes are distributed to the winners among those persons who have paid for a chance to win them usu. as determined by the numbers on tickets as drawn at random." Id. at 1338.

The plain dictionary meaning of the words can lead to no other conclusion than that the plain and ordinary meaning at the time the people voted on the amendment is that "a Missouri state lottery" means a lottery operated within this state.

The trial court should be reversed.

[The dissenting opinion of Judge Donnelly is omitted.]

Notes

1. Lotteries have long been felt to prey upon the poor and produce a host of ills. *See generally* Ronald J. Rychlak, *Lotteries, Revenues and Social Costs: A Historical Examination of State-Sponsored Gambling*, 34 B.C. L. Rev. 11 (1992). When King William III outlawed lotteries in 1699, for example, the legislation's preamble declared:

> Whereas several evil-disposed persons, for divers years last past, have set up many mischievous and unlawful games, called lotteries . . . in most of the eminent towns and places in England . . . and have thereby most unjustly and fraudulently got themselves great sums of money from the children and servants of several gentlemen, traders and merchants, and from other unwary persons, to the utter ruin and impoverishment of many families, and to the reproach of the English laws and government, by color of several patents or grants under the

great seal of England . . . which said grants or patents are against the common good, trade, welfare and peace of his Majesty's kingdoms: for remedy whereof be it enacted, adjudged and declared . . . . That all such lotteries, and all other lotteries are common and public nuisances, and that all grants, patents and licenses for such lotteries, are void and against law.

Despite such sentiments, between 1746 and the start of the Civil War, American lotteries were used to support a wide variety of institutions and projects, including fraternal organizations, schools, hospitals, lighthouses, jails, churches, and roads. In addition, lotteries played a critical role in the early development of numerous universities (including Harvard, Princeton, and Yale) and helped pay for fortifications in New York City and Philadelphia (the latter effort being led by Benjamin Franklin). Because of their revenue-generating ability, England eventually banned many colonial lotteries to maintain its authority. *See further* Herbert Asbury, *Sucker's Progress: An Informal History of Gambling in America from the Colonies to Canfield* (1969).

2. Notable early winners of European lotteries included Voltaire, who, in addition to being a gifted philosopher and writer, was a brilliant mathematician. In 1729, he discovered a miscalculation in a town's lottery (the prize far exceeded the total cost to play). He therefore borrowed money from his friends and purchased every ticket; by shrewdly investing his winnings, he was able to achieve financial independence. Similarly, the artist Claude Monet won 100,000 francs in the 1891 French National Lottery, and thereafter was able to devote himself completely to his art. Robert Hendrickson, *The Literary Life and Other Curiosities* 54-55 (1981).

3. The most notorious American lottery was the Louisiana Lottery, which began operating in 1868. According to the New Orleans *Times-Picayune*, it was "conceived in the miscegenation of reconstruction and born in inequity." Because its books were kept secret, exact numbers are hard to come by; nevertheless, it has been estimated that at the height of its popularity, the Louisiana Lottery paid out more than $3 million annually and generated yearly profits of $13 million. Despite mounting pressure, Louisiana lawmakers were either unwilling or unable to close the lottery down; its practice of making generous donations to various state projects also helped assure its longevity. In 1879, an amendment to the Louisiana state constitution reauthorized the lottery through 1895.

By this time, every other state prohibited lotteries. Yet such laws were generally unsuccessful in keeping the Louisiana Lottery at bay; indeed, 93% of the lottery's gross revenue came from outside its home state. Accordingly, reformers, churches, and newspapers all lobbied for federal intervention. President Benjamin Harrison also called for action. After several false starts, Congress finally banned all lottery materials from the mails in 1890 and from interstate commerce in 1895. When the United States Supreme Court subsequently upheld both statutes (and also reaffirmed the states' use of their police powers to control gambling), the Louisiana Lottery was effectively shut down. *See further Ex parte Rapier*, 143 U.S. 110 (1892) (upholding postal ban) and *Champion v. Ames*, 188 U.S. 321 (1903) (upholding interstate commerce ban). *See also* Lawrence Curtin & Karen Bernardo, *The History of Sweepstakes* (1997).

4. To overcome the foregoing history, modern proponents regularly push lotteries as an easy way to raise money for worthwhile social programs. Yet more often than not, the bright promises have not been fulfilled. *See generally* David Nibert, *Hitting the Lottery Jackpot: Government and the Taxing of Dreams* (2000).

The *Carroll* case provides a good example: by claiming the lottery would enhance public education, Florida's voters put aside their longstanding opposition to lotteries and agreed to amend the state constitution. Yet after the lottery was approved, the legislature took money previously earmarked for education and used it elsewhere. As a result, Florida's public schools remain starved for money. *See further* Jon Mills & Timothy Mclendon, *Setting a New Standard for Public Education: Revision 6 Increases the Duty of the State to Make "Adequate Provision" for Florida Schools*, 52 Fla. L. Rev. 329, 359 n.145 (2000) ("Although total distributions by the Florida lottery to the Department of Education amounted to some $793.1 million in 1996-97, education-related appropriations declined from over 40% in 1985-86, prior to adoption of the lottery, to 31% in 1995-96 and 33% in 1996-97.").

5. When voters in Colorado approved a lottery in 1980, they were told it would pay for parks and outdoor recreation. The "fine print," however, gave lawmakers the right to spend the proceeds as they saw fit, and increasingly they opted for capital improvements such as prisons (due to the state's burgeoning inmate population); by 1992, construction projects accounted for 62% of lottery revenues. As the *van Westrum* case explains, when a proposed tax hike to deal with a looming crisis in the public schools ran into furious opposition, the legislature began looking into diverting even more funds from the lottery.

Fed up with the escalating raids, Governor Roy Romer launched a campaign dubbed "Great Outdoors Colorado." This effort culminated in the passage of a constitutional amendment (known as Amendment 8) at the 1992 elections. As a result, nearly all of Colorado's lottery proceeds must now be used for their original purpose. *See further In re Great Outdoors Colorado Trust Fund*, 913 P.2d 533 (Colo. 1996).

6. In addition to raising money for social programs, proponents argue that having a state lottery fights crime by cutting into illegal "numbers" games (which are essentially daily lotteries). In fact, a state lottery may have the opposite effect. First, legal gambling tends to remove some of the taint from illegal games. Second, the legal game makes the illegal game simpler to operate because the latter can use the state's numbers (thereby assuring players that it is not rigged and making it easy to find out if one is a winner). Third, the legal game gives the illegal operator a ready means of "laying-off" (i.e., insuring against heavy losses) on a popular number. *See further* Don Liddick, *The Mob's Daily Number: Organized Crime and the Numbers Gambling Industry* (1999).

7. In addition to indirectly encouraging illegal gambling, state lotteries create new crimes as people seek to steal, forge, or alter lottery tickets, or tamper with the games themselves. *See, e.g., United States v. Bae*, 250 F.3d 774 (D.C. Cir.), *cert. denied*, 534 U.S. 1062 (2001); *Commonwealth v. Deans*, 610 A.2d 32 (Pa. 1992); *Baker v. State*, 507 S.E.2d 475 (Ga. Ct. App. 1998);

Carlton v. Commonwealth, 478 S.E.2d 730 (Va. Ct. App. 1996); *Jones v. State*, 629 So. 2d 715 (Fla. Dist. Ct. App. 1993). *See also State v. Kiminski*, 474 N.W.2d 385 (Minn. Ct. App. 1991) (fact that accused might be sentenced to 10 years for redeeming $69 worth of stolen lottery tickets did not raise a colorable constitutional claim of excessive punishment).

8. To date, the only serious case of fraud that has been uncovered in connection with a state lottery occurred in Pennsylvania on April 24, 1980. In a scheme involving a state lottery official and a local television announcer, latex paint was injected into most of the ping-pong balls used to determine the day's winning number, thereby throwing off the normal operation of the air-powered drawing machine. The subterfuge was quickly discovered and the men sent to prison. *See Commonwealth v. Katsafanas*, 464 A.2d 1270 (Pa. Super. Ct. 1983). In 2000, *Lucky Numbers*, a movie loosely based on the incident, was made starring Lisa Kudrow and John Travolta; a short time earlier, the same trick was used by lawyer-turned-author David Baldacci in his novel *The Winner* (1997).

Despite the admirable record of modern state lotteries, some suspicion about their honesty still remains. On the one year anniversary of the World Trade Center attacks, for example, the winning number in the New York State lottery turned out to be "9-1-1." Lottery officials quickly issued a press release defending the game and insisting the numbers had not been rigged. *See* Bryan Virasami & Pete Bowles, *No Need for Alarm in Lottery's 9-1-1*, Newsday, Sept. 13, 2002, at A3.

9. In *Cooper v. Department of the Lottery*, 640 N.E.2d 1299 (Ill. App. Ct. 1994), *appeal denied*, 647 N.E.2d 1007 (Ill. 1995), the plaintiff filed a Freedom of Information Act request to obtain the lottery's advertising plans and marketing strategies, hoping to show that low income people were being unfairly targeted. The trial court ruled the data was exempt from disclosure, but the appellate court reversed.

The argument that the lottery disproportionately affects the poor and represents a highly regressive form of taxation is an oft-made one. *See, e.g.*, Todd A. Wyett, Note, *State Lotteries: Regressive Taxes in Disguise*, 44 Tax Law. 867 (1991). Indeed, while serving as governor of California, Ronald Reagan called lotteries "the very worst form of taxation." Recently, however, an economist-turned-law professor has challenged the common wisdom:

> But is the monopoly rent extracted by lotteries actually regressive? The answer is not nearly as obvious as most commentators assume. The regressivity or progressivity of the tax implicit in the monopoly rents collected by the state turns on the question of whether it is the universe of lottery players who pay the tax or just the winners. Imagine that $10,000,000 is wagered at $10 a person from 1,000,000 people and a single winner is paid $4,000,000 and the state keeps $6,000,000 as a tax/rent. Who has paid this $6,000,000, the 1,000,000 purchasers or the one winner? The answer is not a matter of mere semantics. Just as it is a fiction when the federal government pretends that half the social security tax is paid for by the employer and half by the employee, so too it would be a fiction to resolve the question of tax incidence merely by labeling it as a 50% levy on each ticket sold

(regressive), or, alternatively, a 50% levy on the winning ticket (progressive). Both in the case of social security and the lottery, in order to determine the incidence of the tax, one must ask what the world would look like without the tax. If with no tax the public would continue to wager $10,000,000 with all revenues going to a single winner, then the tax is extremely progressive; the winner is paying all of the tax. On the other hand, if the public would, in the tax-free world, wager only $4,000,000 with the revenues going to the winner, then the tax is regressive; it is being paid for by the players.

Lloyd R. Cohen, *The Lure of the Lottery*, 36 Wake Forest L. Rev. 705, 711 (2001). For a further discussion, *see* Mary O. Borg et al., *The Economic Consequences of State Lotteries* (1991); Lawrence Zelenak, *The Puzzling Case of the Revenue-Maximizing Lottery*, 79 N.C. L. Rev. 1 (2000); Edward J. McCaffery, *Why People Play Lotteries and Why It Matters*, 1994 Wis. L. Rev. 71.

10. There are four basic types of games used in virtually all modern lotteries: (1) drawings, (2) instant scratch-off games, (3) numbers, and (4) lotto. Yet as the *Ecumenical Ministries* and *Tichenor* cases illustrate, lottery officials are under tremendous pressure to keep people playing the lottery. As a result, it is common for them to push the development of new games that may go beyond what the electorate has authorized, especially where what is permissible has not been clearly delineated.

11. As explained, the *Tichenor* case involved the Multi-State Lottery. On Christmas Day 2002, this lottery (which now covers 25 jurisdictions) produced the largest prize ever won by a single individual: $314.9 million. The winner, Andrew J. Whittaker, Jr. of Hurricane, West Virginia, chose to take his prize in one lump sum, which, after taxes, came to $113.4 million. *See* David M. Halbfinger, *After Winning $315 Million, Man Vows to Spread Wealth*, N.Y. Times, Dec. 27, 2002, at A1.

12. For a further look at state-run lotteries, *see* Jeff Dense, *State Lotteries, Commercial Casinos, and Public Finance: An Uneasy Relationship?*, 3 Gaming L. Rev. 317 (1999), as well as the web site of the North American Association of State and Provincial Lotteries (www.naspl.org), which contains an array of information as well as dozens of useful links.

Problem 4

During the last election, voters approved a state lottery "subject to the prescription and regulation of the legislature." In response, lawmakers passed a bill creating a nine-member state lottery commission. If a taxpayer sues, arguing that the legislature itself must oversee the lottery, how should the court rule? *See Almond v. Rhode Island Lottery Commission*, 756 A.2d 186 (R.I. 2000).

D. SUITS AGAINST LOTTERY OFFICIALS

HAYNES v. DEPARTMENT OF LOTTERY
630 So. 2d 1177 (Fla. Dist. Ct. App.),
review denied, 642 So. 2d 746 (Fla. 1994)

MICKLE, Judge.

Appellants, Betty Haynes and Linda Courson, appeal a final judgment rendered in favor of appellees, on appellants' claims for breach of contract, negligent breach of contract and negligence arising out of appellants' purchase of lottery tickets. We affirm.

Appellants alleged in their complaint that on December 10, 1988, as part of a joint venture between them, Haynes went to Johnson & Johnson # 9 convenience store to purchase 50 Lotto tickets for the $28,000,000.00 drawing to take place later that night. After standing in line for over an hour, Haynes submitted ten play slips, each containing five selections of six numbers each. While the clerk processed Haynes' tickets, the on-line terminal went off-line for several minutes, refusing to accept any play slips. Haynes was subsequently issued 50 Lotto tickets. On one of the play slips, Haynes had selected the following six numbers: 8-12-13-18-36-44. When Haynes returned home and learned that these six numbers had been selected, she inspected her tickets only to discover none contained the aforementioned six numbers. Instead, two previous play slips had been duplicated resulting in the duplication of several tickets. Appellants contend this error occurred either through the actions of the store clerk or as a result of computer malfunction. Appellants' claim for payment made to the Department of the Lottery was denied.

Appellants sued the Department of the Lottery (Lottery), Johnson & Johnson, Inc. (doing business as Johnson & Johnson # 9), and Control Data Corporation (the firm selected by the Lottery to install, operate, and maintain the computer equipment), seeking damages on three theories: (1) breach of contract; (2) negligent breach of contract; and (3) negligence. The lower court granted the Lottery's motion for summary judgment and dismissed the second amended complaint against Johnson & Johnson and Control Data Corporation, essentially on the ground that, since appellants had not presented the winning ticket, they failed to state a claim upon which relief could be granted. We affirm for the reasons set forth below. (At oral argument, counsel for appellants announced appellants' intent to withdraw the negligence claims. We therefore address solely the remaining contract theories.)

We begin first with the breach of contract claim against the Lottery. We note at the outset, adopting the conclusion reached by numerous courts of foreign jurisdictions, that a lottery winner's entitlement to a prize is governed by the principles of contract law. See e.g., Parsons v. South Dakota Lottery Commission, 504 N.W.2d 593 (S.D.1993); Thao v. Control Data Corporation, 57 Wash.App. 802, 790 P.2d 1239 (1990); Driscoll v. Department of Treasury, 265 N.J.Super. 503, 627 A.2d 1167 (1993). In the instant case, the Lottery made an offer that the purchaser of a Lotto ticket would have a chance to win prize monies according to the rules and procedures of the lottery. Herein, in buying their tickets, appellants accepted that offer and agreed to the announced rules for determining prize winners. Section 24.115 of the Florida Public Education Lottery Act, Florida Statutes (1987), is entitled "Payment of prizes" and provides in pertinent part:

> (c) No prize may be paid arising from claimed tickets that are stolen, counterfeit, altered, fraudulent, unissued, produced or issued in error, unreadable, not received or not recorded by the department by applicable deadlines . . . .

Further, on the back of Lotto play slips the following language is printed: "In purchasing a LOTTO ticket, the player agrees to abide by all rules and procedures of the Florida Lottery. The play slip is not a valid receipt." Thereby, the existence of the law, although not its provisions, is specifically called to the ticket holder's attention and made a part of the contract. Appellants herein were adequately placed on notice of their duty to ensure that the tickets issued them accurately reflected the number combinations selected.

By restricting payment of prize money to holders of winning tickets, the clear legislative purpose is to keep the administrative machinery geared for the payment of winnings as simple and efficient as possible. A reading of the Florida Public Education Lottery Act reveals no intent on the part of the legislature to create liability on the part of the Lottery in the event that terminals malfunction or are improperly maintained.

Further, nothing in the Lottery act lends color to the proposition that the Lottery must bear the consequences for the actions of retail clerks. This result finds support in a Florida case dealing with the subject of pari-mutual betting wherein the court denied recovery for the alleged failure to deliver a winning ticket due to a machine malfunction, Valois v. Gulfstream Park Racing Ass., Inc., 412 So.2d 959 (Fla. 4th DCA 1982), and in foreign jurisdictions where recovery is uniformly denied to winning players who lose their tickets. See Karafa v. New Jersey State Lottery Commission, 129 N.J.Super. 499, 324 A.2d 97 (1974).

Appellants' contention that they were not adequately placed on notice that they should have checked their tickets with the corresponding numbers on the play slip is not well taken. Similarly unsound is appellants' argument that the Lottery prevented them from performing their part of the contract. Nothing or no one prevented or hindered appellants from double-checking the numbers on the tickets with the corresponding play slips. Lastly, we reject appellants' argument that the Lottery's statutes and rules are inapplicable in view of the fact that appellants are not claiming their rightful prize winnings but rather sue for money damages.

We turn next to the breach of contract claim against Johnson & Johnson. Appellants contend that, even if they have no claim against the Lottery under the statute, rules and regulations, vendors are not similarly insulated from liability for their own fault. We disagree. Like the Lottery, Johnson & Johnson is also exempt from liability for fault in failing to deliver a requested ticket. Appellants' contention that Johnson & Johnson is not protected by the applicable statute and rules is belied by the aforementioned express language mandating that a winning ticket must be presented before a player may be adjudged a winner. Further, and perhaps most importantly, appellants failed to identify a recognizable contract between themselves and Johnson & Johnson.

Turning now to the allegations against Control Data Corporation, appellants claimed below that Control Data Corporation and the Lottery entered into a contract to sell lottery tickets to the public, that the contract was intended to benefit appellants as members of the public, and therefore that appellants have a claim against Control Data Corporation as third-party beneficiaries. Appellants stretch the credulity of the court with their claim that any agreement between the Lottery and the mechanism for selling tickets which effectuates its intent renders each member of the ticket buying public a third-party beneficiary. Clearly, the purpose of the contract between Control Data Corporation and the Lottery is to give effect to the mandate underlying the lottery itself, which is to benefit the State's public education system. Section 24.102, Florida Statutes (1987), entitled "Purpose and intent" provides:

> (1) The purpose of this act is to implement s. 15, Art. X of the State Constitution in a manner that enables the people of the state to benefit from significant additional moneys for education and also enables the people of the state to play the best lottery games available.

Appellants cannot enforce the contract between Control Data Corporation and the Lottery because they, at best, derive only a remote and incidental benefit from it.

As a final note, as pointed out by numerous courts of foreign jurisdictions, any enforceable right arising out of the alleged failure to issue appellants a correct ticket must fail for policy reasons. The concerns of fraud and protracted litigation militate against imposing liability on either the Lottery or its vendors, retailers and contractors under the instant scenario. Without the implication that appellants herein participated in such a fraudulent scheme, what is to prevent someone from completing a play slip moments after learning of the winning numbers and thereafter claiming that through the fault of a third party no corresponding ticket was issued? While appellants' plight is certainly lamentable, to recognize a viable cause of action in this case would open the door to innumerable and unenforceable deceptive practices.

AFFIRMED.

TRIANO v. DIVISION OF STATE LOTTERY
703 A.2d 333 (N.J. Super. Ct. App. Div. 1997)

SHEBELL, Presiding Judge.

On March 20, 1996, Teresa Triano and Susan Kerlin filed a complaint in the Law Division against defendants, Division of State Lottery ("State Lottery"), Virginia E. Haines, its Executive Director, and John Gallagher, its controller. In their complaints, plaintiffs alleged they were winners of the New Jersey Lottery Lucky Anniversary game, but that the defendant State Lottery breached its agreement with [each plaintiff] when it advertised and offered [them] and other members of the public the opportunity to win various amounts up to and including $250,000.00, with the purchase of the Lucky

Anniversary Lottery Ticket and when it thereafter failed to pay [them] the [amount] which [was] revealed on [the ticket].

Plaintiffs also alleged that defendants, Haines and Gallagher, "failed to properly manage, direct or oversee the Lucky Anniversary Lottery game to ensure that false and misleading information was [not] presented to the public as an inducement to purchase lottery tickets."

On December 26, 1996, defendants moved for summary judgment seeking dismissal because the Law Division was not the proper forum to review the matter; plaintiffs failed to exhaust their administrative remedies; plaintiffs failed to file notices of claim as required under the Tort Claims Act and Contractual Liability Act; and plaintiffs' claim for negligent misrepresentation against Haines and Gallagher must fail under N.J.S.A. 59:3-10. Defendants asserted that to exhaust their administrative remedies, plaintiffs were required to bring their claims to the Executive Director of the State Lottery for a final review, and that only after obtaining a final decision, could plaintiffs appeal to this court.

On February 7, 1997, the Law Division judge granted defendants' motion holding that the plaintiff failed to exhaust all administrative remedies prior to filing their complaint. The motion judge observed:

> I think it requires the . . . head of the Lottery Commission to make a ruling . . . . In that way the expertise of the Commission, which is substantial, they're the ones that devise all the rules for these games . . . . And it's an important function here because not only are we dealing with these people who claim to be winners, but a lot of other people . . . . So it's an important issue. And I think the Lottery Commissioner should deal with it first. And then there's an appeal to the Appellate Division. There is no stop at the Law Division. The Law Division doesn't get involved. It's straight Commission decision and then to the Appellate Division. The Appellate Division can then deal on the legal issue that the Lottery Commission may or may not decide. I can't say that this [is] a foregone conclusion. There may be enough . . . confusion about this ticket so that the Director might make an exception or might decide that certain people were misled by the rules. It doesn't seem that way. But . . . I don't think it's inconceivable.

The judge also held that plaintiffs' claim was not cognizable under the Tort Claims Act and the Contractual Liability Act, and that Haines and Gallagher had immunity from plaintiffs' negligent misrepresentation claim. Plaintiffs appeal and we affirm.

Between January 1995 and April 1995, plaintiffs purchased Lucky Anniversary tickets from the State Lottery for five dollars each. Among the rules contained on each ticket, it was provided that "all winners, tickets and transactions are subject to New Jersey Lottery rules and regulations and State Law. All prize awards are subject to claim procedures, validation tests, and other applicable requirements of the New Jersey Lottery." After purchasing a ticket, the player had to scratch off an opaque material to reveal certain hidden symbols and dollar amounts. Each ticket contained three games, one of which was the bonus game. The following appeared on the tickets: "Scratch off Bonus area, reveal a 25th symbol and win prize shown below automatically."

Plaintiffs claim that defendants issued an advertising brochure which stated, "Find our Anniversary symbol and win prize shown instantly." Plaintiffs claim that as a result of the brochure they were "induced to purchase the ticket."

When plaintiffs scratched off the bonus section, their tickets revealed a symbol (present, candle, cake, hat) and the amount of their prize ($5,000 to $250,000). Plaintiffs claimed that in accordance with the rules, they won the amount revealed in the bonus section, but when they went to the State Lottery to claim their winnings, defendants claimed they did not possess winning tickets because none revealed the "25th" symbol. Plaintiffs argued that since the wording on the ticket provided that a person only had to reveal a 25th symbol, any symbol that appeared in the bonus area was a winning symbol.

In August 1995, [plaintiffs] sent a letter to the State Lottery seeking payment for their alleged winning tickets. In the letter, they argued that the bonus language was misleading, and should have stated, "reveal the symbol '25th' and win a prize." They argue that it would have been clear then that the "only manner in which a person could win anything in the bonus area is if the symbol '25th' is revealed." They further argued that if the only way to win the bonus award is to reveal the "25th" symbol, "then the game itself is misleading and fraudulent."

In August 1995, the State Lottery responded to the letter:

> In order to win this particular game the graphic "25th" must appear in the bonus circle in order to win . . . . The ticket purchased by your client is not a winner as it lacks the graphic "25th" in the bonus play area . . . . The statement appearing on the face of the ticket adjacent to the Bonus play circle establishes that the "25th" symbol graphic is the only winning symbol for the Bonus game.

Plaintiffs did not seek to have their claim heard by the Executive Director of the State Lottery. They contend that since only the interpretation of ambiguous contract language is involved, they did not have to exhaust their administrative remedies before filing their complaint, and that the Law Division should have heard the matter.

The State Lottery Law, N.J.S.A. 5:9-1 to -25, (the "Act") empowers the State Lottery to promulgate rules and regulations regarding, among other things:

> (4) The manner of selecting the winning tickets or shares . . . .

> (12) Such other matters necessary or desirable for the efficient and economical operation and administration of the lottery and for the convenience of the purchasers of tickets or shares and the holders of winning tickets or shares. [N.J.S.A. 5:9-7(a).]

Pursuant to the above, the Lottery Commission promulgated regulations covering the procedures and safeguards that must be followed in order to claim a prize. N.J.A.C. 17:20-3.1 provides:

> In the event that a dispute arises involving the ownership of a winning lottery ticket or the validity of such a ticket, the Director [of

the Division of the State Lottery] shall schedule and hold a hearing in accordance with N.J.A.C. 1:1.

We do not consider § 3.1 to grant the Director the authority to resolve the issues presented in this dispute, as it involves neither the ownership or validity of the tickets. However, the Lucky Anniversary game rules clearly state under Section 12-Final Decision, that "the Director shall make all final decisions regarding the awarding of prizes." We deem this to be a sufficient grant of authority to empower the Director to hear and decide this matter on behalf of the State Lottery.

The general rule regarding a party's obligation to exhaust the administrative remedies of a state agency is codified in R. 2:2-3(a)(2):

> Appeals may be taken to the Appellate Division as of right . . . (2) to review final decisions or actions of any state administrative agency or officer . . . except that review pursuant to this subparagraph shall not be maintainable so long as there is available a right of review before any administrative agency or officer, unless the interest of justice requires otherwise.

The following three goals are served by the exhaustion requirement:

> (1) the rule ensures that claims will be heard, as a preliminary matter, by a body possessing expertise in the area; (2) administrative exhaustion allows the parties to create a factual record necessary for meaningful appellate review; and (3) the agency decision may satisfy the parties and thus obviate resort to the courts. [City of Atlantic City v. Laezza, 80 N.J. 255, 265, 403 A.2d 465 (1979).]

The first goal is particularly important where the ultimate decision rests upon the factual determinations lying within the expertise of the agency or where agency interpretation of the relevant statutes or regulations is desirable. The second goal is significant, as we are not a court of record and must depend on a record developed below. The third goal requires the parties to pursue available procedures to their appropriate conclusion and correlatively await their final outcome before seeking judicial intervention. This is so because interruption of the administrative process is not justifiable to any greater extent than interference with the trial process by interlocutory appeals. The expertise of an administrative agency may not be exercised or known until it renders its final decision and usually due deference is accorded such expertise upon judicial review.

The preference for exhaustion of administrative remedies is one of convenience, and not an indispensable pre-condition. Generally, the exhaustion rule will not be applied in the following circumstances: (1) when only a question of law exists; (2) when administrative remedies would be futile; (3) when irreparable harm would result; (4) when jurisdiction of the agency is doubtful; or (5) when an overriding public interest calls for a prompt judicial decision. However, even in cases involving only legal questions, jurisdiction should remain with the agency where the agency is in a special position to interpret its enabling legislation, can conclusively resolve the issue or issues, and can provide relief for the plaintiff.

Plaintiffs argue on appeal that it would be futile to bring the matter to the State Lottery for adjudication, since it constructed the ambiguous language and has an inherent interest in ruling in its own favor. Plaintiffs characterize Magliochetti v. State, 276 N.J.Super. 361, 647 A.2d 1386 (Law Div. 1994), as a case in which the trial court "ruled that the exhaustion of administrative remedies was not required in light of the fact that the interpretation of a statute was at issue." 276 N.J.Super. at 365, 647 A.2d 1386. However, in Magliochetti, the Commissioner of Transportation did not have the ability to administratively determine the eminent domain issues, as such power was vested with the Law Division under the Eminent Domain Act. Id. at 366, 647 A.2d 1386.

Here, the Legislature has granted the State Lottery control over the economical operation and administration of the lottery, N.J.S.A. 5:9-7(a), and has also granted it the power to issue subpoenas to compel witness attendance and the production of documents. N.J.S.A. 5:9-10. The State Lottery has, in turn, under the rules for the game in question empowered its Director to render a final decision on the claims presented.

Plaintiffs nonetheless argue that "defendants lack the requisite expertise and most importantly objectivity to render a fair and impartial determination," and that the issue to be determined is one of contract law to be determined by the Law Division. Plaintiffs cite Matawan Borough v. Monmouth County Tax Bd., 51 N.J. 291, 240 A.2d 8 (1968), in which the Borough brought an action against the County Board of Taxation maintaining that the Board's application of a statute was unconstitutional. The Supreme Court held that the borough did not have to exhaust its administrative remedies because the "instant case includes the interpretation of a statute and a constitutional question, matters for which the courts are uniquely suited." The Court also noted that use of "administrative expertise" would be an "idle gesture" because the administrative body "would be asked to declare illegal its own actions under the statute."

In the present case, we are not dealing with a matter of statutory interpretation. Plaintiffs are questioning the interpretation and application of language crafted by the State Lottery. In our view, having the agency determine the issue would not be an "idle gesture," because as the motion judge noted, the Director might decide that there was confusion about the language on the ticket. If the Director were given the opportunity to resolve the matter with the plaintiffs, it could obviate the need to resort to the courts.

Our Supreme Court in Roadway Express, Inc. v. Kingsley, 37 N.J. 136, 139, 179 A.2d 729 (1962), noted that there is a strong policy in favor of exhaustion of administrative remedies, and stated:

> we are not particularly concerned with the label or description placed on the issue but are concerned with the underlying considerations such as the relative delay and expense, the necessity for taking evidence and making factual determinations thereon, the nature of the agency and the extent of judgment, discretion and expertise involved, and such other pertinent factors as may fairly serve to aid in determining whether, on balance, the interests of justice dictate the extraordinary

course of by-passing the administrative remedies made available by the Legislature. Id. at 141 (citations omitted).

In Driscoll v. Department of Treasury, Div. of Lottery, 265 N.J. Super. 503, 627 A.2d 1167 (Law Div. 1993), the judge observed that there "is little case law in New Jersey regarding the viability of a cause of action on behalf of a lottery ticket holder arising out of a statewide lottery scheme." The court further noted that the relationship arising out of the lottery system is primarily contractual in nature, and, from a contractual perspective, "the terms of the contract are subject to the lottery law, and the rules and regulations promulgated pursuant to that authority." Therefore, "the rights and obligations of the contracting parties arising out of a lottery ticket purchase cannot contravene the rules and regulations of the Commission."

Plaintiffs, in purchasing the tickets, agreed to abide by the rules of the State Lottery. The rules provided, among other things, that "all determinations regarding prize awards are subject to the decision of the Director and all rules and regulations of the State Lottery Commission which apply to this game." Since the State Lottery created the tickets and the language thereon, it possesses the expertise involved in interpreting the language.

In balancing the pertinent factors as to whether to by-pass the available administrative remedy, we must also consider plaintiffs' contention that since the State Lottery has a "direct financial stake in the outcome," it could not render a fair and impartial ruling with respect to the interpretation of the bonus language on the tickets. In support of this argument, plaintiffs rely on Karafa v. New Jersey State Lottery Comm'n, 129 N.J.Super. 499, 501, 324 A.2d 97 (Ch.Div. 1974), and Scott v. State, 265 N.J. Super. 591, 598, 628 A.2d 379 (App.Div. 1993).

In Karafa, the plaintiff maintained he was the winner of the weekly lottery drawing, but was unable to produce his ticket. After the Lottery Director rejected plaintiff's claim, plaintiff brought an action in the Chancery Division. The judge noted that the State Lottery had promulgated regulations governing the procedures and safeguards that must be followed in order to claim a prize, and that "these regulations, being substantive in nature, have the force and effect of law." After analyzing the State Lottery Law, the judge dismissed plaintiff's complaint, as it failed to state a claim.

Plaintiffs submit that as in Karafa, their case should receive judicial review because the issue involves a question of law which does not require the special expertise of the State Lottery. However, in Karafa, the judge specifically held that courts must follow the legislative mandate, and that "a lost lottery ticket may not be established by judicial declaration."

In Scott, 265 N.J. Super. at 594, a foster parent submitted a claim under the state-funded liability program seeking indemnification for the damage to her home suffered when a foster child left a hot iron on a bed. A claims investigator denied plaintiff's claim, and plaintiff appealed to the Attorney General. After waiting fourteen months, plaintiff filed a complaint in the Law Division. The judge denied the State's motion to transfer the matter to the Office of Administrative Law, and the State appealed arguing that plaintiff failed to exhaust administrative remedies. We affirmed, stating:

First of all, as a practical matter, she did everything she could to exhaust her administrative remedies. She followed the agency's instructions to appeal from an adverse decision to a deputy attorney general. She waited for a decision until further delay might have jeopardized her claim . . . .

Secondly, the doctrine of exhaustion of administrative remedies assumes the existence of a valid administrative procedure, and we have rejected that assumption. Thirdly, in the absence of an express statutory or contractual exhaustion requirement, exhaustion of administrative remedies is not a prerequisite to a contract suit against the State under the Contractual Liability Act. [Id. at 598.]

In determining that there was no valid administrative procedure, we considered the liability program to have created a unilateral contract, and found that the State bound itself to indemnify plaintiff under the terms of the program. Thus, in accordance with the New Jersey Contractual Liability Act, plaintiff had a statutory right to have her claim for indemnification heard in the Law Division. We noted that the State could have established the program by administrative rules and could have provided for agency adjudication of claims.

In the instant case, the State Lottery did specifically provide through the game rules that the Director would make all final decisions regarding the awarding of prizes, and ticket purchasers are bound by those rules. Therefore, plaintiffs are required to obtain a final determination by the State Lottery, before the matter may be appealed to this court.

Upon consideration and balancing of all pertinent factors, we are convinced that the interests of justice do not require by-passing the administrative remedies available to plaintiffs. We, therefore, affirm the Law Division's dismissal of their complaint and remand directly to the Division of State Lottery for further proceedings to be scheduled by the Director of the Division.

FULLERTON v. DEPARTMENT OF REVENUE SERVICES, GAMING POLICY BOARD
714 A.2d 1203 (Conn. 1998)

CALLAHAN, Chief Justice.

The sole issue in this administrative appeal is whether the plaintiffs, James Fullerton and Mary Fullerton, the holders of one of two Lotto tickets with all six winning numbers from the December 21, 1993 Lotto drawing, are entitled to the entire first level prize from that drawing because the holder of the other ticket did not come forward within one year of the drawing. The plaintiffs claim that they are entitled to the entire prize, rather than one half of the prize, because: (1) they were the only "winners" of the drawing in that the holder of the second ticket never came forward; and (2) failure to award them the entire first level prize would violate § 12-568-1(e)(1) of the Regulations of Connecticut State Agencies, which provides that "[a]t least forty-five percent (45%) of the total gross sales in any lottery game shall be returned as prizes to holders of winning tickets." We disagree with the plaintiffs' claim and conclude that the trial court properly dismissed their administrative appeal.

The parties stipulated to the following facts. James Fullerton purchased a Lotto ticket at G & S Video in Wallingford on December 21, 1993. There was a Lotto drawing that evening, and the six winning numbers selected matched those on the plaintiffs' ticket. On May 10, 1994, the plaintiffs presented their winning ticket to the lottery claims center in Newington and were informed that two tickets containing the six winning numbers had been sold for the December 21, 1993 drawing. The second ticket containing the same six winning numbers as the Fullertons' ticket had been purchased on December 21, 1993, at the Depot Deli in Roxbury (Roxbury ticket). The plaintiffs were told, therefore, that they were entitled to only one of the two shares of the first level prize pool of $5,618,438.86. Thus, the plaintiffs' share of the first level prize pool was valued at $2,809,219.43, payable in twenty annual installments of $94,809.97. A check was issued for $94,811 ($140,461 less federal and state taxes) representing the first installment payment of the plaintiffs' share of the prize, with nineteen additional annual installments of $94,809.97 due on or about May 10 of each year.

Three weeks prior to the expiration of the claim period for the Roxbury ticket, a "Search for the Missing Millionaire" media promotion was conducted. When the holder of the Roxbury ticket failed to claim his or her share of the prize within the one year claim period, which expired December 21, 1994, the unclaimed share of the prize reverted to the prize structure for the December 23, 1994 Lotto drawing, pursuant to § 12-568-5(p) of the Regulations of Connecticut State Agencies.

On December 23, 1994, the plaintiffs sent a facsimile to John B. Meskill, executive director of the division of special revenue (division), making a demand for immediate payment of the unclaimed one-half portion of the first level prize for the December 21, 1993 Lotto drawing. Meskill sent a letter to the plaintiffs denying their demand for payment on the basis of his opinion that the plaintiffs were entitled to and had received only one of the two shares of the first level prize pool for the December 21, 1993 Lotto drawing. Meskill stated in his letter that the failure of the other winning ticket holder to present that ticket for validation did not convert the plaintiffs' ticket into the one winning ticket for the December 21, 1993 Lotto drawing. Rather, he stated that "[t]he number of winners and the portion of their share of the prize pool is determined very shortly after the drawing . . . ."

The plaintiffs appealed to the gaming policy board (board), which held a hearing regarding the plaintiffs' claim to the other one half of the first level prize pool. The board upheld Meskill's ruling. The plaintiffs thereafter appealed to the trial court, which dismissed the plaintiffs' appeal, concluding that the board's decision was not illegal, arbitrary or an abuse of its discretion, and that the lottery regulations were neither vague nor standardless. Furthermore, the court concluded that the 45 percent payout requirement of § 12-568-1(e)(1) applies to the lottery in general, rather than to the individual games, and that the board's interpretation comports with the regulatory requirements. The plaintiffs appealed from the judgment of the trial court to the Appellate Court, and we transferred the appeal to this court pursuant to Practice Book § 4023, now § 65-1, and General Statutes § 51-199(c).

I

"The standard of review of an agency decision is well established. Ordinarily, this court affords deference to the construction of a statute applied by the administrative agency empowered by law to carry out the statute's purposes . . . . [A]n agency's factual and discretionary determinations are to be accorded considerable weight by the courts . . . . Cases that present pure questions of law, however, invoke a broader standard of review than is ordinarily involved in deciding whether, in light of the evidence, the agency has acted unreasonably, arbitrarily, illegally or in abuse of its discretion . . . . Furthermore, when a state agency's determination of a question of law has not previously been subject to judicial scrutiny . . . the agency is not entitled to special deference . . . . [I]t is for the courts, and not administrative agencies, to expound and apply governing principles of law." Assn. of Not-for-Profit Providers for the Aging v. Dept. of Social Services, 244 Conn. 378, 389, 709 A.2d 1116 (1998). Because our review of questions of law is plenary, we address the substantive merits of the plaintiffs' appeal. Id., at 390, 709 A.2d 1116.

The plaintiffs first assert that, under the applicable lottery regulations, they are the only "winners" of the December 21, 1993 Lotto drawing, and, therefore, are entitled to the entire first level prize. Specifically, the plaintiffs argue that, although the regulations refer to "winners" and "holders of winning tickets," they do not define the term "winner." The plaintiffs contend that when § 12-568-1(e)(1) and § 12-568-5(p) are read together, the term "winner" must mean a person holding a ticket containing all six of the winning numbers drawn who presents the ticket to the claims center for payment. In other words, the plaintiffs maintain that in order to be a winner one must not only hold a winning ticket, but must also present the winning ticket to the claims center.

According to the defendants' contrary interpretation of the relevant regulations and the Lotto game procedures, a winner is any ticket holder whose ticket matches all six of the winning numbers drawn. They do not interpret the regulations to require that a winner be a person who has presented a ticket to the claims center for payment. In support of their argument, the defendants rely on § V(A)(1) of the Lotto game procedures, which provides in part that "[w]inner(s) matching all six (6) of the winning numbers in any order will equally share the first-level prize pool." The defendants contend that § V(A)(1) of the game procedures contemplates that there may be more than one winning ticket because the first level prize pool is divided equally by the number of winners. Furthermore, the defendants claim that § 12-568-5(p) provides for the reversion of unclaimed prize money if winning ticket holders fail to present their claims for the prize within the claim period. We agree with the defendants.

The division of special revenue has broad statutory authority to adopt regulations pertaining to the state lottery, including regulations relating to prize payments. See General Statutes § 12-562 and General Statutes (Rev. to 1995) § 12-568(a). "Our rules of statutory construction apply to administrative regulations." Preston v. Dept. of Environmental Protection, 218 Conn. 821, 829 n.9, 591 A.2d 421 (1991). Although the plaintiffs are correct that the regulations do not contain an express definition of the term winner, we conclude that the regulations establish that a winner is determined at the time of the drawing.

One who purchases a ticket for an authorized lottery game agrees to abide by the lottery regulations and is bound by the official procedures of that particular game. Regs., Conn. State Agencies § 12-568-5(a) and (b). Section V(A)(1) of the Lotto game procedures provides in part that "[w]inner(s) matching all six (6) of the winning numbers in any order will equally share in the first-level prize pool." Section V(A)(1) also provides that the first level prize pool, in addition to being funded by 34.182 percent of the Lotto sales applicable to that drawing, also is funded by unclaimed lottery prizes. Section 12-568-5(p) requires the division to "retain for the holder of a winning ticket any prize which that holder has not claimed . . . ." If at the expiration of the claim period any prize remains unclaimed, it "shall revert to the prize structure of future lottery games to be distributed to future winners . . . ." Regs., Conn. State Agencies § 12-568-5(p).

The provisions of § 12-568-5(p) and § V(A)(1) of the game procedures clearly contemplate that a winner is determined at the time of the drawing. After the drawing, the division is required to divide the prize pool into as many shares as there are winners, and retain each share until it is claimed. Upon a winning ticket holder's failure to claim the prize within the applicable claim period, the prize reverts to the prize structure of future games to be distributed to future winners.

Further support for the defendant's interpretation of the term winner is found in the definitions set forth in the lottery regulations. Pursuant to § 12-568-2(a)(11) of the Regulations of Connecticut State Agencies, a "drawing" is defined as the "process as established in the procedures whereby winners in a lottery game are conclusively determined." Although the term winner is not defined expressly, § 12-568-2(a)(11) makes it clear that a winner is "conclusively determined" at the time of the drawing.

Applying the plain language of the regulations and the Lotto game procedures, we are persuaded that the term winner means the holder of a ticket that matches all six of the winning numbers selected. Thus, contrary to the plaintiffs' position, winners are conclusively determined at the time of the drawing, not at the time of presentment of the ticket. We conclude, therefore, that because there were two winning tickets drawn in the December 21, 1993 Lotto game, there were two winners. The plaintiffs therefore are entitled to one half of the first level prize pool. The trial court properly concluded that the plaintiffs have been awarded their one-half share and are not entitled to the share that was payable to the holder of the Roxbury ticket. See Booker v. Rogers, 256 Ill.App.3d 605, 195 Ill.Dec. 728, 628 N.E.2d 1192 (1994) (holder of one of two winning Lotto tickets not entitled to entire prize when other ticket is not presented for collection).

II

The plaintiffs also contend that adoption of the defendants' construction of the regulations will result in a violation of § 12-568-1(e)(1), which provides that "[a]t least forty-five percent (45%) of the total gross sales in any lottery game shall be returned as prizes to holders of winning tickets." The plaintiffs argue that at least 45 percent of the total gross sales for a given Lotto drawing must be distributed to winners of that Lotto drawing, rather than to winners of future drawings. We disagree.

Section 12-568-1(e)(1) requires that at least 45 percent of the total gross sales in any lottery game shall be returned as prizes to the holders of winning tickets. The plaintiffs are confusing the broader term "game" with the more narrow term "drawing." The term "game" as used in the lottery regulations refers generally to the "different types of lottery games" established by the executive director with the advice and consent of the board. Regs., Conn. State Agencies § 12-568-1(b).

Thus, § 12-568-1(e)(1) applies to the distribution of the sales of the games in general, rather than to any individual drawing. Therefore, the 45 percent distribution requirement applies, in general, over time, to the various "games" run by the agency, and not to any particular drawing of any game.

Moreover, if we were to adopt the interpretation urged by the plaintiffs, after the expiration of each claim period, the defendants would be required to supplement the winnings of all levels of winners who had claimed their prizes by the amount of the unclaimed prize. If the division intended to take on this substantial burden, it could have drafted the regulation so that the 45 percent requirement applied to each "drawing." Furthermore, § 12-568-5(p) provides that unclaimed prizes "shall revert to the prize structure of future lottery games to be distributed to future winners." Thus, § 12-568-5(p) clearly contemplates that unclaimed, undisbursed portions of the 45 percent prize payout should be paid not to winners of a particular drawing, but to future lottery game winners.

When interpreting a regulation, we must use common sense. Citerella v. United Illuminating Co., 158 Conn. 600, 609, 266 A.2d 382 (1969). "Courts must assume that a reasonable and rational result was intended and construe the regulation accordingly." Id. When confronted with two possible interpretations, courts will adopt the interpretation that makes the regulations effective and workable, and not the one that leads to unreasonable results. Red Hill Coalition, Inc. v. Town Plan & Zoning Commission, 212 Conn. 727, 737-38, 563 A.2d 1347 (1989). "The unreasonableness of the result obtained by the acceptance of one possible alternative interpretation of an act is a reason for rejecting that interpretation in favor of another which would provide a result that is reasonable." Maciejewski v. West Hartford, 194 Conn. 139, 151-52, 480 A.2d 519 (1984). We must presume that a reasonable and rational result was intended by the division in adopting § 12-568-1(e)(1). See id., at 152, 480 A.2d 519.

The unreasonableness of the plaintiffs' interpretation of § 12-568-1(e)(1) compels us to reject that interpretation in favor of the interpretation advanced by the division and affirmed by the trial court. See id. The trial court correctly concluded that an adoption of the plaintiffs' interpretation would lead to confusion and an administrative burden that would interfere with the defendants' ability effectively to operate the lottery. The division has interpreted the 45 percent requirement to apply to lottery distribution as to particular categories of games in general, over time, not to each lottery drawing. This interpretation provides for an effective and workable method of distributing the regulatory 45 percent mandate.

The judgment is affirmed.

CONVERSE v. LOTTERY COMMISSION
783 P.2d 1116 (Wash. Ct. App. 1989)

PEKELIS, Judge.

The Washington State Lottery Commission (Commission) appeals the trial court's order directing the Commission to pay Seattle-First National Bank (Seattle-First) the annual net prize payment of lottery winner Michael J. Converse. The Commission contends that the trial court's order approving Converse's voluntary assignment of his annual installment to Seattle-First as collateral for a business loan is not an "appropriate judicial order" within the meaning of RCW 67.70.100. We reverse.

The essential facts are not in dispute. In March of 1986, Converse won the Washington State Lottery. As the winner, he is entitled to receive 20 annual payments of $100,000.

After winning the lottery, Converse decided to establish a business to manufacture insulating underwear for scuba divers. In order to do so, he arranged to borrow $350,000 from Seattle-First. The loan was to be secured by the physical assets of the business and Converse's annual lottery winnings for the calendar years 1989 through 1994.

On October 4, 1988, Converse and Seattle-First jointly petitioned the Snohomish County Superior Court for an order assigning Converse's annual lottery winnings to Seattle-First for the years 1989 through 1994. The trial court signed the order as presented. The Commission did not receive notice and was not made a party to this proceeding.

Thereafter, Converse and Seattle-First submitted the agreed order to the Commission, but the Commission refused to honor it, contending that it violated RCW 67.70.100. The petitioners then filed a motion seeking an order of contempt against the Commission for its refusal to comply with the order. The Commission was then allowed to intervene in the proceeding.

On November 8, 1988, the trial court heard the petitioners' contempt motion. The court declined to find the Commission in contempt, but after entering findings of fact and conclusions of law, affirmed the prior order confirming the partial assignment of Converse's annual lottery payments.

The Commission appeals from both rulings, contending that RCW 67.70.100 prohibits a lottery prize winner from voluntarily assigning his winnings. It argues that the exception permitting assignments does not convert voluntary assignments approved by the court pursuant to an agreed order into an assignment "pursuant to an appropriate judicial order." Rather, the Commission argues, the exception applies to judicial orders which, for example, arise from garnishment and bankruptcy proceedings.

RCW 67.70.100 provides:

> No right of any person to a prize drawn is assignable, except that payment of any prize drawn may be paid to the estate of a deceased

prize winner, and except that any person pursuant to an appropriate judicial order may be paid the prize to which the winner is entitled. The commission and the director shall be discharged of all further liability upon payment of a prize pursuant to this section.

No Washington court has yet interpreted RCW 67.70.100. We do so now according to general principles of statutory construction. If a statute is unambiguous, its meaning must be derived from its language alone. Only if the statute is ambiguous will the reviewing court look to other sources to determine its meaning.

RCW 67.70.100's general prohibition against assignments is clear and unambiguous. It is the exception permitting assignments "pursuant to an appropriate judicial order" which is arguably ambiguous. However, exceptions to the general rule, especially when the general rule is unambiguous, should be strictly construed with any doubts resolved in favor of the general provision, rather than the exception.

Converse concedes that the general prohibition against assignments of lottery winnings should be narrowly construed. He nevertheless maintains, however, that any lawful judicial order which confirms an assignment is permissible under the exception. If this court were to accept Converse's interpretation of RCW 67.70.100, any person who wished to assign his lottery winnings for any reason could petition the court for an order affirming the agreed to assignment and avoid RCW 67.70.100's general prohibition. In addition, nothing would prevent a lottery winner from assigning his winnings to a number of parties, thereby burdening the Lottery with the administrative expense involved in parceling out the winner's annual payment to various assignees. In short, Converse's interpretation of the exception would swallow the rule. RCW 67.70.100 must be read to prohibit all voluntary assignments, including those which are confirmed by court order.

This construction of RCW 67.70.100 is in accord with the only court case interpreting an identical provision in the New Jersey State Lottery Law. In McCabe v. Director of New Jersey Lottery Comm'n, 143 N.J. Super. 443, 363 A.2d 387 (1976), the court held that the New Jersey State Lottery Law prohibited voluntary assignments confirmed by judicial order, noting that the lottery winner's request for a court order was:

> an exception to an exception; i.e., a request for a court-ordered sanction of an assignment of winnings which would run counter to the general statutory prohibition against assignments, all within the framework of a statute which itself is an exception to the State's general public policy against gambling.

McCabe, 143 N.J. Super. at 448.

The Lottery Commission has adopted rules interpreting RCW 67.70.100 which are consistent with our reading of the statute. WAC 315-06-120(7) prohibits any person from assigning his right to a lottery prize except:

> (a) That payment of a prize may be made to any court appointed legal representative, including, but not limited to, guardians, executors, administrators, receivers, or other court appointed assignees; or

(b) For the purposes of paying federal, state, or local tax.

Courts are to accord great deference to an agency's interpretation of a statute when the statute is within the agency's field of expertise. Where the Legislature has specifically delegated rule-making power to an agency, its regulations are presumed valid. One asserting invalidity has the burden of proof, and the challenged regulations need only be reasonably consistent with the statutes they implement. Only compelling reasons demonstrating that the regulation is in conflict with the intent and purpose of the legislation warrant striking down a challenged regulation.

Converse has demonstrated no compelling reason to justify striking down WAC 315-06-120(7). WAC 315-06-120(7)'s strict limitations on assignments are reasonable and consistent with RCW 67.70.100's general prohibition against assignments. In addition, RCW 67.70.040 directs the Commission to promulgate rules governing the operation of the state lottery that are for both the "convenience" of ticket holders and "the efficient and economical operation and administration of the lottery." RCW 67.70.040. While WAC 315-06-120(7)'s narrow interpretation of RCW 67.70.100 may not be "convenient" to Converse, it certainly minimizes the Lottery's administrative costs.

More importantly, this narrow interpretation is faithful to the obvious intent of our Legislature, and that of many other states, to extend its parens patriae protection to lottery winners in order to insulate them from their own human frailties and the possible excesses to which they might be subjected. This intent is clearly evidenced by the Legislature's decision to parcel out lottery winnings in installments and to prohibit lottery winners from putting themselves into debt by assigning excessive amounts of their winnings to creditors.

Having failed to articulate any compelling reasons to invalidate WAC 315-06-120(7), the Commission's narrow interpretation of RCW 67.70.100 as prohibiting voluntary assignments confirmed by court order should be upheld.

In conclusion, we hold that a plain reading of RCW 67.70.040 and the public policies underlying it compels the interpretation expressed in WAC 315-06-120(7). RCW 67.70.100 clearly prohibits Converse from voluntarily assigning his lottery winnings and the exception permitting assignments pursuant to "appropriate" judicial orders does not extend to such voluntary assignments.

Reversed.

Notes

1. For a further sampling of cases involving players suing lottery officials, see *Molina v. Games Management Services*, 449 N.E.2d 395 (N.Y. 1983) (neither state nor independent ticket agent liable where latter's failure to keep records caused winner's disqualification); *Georgia Lottery Corporation v. Sumner*, 529 S.E.2d 925 (Ga. Ct. App. 2000) (innocent error that resulted in "misprint" on ticket relieved state of duty to pay); *Horan v. State*, 270 Cal. Rptr. 194 (Ct. App. 1990) (plaintiff who neither purchased nor played winning scratch-off ticket could recover nothing); *Stern v. State*, 512 N.Y.S.2d 580 (App. Div.), *appeal dismissed*, 514 N.E.2d 390 (N.Y. 1987) (state had no responsibility where winner threw away his ticket instead of waiting for official results

to be posted); *Madara v. Commonwealth*, 323 A.2d 401 (Pa. Commw. Ct. 1974) (state's obligation extinguished where winning ticket turned in two days late); *Rice v. Ohio Lottery Commission*, 708 N.E.2d 796 (Ohio Ct. Cl. 1999) (winner who opted for immediate rather than extended payout was not deceived by state's method of calculating amount due him); *Ramesar v. State*, 617 N.Y.S.2d 259 (Ct. Cl. 1994), *aff'd*, 636 N.Y.S.2d 950 (App. Div.), *leave to appeal denied*, 672 N.E.2d 604 (N.Y. 1996) (state had no liability for failing to enter subscription to lottery until after winning ticket, which happened to be plaintiff's number, was drawn). *See also* Michael Jones, *Lotteries Must Strike Balance Between Letter of the Law and Unwritten Contract with Players*, 2 Gaming L. Rev. 9, 9 (1998) ("Most players believe they have sort of a social contract with the lottery . . . . The contract has nothing to do with procedures and processes; it is based upon the perceptions of what consumers believe about a lottery and how it should operate.").

2. Anti-assignment provisions, like the one at issue in *Converse*, are a common feature of state-run lotteries. Designed to protect winners and avoid burdening the government with endless paperwork, they are routinely upheld by the courts. *See, e.g., In re Koonce*, 262 B.R. 850 (Bankr. D. Nev. 2001); *In re Keim*, 212 B.R. 493 (Bankr. D. Md. 1997); *Lotto Jackpot Prize of Dec. 3, 1982, Won by Marianov*, 625 A.2d 637 (Pa. 1993); *Midland States Life Insurance Company v. Hamideh*, 724 N.E.2d 32 (Ill. App. Ct. 1999), *appeal denied*, 731 N.E.2d 765 (Ill. 2000); *Michigan Basic Property Insurance Association v. Ware*, 583 N.W.2d 240 (Mich. Ct. App. 1998), *appeal denied*, 591 N.W. 2d 32 (Mich. 1999); *Petition of Singer Asset Finance Company, L.L.C.*, 714 A.2d 322 (N.J. Super. Ct. App. Div. 1998); *R & P Capital Resources, Inc. v. California State Lottery*, 37 Cal. Rptr. 2d 436 (Ct. App. 1995). *But see Peterson v. District of Columbia Lottery and Charitable Games Control Board*, 673 A.2d 664 (D.C. 1996) (recently-adopted anti-assignment rules could not be applied retroactively).

Generally speaking, the anti-assignment rules have no bearing in "contested judicial proceedings." Thus, a lottery winner ordinarily will be subject to a forced assignment if he or she owes alimony or child support. *See, e.g., In re Marriage of Bohn*, 8 P.3d 539 (Colo. Ct. App. 2000); *Ware v. Ware*, 748 A.2d 1031 (Md. Ct. App. 2000); *Green v. Scott*, 687 So. 2d 655 (La. Ct. App. 1997); *DeVane v. DeVane*, 655 A.2d 970 (N.J. Super. Ct. App. Div. 1995). *See also* Dennis M. LaRochelle, *The Lottery and Divorce: It Could Happen to You . . .* , 2 Gaming L. Rev. 291 (1998), and Jennifer L. Reas, Note, *His, Hers, and Ours: Determining How Courts Will Characterize Lottery Winnings Won Prior to Marriage*, 37 Brandeis L.J. 843 (1998-1999).

Problem 5

During a weekly "Super Drawing" of the state lottery, a woman was erroneously proclaimed the winner of the grand prize. Several days later, when she went to the lottery's headquarters to claim her prize, she was informed of the mistake. If she sues, arguing that when her name was called an irrevocable contract was formed, how should the court rule? *See Coleman v. State*, 258 N.W.2d 84 (Mich. Ct. App. 1977).

E. SUITS AGAINST OTHER PLAYERS

FITCHIE v. YURKO
570 N.E.2d 892 (Ill. App. Ct. 1991)

BOWMAN, Justice.

Plaintiffs, Judy Fitchie, Phyllis Huisel, and Frances Vincent, brought this action seeking a declaration of their rights to a $100,000 prize claimed by defendant, Richard Yurko, from the Illinois Department of the Lottery (Lottery). The trial court held that plaintiffs and defendant were entitled to equal shares of the prize money. Defendant contends on appeal that the court erred in that (1) the court lacked jurisdiction to hear the claim since plaintiffs failed to exhaust their administrative remedies, (2) plaintiffs were improperly allowed to amend their pleadings, (3) the court's findings were inconsistent, and (4) the court's decision was not supported by the evidence. We affirm.

The trial testimony revealed the following sequence of events. Plaintiff Phyllis Huisel and her husband, Robert, owned a combination service station and coffee shop, which they called Hitching-A-Ride, in Burlington. Phyllis operated the coffee shop, and, as a part of the coffee shop business, she sold lottery tickets. Defendant Yurko started coming into the coffee shop in November 1989 to have a cup of coffee or pancakes and to socialize. Sometimes Phyllis would play the lottery with Yurko. Phyllis indicated, but Yurko disputed, that they would share equally in any winnings even when only one of them supplied the money to buy lottery tickets. Plaintiff Judy Fitchie had known Phyllis for a number of years and sometimes helped her in the coffee shop. Judy was acquainted with Yurko only because she saw him occasionally at Hitching-A-Ride.

During the second or third week of February 1990 Phyllis and Judy were both in the coffee shop when Yurko came in and said he wanted to play the lottery. While there were inconsistencies between plaintiffs' and defendant's testimony, as well as minor differences even in the testimony of the various plaintiffs, it appears clear the following events occurred. Phyllis was behind the counter, waiting on customers. Judy, along with plaintiff Frances Vincent, was sitting at the counter. Yurko purchased lottery tickets which needed to have film scratched off the front of them in order to reveal whether a prize had been won. While Phyllis evidently took the money for the tickets, she allowed Yurko to take the tickets themselves from the box, where they were kept behind the counter. Yurko testified that he initially bought $100 worth of tickets, but all of the plaintiffs indicated that he first purchased only two, $1 tickets, which he immediately scratched off. One of the two was a $5 winner, which he redeemed for five more tickets.

At some point Yurko asked Phyllis if she wanted to help him scratch the film off the tickets, but Phyllis suggested that he ask Judy to help because she was the luckier one. Subsequently Yurko placed a number of tickets in front of both Judy and Frances and invited them to help him scratch them off. Yurko had not previously met Frances and was not formally introduced to her on the day in question. While Yurko repeatedly denied it, all three plaintiffs testified that Yurko indicated to them that if they would help him scratch off the lottery tickets they would be his partners and would share in any winnings which resulted from those tickets. After playing for some time, Judy uncovered three television sets and announced that she had a winner. At the time, the parties were playing the Fortune Hunt lottery game, and the ticket scratched by Judy gave the owner a chance to compete for a $100,000 prize.

The back of the Fortune Hunt tickets had a line for the name, address, and phone number of the ticket holder. Completed tickets were to be mailed to the Lottery. On Thursdays, 100 tickets were drawn from all of the winning tickets which had been mailed in. From those 100 tickets, six were drawn on the Lottery television show on Saturday, and those six ticket owners would be the contestants on the television show the following week. The grand prize in the Fortune Hunt game was $100,000, but other prizes were also awarded. There is indication in the record that a winning ticket holder would receive at least $1,500 if he appeared on the television show.

All of the plaintiffs gave very similar testimony as to what occurred after the winning ticket was scratched. Judy placed the ticket on the counter near Phyllis. Yurko urged Phyllis to fill it out, but she said she did not want to go on television. Yurko indicated he was willing to be on the television show, and, after some discussion, all the parties agreed that Yurko should be their representative and go on television. Yurko then printed "F.J.P. Rick Yurko," representing the first initial of each plaintiff and his own name, on the line provided on the back of the ticket for the name of the ticket holder. He also gave his address and phone number. According to Phyllis, when Yurko started filling out the ticket he told her he was going to put all of the plaintiffs' initials and his name on the ticket and indicated once again that they would be partners no matter what they might win.

During the time Yurko and the plaintiffs were playing the lottery, Robert Huisel and Thomas Vincent, Frances' husband, were having coffee in a booth in the coffee shop. Both spouses testified that after Judy declared she had a winner they heard Yurko ask the three plaintiffs for their initials. He indicated he wanted to put their initials on the ticket because they were partners. Shortly afterwards, Frances and her husband left Hitching-A-Ride, and, while defendant may have bought more tickets, Phyllis and Judy essentially stopped playing. All of the plaintiffs admitted that they did not pay out of their own pockets for any of the lottery tickets that were purchased that day.

Yurko acknowledged that he placed plaintiff's initials on the back of the winning ticket. He said he did so because he wanted to remember who helped him scratch the ticket. Then, if he won, he could take them out to dinner or give them something for helping him. He indicated that he had uncovered and sent to the Lottery three similar tickets in the past, and the initials would identify the particular ticket involved here. He could not recall who scratched off the winning ticket, and he did not know why he placed plaintiffs' initials on the same line with his name as opposed to some other part of the ticket.

Yurko subsequently mailed the ticket to the Lottery and it was one of the six tickets drawn on March 10, 1990. On March 11 Yurko stopped at Hitching-A-Ride to see the Huisels. Phyllis' daughter, Sherry Payne, was there at the time. Sherry testified that Yurko gave her a nudge in the arm and said, "We are going to be rich." She knew he was referring to the lottery because her mother had told her about the winning ticket. Phyllis also testified that she heard Yurko make the comment about all of them getting rich. She also said Yurko remarked that Judy would probably use her share to put a down payment on her house and that he was going to go to Las Vegas with his share. Yurko testified that he consulted an attorney regarding the ownership of the ticket about two days before he went on the television show.

The Lottery show on which Yurko appeared as a contestant was taped on March 16 and aired on the evening of March 17. Yurko won the $100,000 prize and placed only his own name on the claim form for the prize. Over the next several days plaintiffs tried unsuccessfully to reach Yurko. On March 22, 1990, they filed this suit, naming both Yurko and the Lottery as defendants. The complaint prayed for a declaration of rights as to the $100,000 lottery prize and sought damages for conversion of the prize money. Plaintiffs were granted a temporary restraining order to prevent the Lottery and Yurko from paying out or collecting on any claim to the prize. On April 2, pursuant to a court order, the Lottery deposited $77,000 with the clerk of the Kane County circuit court.

The amount deposited represents the $100,000 lottery prize, minus applicable Federal and State taxes. The Lottery also interpleaded Yurko's wife, Penny Yurko, who was the plaintiff in a suit in De Kalb County seeking dissolution of her marriage to Richard Yurko.

At the conclusion of the trial the court declared that plaintiffs and Richard Yurko were each entitled to an equal share of the lottery prize and denied plaintiffs' prayer for damages for conversion.

In this court Yurko initially raises a challenge to the jurisdiction of the trial court to hear this cause on the ground that plaintiffs failed to exhaust their administrative remedies. He argues that plaintiffs should have presented their claim to the Lottery before seeking the aid of the court. Defendant's position cannot be sustained.

First of all, defendant relies on section 7.3 of the Lottery Act (Act) (Ill.Rev.Stat.1989, ch. 120, par. 1157.3) for the proposition that the Act grants primary jurisdiction over matters relating to the Illinois lottery to the Illinois Department of Revenue and the Lottery Control Board. Section 7.3 provides for hearings upon complaints charging violations of the Act or regulations promulgated under the Act. However, there are no allegations in the instant case that the Act or any relevant regulations have been violated. Thus, section 7.3 is inapplicable.

Defendant next asserts that section 13 of the Act (Ill.Rev.Stat.1989, ch. 120, par. 1163) provides that no prize awarded to a person shall be assignable. While this may be true, it is a nonissue in this case since no claim has been made that Yurko assigned any portion of the prize money to plaintiffs.

Finally, defendant contends that under section 19 of the Act (Ill.Rev.Stat.1989, ch. 120, par. 1169) all claims for prizes from a lottery game must be made to the Department of the Lottery. While defendant correctly states the content of section 19, it is readily apparent the section is intended only to spell out the procedures to be followed when a lottery game involves the purchase of a physical lottery ticket and the ticket must be presented in order to claim a prize. Section 19 does not address multiple claims to ownership of a winning ticket.

Yurko's next contention is that the trial court abused its discretion by allowing plaintiffs, at the close of their case, to amend their complaint in order to conform it to the proofs they had presented. Specifically, defendant asserts that, while plaintiffs' original complaint sought recovery on a conversion theory, the amended complaint sought recovery on a partnership theory.

The Code of Civil Procedure specifically provides for amendment of pleadings at any time for the purpose of conforming the pleadings to the proofs. (Ill.Rev.Stat.1989, ch. 110, par. 2-616(c).) It is within the sound discretion of the trial court to decide whether to allow amendments after the evidence has been presented, and the court's decision will not be disturbed absent a clear abuse of discretion. (Servbest Foods, Inc. v. Emessee Industries, Inc. (1980), 82 Ill.App.3d 662, 673, 37 Ill.Dec. 945, 403 N.E.2d 1; Lawson v. Hill (1979), 77 Ill.App.3d 835, 844-45, 33 Ill.Dec. 228, 396 N.E.2d 617.) Amendment of pleadings cannot be allowed where the amendment alters the nature of the proof required to defend (Blazina v. Blazina (1976), 42 Ill.App.3d 159, 165, 1 Ill.Dec. 164, 356 N.E.2d 164) or if the other party would be prejudiced or surprised (Trident Industrial Products Corp. v. American National Bank & Trust Co. (1986), 149 Ill.App.3d 857, 866, 103 Ill.Dec. 252, 501 N.E.2d 273). Examination of the facts of this case in light of these principles reveals no abuse of discretion.

Plaintiffs initially sought both declaratory and damages relief on a theory of conversion. In order to establish their rights and sustain their claim, plaintiffs needed to plead facts showing, among other things, that they had an ownership interest in, and a right to possession of, the winning ticket. (See Illinois Education Association v. Illinois Federation of Teachers (1982), 107 Ill.App.3d 686, 689, 63 Ill.Dec. 343, 437 N.E.2d 1265 (setting forth the elements of conversion).) Plaintiffs attempted to make the requisite showing by relating facts which, if proved, would establish either that defendant gave the ticket to plaintiffs as a gift or that the parties had entered into an agreement whereby they were entitled to equal shares of any winnings. For the most part the amendments sought by plaintiffs merely expanded on these facts. More precisely, the amendments set forth more accurately and in greater detail the sequence of events surrounding the discovery of the winning ticket. The facts as amended were still directed only toward establishing a gift or an agreement for the purpose of showing plaintiffs' interest in the ticket. Thus, what defendant calls a change in theory of recovery or, perhaps, addition of a new theory, is in reality merely part and parcel of the ownership element of plaintiffs' claim.

The "partnership theory of recovery" attacked by defendant was not new but had been part of plaintiffs' complaint from the start. Indeed, defendant must have recognized the pleading of an agreement since, in his answer, he denied any implication that the parties "reached any kind of agreement with respect to the proceeds of any winnings." Since the amendments did not add any new theories, and an agreement was pleaded by plaintiffs from the outset, the nature of the proof required to defend was not altered. Furthermore, in light of the nature of the amendments, defendant's claim of surprise, and implication of prejudice to himself, is not persuasive. In our view the modifications to plaintiffs' complaint constitute proper amendments to conform the pleadings to the proof.

We turn now to defendant's challenge to the trial court's findings. At the conclusion of the trial the court found that plaintiffs' evidence supported theories of both partnership and gift. Defendant points out that consideration, while an inherent element of a partnership, is not necessary to the making of a gift. He concludes that the concepts of gift and partnership are contradictory and insists that the court's inconsistent findings require that the judgment in favor of plaintiffs be vacated and the matter be remanded. We agree with defendant that the two concepts in question present certain inconsistencies but do not agree that such inconsistencies require vacation of the judgment in this case.

As we have mentioned, plaintiffs needed to show that they had a protectable interest in the winning ticket and/or the prize money won by the ticket. They sought to establish that interest by offering evidence of both a gift and an agreement. We recognize that the complaint does not set forth separate counts or a separate set of facts in support of each of the separate theories of recovery. Nor does it draw a clear distinction within itself between allegations directed toward a gift theory and those directed toward an agreement theory. However, there is no doubt the two propositions could have been presented as alternatives. It is permissible to argue in the alternative, even when such arguments are based on inconsistent facts and no individual argument is affected by any other. Hillblom v. Ivancsits (1979), 76 Ill.App.3d 306, 311-12, 32 Ill.Dec. 172, 395 N.E.2d 119.

Had defendant made two separate and distinct arguments, the trial court could have responded in kind. In the absence of a clear delineation we think the trial court, in essence, merely acknowledged that evidence had been offered to support both theories and then, without clearly embracing one proposition as opposed to the other, concluded that plaintiffs had established their right to the prize money. While it would have been more desirable for the trial judge clearly to delineate what he found to be the controlling facts, his failure to do so is not fatal to plaintiffs' cause. Defendant has not demonstrated how he has been prejudiced by the lower court's findings. Indeed, we do not believe he could show prejudice since the result would have been the same if the court had resolved the issue solely on the basis of either gift or agreement.

As a final matter defendant attacks the judgment on the ground that the evidence does not support the court's findings of either gift or partnership. As explained below, after reviewing the record we conclude that the finding of partnership was justified. Accordingly, we need not address defendant's challenge to the finding regarding gift.

After all the evidence had been presented and closing arguments completed, the trial court made the following remarks: "In my opinion and the Court finds there is ample evidence in the record to support a theory of both partnership based on consideration and mutual amount of obligation and gift outright." The trial judge expanded on his initial statement as follows: "The defendant, whether viewed as a fiduciary or a partner or as a simple agent of a partnership, had a continuing duty to these plaintiffs." And again, the court added: "[I]t is very plausible that is indeed what happened. There was a joint enterprise, venture, or at least donated partnership under these circumstances."

While it is clear from these statements the court did not perceive the relationship between plaintiffs and defendant as a formal, legal partnership in the business sense, it is also clear the court decided that the parties had entered into a binding agreement which gave rise to rights and duties which the court could recognize and enforce. The court's conclusion is supported by the record.

Whether a partnership exists is generally a question of fact to be resolved by the fact finder. (Peterson v. Prince (1981), 102 Ill.App.3d 220, 224, 58 Ill.Dec. 355, 430 N.E.2d 297.) In a bench trial, the judge, as the trier of fact, is in a better position to determine the credibility of the witnesses and the weight to be given their testimony. (Aetna Insurance Co. v. Amelio Brothers Meat Co. (1989), 182 Ill.App.3d 863, 865, 131 Ill.Dec. 332, 538 N.E.2d 707.) Accordingly, a reviewing court will not reverse a judgment unless the findings of the trial court are clearly contrary to the manifest weight of the evidence. (Amoco Realty Co. v. Montalbano (1985), 133 Ill.App.3d 327, 333, 88 Ill.Dec. 369, 478 N.E.2d 860; In re Estate of Elson (1983), 120 Ill.App.3d 649, 655, 76 Ill.Dec. 237, 458 N.E.2d 637.) A finding is against the manifest weight of the evidence only when an opposite conclusion is clearly evident. (Commonwealth Edison Co. v. Department of Revenue (1989), 179 Ill.App.3d 968, 975, 128 Ill.Dec. 816, 535 N.E.2d 30.) A court of review may not overturn a judgment merely because it disagrees with it or might have reached a different conclusion had it been presented with the issue in the first instance. (Schulenberg v. Signatrol, Inc. (1967), 37 Ill.2d 352, 356, 226 N.E.2d 624; In re Estate of Elson (1983), 120 Ill.App.3d 649, 655, 76 Ill.Dec. 237, 458 N.E.2d 637.) In this case the trial court found that the parties had formed a partnership of some sort. In our opinion the evidence indicates that the arrangement between defendant and plaintiffs constituted a joint venture.

A joint venture is an association of two or more persons to carry out a single enterprise for profit. (In re Johnson (1989), 133 Ill. 2d 516, 525-26, 142 Ill.Dec. 112, 552 N.E.2d 703; Smith v. Metropolitan Sanitary District (1979), 77 Ill.2d 313, 318, 33 Ill.Dec. 135, 396 N.E.2d 524.) Whether a joint venture exists is a question of the intent of the parties. (United Nuclear Corp. v. Energy Conversion Devices, Inc. (1982), 110 Ill.App.3d 88, 109, 65 Ill.Dec. 649, 441 N.E.2d 1163.) The elements to be considered in determining the parties' intent are: an agreement, express or implied, to carry on an enterprise; a demonstration of intent by the parties to be joint venturers; a joint interest, as reflected in the contribution of property, finances, effort, skill or knowledge by each party to the joint venture; a measure of proprietorship or joint control over the enterprise; and a provision for sharing of profits and losses. (Dawdy v. Sample (1989), 178 Ill.App.3d 118, 126, 127 Ill.Dec. 299, 532 N.E.2d 1128; Ambuul v. Swanson (1987), 162 Ill.App.3d 1065, 1068, 114 Ill.Dec. 272, 516 N.E.2d 427.) A formal agreement is not essential to establish a joint venture. (Barton v. Evanston Hospital (1987), 159 Ill.App.3d 970, 973, 111 Ill.Dec. 819, 513 N.E.2d 65.) Rather, the existence of a joint venture may be inferred from facts and circumstances demonstrating that the parties, in fact, undertook a joint enterprise. Ambuul, 162 Ill.App.3d at 1068, 114 Ill.Dec. 272, 516 N.E.2d 427.

It could be inferred that the parties entered into an agreement and showed their intent to be joint venturers when they started playing the lottery together. Yurko invited plaintiffs, both verbally and by placing tickets in front of them, to play the lottery with him. Although it was refuted by Yurko, plaintiffs testified that he told them if they would help him scratch tickets they would be his partners and would share in any prize winnings. Plaintiffs expressed agreement with this proposal when they began scratching off the tickets.

The parties' intent to act jointly could be gleaned also from their subsequent conduct. There was testimony that both Judy and Frances uncovered tickets which were good for small cash prizes or more tickets. Neither defendant nor any of the plaintiffs tried to claim any of those prizes as their own. Rather, the tickets were turned in for more tickets, and plaintiffs kept on scratching. Also, all three plaintiffs testified that, after the winning ticket was revealed, there was a discussion amongst all the parties as to who would appear on the television show. Together, not individually, they decided that Yurko would be the one to go. Finally, although vehemently denied at trial, defendant himself impliedly acknowledged a joint effort when he printed the plaintiffs' initials right alongside his own name on the back of the winning ticket, again amidst talk that he and the plaintiffs were partners.

A joint interest in the effort to win the lottery, as shown by the parties' various contributions, could also be found from the evidence. Although there was a wide divergence as to how much money he actually spent, it is undisputed that Yurko paid for the tickets that were purchased. As for their contribution to the venture, Frances and Judy expended their time and energy and put forth effort to scratch the tickets. While Phyllis' part in this is not altogether clear, her unrefuted testimony was that she scratched off a couple of tickets, and it is evident the other parties considered her part of the enterprise.

Finally, with regard to provision for sharing of profits, plaintiffs testified that Yurko told them they would share in anything that was won if they helped scratch the tickets. While Yurko denied this, he nevertheless later wrote plaintiffs' initials next to his own name on the line provided on the lottery ticket for the ticket holder's name. From this evidence the court could have found that the joint venturers had planned to share equally in any lottery prize ultimately won.

The accumulated evidence favorable to plaintiffs, if believed, warrants the conclusion that all the parties intended and agreed to the joint pursuit of a single enterprise, i.e., a lottery prize. There is no question that the resolution of this dispute turned heavily on the credibility of the witnesses. Nor is there a question that the trial court found plaintiffs to be more credible than defendant. The judge referred to defendant's evidence as "extremely vague and inconsistent" and remarked that "defendant's story is not plausible under these circumstances." After emphasizing that he was well aware of the atmosphere and circumstances of the parties' gathering at Hitching-A-Ride, and of the results of things said freely and clearly in those circumstances, the court added, "there is no doubt what was intended, and I think that the Defendant's memory has failed him." Of plaintiffs' theory of the case the court remarked, "it is very plausible that is indeed what happened." In light of the trial court's determination regarding defendant's and plaintiffs' respective credibility, we cannot say a conclusion opposite to the one reached by the court is clearly evident. We see no reason to disturb the findings of the court below.

Affirmed.

REINHARD, Presiding Justice, dissenting.

Because the record shows the existence of neither a partnership nor a valid gift, I respectfully dissent from the majority's affirmance of the trial court's judgment for plaintiffs.

The majority concludes that the parties here were engaged in a joint venture. A joint venture is essentially a partnership carried on for a single enterprise, and joint ventures are governed by partnership principles. (Bachewicz v. American National Bank & Trust Co. (1986), 111 Ill.2d 444, 448, 95 Ill.Dec. 827, 490 N.E.2d 680.) Because a partnership is a contractual relationship, the principles of contract law fully apply to it. (In re Estate of Johnson (1984), 129 Ill.App.3d 22, 25, 84 Ill.Dec. 322, 472 N.E.2d 72.) Consideration is a basic element for the existence of a contract. (Steinberg v. Chicago Medical School (1977), 69 Ill.2d 320, 331, 13 Ill.Dec. 699, 371 N.E.2d 634.) Accordingly, a partnership agreement must be based on valid consideration between the partners. 59A Am.Jur.2d Partnership § 112 (1987).

Valid consideration for a contract centering on the purchase of legal lottery tickets has been found where each of the parties contributed tickets (Miller v. Radikopf (1975), 394 Mich. 83, 228 N.W.2d 386) or in the context of a long-standing pattern of joint ticket purchases (Pearsall v. Alexander (D.C.App.1990), 572 A.2d 113). Here, where it is conceded that defendant alone purchased the lottery tickets, the majority's only suggestion of what might constitute consideration is the fact that plaintiffs "expended their time and energy and put forth effort to scratch the tickets." However, the consideration supporting a unilateral promise such as the one present here must be that which is bargained for as consideration by the promisor. Bank of Marion v. Robert "Chick" Fritz, Inc. (1974), 57 Ill.2d 120, 124, 311 N.E.2d 138.

The record simply does not support the conclusion that defendant bargained for plaintiffs' "time and energy" in scratching the tickets as their contribution to a joint venture or partnership. The evidence viewed most favorably to plaintiffs shows that defendant promised to share in the lottery winnings if plaintiffs helped him scratch the tickets. The question, then, is whether the scratching of the tickets was intended to be consideration for a contract or merely a condition upon a gratuitous promise.

A promise may propose either a bargain or a gift, and in either case a condition may be imposed using the same words. (L. Simpson, Handbook of the Law of Contracts § 53, at 84 (2d ed. 1965).) As a general rule, "if the happening of the condition will not only be of no benefit to the promisor but it is obviously merely for the purpose of enabling the promisee to receive a gift, the happening of the event on which the promise is conditional, though brought about by the promisee in reliance on the promise, will not properly be construed as consideration." 17A Am.Jur.2d Contracts § 115, at 131 (1991).

Here, I believe that defendant's invitation to plaintiffs to help him scratch the tickets was intended as simply a condition to their receipt of defendant's gift of lottery winnings. It strains credulity to find that plaintiffs' scratching of tickets was viewed by the parties as consideration supporting a partnership contract. I note that this conclusion does not contravene the general rule against inquiring into the adequacy of consideration, because that rule operates only where the parties actually intended a bargain. (L. Simpson, Handbook of the Law of Contracts § 53, at 85 (2d ed. 1965).) Here, the evidence supports, at most, that defendant's promise constituted a conditional promise to make a gift of lottery winnings.

I further believe, however, that no valid gift has been effectuated. In addition to donative intent, the making of a valid gift requires the donor to part with exclusive dominion and control over the subject of the gift, and there must also be delivery. (Frey v. Wubbena (1962), 26 Ill.2d 62, 72, 185 N.E.2d 850.) Here, whether the gift is viewed as the lottery ticket itself or the winnings it produced, defendant never parted with exclusive dominion and control. Moreover, even if the promise to share in the future lottery winnings could be construed as an attempt to effectuate a gift of those winnings, a promise to make a future gift is generally unenforceable (Hux v. Woodcock (1985), 130 Ill.App.3d 721, 724, 86 Ill.Dec. 44, 474 N.E.2d 958) and is revocable at any time until the gift is executed (Meyer v. Meyer (1942), 379 Ill. 97, 104, 39 N.E.2d 311).

Accordingly, I would reverse the judgment of the trial court.

PANDO v. DAYSI
499 N.Y.S.2d 950 (App. Div. 1986)

MEMORANDUM DECISION.

At issue is plaintiff-appellant Christopher Pando's right to share lottery winnings amounting to $2.9 million equally with defendant Daisy Fernandez. Plaintiff alleges that in June 1981 when he was 14 years old he made an oral agreement with defendant in Spanish, the parties' native tongue. According to the agreement, defendant would give plaintiff four dollars with which he would purchase New York State lottery tickets bearing numbers selected by him. During the purchase of the tickets and thereafter plaintiff, a devotee of Saint Eleggua, would pray to the saint for help in the selection of a winning number. If the winning number was selected the parties allegedly agreed to divide the proceeds evenly. In fact, plaintiff did select a winning number. Upon informing defendant of this fact, defendant reportedly made numerous public declarations that plaintiff's prayer had brought about the happy result and that she and plaintiff would share the winnings as partners. Subsequently, defendant denied the existence of any agreement with plaintiff, represented that she was the sole owner of the winning lottery ticket in her possession, and sought to claim the entire prize for herself.

This action followed. Plaintiff ultimately seeks a declaration that the winning lottery ticket was jointly owned pursuant to the parties' agreement and that a constructive trust be impressed upon plaintiff's share of the lottery proceeds. Assuming the existence of a partnership agreement, plaintiff also seeks an accounting from defendant for half of all lottery winnings received by her. Defendant has asserted counterclaims for fraud and harassment.

Discovery in this action has proceeded with great difficulty. Although the parties, on September 9, 1981, stipulated before Justice Klein, inter alia, to the timely exchange of bills of particulars, plaintiff still had not received a complete set of answers to his demand in June 1982. At that time Justice Tyler denied defendant's motion to vacate plaintiff's demand for a bill of particulars. Despite Justice Tyler's order, plaintiff was forced to return to court in September 1982 to obtain an order by Justice Ascione directing that the items demanded by plaintiff be furnished within 30 days.

Rather than comply with Justice Ascione's order defendant moved in October 1982 to dismiss the complaint pursuant to CPLR 3211(a)(7) and 3211(c). Plaintiff cross-moved to obtain the discovery already directed, and for imposition of sanctions for defendant's failure to abide by the above mentioned court orders. Special Term treated defendant's motion as one for summary judgment. In doing so, it found that proof of the alleged agreement was not barred by the Statute of Frauds and that section 1610 of the Tax Law prohibiting the sale of lottery tickets to minors did not prevent plaintiff from asserting a claim to part of the prize. We agree with Special Term for the reasons stated in its opinion that neither of these grounds warranted dismissal of the complaint. We do not agree, however, that there was any greater cause to dismiss the action for impossibility of proof, as was done.

Citing a version of the alleged oral partnership agreement advanced by plaintiff in support of an earlier motion for a preliminary injunction, Special Term opined that to prove his performance of the agreement plaintiff would have to show that Saint Eleggua had in fact interceded at his request to bring about the desired result. The court reasoned that since divine intercession did not admit of forensic proof, plaintiff could not demonstrate that he had discharged his end of the bargain and, therefore, could not have the agreement enforced.

While it is true that saintly intervention is not provable in a court of law, it is far from evident that the alleged agreement requires such intervention as a condition of enforceability, much less makes it, as Special Term argued, "its essence, its very heart and soul."

In at least three places in the record not cited by Special Term (i.e., in plaintiff's affidavit in opposition to summary judgment, plaintiff's amended answers to interrogatories and in plaintiff's verified complaint), plaintiff describes the agreement in terms imposing no condition of saintly intervention for enforcement. According to these versions, plaintiff was obligated only to use his best efforts to enlist Saint Eleggua's help in exchange for which defendant agreed to pay for the tickets and split the prize should it be won. If, as is possible, defendant bargained simply for the assistance of plaintiff whose help she believed would be efficacious, having received that assistance she cannot now disown her obligations under the agreement by imposing the additional condition that plaintiff prove the effect of his prayers. Plaintiff's prayers in this scenario had value to defendant because she believed in their power to help effectuate the desired end; the prayers having been made, the sought after consequence, she believed, was at least more likely to follow. It is then entirely possible that defendant bargained simply for the benefit of those acts which if performed by plaintiff she felt would enhance her chances of winning the lottery. Under this version of the agreement plaintiff was required to do no more than purchase the tickets, select the numbers, and pray to the Saint in order to fulfill his end of the bargain. Certainly, none of these actions is impossible to prove in a court of law.

While there remained an account of the parties alleged agreement supportable in the record and susceptible of proof it was error for Special Term to dismiss the complaint for impossibility of proof. In so doing, the court resolved the central factual issue of the case; it determined what the parties agreed to. It bears repetition that issue resolution is not the court's function on a motion for summary judgment. (Sillman v. Twentieth Century Fox, 3 N.Y.2d 395, 404, 165 N.Y.S.2d 498, 144 N.E.2d 387 [1957].) Once a material question of fact arises as it has here, summary judgment must be denied. (Id.) Given the inconclusiveness of the record, no doubt largely attributable to the parties' apparent lack of sophistication in contractual matters, and the imprecision which easily intrudes when informal agreements reached orally in a foreign language are recounted, translated and documented for forensic purposes, we think the grant of summary judgment was unwarranted. The circumstances of this case render the factual questions raised over the agreement's terms difficult if not impossible to resolve in advance of trial.

Since the complaint is to be reinstated, plaintiff's cross-motion for discovery related relief is not moot. Having noted above defendant's unacceptable delay in meeting plaintiff's legitimate discovery requests we think it appropriate to require defendant to comply with previously ordered discovery within 30 days or face sanctions.

DICKERSON v. DENO
770 So. 2d 63 (Ala. 2000)

MADDOX, Justice.

The parties to these proceedings dispute whether the holder of a winning Florida lottery ticket must share the winnings with others because of an alleged prior oral agreement they all had made to share the winnings if any one of them was a winner. The trial court held that the one had to share the winnings with the others. The resolution of that question raises at least two legal questions:

(1) Given the evidence presented, did the trial judge err in finding that the holder of the winning lottery ticket had orally agreed to share any winnings equally with four other persons?

(2) Assuming, arguendo, that the proof was sufficient to establish an oral agreement, was the agreement unenforceable on the basis that it was a contract made in Alabama and was "founded . . . on a gambling consideration," as that term is used in Ala.Code 1975, § 8-1-150?

We conclude that the agreement constituted a contract "founded . . . on a gambling consideration" and, therefore, that it was unenforceable; consequently, we reverse the judgment of the trial court and render a judgment for the defendant Tonda Dickerson.

The facts are basically undisputed. The plaintiffs—Sandra Deno, Angie Tisdale, Matthew Adams, and Jackie Fairley—and the defendant Tonda Dickerson were all employees at the Waffle House restaurant in Grand Bay, Alabama. Edward Seward, who is not a party to this action, was a regular customer of the Waffle House. On several occasions Seward would travel to Florida and purchase lottery tickets and upon his return would give the tickets to various friends and family members, including the employees of the Waffle House. Seward did not expect to share any potential lottery winnings based on the tickets he gave away, but he claimed that he was promised a new truck by the employees of the Waffle House if one of the tickets he distributed there was a winning ticket. Several employees of the Waffle House received lottery tickets from Seward during the several weeks that he gave out the tickets.

A drawing for the Florida lottery was scheduled for Saturday night, March 6, 1999. During the week before that drawing, Seward traveled to Florida and purchased several lottery tickets. He placed each individual ticket in a separate envelope and wrote the name of the intended recipient on the outside of the envelope. On March 6, 1999, before the lottery drawing, Seward presented the plaintiffs Deno, Tisdale, and Adams each with an envelope containing one lottery ticket. The drawing was held as scheduled. The numbers on the lottery tickets held by Deno, Tisdale, and Adams did not match the numbers drawn in the March 6 drawing.

On March 7, 1999, after the March 6 drawing had already been concluded and the winning numbers had been determined, Seward presented a ticket to the plaintiff Fairley, who had never previously received a ticket from Seward; he also on that date presented the defendant Dickerson with a ticket. Each of those tickets was for the March 6 drawing, and each was presented in a separate envelope. Upon opening her envelope, Fairley determined that the numbers on her ticket did not match the winning numbers. Subsequently, Dickerson opened her envelope and determined that the numbers on her ticket matched the winning numbers drawn in the lottery the night before. The ticket won a prize of approximately $5 million. (The total prize awarded for the March 6, 1999, Florida lottery was $10 million. However, two winning tickets were presented for that award.)

Shortly thereafter, on March 18, 1999, the plaintiffs sued Dickerson, alleging that they and Dickerson had orally contracted with each other that if any one of them should win, then the winner would share any lottery winnings with the other ticket recipients. The plaintiffs asked the court to issue a preliminary injunction enjoining distribution of the winnings until a declaration of their rights could be made, and on March 19, 1999, the trial court ordered all parties to refrain from any further efforts or attempts to collect any funds from the State of Florida Department of Lottery that were, or might be, the subject of a dispute between the parties. This order remained in effect throughout the trial of the case. The plaintiffs sought to have the alleged oral agreement specifically performed, and they also asked the trial court to declare that a constructive trust had been created by the parties.

Dickerson filed a motion to dismiss the complaint, with an accompanying brief, and she later filed an answer. In the motion and in the answer, she alleged that enforcement of any oral agreement would be barred by the Statute of Frauds. She also averred that any oral agreement made by the parties was a gambling contract and could not be enforced under Alabama law.

The trial court refused to dismiss the complaint. Instead, it ordered that the case be tried before an advisory jury on the plaintiffs' claim for declaratory relief. Following the trial, the advisory jury returned a verdict for the plaintiffs, and the trial court entered a final judgment in the plaintiffs' favor. It issued a written order holding that there was an oral contract and that each party was entitled to 20% of the proceeds of Dickerson's Florida lottery ticket. Dickerson appeals.

Dickerson argues on appeal that the alleged oral agreement testified to by the plaintiffs was unenforceable because, she says, it lacked the necessary elements of a valid and enforceable contract. She also argues that, assuming, arguendo, that the alleged oral agreement did have all the elements ordinarily necessary for a contract, it was void as a gambling contract, because, she argues, it was an agreement made in Alabama and § 8-1-150 specifically provides that "[a]ll contracts founded in whole or in part on a gambling consideration are void."

The plaintiffs make several arguments, including: (1) that this Court must apply the ore tenus rule of review because much of the testimony was presented orally to the trial court, and that under that rule the trial court's findings of fact are presumed to be correct; (2) that Dickerson waived her defenses based on the proposition that the contract was unenforceable, because she did not raise those defenses in the trial court; and (3) that other jurisdictions have held that agreements to share lottery winnings are enforceable and do not violate public policy.

We have examined the plaintiffs' arguments and have thoroughly reviewed the record. However, we agree with Dickerson that she presented to the trial court each of the issues that she argues on appeal.

Dickerson argues at some length that the plaintiffs failed to prove that the parties made an oral agreement. However, we conclude that the parties presented sufficient evidence to support a finding that the parties did orally agree that if any one of them should win the lottery, then they all would divide the proceeds. But, assuming they entered into such an agreement, was that agreement void and unenforceable as a "contract[] founded . . . on a gambling consideration"? See Ala.Code 1975, § 8-1-150. We now address the parties' arguments on that question.

The plaintiffs concede that § 8-1-150 seeks to prohibit the enforcement of any payment for actual wagering or gambling, or on games of chance, but they argue that the oral agreement in this case is not void, because, they contend, "[a]n agreement to share proceeds from a legal winning lottery ticket is simply not a wager between the parties to the agreement in the State of Alabama." They cite several cases they contend support their argument that the oral agreement made in this case was not founded on a gambling consideration.

They first cite Talley v. Mathis, 265 Ga. 179, 453 S.E.2d 704 (1995), as being a "strikingly similar case." In that case, the complaint alleged that two friends, both residents of Georgia, had agreed to jointly purchase tickets from the State of Kentucky lottery and to share the proceeds if they won. Mathis made the same argument in that case that Dickerson makes here: that the alleged agreement was against the public policy of the State where it was made and therefore was unenforceable. The Georgia Supreme Court, as the plaintiffs correctly argue, not only held that the alleged agreement would not violate Georgia public policy but stated that "the public policy of this state would be violated if appellant were denied the opportunity to seek to enforce the alleged agreement against appellees." 265 Ga. at 181, 453 S.E.2d at 706. The plaintiffs also argue that the facts of Talley are similar to the facts in Gipson v. Knard, 96 Ala. 419, 11 So. 482 (1892), because in both cases the parties were joint owners of out-of-state lottery tickets.

In further support of their argument for the validity of the oral agreement, the plaintiffs cite Pearsall v. Alexander, 572 A.2d 113 (D.C.1990), which the District of Columbia Court of Appeals described as "the story of two friends who split the price of a lottery ticket only to have the ticket win and split their friendship." 572 A.2d at 114. In Pearsall, the court held that the agreement did not constitute a gambling contract.

The plaintiffs also cite Kaszuba v. Zientara, 506 N.E.2d 1 (Ind.1987); Miller v. Radikopf, 394 Mich. 83, 228 N.W.2d 386 (1975); Pineiro v. Nieves, 108 N.J.Super. 51, 259 A.2d 920 (1969); Campbell v. Campbell, 213 A.D.2d 1027, 624 N.Y.S.2d 493 (1995); Stepp v. Freeman, 119 Ohio App.3d 68, 694 N.E.2d 510 (1997); Welford v. Nobrega, 411 Mass. 798, 586 N.E.2d 970 (1992); and Fitchie v. Yurko, 212 Ill.App.3d 216, 570 N.E.2d 892, 156 Ill.Dec. 416 (1991).

Dickerson answers the plaintiffs' argument by contending that "[e]very case cited by plaintiffs in support of their argument involves, unlike the instant case, the issue of whether jointly purchased and jointly held lottery tickets are enforceable." Dickerson says that "[t]he parties in those cases did not attempt to increase their odds of winning the foreign lottery by entering into a separate contract with each other" and that "the cases cited by plaintiffs generally hold that individuals may cross state lines and jointly purchase a lottery ticket in a state where such lotteries are legal, and the parties may enforce their rights in the jointly owned ticket," but, she says, "[that] fact situation is not present in this case." Dickerson further points out that in the cases cited by the plaintiffs the courts relied heavily on the fact that the parties did not gamble among themselves, but, rather, jointly gambled with a foreign lottery. Dickerson notes that in Talley the court specifically pointed out that the complaint alleged that "the ticket was legally purchased with joint funds in Kentucky," 265 Ga. at 180, 453 S.E.2d at 705, and that in Gipson v. Knard the transaction alleged was a joint purchase of lottery tickets in New Orleans.

In her concluding argument, Dickerson says:

> Every single case cited by Plaintiffs on the gambling issue, without exception, is a case in which the parties were joint owners of lottery tickets, even as Plaintiffs concede that the parties to this suit were not joint owners of the tickets, but were instead owners of individual tickets. Plaintiffs could only be entitled to a share of the winning tickets by virtue of their alleged side agreement with each other to

hedge their bets, made in Alabama, not as a result of an ownership interest in the winning ticket.

We agree with Dickerson that the facts in this case show that there was no agreement to jointly purchase or to jointly hold the lottery tickets. Each lottery ticket was purchased by Seward in Florida and was presented by him to one or the other of the parties, separately. The alleged oral contract in this case was an exchange of promises to share winnings from the parties' individually owned lottery tickets upon the happening of the uncertain event that the numbers drawn in the Florida lottery matched the numbers on one of the tickets held by the five individuals. Consequently, the agreement between the parties was nothing more than an attempt by each of the five lottery-ticket holders to increase his or her odds of winning some portion of the Florida lottery. Stated differently, the agreement, according to the plaintiffs' own evidence, was that Dickerson would pay the plaintiffs a sum of money upon the happening of an uncertain event over which no party had control, that is, upon Dickerson's ticket winning the Florida lottery. Consequently, we conclude that the agreement at issue here was "founded . . . on a gambling consideration," within the meaning of that phrase in § 8-1-150 and that it was, therefore, void.

The judgment of the trial court is due to be reversed and a judgment rendered for the defendant Dickerson.

JOHNSTONE, Justice, dissenting.

I respectfully dissent. The substance of the agreement among the parties is that each agreed that the lottery ticket held by him or her was jointly owned by all the parties. The consideration to each of the parties for his or her agreement in this regard consists of the mutual agreements to the same effect made by all of the other parties. That is, each party received the acknowledgment of each other party that such other's ticket was jointly owned by all the parties. The consideration consisted not of the uncertain event (the lottery) or the possible winnings from the lottery but rather of the mutual agreements among the parties. Likewise, none of the parties agreed to pay money upon the happening of the uncertain event; but, rather each agreed to acknowledge the joint ownership of his or her ticket by all the parties regardless of the happening of the uncertain event.

Thus the agreement, or contract, at issue is not "founded in whole or in part on a gambling consideration" as outlawed by § 8-1-150, Ala.Code 1975. Accordingly, the judgment of the trial court should be affirmed.

Notes

1. The facts in *Fitchie* are reminiscent of the 1994 movie *It Could Happen to You*. In that film, Nicolas Cage starred as kind-hearted New York City cop Charlie Lang. After a meal, Lang discovered he did not have enough money to tip the waitress (Yvonne Biasi, played by Bridget Fonda), so he promised to split his lottery ticket with her. When the ticket turned out to be worth $4 million, Charlie's scheming wife Muriel (Rosie Perez) sought to keep all the money for herself. In typical Hollywood fashion, Charlie and Yvonne ended up with each other and the cash.

2. Cases like *Fitchie*, *Pando*, and *Dickerson* obviously are driven by greed, and show how even the best relationships can quickly sour in the face of a winning lottery ticket. In one particularly nasty example, a woman sued her mother after the latter won a $1.5 million jackpot. To prove the lottery ticket actually belonged to her, the woman enlisted the aid of her two young children, who lied in open court against their grandmother. Although a jury returned a verdict for the woman, the mother eventually was able to have it set aside by presenting evidence that she had been playing the winning number for months. *See Curtis v. Counce*, 32 P.3d 585 (Colo. Ct. App. 2001). For a further look at suits between players, *see* Matthew L. Gries, Note, *Judicial Enforcement of Agreements to Share Winning Lottery Tickets*, 44 Duke L.J. 1000 (1995), and Steven F. Thompson, Comment, *Contracts to Split Lottery Prizes: What Happens When the Ticket is a Winner?*, 18 Am. J. Trial Advoc. 201 (1994).

3. While reading the *Pando* decision, you may have wondered about Saint Eleggua. In fact, as the trial court explained in granting summary judgment, there is no such saint:

> In attempting to ascertain the identity of "St. Eleggua," the closest the court could come in its research was a saint with the Latin name of St. Eligius (immortalized on television as St. Elsewhere), the patron saint of goldsmiths, who before his canonization served under French kings in the 7th Century as master of the mint, and who showered his riches on the poor who turned to him in overwhelming numbers. He possessed the gifts of miracles and prophecy, and is reputed to have broken open the chains of prisoners by his prayers. 2A Dictionary of Christian Biography, p. 93, 1967 ed.; Butler's Lives of the Saints, rev. ed. of 4 Thurston & Attwater, pp. 455-458. No wonder defendant sought to invoke his aid as the means to overwhelming riches!

Pando by Pando v. Fernandez, 485 N.Y.S.2d 162, 167 n.* (Sup. Ct. 1984). What impact, if any, does the non-existence of Saint Eleggua have on the plaintiff's claim for a share of the winnings?

4. At the time the dispute between Tonda Dickerson and her co-workers arose (March 1999), Alabama did not have a state lottery, thereby leading to out-of-state trips like those taken by Edward Seward. That summer, however, Governor Don Siegelman, who had been elected on a pro-lottery platform, convinced the Alabama legislature to pass a lottery bill. He then proposed an amendment to the state constitution to permit the bill to become operational, using a television spot called "Thank you, Alabama," which depicted Georgians thanking Alabamians for crossing their border to play the Georgia lottery and help fund its educational programs.

Like the Georgia lottery, the Alabama lottery pledged that the money it raised would be spent on education, and for a time it appeared the constitutional amendment would pass easily. But when the votes were counted in October 1999, the amendment had failed by a margin of 54%-46%. In the post-mortems, it quickly became clear why: voters were upset that the lottery's merit-based scholarships would not be available to students who qualified for federally-funded Pell grants, which are based on economic need. To many people, this smacked of economic elitism: while poor people would play the lottery, only middle-and upper-class children would benefit. *See* Patricia

Kathryn Carlton, Comment, *All Bets Are Off: An Examination of Alabama's Proposed Lottery and the Educational Inadequacies It Was Intended to Remedy*, 51 Ala. L. Rev. 753 (2000).

Despite the foregoing, voters in Tennessee handily approved creation of a state lottery when the question was put to them in November 2002. As in Alabama, proponents argued that a lottery would raise money for college scholarships while keeping millions of dollars from flowing into Georgia's coffers. But to avoid the sort of contentious debate that had derailed Alabama's effort, the Tennessee proposal was written in bare-bones fashion and left the details to be worked out by the legislature if the measure passed. *See further* Deborah S. Hayden, *Will Tennessee Take a Chance on a Lottery?*, 38 Tenn. B.J. 12 (May 2002).

5. Many people dream about winning the lottery—the final season of the television series *Roseanne*, for example, revolved around Roseanne's fantasy that she and her sister Jackie had won $108 million in the Illinois state lottery. In real life, however, winners often find that hitting it big brings nothing but grief. Friends and relatives suddenly begin asking for money, ex-spouses go to court demanding increased alimony and child support, salespeople become relentless, and neighbors turn jealous. In addition, many winners go on buying binges that quickly deplete their fortunes (as was powerfully depicted during the fourth season of the television show *Hill Street Blues* in a multi-episode story line involving officer Bobby Hill). Then, too, there is the matter of taxes, which come off the top. For a further look at the ups and downs of winning the lottery, *see, e.g.*, Pam Labert et al., *After the Jackpot—Shock, Elation and Phone Calls from Long-Lost Cousin Ed: Lottery Winners Tell How They Coped with Windfall Wealth*, People, June 10, 2002, at 82, and Lisa Hoffman & Tera Copp, *The Trials and Tribulations of Lottery Winners: Coping with Success: Expect Pleas for Help, Lawsuits and Bouts of Boredom*, Nat'l Post, Sept. 1, 2001, at D6. *See also* Linda Suzzanne Griffin, *The Lottery: A Practical Discussion on Advising the Lottery Winner*, 72 Fla. B.J. 84 (Apr. 1998), and David L. MacGregor & Chris K. Gawart, *Advising Lottery Winners*, 67 Wis. Law. 17 (July 1994).

6. The heartbreak the lottery often produces was cleverly exploited in a 2002 commercial for Miller Genuine Draft beer entitled "Lottery." It begins by showing a young man in a car telling his girlfriend Shannon that he is not ready for marriage. The woman says she understands and then casually mentions that she has just won $63 million in the lottery. The commercial cuts to a scene of the man relating the story to two of his buddies while shooting pool and drinking beer. Steve, one of the friends, consoles the man by pointing out that after taxes, Shannon will take home no more than $28-$30 million. The commercial then ends with Steve sneaking away to call Shannon for a date.

Problem 6

A mother and daughter played the lottery together for years; finally, they got lucky and won a $150,000 jackpot. Although they had contributed equally to the cost, the state recognized only the daughter as the winner because she had purchased the ticket.

After collecting three of the 20 annual installments and splitting them with her mother, the daughter and her husband went bankrupt. The trustee subsequently asked the court for an order declaring the remaining 17 installments to be part of the couple's estate and therefore available to pay their creditors. If the mother intervenes and claims that half the money is hers, how should the court rule? *See In re Dalton*, 146 B.R. 460 (Bankr. D. Ariz. 1992).

Chapter 3

CHARITABLE GAMING

A. OVERVIEW

Many states permit charitable organizations to raise money for their causes by offering games of chance. Although bingo and raffles are the most commonly-authorized types of betting, some jurisdictions also allow charities to host "Vegas Nights" at which casino-style games are available on a limited scale.

B. DEFINITIONS

KNIGHT v. STATE ex rel. MOORE
574 So. 2d 662 (Miss. 1990)

PRATHER, Justice.

I. INTRODUCTION

Factual Background

On January 10, 1990, the Office of Attorney General ("AG") filed a complaint at the Hinds County Chancery Court against nine bingo operators and operations seeking a declaration: (1) "that the game of bingo fits the definition of lottery"; (2) that bingo, a form of lottery, is prohibited by the Mississippi Constitution; and (3) that Miss. Code Ann. § 97-33-51, which exempts bingo, is therefore unconstitutional.

II. ANALYSIS

A. The Primary Issue: Whether Bingo is a Lottery?

> No lottery shall ever be allowed, or be advertised by newspapers, or otherwise, or its tickets be sold in this state; and the legislature shall provide by law for the enforcement of this provision; nor shall any lottery heretofore authorized be permitted to be drawn or its tickets sold.

Miss. Const. art. IV, § 98. If bingo is a lottery or a form of lottery, then this section of the constitution makes bingo illegal, and the legislature may not exempt it via simple majority vote. And if bingo is illegal, then § 97-33-51 must be struck down as unconstitutional.

1. The Chancellor's Opinion

The chancellor issued a lengthy opinion from the bench:

113

The Court is well aware that there are numerous forms of bingo and it is also called by different names and described differently, but under the authorities of this state, namely, Naron v. Prestage, 469 So. 2d 83 (Miss. 1985), the Supreme Court of this state defined "lottery" as: "(1) The offering of a prize; (2) The awarding of a prize by chance; (3) The giving of a consideration for the opportunity to win a prize; and all three of these elements must concur in order to constitute a lottery."

And the principal case which removes any question in legal definitions or precedents is found in our sister state of Tennessee which just this past year, construing its constitution and a charitable form of bingo in the case of Secretary of State v. St. Augustine Church, 766 S.W.2d 499 (Tenn. 1989), said: "This Court is firmly of the opinion, however, that the constitutional provision in its present form completely prohibits the General Assembly from undertaking to legalize or authorize the game of bingo for any commercial purpose, charitable or otherwise."

2. The Bingo Operators' Position

The operators cite for support the "Mississippi Gaming Control Act" as support for their belief that the framers did not intend to prohibit bingo when they drafted Miss. Const. Art. IV, § 98 (1890). The Act construes § 98 by defining "lottery" in such a way that one could logically conclude that bingo must not be a lottery:

(a) The player or players pay or agree to pay something of value for chances, represented and differentiated by tickets, slips of paper or other physical and tangible documentation upon which numbers, symbols, characters or other distinctive marks used to identify and designate the winner or winners; and

(b) The winning chance or chances are to be determined by a drawing or similar selection method based predominantly upon the element of chance or random selection rather than upon the skill or judgment of the player or players; and

(c) The holder or holders of the winning chance or chances are to receive a prize or something of valuable consideration; and

(d) The activity is conducted or participated in without regard to geographical location, with the player or players not being required to be present upon any particular premises or at any particular location in order to participate or to win.

The operators conclude that, clearly, the framers did not intend to prohibit such games as bingo—which did not exist at the time when § 98 was drafted.

3. The AG's Position

The AG posits that § 98 prohibits any and all lotteries by whatever name, and bingo is substantially similar in many respects to so-called traditional lotteries. The AG explains that the overwhelming majority of other states which have confronted this issue has held that bingo is a lottery. The AG suggests that this Court should look to the plain meaning of § 98 and hold that bingo is simply another form of lottery. The AG concludes that the legislature was without authority to exempt bingo from § 98's prohibition of lotteries and that this Court should strike down as unconstitutional Miss. Code Ann. § 97-33-51.

4. Disposition

This Court declines to adopt either of the parties' premises, but concurs in the operators' conclusion.

Close scrutiny of the opinions of the "weight of authority" reveals its employment of "loopified" or circular reasoning. Restated, courts in other jurisdictions have generally reasoned that bingo is a lottery simply "because that's what other courts have concluded." In short, most courts which have addressed the issue have merely cross-referenced one another for authoritative support. This Court cannot in clear conscience blindly concur in the conclusion that bingo is a lottery simply because other courts have so concluded. Cf. O.W. Holmes, Jr., The Path of the Law, 10 Harv. L. Rev. 456, 469 (1897) ("It is revolting to have no better reason for a rule of law than that so it was laid down in the time of Henry IV. It is still more revolting if the rule simply persists from blind imitation of the past.").

This Court believes it should look to the popular meaning of "lottery" and "bingo" in order to determine whether the terms are one and the same or sufficiently similar to justify striking down § 97-33-51 as unconstitutional. Over 100 years ago, Massachusetts Supreme Court Justice O.W. Holmes, Jr. similarly concluded that disposition of the issue—whether a so-called "envelope game" was a lottery—required comprehension of the "popular use of the word as shown by the dictionaries." Commonwealth v. Wright, 137 Mass. 250, 251-52 (1884). In addition to dictionaries, experience should help to enlighten this Court. See O.W. Holmes, The Common Law 1 (1881) ("The life of the law has not been logic: it has been experience. The felt necessities of time, the prevalent moral and political theories, institutions of public policy, avowed or unconscious, even the prejudices which judges share with their fellow-citizens, have had a good deal more to do than the syllogism in determining the rules by which citizens should be governed.").

This Court has perused dictionaries and other sources (e.g., experience) in search of the "popular" meaning of "lottery" and "bingo." Both games unquestionably inhere the elements of chance, consideration, and prize; however, this premise alone does not lead to the conclusion that both are one and the same. Indeed, the game of poker inheres the elements of chance, consideration, and prize. Does this mean that poker is a lottery? The AG contends (as does the "weight of authority") that any game which inheres the three elements is a lottery; therefore, the AG presumably would conclude that poker is a lottery. Indeed, under this broad definition, the stock market, life insurance, and other business enterprises involving the three elements could be deemed a lottery. Such logic seems no less absurd than that which equates a horse, dog, and cat with one another simply because each specie has four legs, two eyes, and one tail.

The absurdity stems from the unexplained recognition that the term "lottery" should be deemed the generic "umbrella" which encompasses any game (or business enterprise?) inhering the three elements. This Court is unconvinced that the term "lottery" is a generic umbrella. The term "gambling" would seem to be the appropriate umbrella; this would be consistent with the popular meaning of all terms concerned "as shown by the dictionaries" and experience.

In sum, disposition of this case is not reached by purporting to know what the framers intended nor by utilizing Pythagorean logic. Instead, this Court concludes that, pursuant to the "popular" meaning of the terms, bingo is not a lottery. The provision twice prohibits selling lottery "tickets"—i.e., (1) "or its tickets be sold in this state," and (2) "or its tickets sold." This rather clearly connotes a particular kind of lottery: one with tickets. The provision strongly suggests a restrictive definition—that not all forms of lottery (assuming bingo is even a form) are banned (i.e., only those with tickets). This Court has long held that, in construing the constitution, no words may be regarded as surplusage but should instead be given meaning and effect. Few commonly consider bingo as having tickets that are sold, and any attempt to equate a bingo card with a lottery ticket would be superficial at best and unpersuasive at worst. Therefore, § 97-33-51 is hereby declared constitutional, and the chancellor's decision is reversed.

LEE, Chief Justice, dissenting.

I respectfully dissent from the majority action upholding Miss. Code Ann. § 97-33-51, the bingo exemption statute. I specifically take issue with the rationale which concludes that bingo is not a lottery within the definition of Miss. Const. Art. 4, § 98. Clearly, if bingo is a form of a lottery (which I submit it is), this section of the constitution makes bingo illegal, and the legislature may not exempt it via simple majority vote. And, if bingo is illegal, then § 97-33-51 must be struck down as unconstitutional.

As early as 1927, this Court defined "lottery" as any game which inheres the three elements of consideration, chance, and a prize. This definition is substantially equivalent to those provided by other courts. For today's purpose, I find it unnecessary to consider the effect of this definition on games or activities other than bingo. For example, I deem it inappropriate to address the effect of this constitutional section on gambling. For while all lotteries may be forms of gambling, all gambling is not a form of lottery. In short, it is appropriate today to consider only whether bingo is a lottery.

Virtually all jurisdictions which have addressed the issue have concluded, without equivocation, that bingo inheres the elements of a lottery and, thus, bingo is a lottery prohibited by their state constitutions. In the face of such authority, I find the majority's holding that bingo is not a lottery to be both unpersuasive and disingenuous.

HARRIS v. ECONOMIC OPPORTUNITY COMMISSION OF NASSAU COUNTY, INC.

575 N.Y.S.2d 672 (App. Div. 1991)

MILLER, Justice.

The question before us on this appeal, while seemingly innocuous at first blush, severely affects a fundraising practice widely utilized by charitable organizations. Simply stated, we are called upon to determine whether a charitable organization may interpose the defense of illegality to defeat the claim by the winner of a raffle who was denied his winning prize. For the reasons that follow, we are constrained to hold that such a raffle constitutes an illegal contract in violation of General Obligations Law § 5-417 and, hence, the defendant charitable organization is not compelled to award the winning prize or the value thereof.

The facts underlying this appeal are not in substantial dispute. The defendant Economic Opportunity Commission of Nassau County, Inc. (hereinafter the EOC) is a charitable organization which provides various services to needy citizens in Nassau County. Among those services is the Martin Luther King Scholarship Fund, a privately-funded endeavor which provides educational aid for qualified area students. In 1986 the EOC conducted a charitable raffle to raise money for this scholarship fund.

The plaintiff Ray Harris, vice president of the appellant corporation B.W. Harris, Inc., operated a pharmacy in West Hempstead. In May 1986 a man whom Mr. Harris recognized as a customer entered the pharmacy to sell raffle tickets on behalf of the EOC to raise money for the Martin Luther King Scholarship Fund. Mr. Harris, recognizing an opportunity to enhance the good will of his business, purchased five raffle tickets at a cost of $2 each. Rather than write out his name and address on each of the tickets, Mr. Harris used a rubber stamp identifying the corporation as the purchaser of the tickets. The seller of the tickets left the store, thanking Mr. Harris for his "contribution." The prize being raffled was a 1986 Chevrolet Camaro.

At the very time Mr. Harris purchased the raffle tickets, he was negotiating the sale of the corporation's pharmacy. After concluding those negotiations, he began a vacation. During his absence, on June 7, 1986, the EOC held its drawing. One of the tickets purchased by Mr. Harris on behalf of the corporation was selected as the winner of the automobile.

The one area in which the factual allegations of the parties were in significant dispute concerned the time frame in which Mr. Harris allegedly claimed his prize. It is conceded by all that the drawing on the raffle occurred on June 7, 1986. Mr. Harris testified that he was on vacation at that time, but he returned during the second week of June and was informed by the pharmacist who had purchased the business that EOC representatives had visited the pharmacy to inform him of his good fortune. Mr. Harris claimed that he called the EOC on June 8 or 9, 1986, to claim his prize. He claimed he was given a "run-around" until he finally spoke with the Chief Executive Officer of the EOC John Kearse, who asked him to come to the EOC offices for a meeting the following Saturday. At that meeting, which Mr. Harris estimated occurred on June 11, 1986, Mr. Kearse reportedly told him that the

EOC had attempted to award his prize, but, because of his absence following the drawing, the prize had been withdrawn. In lieu thereof, Mr. Kearse reportedly offered a letter to Mr. Harris which would entitle him to a tax deduction for the value of the car. Mr. Harris rejected this offer.

In stark contrast, John Kearse testified that following the raffle drawing on June 7, he and another EOC representative visited the pharmacy on June 10, 1986, to award the car. On that date they met Craig Niederberger, the pharmacist who had purchased the business, and Mr. Niederberger informed them that Mr. Harris was unavailable and that his whereabouts were unknown. Mr. Kearse left his business card with Mr. Niederberger and the latter agreed to convey the good news to Mr. Harris. Mr. Kearse further testified that he did not hear from Mr. Harris until some time in early August 1986. By that time, however, to take advantage of a limited refund offer, the EOC had returned the car to the dealer from which it was purchased. The refund that was obtained was added to the scholarship fund.

The only documentary evidence concerning the actual sequence of events was a letter from Mr. Kearse dated June 17, 1986, memorializing his June 10, 1986, visit to the pharmacy. Mr. Kearse testified that at the time he sent this letter, the car was still available for delivery. Mr. Harris, however, insinuated that the letter was written after the return of the car in June 1986 in anticipation of litigation. Curiously, no documentation was presented as to when the car was returned to the dealer, information presumably available to the defendant.

In any event, this action was commenced on or about August 26, 1986, and was tried in the District Court of Nassau County, First District. Rejecting the defendant's argument that the raffle of the car was an illegal lottery, the court submitted the case to the jury, which returned a verdict in the plaintiffs' favor in the amount of $15,000. On appeal to the Appellate Term, however, the award to Ray Harris was stricken, and the award to the appellant was reduced to $20—representing twice the cost of the wager—on the ground that the raffle was illegal and hence void. We affirm.

As a logical starting point for our discussion, N.Y. Constitution, article I, § 9 provides in pertinent part:

> no lottery or the sale of lottery tickets, pool-selling, bookmaking, or any other kind of gambling except as otherwise provided herein shall hereafter be authorized or allowed within this state; and the legislature shall pass appropriate laws to prevent offenses against any of the provisions of this section.

The exceptions to the foregoing authorize State-operated lotteries, parimutuel wagering on horse races, and certain specified games of chance, which under the auspices of local governments, are run by charitable organizations and which, unless otherwise provided by law, offer individual prizes which do not exceed $250 and aggregate prizes which do not exceed $1,000 (N.Y. Const. art. I, § 9[2]). It is uncontroverted that the raffle of a new automobile in the case at bar does not fall within the above constitutional exceptions to the prohibitions against illegal gambling.

Among the "appropriate laws" enacted by the Legislature in furtherance of the constitutional prohibition against gambling is Penal Law article 225, which supplies the definitions of proscribed gambling activities. Penal Law § 225.00(2) provides:

> a person engages in gambling when he stakes or risks something of value upon the outcome of a contest of chance or a future contingent event not under his control or influence, upon an agreement or understanding that he will receive something of value in the event of a certain outcome.

Furthermore, Penal Law § 225.00(10) defines a lottery as:

> an unlawful gambling scheme in which (a) the players pay or agree to pay something of value for chances, represented and differentiated by numbers or by combinations of numbers or by some other media, one or more of which chances are to be designated the winning ones; and (b) the winning chances are to be determined by a drawing or by some other method based upon the element of chance; and (c) the holders of the winning chances are to receive something of value.

"Unlawful" means anything "not specifically authorized by law" (Penal Law § 225.00[12]). Clearly, the instant raffle in which a "contribution" of $10 purchased five chances to win an automobile constitutes a lottery proscribed by the Penal Law.

Throughout the course of this action, the appellant has taken the position that Mr. Harris did not wager $10 on five chances to win a car, but rather that he made a donation or charitable contribution in this amount to the EOC in return for which he was permitted to enter a raffle, run by a benevolent organization, seeking to raise funds for a worthy cause. Characterization of the EOC's motivations aside, the appellant asserts that a mere "donation" having been made, the entry in the raffle was incidental thereto and no illegal wager was made for consideration. The appellant thus seeks to bring this case within what it claims is the rule of Johnson v. New York Daily News, 467 N.Y.S.2d 665 (App. Div. 1983), aff'd 462 N.E.2d 152 (N.Y. 1984), which, it asserts, stands for the proposition that a contest winner may sue to recover the value of the winning prize. The appellant's reliance thereon, however, is misplaced, as the facts of that case have no application to the matter presently before us.

The issue before the court in the Johnson case was not whether the contest was illegal. In Johnson, the issue to be decided was whether or not the plaintiff, who had entered a newspaper promotional contest by submitting the name of her 14-year-old grandson, had violated contest rules which provided that the contest was open to persons 18 years of age and older. The court held that the contest rule had been violated, and that the Daily News was not obligated to award the prize to the plaintiff. The issue of the legality or illegality of the contest was not raised before the court in that case and thus the opinion therein provides no authority for the plaintiffs' present argument, as "opinions must be read in the setting of the particular cases and as the product of preoccupation with their special facts" (see, e.g., Matter of Curcio v. Boyle, 542 N.Y.S.2d 1009 (App. Div. 1989), quoting from Danann Realty Corp. v. Harris, 157 N.E.2d 597 (N.Y. 1959)).

Having determined that the raffle in this case constitutes an unlawful gambling scheme, we note that General Obligations Law § 5-417 provides:

> All contracts, agreements and securities given, made or executed, for or on account of any raffle, or distribution of money, goods or things in action, for the payment of any money, or other valuable thing, in consideration of a chance in such raffle or distribution, or for the delivery of any money, goods or things in action, so raffled for, or agreed to be distributed as aforesaid, shall be utterly void.

It is clear, pursuant to the plain meaning of this statute, that the parties agreed to participate in an unlawful raffle and that that agreement is void and unenforceable. "All contracts and dealings in respect to lotteries, and tickets in lotteries, being illegal, no right of action can accrue to a party, by reason of such contracts and dealings." Thatcher v. Morris, 11 N.Y. 437, 438 (1854); Holberg v. Westchester Racing Ass'n, 53 N.Y.S.2d 490 (Sup. Ct. 1945).

This result is in accord with the law of this and other states as well as it is a widely held principle of common law that a party to an illegal contract may not obtain the aid of a court of law to further its illegal purpose.

The defendant acknowledges that its invocation of the defense of illegality poses a threat to its future ability to conduct raffles to raise funds, and that a similar predicament will befall other charitable institutions. It is clearly not unreasonable to assume that the knowledge that an organization may, with impunity, refuse to award a prize to its contest winner, will have a chilling effect upon future solicitations of this nature.

Virtually everyday charitable and nonprofit institutions conduct raffles to finance their essential services. While some of these groups may themselves prefer to continue their fundraising activities without local governmental regulation, the law is clear: charitable raffles entered for consideration are illegal gambling contracts, void under the law. Surely some compromise can be achieved to legalize these essential and beneficial fundraising activities without subjecting their sponsors to overly burdensome governmental regulation. A spin of a wheel of chance need not unravel a roll of bureaucratic red tape!

In sum, while we do not presume to dictate a specific course of action for a co-equal branch of government to follow, we nevertheless accept the invitation to point out to the Legislature that the law should be brought in line with the current state of affairs. Charitable and nonprofit organizations should no longer be forced to conduct their worthy fundraising activities outside of the law. Under the auspices of local governments administrating fundraising activities in a manner similar to that sanctioned by General Municipal Law article 9-A, there seems to be little reason to resist the legalization of charitable raffles. By so doing, the defense of illegality may never again be interposed to deprive a rightful winner of the prize to which he or she is entitled. More importantly, however, a profitable and tacitly approved form of charitable fundraising will receive an official stamp of approval, consistent with the express public policy of this State, so that its beneficent results will no longer run afoul of the law.

ORDERED that the order is affirmed insofar as appealed from, without costs or disbursements.

Notes

1. In discussing *Knight*, one exasperated commentator has written:

> The Knight decision is particularly troublesome. It is difficult to justify using traditional legal principles. Furthermore, its reasoning and the rule it adopts are not based in traditional legal reasoning, and seem internally inconsistent. The best explanation for the case seems to be that its author wanted to adapt the reasoning of critical legal studies ("CLS") to this issue of state constitutional law. If that is so, the decision may show how much or how little CLS ideas have to offer to the jurisprudence of state constitutions and the art of writing appellate opinions.

See Val D. Ricks, *Knight v. State ex rel. Moore: How Bingo Won the Mississippi Lottery*, 61 UMKC L. Rev. 463, 464 (1993) (footnote omitted). Do you agree with this assessment?

2. Was the defendant in *Harris* a bona fide charity? Perhaps, although bogus philanthropies regularly prey on the public. Even Lucy and Ethel, in Episode 137 ("Ricky's European Booking") of *I Love Lucy*, briefly organized their own charity—the "Ladies Overseas Aid" —to raffle off a donated television set. When Ethel expressed doubts about the legality of their plan, Lucy reassured her by explaining: "We're ladies. We want to go overseas. And, boy, do we need aid!" (A subsequent visit by the District Attorney, however, caused Lucy to see matters in a different light.)

3. Bingo traces its roots to "Lo Giuoco del Lotto d'Italia," a form of lottery organized in Italy in 1530. By 1778, the game had migrated to France, where it became a favorite of the learned classes. During this time the playing card began to take on its current form, being divided into both horizontal and vertical rows with numbers ranging from 1 to 90. During the 19th century, educational versions of the game became popular; in Germany, for example, it was used to help children learn their multiplication tables.

While on a trip to Georgia in December 1929, a New York toy salesman named Edwin S. Lowe visited a county carnival. There, he observed a large crowd gathered around a horseshoe-shaped table. A pitchman (now usually referred to as a "caller") was pulling small numbered wooden disks from an old cigar box and announcing the results; each time a player found a match on his or her card, a bean would be placed over the number. This cycle continued until a contestant managed to fill an entire row—horizontally, vertically, or diagonally—and yelled "Beano." The winner would receive a small doll as a prize and a new game would be started.

Upon his return home, Lowe began operating a beano game in his apartment. One guest who won became so excited that instead of shouting "Beano" she yelled "Bingo." Sensing the new name would have greater appeal, Lowe immediately adopted it and soon was marketing a commercial version of bingo.

Due to the small number of cards, Lowe's invention tended to produce multiple winners, thereby limiting the amount of money that could be raised by the game's operators. When a priest in Wilkes-Barre, Pennsylvania pointed this out, Lowe hired Carl Leffler, a Columbia University mathematics professor, to produce 6,000 uniquely-numbered cards. With this greater variety, bingo took off as a fundraising device; within just a few months, the E.S Lowe Company was publishing a monthly bingo newsletter for 37,000 subscribers. For a further look at the early history of bingo, *see* Roger Snowden, *Gambling Times Guide to Bingo* (1986).

4. Today, some form of bingo is legal in 47 states, and it is estimated that on any given day 2.5 million Americans play bingo. Overall, 65 million Americans enjoy bingo at least once a year, and United States bingo parlors report 1.7 billion annual visitors. Seventy percent of bingo players are women.

Gross bingo wagers are estimated at $10.8 billion in North America, generating $1.9 billion in revenues for bingo operators. Contrary to popular belief, bingo's appeal is not limited to senior citizens: while 23% of avid bingo players are over the age of 65, 25% are 18 to 34 years old. Although bingo enjoys its greatest following in the Northeast and Midwest, games can be found throughout the country as well as on-line. *See further* www.bingobugle.com.

5. In addition to bingo, a number of states allow charities to hold "Vegas Nights" (alternately known as "Monte Carlo" events). Typically, a person begins with a stake issued for a donation to the charity and then "gambles" for the duration of the event, being paid for successful wagers in the imitation currency of the evening. At the end of the night, the person with the most "money" wins a prize. *See generally* William N. Czuckrey, *Games for Fundraising* (1998).

Problem 7

Not knowing that raffles were illegal, the executive director of a charity had tickets printed up, took out advertisements, and arranged to have the organization's members drum up sales. Just as these activities were getting under way, the district attorney learned of them and advised the director that raffles were forbidden. Although she immediately called off the drawing, several tickets already had been sold. Is the charity subject to criminal prosecution? *See Koster v. Seney*, 68 N.W. 824 (Iowa 1896).

C. VARIATIONS

CITATION BINGO, LTD. v. OTTEN
910 P.2d 281 (N.M. 1995)

RANSOM, Justice.

We issued a writ of certiorari to the Court of Appeals to review whether a hand-held electronic device known as "Power Bingo" is a permissible piece of gaming equipment under the Bingo and Raffle Act, N.M.S.A. 1978, §§ 60-2B-1 to -14. The Superintendent of the New Mexico Regulation and Licensing Department and the Director of the Alcohol and Gaming Division each had made an administrative determination that Power Bingo is not permissible equipment under the Act, and the Department issued a memorandum to all bingo licensees directing them to discontinue use of such devices. Citation Bingo, a supplier of Power Bingo units, thereafter filed a complaint for declaratory relief and sought an injunction against the Department. The trial court entered a declaratory judgment determining that the devices are not excluded under the Act.

Following an appeal by the Department, the Court of Appeals issued a memorandum opinion in which it affirmed the trial court's determination. Relying solely on its earlier decision in Infinity Group, Inc. v. Manzagol, 884 P.2d 523 (N.M. Ct. App.), cert. denied, 882 P.2d 1046 (N.M. 1994), the Court reasoned that both a player using a Power Bingo unit and a player using a paper bingo card "would be playing the same game even though the skills of one would not be as tested as the skills of the other." We conclude that Power Bingo units are "gambling devices" within the meaning of N.M.S.A. 1978, § 30-19-2(B) (proscribing play of gambling device) and N.M.S.A. 1978, § 30-19-3(F) (proscribing set up of gambling device). Further, consistent with this state's policy against gambling, we narrowly construe the terms of the Act, and finding no statutory provision that would authorize use of Power Bingo units, we conclude that such units may not be used in New Mexico. We therefore reverse the Court of Appeals and remand to the trial court for entry of a judgment for the Defendants.

Facts

Power Bingo consists of a plastic case, a keypad with numbers zero through nine, a small black and white display, a connection that allows the unit to accept data from a computer, and a computer chip capable of storing as many as two hundred simulated bingo "cards." These simulated cards are created using a program that randomly generates twenty-four numbers between one and seventy-five. All simulated cards are generated by a single computer and then downloaded into individual Power Bingo units. The precise number of cards a given unit will contain at any one time is determined by the number of cards purchased by the player using that unit.

Before the advent of the Power Bingo unit, the game of bingo was played using only paper or hardboard cards. During the game, the caller draws from a bin one ping pong ball every twelve to fourteen seconds and announces to the hall the letter and number appearing on that ball. The letter is announced only to aid players in finding the correct column. After the letter and number are announced, each player must check all cards he or she is playing to see if there are any matches. If there are, the player marks each match using an ink dauber. As each mark is made, the player must determine whether it completes a pattern that matches a pre-established winning pattern. If it does, the player must call out "bingo" before the next letter and number are announced.

Power Bingo does not change the rules of the game, but it does change the method of play. When a letter and number are called, Power Bingo users simply enter the two-digit number into their device using the keypad. For example, if the caller announces "B-6," Power Bingo users simply press "06." The unit then compares the number entered with each of its currently stored numbers, placing the entered number in memory if there is a match. The unit also compares any pattern formed by all numbers so stored against the pre-established winning pattern to see if there is a match. If there is, the unit immediately notifies the user. Thus Power Bingo differs from traditional bingo in that players of Power Bingo cannot see the cards they have purchased, need not locate and mark numbers on their cards, and need not visually identify any winning pattern.

Discussion

With limited exceptions, gambling is a crime in New Mexico. Specifically, the legislature has made it a misdemeanor to make a bet (to agree to chance anything of value) or even to be in a gambling place with the intent to make a bet, participate in a lottery, or play a gambling device.

There are, of course, exceptions. Licensed pari-mutuel wagering on horse races has been legalized. Under New Mexico's permissive lottery statute, the "sale" or drawing of any prize at a fair is permitted "when all the proceeds of such fair shall be expended in this state for the benefit of any church, public library, religious society or charitable purpose and when no part of such proceeds go to any individual member or employee thereof." Religious, educational, benevolent, and other not-for-profit organizations may operate lotteries twice in any calendar year for the exclusive benefit of such organization or other public purposes.

In addition to the exceptions created by the permissive lottery statute, the New Mexico Lottery Act authorizes, for the support of public educational institutions, the conduct of "an instant win game in which disposable tickets contain certain pre-printed winners," and "an on-line lottery game in which a player selects a specified group of numbers or symbols out of a predetermined range of numbers or symbols and purchases a ticket bearing the player-selected numbers or symbols for eligibility in a regularly scheduled drawing." Video forms of these authorized lotteries are expressly prohibited.

Finally, under the Bingo and Raffle Act, any licensed organization may conduct games of chance commonly known as "bingo" or "raffles" for educational, charitable, patriotic, religious, or public-spirited purposes. Such games may not be conducted more than five times in any calendar week, more than four hours on any occasion, or more than twice in one day. In bingo, as we have described, the prizes are awarded on the basis of numbers selected at random to form on the participant's card one or more of seventeen different designated patterns, whereas in raffles the prizes are awarded on the basis of winning names or numbers being "drawn." Any attempt to distinguish "raffles" and "lottery" is superficial at best. What either the courts or legislature has said of the one is applicable to the other.

Power Bingo is a prohibited gambling device. Citation Bingo asks this Court to determine that use of Power Bingo is authorized under the Bingo and Raffle Act because it "does not alter the statutory directives on how the game of bingo is to be played." As support for its argument, Citation Bingo principally relies on Infinity Group and State ex rel. Rodriguez v. American Legion Post No. 99, 750 P.2d 1110 (N.M. Ct. App.), cert. denied, 746 P.2d 1120 (N.M. 1987), and cert. denied, 751 P.2d 700 (N.M. 1988).

In Infinity Group, the Court of Appeals held that machines which electronically simulate the game of pull tabs are permissible under the Bingo and

Raffle Act. There, the Regulation and Licensing Department had refused to allow the operation of electronic pull-tab simulations under its definition of pull tabs as "printed tickets that have a pull tab or seal to be opened by the purchaser where a winning combination is printed on each ticket or on a separate card." We agree with the Court of Appeals that paper pull-tab games were contemplated by the legislature as a form of the game of chance commonly known as raffles. We also agree with its memorandum opinion in this case that the question of the legality of the electromechanical device used in Power Bingo is governed by the real question identified in Infinity Group, namely, "whether electronic simulations of pull-tab games are allowed by the Act." Consequently, we here review the Infinity Group resolution of that question.

As in New Mexico, a majority of states continue to prohibit the use or possession of "gambling devices." Courts in these jurisdictions routinely have applied their respective statutory provisions to hold that use of electromechanical devices simulating games of chance is prohibited.

No other state has authorized electromechanical gaming under an extended interpretation of machines intended or used for raffles. We [therefore] overrule Infinity Group and hold that electronic pull-tab simulations are prohibited electromechanical gambling devices. If the legislature should intend otherwise, it may provide for specific exceptions for electromechanical gaming as other states have done.

Power Bingo is inconsistent with the Bingo and Raffle Act. In American Legion Post No. 99 the Court reasoned:

> If we were to adopt the Clubs' broad definition of "raffles," any game in which a prize is awarded by chance would qualify as a raffle. Organizations licensed under the Act could operate slot machines, roulette wheels, many types of card games, and, in fact, virtually any sort of gambling device as long as the net profits were spent for lawful purposes as defined in the Act. We reject this interpretation. It is not reasonable to assume that the legislature would authorize such widespread gambling without explicitly saying so, and this court must presume that the legislature acted reasonably.

We agree with this reasoning, and thus we must reject Citation Bingo's argument that use of Power Bingo units is consistent with the Bingo and Raffle Act because such use does not alter the "essential elements of the game." Our conclusion in this regard is buttressed by decisions from other jurisdictions. For example, the Indiana Court of Appeals also applied a criminal prohibition against "gambling devices" to strike down a proposed offer of tickets for out-of-state lotteries by use of "vending machines" at various Indiana locations.

Section 30-19-1(D) defines a gambling device as "a contrivance other than an antique gambling device that, for a consideration, affords the player an opportunity to obtain anything of value, the award of which is determined by chance, even though accompanied by some skill and whether or not the prize is automatically paid by the device." Section 30-19-2(B) proscribes "entering or remaining in a gambling place with intent to play a gambling device" and § 30-19-3(F) proscribes "setting up for use, for the purpose of gambling, or collecting the proceeds of, any gambling device." Reading § 60-2B-3(L) together with these two criminal prohibitions leads us to the conclusion that Power Bingo units are prohibited gambling devices and cannot be used. While we do not have the benefit of specific electromechanical gaming proscriptions in the Bingo and Raffle Act, the fact that in its most recent Lottery Act the legislature chose to specifically prohibit video forms of the state lottery indicates to us that video, electromechanical, and computer forms of specifically authorized games are against public policy. If Power Bingo units are to be used in New Mexico, express authorization of such devices should come from the legislature.

Conclusion

Current legislation and the public policy expressed by that legislation do not favor the accommodation of gambling. Narrowly construing the terms of the Bingo and Raffle Act, and finding no express authorization for any sort of electromechanical device such as Power Bingo, we hold that such devices may not be used. It is for the people acting through their duly elected representatives, and not for this Court, to effect any change in the public policy against gambling.

BINGO BANK, INC. v. STROM
234 S.E.2d 881 (S.C. 1977)

LEWIS, Chief Justice.

The operation of the game "Bingo Bank" upon its premises near Walterboro, South Carolina, by respondent, Bingo Bank, Inc., during December 1975 and January 1976, brought about the arrest of certain of respondent's employees on charges of violation of South Carolina gaming laws. Respondent contended that it was operating the game of bingo as permitted by the South Carolina Constitution and brought this action to restrain the appellant and other agents of the State Law Enforcement Division from taking further action to stop respondent's "Bingo Bank" operations. The lower court granted the restraining order sought, holding that respondent's activities constituted the game of bingo as presently permitted under the South Carolina Constitution. We reverse.

Prior to its amendment in 1975, the Constitution made unlawful the operation of any lottery in this State, but was amended in 1975 to permit "the game of bingo" under certain conditions. As amended, § 7 of Article 17, at the times pertinent to the present issues, was as follows:

> No lottery shall ever be allowed or advertised by newspapers, or otherwise, or its tickets be sold in this State. The game of bingo, when conducted by charitable, religious or fraternal organizations exempt from Federal income taxation or when conducted at recognized annual State and County fairs, shall not be deemed a lottery prohibited by this section.

The sole question for decision is whether the "Bingo Bank" operated by respondent constituted "the game of bingo" permitted by Article 17, § 7, of the Constitution.

Section 7 contains no definition of the game of bingo. However, the record shows that the game of bingo has been played at various churches and organizations for years prior to the 1975 amendment to § 7. Appellant properly concludes from the testimony and common knowledge that it was "because of the illegality of the game of bingo and its general social acceptance" that the amendment in question was adopted.

The 1975 amendment refers to the "game of bingo, when conducted by charitable, religious or fraternal organizations or at recognized State and County fairs." The conclusion is inescapable, therefore, that "the game of bingo" under the 1975 amendment refers to the game previously played illegally by charitable organizations throughout the State. The testimony clearly describes the game of bingo customarily played in this State by such organizations and is the "bingo" referred to in the constitutional provision in question.

The "game of bingo" is played by the use of a card on which is printed twenty-five squares arranged in five rows of five squares each. The word "Bingo" is at the top of the card, with one letter at the top of each column. The squares on the card contain twenty-four numbers and one free space. The numbers in the five squares under the letter "B" range from one to fifteen, under the letter "I" from sixteen to thirty, under the letter "N" from thirty-one to forty-five, under the letter "G" from forty-six to sixty, and under the letter "O" from sixty-one to seventy-five. Each card used by the players contains a different arrangement of the numbers and the card is indispensable to the play of the game. The player, to enter the game, purchases a card at a set price and no further bets or payments are made. There are always numerous players and they are notified beforehand of the prize they will win if they are successful. The payment for the card and the value of the prize to the winner remain the same throughout the game.

The game of bingo is played by the use of a "Caller" who announces, one at a time, numbers drawn at random from a container into which has been placed numbered balls or objects for that purpose. A total of seventy-five numbers are used. When a number is called, any player having that number would cover that square on his card with some small previously designated object. The winner of the game is the first player who covers a row of squares in accordance with a previously set configuration, such as a vertical, horizontal, or diagonal row of numbers from those drawn and announced. Each game has a winner.

The above described game is the "game of bingo" customarily played illegally throughout the State prior to the amendment in 1975 of Article 17, § 7 and is the "game of bingo" exempted therein from the prohibition against lotteries.

There are material differences between the game of "Bingo Bank" and the "game of bingo" as above described. Bingo Bank is played with one player. While several may play, no one would play in conjunction with the others. The cards used are all identical and the winner does not depend upon covering the squares in any configuration. In fact, the shape of the card and the arrangement of the figures is of no significance. The Bingo Bank player must make additional wagers as the game continues and the prize varies according to the length of the game and the odds at which the management places its bets. The prize in Bingo Bank may be won on the first roll of the dice or draw of a number, or the game may continue indefinitely if the player fails to roll or draw the winning number.

The foregoing method of playing Bingo Bank is at variance with the described manner in which the game of bingo is played and clearly distinguishes Bingo Bank from the game of bingo as contemplated by Article 17, § 7.

The judgment of the lower court is accordingly reversed.

Note

In *Treasure State Games, Inc. v. State*, 551 P.2d 1008 (Mont. 1976), the Montana Supreme Court held that both electronic bingo and keno (a game brought to America in the 19th century by Chinese railroad laborers that is somewhat akin to lotto) are legal forms of bingo because they have the same essential characteristics as traditional bingo. In so holding, the court wrote:

> In ascertaining whether plaintiff's mechanical-electronic games satisfy these definitional requirements, we first note that defendant concedes in its brief one of the key requirements, that plaintiff's machines do operate so as to select winning numbers or symbols at random. There was an extended examination of the electronic method of number selection in the record, which reveals the selection is random if the winning numbers cannot be predetermined by the game owner or operator and there is no method by which the house or game operator has any control over the selection of winning numbers during play or operation of the games.
>
> As to the mechanical or electronic nature of plaintiff's bingo and keno games, we see no violation of the statutory definition for section 62-716(2)(a), [which] provides for various items of bingo equipment 'however operated'. In addition, raffle equipment defined in the same statutory section, section 62-716(2)(b), includes '* * * implements, devices, and machines * * *'. Such language clearly indicates there is no legislative intent demonstrated in the statute to prohibit the use of mechanical or electronic operated bingo machines or devices.
>
> Finally, none of defendant's other suggested differences are factors to be considered in construing the statutory definition of bingo. Thus the language of section 62-716, R.C.M.1947, is unambiguous and clearly contemplates plaintiff's Bonus Bingo and Raven Keno as being games 'commonly known as bingo.' We therefore hold that it is unnecessary to apply any rules of statutory construction . . . .

Id. at 1010.

Problem 8

Recently, a state legislature amended its bingo law to permit charities to offer "instant bingo." The statute describes instant bingo as a "game in which players buy disposable tickets containing tabs, which they pull back to see if they have won a prize, typically by matching three or more symbols, numbers, or letters." If the amendment is challenged on the ground that instant bingo is fundamentally different from traditional bingo, and therefore prohibited by the state's constitution, how should the court rule? *See State ex rel. Stephan v. Parrish*, 887 P.2d 127 (Kan. 1994).

D. OPERATORS

THERE TO CARE, INC. v. COMMISSIONER OF THE INDIANA DEPARTMENT OF REVENUE
19 F.3d 1165 (7th Cir. 1994)

EASTERBROOK, Circuit Judge.

Indiana permits charitable organizations to conduct a limited number of gambling events. In 1992 the state amended its Charitable Gaming Act, adding restrictions that curtailed the bingo games being held in Mishawaka by There to Care (TTC), a charitable corporation. In October 1992 the state directed it to cease operating bingo games, giving several reasons: TTC had not been doing business in Indiana for five years (Indiana Code § 4-32-6-20(a)(1)(C)); it ran bingo too frequently (the limit is three events a week, I.C. § 4-32-9-18, no more than two of which may be held in the same rented facility, I.C. § 4-32-9-20(b)); it rented too opulent a hall (the statute sets a limit of $200 per day, I.C. § 4-32-9-20(a)(2), and there is an administrative limit on rental paid for property used to run the game); and the same persons were conducting bingo for multiple charities (TTC had a sister charity, Extend-A-Hand Association, Inc., hold bingo games in the same hall, an obvious device to evade the weekly limit). TTC filed this suit under 42 U.S.C. § 1983, contending that the state violated the first amendment by limiting the effective size of the bingo operation and thus cutting down on opportunities for speech, and state law.

Is bingo speech? People buy cards in the hope of winning back more than they spend. A voice at the front of the hall drones "B-2" and "G-49"; after a while someone at the back of the hall shouts "BINGO!" and gets a prize. These words do not convey ideas; any other combination of letters and numbers would serve the purpose equally well. They employ vocal cords but are no more "expression" than are such statements as "21" in a game of blackjack or "three peaches!" by someone who has just pulled the handle of a one-armed bandit. Statements promoting gambling are speech, albeit without the first amendment protection accorded to political speech, see United States v. Edge Broadcasting Co., 509 U.S. 418 (1993); Posadas de Puerto Rico Associates v. Tourism Co. of Puerto Rico, 478 U.S. 328 (1986); cf. Barnes v. Glen Theatre, Inc., 501 U.S. 560 (1991), but wagering money is an activity—just as the business of leasing property is not speech and may be regulated by zoning laws and the like, even if the lessee wants to put on a play or open a newsstand. Cf. Graff v. Chicago, 9 F.3d 1309 (7th Cir.1993) (en banc). Gambling has traditionally been closely regulated or even forbidden, without anyone suspecting that these restrictions violate the first amendment.

According to the complaint, TTC uses bingo games to spread the word about its activities. Posters on the walls proclaim its mission; during the games organizers recruit volunteers; net proceeds of the games support charitable endeavors that may include speech. But persons who seek to engage in speech cannot avoid the application of state laws that are neutral with regard to the content and viewpoint of their expression. The state may collect income taxes, which reduce the resources at the command of speakers, but laws indifferent to the content or even existence of speech pose no constitutional difficulties. Indiana does not distinguish between bingo parlors that have posters on the walls and those that do not; its statute regulates the process of wagering rather than expression that may accompany gambling.

To put this in doctrinal terms:

> A regulation that serves purposes unrelated to the content of expression is deemed neutral, even if it has an incidental effect on some speakers or messages but not others. Government regulation of expressive activity is content neutral so long as it is "justified without reference to the content of the regulated speech."

Ward v. Rock Against Racism, 491 U.S. 781, 791 (1989) (quoting from Clark v. Community for Creative Non-Violence, 468 U.S. 288, 293 (1984)). Indiana's regulation of gambling is unrelated to the content of any expression. It is justified without reference to that expression. Indiana invokes the usual arguments against gambling, paternalistic but assuredly content-neutral. Perhaps these days the real reason for limiting bingo parlors and the like is to protect the public fisc; Indiana now conducts a state lottery. But whether the statute serves to shelter improvident citizens from lures to part with their money, or to protect the state's gambling juggernaut from competition, is irrelevant; neither justification depends on the content or viewpoint of any charitable organization's speech.

Three opinions serve as the mainstays of TTC's case. In Schaumberg v. Citizens for a Better Environment, 444 U.S. 620 (1980); Maryland v. Joseph H. Munson Co., 467 U.S. 947 (1984); and Riley v. National Federation of the Blind of North Carolina, Inc., 487 U.S. 781 (1988), the Court held that the first amendment places severe limits on states' ability to regulate charitable fundraising. Games of chance are effective in fundraising and so, according to TTC, are protected by the first amendment. On this understanding, TTC is entitled to run bingo games seven nights a week in the largest hall it can find. When asked at oral argument how far this principle extends, TTC's lawyer ventured that the first amendment would entitle it to stage a bullfight in the Hoosier Dome, if in its view that contest would raise money for its endeavors and be a good forum for the dissemination of its views. Charities do not have special privileges under the first amendment; by parallel reasoning, then, political and educational organizations, the press, and speakers in general also could engage in gambling and other proscribed activities to raise funds.

What TTC fails to appreciate, however, is that the statutes at issue in Schaumburg and its successors were directed only against organizations engaged in expression. Schaumberg prohibited fundraising activities that did not return at least 75% of gross proceeds to the charities. But it did not forbid, say, the manufacture and sale of automobiles when the costs of the business exceeded 25% of the gross income. Because the regulation was targeted at organizations that were distinguished by their manner of expression, the governments could not avail themselves of the principle that regulation unrelated to expression is not doomed by incidental effects. In Munson the Court understood the law as "a direct restriction on the amount of money a charity can spend on fundraising activity" and therefore as "a direct restriction on protected First Amendment activity." 467 U.S. at 967 & n. 16. The other two cases approached the subject in the same way. Indiana has not enacted a law that disfavors or heaps special regulation on charitable expenditures for solicitation; charities may spend as much as they want to raise money and engage in expression. True enough, a charity may not spend more than $200 a night to rent a hall for bingo, but a non-charity may not spend a penny on this endeavor. Only charities are entitled to conduct games of chance under the Charitable Gaming Act. TTC has been favored over, say, Hilton Hotels, which would dearly love to open casinos in underused ballrooms; that charities have not been favored by as much as they would prefer does not create a problem under the first amendment. Schaumburg, Munson, and Riley do not create exemptions from rent-control statutes, even though those statutes disable charities (and other speakers) from outbidding other potential lessees.

Charities in Indiana have a protected market in gambling. Having barred commercial enterprises from this business, and thus created some monopoly rents for the plucking, the state did not violate the first amendment by setting limits on charities' endeavors. The statute is indifferent to the content and viewpoint of charities' expression; no more is required.

AFFIRMED.

ARMY NAVY BINGO, GARRISON NO. 2196 v. PLOWDEN
314 S.E.2d 339 (S.C. 1984)

HARWELL, Justice.

This action challenges the constitutionality of the prize limitations and the residence requirement for bingo operators found in S.C. Code Ann. § 12-21-2590 (1983). The bingo operators assert that the statute violates the Fourteenth Amendment due process clause. We disagree.

The trial judge held the prize limitations constitutional and the residence requirement unconstitutional. We hold that neither the limits on prizes nor the residence requirement denies the bingo operators due process of law.

S.C. Code Ann. § 12-21-2590 (1983) provides in pertinent part:

> Any person or organization operating a game of bingo . . . must obtain [an] annual Class B License from the South Carolina Tax Commission at the cost of Five Hundred Dollars per year. The holder of a Class B License is restricted to a maximum of three sessions per week. No license shall be issued to any charitable, religious, or fraternal organization that has not been domiciled in South Carolina for at least three years.

An analysis of the propriety of state bingo regulation must begin with the recognition that bingo was until 1975 prohibited by our State Constitution, Article XVII, § 7. The Constitution was amended to allow certain organizations to conduct bingo. Section 7 now provides:

No lottery shall ever be allowed or be advertised by newspapers, or otherwise, or its tickets be sold in this State. The game of bingo when conducted by charitable, religious or fraternal organizations exempt from federal income taxation or when conducted at recognized annual State and County fairs, shall not be deemed a lottery prohibited by this section.

Section 7 is not a self-executing constitutional grant of power to conduct bingo. On the contrary, the Section indicates that bingo is no longer constitutionally prohibited. The State Constitution is a limitation upon and not a grant of power to the General Assembly.

Bingo is a lottery and it is gambling. There is no right to conduct bingo under the State Constitution. Nor is there a fundamental right to gamble protected by the Federal Constitution. In fact, the State's power to suppress gambling is practically unrestrained.

Organizations may conduct bingo in this state only by license. The license confers no property right. It is a permit issued pursuant to the State's police power. Unlicensed bingo is punishable under Code § 16-19-10 as a crime. Bingo may only be conducted in accordance with the restrictions imposed by the legislature.

We also note that the bingo licensing scheme is part of our state's tax law. An admissions tax must be collected under Code § 12-21-2600 (1983). The United States Supreme Court has held that a tax does not violate the Fourteenth Amendment due process clause when its enforcement may result in destroying a particular business.

Likewise, the fact that the residence requirement may put certain operators out of business and that the prize limitations may reduce their business does not necessarily offend due process.

The bingo operators carry a substantial burden of establishing the unconstitutionality of the statute. We conclude that the state interests here override the interest of the bingo operators in a going concern and in offering unlimited prizes.

First, the State has a legitimate interest in limiting the monetary value of prizes. Crowds throng to events that promise large prizes. The record reflects that over forty-two hundred persons attended one session in which the proceeds exceeded three hundred thousand dollars ($300,000). Crowd control is a governmental function. Traffic must be regulated and public peace maintained.

The State also has an interest in protecting its people from unlimited lotteries. The prize limitations reduce the likelihood of extensive gambling sessions being held under the guise of raising funds for charity.

The State's policy interests also amply support the residence requirement. In order to conduct bingo, our Constitution requires that organizations be charitable, religious or fraternal. The earnings or income from bingo must be used for those purposes. The organizations are prohibited from employing persons who have been convicted of certain crimes. The record establishes that the durational domicile aids in the enforcement of these requirements. In addition, the requirement helps discourage out-of-state groups from coming into the state for the sole purpose of taking advantage of our constitutional exemption.

The exemption for charitable bingo operators in the general prohibition of gambling has been taken far beyond its intended purpose of giving South Carolina charities a means for additional revenue. Certainly, the operation of bingo should not be the primary purpose for the existence of the exempted groups in South Carolina.

The bingo operators additionally assert that the residence requirement denies them equal protection of the laws. The record does not reveal, however, that the issue was properly before the trial court. The pleadings raise no equal protection issue.

Thus, we conclude that the prize limitations and the residence requirement do not deny the bingo operators due process of law. The trial court's order is, accordingly,

Affirmed in Part; Reversed in Part.

DURHAM HIGHWAY FIRE PROTECTION ASSOCIATION, INC. v. BAKER
347 S.E.2d 86 (N.C. Ct. App. 1986),
review denied, 351 S.E.2d 744 (N.C. 1987)

PHILLIPS, Judge.

When this action was filed each of the plaintiffs, as an "exempt organization" under G.S. 14-309.6(1), was licensed to conduct bingo games and each had been conducting its games immediately after the games of another exempt organization in the same building. On 13 August 1984 the defendant Sheriff advised each of the plaintiffs that conducting two sessions of bingo during a 48-hour period violated G.S. 14-309.8 and that future violations would result in prosecution. Plaintiffs sued to declare the cited statute unconstitutional and obtained orders temporarily and preliminarily restraining the defendants from arresting or prosecuting them because of the violations alleged. Later, pursuant to defendants' motion, an order of summary judgment was entered dissolving the injunction and dismissing plaintiffs' action. The only question presented by plaintiffs' appeal is the constitutionality of G.S. 14-309.8, which reads as follows:

> The number of sessions of bingo conducted or sponsored by an exempt organization shall be limited to two sessions per week and such sessions must not exceed a period of five hours each per session. No two sessions of bingo shall be held within a 48-hour period of time. No more than two sessions of bingo shall be operated or conducted in any one building, hall or structure during any one calendar week and if two sessions are held, they must be held by the same exempt organization. This section shall not apply to bingo games conducted at a fair or other exhibition conducted pursuant to Article 45 of Chapter 106 of the General Statutes.

Plaintiffs contend on appeal, as they alleged in the complaint, that the 48-hour proviso violates the due process, free speech, and equal protection of the law guarantees contained in both the United States and North Carolina Constitutions. These contentions have no merit and require little discussion.

The theory of plaintiffs' due process claim is that the statute is too vague to be generally followed or enforced because the words "session" and "sessions" are not defined by the statute and can mean different things to different people. But in the context of the statute as a whole, which is what we are concerned with, the meaning of these words is quite plain to anyone of common understanding and the statute is not unconstitutionally vague. A "session" of bingo as used in the statute means a period of time in which bingo is conducted or sponsored by a particular exempt organization in one location, and "sessions" is more than one session. Thus, it is quite clear that plaintiffs were violating the statute by conducting a bingo session immediately after a similar session by another organization at the same location.

The First Amendment free speech theory is that since plaintiffs raise money for charity through bingo, limiting them to one session of bingo during a 48-hour period unduly restricts their right to solicit charitable contributions. While soliciting contributions is certainly protected by the First Amendment, Village of Schaumburg v. Citizens for a Better Environment, 444 U.S. 620 (1980), this statute does not impinge upon plaintiffs' right to solicit contributions, charitable or otherwise, from whomever they desire. The statute restricts only the conducting of bingo, which is gambling, and no one has a constitutional right to operate a gambling business. Marvin v. Trout, 199 U.S. 212 (1905).

The equal protection argument is that the 48-hour provision creates a favored and unfavored class because the first organization to conduct its bingo session in a given location during that period is not subject to prosecution but the second organization is, and that no rational basis exists for creating these two classes. Statutes are always creating classes and making distinctions, and it is lawful to do so as long as the distinction is reasonably related to the accomplishment of a purpose that the Legislature has the power to reach. Obviously, one purpose of the distinction in question, a laudable and proper one, is to limit gambling, an offense against public morals when not conducted as the statute specifies. Except for this or some similar limitation licensed bingo, instead of providing brief and occasional opportunities for harmless recreation, could fill the weekends of many people to their ruinous cost in money and otherwise.

Affirmed.

Notes

1. In addition to residency requirements, frequency and duration rules, spending caps, advertising bans, and prize limits, some states also restrict the kind of goods that can be awarded by a charity. *See, e.g.*, Ariz. Rev. Stat. § 5-406(L) (alcoholic beverages prohibited), and N.C. Gen. Stat. § 14-309.15(d) (real property prohibited).

2. States typically limit bingo and raffle licenses to charitable, educational, fraternal, religious, and other non-profit organizations. As such, courts sometimes are called upon to decide whether a particular applicant's activities

qualify. *See, e.g., Lake Brady Spiritualists Camp Association v. Brown*, 402 N.E.2d 1187 (Ohio 1988) (group's summer gatherings were religious in nature); *Oklahoma State Navy Ladies Auxiliary and Marine Corps v. Macy*, 821 P.2d 397 (Okla. Ct. App. 1991) (recognition of non-profit status by IRS not determinative); *Exotic Feline Survival Association, Inc. v. City of Hammond*, 479 So. 2d 645 (La. Ct. App. 1985) (denying license to animal welfare shelter); *State v. Opelousas Charity Bingo, Inc.*, 462 So. 2d 1380 (La. Ct. App. 1985) (finding insufficient connection to charitable causes); *Cadet-Ettes Corporation v. Brown*, 406 N.E.2d 538 (Ohio Ct. App. 1977) (baton-twirling school deemed ineligible).

3. For a further look at bingo operations, *see, e.g., Home Health Service, Inc. v. South Carolina Tax Commission*, 440 S.E.2d 375 (S.C. 1994) (improper for operator to have its employees "sit in" for patrons while they temporarily left the playing hall); *Ginny's Kids International, Inc. v. Office of Secretary of State*, 29 P.3d 333 (Colo. Ct. App. 2000) (five-year residency requirement could only be met by in-state activities); *State ex rel. Macy v. Items and Money Seized from Flamingo Bingo*, 738 P.2d 1384 (Okla. Ct. App. 1987) (conducting bingo game without a license did not authorize state to forfeit equipment); *State ex rel. McLeod v. Coates*, 313 S.E.2d 642 (S.C. Ct. App. 1984) (contract by which operator guaranteed set amounts to charity based on how many people attended its bingo games was not illegal gambling contract); *Joseph Brothers Company v. Brown*, 415 N.E.2d 987 (Ohio Ct. App. 1979) (rent maximum of $250 per bingo session was valid exercise of state's police power). *See also* Richard J. Van Wagner & Bernadette Fallows Davidson, *Bingo and Raffles: Nonprofits and Games of Chance*, N.J. Law., Feb. 1998, at 19, and Daniel J. Guinan, Note, *An Unlawful Interpretation of the "Lawful Purpose" Provisions of the Nebraska Bingo and Pickle Card Lottery Acts*, 31 Creighton L. Rev. 347 (1997).

Problem 9

A state's bingo statute prohibits licensees from giving door prizes. If the owner of a building in which bingo is conducted by various charities decides to award such a prize, has the law been violated? *See Lyon v. State*, 766 S.W.2d 879 (Tex. Ct. App. 1989).

E. SUPPLIERS

BOBBIE PREECE FACILITY v. COMMONWEALTH
71 S.W.3d 99 (Ky. Ct. App. 2001)

COMBS, Judge.

Bobbie Preece Facility appeals from the opinion and order of the Franklin Circuit Court which affirmed the decision of the appellee, Commonwealth of Kentucky, Department of Charitable Gaming ("the Department"), to deny the facility's renewal application for a license to operate a charitable gaming establishment. Preece challenges the constitutionality of Kentucky Revised Statute (KRS) 238.530(3), pursuant to which the Department denied its renewal application. Preece argues that its property has been taken without just compensation. After our review of the record, the arguments, and the legal authorities relied upon by Preece, we affirm.

The facts are undisputed and were largely stipulated to by the parties during the administrative proceeding conducted by the Department. Bobbie Preece Facility, a sole proprietorship owned by Bobbie Preece, includes a building in Catlettsburg, Kentucky, in which charitable gaming activities (bingo games) are conducted. Preece has owned the building since 1985. She is also the President and owner of at least 10% of Preece Wholesale, Inc., involving the distribution of gaming supplies and equipment—a business in which she and her husband have been involved for more than thirty years.

After the passage of the Charitable Gaming Act in 1994, Preece applied for and was issued a license by the Department to operate a charitable gaming facility. Preece Wholesale, Inc., also applied for and was granted a license to distribute charitable gaming supplies and equipment. Both licenses were renewed annually through February 1999. However, in 1998, the General Assembly amended KRS 238.530(3), a portion of the Charitable Gaming Act, effective April 1, 1998, to read as follows:

> No person who is licensed as a charitable organization, and no owner, officer, employee, or member of the immediate family of an owner, officer, or employee of a licensed charitable gaming facility shall be eligible for licensure as a distributor or manufacturer. No affiliate of an owner, officer, or employee, or member of the immediate family of an owner, officer, or employee of a licensed charitable gaming facility shall be licensed as a distributor or manufacturer.

In April 1998, the Department notified Preece of the change in the statute and informed her that when her facility and distributor licenses expired, she would not be eligible to have both of them renewed. Nevertheless, Preece sought renewal of both licenses. On January 29, 1999, she was notified that the renewal of her license to operate a charitable gaming facility (the first to expire) had been denied. The distributor license was renewed. At Preece's request, a hearing was conducted before a hearing officer, who determined that he was without authority to address Preece's argument that KRS 238.530(3) was unconstitutional. A final order of the Department was rendered affirming the denial of the facility license, and Preece appealed to the Franklin Circuit Court.

Preece argued that her rights pursuant to the Due Process Clause of the Fourteenth Amendment of the United States Constitution had been violated by the non-renewal of her license. The court disagreed and upheld the constitutionality of KRS 238.530(3), discussing the statutory restrictions on holding multiple licenses as follows:

> This Court finds that the extended restrictions are rationally related to the legitimate state interest of preventing commercialization of charitable gaming and are necessary to avoid commingling of functions among licensees, and to prevent a handful of individuals from controlling the entire activity of charitable gaming.

As to Preece's argument that the non-renewal constituted an unconstitutional taking of her property without just compensation, the Franklin Circuit Court concluded as follows:

This Court cannot find that the interest Ms. Preece has in her charitable gaming licenses is one of entitlement that affords her the due process protection she seeks. Ms. Preece has no constitutional right to engage in charitable gaming. In fact, her right is solely created by statute, and is then heavily regulated. Accordingly, the Legislature may prohibit charitable gaming altogether, or it may place restrictions on licensing as it sees fit to create them. This Court finds that an interest in a charitable gaming license is more akin to a privilege than to a property right. Therefore, we cannot agree that KRS 238.530(3) rises to the level of leaving property without beneficial use as that contemplated in Lucas v. South Carolina Coastal Council, 505 U.S. 1003 (1992). We find a distinct difference in rights and protection between the actual physical use of land, and the acquiring of a license to perform a specific function on the land, the latter requiring a lower level of protection. Accordingly, this Court finds that KRS 238.530(3) has not constituted a taking of Ms. Preece's property interests within the meaning of the Fifth Amendment's Takings Clause.

In this appeal, Preece argues that the Franklin Circuit Court erred in failing to find a violation of her substantive due process rights as guaranteed by the Fourteenth Amendment to the United States Constitution by virtue of the application of the amended version of KRS 238.530(3) to deny her license. She contends that the statute forces her "to choose between the deprivation of two (2) property interests" and that it has resulted in the "taking" of her property. Preece observes that in a town the size of Catlettsburg, there are very few other uses for a bingo hall—and certainly none that "would provide as significant a source of revenue as a charitable gaming facility."

A party challenging governmental action as amounting to an unconstitutional taking bears a rather hefty burden. The alleged "violation of the Constitution must be clear, complete and unmistakable" in order to succeed on a claim that the law is unconstitutional. Kentucky Industrial Utility Customers, Inc. v. Kentucky Utilities Company, 983 S.W.2d 493, 499 (Ky. 1998). With respect to claims of substantive due process affecting "economic and business rights rather than fundamental rights," the statute at issue must be evaluated by the rational basis test—and the analysis is deferential in nature. Stephens v. State Farm Mutual Automobile Ins. Co., 894 S.W.2d 624, 627 (Ky. 1995).

Preece has no "fundamental right" to a license to operate a charitable gaming facility as noted in Commonwealth v. Louisville Atlantis Community/ Adapt, Inc., 971 S.W.2d 810, 816 (Ky. Ct. App. 1997), where this Court stated: "There is no constitutional right to engage in charitable gaming." Additionally, Preece has failed to establish that the statute is either arbitrary or unreasonable so as to render it unconstitutional on its face. As was stressed repeatedly in Louisville Atlantis, the Legislature has a legitimate objective of "keeping charitable gaming from becoming commercial, preventing participation by criminals, and preventing the diversion of funds from legitimate charitable purposes." By denying multiple licenses to an individual, KRS 238.530(3), as altered by the 1998 amendment, promotes the Legislature's goal of preventing the commercialization of charitable gaming, of preventing the concentration of profits in one individual, and of "insuring that funds raised by charitable gaming actually benefit charitable works." Pigeons' Roost, Inc. v. Commonwealth, Division of Charitable Gaming, 10 S.W.3d 133, 135 (Ky. Ct. App. 1999). We hold that the statute is rationally related to a legitimate state objective and thus that it does not violate Preece's substantive due process rights.

Preece vigorously argues in the alternative that even if a legitimate basis for the statute exists, the Department has taken her property without just compensation. The "Takings Clause" of the Fifth Amendment to the United States Constitution provides: "Nor shall private property be taken for public use, without just compensation." Section 13 of the Kentucky Constitution mirrors that provision: "Nor shall any man's property be taken or applied to public use without the consent of his representatives, and without just compensation being previously made to him." Preece correctly argues that the concept of "taking" has evolved over the years to include regulatory interference with one's use or enjoyment of his property in addition to the more traditional notion of a taking as a physical seizure of property. "When the owner of real property has been called upon to sacrifice all economically beneficial uses in the name of the common good, that is, to leave his property economically idle, he has suffered a taking." Lucas v. South Carolina Coastal Council, 505 U.S. 1003, 1019 (1992). Preece argues that she has suffered the very type of regulatory taking described and denounced in Lucas and that the denial of a charitable gaming license essentially has resulted in a substantial loss in value of her real estate and the loss of income, amounting to a "taking without compensation."

We agree with the Franklin Circuit Court that the denial of Preece's license to operate a charitable gaming facility has not resulted in a "taking" as contemplated by Lucas or as encompassed within the meaning of either the United States or the Kentucky constitutions. There is no evidence that the real property owned by Preece has been diminished in value by the enforcement of the statute and the denial of the facility license. Preece has not argued that she has been denied all beneficial uses of the property—only the most profitable one. However, lost profits are "not a proper element of compensation for land taking in condemnation proceedings." Siding Sales, Inc. v. Warren County Water District, 984 S.W.2d 490, 494 (Ky. Ct. App. 1998).

Furthermore, it is significant that at the time Preece obtained the property in 1985, charitable gaming was not a legal enterprise in Kentucky. In order to be entitled to compensation under the Takings Clause of the Fifth Amendment, the owner must be deprived of a portion of the "bundle of rights" in the property that existed when he obtained title to the property. Lucas, 505 U.S. at 1027.

Finally, we agree with the conclusion of the lower court that Preece does not have an enforceable property interest in the facility license that would support a claim under the Takings Clause of either constitution. As explained in Mitchell Arms, Inc. v. United States, 7 F.3d 212, 215-216 (Fed. Cir.1993), cert. denied, 511 U.S. 1106 (1994), an interest which depends totally on regulatory licensing is not a property interest that is compensable under the Takings Clause:

The chief and one of the most valuable characteristics of the bundle of rights commonly called "property" is "the right to sole and exclusive possession—the right to exclude strangers, or for that matter friends, but especially the Government." Hendler v. United States, 952 F.2d 1364, 1374 (Fed. Cir.1991) (citation omitted). In this case, Mitchell did not possess such a right.

Enforceable rights sufficient to support a taking claim against the United States cannot arise in an area voluntarily entered into and one which, from the start, is subject to pervasive Government control" (citation omitted). The reason "enforceable rights sufficient to support a taking claim" cannot arise in such an area is that when a citizen voluntarily enters such an area, the citizen cannot be said to possess "the right to exclude." Hendler, 952 F.2d at 1374. And the reason the citizen cannot be said to possess "the right to exclude" is that the citizen is in an area subject to government control. Mitchell voluntarily entered the firearms import business, thereby knowingly placing itself in the governmentally controlled arena of firearms importation under the Gun Control Act. Under these circumstances, Mitchell's expectation of selling the assault rifles in the United States—which expectation necessarily flowed from the ATF permits—could not be said to be a property right protected under the Fifth Amendment.

As the Franklin Circuit Court correctly found, the subject of charitable gaming is highly regulated. Those who hold licenses must seek renewal annually or biennially. KRS 238.525. Preece first voluntarily entered the charitable gaming arena when it was an illegal activity. Since it was legitimized in 1994, charitable gaming has been subjected to strict governmental regulation. For these reasons, we agree with the Franklin Circuit Court that Preece's license is more akin to a privilege than a license. Preece could reasonably expect that the privilege could be taken away or encumbered as a means of meeting the legitimate goals of the Legislature. Lucas, supra, at 1027-1028. In this vein, the United States Supreme Court aptly summarized that:

> in the case of personal property, by reason of the State's traditionally high degree of control over commercial dealings, the owner ought to be aware of the possibility that new regulation might even render his property economically worthless.

We conclude that the refusal of the Department to renew Preece's facility license did not trigger the right to compensation guaranteed by the Fifth Amendment to the United States Constitution and by § 13 of the Kentucky Constitution.

The judgment of the Franklin Circuit Court is affirmed.

WISCONSIN BINGO SUPPLY & EQUIPMENT COMPANY, INC. v. WISCONSIN BINGO CONTROL BOARD
276 N.W.2d 716 (Wis. 1979)

HANSEN, Justice.

Pursuant to the provisions of §§ 163.21 and 163.22, the appellant filed an application for a bingo supplier's license with the Wisconsin Bingo Control Board on June 26, 1974. This application was denied pursuant to §§ 163.27(2) and 163.27(4), which provide:

> 163.27 Persons not eligible for supplier's license. The following persons shall not be eligible for a supplier's license . . . .
>
> (2) A person who is or has been a professional gambler or gambling promoter or who is not of good moral character as defined in § 139.34
>
> . . . .
>
> (4) A business in which a person disqualified under sub. (1), (2) or (3) is employed or active or in which a person is married or related in the first degree of kinship to such person who has an interest of more than 10% in the business.

Ned E. Torti, Jr., is the president of the appellant corporation and fifty percent shareholder. His father, Ned E. Torti, Sr., is vice-president of the corporation and owns the remaining fifty percent of the capital stock.

At the hearing before the Board on November 20, 1974, the parties stipulated that the only issue was whether Ned E. Torti, Sr., was a gambling promoter. Following the hearing, the Board denied the application for a bingo supplier's license. On review, the circuit court affirmed the determination of the Board, and this appeal follows.

At the hearing, Ned E. Torti, Sr., testified that his family began a novelty store business in 1919 and that he became a partner in the business in the late 1930's or early 1940's. The business is now known as Wisconsin Deluxe Premium & Novelty, Inc., and he has been the president and general manager of this family corporation for about ten years. He admitted they rented roulette wheels and chuck-a-luck cages and sold play money to churches and other organizations for Las Vegas nights; that they sold small, toy versions of roulette wheels and might have sold some of the larger type that they rented. He also admitted that prior to a 1951 raid by law enforcement officers, they sold punch boards, number jars and tip tickets, but said they discontinued such sales after the raid.

He also testified they no longer stocked tip tickets here in Wisconsin but would order them from an out-of-state supplier and have them shipped directly to the customer. The customer would pay his company for the tip tickets. He said he understood it was illegal to have tip tickets on the premises, but thought it was permissible to sell them in this manner. He said the sale of such tip tickets represented but a small portion of the total gross sales of Wisconsin Deluxe Premium & Novelty, Inc.

Richard R. Puchter, of the criminal investigation division of the state department of justice, testified that he and another agent drove to Wisconsin Deluxe Premium & Novelty, Inc., on May 1, 1972. His partner went into the place of business, purchased and paid for some tip tickets. They both returned on June 26, 1972, to purchase some more tip tickets and both went into the place of business and approached an employee who told them "We don't sell those here." Puchter then told the employee they had previously purchased tip tickets there. The employee found the file under the name of Tom Nelson and acknowledged a previous sale of single tip tickets instead of "Big Seven Dixie Special" which he now wanted to order. At this point, Torti entered into the conversation and finally instructed the employee to "Go ahead and order for them." At the suggestion of Torti he ordered two boxes of the tip tickets because he was told he could save by ordering in a larger quantity and when asked how much he could expect selling these tip tickets, Torti stated approximately $140.

The tip tickets were ultimately delivered to Puchter at his residence address by United Parcel Service. He received a statement for the tip tickets in the amount of $23.78 from Wisconsin Deluxe Premium & Novelty, Inc., and paid it by check. The invoice, cancelled check and one of the tip tickets were admitted into evidence. Torti testified the tip ticket was not similar to the ones he had ordered and that he had never seen one used and didn't know how to use it.

Milwaukee county circuit court records were introduced in evidence which reflect that on October 6, 1972, Ned E. Torti, Sr., was arrested for dealing in gambling devices (party to a crime). The complaint was amended to name Wisconsin Deluxe Premium & Novelty Co. as defendant, a plea of no contest was entered to a misdemeanor gambling charge contrary to § 945.02(3), and the defendant was fined $100.

On the basis of this record the Board made the following findings of fact: That Ned E. Torti, Sr., sold tip tickets to an agent of the Wisconsin Department of Justice for valuable consideration at a business establishment known as Wisconsin Deluxe Premium & Novelty, Inc.; that the company was fined $100 for possession of gambling devices; that at all times material thereto Ned E. Torti, Sr., was the principal officer and managing agent of Wisconsin Deluxe Premium & Novelty, Inc.; that Ned E. Torti, Sr., was vice-president and fifty percent owner of Wisconsin Bingo Supply & Equipment Company, Inc.; that over the past five years Wisconsin Deluxe Premium & Novelty, Inc., has sold and leased gambling devices for profit in the state.

On the basis of these findings the Board concluded that Wisconsin Deluxe Premium & Novelty and Ned E. Torti, Sr., had been engaged in the promotion of gambling and that Wisconsin Bingo Supply & Equipment Company was therefore not eligible for a bingo supplier's license.

On this appeal the appellant challenges the judgment on the following grounds:

1. Sec. 163.27 is unconstitutional because it is vague, it is a bill of attainder, an ex post facto law and a retrospective law and it violates the equal protection clause.

2. The evidence is insufficient to support the Board's conclusion that the appellant and Ned E. Torti, Sr., have been gambling promoters.

CONSTITUTIONALITY

Appellant contends § 163.27 is void because the term "gambling promoter" has not been and cannot be defined with any definiteness and certainty and the statute is therefore unconstitutionally vague. The Board denied the corporation's license application under subsection (4) because Ned E. Torti, Sr., was found to be a gambling promoter under subsection (2).

This court set forth the following guidelines when considering constitutional attacks on a civil statute for vagueness:

> A statute is not necessarily void merely because it is vague, indefinite, or uncertain, or contains terms not susceptible of exact meaning, or is stated in general terms, or prescribes a general course of conduct, or does not prescribe precise boundaries, or is imperfect in its details, or contains errors or omissions, or because the intention of the legislature might have been expressed in plainer terms, and questions may arise as to its applicability, and opinions may differ in respect of what falls within its terms, or because the statute is difficult to execute. Unless a statute is so vague and uncertain that it is impossible to execute it or to ascertain the legislative intent with reasonable certainty, it is valid.

Forest Home Dodge, Inc. v. Karns, 138 N.W.2d 214 (Wis. 1965).

The statute on its face appears to be a proper exercise of the police power and is presumptively constitutional.

The legislative purpose behind chapter 163 is set forth in § 163.02:

> 163.02 Purpose. The purpose of this chapter is to implement § 24 of Article IV of the state constitution, as amended by vote of the people at the general election in April, 1973. The legislature hereby declares that:
>
> (1) All phases of the conduct of bingo, except bingo games using free cards and donated prizes for which no payment of consideration is made by participants, should be closely controlled by appropriate laws and rules which should be strictly and uniformly enforced throughout this state.
>
> (2) The conduct of bingo and all attendant activities, except bingo games using free cards and donated prizes for which no payment of consideration is made by participants, should be so regulated as to discourage commercialization of bingo in all its forms, including the rental of commercial premises for bingo, and to ensure the maximum use of the profits of bingo exclusively for the lawful purposes specified in this chapter.
>
> (3) It is a matter of statewide concern to foster and support such lawful purposes and to prevent commercialized gambling, participation by criminal and other undesirable elements and diversion of funds from the lawful purposes herein authorized.

The term "promoter" has been defined using the following definition from Black's Law Dictionary (rev. 4th ed. 1968), "a person 'who promotes, urges on, encourages, incites, advances, etc.' "

Sec. 163.03(6m) expressly refers to § 945.01(4)(a) for its definition of a "gambling place." By specifically prohibiting both commercial gambling and gambling promoters from obtaining bingo supplier licenses the legislature clearly intends to bar not only those actively engaged in commercial gambling from obtaining licenses, but also those who facilitated such gambling by promoting it with the sale and lease of equipment necessary to carry it on.

Based upon the record before us there is substantial evidence to support the findings and conclusions of the Board that Ned E. Torti, Sr., was a gambling promoter. When one is engaged in the commercial sale and lease of gambling devices which are illegal in Wisconsin, he is fostering gambling activities and is a gambling promoter.

The reference to chapter 945 and the declaration of legislative intent and purpose as contained in chapter 163 provide the Bingo Control Board with guidelines to apply the term gambling promoter with sufficient definiteness to satisfy the constitutional requirements of due process.

Appellant next contends § 163.27 is a bill of attainder or ex post facto law. A bill of attainder is a legislative act which inflicts punishment without a judicial trial. An ex post facto law is one which imposes a punishment for an act which was not punishable at the time it was committed or imposes an additional punishment to that then prescribed. These constitutional provisions apply only to statutes which impose penalties. Where the disability is imposed to accomplish some other legitimate governmental purpose these doctrines do not apply.

Appellant is not being punished here. It is merely being denied a license because it does not qualify under the standards established by the legislature in the valid exercise of its police power to regulate the issuance of bingo suppliers' licenses. This court has held that statutes which set up qualifications for obtaining a license for a particular trade or profession are not ex post facto laws.

SUFFICIENCY OF THE EVIDENCE

The Board's conclusion that Torti was a gambling promoter was based on the findings that he or his corporation sold tip tickets, had been fined for the possession of gambling devices and sold and leased gambling devices for profit. These findings are supported by the evidence set out above. The Board did not attempt to convict appellant of a violation of § 945.05, nor did it apply an irrebuttable presumption that a conviction under § 945.05 would make one a gambling promoter. The Board had more than the 1972 conviction on which to base its conclusion. A party who sells and rents illegal gambling equipment and supplies to others clearly is engaged in the promotion of gambling and falls within that class of persons the legislature intended to exclude from participation in legalized bingo. The Board's application of §§ 163.27(2) and (4) to appellant was correct and the judgment is affirmed.

Notes

1. Most states require bingo suppliers and manufacturers to be licensed and keep detailed sales records. For many years, Ohio was a notable exception,

due in part to a ruling by the state supreme court that permitted unregulated bingo to be played in bars and taverns. *See Freedom Road Foundation v. Ohio Department of Liquor Control*, 685 N.E.2d 522 (Ohio 1997). *See also* Tom Breckenridge, *Charities Not Cashing in on Bingo Jackpots*, Cleve. Plain Dealer, June 27, 1999, at 1A. In December 2002, the legislature finally passed a reform package that closed many of the loopholes in the old law and, for the first time, required bingo suppliers and manufacturers to be licensed. *See* Lee Leonard & Jon Craig, *Veto Request Ignored; Legislation Increases Regulation of Bingo*, Columbus Dispatch, Jan. 3, 2003, at 1C.

2. For an interesting patent case pitting two bingo suppliers and their respective electronic "card management" devices against one other, *see Bingo Brain, Inc. v. California Concepts, Inc.*, 2002 U.S. Dist. LEXIS 1209 (N.D. Ill.), *aff'd mem.*, 2002 U.S. App. LEXIS 25401 (7th Cir. 2002).

Problem 10

When a bingo supply company had its license revoked, regulators in another state immediately took the same action. If the company appeals the second order on due process grounds, how should the court rule? *See Bullock v. Bingo King Company, Inc.*, 714 S.W.2d 320 (Tex. Ct. App. 1986).

F. TAXES

ARDEN CARMICHAEL, INC. v. COUNTY OF SACRAMENTO
113 Cal. Rptr. 2d 248 (Ct. App. 2001)

KOLKEY, Justice.

In Arden Carmichael, Inc. v. County of Sacramento (Arden Carmichael), 94 Cal. Rptr. 2d 673 (Ct. App. 2000), this Court held that a fee imposed on nonprofit organizations by the County of Sacramento (the County) based upon a percentage of their gross receipts earned from bingo games violated article XIII, § 26, subdivision (d) of the state Constitution ("subdivision (d)"). Subdivision (d) provides that a nonprofit organization "is exempt from any business license tax or fee measured by income or gross receipts that is levied by a county."

In an effort to conform with the law, the County changed its fee structure. It now imposes a fee based upon a percentage of the prize payouts from the bingo games.

Plaintiffs, a group of 34 nonprofit organizations that operate licensed bingo games within the County, brought this action challenging the County's new fee structure, arguing that "prize payouts track the gross income closely enough to be considered inextricably linked" and that a fee based thereon is therefore violative of the state Constitution's prohibition against fees measured by income or gross receipts. Plaintiffs also argue that the new fee violates Penal Code § 326.5, subdivision (l)(2), which authorizes the imposition of a license fee in the amount of $50, plus an additional fee that may not exceed the actual costs of law enforcement and public safety directly related to the bingo activities.

The County moved for summary adjudication, and the trial court ruled that the County's new fee complied with the state Constitution and Penal Code § 326.5.

In the published portion of our opinion, we conclude that the County's fee does not violate the state Constitution because a fee measured by prize payouts—which is an expense of the bingo operations—cannot be deemed a fee based on income or gross receipts. Neither the plain language of the constitutional provision nor its purpose supports an extension of the prohibition to fees based on expenses. However, we reverse and remand because the County has failed to sustain its burden of persuasion that there is no triable issue of material fact whether the County is charging plaintiffs a fee that exceeds that permitted by Penal Code § 326.5, subdivision (l)(2).

I. BACKGROUND

In June 1994, the voters adopted Proposition 176, which amended and limited the reach of article XIII, § 26 of the state Constitution—which authorizes, with some exceptions, the imposition of taxes measured by income—by adding another exception, subdivision (d). Subdivision (d), which exempts nonprofit organizations from any local business license tax or fee measured by income or gross receipts, states in relevant part: "A nonprofit organization is exempt from any business license tax or fee measured by income or gross receipts that is levied by a county or city, whether charter or general law, a city and county, a school district, a special district, or any other local agency."

Notwithstanding the passage of Proposition 176, between June 1994 and December 1996, the County collected from nonprofit organizations $905,134.37 in fees based on one percent of each organization's gross receipts over $5,000 earned from bingo games, as authorized by a former version of Penal Code § 326.5 and a former County ordinance. Given the clear and unambiguous language of subdivision (d), we concluded in Arden Carmichael that the County's imposition of a "fee based on the gross receipts of the bingo games was unconstitutional."

Effective January 1, 1997, Penal Code § 326.5 was amended ("§ 326.5") to conform with the requirements of subdivision (d). Section 326.5, subdivision (l), now states in relevant part:

(1) A city, county, or city and county may impose a license fee on each organization that it authorizes to conduct bingo games. The fee, whether for the initial license or renewal, shall not exceed fifty dollars ($50) annually.

(2) In lieu of the license fee permitted under paragraph (1), a city, county, or city and county may impose a license fee of fifty dollars ($50) paid upon application. An additional fee for law enforcement and public safety costs incurred by the city, county, or city and county that are directly related to bingo activities may be imposed and shall be collected monthly by the city, county, or city and county issuing the license; however, the fee shall not exceed the actual costs incurred in providing the service.

Also effective January 1, 1997, the County amended County Code § 4.26.050 to conform with § 326.5, modifying the basis for its bingo fee from one percent of gross receipts to a $50 fee plus an additional fee, to be prescribed by the County Board of Supervisors, to recover law enforcement and public safety costs in accordance with § 326.5. That fee, as set by the Board of Supervisors, has varied from 1.225 percent of monthly prize payouts (less an exemption of $2,000 monthly) for the period of January-March 1997, to a fee of 1.2 percent for April-December 1997, to a fee of 1.15 percent effective January 1, 1998.

In deciding to base a fee on prize payouts, the County reasoned that not only was the amount of prize payouts steady, thereby offering "a consistent source of monies for the County to fully recover its costs," but that "prize payouts generally correlated to the amount of time involved by the County in regulating licensees": "Usually, with greater sums in prizes and payouts, a charity conducts more games thereby attracting a larger number of gamblers."

In their first cause of action, plaintiffs charged that because prize payouts are linked to gross receipts, the County's new fee structure violated the state Constitution. They also contended that the amount of fees did not reflect the actual law enforcement and public safety costs incurred by the County to oversee the operation of the bingo games.

Following hearing and argument, the trial court granted the County's motion for summary adjudication. The court concluded that the fee complied with the state Constitution and § 326.5. The court also granted the County's motion for judgment on the pleadings with respect to the second and fourth causes of action for declaratory relief. The action was dismissed in its entirety. Plaintiffs appeal.

II. DISCUSSION

It is undisputed that the County's fee is calculated on the basis of prize payouts, and the relevant question is whether this violates subdivision (d)'s prohibition against fees "measured by income or gross receipts." This issue was thus properly subject to a summary judgment determination.

Plaintiffs argue that a fee measured by prize payouts is illegal because "prize payouts track the gross income closely enough to be considered inextricably linked." They observe that "prize payouts have historically amounted to about 77 percent of gross receipts," and thus claim that the County adjusted its fee from one percent of gross receipts under the former (and now unconstitutional) County ordinance to roughly 1.298 percent of prize payouts under the new County code section to achieve the same result. Plaintiffs argue that the County cannot do indirectly what it is prohibited from doing directly.

This analysis misses its target. The issue in this case is not whether the County is legally permitted to devise a new measure for its fee that recovers the same amount of revenue as before, but whether the particular measure developed by the County is constitutional. We have little doubt that as long as the County is legally entitled to recover all of its law enforcement and public safety costs—and it is—it will eventually find a constitutional formula to collect them. Thus, the question becomes whether the state Constitution prohibits a fee calculated as a percentage of prize payouts, simply because prize payouts can be shown to be a roughly constant percentage of gross receipts—a measure that the Constitution prohibits.

In this case, article XIII, § 26 generally permits "taxes on or measured by income," but makes specific exceptions, including that specified under subdivision (d). Subdivision (d) provides that "a nonprofit organization that is exempted from federal or state income taxation is exempt from any business license tax or fee measured by income or gross receipts that is levied by a county or city, whether charter or general law, a city and county, a school district, a special district, or any other local agency." Accordingly, the provision does not exempt nonprofit organizations from all business license taxes or fees, but only those measured by income or gross receipts.

Prize payouts are, however, not income but an expense to the nonprofit organization. They are ultimately deducted from the gross income realized by the nonprofit organization to determine the net income that it has derived from its bingo games. Does a fee based on an expense that is deducted from gross receipts constitute a prohibited fee measured by income or gross receipts under subdivision (d)? We think not.

In this case, the plain language of subdivision (d) does not prohibit fees that are measured on the basis of expenses, although it certainly could have. Adherence to the natural and ordinary meaning of "income" and "gross receipts" in subdivision (d) supports the conclusion that the County's fee, measured instead by a type of expense, does not violate the constitutional provision. A court that speculates over what a provision might have said, rather than grounding its interpretation on what the provision has in fact said, oversteps its judicial role.

Our state high court's decision in A.B.C. Distributing Co. v. City & County of San Francisco, 542 P.2d 625 (Cal. 1975) supports our conclusion that a fee based on an expense incurred by a taxpayer does not constitute a fee measured by income or gross receipts. There, the plaintiffs—wholesale liquor and beer distributors—contended that San Francisco's ordinance, which imposed a one percent payroll expense tax on persons hiring employees to perform services in San Francisco, violated § 17041.5 of the Revenue and Taxation Code, which provides that no city may levy or collect any tax upon the income of any person. Although the payroll expense tax was measured by the wages paid to employees, the California Supreme Court rejected the challenge: "The short answer to plaintiffs' contention is that the payroll expense tax is not a tax on or measured by their income. Instead, the tax is imposed upon plaintiffs by reason of their employment of labor within the city and county, measured by the expense incurred by plaintiffs in conducting this aspect of their business. The fact that the tax is measured by wages paid to the employees would not convert the tax to an income tax." Thus, the state Supreme Court distinguished a tax measured by an expense incurred by plaintiffs from one measured by their income. In response to plaintiffs' suggestion that a payroll expense tax was, in essence, an income tax because it was paid from plaintiffs' income—a suggestion similar to that of plaintiffs in this case—the state high court observed that "all taxes necessarily involve some reduction of and relationship to available revenues."

Our construction is also supported by the canon of statutory construction, expressio unius est exclusio alterius. This maxim "expresses the learning of common experience that when people say one thing they do not mean something else." Here, subdivision (d)'s specific listing of prohibited measures for taxation—income or gross receipts—permits the others.

Nor can a fee based on prize payouts be deemed a mere subterfuge to circumvent subdivision (d)'s prohibition on the use of income or gross receipts as a measure for fees. We suppose that plaintiffs could argue that subdivision (d)'s exemption should be construed to extend beyond income-based fees on the ground that it also includes a ban against fees based on gross receipts, thereby also prohibiting income-like measurements. However, to the extent that the reference to gross receipts is argued to create an ambiguity, it is appropriate to consider indicia of the voters' intent in construing the provision—which was an initiative measure, Proposition 176. This includes the analysis and arguments contained in the official ballot pamphlet. The argument in favor of Proposition 176 in the ballot pamphlet stated that it would "protect community service groups from having their contributions taxed which were originally intended to aid many of the community health and human services such as those for children, the disabled, the poor or those displaced by natural disasters." Proponents further argued that "nonprofit organizations should be exempt from any business license tax or fee measured by income or gross receipts because they would need to reduce services, raise fees, or divert staff and volunteer time to raising more funds to pay these taxes."

These ballot arguments demonstrate two points. First, the exemption from fees measured by income or gross receipts was intended to protect contributions and other categories of revenue from direct taxation, which would directly reduce those revenues and the services they fund. Taxing an expense, however, has the opposite effect: It encourages a reduction in expenses, with an accompanying benefit to revenues. Second, nothing expressly stated in the ballot arguments supports a reading of subdivision (d) that is different from its plain language. Neither the subdivision's plain language nor the interpretive materials suggest an intent to prohibit all fees or any fees other than those based on a measurement that is expressly prohibited. To go beyond the express words of this constitutional provision, when no express intent to do so appears in either the text or interpretative materials, would trespass into the province of policy, which is the prerogative of the lawmaker, not the judge.

Finally, by limiting our construction of subdivision (d) to its plain language, we promote predictability in the law, which is of particular value in laws affecting economic activity: Where a provision, as here, is meant to guide the future behavior of governments and the public alike in making tax and economic decisions, respectively, reliance on the provision's plain language allows interested parties to gear their actions to the law's objective text, rather than wager their future on an uncertain quest in the courts for the law's inner meaning. We conclude that the County was entitled to rely on subdivision (d)'s text in determining to base its fee on an expense of the bingo operations—prize payouts—in lieu of one of the income-based measurements prohibited by that provision.

STATE v. CRAYTON
344 So. 2d 771 (Ala. Civ. App.),
cert. denied, 344 So. 2d 775 (Ala. 1977)

BRADLEY, Judge.

The State Revenue Department ("State") entered a final sales tax assessment against Roosevelt Crayton pursuant to Title 51, § 786(3)(b), Code of Alabama 1940. Crayton appealed to the Circuit Court of Macon County where judgment was rendered absolving him of any liability for payment of the taxes. The State appeals.

The evidence shows that Crayton operates a business that may be properly termed a "bingo parlor." Bingo games are conducted at the parlor twice each week; at least ten games of bingo are played each night of operation. Prize money amounting from $25 to $100 is awarded to the game winners. Additionally, each night a jackpot of up to $1,000 is awarded. The amount of prize money to be given away on a particular night is announced on the next preceding bingo night. For example, the amount of prize money for a Saturday night is announced on the preceding Wednesday night.

Customers may either bring their own bingo cards to the game or use cards provided by the taxpayer. No admission fee is charged; however, in order to win the prize money or the jackpot, a customer must register each card he or she intends to play with Crayton and pay a fee of $1.00 per card played. The prize money is paid out of the money collected from the customers or from Crayton's own funds. Crayton operates the bingo business for profit.

During intermissions between bingo games, Crayton sells punchout boards; cash prizes are distributed to the winners of the punchout games. Crayton does not dispute the tax assessed on revenues from the punchout boards.

Title 51, § 786(3)(b), provides in pertinent part:

> There is hereby levied a privilege or license tax against the person [on] account of the business activities and in the amount to be determined by the application of rates against gross sales, or gross receipts, as the case may be, as follows:

> (b) Upon every person, firm or corporation engaged, or continuing within this state, in the business of conducting, or operating, places of amusement or entertainment, or any other place at which any exhibition, display, amusement or entertainment is offered to the public an amount equal to four percent of the gross receipts of any such business.

On April 15, 1975 the State Department of Revenue entered sales tax assessments against Crayton based on the gross receipts of the bingo operation. Both parties stipulated that the amount of the final assessments entered against the taxpayer is correct and that if the sales tax is in fact due, it is due in the amounts as assessed, as follows:

State of Alabama: $13,174.71

Macon County: 3,293.68

City of Tuskegee: 3,293.68

The Circuit Court of Macon County, following Otto v. Kosofsky, 476 S.W.2d 626 (Ky. App. 1971), cert. den. 409 U.S. 912 (1972), found that bingo is a lottery and set aside the tax assessed against Crayton under Title 51, § 786(3)(b). The court's reasoning was twofold. The court first concluded that since bingo is a lottery, and a lottery is gambling, bingo is therefore not amusement. The court apparently felt that bingo is played in order to win money and not merely for enjoyment, and that only the winners were amused by the activity. Playing bingo, said the court, is more like placing bets in a pool parlor or at a domino table than attending a theatre, restaurant, or amusement park. The second basis for the circuit court's ruling was that by collecting a tax based on playing bingo, the State is in effect condoning the operation of a lottery, which is prohibited by § 65, Constitution of Alabama 1901.

In its brief here, the State argues that the legislature did not define the meaning of the term "place of amusement or entertainment" in the statute; therefore, this court should give to that term its "commonly understood meaning." The State goes on to say that a place of amusement is commonly understood to be a place where people go for enjoyment, recreation, fun, sport, or any other type of pleasurable diversion. Thus, the patrons of Crayton's bingo parlor go there because they like to play bingo; they derive enjoyment from the game and from the chance of winning prizes. The State adds that bingo is a game and people play games for amusement or entertainment.

Crayton replies by saying that bingo, played for a prize, is a game of chance and a lottery. A lottery is prohibited by § 65 of the Alabama Constitution of 1901. Consequently, playing bingo is gambling and therefore evil. Since gambling is a vice which corrupts the morals of the public, playing bingo cannot be considered fun, pleasurable or amusing within the context of the phrase "place of amusement or entertainment," as used in § 786(3)(b). Crayton concedes that gambling can be taxed but insists that such tax must be by a specific statute and that the words "amusement or entertainment" are too broad to permit a lottery to be taxed.

The sole issue for our decision is whether or not the proceeds from the operation of a bingo parlor where people congregate for the purpose of paying money to play bingo with the hope of winning a prize—an activity admittedly contrary to the State's criminal laws—can be taxed as a "place of amusement or entertainment" as provided in § 786(3)(b).

As already noted, § 65, Constitution of Alabama 1901, prohibits a lottery. The elements of a lottery are a prize awarded by chance for a consideration. Opinion of the Justices, 251 So. 2d 751 (Ala. 1971). The evidence shows that one playing bingo at Crayton's bingo parlor pays a consideration to take a chance on winning a prize or the jackpot for that evening, and the patrons know in advance what the jackpot amount will be for the next gaming night. The evidence supports the conclusion that the manner of playing bingo at Crayton's constitutes a lottery; therefore, those who play bingo at Crayton's are gambling contrary to the criminal laws of this state. The evidence showed that this gambling operation has been in operation for at least nine months and, for this period, has grossed approximately $330,000.

The question that immediately arises is whether the State can tax an illegal activity. The answers is without doubt in the affirmative. Casmus v. Lee, 183 So. 185 (Ala. 1938). In this case the supreme court clearly held that an illegal activity may be taxed, and settled the apparent incongruity between the State's outlawing an activity and turning right around and taxing it. In Department of Public Safety v. Freeman Ready-Mix Co., 295 So. 2d 242 (Ala. 1974), the supreme court reiterated that "a tax of an illegal activity does not in any manner legalize the taxed activity." We therefore conclude that bingo as played at Crayton's, although an illegal activity, could nevertheless be taxed.

It is true that in Casmus the supreme court was concerned with a statute which specifically levied a tax on punchboards, which were a form of lottery. However, the court did not restrict its holding to only those statutes which specifically levy a tax on an illegal activity. And, in Department of Public Safety v. Freeman Ready-Mix Co., the taxing statute was not specifically directed to an illegal activity; yet the supreme court said that if the activity is illegal, it can nevertheless be taxed. Crayton's argument that only statutes specifically levying a tax on an illegal activity can be enforced is not persuasive.

The next question to be answered is whether bingo, as played at Crayton's, can be construed as entertaining and amusing so that the proceeds of the bingo operation can be taxed under § 786(3)(b). We think the answer is obviously in the affirmative.

When we examine Title 51, § 786(3)(b), we do not find any legislative intent to delineate the term "place of amusement." A broad range of activities is specifically enumerated within the statute, including race tracks where pari-mutuel betting will be allowed. Since the statute does not define "place of amusement," and since there does not appear to us to be legislative intent to the contrary, we give the term "place of amusement" its commonly understood meaning.

As suggested by the State, we believe that Crayton's patrons were there because they wanted to be entertained and amused and that the majority of them received exhilaration, pleasure and enjoyment from the prospect of winning a prize or the jackpot. The mere fact that playing bingo Crayton style is gambling and possibly morally corrupting does not necessarily mean that such activity cannot be pleasurable and entertaining. After careful examination of the evidence we consider that Crayton's bingo parlor is a "place of amusement or entertainment" as that term is used in § 786(3)(b) and the proceeds of its operation are subject to the gross receipts tax provided by that law.

The judgment of the trial court is reversed and the case is remanded for the entry of a judgment affirming the State's final tax assessment against Roosevelt Crayton.

Note

Many state constitutions expressly prohibit taxes on charitable gaming revenues. In the absence of such a clause, however, the government may levy assessments. *See Aerospace Optimist Club of Fort Worth v. Texas Alcoholic Beverage Commission*, 886 S.W.2d 556 (Tex. Ct. App. 1994) (holding that statute requiring all bingo proceeds to be used for charitable purposes had to be interpreted as referring to amounts left after paying reasonable operating expenses, including taxes).

Problem 11

A state constitution enjoins the collection of "all personal and corporate income taxes." Given this wording, would a bingo license fee equal to one percent of gross revenues be legal? *See Bingo Games Supply Company, Inc. v. Meyer*, 895 P.2d 1125 (Colo. Ct. App. 1995).

Chapter 4

PARI-MUTUEL GAMING

A. OVERVIEW

Pari-mutuel wagering has existed for centuries; today, its principal forms are greyhound racing, horse racing, and jai-alai. Although similar to other types of gaming in many respects, pari-mutuels are notable because payouts are tied to the number of players and the amount of their bets.

B. CHARACTERISTICS

LONGSTRETH v. COOK
220 S.W.2d 433 (Ark. 1949)

SMITH, Justice.

The question presented by this appeal is whether Act 46 of the Acts of 1935, legalizing pari-mutuel betting on horse races, violates § 14 of Article 19 of the State Constitution and is void for that reason. This section of the Constitution reads as follows: "No lottery shall be authorized by this State, nor shall the sale of lottery tickets be allowed." Act 46 of 1935 created the Arkansas Racing Commission, and, among other things, provided that the Commission shall promulgate rules and regulations for horse racing and for the issuance of permits to operate race tracks and licenses to hold racing meetings under the terms and conditions therein specified.

The Act is a lengthy and very comprehensive one, and contains specific directions for the exercise of the license which the Commission is authorized to issue. Since the passage of the Act in 1935, the Racing Commission has issued annually a permit or license to hold racing meetings under its provisions in the City of Hot Springs, and it is sought by this suit to restrain the Commission from renewing this license or permit.

Unquestionably Act 46 has authorized and legalized and possibly given encouragement to a form of gambling, but the question here presented is whether it has done so by authorizing a lottery. If it does, the Act is unconstitutional, as the provisions of the Constitution quoted above denied the General Assembly the power to authorize a lottery. So that the question for decision is whether Act 46 authorizes a lottery.

The owners bring their horses to the meeting and are accompanied by their trainers, who keep the horses in condition and accustom them to the tracks on which the races will be run. The horses are ridden by riders called jockeys, whose training, skill and ability are known to the owners who compete for the prizes offered in each race, and it is these prizes paid in money which compensate the owners for racing their horses. They receive no part of the money bet on the races. Admission fees to the race track are charged but the owners of the horses have no share therein.

After the deduction of the fifteen per cent as payments for the track and for the State has been made the balance in each pool is paid to the holder of tickets bet on the horses in the respective pools. The bettors do not bet against each other. The Act makes it unlawful to do so. The bet is between the bettor and the Jockey Club or the Association.

Horses are selected for entrance in a particular race by the Association, and the horses names are listed or lined up on a daily racing card, and there is sold a racing form which shows the weight carried by each horse and its handicap depending on the past performances of the horse in previous races at that or other tracks. This weight handicap is intended in some measure to equalize the speed of the horses, and the amount thereof depends upon the horse's record in prior races run within the preceding twelve months.

The owners have trainers who are skilled in handling horses with the purpose of increasing their speed and making them more responsive to the control of the jockeys.

Many persons attend the races for the thrill of witnessing the horses as they cross the finish line, and add to the thrill and interest by betting on some horse without knowledge of the information disclosed by the form sheets. For instance, a lady might bet the minimum amount permissible on a horse having the same name as her kitchen range. But sources of information now are provided, as stated above, by which bettors may bet with more discrimination and with improved chances of selecting or picking a winner.

These form sheets designate whether upon previous performances a particular horse is a fair mud runner, a good mud runner, or a superior mud runner, which information is of value when the track upon which the races are to be run on the day of the issue of the form sheet is muddy.

Followers of racing who for long periods of time have studied the records of the horses choose as their selections the horse which in their opinion will be most likely to win and these are for sale and may be purchased at the track. Neither the Jockey Club nor any one connected with it fixes the odds which will prevail on any horse. The bettors themselves do this and it is done through the number of bets made and the amount thereof on particular horses.

The animal equation enters into these races just as the human equation enters into sports between men and women. A horse may run better on one day than on another depending on the condition of the horse and it is the function of the trainer to see that the horses are in the best possible condition and properly trained. The element of chance necessarily enters into these races but it is by no means controlling. Other elements of more importance are the condition and the power of endurance of the horse and the skill and daring of its rider. Some jockeys win more races and a higher percentage of the races in which they participate than others. The services of these jockeys are of course in greater demand by the horse owners who must win the races to obtain the money prizes for which they race.

Under the facts above stated, is the horse race a lottery conducted under the pari-mutuel system herein described? It must be admitted that courts have differed in their conclusion, but an examination of many of these cases leads to the conclusion that the great weight of authority is that such races are not lotteries and we think the sounder reasoning supports that conclusion.

In our case of Burks v. Harris, 120 S.W. 979, 980 (Ark. 1909), the following definition was given: "A lottery is a species of gaming which may be defined as a scheme for the distribution of prizes by chance among persons who have paid, or agreed to pay, a valuable consideration for the chance to obtain a prize."

It appears that to constitute a lottery it is essential not only that the element of chance is present but also that it controls and determines the award of the prize whatever it may be.

The briefs of opposing counsel collect cases from which it appears to have been more frequently held that the pari-mutuel system of waging does not constitute a lottery. An opinion would be of interminal length which undertook to review all of them.

In People v. Monroe, 182 N.E. 439, 442 (Ill. 1932), with one member of the Court dissenting upon a ground not stated, the Supreme Court of Illinois held that a statute not essentially different from our Act 46 had not authorized a lottery. "The winning horse is not determined by chance, alone, but the condition, speed, and endurance of the horse, aided by the skill and management of the rider or driver, enter into the result." As showing that the horse race is not a game of chance the Court pointed out that in such races the horses engaged in the race are subject to human guidance and management, and it may be added that whip and spur are used to incite the horses to put forth their best efforts to win.

The cases cited and relied upon as supporting the contention that a lottery has been authorized are State v. Ak-Sar-Ben Exposition Co., 226 N.W. 705 (Neb. 1929), and Pompano Horse Club v. State, 111 So. 801 (Fla. 1927).

The Nebraska opinion above cited, delivered in 1929, supports appellant's contention, but it may be said of it that this opinion led to the adoption of an amendment to the Constitution of that State, which nullified the opinion. The Pompano case, supra, did not involve the question of whether a horse race was dependent on chance or not, the issue there being whether betting on a horse race was prohibited by the Florida game statute. The Court held that it was and so would we hold if the question was merely whether it was gambling. The Florida Court said: "The question before us is whether or not the buying, selling, and redeeming of certificates in the manner and for the purpose stated, constitutes gambling, or a game of chance." The Court merely held that it was gambling, and so it is. So also is betting by the pari-mutuel system gambling, but it is not a lottery, and Act 46 provides that such betting shall not be unlawful.

The use of the pari-mutuel machine does not make the betting a lottery, if it is not otherwise so, as it makes no determination of what horses are winners. It is merely a wonderful machine which expedites calculations which could laboriously be made without its use. Its use in no manner affects the results of a race as it merely calculates the results of the betting after the races have been run and the respective winners announced.

We conclude, therefore, that while the element of chance no doubt enters into these races, it does not control them, and that there is therefore no lottery.

The decree so holding is affirmed.

[The dissenting opinions of Chief Justice Smith and Justice Robins are omitted.]

OPINION OF THE JUSTICES
385 A.2d 695 (Del. 1978)

To His Excellency
Pierre S. duPont, IV
Governor of Delaware:

Reference is made to your letters dated November 21 and December 2, 1977, containing a request for the opinions of the Justices of the Supreme Court, under Del.C. § 141, upon the constitutionality of Senate Bill No. 379, as amended by Senate Amendment No. 1.

Your request contains the following background information:

On August 9, 1977 the General Assembly passed Senate Bill Number 379, as amended by Senate Amendment Number 1, which authorizes the performance of the Spanish game of jai-alai and wagering thereon, and provides for a Delaware Jai-Alai Commission to regulate the game. I had previously vetoed House Substitute Number 1 for House Bill Number 417, as amended, which also permitted the playing of jai-alai in Delaware, because of my concern that the bill did not contain adequate regulatory procedures.

As you are undoubtedly aware, this legislation has provoked great discussion among citizens of the State about whether wagering on jai-alai exhibitions is permitted in light of the provisions of Article II, Section 17 of the Delaware Constitution of 1897 which prohibits all forms of gambling in the State except for lotteries under State control, horse racing and bingo. Additional concern has been voiced about whether the legislation required the concurrence of two-thirds of all members elected to each House of the General Assembly pursuant to Article IX, Section 1 of the Constitution, because it may have the effect of amending the Wilmington City Charter.

Although many comments on the effect of these constitutional provisions on Senate Bill Number 379 were presented to me during the time I was considering the bill, I felt that, as the ultimate test of constitutionality must be decided in the courts, it would not be appropriate for me to make such a determination.

I signed Senate Bill Number 379 on August 12, 1977 (Chapter 189, Volume 61, Laws of Delaware) and on October 12, 1977 I appointed members of a Delaware Jai-Alai Commission, as I am directed to do by Section 4822 of the Act.

However, public speculation over the constitutionality of the Act has continued. In addition, the newly designated members of the Jai-Alai

Commission have expressed to me their concern that the constitutional issue be resolved before they proceed to embark on any of their activities or even formally convene. To underscore their concern, the membership has chosen to postpone taking their oaths of office and recordation of their commissions until the probability of final resolution of the subject constitutional questions is assured.

As head of the Executive Branch, it is incumbent upon me, in order that I might faithfully discharge the duties of my office, to resolve these fundamental, constitutional concerns before the Executive Department must commit funds and hire personnel and before private individuals make substantial personal and financial commitments as Commissioners. Under Senate Bill Number 379, the Delaware Jai-Alai Commission is not placed within any executive department of State government; and therefore, is necessarily directly responsible to, and part of the Office of the Governor. I recognize, therefore, a special legal responsibility for assuring that the new Commission, whose regulatory and supervisory functions are crucial to protect the citizens of Delaware from potential abuse, begins its operations and activities free of any cloud about its authority.

Upon the basis of the foregoing, we find the request within the purview of 10 Del.C. § 141.

The questions presented are as follows:

In summary, then the three questions relating to the constitutionality of Senate Bill 379 upon which I have requested your opinion are as follows:

1. Is pool or pari-mutuel wagering on jai-alai exhibitions a lottery for purposes of Article II, Section 17 of the Delaware Constitution of 1897?

2. Does Senate Bill No. 379, as amended by Senate Amendment No. 1, amend the Charter of the City of Wilmington and is thus required to be enacted by the concurrence of two-thirds of all the members elected to each House of the General Assembly pursuant to Article IX, Section 1 of the Delaware Constitution of 1897?

3. Is Senate Bill 379 in violation of Article VIII, Section 2 of the Delaware Constitution of 1897 which requires that all bills for raising revenue shall originate in the House of Representatives?

Del.Const. Art. II, § 17, as revised in 1973, provides:

§ 17. Lotteries and other gambling.

Section 17. All forms of gambling are prohibited in this State except the following:

(a) Lotteries under State control for the purpose of raising funds,

(b) Wagering or betting on races within the enclosure of any race meeting licensed and conducted under the laws of this State by the use of pari-mutuel machines or totalizators,

(c) Bingo games as conducted under the limitations of Section 17A.

The General Assembly shall enforce this Section by appropriate legislation.

I.

A brief outline of the Act is desirable for clarity.

The purpose of the Act is set forth as follows (§ 4820):

> It is the purpose of this subchapter to permit wagering or betting upon exhibitions of the Spanish game of jai-alai, which exhibitions are to be conducted only by those licensed under this subchapter and in accordance with the provisions hereof. This gambling activity is deemed by the General Assembly to be a lottery and permissible under the Constitution of this State. It is the opinion of the General Assembly that permitting such gambling activity is in the best interest of the citizens of this State. It will raise funds for the State and the City of Wilmington, provide a recreational activity, create numerous job opportunities and will provide the State and political subdivisions thereof with other economic benefits. It is also the purpose of this subchapter to exercise state control over all aspects of the operation of a jai-alai meeting in this State including but not limited to control over the conduct of the game of jai-alai, control over the conduct of the wagering or betting thereon and control over the conduct of any concessionaires providing food, beverages, parking or other goods and services on the premises where any such meeting is conducted.

The Act creates the Delaware Jai-Alai Commission; gives it broad regulatory powers; makes provision for licensing and licensing requirements, the conduct of licensees, and the operation by licensees of jai-alai games and pari-mutuel wagering thereon; and provides for payments to the State and the City of Wilmington from the monies generated by the jai-alai operation. The Commission has three members and they are appointed and removable by the Governor (§§ 4822, 4831). The Commission appoints a Director, experienced in the administration of jai-alai, to be its chief administrator (§ 4824).

The Commission is granted broad powers to enforce the provisions of the Act, including the power to create and enforce regulations for "insuring proper, safe and orderly conduct of jai-alai meetings and for protecting the public against fraud or overcharge" (§ 4827). The Commission has subpoena power (§ 4828), power to compel inspection or production of all books and records of a licensee (§ 4873), and power to require fingerprint submissions of all applicants, licensees and employees of licensees (§ 4829). The Commission is empowered to remove employees, officials and management personnel of licensees (§§ 4852, 4873); and to levy fines and to suspend or revoke licenses (§§ 4857, 4873). Any license granted by the Commission is subject to suspension or revocation by the Commission for "good cause" and any aggrieved licensee may appeal the action of the Commission to the Superior Court (§ 4873).

Potential licensees must submit detailed financial and character information and references (§§ 4829, 4836). Application and annual license fees are required (§ 4870). The Act disqualifies from licensing all persons convicted of felonies or other crimes of moral turpitude, and also any corporation (except a publicly traded corporation) with an officer, director, or stockholder who has been so convicted (§ 4865). Corporate licensees are strictly regulated to prevent hidden interests and to subject the principals of the corporation to the various requirements of the Act (§§ 4838-4863). Licenses are not assignable (§ 4872), and all licensees must furnish annual operating reports (§ 4876). Licensed jai-alai meetings must be held in the City of Wilmington (§ 4835(b)).

Betting or wagering on jai-alai is authorized only within the confines of a licensed fronton and only under "a pari-mutuel system, so called, including standard pari-mutuel, daily double, exacta, quiniela, trifecta, and superfecta betting and such other forms of multiple betting or wagering as the Commission may determine" (§ 4883). From the gross amounts contributed to "all pari-mutuel and totalizator pools", the licensee must pay to the State 5% of the pool, plus one-half of the breakage (the odd cents in excess of 10 as calculated on the basis of each dollar wagered); and the City of Wilmington must receive 3/4% of the pool. The licensee-operator of the game is to receive a commission of 12 1/4% of the pool, plus one-half of the breakage; and the remainder is returned to the bettors (§§ 4884, 4885).

II.

The details of the game of jai-alai and pari-mutuel wagering thereon have been furnished by mutual agreement of counsel as follows:

> The game of jai-alai is played between individuals or two-man teams. It is initiated by one player hurling a ball, called a "pelota", against the front wall, with a long basket, called a "cesta", strapped to his right arm. The ball is slightly smaller than a baseball and is as hard as and livelier than a golfball. On the serve the ball must rebound from the front wall and strike the floor within a designated service area. The opposing player must then return the ball to the front wall before the second bounce. Play continues with each player (or team) alternately being required to catch the ball in his cesta before the second bounce and to return it to the front wall. A point is lost when a player fails to so catch the ball or return it to the front wall. The ball is permitted to carom off the side or back wall before being returned to the front wall. The catch and return must be made in one continuous motion; any hesitation results in the loss of the point.

> Jai-alai has been called the world's fastest sport because the ball routinely achieves speeds of 150 miles per hour. It is said that, because of the shape of the cesta, the ball is also delivered with more spin and resulting curve than in any other sport. Moreover, since the ball must strike the front wall and may carom off the side wall, back wall, and floor before being caught and since each impact alters the spin on the ball, the ball may display four different curves on any given shot. This presents difficulties not only for the player who must make the catch but also for the player making the shot who must be sure that the ball does not carom out of bounds before striking the floor. The game is one of great quickness and precision where the failure to judge speed and spin instantly usually results in the loss of a point.

> In the traditional form of the sport played in Spain, jai-alai is a contest between two players or two-man teams competing in a game

of from 10 to 40 individual points. In the United States, however, this form has been significantly modified to adapt it to pari-mutuel betting. Here, jai-alai is a contest among eight players or teams competing in a game of seven points. Moreover, in the American form of scoring, called the "Spectacular Seven" system, all volleys after the first round of play yield two points rather than one.

The competition among the eight players or teams (hereinafter "team") is conducted on a round-robin basis. The game is initiated with the team designated for post position No. 1 serving to the team designated for post position No. 2. The winner of that volley remains on the court to serve to team No. 3; the loser retires behind team No. 8 and returns to the court to play following team No. 8. Play continues in this fashion with the winner of each volley remaining on the court to play the next team in line and the loser retiring to the end of the line. During the first round of play, i.e. until team No. 8 has played for the first time, the winner of each volley receives one point; thereafter the winner receives two points. The first team to accumulate seven points wins the game. Thus, in order to win, a team need win no more than seven volleys and may win as few as four. When one team has won, second and third places are awarded to the teams having the second and third highest point totals at that time. Ties are played off between the tied teams.

We are told that pari-mutuel wagering on jai-alai games is "the same as wagering at horse tracks, with several innovations": A wager may be made that a team (or player) will win the game, or will "place" by finishing first or second, or will "show" by finishing at least third. There is a "quiniela" wherein the bettor selects two teams to finish first and second in any order; a "perfecta" in which two teams are selected to finish first and second in that order; and a "trifecta" in which three teams are selected to finish first, second and third, in that exact order. There is also a "double" in which the winners of two consecutive games must be selected.

Programs sold at jai-alai games are much the same as those sold at race tracks. Bettors are provided with detailed statistics of the past performances of the players and teams, together with data as to the height and weight of each player and the opening odds on each single or team. Monthly and yearly performance charts and result books on players and teams are also available to the bettor, as well as seasonal quiniela, perfecta, post position, and daily double records and statistics on the players and teams.

Official programs made available to bettors contain the following prominent statements:

"Jai-alai is known as the world's fastest ball game—a game which sport's experts agree requires more skill, speed, endurance, and nerve than any other."

"Pari-mutuel wagering rules * * * state that * * * jai-alai being a game of skill, the winning or losing of a point depends entirely on the individual player's skill and ability or lack of it, * * *."

"Players salaries for the next year depend on their respective performances this year."

"Players are given purses for win, place, and show, in addition to their regular salary."

III.

A.

The ultimate question is whether pool or pari-mutuel wagering is a "lottery" under Art. II, § 17(a). In our opinions, it is not.

It is agreed by all involved that pari-mutuel betting is a form of pool selling. For example, in horse racing, all money wagered is initially divided into several pools, such as the win, place, and show pools, and after the deduction of a percentage for the operators and the State, the remainder is distributed to the successful bettors in proportion to their contributions to the various pools. See e.g., Utah State Fair Ass'n. v. Green, Utah Supr., 68 Utah 251, 249 P. 1016 (1926); Ginsburg v. Centennial Turf Club, Colo.Supr., 126 Colo. 471, 251 P.2d 926 (1952).

The original 1897 version of Art. II, § 17 provided:

Lotteries, the sale of lottery tickets, pool selling and all other forms of gambling are prohibited in this State. The General Assembly shall enforce this section by appropriate legislation.

It appears that the 1897 drafters distinguished lotteries and pool-selling as separate types of gambling sufficiently objectionable to be specified by name, and that pool-selling, unlike lotteries, was a form of gambling generally understood to be related to horse racing. 1897 Delaware Constitutional Debates, Vol. 4, pp. 2871-2885. In common usage and by definition, this understanding of a basic difference between lotteries and pool-selling was general then, as it is now.

A lottery is defined [as]:

A gambling game or method of raising money, as for some public, charitable purpose, in which a large number of tickets are sold, and a drawing is held for certain prizes; any scheme for the distribution of prizes by chance; * * *. The Random House Dictionary of the English Language. (Unabridged Ed.) p. 848.

Sports pool betting is defined in Black's Law Dictionary, p. 1321 [as]:

In various methods of gambling, a 'pool' is a sum of money made up of the stakes contributed by various persons, the whole of which is then wagered as a stake on the event of a race, game, or other contest, and the winnings (if any) are divided among the contributors to the pool pro rata. Or it is a sum similarly made up by the contributions of several persons, each of whom then makes his guess or prediction as to the event of a future contest or hazard, the successful bettor taking the entire pool.

And a betting "pool" is defined in Webster's Third New International Dictionary p. 1764 as:

All the money bet by a number of persons on the result of a particular event with the aggregate to be paid to the winner or divided among several winners according to conditions established in advance.

The three elements of a lottery, as a matter of law, are generally stated to be: prize, consideration, and chance. Affiliated Enterprises, Inc. v. Waller, Del.Super., 5 A.2d 257, 259 (1939). However, there is contrariety of judicial opinion as to whether a game that incorporates an element of skill as well can qualify as a lottery. Under the English rule, if skill plays any part in determining the prize winner, there is no lottery. Under the prevailing American rule, it is sufficient if chance is the dominant or controlling factor. See National Football League v. Governor of State of Delaware, D.Del., 435 F.Supp. 1372, 1382-3 (1977). The decision as to which rule applies often seems to depend upon whether the case is a tax case or a regulation case. The Courts of this State have not ruled on whether the "pure chance" or "dominant factor" rule applies in Delaware. Fortunately, we are not obliged to adopt and apply either one or the other of these two rules in this expedited, quasi-judicial proceeding.

The express prohibition of pool-selling remained in Art. II, § 17 until 1973 when the Article was revised and entirely rewritten upon the advent of the Lottery Exception as § 17(a). (59 Del.L. Ch. 143). In the intervening years between 1897 and 1973, however, the express prohibition against pool-selling remained in Art. II, § 17, throughout the 1935 amendment (40 Del.L. Ch. 1) excepting on-track pari-mutuel betting on races, and the 1957 amendment (51 Del.L. Ch. 61) excepting the game of bingo, from the general prohibition of the Section against "all forms of gambling."

In the 1973 Revision of the Section, pool-selling was omitted as the only remaining itemized form of prohibited gambling after the Lottery Exception was created. But its omission did not constitute a general exception of pool-selling, express or implied, to the general prohibition against "all forms of gambling." The omission of specifics, especially one remaining specific, was good, modern constitutional draftsmanship.

As presently written, Art. II, § 17 prohibits "all forms of gambling" except those expressly authorized, i.e., on-track pari-mutuel betting on racing, bingo, and lotteries. Any exception to such general constitutional prohibition must be narrowly and strictly construed. U.S. v. Allen, 163 U.S. 499, 16 S.Ct. 1071, 41 L.Ed. 242 (1895); E.I. DuPont De Nemours & Co. v. Clark, Del.Supr., 88 A.2d 436 (1952); County Council, etc. v. Supervisor of Assessments, etc., Md.Ct.App., 274 Md. 116, 332 A.2d 897 (1975); Karafa v. N.J. State Lottery Commission, 129 N.J.Super. 499, 324 A.2d 97 (1974).

Except for on-track pari-mutuel betting authorized by § 17(b), pool-selling is not excepted from the general anti-gambling prohibition of Art. II, § 17 by any express provision. We are of the opinion, therefore, that all other forms of pari-mutuel betting remain constitutionally banned. It strains established rules of constitutional construction too far to say, as do the proponents of the Act, that unlimited pool-selling was excepted from the general anti-gambling prohibition of § 17 by implication. It is unreasonable to assume that the drafters of the 1973 Revision intended by implication to legalize unlimited pool or pari-mutuel betting, including, for example, off-track pari-mutuel betting on racing, in the face of the continuing provisions of § 17(b) expressly and carefully delimiting pari-mutuel betting to on-track wagering.

The proponents contend that § 4805(b)(4) of the State Lottery Act is persuasive evidence that the drafters of the 1973 Revision intended, by implication, to remove the 75 year old constitutional prohibition against pool-selling and pari-mutuel betting. We find this contention wholly untenable.

29 Del.C. § 4805(b)(4) empowered the State Lottery Director:

> (4). Enter into contracts for the operation of any game or part thereof and into contracts for the promotion of the game or games. This authorization is to be construed to include, but not be limited to, contracting with any racing or other sporting association to conduct sporting events within any race-track or sports field in the State the outcome of which shall determine the winners of a state game or, as an alternative, to affiliate the determination of the winners of a game with any racing or sporting event held with or without the State . . . .

The history of the present State Lottery has demonstrated various possible interrelationships between State games and sporting events, none of which involved pari-mutuel betting. To accept the proponents' contention on this point would be to see implied in § 4805(b)(4) of the State Lottery Act an unlimited authorization for the State, under the guise of a § 17(a) lottery, to operate a pari-mutuel system of betting on any type of sporting event, on or off the premises in the face of the general constitutional ban against "all forms of gambling" and in conflict with the express provision of § 17(b) unequivocally limiting pari-mutuel betting to on-track racing. To state the proposition is to demonstrate its absurdity.

In our opinions, therefore, it is unreasonable to assume, as the proponents urge, that the drafters of the 1973 Revision intended to include unlimited sports pool-selling or pari-mutuel wagering within the word "lottery" as an exception to the general prohibition against "all forms of gambling." Several reasons support this conclusion: (1) Historically, as has been noted, the word "lottery" did not include "pool selling" and the two forms of gambling were distinguished at the Constitutional Convention of 1897; (2) by common usage and ordinary definition, the two forms of gambling have been clearly differentiated; (3) following the lead of the 1897 Constitutional drafters, later constitutional drafters have consistently distinguished between lotteries and pool-betting and other types of gambling, expressly maintaining the distinction in both the 1935 Racing Amendment and the 1957 Bingo Amendment; and (4) prevailing case law would have guided the 1973 drafters away from the word "lottery" and along other lines if they had intended to legalize unlimited pool-selling and pari-mutuel wagering in this State.

It is our conclusion that the pool or pari-mutuel system of wagering has never been considered a "lottery" by the constitutional draftsmen of our State either in 1897 or in 1973 and that it may not be made so now either by legislative act or judicial fiat. Common and ordinary understanding of the word "lottery", then and now, rejects the concept of pari-mutuel betting on sporting events. Moreover, the historical evolution of Art. II, § 17 and the great weight of authority are in harmony with this result and lead inescapably to the conclusion that a sound basis in reason, logic, and experience exists in support of the result we reach.

Specifically, therefore, we are of the opinion that pool or pari-mutuel wagering on jai-alai exhibitions under the Act would not be a "lottery" within the meaning of Art. II, § 17(a).

[The remainder of the court's opinion is omitted.]

McNEILLY, Justice, dissenting.

My response to question number 1 is in the affirmative, as I am of the opinion that pari-mutuel wagering on jai-alai as envisaged by the Act constitutes a lottery under Delaware law, compare Affiliated Enterprises v. Waller, Del.Super., 5 A.2d 257 (1939).

When determining that the proposed pari-mutuel wagering on jai-alai is not a lottery, the majority provides a learned review of Delaware constitutional history of anti-gambling provisions, and the exceptions thereto. According to the majority, pool wagering cannot be encompassed within the word lottery because (1) historically lottery did not include pool selling, as the two forms of wagering were distinguished at the Constitutional Convention of 1897, (2) by common usage the two forms of betting are distinguished, (3) following the lead of the 1897 constitutional drafters, later constitutional writers, in drafting the 1935 Racing Amendment and the 1957 Bingo Amendment, recognized and maintained the distinction between pool wagering and lotteries, and (4) prevailing case law, which recognizes the distinction, would have guided the 1973 amendment writers away from the word "lottery" if they intended to legalize pool-selling and pari-mutuel wagering. While I find the majority's analysis interesting, my opinion is that the definition of lottery at which the majority eventually arrives is outmoded, and inapplicable to the case sub judice. I believe that the majority misdirects its attention to ancient history, dictionary definitions, and certain case law which it considered to be prevailing, while ignoring modern pronouncements of the Delaware Legislature concerning the definition of "lottery."

I examine first the majority's exposition of case law dealing with the term "lottery." The majority states: "For decades, by the great weight of authority, pari-mutuel betting has been held not to be a lottery." A series of citations to cases follows in support of the above-quoted assertion. I submit that one must examine the context in which these authoritative cases were decided. Each case cited by the majority dealt with the question of whether pari-mutuel betting on races fell within the constitutional proscription of lotteries, when the legislature had chosen to declare that the activity was not a lottery by the enactment of publicly desired racing legislation. See, e.g., Engle v. State, Ariz.Supr., 53 Ariz. 458, 90 P.2d 988 (1939); Longstreth v. Cook, Ark.Supr., 215 Ark. 72, 220 S.W.2d 433 (1949); Ginsberg v. Centennial Turf Club, Colo.Supr., 126 Colo. 471, 251 P.2d 926 (1952); People v. Munroe, Ill.Supr., 349 Ill. 270, 182 N.E. 439 (1932); Commonwealth v. Kentucky Jockey Club, Ky.Supr., 238 Ky. 739, 38 S.W.2d 987 (1931); Gandolfo v. Louisiana State Racing Commission, La.Supr., 227 La. 45, 78 So.2d 504 (1954); Rohan v. Detroit Racing Ass'n., Mich.Supr., 314 Mich. 326, 22 N.W.2d 433 (1946); People, etc. v. Fallon, N.Y.Supr., 4 App.Div. 82, 39 N.Y.S. 865 (1896); Utah State Fair Ass'n v. Green, Utah Supr., 68 Utah 251, 249 P. 1016 (1926); Oneida County Fair Board v. Smylie, Governor, Idaho Supr., 86 Idaho 341, 386 P.2d

374 (1963); Opinion of the Justices, Ala.Supr., 287 Ala. 334, 251 So.2d 751 (1971).

The Idaho Supreme Court in Braddock v. Family Finance Corporation, Idaho Supr., 95 Idaho 256, 506 P.2d 824 (1973) analyzed its decision in Oneida County Fair Ass'n. v. Smylie, supra, as "an attempt to reconcile the constitutional prohibition against lotteries with the legislative desire to legitimize horse racing." The cases cited involve constitutional or statutory bans on lotteries, while here we deal with a constitutional prohibition on most forms of gambling, lotteries being one of the exceptions to the general prohibition. Thus in the cases upon which the majority relies, a judicial finding that pari-mutuel wagering on races was a lottery would have necessitated a ruling striking down an enactment of the legislature, whereas, the converse is true here.

The distinction, I believe, is critical, because of the general rule of law that legitimately enacted laws of a Legislature are accorded a presumption of constitutionality. As the Court stated in Rohan v. Detroit Racing Ass'n., supra: "The statute is presumed to be constitutional, and every reasonable presumption or intendment must be in favor of its constitutionality." Therefore, an important, if not controlling, factor in each of the cases cited was the rule of presumption of constitutionality. The conclusion I reach in my analysis of the cited cases is that the term "lottery" is ambiguous, and, as a proposition of law, where an ambiguous term is used, the legislative interpretation of a word is well-nigh conclusive upon judicial review. I believe the majority misses the point of the cases when they merely examine the result reached, and not the reasoning behind the result.

I turn now to what I believe is a more rational analysis of what the Delaware Legislature meant when it used the term "lottery" in the 1973 Constitutional Amendment. Judge Stapleton of the Federal District Court in Delaware addressed the issue of what the term "lottery" as used in the Delaware Constitution means in the case of Nat. Football League v. Governor of the State of Delaware, D.Del., 435 F.Supp. 1372 (1977). I adopt Judge Stapleton's cogent analysis of the Constitutional Amendment, and his definition of lottery derived from the amendment and contemporaneous legislation dealing with lotteries. I can say it no better than he, and I quote those portions of Judge Stapleton's opinion which are on point:

> The 1974 Amendment to Article II, Section 17 of the Delaware Constitution authorizes lotteries under State control. It does not define the term 'lottery'.
>
> It is unquestioned that there are three elements necessary to a lottery: prize, consideration and chance (citing Affiliated Enterprises v. Waller, Del.Super., 5 A.2d 257 (1939)). However, there is a split of authority as to whether a game that incorporates an element of skill as well can qualify as a lottery. Two approaches to the question have developed: Under the English rule, a lottery consists in the distribution of money or other property by chance, and nothing but chance, that is, by doing that which is equivalent to drawing lots. If merit or skill play any part in determining the distribution, there is no lottery
>
> . . . .

In the United States, however, by what appears to be the weight of authority at the present day, it is not necessary that this element of chance be pure chance, but it may be accompanied by an element of calculation or even of certainty; it is sufficient if chance is the dominant or controlling factor. However, the rule that chance must be the dominant factor is to be taken in the qualitative or causative sense.

I favor adoption of the "dominant factor rule" as suggested by Judge Stapleton. To apply the rule to the game of jai-alai, I rely upon the statistical analysis of the game derived by counsel from publications printed by the operators of Jai-alai frontons in Bridgeport, Milford, and Hartford, Connecticut, and which all counsel agree are correct. An analysis of player performance over a large number of games shows that no player or players has been able to establish a dominant winning percentage, and that the vast majority of players win approximately one-eighth of the games they play, i.e., the precise winning percentage that statistically should be achieved in a game of pure chance played by eight individuals. Thus, the performance statistics reveal that skillful players cannot dominate the game. An analysis of the wagering results of the general public also confirms the theory that chance is the dominant factor in jai-alai wagering. In a sample of over 6,000,000 bets during a one month period, researchers found that for each category of bet the public did no better selecting winners than they would have in a game governed by pure chance. A seven month analysis of win payoffs demonstrated that in over half of the games the public was able to pick the winners in numbers less than or equal to the amount which statistics show a person would be able to pick winners in a randomly determined game. From these facts I can reach no other rational conclusion than that pari-mutuel wagering on jai-alai contains the predominant element of chance controlling the recovery of a "prize" on the bettor's wager.

In the determination of whether or not pari-mutuel betting on jai-alai contains sufficient chance to qualify as a "lottery", I am of the opinion that we should not only recognize the chance element in the underlying sports event, but we must also view the chance element from the position of the bettor who is one step removed from the actual game, and who faces the variety of pari-mutuel pools in which he may place his money. Common sense alone dictates the conclusion that the multitudes attending the races or jai-alai do so to watch the sport, and to take their chances of coming away with more cash in their pockets than that with which they arrived. The odds on all of the pools change constantly with the ebb and tide of betting, until the bell rings marking the start of the contest. Play your money and take your chance, is the name of the game. Because chance is the dominating factor in the wagering on jai-alai, I conclude that the pari-mutuel system of betting on the jai-alai games as allowed by the Act constitutes a lottery.

Notes

1. Of the $18 billion bet annually on pari-mutuels, $14.5 billion is spent on horse racing. Forty-three states permit wagers on such contests, of which there are several types. While flat racing (also called thoroughbred racing)

is the best known, harness racing (in which the jockey sits behind the horse on a lightweight two-wheel carriage called a sulky) and the steeplechase (which involves racing on an obstacle course) also are popular. *See further* Joan S. Howland & Michael J. Hannon, *A Legal Research Guide to American Thoroughbred Racing Law for Scholars, Practitioners and Participants* (1998); Sharon B. Smith, *The Complete Idiot's Guide to Betting on Horses* (1998); *Storey's Horse-Lover's Encyclopedia: An English and Western A-to-Z Guide* (Deborah Burns ed. 2000). *See also* Peter Langrock, *Reflections of a Harness Racing Senior Lawyer*, 11 Experience 17 (Winter 2001).

2. Fifteen states sanction greyhound racing, although pari-mutuel revenues generated by this part of the industry have declined significantly in recent years. Greyhounds run counter-clockwise (known as "left-hand travel") around a track, following a mechanical lure that often resembles a rabbit. A race may be for a short distance (less than 500 yards), middle distance (525-600 yards), or long distance (over 600 yards). *See further* Roy Genders, *The Encyclopedia of Greyhound Racing: A Complete History of the Sport* (1982); William E. McBride, *The Gambling Times Guide to Greyhound Racing* (1990); George Ignatin & Frank Watkins, *Legal and Economic Issues of Greyhound Racing*, 3 Gaming L. Rev. 59 (1999).

3. Jai-alai accounts for only a small percentage of pari-mutuel activities in this country. In fact, only three states—Connecticut, Florida, and Rhode Island—authorize such betting, and only the latter two currently have operating frontons. As a result, the amount bet has dropped by more than half from its peak in the early 1980s. *See further* William R. Keevers, *Gambling Times Guide to Jai Alai* (1984); Don Lostritto, *Jai Alai Wagering to Win: The Complete Book for Jai Alai* (1985); Steven Skiena, *Calculated Bets: Computers, Gambling, and Mathematical Modeling to Win* (2001).

4. At the heart of any pari-mutuel betting operation is the "totalisator" (also spelled "totalizator"), which the court in *Longstreth* described as that "wonderful machine which expedites calculations." In *United States v. United Tote, Inc.*, 768 F. Supp. 1064 (D. Del. 1991), the totalisator's mechanics were explained as follows:

> Pari-mutuel wagering is the most common form of wagering at horse races, greyhound races and jai alai contests in the United States. The essential characteristic of pari-mutuel wagering is that the wagers of the betting patrons are combined into pools from which the successful bettors recover. As a result, wagering odds are determined by the size of the pools established by the patrons' wagers. The odds, conveyed to the bettors at frequent intervals, change continually until betting closes at the start of a race or event.

> A totalisator system supports pari-mutuel wagering by controlling the acceptance of wagers, calculating odds and payout, cashing winning tickets, and performing assorted management, accounting and reporting functions. Totalisator systems can be used to serve on-track, off-track and inter-track wagering. On-track wagering is conducted on the premises of a racetrack while that event is taking place.

> Off-track wagering takes place somewhere other than the racetrack. Most commonly, it takes place at off-track betting "parlors", some of

which televise the event taking place. An off-track totalisator system generally combines or "commingles" wagers from the remote locations into a common pari-mutuel pool maintained at the host track. In some instances, the combination of pools and the calculation of payout amounts are done by the off-track betting system itself.

Inter-track wagering is similar to off-track wagering in that it entails the combination of wagering pools from different locations into a common pool at the host track. The only significant difference is the location where the wagering occurs. Inter-track wagering occurs at one racetrack when it accepts bets on a live racing event at another track. In many cases, the racing event is televised from the host track where the contest is conducted to one or more "guest" or "satellite" tracks. Inter-track wagering then occurs when the wagers from the guest tracks are transmitted to the host track and combined with the host track's pari-mutuel pool. The host track's central computer calculates the resulting odds and returns that information to the guest tracks. As a result, betting patrons at the guest tracks share in the pari-mutuel pool of the host track and they receive the same payout for winning wagers as they would have received had they attended the live racing event. (Until 1990, wagering pools were only combined on an intrastate basis because it was commonly thought that federal law precluded the commingling of wagering pools across state lines. In the spring of 1990, however, the racing industry reached an understanding with the Department of Justice as to the legality of interstate commingling. Since then, interstate commingling of wagering pools has increased dramatically.)

By far, the most common form of totalisator system used in North America is the computerized "cash/sell" system that allows patrons to place bets and to cash winning tickets at the same window. A typical cash/sell system consists of a central computer, ticket issuing terminals, display equipment and associated peripheral equipment. The system also includes proprietary software to carry out the complex, high speed wagering functions required by modern pari-mutuel betting.

The interface between the totalisator system and pari-mutuel customer is the totalisator terminal. Totalisator terminals are most commonly operated by pari-mutuel tellers or clerks although a number of companies supply terminals that are operated manually by the patrons as well as some that accept pre-marked betting slips the patrons have prepared. After the terminals accept the wagering information, the terminal transmits it to a central computer system.

Terminals at a pari-mutuel facility are linked to one or more central processing units ("CPUs") which perform the bulk of the computer calculations for the system. The CPUs verify each bet and authorize the issuance of a printed ticket, aggregate the wagers into pools and calculate the resulting odds. The CPUs also commonly communicate the calculated odds for display on video devices or totalisator boards and calculate the final odds and payout amounts when the racing event is complete and the results are official. At that point, the winning bettors can present their tickets to the pari-mutuel tellers or clerks who enter them into the terminals. The terminals read and confirm the ticket as a winning ticket. The terminals then communicate information from the winning tickets to the CPUs, which calculate and display the payout amount to the clerk, who pays the patron.

Totalisator systems are typically supplied pursuant to lease agreements. Under the agreement, a totalisator supplier provides and operates the totalisator system and guarantees that the system will perform accurately and reliably. Employees of the totalisator company operate, service and maintain the totalisator system. Because of the extreme importance of the totalisator function, a totalisator company must be prepared to prevent breakdowns and quickly repair any problems. For example, computer operators and maintenance personnel are typically located on-site at the racetrack to ensure that the system functions smoothly and reliably. In addition, all major totalisator systems include backup computers that take control in the event that the primary computer malfunctions. Finally, the totalisator company often provides an uninterrupted power supply to protect against power failures. Totalisator suppliers usually assume liability for wagering revenues that are lost by the racetracks as a result of a totalisator system malfunction.

Prior to 1976, all totalisator systems in the United States market were "sell-only" systems that required the patron to purchase wagering tickets from one location and return to a different window to cash winning tickets. In 1976, American Totalisator ("AmTote") introduced the first cash/sell North American totalisator system at the Ontario Jockey Club in Canada. The primary innovation of the cash/sell totalisator system was that it allowed wagering patrons to return to the same terminal from which they placed their bets to cash their tickets. This development not only resulted in greater convenience to the wagering customer but also reduced labor costs to the track. The cash/sell totalisator system was immediately recognized as offering a number of advantages over the sell-only system and, at the present time, all but the smallest tracks and state fair events have converted to cash/sell systems.

Id. at 1065-67.

Despite having invented both the original totalisator (in 1933) and the cash/sell totalisator, in recent years AmTote (www.amtote.com), located in Hunt Valley, Maryland, has been eclipsed by Autotote Systems, Inc. Based in Newark, Delaware, Autotote (www.scientificgames.com) now supplies totalisators to two out of every three American race tracks.

Problem 12

To cash in on his horse's racing success, an owner hired a public relations firm. In addition to creating an official web site, it entered into product licensing agreements with various manufacturers. Recently, the firm discovered that an artist is selling unauthorized paintings of their client's horse.

If it sues him, how should the court rule? *See Cortez v. CMG Worldwide Inc.*, 962 F. Supp. 308 (N.D.N.Y. 1997).

C. VENUES

LIVINGSTON DOWNS RACING ASSOCIATION, INC. v. JEFFERSON DOWNS CORPORATION
192 F. Supp. 2d 519 (M.D. La. 2001)

BRADY, District Judge.

Before the Court is the Defendants' motion for summary judgment urging dismissal of both the Plaintiffs' antitrust and civil Racketeering Influenced and Criminal Organizations (RICO) claims. Regarding the antitrust claims, the Defendants assert that their actions, though admittedly anticompetitive, represent a good-faith effort to petition the Government for favorable action. As a result, these actions come within the aegis of the Noerr-Pennington doctrine, which shields from antitrust liability a private party's efforts to obtain, through government action, a competitive advantage over business rivals. The Plaintiffs counter that the Defendants undertook a campaign of repetitive, baseless litigation, the sole purpose of which was to burden the Plaintiffs with the costs and delays which attend the litigatory process. The Defendants' actions thus fall under the "sham litigation" exception to the Noerr-Pennington doctrine and are subject to antitrust liability, the Plaintiffs contend.

As to the civil RICO claims, the Defendants argue that the Plaintiffs, having suffered no concrete injury as a result of the Defendants' actions, lack standing to bring such a claim. The Defendants also urge that any such claims are barred by the doctrine of res judicata.

BACKGROUND

This hoary case stems from the Plaintiffs' failed efforts to open a racetrack for live horse racing in Livingston Parish, Louisiana, and to obtain a license to conduct off-track betting (OTB) operations. This enterprise required the Plaintiffs not only to obtain the appropriate licenses from the Louisiana State Racing Commission (the Commission), but also to secure the voters' approval for horse racing in Livingston Parish through a referendum election. The Plaintiffs aver that they found their efforts to satisfy these requirements opposed at every turn by the Defendants, Bryan and Marie Krantz. According to the Plaintiffs, the Defendants pursued four main avenues in their efforts to thwart the Plaintiffs' bid to enter the market for live horse racing. These include lobbying the Commission and the Louisiana legislature to oppose the Plaintiffs' applications for racing and gaming licenses; campaigning against the new racetrack in the referendum election; filing lawsuits contesting the legitimacy of both the referendum election and the Plaintiffs' racing and gaming licenses; and intervening in the various lawsuits the Plaintiffs filed in an attempt to obtain racing and gaming licenses. The delays engendered by the Defendants' incessant legal challenges and lobbying, the Plaintiffs argue, caused the financing for the proposed racetrack to fall through, eventually scuttling their plans entirely.

LDRA's Efforts to Obtain a Racing License

Marie and Bryan Krantz owned Jefferson Downs Corporation (Jefferson Downs), a racetrack for live horse racing in Jefferson Parish. Jefferson Downs also possessed an OTB license, which allowed it to conduct off-track wagering both at the racetrack and at other facilities. In 1990, the Krantzes acquired an interest in Fair Grounds Corporation, a racetrack in Orleans Parish which also had an OTB license. In 1992, after the Krantzes had obtained a majority interest in Fair Grounds, they elected to consolidate their operations by shuttering the racetrack in Jefferson Parish and transferring Jefferson Downs's OTB license to Fair Grounds.

Under state regulations, Jefferson Downs and Fair Grounds could not, owing to their geographical proximity, hold races on the same dates. See La.Rev.Stat. §§ 4:147(1) & 4:215(b). Accordingly, prior to its closing, Jefferson Downs had conducted races in the Spring and Summer, whereas Fair Grounds had held races only in the Fall and Winter. The closing of Jefferson Downs thus left a void for live horse racing in Louisiana during the spring and summer months. In hopes of exploiting this opening, Al Ransome formed Livingston Downs Racing Association, Inc. (LDRA) in December 1992. LDRA's business plan called for building a racetrack in Livingston Parish and obtaining an OTB license therefor. LDRA applied to the Commission for a license to conduct horse races on Jefferson Downs' erstwhile race dates. See Livingston Downs Racing Ass'n v. State, 96-2890 (La.12/2/97), 705 So.2d 149, 150-51 (recounting the circumstances leading up to the formation of LDRA and its efforts to obtain racing dates).

The Commission approved LDRA's application and voted, on December 12, 1992, to grant it a permit to conduct pari-mutuel horse racing on the dates abandoned by Jefferson Downs. The next step for LDRA was to secure popular approval for live horse racing in Livingston Parish through a referendum election. See La.Rev.Stat. § 4:181. But before the Commission could issue LDRA's permit, Jefferson Downs and Fair Grounds obtained an order in state court staying the Commission's decision to grant the permit. Jefferson Downs and Fair Grounds subsequently amended their complaint to request an injunction prohibiting the referendum election. The election, they argued, was precipitous in light of the stay on LDRA's license. See Original Complaint ¶¶ 41, 43.

LDRA appealed the order staying the issuance of its license. It prevailed, and the state appellate court ordered the license issued. Jefferson Downs and Fair Grounds, however, appealed to the Louisiana Supreme Court, which reinstated the original order staying the issuance of LDRA's racing permit. Because Jefferson Downs and Fair Grounds omitted to request a stay while they took this appeal to the Louisiana Supreme Court, however, the Commission issued LDRA's permit while the appeal was pending. Since the permit had been issued, the police jury for Livingston Parish added the proposition on live horse racing to an election scheduled for January 16, 1993. See Def.'s Exh. I, Ransome v. Secretary of State for the State of Louisiana, No. 67,710, slip op. at 2-3 (Jan. 11, 1993) (detailing the circumstances surrounding the referendum election in Livingston Parish).

LDRA believed that the pendency of the suit challenging its racing license cast doubt upon the propriety of the referendum election. To remove this taint, Al Ransome filed suit seeking a writ of mandamus to compel the Secretary of State to permit the referendum election to proceed. The Krantzes intervened in this suit, urging that the referendum be halted. To obtain standing to challenge the referendum, the Krantzes' attorney, Larry Bankston, solicited the aid of Karen Thomas, a legal secretary in his firm and a resident of Livingston Parish. Ms. Thomas agreed to serve as the titular plaintiff for the petition to intervene, which alleged various procedural improprieties in noticing the referendum election. Also at the behest of the Krantzes' attorney, Ms. Thomas served as the plaintiff in a separate lawsuit which sought a writ of mandamus prohibiting the Secretary of State from holding the referendum election in Livingston Parish. This suit was also predicated in part upon alleged procedural irregularities in noticing the referendum. See Depo. of Karen Thomas at 11-12; see also Def.'s Exh. I, Thomas v. Secretary of State, No. 67,728, Division B, 21st Judicial District Court, Parish of Livingston.

The independent suit filed under Ms. Thomas's name was consolidated with Ransome's suit seeking a writ of mandamus. The state trial court concluded that, although there were some troubling deficiencies in noticing the referendum, they were too trifling to warrant cancelling the election. In light of the substantial media coverage the election had received, the court remarked, there was little danger that the "plaintiff was trying 'to pull a fast one' as alleged." More nettlesome in the trial court's view was Thomas's assertion that the election could not proceed because the Louisiana Supreme Court's ruling effectively abrogated the Commission's decision to issue LDRA a racing license. The trial court determined, however, that as the Commission issued LDRA's license before the Louisiana Supreme Court had ruled, and as there was no stay in place when the Commission issued the license, the license was valid. Accordingly, the district court granted Ransome's writ request and directed the Secretary of State to conduct the referendum election on January 16, 1993. See Thomas, slip op. at 2-5 (Def.'s Exh. I).

Thomas petitioned for an emergency stay of this ruling. She was unsuccessful, and appealed to the Louisiana Supreme Court. She was again rebuffed and requested rehearing before that court; the request was denied. According to the Plaintiffs, Thomas pursued this suit until October 13, 1995, when it was dismissed as moot by Louisiana's First Circuit Court of Appeal. See Original Complaint ¶¶ 64-66.

Having failed to stop the referendum from taking place, the Krantzes undertook to defeat the proposition to allow horse racing in Livingston Parish. To this end, they formed the Committee to Control Gambling, Inc. (CCG), a non-profit organization devoted to campaigning against LDRA in the election. See Plaintiff's Exh. 10. As part of this campaign, CCG allegedly aired a television commercial depicting a child, perched atop an adult's lap, playing video poker. The commercial served to remind voters that approving horse racing would also permit the introduction of OTB parlors into the Parish. CCG also ran print ads and conducted a mass mailing urging voters to reject live horse racing in their parish, but to no avail. See Plaintiff's Exh. 9. The proposition passed. See id. ¶¶ 49, 52-59, 69.

On February 23, 1993, approximately one month after the referendum election, the Krantzes filed another lawsuit. Fashioned as an election challenge, the suit sought to nullify the election based upon the same procedural anomalies that had been raised in the Thomas lawsuit. Terrance Lee Odom, the husband of another of Bankston's legal secretaries and a resident of Livingston Parish, agreed to serve as the titular plaintiff in this suit, which was filed in Livingston Parish. See Depo. of T. Odom at 9-10. The state district court, observing that the legitimacy of LDRA's racing license was already being contested in a separate lawsuit in Orleans Parish, dismissed Odom's election contest as premature. Odom successfully challenged this ruling on appeal and, more than a year later, the case was remanded for trial. See Odom v. Livingston Parish Police Jury, 637 So.2d 1323 (La.App. 1 Cir.1994).

On remand, Odom obtained court orders prohibiting the Plaintiffs from deposing him and from conducting discovery. This latter order remained in place until December 5, 1996, when LDRA succeeded in having it lifted. After discovery was completed, LDRA moved for summary judgment. The trial court granted the motion on April 1, 1997, and dismissed the suit. Odom appealed once again, but he withdrew the appeal nearly a year later, on August 18, 1998. See Original Complaint ¶¶ 70, 72-73.

While the first appeal of Odom's election contest was pending, LDRA renewed its application to the Commission for a racing license and requested racing dates for the upcoming season. According to the Plaintiffs, the Commission refused to consider this application until after Jefferson Downs had successfully transferred its OTB license to Fair Grounds. The Plaintiffs ascribe the Commission's temporizing to a fear that granting LDRA a racing license before the transfer was complete would entitle LDRA to compete with Fair Grounds for the right to assume Jefferson Downs' OTB license. LDRA alleges that the Committee conspired with the Krantzes to postpone considering LDRA's license application in order to safeguard the Krantzes' financial interests and to delay LDRA's entry into the market for live horse racing. See Original Complaint ¶¶ 83-85.

Frustrated with the lack of progress on its application for a racing license, LDRA filed suit seeking a writ of mandamus to compel the Commission to consider the application. Odom intervened in this suit as well. According to LDRA, he was again being used by the Defendants as the putative interested party. Bankston was Odom's attorney of record in this action. As Bankston was also a member of the state legislature, he attempted to invoke his privilege under La.Rev.Stat. § 13:4163 to request that the suit be postponed until the end of the year's legislative session. Bankston's stay request was denied, and the state district court ordered the Commission to consider LDRA's license application at its May 27, 1993, meeting. The Commission granted LDRA a 10-year racing license at that meeting, but not until after it had voted to permit Jefferson Downs to transfer its OTB license to Fair Grounds. The Commission also assigned LDRA racing dates for the 1993-94 racing season. See id. ¶¶ 87-88, 92.

LDRA's Efforts to Obtain a Gaming License

At the time LDRA received its racing license, Louisiana's gaming statutes conferred the right to operate OTB facilities to anyone holding a primary racing license. See La.Rev.Stat. § 213 (West 1993). A separate statutory provision, however, restricted the right to operate OTB facilities to those race tracks in existence during the 1986-87 racing season. See La.Rev.Stat. § 4:211(5) & (7) (West 1993). Because LDRA had not received a racing license until 1993, this latter statutory provision ostensibly proscribed it from conducting OTB operations. LDRA petitioned the Commission to resolve this statutory ambiguity in its favor and to issue it an OTB license. LDRA made three such license applications, in June and December 1993, and again in January 1994. The Commission, however, refused even to place LDRA's applications on its agenda. See Original Complaint ¶ 95; see also Livingston Downs Racing Ass'n v. State, 653 So.2d 1311, 1313 (La.App. 1 Cir.1995), rev'd in part, vacated in part, 96-2890 (La.12/2/97), 705 So.2d 149, rehearing denied (1/9/98).

Unable to obtain an OTB license from the Commission, LDRA filed suit in state court challenging the statute that reserves the right to operate OTB parlors to only those race tracks in operation during or prior to the 1986-87 racing season. See Livingston Downs, 653 So.2d at 1313. This restriction, it was argued, violated LDRA's constitutional guarantee to equal protection. LDRA requested the court to declare the statute invalid and to enjoin the Commission from enforcing it. Fair Grounds intervened in this suit and filed a motion for summary judgment, which motion was joined by the Commission. The trial court granted the summary judgment motion and dismissed the suit on January 19, 1994. LDRA prevailed on appeal, and the matter was remanded for trial. See Livingston Downs Racing Ass'n, Inc. v. State, 653 So.2d 1311, 1313, 1318 (La.Ct.App.1995).

While LDRA's appeal was pending, it filed a second lawsuit challenging the validity of the statutes establishing limits for payouts on video poker machines. These statutes also favored race tracks in operation during or prior to the 1986-87 season by permitting them to make higher payouts than other facilities. This suit was consolidated with LDRA's already pending declaratory judgment action. See Livingston Downs, 705 So.2d at 151; see also original complaint ¶¶ 128, 130.

On remand, the Defendants filed numerous pretrial exceptions and were, according to the Plaintiffs, generally intransigent during discovery. The case proceeded to trial nonetheless, with the court declaring the statutes in question unconstitutional. Fair Grounds and the Commission appealed this ruling directly to the Louisiana Supreme Court, where they prevailed. See Livingston Downs, 705 So.2d at 156-57. By the time the Louisiana Supreme Court issued its ruling, however, the case had consumed nearly four years. See id. at 149; see also Original Complaint ¶¶ 130, 132.

The Krantzes, meanwhile, were not idle. During the pendency of LDRA's suit, Fair Grounds filed a letter with the Commission urging it to deny LDRA's application for a gaming license. This letter, the Plaintiffs contend, was rife with misrepresentations, such as that the Governor of Louisiana was himself opposed to LDRA's license application. Additionally, when LDRA requested a hearing before the Commission to discuss the OTB statutes and issued subpoenas for this hearing, Fair Grounds moved the Commission to quash the subpoenas and to postpone the hearing indefinitely. Any such hearing, Fair Grounds argued, should be delayed until LDRA's lawsuit challenging the constitutionality of these statutes concluded. See Original Complaint ¶¶ 99-102.

The Commission granted LDRA a hearing on January 24, 1994. The Plaintiffs, however, allege that this hearing was merely pro forma. LDRA avers that it was permitted neither to call its witnesses nor to present its full arguments. Rather, it was limited to a short period for argument and to reading into the record the questions it would have asked its witnesses. After the hearing, the Commission elected to take no action on the license application until LDRA's legal challenge to the statutes in question was finally resolved. See Original Complaint ¶¶ 103-106.

The Revocation of LDRA's Racing License and Subsequent Litigation

At its April 24, 1994, meeting, the Commission resolved to cancel LDRA's racing license. The chief justification for the revocation was that LDRA had not met its obligations as a primary licensee, which obligations included a duty to construct and operate a race track in Livingston Parish. The Plaintiffs contend, however, that the Commission was acting at the Krantzes' behest and that the revocation was aimed at depriving LDRA of standing in its lawsuit contesting the statute that denies OTB licenses to race tracks not in existence during the 1986-87 racing season. See Original Complaint ¶¶ 107-08.

The revocation of LDRA's racing license also prompted Odom to file, as part of his lawsuit challenging the referendum election in Livingston Parish, a new motion urging that the election be declared a nullity. This motion was denied and Odom's suit later dismissed upon LDRA's motion. See id. ¶ 109.

On April 29, 1994, LDRA filed suit in state court challenging the cancellation of its racing license. The Commission responded with a motion to dismiss LDRA's suit due to improper venue. Although the Commission was unsuccessful at both the trial and appellate levels, the Louisiana Supreme Court granted its motion and ordered LDRA's suit transferred to Orleans Parish. According to the Plaintiffs, the Commission's motion to dismiss was filed at the Krantzes' request and was designed solely to defeat or to delay LDRA's entry into the market for live horse racing. See id. ¶¶ 110, 113, 144.

On December 2, 1994, while LDRA's suit contesting the cancellation of its license was still pending, LDRA petitioned the Commission to reinstate the license. Citing the pendency of LDRA's lawsuit, the Commission declined to consider the petition. LDRA alleges that, owing to the Commission's refusal to reinstate its license, its lender withdrew the $10 million commitment to finance the proposed race track at Livingston Downs. See Original Complaint ¶¶ 136-37.

LDRA's suit contesting the revocation of its racing license culminated in a settlement agreement and the entry of a consent judgment in November 1996. See Def.'s Exh. C. Under the agreement, the Commission agreed to

commute the revocation of LDRA's racing license to a two-year suspension
and to give LDRA until October 31, 1998, to submit a new license application.
See id. ¶ 3. The agreement specified that any such application must include
a letter of commitment for $10 million in financial backing; it also provided
that the Commission must approve of LDRA's proposed financier. See id.
¶¶ 6-7. The agreement contained a proviso allowing the Commission to declare the agreement void and to move to have the consent judgment dismissed
if LDRA failed to submit an application by the deadline. See id.

LDRA requested an extension in which to file its application, which request
the Commission denied. LDRA was nevertheless able to file a new application,
complete with a letter of commitment for $10 million, one day before the
deadline. On November 10, 1998, the Commission filed a motion to dismiss
the consent judgment, arguing that Livingston Downs had failed to satisfy
the terms and conditions of the agreement. See Def.'s Exh. E. Specifically, it
argued that LDRA's commitment for financing was not a binding, enforceable
commitment as the agreement required. It also argued that LDRA's financial
commitment traduced La. R.S. § 4:147(4) because it conferred upon LDRA's
financial backer, Remington Financial Group, the unfettered discretion to
appoint owners of Livingston Downs. The Racing Commission also objected
to the application because it was in the name of Livingston Downs Racing
Association, L.L.C. rather than Livingston Downs Racing Association, Inc.,
the named plaintiff in the suit and consent judgment. The trial court ruled
in favor of the Commission, and the Court of Appeal affirmed. See Jefferson
Downs Corp. v. Louisiana State Racing Comm'n, 751 So.2d 465 (La.App. 4
Cir.2000), writ denied, 2000-1067 (La.5/26/00, 762 So.2d 1112).

Efforts to Influence the State Legislature and the Commission

LDRA also asserts that its entry into the relevant market was obstructed
by the Defendants' extensive lobbying of the state legislature and the Commission. With regard to the legislature, LDRA maintains that the Defendants
were able to obtain changes in proposed legislation that hindered the Plaintiffs' competitiveness. LDRA refers to proposed amendments to state gaming
laws that would have increased substantially the maximum payout for video
poker devices located at race tracks. The Plaintiffs aver that the Defendants
directed Bankston, their attorney and the chairman of the legislative committee that oversees gambling in Louisiana, to modify the new legislation to limit
the right to make higher video poker payouts to only those race tracks in
existence during the 1986-87 racing season.

The Plaintiffs further maintain that the Defendants successfully lobbied the
Commission to take numerous actions that ultimately defeated LDRA's entry
into the market for live horse racing. As well as convincing the Commission
to revoke LDRA's racing license and to oppose any efforts to reinstate the
license, the Plaintiffs contend that the Defendants influenced the Commission
to take the following anticompetitive steps: extending preferential treatment
to other racetracks, including Jefferson Downs, Louisiana Downs, and Sawyer
Downs; delaying LDRA's license application so as not to jeopardize the
transfer of Jefferson Downs' OTB license to Fair Grounds; rejecting LDRA's
application for an OTB license; fining LDRA over $200,000 for failing to hold

races on the dates it was given; withholding the deposit on LDRA's license application; instituting harassing audits of LDRA's business records; and rejecting, mala fide, the new license application submitted by LDRA pursuant to the consent agreement. See generally Original Complaint ¶¶ 142-212.

Federal Court Proceedings

The Plaintiffs filed this action on August 30, 1996. See Original Complaint. Named as defendants were Jefferson Downs; Fair Grounds; CCG and its officers; Bryan and Marie Krantz; Finish Line Management, Inc. (the company that operates the Krantzes' OTB parlors); Terrance Odom and Karen Thomas; Larry Bankston, in his official and personal capacities; and various members of the Commission. See id. ¶ 5. The original complaint asserted claims under the Sherman Antitrust Act, 15 U.S.C. § 1; various federal civil rights statutes, 42 U.S.C. §§ 1983, 1985, and 1986; and state law. See id. ¶ 1. The Plaintiffs later amended their complaint to assert civil claims under federal RICO statutes, see 18 U.S.C. §§ 1961-1968, against all defendants save the Commission. See First Supplemental and Amended Complaint ¶¶ 219, 233, 247 (doc. no. 69).

The Defendants variously moved, under Fed.R.Civ.P. 12(b)(6), for dismissal of all claims. See doc. nos. 12, 15, 38, 46. As the Plaintiffs had already dismissed the individual members of the Commission from the suit, the court granted the motion as to the claims under §§ 1983, 1985, and 1986. The court, however, declined to dismiss any of the other claims. See doc. no. 66. The Plaintiffs subsequently dismissed Defendants Terrance Odom and Karen Thomas from the action. See doc. nos. 249, 277.

The remaining Defendants filed an answer which invoked, as affirmative defenses, res judicata, statute of limitations, and the Noerr-Pennington and Parker doctrines. The Defendants have now moved for summary judgment on all remaining claims. See doc. nos. 295, 305. The Plaintiffs oppose.

Also pending before the Court is an unopposed motion by the Plaintiffs to withdraw selected factual representations from their first amended complaint. See doc. nos. 358-59. This brings to six the total number of motions pending before the Court in this matter.

ANALYSIS

LDRA asserts that the Defendants violated federal antitrust and racketeering laws when they undertook to defeat or to delay substantially LDRA's efforts to enter the market for live horse racing in Louisiana. The Defendants contend that the Noerr-Pennington and Parker doctrines shield from antitrust liability their efforts to hinder, through litigation, campaigning, and lobbying, LDRA's entry into the relevant market.

The Plaintiffs counter that the Defendants were not concerned with securing favorable Government action. Rather, their true goal was to entangle LDRA in such a quagmire of litigation and regulatory red tape that LDRA could not obtain financing for its proposed race track. As a result, LDRA argues, the "sham litigation" exception to Noerr-Pennington immunity applies, and summary judgment is inappropriate.

Noerr-Pennington Doctrine

The Court begins with first principles. Section 1 of the Sherman Act prohibits "[e]very contract, combination . . . or conspiracy" that unreasonably restrains interstate or foreign trade. See 15 U.S.C. § 1 (West 2000); State Oil Co. v. Khan, 522 U.S. 3, 10, 118 S.Ct. 275, 139 L.Ed.2d 199 (1997) (the Sherman Act prohibits only unreasonable restraints on trade). In Eastern R.R. Presidents Conference v. Noerr Motor Freight, Inc., 365 U.S. 127, 81 S.Ct. 523, 5 L.Ed.2d 464 (1961), the Supreme Court carved out an exemption to the antitrust laws for efforts by private individuals to petition the Government for action that may have anticompetitive consequences. Id. at 136, 81 S.Ct. 523; see also Mine Workers v. Pennington, 381 U.S. 657, 669, 85 S.Ct. 1585, 14 L.Ed.2d 626 (1965). This exemption, known as Noerr-Pennington immunity, protects efforts to influence government officials regardless of the petitioner's anticompetitive motives or the efficacy of those efforts. See Noerr, 365 U.S. at 138, 143, 81 S.Ct. 523. The doctrine, moreover, encompasses attempts to influence legislative, executive, and administrative bodies, as well as efforts to obtain favorable court action through the filing of lawsuits. See Noerr, 365 U.S. at 136, 81 S.Ct. 523 (legislative action); Pennington, 381 U.S. 657, 85 S.Ct. 1585, 14 L.Ed.2d 626 (administrative processes); California Motor Transp. Co. v. Trucking Unlimited, 404 U.S. 508, 510-11, 92 S.Ct. 609, 30 L.Ed.2d 642 (1972) (state and federal agencies and courts). This broad application is mandated by the doctrine's roots in the First Amendment's guarantee of the right to petition the Government for redress. See Noerr, 365 U.S. at 138, 81 S.Ct. 523; see also California Motor, 404 U.S. at 510-11, 92 S.Ct. 609.

The Noerr-Pennington doctrine admits of one exception: it does not shield petitioning activity that is "a mere sham to cover what is actually nothing more than an attempt to interfere directly with the business relationships of a competitor." See Noerr, 365 U.S. at 144, 81 S.Ct. 523. Under this sham exception, if the petitioner seeks "to use the governmental process—as opposed to the outcome of that process—as an anticompetitive weapon," the petitioning activity will not be protected from antitrust liability. Columbia v. Omni Outdoor Adver., Inc., 499 U.S. 365, 380, 111 S.Ct. 1344, 113 L.Ed.2d 382 (1991). The sham exception governs situations in which the petitioner's "activities are not genuinely aimed at procuring favorable governmental action." See Allied Tube & Conduit Corp., 486 U.S. 492, 500 n. 4, 108 S.Ct. 1931, 100 L.Ed.2d 497 (1988) (internal citation omitted). The absence of a genuine desire for governmental action may be evidenced by "a pattern of baseless, repetitive claims" indicating that "the administrative and judicial processes have been abused." See California Motor, 404 U.S. at 513, 92 S.Ct. 609 (internal citation and quotation marks omitted).

1. Political Activities

A. Lobbying the Legislature

LDRA asserts that the Defendants successfully lobbied the Louisiana Legislature to alter proposed legislation to LDRA's detriment. By denying LDRA the right to make larger payouts on video poker devices, LDRA contends, the Defendants directly impaired LDRA's ability to enter the market for live horse racing.

This claim is without merit, for the Defendants' attempt to obtain legislation inimical to LDRA's interests is precisely the sort of petitioning activity Noerr-Pennington immunity was designed to protect. See Noerr, 365 U.S. at 135, 81 S.Ct. 523 ("no violation of the [Sherman] Act can be predicated on mere attempts to influence the passage . . . of laws."). The plainly anticompetitive goal that underlay the Defendants' actions does not alter this conclusion. Nor does the efficacy of the Defendants' lobbying efforts or the degree of actual harm suffered by LDRA. See id. at 139-40, 81 S.Ct. 523 ("it is not . . . illegal for people to seek action on laws in the hope that they may bring about . . . a disadvantage to their competitors.").

Antitrust liability would be warranted only if LDRA asserted that the Defendants did not genuinely seek the legislation they argued for and sought simply to delay or defeat LDRA's entry through the lobbying process itself. See Omni Outdoor Adver., 499 U.S. at 381, 111 S.Ct. 1344. LDRA makes no such claim as, indeed, it cannot. The Defendants clearly desired the governmental action they advocated: denying the competitive advantage of higher video poker payouts to any would-be rivals.

B. Campaigning in the Referendum Election

LDRA likewise complains that the Defendants ran afoul of the Sherman Act when they formed CCG and mounted a publicity campaign against LDRA in the referendum election. LDRA contends that the Defendants used deceptive tactics in order to mislead the public. These tactics included forming and surreptitiously funding CCG to make it appear that the views expressed during the campaign were those of independent persons and groups. These clandestine tactics, LDRA contends, deprived the Defendants' activities of legitimacy.

This argument is likewise foreclosed by Noerr. In that case, the Supreme Court concluded that political activities such as publicity campaigns are beyond the remit of the antitrust laws even when the defendants resort to "unethical tactics" during the campaign. See Noerr, 365 U.S. at 140-41, 81 S.Ct. 523 (noting that it is inapposite for purposes of antitrust liability that the defendants used unethical tactics in a publicity campaign because the antitrust statutes do not regulate political activities). The Defendants' efforts to sway public sentiment against the proposed race track are plainly within the scope of Noerr-Pennington immunity. This remains true even if, as the Plaintiffs allege, the Defendants used misleading or underhanded methods. See id.

2. Administrative Hearings

A closer question is posed by the Defendants' efforts to influence the Commission. It is clear that Noerr-Pennington immunity extends to efforts to influence all branches of government, including state administrative agencies. See California Motor Transp., 404 U.S. at 510-11, 92 S.Ct. 609. [H]owever, the Supreme Court has intimated that the scope of the sham exception varies depending upon the branch of government involved. See id. at 513, 92 S.Ct. 609. In the legislative or political arenas, the Court has explained, Noerr-Pennington immunity enjoys its broadest sweep, and the sham exception is at its nadir. Hence, even "misrepresentations and other forms of unethical conduct" will not incur antitrust liability when directed toward lawmakers. See id. at 513, 92 S.Ct. 609. But when a court of law is the object of the challenged petitioning, the sham exception is given a much broader compass. Thus, unethical or illegal conduct that would be condoned in the political context is proscribed when it is used to inveigle an adjudicatory tribunal. See id.

As a necessary prologue to any Noerr-Pennington immunity analysis, therefore, the Court must determine whether the Commission, an executive agency, is more akin to a political entity or to a judicial body. Such a distinction is a difficult one to draw, for, as the Ninth Circuit has observed, "the executive branch is radically diverse," encompassing everything from administrative bodies that hold formal hearings and are bound by regulations to entities that are "unapologetically political." See Kottle v. Northwest Kidney Ctrs., 146 F.3d 1056, 1061 (9th Cir.1998).

The Court concludes that the Committee's discretion was adequately circumscribed that it should be regarded as an adjudicatory body for purposes of the sham exception. The Commission is governed both by Louisiana's Administrative Procedures Act and the Open Meeting Law. See Jefferson Downs, 751 So.2d at 468. Accordingly, the Commission was required not only to hold public hearings to consider LDRA's various license applications, but also to permit LDRA to present arguments and witnesses at such hearings and to be represented by counsel. Moreover, Louisiana's racing statutes enumerate several criteria the Commission was obligated to weigh in evaluating LDRA's license applications. See La.Rev.Stat. Ann. §§ 4:159, :214. Those statutes also limit the Commission's authority to revoke a racing license, permitting such action only for just cause. See La.Rev.Stat. Ann. § 4:160. LDRA further had a statutory right to judicial review of the Committee's decisions to deny and to revoke its licenses. See La.Rev.Stat. Ann. § 4:158. Insofar as the LDRA's license applications are concerned, therefore, the broader sham exception that obtains in the context of judicial proceedings is applicable.

LDRA's pleadings contain assertions of fraud and denial of access to regulatory agencies. LDRA contends, for instance, that the Defendants submitted a letter to the Commission which represented, falsely, that the Governor of Louisiana opposed LDRA's racing license. Furthermore, LDRA alleges that the Defendants curtailed its access to the Commission by inducing the Commission to take the following steps: delay consideration of LDRA's racing-license until after Jefferson Downs had successfully transferred its OTB license to Fair Grounds; quash subpoenas LDRA had issued for a hearing before the Commission; and deny LDRA the opportunity to present witnesses or arguments in support of its bid for an OTB license. LDRA argues that the sole aim of these exclusionary tactics was to hinder LDRA's efforts to obtain redress from the Commission.

The record, as it currently stands, fails to raise a genuine issue with regard to LDRA's claims of fraud. LDRA has adduced no evidence to substantiate its contention that the Defendants made misrepresentations to the Commission. See Stearns Airport Equip. Co. v. FMC Corp., 170 F.3d 518, 521 (5th Cir.1999) (to avoid summary judgment, the nonmoving party must produce or identify in the record evidence sufficient to sustain a finding in its favor respecting those facts as to which it bears the burden of proof). The letter containing the supposed misrepresentations is not included in the record, and, with one exception, LDRA has failed even to allege what untruths the letter contained. See Kottle, 146 F.3d at 1063-64 (holding that the plaintiff's failure to specify the misrepresentations allegedly made by the defendant before the state licensing agency precluded it from invoking the sham exception). As for the assertion that the letter falsely indicated that the Governor opposed LDRA's license, LDRA has not shown that this assertion, which was not even set forth in an affidavit, was material to the Commission's decision or that this assertion so tainted the proceedings as to deprive them of all legitimacy.

Less certain is whether LDRA has raised a genuine issue with regard to its contention that it was denied meaningful access to the Commission. LDRA asserts that, although it was afforded a hearing on its second application for a racing license, this hearing was itself a sham. LDRA alleges that the Defendants used their influence with the Commission to delay the hearing on LDRA's application. LDRA also asserts that, when the application was finally heard, the Commission quashed its subpoenas, prohibited it from calling its witnesses, and refused to allow LDRA to present its arguments fully, all at the Defendants' behest. These assertions, if believed, could lead a reasonable factfinder to conclude that the Defendants were using their "power, strategy, and resources . . . to harass and deter [LDRA] in its use of administrative . . . proceedings so as to deny [it] free and unlimited access" to the Commission. See California Motor, 404 U.S. at 511, 92 S.Ct. 609. As a result, genuine issues of fact remain as to whether "the machinery of [the Commission] was effectively closed" to LDRA and whether that the Defendants usurped the Commission's decision-making authority. See id. Summary judgment on this claim is therefore inappropriate.

Moreover, it is clear that, in certain respects, the Commission was acting as an executive body as opposed to an adjudicatory one. For example, the Commission, pursuant to its role as the agency responsible for enforcing gaming statutes, initially revoked LDRA's racing license because it had failed to hold races during the required period. The Commission, also in its enforcement capacity, cancelled the race dates LDRA was later granted; rejected the license application LDRA submitted pursuant to the consent judgment because of supposed inadequacies; withheld LDRA's application fees; audited LDRA's financial and business records; and extended preferential treatment to other race tracks. Even if the Commission took all these actions at the Defendants' bidding as LDRA claims, however, LDRA cannot prevail. The Commission was acting in an executive or enforcement capacity when it took these actions, and hence the Noerr-Pennington doctrine was at its broadest reach. See California Motor, 404 U.S. at 510, 92 S.Ct. 609 (noting that Noerr precludes any cause of action for efforts to influence the Executive Branch for the enforcement of laws). Furthermore, the efficacy of the Defendants' efforts to persuade the Commission to take these various steps renders them immune from antitrust liability.

LDRA's allegations further imply that various members of the Commission colluded with the Defendants to prevent LDRA from obtaining the racing and OTB licenses necessary to enter the relevant market. These claims, even if true, would not deprive the Defendants of their immunity under Noerr-Pennington, however, for the Supreme Court has emphatically rejected the notion that there is a conspiracy exception to this doctrine. See Omni, 499 U.S. at 374, 383-84, 111 S.Ct. 1344 (also denying the existence of such an exception to state-action or Parker immunity). Thus, even if the Defendants did conspire with the members of the Commission to delay or otherwise hinder LDRA's license applications, the Defendants would nevertheless be entitled to summary judgment.

3. Litigation

LDRA also asserts that the Defendants repeatedly engaged in sham litigation in the state courts in an effort to prevent or delay its entry into the market for live horse racing and gambling. Accordingly, the Court will examine the lawsuits in an effort to discern whether, as a whole, they signify a pattern of frivolous claims that were initiated with no regard for the merits.

Clearly, those suits in which the Defendants prevailed do not support a finding that the judicial process was abused. Yet there is some evidence that the Defendants engaged in repetitive litigation. For example, the Defendants, through Karen Thomas, intervened in an action initiated by LDRA in which LDRA sought to compel the Secretary of State to hold the referendum election in Livingston Parish. The Defendants argued that procedural irregularities in noticing the election precluded its being held. Notwithstanding this intervention, the Defendants, through Terrence Odom, filed a separate lawsuit seeking to enjoin the Secretary from holding the election. This action was based on the same grounds as the Defendants' intervention. Moreover, when LDRA prevailed and the election went ahead, the Defendants challenged the election's legitimacy. This action was also based on supposed procedural irregularities in noticing the election. Clearly, the Defendants pursued the same claim on several occasions.

There is also some evidence that the Defendants abused the judicial process. After their request for an injunction to stop the election was denied, the Defendants unavailingly appealed to the Louisiana Supreme Court. Though rebuffed there, the Defendants maintained the suit for nearly two years, until, the election long over, it was dismissed as moot. Additionally, there is evidence suggesting that the Defendants attempted to delay adjudication of their own lawsuits. For example, in the election challenge filed by Odom, the Defendants attempted to stay discovery and to prevent Odom's and Thomas's depositions. The Defendants also intervened in LDRA's April 1993 action seeking to compel the Commission to hold a hearing to consider its application for racing dates. Upon being admitted to that action, the Defendants' attorney, Bankston, attempted to stay the suit until the end of the legislative session.

The Defendants' apparent temporizing, coupled with their seemingly over-zealous pursuit of certain actions, gives rise to an inference that they were attempting to "use [the litigation] process—as opposed to the outcome of that process—as an anticompetitive weapon." See Omni, 499 U.S. at 380, 111 S.Ct.

1344; but see St. Joseph's Hosp. v. Hospital Corp. of Am., 795 F.2d 948, 955 (11th Cir.1986) (noting that the defendants were entitled to use every available means to delay the issuance of the plaintiff's license). This inference is confirmed by two complementary factors: (1) the insubstantial nature of the election challenge reiterated by the Defendants; and (2) the evidence that the Defendants were aware of the pejorative effects any pending lawsuit would have upon LDRA's ability to obtain the requisite financing.

Given that the state courts uniformly rejected the Defendants' argument that the referendum had been improperly noticed, the Defendants' dogged pursuit of that claim cannot easily be reconciled with a genuine desire to obtain judicial relief. The Defendants continued to press the Thomas suit, which sought injunctive relief, until well after the election concluded. The same is true of the Odom election contest, which was pursued for years after the election was held. The Defendants' persistence with regard to claims that were manifestly tenuous suggests that the Defendants sought merely to keep the lawsuits pending as long as possible. This inference, when coupled with LDRA's evidence that the Defendants were aware that a pending lawsuit could scuttle LDRA's efforts to obtain financing, see Plaintiff's Exh. 12, could lead a reasonable factfinder to conclude that the Defendants sought not to obtain judicial relief but rather to hamper LDRA with the litigatory process itself.

The assertion that the Defendants sought to inflict injury collateral to the lawsuits themselves renders summary judgment inappropriate on LDRA's sham litigation claims. See Westmac, Inc. v. Smith, 797 F.2d 313 (6th Cir.1986) (indicating that evidence suggesting that the challenged lawsuits, though not frivolous, were instigated in order to prevent the plaintiff from obtaining financing was sufficient to rebut the presumption that the defendants were immune).

In sum, the Court concludes that the Defendants are entitled to summary judgment on LDRA's claim that they violated the Sherman Act by lobbying the Louisiana Legislature and by engaging in a publicity campaign to defeat the referendum. The Court further concludes, however, that the Defendants are not entitled to summary judgment on LDRA's claims that the Defendants' sham petitioning denied them meaningful access to the Commission or that the Defendants engaged in sham litigation.

Parker or State Action Doctrine

The Defendants further assert that their actions are shielded from antitrust liability by the state action or Parker doctrine. This doctrine has been construed to exempt both state agencies and private individuals from liability for activities that might otherwise violate federal antitrust law. See, e.g., Southern Motor Carriers Rate Conference, Inc. v. United States, 471 U.S. 48, 56-57, 105 S.Ct. 1721, 85 L.Ed.2d 36 (1985). The parties concur, however, that, since the individual members of the Commission have been dismissed from this suit, the state is no longer party to this action. If the Parker doctrine is to find any application in the instant circumstances, therefore, it must shield the Defendants as private individuals.

When the Parker exemption is invoked by a defendant other than the state, the allegedly anticompetitive activity is subjected to greater scrutiny before state action immunity will be granted. See Hoover v. Ronwin, 466 U.S. 558, 569, 104 S.Ct. 1989, 80 L.Ed.2d 590 (1984). In California Retail Liquor Dealers Ass'n v. Midcal Aluminum, 445 U.S. 97, 100 S.Ct. 937, 63 L.Ed.2d 233 (1980), the Supreme Court articulated a two-pronged test to determine whether private individuals are entitled to the Parker exemption: (1) the alleged anticompetitive conduct must have been taken pursuant to a clearly articulated and affirmatively expressed state policy to displace competition with state regulation; and (2) the state must actively supervise the implementation of its policy. See id. at 105, 100 S.Ct. 937; see also Earles v. State Bd. of Certified Public Accountants of Louisiana, 139 F.3d 1033, 1040-41 (5th Cir.1998) (applying the Midcal test).

The Defendants claim to have satisfied the Midcal criteria because their actions were all taken within the context of the state's regulatory scheme that displaces competition in the market for live horse racing. This construction of the Midcal test, however, is a strained one. The state's regulatory scheme may well displace competition in the market for live horse racing, but the Defendants played no role in implementing or enforcing that regime. See DFW Metro Line Servs. v. Southwestern Bell Tel. Corp., 988 F.2d 601, 603 (5th Cir.1993) (holding that a private utility's enforcement of rates set by the state, which it was required to do under the state's regulatory scheme, was protected by Parker). Nor were the Defendants' anticompetitive actions "actively supervised" or even endorsed by the state. See FTC v. Ticor Title Ins. Co., 504 U.S. 621, 633-34, 112 S.Ct. 2169, 119 L.Ed.2d 410 (1992). The Defendants herein did nothing more than to urge the government to take anticompetitive action. Therefore, their efforts are shielded, if at all, by the Noerr-Pennington doctrine.

Civil RICO Claims

LDRA also brings claims against the defendants under the civil RICO statutes. It contends that the Defendants' concerted efforts to obstruct its entry into the market for live horse racing and gambling constitute such a violation. The Defendants offer several defenses to this claim, including, inter alia, res judicata. Specifically, the Defendants assert that LDRA's RICO claims are all predicated on the same occurrences giving rise to LDRA's 1993 action in state court alleging violations of Louisiana's Unfair and Deceptive Trade Practices Act. The final judgment against LDRA in that case, entered April 27, 1995, the Defendants urge, bars relitigation of these claims under La.Rev.Stat. § 13-4231.

Apparently conceding that some of its claims are res judicata, LDRA argues that the Thomas and Odom lawsuits form the exclusive basis of its RICO action. See Plaintiff's Opposition to Summary Judgment at 69-70. LDRA asserts that these two claims are not res judicata because they were not known to them at the time it filed the 1993 state court action. In this regard, LDRA alleges that it did not discover that the Defendants were the impetus behind the Thomas and Odom lawsuits until it was able to depose Thomas and Odom in 1997. See id. at 70.

When a defendant in Louisiana prevails in a civil action, § 13:4231 bars a second action between the parties on any cause of action "existing at the time of final judgment arising out of the transaction or occurrence that is the subject matter of the [prior action]." See La.Rev.Stat. Ann. § 13:4231(2) (West 2001). The Court need not decide whether the Thomas and Odom lawsuits satisfy the "same occurrence or transaction" criterion, however, for § 13:4232 enumerates several exceptions to § 13:4231's broad application of the doctrine of res judicata. Among these exceptions is that a judgment does not bar a successive action by a plaintiff "[w]hen exceptional circumstances justify relief from the res judicata effect of the judgment . . . ." La.Rev.Stat. § 13:4232A(1) (West 2001). The official comment to § 13:4232 explains that this provision gives courts the authority to exercise their equitable discretion to balance the principle of res judicata with the interests of justice.

The Court concludes that the Defendants' alleged use of straw plaintiffs, coupled with the Defendants' successful efforts to delay the depositions of Thomas and Odom, abates the principles of judicial economy and finality that underlie the doctrine of res judicata. See Tate v. Prewitt, 33,895 (La.App. 2 Cir. 9/27/00), 769 So.2d 800, 803 (noting that res judicata promotes judicial efficiency and final resolution of disputes). This is certainly not a case in which a plaintiff has simply failed to assert a right or claim through oversight or lack of proper preparation. See La.Rev.Stat. § 13:4232 cmt. (West 2001). Accordingly, the court will exercise its discretion and permit LDRA's claims to proceed.

The Defendants further contend that LDRA lacks standing to bring its RICO claims because it has failed to allege a concrete injury to its business or property resulting from the Defendants' purported racketeering activities. The losses identified by LDRA thus far, note the Defendants, include expenses in dealing with the Thomas and Odom litigation and lost profits from the inability to enter the market for live horse racing. The Defendants characterize the first category of losses as normal business expenses that are beyond the ambit of RICO. They also assert that the latter type of injury is too speculative to support a RICO claim. Alternatively, the Defendants maintain that LDRA cannot establish that its alleged racketeering activities were the proximate cause of its alleged injuries.

The Court concludes that LDRA has established an injury to its business or property sufficient to confer standing. In Khurana v. Innovative Health Care Systems, Inc., the plaintiff alleged that the defendant had damaged his professional reputation by fraudulently inducing the plaintiff to accept employment with the defendants, who were engaged in a conspiracy to defraud Medicare. See 130 F.3d 143, 150 (5th Cir.1997), vacated on other grounds sub. nom. Teel v. Khurana, 525 U.S. 979, 119 S.Ct. 442, 142 L.Ed.2d 397 (1998). The plaintiff also asserted that, in fraudulently inducing him to work for them, the defendants had deprived him of other, legitimate business opportunities. See id. The Fifth Circuit concluded that these injuries were sufficient to confer standing upon the plaintiff.

LDRA asserts that, as a result of the Defendants' maintenance of the Thomas and Odom lawsuits, it was required to expend substantial sums contesting those lawsuits. It further alleges that these lawsuits were the principal barrier to their entry into the market for live horse racing and gambling. These losses are palpable enough to satisfy the "injury to business or property" requirement for RICO standing.

Less clear, however, is whether LDRA can fulfill [RICO's proximate cause requirement]. Defining the scope of proximate cause for purposes of RICO standing has proven an elusive task. See, e.g., Holmes v. Securities Investor Protection Corp., 503 U.S. 258, 112 S.Ct. 1311, 117 L.Ed.2d 532 (1992) (noting that "the infinite variety of claims that may arise [under RICO] make it virtually impossible to announce a black letter rule [of proximate causation] that will dictate the result in every case."). In Holmes, the Supreme Court directed courts to look to "the many shapes this concept took at common law." Id. at 268, 112 S.Ct. 1311. The Fifth Circuit has interpreted Holmes as holding merely that "common law ideas about proximate causation inform the understanding of RICO." Procter & Gamble Co. v. Amway Corp., 242 F.3d 539, 565 n. 53 (5th Cir.2001) (citing Israel Travel Advisory Serv., Inc. v. Israel Identity Tours, Inc., 61 F.3d 1250, 1257 (7th Cir.1995)). Accordingly, it has been held that the pertinent inquiry in determining the existence of proximate cause is "whether the conduct has been so significant and important a cause that the defendant should be held responsible." Chisolm v. TransSo. Fin. Corp., 95 F.3d 331, 336 (4th Cir.1996) (quoting Prosser & Keeton on Torts § 42, p. 272 (5th ed.1984)). The proximate cause determination for RICO standing is guided by indications of preconceived purpose, specifically intended consequence, necessary or natural result, reasonable foreseeability of result, the intervention of independent causes, whether the defendant's acts are a substantial factor in the sequence of responsible causation, and the factual directness of the causal connection. See, e.g., Chisolm, 95 F.3d at 338; In re Am. Express Co. Shareholder Litig., 39 F.3d 395, 400 (2d Cir.1994); Standard-bred Owners Ass'n v. Roosevelt Raceway Assocs., 985 F.2d 102, 104 (2d Cir.1993).

Applying these principles to the instant case, it would seem clear that the expenses LDRA incurred in fighting the Thomas and Odom suits were a direct and foreseeable consequence of those suits. As LDRA alleges that the Defendants intended to inflict these expenses as part of their conspiracy to exclude LDRA from the market for live horse racing, these injuries satisfy the proximate cause requirement for RICO standing.

Yet as to LDRA's claim that the lawsuits deprived them of future income by preventing them from operating a race track, it would seem that several intervening factors irretrievably shatter the chain of causation. It is true that LDRA was unable to obtain financing until after the Odom suit was dismissed, but it is unclear to what extent that the Odom suit was responsible for this. LDRA has presented affidavits suggesting that the Odom suit was a concern for potential investors, see Plaintiff's Exh. 13, but it would seem axiomatic that other concerns would also have played a role in these potential investors' decisions not to finance Livingston Downs. Moreover, it is indisputable that LDRA's entry into the market for live horse racing was ultimately foreclosed not by the Odom lawsuit, but rather by the Commission's rejection of LDRA's renewed racing application. The basis for the Commission's rejection of this application was the inadequacy of LDRA's financial backing; it had nothing to do with the Odom lawsuit. In the end, it was LDRA's own inability to satisfy the criteria of the consent agreement that scuttled its efforts to enter the market for live horse racing.

Because there are too many intervening factors to establish proximate causation as to LDRA's ultimate failure to enter the market for live horse racing, the Court concludes that LDRA lacks standing to pursue a RICO claim on this ground. See Procter & Gamble, 242 F.3d at 565. Because LDRA has established a direct harm stemming from the expense of defending the Thomas and Odom lawsuits, however, it does have standing to pursue that claim.

CONCLUSION

For the foregoing reasons, the Court hereby GRANTS the Defendants' Motion for Summary Judgment (doc no. 295) insofar as it seeks dismissal, under the Noerr-Pennington doctrine, of LDRA's claims that its efforts to influence the Louisiana State Legislature and the Commission were violative of the Sherman Act. The Court, however, DENIES the Defendants' Motion for Summary Judgment (doc. no. 295) insofar as it seeks dismissal of LDRA's claims that the Defendants violated the Sherman act through sham petitioning before the Commission and through sham litigation in the state courts. The Court also GRANTS the Defendants' Motion for Summary Judgment (doc no. 295) to the extent that it seeks dismissal of LDRA's RICO claim for lost profits but DENIES the motion to the extent that it seeks dismissal of LDRA's RICO claim for the expenses incurred as a result of the purportedly sham litigation.

MOTION GRANTED IN PART, DENIED IN PART.

BALMORAL RACING CLUB, INC. v. ILLINOIS RACING BOARD
603 N.E.2d 489 (Ill. 1992)

CUNNINGHAM, Justice.

Appellants in this case, Balmoral Racing Club, Inc. (Balmoral), and Chicago Division of the Horsemen's Benevolent and Protective Association, Inc. (the Horsemen's Association), separately initiated this action against numerous defendants to contest a decision rendered by the Illinois Racing Board (Board) pursuant to the Board's 1991 dates hearing. Their cases were consolidated for purposes of this appeal.

The decision of the Board denied Balmoral's request for thoroughbred racing dates in 1991. The circuit court of Will County reversed the decision of the Board and awarded Balmoral 62 thoroughbred racing dates during the summer of 1991. The appellate court reversed the decision of the circuit court. (214 Ill.App.3d 112, 157 Ill.Dec. 888, 573 N.E.2d 306.) We granted Balmoral's petition for leave to appeal to this court (134 Ill.2d R. 315). In the instant case, we reverse the judgments of the appellate and circuit courts, and remand this cause to the circuit court for action consistent with this opinion.

Before reviewing the facts giving rise to this action, it is helpful to address the identity of the parties involved. Balmoral is an organization whose principal place of business is Balmoral Park, located in Crete, Illinois. Balmoral is in the business of conducting horse races. The Horsemen's Association is a not-for-profit organization whose membership is comprised of owners or trainers of thoroughbred racehorses licensed to race in the United States or Puerto Rico.

The defendants were numerous and consisted of all participants in the 1991 dates hearing conducted by the Board. However, for purposes of this appeal, only Arlington Park Racetrack, Ltd., d/b/a Arlington International Racecourse, Ltd., and Washington Park Thoroughbred Racetrack, Ltd. (collectively, Arlington), and the Illinois Racing Board remain as appellees. (Hawthorne Race Course, Inc. (Hawthorne), did file a motion to dismiss this appeal due to mootness and did participate in the proceedings before the appellate court. However, in this action, Hawthorne did not file a response to Balmoral's petition for leave to appeal, did not brief any of the issues and did not participate in oral argument. For all intents and purposes, Hawthorne is no longer a party to this appeal.)

The Board is an administrative agency whose actions are authorized and restricted by the Illinois Horse Racing Act of 1975 (the Racing Act) (Ill.Rev.Stat.1989, ch. 8, par. 37-1 et seq.). The Board is responsible for executing the mandates of this act, including assigning horse racing dates to the various racing entities requesting such and regulating the horse racing industry of Illinois.

The remaining defendants-appellees are entities responsible for conducting horse racing meetings in the State of Illinois. The principal place of business of the Arlington defendants is Arlington Racetrack, which is located in Cook County.

THE 1991 RACING DATES HEARING

The parties convened in Chicago on September 18, 1990, for purposes of conducting the 1991 dates hearing. During this meeting, racing dates to conduct thoroughbred and harness races in 1991 were to be assigned to various racing entities. The parties had been required to submit applications for racing dates to the Board no later than the end of August. These applications were ostensibly used to assist the Board in the award of racing dates.

In its application, Arlington requested dates for summer thoroughbred racing. Balmoral requested dates be awarded to it to conduct its own thoroughbred race meet during overlapping summer months. Balmoral also requested dates to hold harness races at Balmoral racetrack at other times of the year.

At 6 a.m. on September 18, 1990, the Board posted a proposed schedule of racing dates for 1991 along with a preliminary statement. This schedule did not include any thoroughbred racing dates to be conducted at Balmoral Park and instead awarded year-long harness racing to be conducted at the Balmoral track. A year-long harness racing meet was not requested by Balmoral.

The meeting began later that morning with the Board chairman reading the preliminary statement which was posted at 6 a.m. After disposing of preliminary matters, the Board invited representatives from various horsemen's associations to speak. The first speaker was a representative from the Horsemen's Association. The Horsemen's Association indicated a preference for racing at Balmoral, as Balmoral had exhibited a greater commitment to Illinois thoroughbred racing than had Arlington.

After several more speakers, the Board proceeded to admit into evidence, among other things, past dates orders establishing racing dates from as early as 1985, annual reports of the Board from the last five years, and an evidentiary submission from Balmoral. Additional evidence was presented to the Board and admitted into the record as the hearing progressed. This included admitting all the applications received from those requesting racing dates.

After admitting this evidence, the chairman asked a representative from each racing entity to address the Board's proposed schedule. The representatives were "sworn in" and their sworn statements became part of the record.

One of the first speakers was a representative from Arlington International Racecourse. Arlington indicated its willingness to accept the dates which the Board had assigned to it and the conditions which the Board had imposed upon Arlington. The Arlington representative then addressed the concerns expressed by the Horsemen's Association and indicated that it was Arlington's intention to provide racing opportunities for many Illinois horses, owners and trainers. The Board asked several more questions of the Arlington representative; the representative's answers all indicated Arlington's commitment to ensuring excellence in racing and providing quality horse races and its dedication to Illinois racing.

During the testimony provided by Arlington, the Board noted it had received a six-page statement from the representative and asked if the racetrack would like to have this statement made part of the record. The representative responded affirmatively. This unsigned and unsworn statement alleges that contemporaneous races held at Balmoral the previous year had harmed Arlington revenues and races.

After testimony from Fairmount Park was presented, the representative from Hawthorne Race Course was asked to speak. The representative expressed consternation over the fact that Hawthorne was given the fewest number of days of racing, was given dates to race during the winter months, the "worst time of the year," and was given the fewest wagering opportunities. The representative exclaimed that the assignment of dates was not "fair." An amendment to the racing schedule was proposed by the representative which would give Hawthorne additional racing opportunities during better racing times.

The next speakers were representatives from Balmoral, who expressed their dissatisfaction with the proposed schedule, maintaining that the schedule as proposed would reduce its income by as much as one-third and would ultimately decrease State revenue. In rendering this opinion, the Balmoral representative stated, "I cannot believe that we are put in the position of fighting for our thoroughbred life without warning." Balmoral also addressed the issue of "short fields" (not having enough eligible horses to run particular races at certain tracks). The Balmoral representative contended that the problem of "short fields" was not caused by running races on the same days at both Balmoral and Arlington, as was suggested during the meeting, but was rather the product of a number of other factors beyond Balmoral's control, including the strict eligibility requirements which Arlington placed upon horses before they were allowed to participate in a particular race. The representative also addressed the reasons Arlington's handle was down the year before, presenting numerous reasons which, it was alleged, had all been previously noted by Arlington or other entities. ("Handle," in the racing industry, is generally recognized as referring to the total amount of money wagered.) Balmoral concluded that none of these reasons could be attributed to contemporaneous Balmoral race meets.

During their presentation, the Balmoral representatives indicated that they had become suspicious that the Board would deny Balmoral summer thoroughbred racing dates. Therefore, before the meeting had taken place, Balmoral requested of the Board a copy of Arlington's application for racing dates. Balmoral asserted that this application would enable it to prepare responses to any contentions raised by Arlington that Balmoral should not receive thoroughbred dates. Balmoral testified that it had been shown the applications before the dates hearing in the past. However, on this occasion, the representatives were denied access to Arlington's application. Therefore, Balmoral asserted, it could not affirmatively refute any arguments made by Arlington against awarding Balmoral racing dates.

The Board discussed this and, noting that the applications had been admitted into the record, determined to make a copy of Arlington's application available to Balmoral. It further acknowledged that the Board representative's failure to allow Balmoral to view this application before the meeting was an inadvertent error. The Board determined, however, that it would have to remove confidential information from the application.

Balmoral was later supplied a redacted copy of Arlington's application, which omitted certain "proprietary information" about Arlington, and was given an opportunity to review this document. In this redacted copy, the Board had deleted the addresses of various Arlington officers and removed certain financial information about the owners.

The Board further notified Balmoral that it had, at the last year's meeting, requested that evidentiary submissions in support of each application be turned over at the end of August, along with the application. The Board indicated that Balmoral had not submitted its evidentiary exhibits until the day before the meeting. Balmoral noted that it did not remember this request but would attempt to comply with the rule in the future.

Balmoral then addressed its request for harness dates. Other entities requesting harness dates were also asked to speak. The speaker from Sportsman's Harness Board noted that the proposed schedule, while losing thoroughbred competition, increased competition for Sportsman's Harness, thereby hurting that harness meet.

After a lunch break, the meeting was reconvened and the representative from Arlington was recalled to provide additional testimony. The representative was asked to give his opinion on the value of "exclusivity" to the horse racing market and, further, whether allowing Balmoral to run thoroughbred races while Arlington is conducting its own thoroughbred race meetings harms Arlington. The Arlington representative responded that exclusivity is the most important thing that could happen for the future of Arlington and Illinois racing. Arlington also addressed the shortage-of-horses issue and indicated that in 1990, when Balmoral was conducting a concurrent race schedule, there had been an average of 7.6 horses per race in the field, compared to 8.7 horses the year before, when Arlington did not have competition from Balmoral, and alleged that this reduction in horses significantly negatively affected wagering at Arlington, decreasing revenues.

While acknowledging agreement with Arlington's comments, one Board member stated:

> And personally, you know, Mr. Duffy, it's my opinion that Arlington Park has the greatest racing facility in the entire world.
>
> I have been to almost every major racing facility in this country and in many foreign countries and I feel definitely that Arlington has the best facility in the entire world . . . . So I believe personally that Arlington does deserve a chance to really succeed.
>
> I am a proponent not only this year but in prior years of the exclusivity of thoroughbred dates."

One of the questions asked of the Arlington representative was: "If we grant market exclusivity to Arlington will we be maximizing revenue [to] the State of Illinois all other things being equal?" The Arlington representative replied, "In my opinion you absolutely will," and explained that Arlington, being located in Cook County, pays higher taxes to the State on racing revenue than Balmoral does. In essence, therefore, Arlington must make half as much revenue as Balmoral in order to earn the State the same amount of money.

The Board then asked Balmoral if it had had an opportunity to review Arlington's application. Balmoral stated that the application did not provide any evidence that Balmoral had harmed Arlington. Balmoral was also given the six-page statement made by Duffy, the Arlington representative, which discusses the harm which competition from Balmoral had allegedly caused Arlington. The representative expressed that there were problems with the statistics presented but felt Balmoral had not been given enough time to review the document and to prepare an adequate rebuttal to the contentions raised, although he could indicate that he felt that some of the statistics were in error. Balmoral repeated that harness racing does not generate as much handle as thoroughbred racing and that this will affect State revenue. The Board agreed that harness handle would mean less revenue for Balmoral but disagreed that awarding harness to Balmoral would negatively affect State revenue.

After the close of the Balmoral testimony, the Board suggested amendments to the schedule, based upon the testimony it had heard. Those amendments did not include Balmoral thoroughbred racing dates. A vote was taken on these modifications; they were unanimously affirmed and the meeting was soon after adjourned.

PROCEDURAL HISTORY

On October 4, 1990, Balmoral and the Horsemen's Association filed a complaint in the circuit court of Will County seeking review of the Board's actions at the 1991 dates hearing.

On October 16, 1990, the Board entered its order assigning racing dates to various entities. This order was based upon the results of the September 18 dates hearing (the order). Pursuant to the Racing Act, the order specified distances between various racing parks in upstate Illinois. (Ill.Rev.Stat.1991, ch. 8, par. 37-19(a)(1).) The Illinois Department of Transportation certified to the Board that the mileage between Arlington International Race Course and Balmoral Park is 63.6 miles. The order also noted that each applicant had filed with the Board an affirmative action plan, outlining plans to recruit, train and upgrade minorities.

The Board then proceeded to award thoroughbred racing dates. The thoroughbred dates were awarded as follows: (1) from February 19 to May 11, races to be held at Sportsman's Park; (2) from May 12 to October 9, races to be held at Arlington Racecourse; (3) from October 10 to December 30, races to be held at Hawthorne Race Course.

All of these tracks are located in Cook County. The harness schedule was also presented. Harness dates were scheduled to be run by Balmoral at Balmoral Park from January 1, 1991, to June 2, 1991, with races to be run at Balmoral Park for the remainder of the year by Balmoral Park Trot, a tenant of the racetrack. Harness dates were also scheduled to be run at Sportsman's Park and Hawthorne Race Course during this same period.

The day after this order was published, an amended complaint was filed by Balmoral and the Horsemen's Association. On February 27, 1991, after extensive hearings, the circuit court rendered a decision in favor of Balmoral. In its order, the circuit court awarded 62 thoroughbred racing dates for 1991 (between May 12, 1991, and December 30, 1991) to Balmoral to be run on consecutive Sunday evenings, Mondays and Tuesdays.

As stated by the circuit court, the sole issue before it was whether the 1991 dates order issued by the Board was contrary to law or against the manifest weight of the evidence. The court found that the Illinois Administrative Procedure Act (Ill.Rev.Stat.1991, ch. 127, par. 1001 et seq.) applied to the Board's proceedings, that the Board had failed to comply with the requirements of various provisions of this act and that much of the Board's order was against the manifest weight of the evidence.

A motion to vacate or reconsider portions of the judgment was filed by Arlington and the Board on March 7, 1991. In response to certain comments of the circuit court in rendering its opinion, the affidavit of Cecil Troy, a member of the Board, was attached to this motion. This affidavit outlined the various procedures adopted by the Board in conducting the date hearings. The motion to vacate was denied.

The decision of the circuit court was then appealed to the appellate court by Arlington, the Board and Hawthorne. The parties sought to have the judgment of the circuit court reversed or reversed and remanded.

In an opinion filed May 30, 1991, the appellate court reversed the circuit court decision and denied Balmoral thoroughbred racing dates. The appellate court also held that the Administrative Procedure Act did not apply to the proceedings of the Board. 214 Ill.App.3d 112, 157 Ill.Dec. 888, 573 N.E.2d 306.

Balmoral sought leave to appeal this decision to this court. The Horsemen's Association filed a separate petition for leave to appeal this judgment. Allowing both parties to appeal, this court ordered that Balmoral's cause be consolidated with that of the Horsemen's Association.

ANALYSIS

Balmoral raises several issues in its argument addressing the procedural propriety of the dates hearing which denied it thoroughbred racing dates. These issues include (1) whether the Racing Act requires the Board to consider the five factors presented in section 21(c) of the Racing Act (Ill.Rev.Stat.1991, ch. 8, par. 37-21(c)) in evaluating each application before it; (2) whether the provisions of the Administrative Procedure Act (Ill.Rev.Stat.1991, ch. 127, par. 1001 et seq.) apply to the racing dates hearings; and (3) whether Balmoral was denied due process during the 1991 dates hearing.

The Racing Act

Initially, Balmoral attacks the Board's interpretation and application of the Illinois Racing Act (Ill.Rev.Stat.1991, ch. 8, par. 37-1 et seq.), contending that the Board's application to Balmoral of the factors set forth in section 21(c) (Ill.Rev.Stat.1991, ch. 8, par. 37-21(c)) is error because Balmoral is more than 35 miles from any other track.

Section 21(c) reads as follows:

(c) Where two or more applicants propose to conduct horse race meetings within 35 miles of each other, as certified to the Board under Section 19(a)(1) of this Act, on conflicting dates, the Board may determine and grant the number of racing days to be allotted to the several applicants. In the granting of organization licenses and in allocating dates for horse race meetings which will, in its judgment, be conducive to the best interests of the public and the sport of horse racing, the Board shall give consideration to an agreement among organizations, as provided in subsection (b) of Section 21 of this Act, and also shall give due consideration to:

(1) the character, reputation, experience and financial integrity of the applicants and of any other or separate person that either:

(i) controls, directly or indirectly, such applicant, or

(ii) is controlled, directly or indirectly, by such applicant or by a person which controls, directly or indirectly, such applicant;

(2) their facilities and accommodations for the conduct of horse race meetings;

(3) the location of the tracks of the applicants in relation to the principal centers of population of the State;

(4) the highest prospective total revenue to be derived by the State from the conduct of such meets;

(5) the good faith affirmative action plan of each applicant to recruit, train and upgrade minorities in all classifications within the association.

Ill.Rev.Stat.1991, ch. 8, par. 37-21(c).

In understanding Balmoral's argument, it is useful to note that section 19(a)(1) of the Racing Act disallows the award of concurrent racing dates to tracks located within 35 miles of one another. (Ill.Rev.Stat.1989, ch. 8, par. 37-19(a)(1).) Balmoral concludes that no conflict exists where two tracks located more than 35 miles apart apply for competing dates and argues that, because section 21(c) begins with a reference to tracks located within 35 miles, those factors listed in the second sentence of section 21(c) are only to be applied when tracks within 35 miles of each other apply for conflicting racing dates. We disagree, holding that the section 21(c) factors should be applied whenever evaluating applications for racing dates.

This court has consistently held that the starting place in interpreting the meaning of a statute is to ascertain and give effect to the legislative intent in enacting the statute. (See, e.g., Fumarolo v. Chicago Board of Education (1990), 142 Ill.2d 54, 96, 153 Ill.Dec. 177, 566 N.E.2d 1283; People v. Madison (1988), 121 Ill.2d 195, 200, 117 Ill.Dec. 213, 520 N.E.2d 374.) " 'This is to be done primarily from a consideration of the legislative language itself, which affords the best means of its [the statute's] exposition * * *.' " (Maloney v. Bower (1986), 113 Ill.2d 473, 479, 101 Ill.Dec. 594, 498 N.E.2d 1102, quoting Franzese v. Trinko (1977), 66 Ill.2d 136, 139, 5 Ill.Dec. 262, 361 N.E.2d 585.) We are also mindful that "[w]e should not attempt to read the statute other than in the manner in which it was written." Kozak v. Retirement Board of the Firemen's Annuity & Benefit Fund (1983), 95 Ill.2d 211, 215, 69 Ill.Dec. 177, 447 N.E.2d

We thus turn to the language of the statute to begin our analysis of the meaning of section 21(c). The statute clearly states: "In the granting of organization licenses and in allocating dates for horse race meetings which will, in its judgment, be conducive to the best interests of the public and the sport of horse racing," the Board shall give consideration to five factors. There is no limitation placed in this sentence that the five factors are only to be considered if the tracks are located within 35 miles from one another.

This sentence further makes reference to section 21(b) of the Racing Act, which provides a general grant of discretion to the Board in awarding racing dates. Section 21(b) does not contain a 35-mile limitation in the award of racing dates. As section 21(c) refers to this general grant of discretion, we must conclude that section 21(c) was meant to guide the exercise of the Board's general discretion.

When the legislature vests discretionary authority within an administrative agency, "intelligible standards must be provided to guide the officer in the exercise of his discretion." (Bio-Medical Laboratories, Inc. v. Trainor (1977), 68 Ill.2d 540, 551, 12 Ill.Dec. 600, 370 N.E.2d 223.) Failure to determine such standards renders the statute void. Krol v. County of Will (1968), 38 Ill.2d 587, 593, 233 N.E.2d 417.

An examination of the legislative history confirms our interpretation. This court has noted that where a statute is susceptible of different interpretations, it is proper to examine things other than the plain language of the statute. (In re Marriage of Logston (1984), 103 Ill.2d 266, 279, 82 Ill.Dec. 633, 469

N.E.2d 167.) In these instances, courts often turn to the legislative history of the statute. People v. Boykin (1983), 94 Ill.2d 138, 141, 68 Ill.Dec. 321, 445 N.E.2d 1174.

The legislative history of this act supports the conclusion we have reached. In 1984, the legislature proposed to amend section 21(c). Originally, the Act created a conflict in the award of racing dates where tracks within 45 miles of each other requested the same racing dates be awarded them. The amendment sought to have this mileage reduced to the current 35-mile limitation.

During the Senate debates when the bill was presented, upon questioning concerning the reasons for reducing the limitation to 35 miles, Senator Phillip Rock addressed the Assembly and noted:

> As you well know, I am probably as friendly to the people who own and . . . and run Sportsman's Park as anybody in the Chamber, but I really believe, given the fact that Balmoral Race Track and all the parimutuel employees and all the concessionaires and their employees and . . . and the . . . I . . . I think they ought to have a chance. Now we can't grant them that chance because we can't, under our law, dictate to the Illinois Racing Board the awarding of dates or times or any of that stuff, that's up to them. All we are . . . we are doing is affording the racing board that opportunity. If they don't want to do it, they don't have to do it, but we are not prohibiting it by law and I think that's a fair chance * * *.

83d Ill.Gen.Assem., Senate Proceedings, June 28, 1984, at 202-03.

The Senate debate indicates that the Senate never meant to remove from the Board the discretion which it had originally been granted. The Senator expressly noted that the Senate would not be prohibiting the award of racing dates to Balmoral based upon the mileage requirement in resolving conflicts but it would also not mandate the award of racing dates to any entity outside of the 35-mile limitation.

Therefore, based upon plain language and legislative history, we conclude that section 21(c) is meant to guide the exercise of the Board's general discretion whenever reviewing any application for horse racing dates. The factors of section 21(c) should be applied regardless of distance between tracks.

Balmoral disagrees with this conclusion and instead sets forth several arguments in support of its position. These arguments ignore the plain language of section 21(c) and the legislative history in enacting it. We shall, however, address those issues of substance which Balmoral raises.

The first of these arguments is that certain provisions of the Racing Act itself require us to read section 21(c) as Balmoral suggests. First, Balmoral states that provisions of the Racing Act, most particularly sections 19(a)(1) through 19(a)(5) (Ill.Rev.Stat.1991, ch. 8, pars. 37-19(a)(1) through (a)(5)), establish standards to guide the Board in awarding racing dates. Therefore, Balmoral argues that, as these provisions already supply standards, to read section 21(c) as we now do would render these provisions superfluous. However, none of these provisions establishes a standard for determining the award of racing dates, as does section 21(c). Particularly, section 19 merely deals with minimal requirements for delineating to whom a license may be granted. Further, these requirements do not duplicate the requirements set forth in section 21(c), as Balmoral suggests.

Balmoral's second argument asserts that a construction which requires the application of the section 21(c) factors to every racetrack would unfairly discriminate against non-Cook County tracks. Because the Racing Act establishes a graduated tax system whereby tracks located in a county of less than 400,000 individuals pay a different tax than do tracks located in a county with more than 400,000 inhabitants, non-Cook County tracks will always generate less State revenue. Therefore, the argument continues, the Board will always favor Cook County tracks.

This argument elevates one factor in section 21(c), the maximization of State revenue, above the remaining four factors. There is no indication that the legislature meant for this result. Furthermore, to adopt Balmoral's theory would mean adopting the theory that the Board is required to award exclusive dates and may not consider awarding concurrent race schedules to tracks located more than 35 miles from each other.

Despite the arguments raised by Balmoral and the Horsemen's Association, we conclude that the award of racing dates, regardless of distance between tracks, remains within the Board's discretion. The Board's discretion is limited by the requirements set forth in section 21(c). Through consideration of these factors, the Board may elect to award concurrent racing dates to tracks located more than 35 miles apart, but is not required to do so.

However, the Board is required to consider all five factors presented in section 21(c) when making this decision. This the Board did not do. Rather, the 1991 dates order indicates that the Board focused exclusively upon one factor: the maximization of State revenue. Ill.Rev.Stat.1991, ch. 8, par. 37-21(c)(4).

In providing a racing schedule which presented "the Board's best effort to fulfill its obligation to maximize State revenue while discharging its obligation to Illinois horsemen," the Board's order read, in pertinent part, as follows:

> In the 1990 Dates Order, the Board found that the 1989 race meeting at Arlington International Racecourse 'was an unprecedented success, setting new Illinois records for handle and attendance.' That meet was unopposed by any other Chicago-area thoroughbred race meeting. During the same year, the thoroughbred race meeting conducted at Sportsman's Park was opposed by a thoroughbred race meeting at Balmoral Park. It was evident that, during the spring of 1989, the thoroughbred horse population was insufficient to support both of these race meetings. The thoroughbred race meetings at Hawthorne Race Course were unopposed during most of 1989 and all of 1990. For calendar year 1990 the Board eliminated thoroughbred competition between Sportsman's Park and Balmoral Park but allowed Balmoral to conduct thoroughbred racing two (2) days per week opposite the race meeting conducted at Arlington International Racecourse. This experiment clearly benefited the thoroughbred race meeting at Sportsman's Park but again resulted in an insufficient horse population for concurrent race meetings at Arlington and

Balmoral. Like Sportsman's 1989 meet, Arlington's 1990 meet has been plagued by short fields which have caused a decline in attendance and handle. It is uncontested that the fewer the number of betting interests in a race, the fewer the number of dollars that will be bet on that race. The supply of available horses for Illinois thoroughbred racing has been further reduced in recent years by the operation of thoroughbred racetracks in Minnesota, Oklahoma, Iowa and the summer thoroughbred meets at Churchill Downs in Kentucky.

The experience of the last two racing years demonstrates a vital need for unopposed race meetings at the three principal Chicago thoroughbred racetracks—Sportsman's Park, Arlington International Racecourse and Hawthorne Race Course. In the exercise of our obligation to maximize state revenue, we conclude that such exclusivity will have a positive affect [sic] on state revenue and, at the same time, will not negatively impact those horsemen who have regularly participated in thoroughbred race meetings at Balmoral Park.

Representatives of Balmoral presented a cogent and forceful argument with respect to its desire to retain thoroughbred dates in competition with Arlington. For purposes of this order, we accept Balmoral's entire factual statements as accurate, but, nonetheless, are required to exercise our discretion in favor of a schedule that provides the greatest financial return to the state treasury. In our judgment, market exclusivity will best accomplish that objective.

Despite this language, the appellate court held that the Board impliedly considered all five factors. (214 Ill.App.3d at 118, 157 Ill.Dec. 888, 573 N.E.2d 306.) This holding is error. The appellate court reasoned that evidence to make a determination about all five factors was possibly present in the record. It is the opinion of this court that the mere fact that the record might contain such evidence is not an indication that the Board has considered the evidence, as required by the statute. (Ill.Rev.Stat.1991, ch. 8, par. 37-21(c)). This conclusion is bolstered by the fact that the Board's own language repeatedly states that its duty is to exercise its discretion to maximize State revenue. The exercise of this duty apparently, by the Board's own order, excludes consideration of the additional four factors.

We recognize, as Arlington points out, that we previously emphasized the maximization of State revenue in People ex rel. Scott v. Illinois Racing Board (1973), 54 Ill.2d 569, 301 N.E.2d 285. In that case, this court stated, "A primary legislative purpose in the regulation of horse racing is the generation of income for the State * * *. * * * The strong public interest in maximizing both revenue to the State and to public charities is apparent, as is the necessity of requiring strict observance * * * of these objectives." (Scott, 54 Ill.2d at 576, 301 N.E.2d 285.) At no point, however, did this court state that this factor was more important than the other factors presented in the Racing Act.

It is our holding today that the Board must consider all five factors listed in section 21(c) when awarding racing dates. There is no evidence in this record that the Board exercised its discretion in the award of 1991 dates so as to do precisely what the statute requires. For purposes of due process, these findings should be made evident in the Board's dates orders.

In considering section 21(c)(4), the Board should take into consideration all the revenue generated by a particular racing establishment. Section 21(c)(4) states that the Board is to consider "the highest prospective total revenue to be derived by the State from the conduct of such meets." (Ill.Rev.Stat.1991, ch. 8, par. 37-21(c)(4).) There is no restriction placed in the statute that only handle tax should be considered. Therefore, among other things, the Board should consider any sales taxes, income taxes and admission taxes which might apply.

[The remainder of the court's opinion is omitted.]

Notes

1. As *Livingston Downs* makes clear, anyone hoping to start a race track faces substantial up-front costs. As a result, some jurisdictions grant pari-mutuel operators "unlimited duration" licenses, thereby eliminating the need for periodic re-certification. Of course, such licenses are still subject to suspension and revocation for improper conduct. *See, e.g.*, Tex. Rev. Civ. Stat. art. 179e, at § 6.18(a) ("A racetrack license issued under this article is perpetual. The commission may suspend or revoke a license as provided by this Act.").

2. Battles for prime racing dates are commonplace, and all tend to resemble the fight in *Balmoral Racing*. Almost certainly, however, the most famous struggle involved three South Florida tracks: Gulfstream Park, Hialeah Park, and Tropical Park. Hialeah opened in January 1925, and at its founding was considered the most beautiful race track in America (it later became famous for its flock of pink flamingos, which the owners imported from Cuba). When horse racing became legal in 1931, Hialeah (which until then had bribed public officials to look the other way) was joined by Tropical. In 1939, Gulfstream commenced operations.

In 1947, the Florida Legislature passed a bill granting to Hialeah in perpetuity the "middle" racing dates (i.e., January to mid-March). This was the prime part of the state's racing season (because it was the height of the tourist season), and assured Hialeah of continuing dominance. In 1971, however, Gulfstream successfully challenged the law on constitutional grounds. *See Hialeah Race Course, Inc. v. Gulfstream Racing Association, Inc.*, 245 So. 2d 625 (Fla. 1971). The Florida Supreme Court subsequently held that future dates should be assigned based on a review of seven distinct factors: the interest of the state in maximizing pari-mutuel revenues, the operator's right to turn a profit, good will, quality of horses, track facilities, geography, and management skill. *See Hialeah Race Course, Inc. v. Board of Business Regulation*, 270 So. 2d 366 (Fla. 1972).

In January 1972, Tropical, the least successful of the three tracks, folded, and its racing dates were transferred to Calder Race Course. Calder had opened in May 1971 as a summer-only track after the Florida Legislature had approved year-round racing.

Beginning in 1973, Hialeah and Gulfstream annually traded the middle dates. Neither track was happy with this arrangement, and in 1980 the Florida Legislature passed a new racing date statute. Because the law failed to provide a method for awarding dates, the Florida Supreme Court decided the Legislature had implicitly approved its seven-factor test. *See Gulfstream Park Association, Inc. v. Department of Business Regulation*, 441 So. 2d 627 (Fla. 1983). In a follow-up opinion, the court ruled that if the test failed to produce a clear choice for the middle dates in a given year, a rotation system should be used. *See Gulfstream Park Racing Association, Inc. v. Hialeah, Inc.*, 453 So. 2d 812 (Fla. 1984).

By 1987, the deteriorating conditions in and around Hialeah made Gulfstream the annual recipient of the middle dates. Hialeah sued, complaining that its geography was being unfairly held against it, but an appellate court found no impropriety. *See Hialeah, Inc. v. Department of Business Regulation*, 509 So. 2d 1290 (Fla. Dist. Ct. App. 1987). As in past years, Hialeah had been given the early dates (mid-November to the end of December), Gulfstream the middle dates, and Calder the late dates (mid-March to the end of April).

In the spring of 2001, the Florida Legislature went ahead with its longstanding plan to deregulate the state's racing dates. This proved to be the end for Hialeah, which now found itself with just one day of unopposed racing. *See* Dave Joseph, *Requiem for a Race Track*, S. Fla. Sun-Sentinel, May 23, 2001, at 1A. Ironically, the demise of Hialeah has undermined Gulfstream by creating an acute shortage of stalls, thereby forcing many owners to winter their horses elsewhere. *See further* Paul Moran, *No Hialeah Hurts Gulfstream*, Newsday, Nov. 15, 2001, at A82.

3. Pari-mutuel facilities are sometimes required to keep a certain distance from each other. In *Ocala Kennel Club, Inc. v. Rosenberg*, 725 F. Supp. 1205 (M.D. Fla. 1989), a law obligating greyhound tracks to be at least 100 miles apart was upheld as a valid exercise of the state's police power:

> The imposition of a 100-mile limitation rule serves to protect Florida's revenue base. It promotes the economic viability of existing pari-mutuel operations and in turn protects the efficacy of Florida's tax structure. Because [the rule] rationally relates to the achievement of these state interests, the Court need not consider defendants' other arguments that the statute preserves the integrity of the industry generally, or that the state has an inherent interest in regulating gambling for the purpose of serving the social welfare.

Id. at 1209. *See also Rodriguez v. Jones*, 64 So. 2d 278 (Fla. 1953) (regulation designating 20 miles as the minimum allowable distance between jai-alai frontons did not violate plaintiff's equal protection rights, even though it provided competing operator with lucrative geographical monopoly).

4. For a variety of reasons, the pari-mutuel industry has failed to attract younger bettors:

> Faced with declining on-track attendance and an unsavory image, racetracks are reinventing themselves as entertainment complexes in an effort to appeal to a generation that grew up on MTV, video games, and NFL football.

That means live music and dancing, cheerleaders, races after dark, cheap suds and drinks, and even fun and games for the kiddies.

"It's not just about being a racetrack anymore, it's about being entertainment and having the full package," said Keith Chamblin, marketing director at Hollywood Park in Inglewood, Calif.

"We want to send a singular message to the marketplace," said Rick Baedeker, senior vice president of marketing for the National Thoroughbred Racing Association (NTRA). "That message is that the track is a great place to have fun."

The NTRA, a coalition of racetracks, owners, breeders, off-track betting sites, trainers, and jockeys, was formed last April with a goal of building the NTRA brand by exposing a broader audience to thoroughbred racing.

Horse racing's popularity and image have waned since its heyday in the '40s and '50s due to a number of factors.

Competition from casinos, state lotteries and other forms of gambling have hurt. So has the racetracks' reputation as a venue frequented by "cigar-chewing guys throwing pieces of paper on the floor."

And while football, basketball and other major sports have flourished in the TV ratings, horse racing has been all but nonexistent on the small screen.

There are also factors inherent in the sport itself—like the 30 minutes of downtime between races—that make it a hard sell for young people who like their fun fast-paced and spoon-fed.

Further, betting on horses is difficult and intimidating for the novice.

Anne Burke, *Racing's Revamped Image*, Int'l Gaming & Wagering Bus., Nov. 1, 1998, at 53. *See also* Andrew Beyer, *Tampa Offers Way to Plan for the Future*, Wash. Post, Dec. 27, 2002, at D1 (decrying the lack of quality racing at most tracks).

Despite marketing themselves as family-oriented entertainment complexes, race tracks have been unable to capture the baby boomer market. As a result, operators have been left to fight over an ever smaller number of aging customers. To try to turn things around, many states have passed legislation allowing other forms of gaming to take place at pari-mutuel facilities (such as the video poker law discussed in *Livingston Downs*). To date, these efforts have failed to make much of a dent in the industry's problems. For a further discussion, *see* Richard McGowan, *Horse Racing and Casino Gambling: Mortal Enemies or Allies*, 2 Gaming L. Rev. 667 (1998), and Cassandra Ferrannini, Note, *The Sport of Kings Gambles on California Breeding Incentives*, 29 McGeorge L. Rev. 439 (1998). *See also In re Advisory Opinion to Attorney General re Authorization for County Voters to Approve or Disapprove Slot Machines Within Existing Pari-Mutuel Facilities*, 813 So. 2d 98 (Fla. 2002) (ordering citizen initiative to be removed from upcoming ballot due to various technical defects).

Problem 13

The operator of a greyhound track submitted a request for 60 racing dates, the maximum permitted by state law, but received approval for only 30. If it sues the state for failing to give it a full slate, how should the court rule? *See State ex rel. Daly v. Montana Kennel Club*, 396 P.2d 605 (Mont. 1964).

D. WORKERS

MURTHA v. MONAGHAN
148 N.Y.S.2d 615 (App. Div. 1956),
aff'd mem., 140 N.E.2d 746 (N.Y.),
cert. denied, 355 U.S. 891 (1957)

BASTOW, Justice.

The Commissioner of Harness Racing appeals from an order directing him to accept petitioner's application for a license as a mutuel clerk and to issue such license. The petitioner is employed by the Board of Education, Union Free School District No. 23, in Nassau County, as a physical education teacher and receives an annual salary of $6,700. Between the years 1947 and 1953, except during absence in the military service, petitioner was employed as a mutuel clerk at Roosevelt Raceway.

In June, 1955, petitioner filed with the New York State Harness Racing Commission a written application for a license to act as a mutuel clerk. On June 28, 1955, by written communication, counsel for the Commissioner informed petitioner that his application could not be accepted for the reason that he was a public employee earning in excess of $5,000 per year and therefore came within the ban of § 63 of the Pari-Mutuel Revenue Law. Thereafter, this proceeding was commenced to compel the issuance of the license.

Directing our attention to § 63, in so far as it applies to harness racing, we find that paragraphs (a) through (c) set up the following prohibitions as to public officers, public employees and party officials. Paragraph (a) is a complete prohibition on holding a license. Paragraph (b) prohibits the ownership or holding of a proprietary interest in a firm, association or corporation doing certain things in connection with pari-mutuel racing as follows: (1) conduct such racing; (2) conduct its occupation, trade or business at such a race meet; (3) own or lease such a race track and (4) manage such a race track. Paragraph (c) prohibits the holding of any office or employment with any firm, association or corporation falling in these four last-described categories. The prohibition of paragraph (c) was relaxed by subdivision 6 to the extent that it was made inapplicable to a public employee of a political subdivision (with certain stated exceptions) whose compensation is less than $5,000 per annum if the appropriate local legislative body authorizes such employment by suitable enactment.

The intent of the Legislature in adopting these laws becomes plain in the light of the history of the licensing statutes applicable to the two racing commissions. There was first imposed a blanket prohibition on licensing public employees. It was apparent, however, that there were many race track jobs for which no license was required or licensing by the commission was permissive. Therefore, the Legislature in effect said that public employees may not hold office or be employed by a firm or corporation that had a proprietary interest in (1) a track, (2) a business conducted at a track, (3) a landlord of a track or (4) the management of a track. However, if the compensation of such public employee was less than $5,000 and he had the approval of his public employer, then he might be employed by an employer falling in one of the four stated categories.

Directing our attention to the petitioner, we find that he is a public employee receiving a compensation of more than $5,000 annually and prior to 1954 he was employed as a mutuel clerk at a harness race track by a corporation which was licensed by the Commission to conduct pari-mutuel racing. Chapter 514 of the Laws of 1954 when enacted contained two prohibitions that prevented him from obtaining a license. First, the absolute prohibition of paragraph (a) of subdivision 1 of § 63, and second, by the indirect prohibition of paragraph (c) thereof because he was employed by a corporation licensed to conduct pari-mutuel racing as provided in paragraph (b)(1) of subdivision one of the same section. Subdivision 6 could give him no relief because his annual compensation was in excess of $5,000.

On March 15, 1954, the Governor sent a message to the Legislature with particular reference to political ownership of race track stock. It was proposed that public officers and employees and political leaders be barred from owning any interest in a racing association licensed to conduct pari-mutuel meetings at harness tracks and running tracks. It was further proposed that such persons be prohibited from selling goods or services to any licensed racing association.

As we have seen, the Legislature, by chapters 510 through 515 of the Laws of 1954, adopted even more stringent prohibitions than those contained in this proposal. The category of described persons was prohibited from holding any license from either commission and from holding any office or employment with any firm, association or corporation having a proprietary interest in a track, a business conducted at a track, the owner of a track or the management thereof. This intent of the Legislature in adopting the latter provision is not difficult to ascertain. In effect, the Legislature said that not only were public officers, public employees and political leaders barred from having a proprietary interest in a race track or its operation but such owners and operators after the purge were barred from doling out jobs to those in the marked group. This is the group in which petitioner finds himself and as to this group the prohibition has not been lifted. Moreover, the Legislature apparently determined that an exception should be made under certain conditions as to local public employees whose annual salary was less than $5,000. Information may have been before the lawmakers that, for the most part, this group obtained employment in minor jobs at a track and generally their influence in public life was not such as to be of value or assistance to the track owners and operators.

On the other hand, the Legislature in 1955 may well have determined that as to participants, such as owners of horses, trainers and grooms, no reason existed for continuing the prohibition against public officials, public employees and party officials. In addition, the Legislature may have determined to insure that persons already benefitted by subdivision 6 of § 63 would not be prohibited from working at a track because the Commission might require licenses for such employment.

The petition is dismissed.

CAMILLO v. STATE

1992 Conn. Super. LEXIS 2005 (Conn. Super. Ct. 1992)

MALONEY, Judge.

Plaintiff John J. Camillo appeals the decision of the defendant Gaming Policy Board (Board) of the defendant Department of Revenue Services (Department) which sustained the decision of the defendant Division of Special Revenue (Division) revoking the plaintiff's license as a jai alai player. The defendants revoked the plaintiff's license pursuant to General Statutes §§ 12-574(i) and (j). He appeals to this court pursuant to § 4-183.

Certain essential facts are not disputed. On March 25, 1991, the Division sent the plaintiff a notice summarily suspending his license to act as a jai alai player at the Bridgeport Jai Alai Fronton. The Division took this action as a result of its investigation of allegations that the plaintiff had wagered on a jai alai game on April 15, 1989, in violation of Regulations of State Agencies § 12-574-D26(k). As required by General Statutes § 12-574(i), the Division scheduled a hearing to be conducted in accordance with the Uniform Administrative Procedure Act, General Statutes § 4-166 et seq., on March 25, 1991. The notice to the plaintiff included the following statement:

> You, of course, may be accompanied by your attorney. If you desire more specifics and/or more time, you may request the same in writing prior to four (4) business days in advance of the scheduled hearing.

The plaintiff did not request a continuance of the hearing, nor did he request a more detailed statement of the charges. He appeared at the hearing pro se and stated that he understood that he had the right to be represented by an attorney.

The hearing was conducted by Edward F. Osswalt, Unit Chief of the Division, as designee of the Executive Director in accordance with General Statutes § 12-574(i). At the hearing, the Division produced evidence in the form of testimony and documents tending to show that on April 16, 1989, the plaintiff requested another individual, Michael Casey, to cash three winning pari-mutuel tickets that the plaintiff owned. This evidence tended to show further that Michael Casey and his brother, John Casey, did cash the tickets and remitted the proceeds, minus a "cashing fee," to the plaintiff. The tickets were on a game in which the plaintiff participated the day before, April 15, 1989, at the Bridgeport Jai Alai Fronton.

Based on the evidence summarized above, Unit Chief Osswalt concluded that the plaintiff had violated state regulations prohibiting licensed jai alai players from wagering on professional jai alai games and recommended that his license be revoked. The Executive Director of the Division adopted the recommendation and issued the final decision on July 1, 1991. On July 17, 1991, the plaintiff requested the Division to reconsider the decision. On August 8, 1991, the Division denied the request. Pursuant to General Statutes § 12-574(j), the plaintiff appealed the Division's decision to the Board. In that appeal, the plaintiff was represented by counsel, who filed briefs and made oral argument. On December 19, 1991, the Board affirmed the Division's decision and dismissed the plaintiff's appeal.

Since the decision of the defendants revoked the plaintiff's license to act as a jai alai player, a significant personal and legal interest, the court finds that the plaintiff is aggrieved within the meaning of General Statutes § 4-183 and Light Rigging Co. v. Dept. of Public Utility Control, 219 Conn. 168, 173 (1991).

In his brief, the plaintiff advances three bases for his appeal to this court. The court considers each contention separately.

The plaintiff first claims that the defendants misinterpreted the state regulation which prohibits wagering by applying it to the facts of this case, where the plaintiff acted through an agent. The applicable regulation, section 12-574-D26(k), reads as follows:

> (k) Wagering prohibited. No player under contract at a fronton, or his wife or blood relatives, may wager money or any other thing of value on the results of games played at any board licensed fronton.

The plaintiff argues that the evidence in the record proves, at most, that any wagering was done by Michael and John Casey acting as the plaintiff's agents. There is no evidence, he argues, to support the finding that he personally wagered. The plaintiff further argues that this regulation, in the context of a license revocation proceeding, is penal in nature and must be strictly construed. Therefore, he claims, the defendants erred in applying the regulation to the facts of this case because it does not specifically prohibit a player from wagering through an agent.

"Judicial review of conclusions of law reached administratively is . . . limited. The court's ultimate duty is only to decide whether, in light of the evidence, the agency has acted unreasonably, arbitrarily, illegally, or in abuse of its discretion." CL & P v. DPUC, 219 Conn. 51, 57-58 (1991). Similarly, "it is the court's practice to accord great deference to the construction given a statute by the agency charged with its construction . . . . This principle applies with even greater force to an agency's interpretation of its own duly adopted regulations." Griffin Hospital v. Commission on Hospitals & Health Care, 200 Conn. 489 (1986).

In the present case, the court concludes that the defendants' interpretation of the regulation is entirely reasonable in view of its obvious, legitimate purpose of preventing players from rigging the outcome of jai alai games for their own profit and at the expense of the public. Virtually all professional sports have similar rules and for the same purpose. Under the plaintiff's restricted interpretation of the regulation, however, whole groups of jai alai players could rig games and "wager" on the results by the simple stratagem of hiring messengers to place their bets and collect their inevitable winnings. Although there is no evidence of any such conspiracy here, the plaintiff's argument that he should be able legally to evade the prohibition merely by hiring a bagman would, if adopted, totally nullify the effect of the regulation. Statutory and regulatory interpretation must meet the test of common sense. Shelby Mutual Ins. Co. v. Della Ghelfa, 200 Conn. 630, 638 (1986). The plaintiff's argument fails that test.

The second basis of the plaintiff's appeal is that, even if the anti-wagering regulation applies to wagering conducted through an agent, the conduct which the defendants allege in this case does not come within the definition of wagering in the regulations. The applicable regulation, section 12-574-D2a(51), provides as follows:

> (51) Wagering. This shall be deemed to include both the purchasing and cashing of tickets.

Again, the plaintiff argues for a restrictive interpretation on the basis that the regulation has a punitive effect in his case. He contends, therefore, that there must be evidence that a person both purchased and cashed a ticket in order to prove that he "wagered" within the meaning of this regulation. He argues further that there is no evidence in the record in this case that shows that he purchased the tickets or how he came into possession of them. Therefore, he argues, the evidence is insufficient to establish wagering.

The plaintiff's second argument, as summarized above, is not persuasive. The defendants' interpretation of the regulation is that either of the two distinct activities, purchasing and cashing tickets, is sufficient to constitute wagering. The court agrees that such interpretation is the more reasonable. First, it best accords with the plain meaning of the text. The use of the word "include" indicates that both purchasing and cashing are contained within the definition of "wagering," so that the term is broad enough in its meaning to cover either activity alone. Secondly, the defendants' interpretation accords best with common sense. Adopting the plaintiff's view would mean that a player could avoid the prohibition against wagering by purchasing tickets and selling them or giving them away, or accepting tickets from someone else and cashing them in. In either scenario, the player would be significantly participating in the gambling enterprise, but the prohibiting regulation would be rendered essentially unenforceable. The plaintiff's interpretation would thus lead to a bizarre and unreasonable result. Under these circumstances, the court must accord great deference to the defendants' interpretation. Griffin Hospital v. Commission, supra.

The plaintiff's third argument is that the evidence was insufficient to support the defendants' finding that the tickets were owned by him. At the administrative hearing, Michael Casey testified that he received the tickets from the plaintiff and that he remitted the proceeds to the plaintiff after cashing them. In opposition, the plaintiff testified that Casey owned the tickets and he brought out that Casey had at one time told the Division's investigator that the tickets belonged to Casey. Casey then testified, again, that he received the tickets from the plaintiff and that his prior statement to the investigator was incorrect.

The plaintiff essentially asks the court to step in and resolve the factual dispute arising from the conflicting testimony of Casey and the plaintiff.

Under statute and case law, however, this court's scope of review of administrative decisions is very limited. General Statutes § 4-183 provides that "[t]he court shall not substitute its judgment for that of the agency as to the weight of the evidence on questions of fact." See also Feinson v. Conservation Commission, 180 Conn. 421, 425 (1980), and numerous cases cited therein, holding that "[t]he credibility of witnesses and the determination of factual issues are matters within the province of the administrative agency." Furthermore, "[t]he court can do no more, on the factual questions presented, than to examine the record to determine whether the ultimate findings were supported, as the statute requires, by substantial evidence." Persico v. Maher, 191 Conn. 384, 409 (1983). As summarized above, there was direct testimony by Michael Casey that he received the tickets from the plaintiff, cashed them at the plaintiff's request, and delivered the proceeds to the plaintiff. This court finds that evidence to be substantial. That being so, the defendants' decision must be affirmed notwithstanding the fact that the plaintiff presented conflicting evidence. It was for the Division's Unit Chief, as trier of the facts, not this court, to weigh the evidence and make findings of fact.

For all of the reasons set forth above, the court affirms the decision of the defendant Board.

The plaintiff's appeal is dismissed.

Notes

1. States normally require those employed at a pari-mutuel facility to undergo a background check. The rules of the Texas Racing Commission, for example, specifically list announcers, chaplains, concessionaires, and tattooers, among several dozen others, as needing licenses. See 16 Tex. Admin. Code § 311.5.

2. Licensing requirements may be general or specific, as well as discretionary or mandatory. The Colorado Racing Commission's age rule, for example, is specific and mandatory: "All applicants for license must have attained the age of 16 years." 1 Code Colo. Regs. § 208-2(10). Pennsylvania's racing regulations contain a general, discretionary statement:

> If the Commission finds that the experience, character and general fitness of the applicant are such that the participation of the person in thoroughbred horse race meets will be consistent with the public interest and with the best interests of racing generally in conformity with the purpose of the act, the Commission may grant a license.

58 Pa. Code § 163.56.

3. In most states, a person's pari-mutuel license will be revoked only because of his or her own transgressions. See, e.g., Levinson v. Washington Horse Racing Commission, 740 P.2d 898 (Wash. Ct. App. 1987). In some jurisdictions, however, violations by spouses or immediate family members are imputed to the licensee. See, e.g., Niglio v. New Jersey Racing Commission, 385 A.2d 925 (N.J. Super. Ct. App. Div. 1978).

4. To ensure that pari-mutuel contests are conducted honestly, broad powers are given to the relevant administrative agencies as well as to race officials.

See, e.g., LeRoy v. Illinois Racing Board, 39 F.3d 711 (7th Cir. 1994), *cert. denied*, 515 U.S. 1131 (1995) (upholding warrantless search of jockey's automobile); *Dimeo v. Griffin*, 943 F.2d 679 (7th Cir. 1991) (en banc) (racing board's random drug testing program did not violate the Fourth Amendment); *Luzzi v. Commonwealth*, 548 A.2d 659 (Pa. Commw. Ct. 1988) (suspension of license for cocaine possession upheld); *Vaccaro v. Joyce*, 593 N.Y.S.2d 913 (Sup. Ct. 1991) (decision to cancel race proper where track suffered computer failure); *Discenza v. New York City Racing Association, Inc.*, 509 N.Y.S.2d 454 (N.Y.C. Civ. Ct. 1986) (race officials had authority to stop wagering). *See also* David J. Marchitelli, Annotation, *Disciplinary Proceedings Against Horse Trainer or Jockey*, 59 A.L.R.5th 203 (1998).

5. Despite the numerous precautions taken to safeguard the pari-mutuel industry, cheating does occur. In October 2002, for example, the largest betting scandal in horse racing history took place when three men, who had known each other since college, correctly picked six winners during the Breeders' Cup, resulting in a $3.2 million payout. It was quickly determined that one of the culprits worked for Autotote and had exploited a flaw in its computer system. *See further* Joe Drape, *3 Charged as Bumblers Who Rigged Big Bet*, N.Y. Times, Nov. 13, 2002, at A1.

Problem 14

A race horse owner refused to pay an out-of-state veterinarian's bill, believing it was excessive. Eventually, the veterinarian went to court and obtained a default judgment against the owner. Upon hearing this, the state racing board revoked the owner's license for "financial irresponsibility." If the owner appeals, how should the court rule? *See Partridge v. State*, 895 P.2d 1183 (Colo. Ct. App. 1995).

E. EXCLUSIONS

BROOKS v. CHICAGO DOWNS ASSOCIATION, INC.
791 F.2d 512 (7th Cir. 1986)

FLAUM, Circuit Judge.

This is a case of first impression on whether under Illinois law the operator of a horse race track has the absolute right to exclude a patron from the track premises for any reason, or no reason, except race, color, creed, national origin, or sex. We find that Illinois follows the common law rule and would allow the exclusion. The court below is thus affirmed.

I

Plaintiffs are citizens of Pennsylvania who have formed a Pennsylvania partnership whose sole purpose is to pool the assets of the partners in order to place bets at horse racing tracks throughout the country. This case is about a bet they were not allowed to make.

The defendant is a private Illinois corporation licensed by the State of Illinois to conduct harness racing at Sportsman's Park race track in Cicero,

Illinois. At various times during the racing season, Sportsman's Park conducts a parimutuel pool known as "Super Bet." In order to win the Super Bet pool, one must select the first two finishers of the fifth and sixth races and the first three finishers of the seventh race. The Super Bet pool is able to increase quickly and substantially because if the pool is not won on any given day, the total amount wagered is rolled over and added to the Super Bet purse for the next racing date. For example, in April of 1985 the plaintiffs, using their method for handicapping horses, placed bets on the Super Bet totaling $60,000. They picked the right horses and took home approximately $600,000.

In late July, 1985 the president of Chicago Downs ordered two of the plaintiffs (Jeffrey Yass and Kenneth Brodie) barred from Sportsman's Park just as they were seeking to place a $250,000 wager in the Super Bet. After the plaintiffs had been barred from Sportsman's Park, the Park's counsel informed them that they would be denied entry to all future racing dates at the Park. The plaintiffs then filed suit seeking injunctive relief that would prohibit the defendant from barring them from entering the race track premises. Sportsman's Park filed a motion to dismiss the complaint on the ground that under Illinois law the operator of a proprietary race track has the absolute right to exclude a patron from the track premises for any reason except race, creed, color, national origin, or sex. The trial court agreed with the defendants and granted their motion to dismiss, from which the plaintiffs now appeal. We affirm.

II

The parties do not contest the Illinois Supreme Court's holding that a race track operator has the right to exclude patrons for good cause. But in this case, the race track argues that it should be able to exclude a patron absent any cause at all, as long as it does not do so on the basis of race, color, creed, national origin, or sex. Under the defendant's theory, because the race track is a privately owned place of amusement it may exclude someone simply for wearing a green hat or a paisley tie. It need give no reason for excluding the patron, under its version of the common law, because it is not a state-granted monopoly, but a state-regulated licensee operating on private property.

The most recent Illinois Supreme Court case to touch on this issue was Phillips v. Graham, 427 N.E.2d 550 (Ill. 1981). In Phillips several harness racing drivers, owners, and trainers were excluded by formal Order of the State Racing Board from all race tracks in the state because they had been indicted for bribery. The Illinois Supreme Court held first that the plaintiffs were not deprived of procedural due process by their exclusion from the race tracks without a prior evidentiary hearing. Second, the Court held that the authority given organization licensees (such as race tracks) to exclude occupation licensees (such as jockeys) from their private property was not an unconstitutional delegation of legislative power. Paragraph 9(e) of the Illinois Horse Racing Act of 1975 states: "The power to eject or exclude occupation licensees trainers, jockeys, owners, and others may be exercised for just cause by the organization licensee race track or Board subject to subsequent hearing by the Board, as to the propriety of said exclusion." The addition of this section to the Act followed closely on the heels of Cox v. National Jockey Club, 323 N.E.2d 104 (Ill. App. Ct. 1974) and apparently codifies its holding.

The Court in Phillips cited the appellate court holding in Cox with approval and an explanation of that case is crucial to an understanding of Phillips. The plaintiff in Cox was a jockey licensed by the Illinois Racing Board. During the course of the defendant race track's annual meeting, it excluded Cox from its track, and thus foreclosed him from accepting mounts on horses he had been under contract to ride during the meet. Cox sought injunctive relief prohibiting the track from continuing to exclude him and directing that it permit him to ride unless the track could prove "just cause" for his exclusion. The race track moved to dismiss the complaint on the ground that as a private corporation it could exclude any person from its premises or deny any person racing privileges for any reason except race, color, creed, sex, or national origin. The trial court granted the relief sought by Cox and the appellate court affirmed.

The Cox court differentiated between the right of a track to exclude a licensee and its right to bar a patron. The track had argued that its common law right to exclude a patron without reason applied equally to a licensee. Although acknowledging precedent which held that the track could exclude a patron without reason or justification, the court refused to extend that authority to cover a licensee.

The Illinois Supreme Court in Phillips found that the codification in 9(e) of the Cox holding was not an unconstitutional delegation of a recognized legislative power because there was in fact no attempted grant of legislative power to an administrative agency or private person. The authority to exclude came from the common law. The court stated:

> There is no such delegation of a recognized legislative power here. The right to exclude patrons from a private enterprise, here a racetrack, has long been recognized at common law. Though it cannot be said that § 9(e), which goes further and permits the exclusion of occupation licensees, is a precise codification of the common law right, it is clear that the authority to exclude here is not derived from some recognized legislative power, unique to the legislature, that has been delegated to organization licensees. It is simply, as the State argues, a grant of authority by the legislature.

The language of Phillips and Cox lead us to conclude that Illinois follows the common law rule regarding the exclusion of patrons, as opposed to the exclusion of licensees which is governed by the "just cause" rule codified in 9(e). Of the cases cited by the Illinois courts as demonstrating the common law rule, Madden v. Queens County Jockey Club, 72 N.E.2d 697 (N.Y.), cert. denied, 332 U.S. 761 (1947), is the most explicit and most cited. The plaintiff, "Coley" Madden, who claimed to be a professional "patron of the races," was barred from the defendant's Aqueduct Race Track under the mistaken belief that he was "Owney" Madden, reputed to be the fabled Frank Costello's bookmaker. Coley Madden brought suit for declaratory judgment and contended that as a citizen and taxpayer he had the right to enter the track and patronize the races. The defendant moved to dismiss on the ground that it had an unlimited right of exclusion. The trial court granted plaintiff's motion and entered an order enjoining the defendant from barring Coley Madden from its race track. The appellate division reversed, and the New York Court of

Appeals affirmed the appellate division's reversal of the trial court. The Court of Appeals framed the question: "Whether the operator of a race track can, without reason or sufficient excuse, exclude a person from attending its races." Its answer: "In our opinion he can; he has the power to admit as spectators only those whom he may select, and to exclude others solely of his own volition, as long as the exclusion is not founded on race, creed, color or national origin."

The court went on to explain the common law:

> At common law a person engaged in a public calling, such as innkeeper or common carrier, was held to be under a duty to the general public and was obliged to serve, without discrimination, all who sought service. On the other hand, proprietors of private enterprises, such as places of amusement and resort, were under no such obligation, enjoying an absolute power to serve whom they pleased. A race track, of course, falls within that classification.

We, too, find that the defendant in this case is not a state granted franchise or monopoly. Section 2 of the Horse Racing Act states in essence that race tracks within 35 miles of each other may not have horse races on the same day. The defendant here is granted only a license for 75 days of racing in any one year. That license is imposed only to regulate and raise revenue, as opposed to a franchise which grants a special privilege that does not belong to an individual as a matter of common right. The court in Cox held that the race track had a "quasi-monopoly" only with regard to a licensee—a jockey who was alleging that he was being denied the right to earn a livelihood—rather than a patron of the offered amusement. While we pass no judgment on the language in Cox, we note again that the relationship between the race track and licensed jockeys is substantially different than the relationship between the race track and its patrons. Any one race track may or may not have a "quasi-monopoly" (a term that is subject to many interpretations) over opportunities available to jockeys, owners, or drivers, but they do not have a true monopoly over opportunities for the plaintiffs to bet on horses. This difference is recognized and emphasized in Phillips, Cox, and the Illinois statute, and is dispositive of this case.

We also choose not to follow the arguable—but not clear—abandonment of the common law rule in New Jersey in the case of Uston v. Resorts International Hotel, Inc., 445 A.2d 370 (N.J. 1982). The defendant operated a gambling casino licensed pursuant to the New Jersey Casino Control Act. The defendant excluded Uston from the blackjack tables in its casino because of Uston's strategy of "card counting." The New Jersey Supreme Court held that the Casino Control Act gave the Casino Control Commission the exclusive authority to exclude patrons based upon their strategies for playing licensed casino games and that any common law right the defendant may have had to exclude Uston for these reasons was abrogated by the Act and outweighed by Uston's right of access.

As a policy matter, it is arguably unfair to allow a place of amusement to exclude for any reason or no reason, and to be free of accountability, except in cases of obvious discrimination. In this case, the general public is not only invited but, through advertising, is encouraged to come to the race track and wager on the races' outcome. But the common law allows the race track to exclude patrons, no matter if they come from near or far, or in reasonable reliance on representations of accessibility. We may ultimately believe that market forces would preclude any outrageous excesses—such as excluding anyone who has blond hair, or (like the plaintiffs) who is from Pennsylvania, or (even more outrageous) who has $250,000 to spend in one day of betting. But the premise of the consumer protection laws that the New Jersey Supreme Court alluded to in Uston recognizes that the reality of an imperfect market allows numerous consumer depredations. Excluding a patron simply because he is named Adam Smith arguably offends the very precepts of equality and fair dealing expressed in everything from the antitrust statutes to the Illinois Consumer Fraud and Deceptive Business Practice Act.

But the market here is not so demonstrably imperfect that there is a monopoly or any allegation of consumer fraud. Consequently, there is no such explicit legislative directive in the context of patrons attending horse races in Illinois—so the common law rule, relic though it may be, still controls. Therefore, we hold that the common law rule is the law of Illinois.

IWINSKI v. COMMONWEALTH
481 A.2d 370 (Pa. Commw. Ct. 1984)

WILLIAMS, Judge.

Michael Iwinski, an assistant horse trainer, has appealed from an order of the Pennsylvania State Horse Racing Commission (Commission) affirming his exclusion, by Eagle Downs Racing Association (Eagle Downs), from the stable area at Keystone Race Track.

On January 19, 1983, the Commission granted Mr. Iwinski a license to work at race tracks in Pennsylvania. The agency described the license as being "temporary in nature." Soon after receiving his license, Iwinski applied to the officials at Keystone Race Track for permission to work there. By a written notice dated January 26, 1983, Eagle Downs, co-owner of Keystone, advised him that he was denied admission to the stable area at the track. One of the reasons for the decision, according to the notice, was the fact that in 1980 Iwinski had been put on criminal probation in the State of Michigan for the offense of marijuana delivery. Another reason stated in the notice was that, when Iwinski applied for permission to work at Keystone, he admitted to the track's security officer that he had actually sold marijuana in connection with the 1980 drug offense.

As was further set forth in the notice from Eagle Downs, Keystone Race Track had a policy which, in part here pertinent, provided as follows: if a person has been convicted of selling or distributing a controlled dangerous substance, including marijuana, or has admitted such conduct, he will not be allowed to work at Keystone for a period of seven years after the conviction or admission.

Eagle Downs' action was appealed by Iwinski to the Commission. When the Commission affirmed following a hearing, he took a further appeal to this Court.

The appellant points to the undisputed fact that, when he was granted his license on January 19, 1983, the Commission had before it and had taken into account a statement of his criminal history—including the 1980 conviction in Michigan for marijuana delivery (his other crimes were larceny and attempted larceny). Asserting that his exclusion by Eagle Downs was for conduct which the Commission itself had considered in adjudging him fit for a license, the appellant argues that the Commission's later order affirming the action of Eagle Downs violated the doctrines of res judicata and collateral estoppel. We must note, perhaps appropriately at this point, that in the adjudication by which the Commission granted Iwinski a license, the agency found that he had "never been charged with a sale of marijuana, only with possession and delivery."

Section 213(c) of the Race Horse Industry Reform Act (Act) empowers the Commission to license a person if it finds that "the experience, character and general fitness of the applicant" are such that his participation in meets is "consistent with the public interest, convenience and necessity, and with the best interests of racing." In addition to the foregoing general standards, another provision of the Act, § 213(d), authorizes the Commission to refuse to issue a license if it finds that the applicant has been convicted of any of certain offenses, or has perpetrated certain others. It seems that Iwinski's criminal record, even with the 1980 marijuana conviction, was not deemed by the Commission to include any of the offenses which would have warranted refusing him a license under § 213(d).

One of the crucial elements of this case arises from the terms of § 215(c) of the Act, upon which Eagle Downs relied for its right to exclude the appellant. Of significance in this regard is the part of § 215(c) which states that:

> A licensed corporation may refuse admission to and eject from the enclosure of the race track operated by the corporation, any person licensed by the Commission under § 213, employed at his occupation at the race track, whose presence there is deemed detrimental to the best interests of horse racing, citing the reasons for that determination.

As is obvious from the above statutory provision, the legal right of Eagle Downs to exclude a licensed person from its track depends upon a reasoned determination that his presence there is "detrimental to the best interests of horse racing."

The appellant observes that the standard for exclusion under § 215(c) is, but for an insignificant difference in its phrasing, essentially identical to one of the factors the Commission itself must consider in the process of granting a license under § 213. That is, by force of § 213(c) of the Act, the Commission may not license a person unless it finds that the applicant's participation in horse race meets is "consistent with the best interests of racing." In his reliance on the doctrines of res judicata and collateral estoppel, the specific nature of the appellant's argument begins as follows: that since the Commission had considered his 1980 marijuana conviction when it granted him a license, the agency's decision in that respect was a binding determination that, even with the conviction, he satisfied the standards for licensing under § 213 of the Act—including the requirement that his participation be "consistent with the best interests of racing." Based on this assertion, he further argues that Eagle Downs could not use the 1980 conviction to conclude that his presence at its track was "detrimental to the best interests of horse racing." According to the appellant, such a determination by Eagle Downs had to rest on a factor that was not considered by the Commission in licensing him.

For a prior judgment to have the effect of res judicata on a subsequent suit or proceeding, there must be a concurrence of four conditions: (1) identity of issues; (2) identity of causes of action; (3) identity of persons and parties to the action; and (4) identity of the quality or capacity of the parties suing or sued. In the matter before us, the doctrine of res judicata could not apply. We need not address all of the defects in the appellant's reliance on that plea, but at least one of them is obvious: there was no identity of parties in the two proceedings before the Commission. In the proceeding that resulted in Iwinski being granted a license, the only parties were he and the Commission itself. Eagle Downs was not a party in that proceeding; and there is no basis for concluding that a relationship of privity existed between the Commission and Eagle Downs. Hence, in the subsequent proceeding concerning Iwinski's exclusion from Keystone Race Track, Eagle Downs could not be affected by a plea of res judicata.

The appellant can fare no better with the doctrine of collateral estoppel. A plea of collateral estoppel is valid if: (1) the issue decided in the prior adjudication was identical with the one presented in the later proceeding; (2) there was a final judgment on the merits; (3) the party against whom the plea is asserted was a party or in privity with a party to the prior adjudication; and (4) the party against whom it is asserted had a full and fair opportunity to litigate the issue in question in the prior proceeding. One of those elements, at the least, is missing in the case at bar. Iwinski's sole party-adversary in the proceeding concerning his exclusion from the race track was Eagle Downs. As we have already stated, Eagle Downs was not a party nor in privity with a party to the antecedent licensing adjudication. That factor alone would preclude Iwinski from asserting a plea of collateral estoppel against Eagle Downs.

One other ingredient of this case deserves mention. Eagle Downs, in exercising the power of exclusion conferred by § 215(c) of the Act, did not base its decision solely on the appellant's 1980 conviction for marijuana delivery. The exclusion was also grounded on his admission to security personnel at Keystone that he had actually sold marijuana in connection with the 1980 offense. The Commission apparently did not have the latter information when it licensed him.

For the reasons set forth in this opinion, the Commission order here for review must be affirmed.

Note

Some states have cut back on the common law right of race tracks to exclude persons. *See, e.g., Burrillville Racing Association v. Garabedian*, 318 A.2d 469 (R.I. 1974). Even in these jurisdictions, however, courts generally permit operators to bar persons whose presence would undermine public confidence. *See, e.g., Bonomo v. Louisiana Downs, Inc.*, 337 So. 2d 553 (La. Ct. App. 1976) (affirming banning from race track of person convicted of illegal bookmaking on football games). For a further discussion, *see* Carol Schultz Vento, Annotation, *Propriety of Exclusion of Persons from Horseracing Tracks for Reasons Other than Color or Race*, 64 A.L.R.5th 769 (1998).

Problem 15

Because of his alleged connections with certain persons reputed to be members of organized crime, an individual was permanently denied entry to three local tracks. If he appeals, claiming his exclusion amounts to "guilt by association," how is the court likely to rule? *See Presti v. New York Racing Association, Inc.*, 347 N.Y.S.2d 314 (Sup. Ct. 1973).

F. STAKES

STATE v. COUNTDOWN, INC.
319 So. 2d 924 (La. 1975)

DIXON, Justice.

The attorney general brought this action by the State of Louisiana to annul the charter of Countdown, Inc. and to enjoin its operation. From adverse judgments dismissing plaintiff's suit in the district court and the Court of Appeal (State of Louisiana v. Countdown, Inc., La.App., 305 So.2d 634), the State applied for writs to this court, alleging two errors:

> I. It was error to find that the business activity of Countdown is not an activity prohibited to corporations by Louisiana law.

> II. It was error to find that the activity of Countdown is not an off-track betting operation prohibited by Louisiana law.

The first specification of error is based on the prohibition of C.C. 441:

> 'A corporation can not be administrator, guardian or testamentary executor, nor fulfill any other office of personal trust. A corporation can not be imprisoned, for its existence being ideal, nobody can arrest or confine it.'

The second specification of error is based on the contention that Countdown, Inc. violates R.S. 4:147 and 149, which prohibit wagering on horse races except by a licensed parimutuel arrangement conducted in the 'race meeting grounds' or the 'enclosure of the licensee.'

Suit was filed February 11, 1974; trial was on March 15, 1974. The ledger sheet for Countdown introduced in evidence showed operations were conducted on twelve days from November 28, 1973 through January 24, 1974. The gross income totaled $611.00, for which the 'messenger fee' was $61.10, derived from an estimated three hundred transactions.

Another exhibit consisted of a collection of forms—an original and two carbon copies in each set. To each set of forms a Fair Grounds betting receipt is stapled. That receipt and the form show the date, the race, the number of the horse and the amount of the bet to win, place or show. The forms were kept for fourteen days; they contained printed 'Rules and Regulations' on the reverse side of each sheet:

1. COUNTDOWN, INC.

Countdown, Inc., is a corporation organized and existing by virtue of the laws of the State of Louisiana.

Countdown, Inc., provides agents to place bets or wagers through the parimutuel wagering system on the result of horse races conducted on the grounds of any enclosed race track which is licensed by the Louisiana State Racing Commission to conduct a race meeting or meetings.

Any money paid to Countdown, Inc., does not constitute a bet or wager but only as a grant of authority to Countdown, Inc., its agents, employees, or servants, to place such money in the parimutuel pool of any enclosed race track which is licensed by the Louisiana State Racing Commission to conduct a race meeting or meetings.

Countdown, Inc., in consideration for providing the messenger service stated above, charges a fee of ten percent (10%) of the amount to be placed in the parimutuel pool of an enclosed race track which is licensed by the Louisiana State Racing Commission to conduct a race meeting or meetings.

(1) The ten percent (10%) messenger service fee shall be collected irrespective of the official result of any horse race or races on which a patron wagers or bets.

(2) Should any such patron win, agents of Countdown, Inc., shall cash in such winning ticket at a cashier's window on the grounds of any such authorized race track and any such patron shall be paid the full sum of any such winnings in exchange for his receipt; except where Social Security Number is required to cash in such winning ticket, in which event agents of Countdown, Inc., shall deliver such winning ticket to patron in exchange for his receipt.

(3) Should any such patron lose, agents of Countdown, Inc., shall, on demand of any such patron, deliver any and all losing tickets to such patron in exchange for his receipt.

RULES AND REGULATIONS

(1) SCRATCHES.

(A) Any horse which is scratched or declared from any race which is conducted on the grounds of an authorized race track after twelve o'clock (12:00) noon on the day when such horse race or races is scheduled to run shall be deemed a 'late scratch.' With respect to a 'late scratch,' the messenger service fee of ten percent (10%) of the amount to be placed in the parimutuel pool of any such authorized race track shall be non-refundable; the amount of the wager or bet shall, however, be refunded to any such patron in exchange for his receipt.

(B) Scratch or declaration of a part of an entry, if scratched or declared after twelve o'clock (12:00) noon on the day when such horse race or races is scheduled to run, shall not revoke the agency of any duly authorized agent, employee, servant, or representative of Countdown, Inc., to place the full amount of the wager or bet on the remaining part of any such entry in the parimutuel pool of an authorized race track.

(2) JOCKEY CHANGES.

No change or transfer of jockey or jockies, if such change or transfer is made after twelve o'clock (12:00) noon on the day when any such horse race or races is scheduled to run, shall revoke the agency of any duly authorized agent, employee, servant or representative of Countdown, Inc., to place the full amount of the wager or bet on the horse selected by the patron.

(3) EQUIPMENT CHANGES.

No change of equipment (e.g., adding blinkers to equipment or discontinuing the use of them, etc.), if such change is made after twelve o'clock (12:00) noon on the day when any such horse race or races is scheduled to run shall revoke the agency of any duly authorized agent, employee, servant, or representative of Countdown, Inc., to place the full amount of the wager or bet on the horse selected by the patron.

(4) WEATHER CHANGES.

No change of weather or change of the condition of the track (e.g., fast, sloppy, good, slow, muddy) shall revoke the agency of any duly authorized agent, employee, servant, or representative of Countdown, Inc., to place the full amount of the wager or bet on the horse selected by the patron.

(5) TIME WITHIN WHICH TO COLLECT WINNINGS AND/OR LOSING TICKETS.

Any patron shall have fourteen days within which to exchange his receipt for either the full amount of his winnings or the losing tickets on the horse or horses which he selected or to claim his refund as provided for in Rule (1)(A) and Rule (6).

(6) DISCLAIMER OF WARRANTY.

For causes over which Countdown, Inc., its agent, employees, servants, or representatives may have no control (e.g., traffic jams, armed robberies, etc.), Countdown, Inc., its agents employees, servants, or representatives cannot and do not guarantee that the amount to be placed through the parimutuel pool of an authorized race track on the results of horse races conducted on the grounds of any such authorized race track will be placed in the parimutuel pool and in such event the patron shall be entitled to a refund of the total amount of his wager as well as the ten percent (10%) messenger service fee within the time period set out in Rule (5).

In the event of a winner, the testimony is that the bettor, on production of the proper receipt, would be given his winning ticket to cash at the track. A bettor who wanted Countdown to retrieve his winnings from the track could sign another form authorizing that transaction. There was only one winner in the course of the operation—an undercover policewoman.

Three police agents testified about the operation of Countdown. There is no dispute about the evidence. The only evidence offered shows that Countdown operated a messenger service only, and did not wager. It took money from customers, transported it to the track, returned with betting tickets obtained at the track, and surrendered the tickets to customers on demand.

Such an operation cannot be characterized as an 'office of personal trust' and the courts below were correct in holding C.C. 441 inapplicable.

Nor is there any merit to the State's contention that Countdown's operation constitutes betting at an off-track site prohibited by R.S. 4:149 and 171. Countdown did not bet or wager. It accepted money, carried to the track, placed the bet at pari-mutuel windows and returned the betting ticket to its office, to be retrieved by the bettor. It takes two to wager, and until Countdown reached the track with the bettor's money and bought the ticket at the parimutuel window, no bet was made.

For these reasons, the judgments of the Court of Appeal and the district court are affirmed.

MARCUS, Justice, dissenting.

I disagree with the majority opinion. In my view, the operation of Countdown, Inc., violates La.R.S. 4:149 and La.R.S. 4:171. La.R.S. 4:149 provides that the State Racing Commission shall make rules governing, permitting, and regulating the wagering on horse races under the form of mutuel wagering by patrons, known as parimutuel wagering. This statute further provides that:

> Only those persons receiving a license from the commission may conduct this type of wagering, and shall restrict this form of wagering to a space within the race meeting grounds. All other forms of wagering on the result of horse races are illegal, and all wagering on horse races outside the enclosure where horse races have been licensed by the commission is illegal.

La.R.S. 4:149 (1950), as amended, La.Acts 1968, No. 554, § 1.

La.R.S. 4:171 provides in pertinent part:

> No person shall directly or indirectly hold any horse race meeting with mutuel pool or pools making wagering on the results, without having first procured a license. No person shall wager upon the results of a horse race, except in the pari-mutuel or mutuel method of wagering when the same is conducted by a licensee and upon the grounds or enclosure of the licensee.

La.R.S. 4:171 (1950), as amended, La.Acts 1968, No. 554, § 1.

In my view, the operation of Countdown, Inc., constitutes a form of wagering on the results of a horse race outside the enclosure where horse races have been licensed by the commission. Hence, its operation violates the above statutes and should be enjoined. Accordingly, I respectfully dissent.

STATE ex rel. STENBERG v. OMAHA EXPOSITION AND RACING, INC.
644 N.W.2d 563 (Neb. 2002)

WRIGHT, Justice.

NATURE OF CASE

In this original action, the Attorney General (relator) asks the court to declare (1) that the conduct of "telephonic wagering" pursuant to Neb.Rev.Stat. §§ 2-1230 to 2-1242 (Reissue 1997) violates Neb. Const. art. III, § 24, and (2) that licenses to conduct telephonic wagering are void due to the unconstitutionality of the statutes under which they were issued. The relator also seeks to permanently enjoin the respondents from acting pursuant to licenses granted by the Nebraska State Racing Commission (Commission).

SCOPE OF REVIEW

The burden of establishing the unconstitutionality of a statute is on the one attacking its validity. Bergan Mercy Health Sys. v. Haven, 260 Neb. 846, 620 N.W.2d 339 (2000).

Statutes are afforded a presumption of constitutionality, and the unconstitutionality of a statute must be clearly established before it will be declared void. Id.

FACTS

The respondents are entities licensed by the Commission to conduct pari-mutuel wagering on live horseracing and on horseracing events conducted both within and outside the state, including simulcast wagering. Named as respondents are Omaha Exposition and Racing, Inc., which operates Horsemen's Park Racetrack in Omaha; the Nebraska State Board of Agriculture, which operates State Fair Park Racetrack in Lincoln; the Hall County Livestock Improvement Association, which operates Fonner Park Racetrack in Grand Island; the Platte County Agricultural Society, which operates Columbus Agricultural Park Racetrack in Columbus; and South Sioux City Exposition and Racing, Inc., which operates Atokad Downs Racetrack in South Sioux City. In May 2001, the Commission, acting pursuant to §§ 2-1232 and 2-1241, approved licenses for the respondents which allow them to conduct telephonic wagering at the respective racetracks. Omaha Exposition and Racing, Inc., began operating telephonic wagering pursuant to its license on October 24.

The relator asserts that a portion of 1992 Neb. Laws, L.B. 718, now codified at §§ 2-1230 to 2-1242, violates article III, § 24, which states in pertinent part:

Nothing in this section shall be construed to prohibit (a) the enactment of laws providing for the licensing and regulation of wagering on the results of horseraces, wherever run, either within or outside of the state, by the parimutuel method, when such wagering is conducted by licensees within a licensed racetrack enclosure . . . .

Sections 2-1230 to 2-1242 purport to authorize telephonic wagering which does not occur within the confines of a licensed racetrack enclosure in the state.

In Nebraska, betting on the outcome of horseraces is authorized when conducted by the parimutuel method. Bettors attempt to predict the outcome of one or more races. All wagers on any of the horses to win in a specific race constitute a pool. After deductions for taxes, for promotion of agriculture and breeder's awards, and for payment to the entity conducting the races, the amount remaining in the pool is paid out to the bettors in proportion to their bets, e.g., the winner who has wagered $20 receives 10 times as much as the winner who wagered $2. A combination of the total amount bet by all bettors and the total amount bet upon the same successful horse or combination of horses determines the amount won. A separate pool is used to collect more complicated bets, such as predicting the exact order of finish of horses in a race or of the winners in two or more races. That pool is divided among the successful bettors.

A computer known as a totalizator is used to manage the wagers. The computer continuously computes and recomputes the amount of each pool, the amount bet upon each prediction for each horse, and the amount that would theoretically be paid out for each $2 bet on each horse if the race is finished and that horse wins, places, or shows.

According to the parties, when telephonic wagering is not available, an individual who wishes to place a bet on a horserace is required to go to a licensed racetrack; select the race, the horse, and the order of finish; and then place the bet at a terminal station, which is either operated by the bettor or a parimutuel clerk at a parimutuel window. When the bet is entered into the totalizator, a ticket showing the transaction is issued and given to the bettor. If the bettor is successful, the ticket is presented to the racetrack for payment.

As a result of the Commission's issuance of licenses for telephonic wagering, a person outside the confines of a licensed racetrack enclosure may place a telephone call to a racetrack and give instructions to an employee of the racetrack concerning the wager of money that the individual has on deposit at a telephone deposit center in his or her own deposit account. After the racetrack employee at the telephone deposit center has received a call and determined that the individual has sufficient funds in the deposit account, the employee places the wager on behalf of the caller. The wager is entered into the totalizator, which records the transaction and places the money in the applicable parimutuel pool. Any winnings are credited to the individual's deposit account, and any losses are deducted from the account. The employee is allowed to enter a wager only if the individual has sufficient funds available in the deposit account at the time the wager is placed by the employee.

ISSUES BEFORE COURT

The court is asked to determine (1) whether the authorization of telephonic wagering on horseraces pursuant to §§ 2-1230 to 2-1242 violates article III, § 24, which authorizes parimutuel wagering on the results of horseraces within or outside the state only "when such wagering is conducted by licensees within a licensed racetrack enclosure"; (2) whether licenses issued by the

Commission authorizing the respondents to conduct telephonic wagering are void due to the unconstitutionality of the statutes under which they were issued; and (3) whether the respondents should be permanently enjoined from acting pursuant to the telephonic wagering licenses issued by the Commission.

ANALYSIS

L.B. 718

The statutes in question were passed by the Legislature as 1992 Neb. Laws, L.B. 718. The Legislature stated that "horseracing, horse breeding, and parimutuel wagering industries are important sectors of the agricultural economy of the state, provide substantial revenue for state and local governments, and employ many residents of the state." § 2-1230(1)(a). Teleracing facilities provide a potential for strengthening the horseracing industry and its economic contributions to the state. § 2-1230(1)(b). The Legislature found that "it is in the best interests of the state to encourage experimentation with parimutuel wagering through licensed teleracing facilities" and telephonic wagering. § 2-1230(1)(b) and (c). The experimentation would determine whether teleracing and telephonic wagering would promote growth of the horseracing industry and provide additional revenue to the state. § 2-1230(1)(d). The Legislature also found that teleracing and telephonic wagering should be authorized and regulated so that it would not jeopardize horseracing or employment opportunities. § 2-1230(1)(e).

Telephonic wagering is defined as "the placing of parimutuel wagers by telephone to a telephone deposit center at a licensed racetrack as authorized by the commission." § 2-1231(5). A teleracing facility is "a detached, licensed area occupied solely by a licensee for the purpose of conducting telewagering and containing one or more betting terminals, which facility is either owned or under the exclusive control of the licensee during the period for which it is licensed." § 2-1231(6). Telewagering is "the placing of a wager through betting terminals electronically linked to a licensed racetrack, which . . . instantaneously transmits the wagering information to the parimutuel pool for acceptance and issues tickets as evidence of such wager." § 2-1231(7).

At the present time, the Commission issues licenses to racetracks for the operation of telephonic wagering facilities. § 2-1232. A licensee may deduct up to 5 percent from the winnings of any winning ticket purchased through telephonic wagering. § 2-1236. A licensed racetrack that conducts live races may establish a telephonic wagering system if the racetrack establishes and maintains a telephone deposit center. All wagers must be entered into the parimutuel pool and are subject to all laws and conditions applicable to any other wagers. § 2-1239.

Under the law, only the holder of the deposit account may place a telephonic wager. § 2-1240. Any violation of that rule constitutes a Class II misdemeanor. Id. Telephonic wagering is allowed at licensed racetracks which conduct either intrastate simulcasting or interstate simulcasting as approved by the Commission. § 2-1241. The racetracks must pay one-half of 1 percent of the amount wagered through telephonic wagering to the Department of Revenue for credit to the Commission's cash fund. § 2-1242.

CONSTITUTIONALITY OF L.B. 718

This court has previously been asked to consider the constitutionality of portions of L.B. 718. In 1994, upon an original action filed by the relator, we held that the provisions of L.B. 718 which authorized teleracing facilities to conduct telewagering were unconstitutional in violation of article III, § 24. See State ex rel. Stenberg v. Douglas Racing Corp., 246 Neb. 901, 524 N.W.2d 61 (1994).

Douglas Racing Corp. was licensed to operate a teleracing facility in Bennington, Nebraska, at which terminals were electronically linked to its totalizator located in Omaha. The bets were entered by either the bettor or the parimutuel clerk and then sent to the totalizator at the racetrack. The bettors received tickets as evidence of their wagers. We held that the relator had met the burden to establish that certain statutes were unconstitutional to the extent they authorized telewagering.

In Douglas Racing Corp., the relator argued that telewagering at a teleracing facility was unconstitutional because parimutuel wagering on horseraces must be conducted within a licensed racetrack enclosure and that telewagering was equivalent to offtrack betting, which was not constitutionally authorized. The respondent unsuccessfully asserted that because the licensee conducted his end of the wagering within the confines of the licensed racetrack, telewagering was constitutional.

We concluded that article III, § 24, was unambiguous and required no construction. State ex rel. Stenberg v. Douglas Racing Corp., supra, citing State ex rel. Spire v. Conway, 238 Neb. 766, 472 N.W.2d 403 (1991). The Constitution's provision that parimutuel wagering is authorized only when conducted within a licensed racetrack enclosure "plainly requires that (1) the wagering must be conducted by an entity licensed to do so and (2) the wagering must be conducted by licensees at a racetrack enclosure which is licensed to operate horseraces." Douglas Racing Corp., 246 Neb. at 906, 524 N.W.2d at 64. Wagering which takes place outside a licensed racetrack enclosure or a detached facility "cannot logically occur within a licensed racetrack enclosure as required by our Constitution." Id. We determined that telewagering at teleracing facilities was the functional equivalent of offtrack betting, which was not conducted within a licensed racetrack enclosure and which violated the state Constitution. Id.

We held that Douglas Racing Corp.'s license for the operation of the Bennington facility was void because it was licensed pursuant to an unconstitutional statute. We enjoined the respondent from acting pursuant to the license issued by the Commission. While we held that Neb.Rev.Stat. §§ 2-1203, 2-1203.01, 2-1207, 2-1208, 2-1216, 2-1221, 2-1222, and 2-1230 through 2-1242 (Cum.Supp.1994) were all unconstitutional to the extent they authorized telewagering at teleracing facilities, we did not address any other portions of L.B. 718.

Here, we are asked to consider the remainder of L.B. 718 as it purports to authorize telephonic wagering. We first address whether the remainder of L.B. 718 is severable from the provisions previously held to be unconstitutional. Several factors must be considered in determining whether an unconstitutional provision is severable from the remainder of a statute:

(1) whether, absent the invalid portion, a workable plan remains; (2) whether the valid portions are independently enforceable; (3) whether the invalid portion was such an inducement to the valid parts that the valid parts would not have passed without the invalid part; (4) whether severance will do violence to the intent of the Legislature; and (5) whether a declaration of separability indicating that the Legislature would have enacted the bill absent the invalid portion is included in the act.

Duggan v. Beermann, 249 Neb. 411, 427-28, 544 N.W.2d 68, 78 (1996), quoting Jaksha v. State, 241 Neb. 106, 486 N.W.2d 858 (1992).

There is no dispute between the parties concerning the severability of L.B. 718. The relator suggests that although L.B. 718 did not include a severability clause, the provisions relating to telephonic wagering are severable because a workable plan remains even if telewagering is prohibited. The provisions related to telephonic wagering are independently enforceable, and it does not appear that passage of telewagering was contingent upon or an inducement to enact the telephonic wagering portions. Experimentation with parimutuel wagering through both teleracing facilities and telephonic wagering was authorized in § 2-1230(2). The relator asserts that the holding in State ex rel. Stenberg v. Douglas Racing Corp., 246 Neb. 901, 524 N.W.2d 61 (1994), does not preclude severing the invalid provisions concerning telewagering from the provisions concerning telephonic wagering. Thus, we conclude that it is possible to sever the telewagering provisions from the telephonic wagering provisions.

We next examine whether telephonic wagering is unconstitutional. The burden of establishing the unconstitutionality of a statute is on the one attacking its validity. Bergan Mercy Health Sys. v. Haven, 260 Neb. 846, 620 N.W.2d 339 (2000). Statutes are afforded a presumption of constitutionality, and the unconstitutionality of a statute must be clearly established before it will be declared void. Id. Constitutional provisions, like statutes, are not open to construction as a matter of course; construction of a constitutional provision is appropriate only when it has been demonstrated that the meaning of the provision is not clear and that construction is necessary. State ex rel. Stenberg v. Douglas Racing Corp., supra.

As noted earlier, article III, § 24, does not prohibit wagering on horseracing by the parimutuel method "when such wagering is conducted by licensees within a licensed racetrack enclosure." The key issue here is whether telephonic wagering occurs within a licensed racetrack enclosure.

Section 2-1231(5) defines telephonic wagering as "the placing of parimutuel wagers by telephone to a telephone deposit center at a licensed racetrack" as authorized by the Commission. For purposes of this opinion, the person placing the wager is not at the racetrack, but is calling from a telephone away from the facility. The parties stipulated that "a person located outside the confines of a racetrack will be allowed to place a call to a licensed racetrack enclosure to give instructions to an employee of the racetrack concerning the wager of money that the individual has on deposit at a telephone deposit center."

In attempting to allow different forms of parimutuel wagering, the Legislature stated that "[w]agers placed . . . by approved telephonic wagering as authorized by sections 2-1230 to 2-1242 shall be deemed to be wagers placed and accepted within the enclosure of any racetrack." See § 2-1207 (Reissue 1997). However, as the relator notes, the Legislature may not circumvent or nullify the constitution by defining terms in statutes. In MAPCO Ammonia Pipeline v. State Bd. of Equal., 238 Neb. 565, 571, 471 N.W.2d 734, 739 (1991), cert. denied 508 U.S. 960, 113 S.Ct. 2930, 124 L.Ed.2d 681 (1993), we held that the Legislature's "power to define [terms] is limited, since (1) the Legislature cannot abrogate or contradict an express constitutional provision and (2) the legislative definition must be reasonable, and cannot be arbitrary or unfounded."

Pursuant to stipulation, under telephonic wagering, the person making the wager calls the licensed racetrack directly to instruct an employee on the placing of a wager. Thus, it is undisputed that the person placing the call is outside the licensed racetrack enclosure.

Nebraska's Constitution is not a grant, but, rather, is a restriction on legislative power, and the Legislature is free to act on any subject not inhibited by the constitution. State ex rel. Stenberg v. Douglas Racing Corp., 246 Neb. 901, 524 N.W.2d 61 (1994). The question is whether the wager is placed within the licensed racetrack enclosure when the telephone call is initiated outside the racetrack enclosure. Simply stated, does the constitution require that the person making the call to the licensee also be located within the licensed racetrack enclosure?

The respondents argue that the constitution requires only that the licensee's activity in conducting wagering on horseraces occur within a licensed racetrack enclosure. This is distinguished from wagers made at a teleracing facility, where at least a part of the licensee's activity occurs outside the racetrack enclosure. They assert that the wager occurs within the confines of the racetrack enclosure because the wager is placed by a racetrack employee pursuant to instructions from a person outside the enclosure. They conclude that it is only the actions of the licensee's employee that constitute the placing of the wager.

The respondents argue that telephonic wagering is substantially different from telewagering. They assert that the only action taken by a person who is outside the racetrack enclosure is to give instructions to an employee of the licensed racetrack, who then places the wager from within the enclosure. In their brief, they claim that telephonic wagering is conducted every day by persons who go to the racetrack with a cellular telephone and place wagers for friends who are located outside the racetrack enclosure. They argue that the wager occurs only when the person inside the racetrack enclosure places the wager with the licensee.

The relator argues that both telephonic wagering and telewagering involve the same conduct—placing wagers on horseraces from an offtrack location. The relator claims that it is the caller who directs the racetrack employee to follow his instructions and that, therefore, it is the offtrack caller who is engaged in wagering on the horserace.

Minnesota has faced a similar challenge to its constitution, which was amended in 1982 to provide that " '[t]he legislature may authorize on-track parimutuel betting on horseracing in a manner prescribed by law.' " Rice v. Connolly, 488 N.W.2d 241, 244 (Minn.1992). In 1985, the Minnesota Racing Commission adopted rules implementing a telephone account wagering system, in which account holders maintained a minimum balance against which wagers were debited and winnings were credited. The account holder telephoned a licensed employee at a racetrack to place and record wagers on behalf of the account holder. "[T]he wagerer need not be present at the racetrack or a teleracing facility—all that is required is access to a telephone." Id. at

When asked whether the constitution "contemplate[d] other than on-track, i.e., on the racetrack premises, parimutuel betting," the Minnesota Supreme Court found that it did not. See id. The court found that "[i]n its literal sense, the word 'on' as a part of the phrase 'on-track' is more precisely defined as 'at' to denote a location for the placement of a parimutuel bet." Id. at 247. The state's voters had specifically approved " 'on-track parimutuel betting on horseracing,' " and the court found, as a practical matter, that "bets not physically placed at the racetrack cannot be, by definition, 'on-track,' no matter how they are transmitted to the track, electronically recorded or accepted into the pool of funds."

The Minnesota court noted, as the respondents had pointed out, that advances in technology facilitated remote wagering. However, the court found that its own mandate required it to "refrain from expansive interpretation by looking beyond the clear, unambiguous and ordinary meaning of the language of the constitutional provision." Id. at 248. It held: "Wagering at facilities remote from the racetrack or by telephonic means are beyond the scope of the activities authorized by the voters and are therefore impermissible." Id.

Following the rationale of the Minnesota Supreme Court, resolution of the case at bar is relatively simple. In the context of telephonic wagering, wagers are not placed by a licensee until the licensee has been instructed to do so by a caller, and the instructions do not originate from within a licensed racetrack enclosure. We conclude the constitution requires that the instructions to place the wager must originate from within the licensed racetrack enclosure.

Nebraska voters have previously rejected an attempt by the Legislature to change the constitutional provisions concerning parimutuel betting. In 1995, the Legislature adopted L.R. 24CA, which placed before the voters a constitutional amendment proposing the elimination of the location requirement in article III, § 24. The amendment provided that parimutuel wagering on racehorses could be conducted by licensees "at such locations and by such means as are authorized by the Legislature." The introducer's statement of intent noted this court's decision in State ex rel. Stenberg v. Douglas Racing Corp., 246 Neb. 901, 524 N.W.2d 61 (1994), and stated that L.R. 24CA would delete the location provision and provide the Legislature with the authority to determine the location and means of wagering on horseraces. See Statement of Intent, L.R. 24CA, General Affairs Committee, 93d Leg., 2d Sess. (Jan. 23, 1995). At the general election in November 1996, the constitutional amendment was defeated by a vote of 388,462 against and 236,600 in favor.

Nebraska's Constitution permits wagers on horseracing when the "wagering is conducted by licensees within a licensed racetrack enclosure." See Neb. Const. art. III, § 24. As this court held in Douglas Racing Corp., the constitutional language allows wagering only by those who are within a racetrack enclosure. Telephonic wagering differs from telewagering only as to the form used to transmit the wager. It is a distinction without a difference. Telephonic wagering violates the constitution because it does not occur within a licensed racetrack enclosure. The relator has met the burden of establishing that the telephonic wagering statutes are unconstitutional.

CONCLUSION

We have held that "[a]n unconstitutional statute is a nullity, is void from its enactment, and is incapable of creating any rights or obligations." Douglas Racing Corp., 246 Neb. at 906, 524 N.W.2d at 65. The statutes purporting to authorize telephonic wagering, §§ 2-1230 to 2-1242, are unconstitutional. The licenses issued to the respondents to conduct telephonic wagering are void because they were issued pursuant to these statutes. The respondents are permanently enjoined from acting pursuant to the licenses issued by the Commission, and judgment is entered for the relator.

Notes

1. For other cases like *Countdown, see* William B. Johnson, Annotation, *Validity, Construction, and Application of Statute or Ordinance Prohibiting or Regulating Use of Messenger Services to Place Wagers in Pari-Mutuel Pool*, 78 A.L.R.4th 483 (1990).

2. Although the court in *Stenberg* did not find them authorized, a number of states have established off-track betting ("OTB") systems that allow patrons to place wagers without having to go to the race track. While the goal of such systems is to make pari-mutuel racing more attractive, the industry has not always supported such efforts. In *Finger Lakes Racing Association, Inc. v. New York State Off-Track Pari-Mutuel Betting Commission*, 282 N.E.2d 592 (N.Y.), *appeal dismissed*, 409 U.S. 1031 (1972), for example, a group of track owners believed the introduction of OTB in New York would reduce their income. They therefore sued, arguing the government's plan constituted an illegal taking of their property. In rejecting this claim, the court noted the statute required tracks to receive a portion of all OTB revenues.

3. "Simulcasting" refers to the practice of broadcasting races being held in remote (usually out-of-state) locations and offering patrons the opportunity to bet on them. Congress enacted the Interstate Horseracing Act of 1978, 15 U.S.C. §§ 3001-3007, to both legalize simulcasting and prohibit it in the absence of local permission. A First Amendment challenge to the statute was turned back in *Kentucky Division, Horsemen's Benevolent & Protective Association, Inc. v. Turfway Park Racing Association, Inc.*, 20 F.3d 1406 (6th Cir. 1994). For a further discussion of the Act, *see* M. Shannon Bishop, Note, *And They're Off: The Legality of Interstate Pari-Mutuel Wagering and Its Impact on the Thoroughbred Horse Industry*, 89 Ky. L.J. 711 (2000-2001).

4. When the New York legislature decided to tax simulcasts, a coalition of licensees filed suit (because the levy made transmissions of their races more

costly and therefore less desirable to out-of-state tracks). Although the attorney general argued the tax simply sought to make interstate commerce bear a burden already borne by intrastate commerce, the court found it to be discriminatory. *See Yonkers Racing Corporation v. State*, 705 N.Y.S.2d 193 (Sup. Ct. 2000).

5. During the 2001 California energy crisis, state power authorities ordered a cut back on the number of horse races (to conserve electricity). This severely crippled the industry and led to an ultimately successful effort to gain additional simulcasting dates. *See* Holly Jo Bohannan, Note, *Horse Racing in the Dark? Legislation to Compensate Horse Racing Associations for Decreased Number of Wager-Accepted Races Due to Power Crisis*, 33 McGeorge L. Rev. 369 (2002).

Problem 16

A jockey, not realizing the race had been declared a "false start," had his horse run the entire length of the track. Although the owner was given the option of scratching the horse when the race was re-run 30 minutes later, she declined, and it finished out of the money. Do these facts give rise to a cause of action on behalf of any patron? *See Shapiro v. Queens County Jockey Club*, 53 N.Y.S.2d 135 (N.Y.C. Mun. Ct. 1945).

G. WINNINGS

REGISTER v. OAKLAWN JOCKEY CLUB, INC.
821 S.W.2d 475 (Ark. 1991)

DUDLEY, Justice.

We grant rehearing in this case and affirm the ruling of the trial court. The facts were accurately set out in the original opinion, Register v. Oaklawn Jockey Club, Inc., 306 Ark. 318, 319, 811 S.W.2d 315, 316 (1991) as follows:

> On February 10, 1989, Mr. Register attempted to place a Classix wager, where the bettor correctly selects the winning horse in six consecutive races, at Oaklawn Park in Hot Springs. When Mr. Register attempted to place his bet, the Amtote machine failed to issue a ticket conforming to his designated selections. Upon inquiry, Mr. Register was erroneously advised by Oaklawn's ticketing clerk that one of the horses he had selected had been withdrawn from its race. Mr. Register subsequently chose another horse and made his bet. At the conclusion of the six races, Mr. Register had correctly selected five winning horses. Apparently, though, the horse that Mr. Register had been told had been withdrawn had not been "scratched" and was in fact the winner of its race. Had Mr. Register's original wager been accepted, he would have been the holder of a winning ticket to a major share in the Classix.

The "Major Share" of the Classix pool (75% of the net amount in the pool) that day was $56,165.40, which was paid to the holder of one winning ticket issued for that wager. Mr. Register filed suit to recover one-half of that amount, $28,082.70. The trial court granted the appellees' motion for summary judgment, and Mr. Register appeals and alleges that the trial court erred in granting the summary judgment on the following bases: 1) Oaklawn and Amtote owed him a duty to use ordinary care, 2) Oaklawn and Amtote owed him a contractual duty on theories of implied contract, quasi-contract, and third party beneficiary, and 3) his cause of action is not barred by the Arkansas State Racing Commission Rules.

We affirmed the trial court's granting of summary judgment on the counts of implied contract, quasi-contract, and third party beneficiary, but reversed the trial court's granting of summary judgment on the count alleging negligence. We held that Oaklawn and Amtote owed Mr. Register a duty to use ordinary care in taking his bet and, as a result, Mr. Register had stated a cause of action sounding in tort.

After reading the briefs submitted to us on the petition for rehearing, we have concluded that we erred in reversing the trial court on the negligence count. That error came about in the following way. The trial court held that statutes and regulations of the Arkansas State Racing Commission barred the negligence count. Mr. Register, in his original appellant's brief, argued that the regulations did not bar the negligence claim, but he failed to abstract the regulations. Both Oaklawn and Amtote cited the statutes and quoted the regulations in the argument part of their original appellees' briefs but, even so, we refused to consider them because appellant Register had not abstracted them. That was error on our part. We should have considered the regulations for either of two reasons. First, they were set out in the appellees' brief, and second, courts take judicial notice of regulations of state agencies which are duly published. Webb v. Bishop, 242 Ark. 320, 413 S.W.2d 862 (1967). Unfortunately, we held: "Finally, Mr. Register argues that his cause of action is not barred by the Arkansas State Racing Commission Rules. However, these rules have not been included in the abstract, and we are unable to address the issue." Register v. Oaklawn Jockey Club, Inc., 306 Ark. at 321, 811 S.W.2d at 317-18 (citing Burgess v. Burgess, 286 Ark. 497, 696 S.W.2d 312 (1985)). Then, instead of affirming the trial court's holding that the statutes and regulations barred the negligence claim, we held that the trial court erred and that Mr. Register had stated a common law claim on that one count. Once the statutes and regulations on the negligence count are considered, it becomes apparent that the trial court ruled correctly, and we are the court that erred. Accordingly, we grant rehearing, modify the original opinion, and now affirm the trial court on the negligence count.

In earlier times all gaming contracts were against the public policy of this State. Our public policy was strong, so strong that since the Revised Statutes of 1838, we have had a statute that provides a losing bettor can maintain a suit to recover his losses, but a winning bettor may not do likewise because his contract is void. Ark.Code Ann. § 16-118-103(a) and (b)(1) (1987). In construing this statute we held that it meant that a winning wager on a horse race is illegal and void. McLain v. Huffman, 30 Ark. 428 (1875). Since a winning wager was illegal and void, there was no common law duty of care owed to a person making a wager.

Our law so continued until 1956, when the voters of Arkansas adopted the 46th Amendment to the Constitution of Arkansas which provides: "Horse racing and pari-mutuel wagering thereon shall be lawful in Hot Springs, Garland County, Arkansas, and shall be regulated by the General Assembly." The General Assembly has now regulated pari-mutuel wagering and has expressly provided for the disposition of wagering money as follows:

> Excepting only the moneys retained for the use and benefit of the franchise holder, the amounts paid to the commission for the use and benefit of the State of Arkansas, the amount paid to the commission for deposit in the Arkansas Racing Commission Purse and Awards Fund, and the amount paid to a city, town, or county as provided in this subchapter, all moneys received by the franchise holder from wagers pursuant to this subchapter shall be paid over to bettors holding winning pari-mutuel tickets in accordance with the provisions and at those times specified in the various race programs written by the franchise holder for the racing meet, as their respective interests may appear, upon presentation of the tickets.

Ark.Code Ann. § 23-110-406(a) (1987). The meaning of the statute is clear. All wagering money received by Oaklawn shall be paid over to bettors holding winning tickets.

In addition, Ark.Code Ann. § 23-110-405(d)(2) (1987), in pertinent part provides, "There shall be no wagering on the results of any races except under the pari-mutuel or certificate method of wagering as provided for in this section . . . ." Again, it is clear that the General Assembly intends for all money received from wagers to be paid over to the bettors, subject to the other provisions of the statute.

Rule 2416 of the Arkansas State Racing Commission Rules and Regulations Governing Horse Racing in Arkansas (1989), provides:

> Any claim by a person that a wrong ticket has been delivered to him must be made before leaving the mutuel ticket window. No claims shall be considered thereafter and no claim shall be considered for tickets thrown away, lost, changed, destroyed or mutilated beyond identification. Payment of wagers will be made only on presentation of appropriate pari-mutuel tickets.

Classix wagers are governed by Rule 2460(D) as follows:

> (1) The net amount in the Classix pari-mutuel pool will be divided into the Major Share (75%) and the Minor (Consolation) Share (25%).

> (a) The Major Share (75%) will be distributed among the holders of Classix tickets which correctly designate the official winner in each of the six races comprising the Classix.

> (b) The Minor Share (25%) will be distributed among the holders of the Classix tickets which correctly designate the most official winners, but fewer than six, of the six races comprising the Classix.

In summary, pari-mutuel wagering is now authorized by the Constitution of the State of Arkansas and "shall be regulated by the General Assembly." The General Assembly has enacted statutes heavily regulating such wagering, has created the Arkansas State Racing Commission, and has authorized it to promulgate rules and regulations. That Commission has promulgated rules and regulations concerning Classix wagering. Under the statutes and regulations, a bettor must hold a pari-mutuel ticket that correctly designates the winner of all six races in order to receive any money from the Classix Major Share Pool.

All other jurisdictions that have considered similar statutes and regulations have concluded that common law negligence claims such as the one now before us are barred. Bourgeois v. Fairground Corp., 480 So.2d 408 (La.App.1985); Seder v. Arlington Park Race Track Corp., 134 Ill.App.3d 512, 89 Ill.Dec. 657, 481 N.E.2d 9 (1985); Valois v. Gulfstream Park Racing Ass'n, 412 So.2d 959 (Fla.App.1982); Hochberg v. New York City Off-Track Betting Corp., 74 Misc.2d 471, 343 N.Y.S.2d 651 (1973), aff'd, 43 A.D.2d 910, 352 N.Y.S.2d 423 (1974).

In holding no liability on a negligence claim in a case almost identical to the one at bar, the court, in Seder v. Arlington Park Race Track Corp., 134 Ill.App.3d 512, 89 Ill.Dec. 657, 659-60, 481 N.E.2d 9, 11-12 (1985), relied on a comparable statute and wrote:

> [T]he only legislatively authorized way for a patron at a racetrack to recover money based upon the outcome of a horse race is through the pari-mutuel or certificate system. (Ill.Rev.Stat.1983, ch. 8, pars. 37-26.) . . . The Act also establishes a board to supervise the pari-mutuel system and to prescribe rules, regulations and conditions governing the conduct of the races. Under the rules and regulations adopted by the board, it is clear that in order to receive any funds from the sweep six wagering pool, a patron must hold a pari-mutuel ticket which correctly designates the winner of the six races. See Illinois Racing Board Rules B5.14, B17.3.

In Valois v. Gulfstream Park Racing Ass'n, 412 So.2d 959, 960 (Fla.App.1982), in affirming the dismissal of a complaint which included a negligence count, the court cited the applicable regulation that provided, "[p]ayment of winning pari-mutuel tickets shall be made only upon presentation and surrender of such tickets. No claims shall be allowed for lost or destroyed winning tickets." It additionally cited, but did not apply, a statute enacted after the occurrence of the alleged negligent act as expressing the public policy of the state that there should be no recovery for such a claim.

In Hochberg v. New York Off-Track Betting Corp., 74 Misc.2d 471, 343 N.Y.S.2d 651, 656 (1973), the court held, "Defendant, in this case, owes no duty to the plaintiff or any other OTB [New York City Off-Track Betting Corporation] bettor with respect to the accuracy of the information and neither plaintiff nor any other bettor is entitled to rely on the information and hold defendant liable for any mistakes therein." In so holding the court relied on a statute which provided that "all sums deposited in any off-track pari-mutuel pools shall be distributed to the holders of winning tickets therein . . . ." Id., 343 N.Y.S.2d at 655.

In conclusion, we erred in not considering the statutes and regulations in our original opinion. Upon considering them we now hold, as have all other jurisdictions having similar statutes and regulations, that without the presentation of a winning Classix ticket, a bettor is precluded from asserting a claim sounding in either tort or contract. Accordingly, rehearing is granted, the original opinion of this court is modified, and the decision of the trial court is affirmed.

HOLT, Chief Justice, dissenting.

The petitioner, American Totalisator Co., Inc. (Amtote), submits its petition for rehearing on the basis that this court should reconsider its analysis of the decisions of courts in other jurisdictions. Amtote makes two assertions: 1) the other courts relied on statutes or rules and regulations virtually identical to those in effect in Arkansas, and 2) the plaintiff in every one of the five cited cases attempted to recover on a negligence theory, as well as a contract theory, and the negligence claim was rejected in each case.

Arkansas Sup.Ct. R. 20(g) states as follows:

> The petition for rehearing should be used to call attention to specific errors of law or fact which the opinion is thought to contain. Counsel are expected to argue the case fully in the original briefs, and the brief on rehearing is not intended to afford an opportunity for a mere repetition of the argument already considered by the court.

Amtote essentially requests that this court reassess its analysis of the decisions of courts in other jurisdictions. In its opinion of July 15, 1991, this court stated, "The existence of a duty depends upon whether a relation exists between the parties that the community will impose a legal obligation upon one for the benefit of the other. Under our well-established principles of common law duty and the facts before us, we find that a duty existed between the appellees and Mr. Register."

In addressing the parties' arguments on appeal, this court also noted that "Oaklawn and Amtote's reliance on cases decided in other jurisdictions is misplaced in that those cases generally had statutes or rules and regulations limiting tort liability or dealt with the contractual theory of liability."

Given the court's phrasing in finding a duty owed by Amtote to Mr. Register, and analysis of the decisions of other jurisdictions, it is apparent to the dissent that this court addressed Amtote's extensive appellate arguments.

In our previous opinion, we declined to reach Mr. Register's final argument that his cause of action was not barred by the Arkansas State Racing Commission Rules inasmuch as he had failed to abstract them and noted that Amtote likewise had failed to properly supplement the abstract with the rules. Granted, we were partially wrong in this regard. Amtote, in its original brief, presented Rules 2416 and 2460(D) of the Arkansas State Racing Commission Rules and Regulations (ed. 1989), covering horse racing in this state, to support its argument that Mr. Register's cause of action is barred by the Racing Commission rules.

Rule 2416 provides as follows:

> Any claim by a person that a wrong ticket has been delivered to him must be made before leaving the mutuel ticket window. No claim shall be considered thereafter and no claim shall be considered for tickets thrown away, lost, changed, destroyed or mutilated beyond identification. Payment of wagers will be made only on presentation of appropriate pari-mutuel tickets.

Rule 2460(D) provides that the Classix pari-mutuel pool shall be handled as follows:

(1) The net amount in the Classix pari-mutuel pool will be divided into the Major Share (75%) and the Minor (Consolation) Share (25%).

(a) The Major Share (75%) will be distributed among holders of Classix tickets which correctly designate the official winner in each of the six races comprising the Classix.

(b) The Minor Share (25%) will be distributed among the holders of Classix tickets which correctly designate the most official winners, but fewer than six, of the six races comprising the Classix.

In its petition for rehearing, Amtote again provided us with Rules 2416 and 2460(D), noting that it had cited "these rules in its brief, and this court may take judicial notice of rules and regulations promulgated pursuant to statutory authorization and brought to the attention of this court."

Taking judicial notice of Rules 2416 and 2460(D), they may well limit contractual liability; however, they do not restrict tort liability. The fact still remains that under our well-established principles of common law duty and the facts before us, a duty existed between Amtote and Mr. Register. Accordingly, I disagree with the court's present finding that our statutes and regulations preclude a claim of tort liability of Oaklawn Jockey Club, Inc. and Amtote.

Consequently, Amtote impermissibly attempts to reargue the interpretation of cases decided in other jurisdictions and does not point out any specific errors of law or fact thought to be contained in this opinion.

I respectfully dissent to the granting of the petition for rehearing.

SZADOLCI v. HOLLYWOOD PARK OPERATING COMPANY
17 Cal. Rptr. 2d 356 (Ct. App. 1993)

ORTEGA, Acting Presiding Justice.

We affirm the summary judgment granted in favor of defendants.

BACKGROUND

James Farenbaugh went to Hollywood Park on June 14, 1989, and put down $4,860 on a "Pick-9" ticket. A Pick-9 requires the bettor to pick the winners of the nine races run that day. Picking all nine winners results in a large return.

But Farenbaugh had something else in mind. He cancelled the ticket and bribed the parimutuel clerk to let him keep the worthless ticket. Farenbaugh then set out to sell shares in the ticket to other patrons at the track. The record does not reveal whether this was an ongoing scam by Farenbaugh. In any event, since the chance of hitting a big winner is remote, any shares sold would result in clear profit to Farenbaugh, who, having cancelled the ticket, had none of his own money at risk.

Plaintiffs Jim Szadolci and Daniel Teich bought into the ticket before the first race started. Each paid approximately $240 for a 5 percent share. Teich left the track shortly thereafter. Plaintiff Mardy Loewy apparently bought in for 5 percent after the day's racing program had commenced. The record is not clear at what point Loewy invested (he said probably after the second or third race) or how much he paid for his share (possibly around $300).

But, lo and behold, Farenbaugh (much to his dismay, we assume) picked all nine winners. A valid ticket would have paid $1,380,000. Farenbaugh's cancelled ticket was worth zero.

Szadolci and Loewy (jubilant, we presume, at the prospect of realizing $69,000 each) accompanied Farenbaugh (feigning aplomb, no doubt) to the pay window, only to learn of the ticket cancellation. Unfortunately, the record does not reveal what happened at that moment.

The three plaintiffs sued Hollywood Park, the parimutuel clerk, another track employee, and Farenbaugh for negligence, conspiracy, and negligent hiring. Defendants secured summary judgment and plaintiffs appeal.

STANDARD OF REVIEW

After examining the facts before the trial judge on a summary judgment motion, an appellate court independently determines their effect as a matter of law. (Bonus-Bilt, Inc. v. United Grocers, Ltd. (1982) 136 Cal.App.3d 429, 442, 186 Cal.Rptr. 357.)

Despite this independent review, the appellate court applies the same legal standard as did the trial court. Code of Civil Procedure section 437c, subdivision (c), requires the trial court to grant summary judgment if no triable issue exists as to a material fact, and if the papers entitle the moving party to a judgment as a matter of law. Emphasizing triable issues rather than disputed facts, summary judgment law turns on issue finding rather than issue determination. (Walsh v. Walsh (1941) 18 Cal.2d 439, 441-442, 116 P.2d 62.)

DISCUSSION

The trial court's ruling was based on the conclusion that the transactions between plaintiffs and Farenbaugh were illegal bets. Since plaintiffs' complaint relied on a theory which put them in pari delicto, the trial court held, they were barred from recovery. " 'The general rule is that the courts will not recognize such an illegal contract [betting] and will not aid the parties thereto, but will leave them where it finds them. This rule has been rigidly enforced in this state to deny any relief in the courts to parties seeking to recover either their stakes or their winnings under a wagering contract which is in violation of law, . . . [Citations.]' " (Bradley v. Doherty (1973) 30 Cal.App.3d 991, 994, 106 Cal.Rptr.

Plaintiffs seek to distinguish themselves from the above rule by arguing that the transactions here did not constitute illegal bets. They argue that the trial court found these to be illegal "lay off bets" by erroneously relying on People v. Oreck (1946) 74 Cal.App.2d 215, 168 P.2d 186, which held that a "lay off man" was engaged in illegal bookmaking. What is a lay off bet/man? "If a customer of a bookie bets $5.00 on horse X to win a certain race, and the track odds are 5-1, if that horse wins the bookie must pay the customer $25, while if it loses the bookie wins $5.00. Now, if before the race, the bookie lays off that $5.00 bet with a lay off man, what is the result? If the horse wins, the bookie must pay the customer $25, but he is reimbursed to the extent of $25 by his bet with the lay off man. In a very real sense the bookie has won that bet with the lay off man, and the lay off man has lost. But if the horse loses, the bookie wins $5.00 from his customer, but he must pay the lay off man $2.50. In a very real sense the bookie has lost and the lay off man has won on that transaction . . . ." (Id. at pp. 220-221, 168 P.2d 186.)

But here, argue plaintiffs, unlike in Oreck, Farenbaugh's bet with the track was legal, so their investments did not constitute lay off bets. Farenbaugh possessed, they claim, a chose in action ("a right to recover money or other personal property by a judicial proceeding" (Civ.Code, § 953)), interest in which could be transferred. (See Mattson v. Hollywood Turf Club (1950) 101 Cal.App.2d 215, 225 P.2d 276, which holds there is at least an implied contract between the track and its bettors. Mattson also aptly points out that whether betting on horses "is a game of skill, as some believe, or of chance, as many have learned, it provides a legal method for getting rid of one's money." (Id. at p. 219, 225 P.2d 276.))

We agree that the transactions between Farenbaugh and plaintiffs did not constitute lay off bets, but for a different reason than proffered by plaintiffs. There was no underlying bet between Farenbaugh and any person or entity. Farenbaugh had withdrawn his legitimate bet and had no stake with the track in the outcome of the race, so he was laying nothing off when he fleeced plaintiffs. Farenbaugh had no chose in action. Plaintiffs bought a share of a worthless ticket, which entitled Farenbaugh and them to recover nothing from the track. If there was any kind of implied contract, it was between plaintiffs and Farenbaugh, who impliedly had offered plaintiffs a return if the selected horses won. A lay off bet provides a bookie with a backup. Farenbaugh, who could have used the help, had no backup.

Business and Professions Code section 19595 provides in part: "Any form of wagering or betting on the result of a horse race other than that permitted by this chapter is illegal." The basic approved betting format is for a bettor to give his money to the track, where it is then placed in the parimutuel pool, out of which winning bettors are paid. (See Bus. and Prof.Code, § 19594— "Any person within the inclosure where a horse racing meeting is authorized may wager on the result of a horse race held at that meeting by contributing his money to the parimutuel pool operated by the licensee under this chapter . . . .") One of the advantages of this system is that it should eliminate the type of problem that occurred here.

Any way we look at it, plaintiffs laid direct wagers with Farenbaugh, who took their money and impliedly agreed to a 5 percent winner's share for each plaintiff. None of the money involved ended up in the parimutuel pool. So, while these were not lay off bets, they were unauthorized direct bets with Farenbaugh, and illegal.

Plaintiffs argue that these were not bets because Farenbaugh received no compensation, had no interest in the outcome of the races, and was on the same side as plaintiffs. But Farenbaugh had a very real stake in the outcome. For his scam to work, the ticket had to be a loser, because he could then offer his condolences to plaintiffs and walk away with their money. Only when the ticket "won" did Farenbaugh's problems arise. So, Farenbaugh was directly betting against plaintiffs. If their horses won, his scam was revealed and he acquired a measure of grief. If they lost, he kept several hundred dollars of plaintiffs' money without having risked one dime.

Plaintiffs offer the example of friends going to the track and pooling their money, with one of them purchasing the ticket. If the purchaser actually takes his friends' money and hands it to the parimutuel clerk, the bet is legal, plaintiffs argue, because the friends' money has been placed in the parimutuel pool. If he spends his own money and is then reimbursed by his friends, the bet is an illegal lay off bet according to defendants' analysis. This, plaintiffs argue, is illogical. But, since we have a different situation here, we need not analyze whether either of the above situations constitutes legal or illegal betting. Here, no one's money was in the parimutuel pool. There was no lay off bet. The transactions were direct and face-to-face between Farenbaugh and plaintiffs. Plaintiffs laid bets with Farenbaugh. The bets were not as authorized by the Business and Professions Code. They were illegal bets. Plaintiffs have no remedy. Whether the trial court relied on the wrong theory or not, its result was correct.

DISPOSITION

The judgment is affirmed.

Notes

1. In *Neifert v. Commonwealth*, 567 A.2d 789 (Pa. Commw. Ct. 1989), a pari-mutuel clerk made a mistake while issuing a twin trifecta ticket. By the time she realized her error, the patron was gone. Hoping he would return, the clerk printed a corrected ticket, which turned out to be a winner. When the patron failed to come back, the clerk attempted to cash in the ticket. Her efforts to do so were rejected because it was clear she had not placed the initial bet.

2. If an operator issues the payout according to the racing board's rules, its contractual liability normally ends. *See, e.g., Ambeault v. Burrillville Racing Association*, 373 A.2d 807 (R.I. 1977) (operator's "daily double" payout following cancellation of second race due to inclement weather complied with applicable administrative regulations). In addition, some states treat vouchers generated by automated pari-mutuel machines as bearer paper. A track takes these as a "holder in due course" and thereby gains a significant measure of immunity from liability. *See Chung v. New York Racing Association*, 714 N.Y.S.2d 429 (Dist. Ct. 2000).

3. "Breakage" in a pari-mutuel pool refers to the odd amount above a multiple that a state sets by statute or regulation. For example, Maryland's regulations establish payouts in multiples of 10 cents. *See* Md. Regs. Code tit. 9, at § 09.10.02.02(2). Thus, if a payout share mathematically comes to $5.53, the payout is lowered to $5.50 and the remaining amount is breakage.

4. Money not claimed by patrons for winning tickets typically goes to the state after a specified period of time. *See, e.g.,* Tex. Rev. Civ. Stat. art. 179e, at § 11.08 (60 days), and *Oregon Racing Commission v. Multnomah Kennel Club*, 411 P.2d 63 (Or. 1966) (seven years).

5. The size of the purse paid to the winning horse (an amount that does not come out of the betting pool) may be established by statute or administrative regulation. In the absence of such a rule, the amount is set by the race track or sponsor and normally cannot be changed after being announced. *See further Horsemen's Benevolent & Protective Association v. Valley Racing Association*, 6 Cal. Rptr. 2d 698 (Ct. App. 1992).

6. Purses are awarded according to a race's official results. If the outcome is later modified (as happens from time to time), the purse may be redistributed to the other contestants. *See, e.g., Jackson v. Arkansas Racing Commission*, 34 S.W.3d 740 (Ark. 2001), and *Maryland Racing Commission v. Belotti*, 744 A.2d 558 (Md. Ct. Spec. App. 1999). But because of the practical problems that would arise if formerly winning bets had to be redistributed, players are estopped by so-called "finality rules." Kentucky's provision is typical:

> Section 17. Official Order of Finish as to Pari-Mutuel Payoff.
>
> When satisfied that the order of finish is correct and that the race has been properly run in accordance with the rules and administrative regulations of the commission, the stewards shall order that the official order of finish be confirmed and the official sign posted for the race. The decision of the stewards as to the official order of finish for pari-mutuel wagering purposes is final and no subsequent action shall set aside or alter such official order of finish for the purposes of pari-mutuel wagering.

810 Ky. Admin. Regs. 1:016, § 17 (2001).

7. To improve bloodlines, some states use a portion of their pari-mutuel pools to support "breed development" programs. Such efforts occasionally have been challenged in court. Florida's program, for example, which was funded by a one percent share of the pool, was declared unconstitutional in *Florida Horsemen Benevolent & Protective Association v. Rudder*, 738 So. 2d 449 (Fla. Dist. Ct. App. 1999). In contrast, New York's program, which utilizes a share of the breakage, has been upheld. *See Saratoga Harness Racing Association v. Agriculture and New York State Horse Breeding Development Fund*, 238 N.E.2d 730 (N.Y. 1968).

Problem 17

A customer placed a bet on a certain horse but had to leave the track before the race was run. Latter that day, the horse won. Before the customer could return to claim her winnings, she inadvertently destroyed the ticket. Does she have any enforceable claim to the money? *See Aliano v. Westchester Racing Association*, 38 N.Y.S.2d 741 (App. Div. 1942).

H. INJURIES

McCURRY v. INVESTMENT CORPORATION OF PALM BEACH
548 So. 2d 689 (Fla. Dist. Ct. App. 1989)

POLEN, Judge.

Appellants were attending the dog races at appellee's facility, Palm Beach Kennel Club, when Mrs. McCurry allegedly slipped and fell on a liquid allowed to accumulate on the floor. Although Mrs. McCurry could not identify the exact substance which caused her to slip, she testified as to the back of her pants being wet immediately after the fall. Mr. McCurry testified that beer and Coca-Cola were on the floor, as well as betting tickets that were allowed to pile up from race to race. Appellants do not contend that Mrs. McCurry slipped on a betting ticket, but offered that evidence to support their theory of constructive notice to appellee.

Appellants offered testimony at trial to the effect that other patrons of the kennel club, on the night of the accident, were walking back and forth across the area where Mrs. McCurry fell with their beverage cups, and were drinking their beverages in the aisles. There was no specific offer of testimony that any particular patron was seen spilling his beverage. The trial court sustained appellee's objection on grounds of relevancy. At the close of appellants' case, the trial court granted a directed verdict in favor of appellee.

We find that this matter is most closely related to the supreme court case of Wells v. Palm Beach Kennel Club, 35 So. 2d 720 (Fla. 1948), and our own opinion in Fazio v. Dania Jai-Alai Palace, Inc., 473 So. 2d 1345 (Fla. Dist. Ct. App. 1985). In the Wells case, the court said:

> One operating a place of amusement like a race course where others are invited is charged with a continuous duty to look after the safety of his patrons. Both sanitary and physical safety of its patrons require that receptacles be provided for bottles and that they be so placed.
>
> We do not mean to imply that they are insurers of the safety of their patrons, but we do say that reasonable care as applied to a race track requires a higher degree of diligence than it does when applied to a store, bank or such like place of business.

35 So. 2d at 721. We find that it was error for the trial court to preclude appellants' offered testimony as to what the other patrons were doing with their beverages on the night of the accident. Such testimony would be clearly relevant to the issue of constructive notice of the dangerous condition to appellee, when taken together with Mr. McCurry's testimony of observing beer, Coca-Cola, and race tickets on the floor.

Upon admission of such testimony, we could not then say it would be proper for the trial court to grant a directed verdict in favor of appellee. This additional evidence, coupled with evidence in favor of appellants that was adduced at the first trial, and the permissible inferences the jury might draw therefrom, may be sufficient upon retrial so as to preclude the granting of a directed verdict.

We therefore reverse and remand for a new trial consistent with this opinion.

ON REHEARING

In its motion for rehearing, appellee correctly identifies error in our opinion dated July 7, 1989, wherein we said: "Mr. McCurry testified that beer and Coca-Cola were on the floor as well as betting tickets that were allowed to pile up from race to race."

While Mr. McCurry did refer to seeing the betting tickets on the floor, our incorrect reference to his testifying to seeing beer and Coca-Cola on the floor was inadvertently derived from the following exchange in the testimony:

> Q. Now, do you know what kind of substance it was that she slipped on?
>
> A. No, I'm not sure what it was. I always thought it was coke or beer.
>
> Q. Why do you say that?
>
> A. Well there was a lot of people around there drinking coke and beer. You hardly ever see anybody drinking water.

Appellants offered testimony that on the night of the accident, other patrons of the Kennel Club were drinking beverages in the aisles and carrying beverage cups while walking back and forth across the area where Mrs. McCurry fell. There was no specific offer of testimony that any particular patron was seen spilling his or her beverage. The trial court sustained appellee's objection to the testimony on grounds of relevancy.

On rehearing, we must recede from that portion of our July 7, 1989, opinion finding it was error for the trial court to exclude such testimony. Appellee having brought to our attention that Mr. McCurry never testified as to having actually seen Coke or beer on the floor, it would have been at best discretionary for the trial court to allow the proffered testimony about what the patrons were doing concerning their beverages.

Having made this correction, we are still of the view that it was error for the trial court to grant a directed verdict in favor of appellee. The testimony that there were betting tickets on the floor would still give rise to an inference that appellee's personnel were negligent as to their maintenance of the area in which Mrs. McCurry fell. We still find Wells v. Palm Beach Kennel Club, 35 So. 2d 720 (Fla. 1948), and Fazio v. Dania Jai-Alai Palace, Inc., 473 So. 2d 1345 (Fla. Dist. Ct. App. 1985), support our conclusion that the question of liability was one for the jury and would preclude the granting of a directed verdict.

Accordingly, the result as stated in our opinion of July 7, 1989, stands. The cause is reversed and remanded for a new trial consistent with this opinion.

TURCOTTE v. FELL
502 N.E.2d 964 (N.Y. 1986)

SIMONS, Judge.

The issue raised in this appeal is the scope of the duty of care owed to a professional athlete injured during a sporting event. The defendants are a coparticipant and his employer and the owner and operator of the sports facility in which the event took place.

Plaintiff Ronald J. Turcotte is a former jockey. Before his injury he had ridden over 22,000 races in his 17-year career and achieved international fame as the jockey aboard "Secretariat" when that horse won the "Triple Crown" races in 1973. On July 13, 1978 plaintiff was injured while riding in the eighth race at Belmont Park, a racetrack owned and operated by defendant New York Racing Association (NYRA). Plaintiff had been assigned the third pole position for the race on a horse named "Flag of Leyte Gulf." Defendant jockey Jeffrey Fell was in the second pole position riding "Small Raja," a horse owned by defendant David P. Reynolds. On the other side of plaintiff, in the fourth position, was the horse "Walter Malone." Seconds after the race began, Turcotte's horse clipped the heels of "Walter Malone" and then tripped and fell, propelling plaintiff to the ground and causing him severe personal injuries which left him a paraplegic.

Plaintiff charges that Fell is liable to [him] because [he is] guilty of common-law negligence and of violating the rules of the New York Racing and Wagering Board regulating "foul riding" (interfering with another horse and rider), that Reynolds is liable for Fell's negligence under the doctrine of respondent superior, and that defendant NYRA is liable because it "negligently failed to water and groom that portion of the racetrack near the starting gate or watered and groomed the same in an improper and careless manner" causing it to be unsafe.

The court below granted the motions of Fell and Reynolds for summary judgment, holding that Turcotte, by engaging in the sport of horseracing, relieved other participants of any duty of reasonable care with respect to known dangers or risks which inhere in that activity. Finding no allegations of Fell's wanton, reckless, or intentional conduct, it dismissed the complaint as to Fell and Reynolds with leave to replead. NYRA subsequently moved for summary judgment and the court below denied its motion because it found there were questions of fact concerning NYRA's negligent maintenance of the track.

I

It is fundamental that to recover in a negligence action a plaintiff must establish that the defendant owed him a duty to use reasonable care, and that it breached that duty. The statement that there is or is not a duty, however, "begs the essential question—whether the plaintiff's interests are entitled to legal protection against the defendant's conduct." Prosser & Keeton, Torts § 53, at 357 (5th ed (1984)). Thus, while the determination of the existence of a duty and the concomitant scope of that duty involve a consideration not only of the wrongfulness of the defendant's action or inaction, they also necessitate an examination of plaintiff's reasonable expectations of the care owed him by others. This is particularly true in professional sporting contests, which by their nature involve an elevated degree of danger. If a participant makes an informed estimate of the risks involved in the activity and willingly undertakes them, then there can be no liability if he is injured as a result of those risks.

Traditionally, the participant's conduct was conveniently analyzed in terms of the defensive doctrine of assumption of risk. With the enactment of the comparative negligence statute, however, assumption of risk is no longer an absolute defense. Thus, it has become necessary, and quite proper, when measuring a defendant's duty to a plaintiff to consider the risks assumed by the plaintiff. The shift in analysis is proper because the "doctrine of assumption of risk deserves no separate existence (except for express assumption of risk) and is simply a confusing way of stating certain no-duty rules." James, Assumption of Risk: Unhappy Reincarnation, 78 Yale L.J. 185, 187-188 (1968). Accordingly, the analysis of care owed to plaintiff in the professional sporting event by a coparticipant and by the proprietor of the facility in which it takes place must be evaluated by considering the risks plaintiff assumed when he elected to participate in the event and how those assumed risks qualified defendants' duty to him.

The risk assumed has been defined a number of ways but in its most basic sense it "means that the plaintiff, in advance, has given his consent to relieve the defendant of an obligation of conduct toward him, and to take his chances of injury from a known risk arising from what the defendant is to do or leave undone. The situation is then the same as where the plaintiff consents to the infliction of what would otherwise be an intentional tort, except that the consent is to run the risk of unintended injury. The result is that the defendant is relieved of legal duty to the plaintiff; and being under no duty, he cannot be charged with negligence." Prosser & Keeton, Torts § 68, at 480-481 (5th ed. 1984).

Defendant's duty under such circumstances is a duty to exercise care to make the conditions as safe as they appear to be. If the risks of the activity are fully comprehended or perfectly obvious, plaintiff has consented to them and defendant has performed its duty. Prosser & Keeton, Torts § 68 (5th ed. 1984). Plaintiff's "consent" is not constructive consent; it is actual consent implied from the act of the electing to participate in the activity. When thus analyzed and applied, assumption of risk is not an absolute defense but a measure of the defendant's duty of care and thus survives the enactment of the comparative fault statute.

II

It would be a rare thing, indeed, if the election of a professional athlete to participate in a sport at which he makes his living could be said to be involuntary. Plaintiff's participation certainly was not involuntary in this case and thus we are concerned only with the scope of his consent.

As a general rule, participants properly may be held to have consented, by their participation, to those injury-causing events which are known, apparent or reasonably foreseeable consequences of the participation. But while the courts have traditionally exercised great restraint in the belief that the law should not place unreasonable burdens on the free and vigorous participation in sports, they have recognized that organized, athletic competition does not exist in a vacuum. Some of the restraints of civilization must accompany every athlete onto the playing field. Thus, the rule is qualified to the extent that participants do not consent to acts which are reckless or intentional.

Whether a professional athlete should be held under this standard to have consented to the act or omission of a coparticipant which caused his injury involves consideration of a variety of factors including but not limited to: the ultimate purpose of the game and the method or methods of winning it; the relationship of defendant's conduct to the game's ultimate purpose, especially his conduct with respect to rules and customs whose purpose is to enhance the safety of the participants; and the equipment or animals involved in the playing of the game. The question of whether the consent was an informed one includes consideration of the participant's knowledge and experience in the activity generally. Manifestly a professional athlete is more aware of the dangers of the activity, and presumably more willing to accept them in exchange for a salary, than is an amateur.

In this case plaintiff testified before trial to facts establishing that horse racing is a dangerous activity. A thoroughbred race horse is the result of years of breeding and that breeding, and all the horse's training, are directed to building speed. A thoroughbred horse weighs about one-half ton and, during the course of the race, will reach speeds of 40 miles per hour or more. Jockeys weighing between 100 and 120 pounds attempt to control these animals, all the while trying to prevail in a race whose very rules require them to exert a maximum effort to win. Plaintiff testified that every professional jockey had experiences when he was not able to keep a horse running on a straight line, or a horse would veer, or jump up on its hind legs, or go faster or slower than the jockey indicated. He further acknowledged that horses in a race do not run in prescribed lanes and it is lawful, under the rules of racing, for horses to move out of their starting lane to other parts of the track provided that the horse does not interfere with other horses when doing so. Indeed, during the course of a race, speeding horses lawfully and properly come within inches of other horses and frequently bump each other. Turcotte conceded that there is a fine line between what is lawful and unlawful in the movement of a horse on the track during a race and that when and where a horse can lawfully change its position is a matter of judgment. Such dangers are inherent in the sport. Because they are recognized as such by plaintiff, the courts below properly held that he consented to relieve defendant Jeffrey Fell of the legal duty to use reasonable care to avoid crossing into his lane of travel.

Plaintiffs nonetheless contend that Fell's alleged violation of the New York Racing & Wagering Board rule prohibiting foul riding is sufficient to sustain their complaint. They assert that the rule is a safety rule and that a participant does not accept or consent to the violation of the rules of a game even though the violation is foreseeable.

The rules of the sport, however, do not necessarily limit the scope of the professional's consent. Although the foul riding rule is a safety measure, it is not by its terms absolute for it establishes a spectrum of conduct and penalties, depending on whether the violation is careless or willful and whether the contact was the result of mutual fault. As the rule recognizes, bumping and jostling are normal incidents of the sport. They are not flagrant infractions unrelated to the normal method of playing the game and done without any competitive purpose. Plaintiff does not claim that Fell intentionally or recklessly bumped him, he claims only that as a result of carelessness, Fell failed to control his mount as the horses raced for the lead and a preferred position on the track. While a participant's "consent" to join in a sporting activity is not a waiver of all rules infractions, nonetheless a professional clearly understands the usual incidents of competition resulting from carelessness, particularly those which result from the customarily accepted method of playing the sport, and accepts them. They are within the known, apparent and foreseeable dangers of the sport and not actionable and thus plaintiffs' complaint against defendant Fell was properly dismissed.

III

The complaint against NYRA should be dismissed. As the owner of the racetrack, it owed the same general duty to those using its property as to owners of real property generally, the duty to exercise reasonable care under the circumstances. Reasonable care may vary, however, depending upon the party seeking relief and his purpose in being on the premises.

NYRA's duty to plaintiff is similarly measured by his position and purpose for being on the track on July 13 and the risks he accepted by being there. In deciding whether plaintiff consented to the conditions which existed at the time, the court should consider the nature of professional horseracing and the facilities used for it, the playing conditions under which horseracing is carried out, the frequency of the track's use and the correlative ability of the owner to repair or refurbish the track, and the standards maintained by other similarly used facilities.

Plaintiffs charge that NYRA was negligent in failing to water the "chute," which leads to the main track, and "overwatering" the main track. Thus, they claim the horses had to run from the dry surface of the chute onto the overly watered, unsafe "cuppy" surface of the main track (the tendency of a wet track surface to stick to the underside of a horse's hoof within the shoe). Plaintiff testified, however, that "cupping" conditions are common on racetracks and that he had experienced them before at Belmont Park and also at many other tracks. Indeed, he testified that he had never ridden on a track where he had not observed a cupping condition at one time or another. Thus, Turcotte's participation in three prior races at this same track on the day of his injury, his ability to observe the condition of the track before the eighth race and his general knowledge and experience with cupping conditions and their prevalence establish that he was well aware of these conditions and the possible dangers from them and that he accepted the risk.

Accordingly, on appeal by plaintiffs, the order of the Appellate Division should be affirmed, with costs, and the certified question answered in the affirmative. On appeal by defendant NYRA, the order should be reversed, with costs, defendant's motion for summary judgment granted and the certified question answered in the negative.

Note

For a further discussion of racing-related injuries, *see, e.g.*, Andrea G. Nadel, *Liability for Injury or Death of Participant in Automobile or Horse Race at Public Track*, 13 A.L.R.4th 623 (1982); Daniel E. Wanat, *Torts and Sporting Events: Spectator and Participant Injuries—Using Defendant's Duty to Limit Liability as an Alternative to the Defense of Primary Implied Assumption of the Risk*, 31 U. Mem. L. Rev. 237 (2001); William Powers, Jr., *Sports, Assumption of Risk, and the New Restatement*, 38 Washburn L.J. 771 (1999).

Problem 18

While attempting to cross a busy highway leading to the defendant's greyhound track, the plaintiff was struck by a car and severely injured. She subsequently sued the owner of the track, claiming it should have constructed a pedestrian bridge or had a traffic light installed. If the owner moves to have the case dismissed, how should the court rule? *See Davis v. Westwood Group*, 652 N.E.2d 567 (Mass. 1995).

I. ANIMAL HEALTH AND TRAINING

GOLDMAN v. MARYLAND RACING COMMISSION
584 A.2d 709 (Md. Ct. Spec. App. 1991)

WILNER, Chief Judge.

Appellants Goldman and Capuano are trainers of thoroughbred horses and are licensed as such by the Maryland Racing Commission. In a consolidated proceeding, the Commission found that they had violated certain regulations proscribing the administration of drugs to horses entered in races and suspended their respective licenses for 15 days. The Circuit Court for Prince George's County upheld the Commission's action whereupon they have brought this appeal complaining that (1) the regulations are unconstitutional both facially and as applied to them and (2) the findings of the Commission are not supported by substantial evidence. We find no merit in either complaint and therefore shall affirm.

The Regulations and Their Implementation

The Maryland Racing Commission was created by the General Assembly and vested with "full power to prescribe rules, regulations and conditions under which all horse races shall be conducted within the State of Maryland." Art. 78B, § 11(a). Among the regulations promulgated by the Commission pursuant to this authority are those codified as COMAR 09.10.01.11, captioned "Corrupt Practices." Paragraph B of that section deals with drugs and provides, in relevant part, that:

> (1) A horse participating in any race may not carry in its body any drug.

> (2) Phenylbutazone, sometimes called "bute," in an amount less than two micrograms per milliliter (μg/ml) of plasma is not regarded

as a drug for purpose of the regulation, but any greater amount of that substance is regarded as a drug.

(3) A person may not administer, or cause to be administered, or participate, or attempt to participate in any way in the administration of any drug to a horse entered to race.

(4) The presence of a drug in the post-race saliva, urine, or other sample taken from the horse shall be prima facie evidence that the horse had been administered and carried the drug in its body during the race.

(5) Whenever the post-race sample taken from a horse discloses the presence of a drug, it shall be presumed that the drug was administered by the person or persons having control, care, or custody of the horse. The presence of any drug in a post-race sample is prohibited.

(6) Every trainer has the duty to be familiar with these drug rules and to be familiar with the substances that are administered to his horse.

(7) The trainer shall be the absolute insurer of, and responsible for, the condition of each horse he enters in a race, regardless of the acts of third parties. A trainer may not start a horse or permit a horse in his custody to be started if he knows, or if by the exercise of reasonable care he might have known or have cause to believe, that the horse has received any drug that could result in a positive test. Every trainer shall guard or cause to be guarded each horse trained by him in such manner and for such period as to prevent any person from administering a drug to the horse that could result in a positive test. If the post-race test reveals the presence of a drug, the trainer may be disciplined.

(8) The stewards may at any time order the post-race taking of a urine or blood specimen for testing from any horse who participated in a race.

(9) The Commission, in its discretion may fine, suspend, or revoke, or all of the above, the license of any person found to have violated these drug rules.

In accordance with these regulations, the Commission requires that blood and urine samples be taken from each horse that finishes a race "in the money." Those samples—one container of urine and two vials of blood—are delivered to the Detention Barn, where the urine is separated into two containers. Each of the four containers is then tagged with a sample number, assigned by the Commission, that identifies the horse from which the sample was taken. One set—i.e., one container of blood and one container of urine—is sent to the Commission laboratory for testing. The other set is placed in a locked refrigerator in the Detention Barn and retained for three to four days.

The normal procedure of the Commission laboratory is to make an initial test only of the urine. If a chemical other than phenylbutazone is detected, that finding is reported to the Stewards without any testing of the blood. If phenylbutazone is found in the urine, however, the blood sample is tested to determine the quantity of the substance. The blood is tested on High

Performance Liquid Chromatography equipment, which the Director of the laboratory described as "more or less state of the art for quantitation." If the test shows an amount of phenylbutazone in excess of what is allowed, it is repeated twice more to confirm the result, but only the lowest reading (if the results differ) is reported to the Stewards. Although under the Regulation (09.10.01.11 B(2)), any quantity of phenylbutazone greater than 2 (μg/ml) of plasma qualifies as a drug, in fact the Laboratory did not, at the time relevant to this case, report quantities less than 2.5 (μg/ml) .

If the Commission laboratory reports the presence of a drug, including a prohibited amount of phenylbutazone, the trainer is given the opportunity to have the samples retained in the Detention Barn tested by an independent laboratory. That, indeed, is the sole purpose for which they are retained. If the Commission laboratory report is negative or the trainer opts not to have the retained samples tested, they are routinely discarded.

This Case

On December 4, 1988, Libra Queen, a horse trained by appellant Capuano, won the fifth race at Laurel Race Course. The blood and urine samples taken after the race were assigned the number 0829. On December 6, Smarterilla, also trained by Capuano, finished second in the second race at Laurel. The samples taken from him were given the number 0204. The ninth race at Laurel on December 6 was won by Baca D'Or, trained by appellant Goldman. His samples were numbered 0133.

In accordance with the procedures noted above, one set of these samples was sent to the Commission laboratory and one set was retained in the Detention Barn. The laboratory tested the samples on December 8, 1988. The urine samples were subjected to an acid urine test and a thin-layer chromographic test, each of which verified the presence of phenylbutazone. The blood samples were then subjected to three separate high performance liquid chromographic tests to determine the quantity of the substance. The test results for Libra Queen (0829) ranged from 2.9829 to 3.3805 (μg/ml) of phenylbutazone. The results for Smarterilla (0204) ranged from 3.1829 to 3.4102; those for Baca D'Or ranged from 2.9589 to 3.4847. As the lowest reading for each horse exceeded 2.5 (μg/ml), those results were reported to the Stewards. On being informed of the laboratory findings, appellants elected to have the retained samples tested by an independent laboratory, in this case the New York State College of Veterinary Medicine. That laboratory reported findings of: (1) for 0829 (Libra Queen), 1.5 (μg/ml); (2) for 0204 (Smarterilla), 2.2 (μg/ml); and (3) for 0133 (Baca D'Or), 2.8 (μg/ml).

Unfortunately, there were two particular problems with sample 0829. At the Commission laboratory, the blood sample first tested was temporarily mislabeled. Eventually, the mislabeling was discovered and the second two tests correctly revealed the origin of the sample. More significant, the blood and urine samples retained in the Detention Barn were discarded prior to December 8, and thus before the positive finding was reported by the Commission laboratory. Testimony before the Commission indicated that, normally, the retained samples are kept for three to four days after the race. The supervisor of the Barn then calls the laboratory to see if it is all right to discard the samples. If permission is given, the samples are thrown in the dumpster near the Barn.

Libra Queen, as noted, raced on December 4, but the laboratory did not test her blood until the evening of December 8. Inadvertently, however, the supervisor threw the retained samples in the dumpster before receiving word from the laboratory. He retrieved them from the dumpster the next day when he learned that the specimens sent to the Commission laboratory had tested positive. Although, by the time of the hearing before the Commission, the supervisor could not remember which sample number was involved, he recalled that he retrieved the one sample he was told to retrieve. The Commission's chief investigator testified that he examined the item recovered from the dumpster and noticed that it contained the number 0829.

Notwithstanding the mishandling of the retained specimen 0829, the Stewards, after a hearing, concluded that Libra Queen, as well as Smarterilla and Baca D'Or, had been administered drugs in violation of the Commission regulation and that appellants Capuano and Goldman were responsible for that administration with respect to the horse(s) under their care. Sanctions appropriate to those findings were imposed, whereupon the trainers appealed to the Commission.

In light of the difficulties raised by the improper discarding of retained specimen 0829, the Commission, as its first order of business, dismissed the charge against Capuano with respect to Libra Queen. After a full evidentiary hearing, however, it concluded that Smarterilla and Baca D'Or had been drugged and that Capuano and Goldman were responsible. Accordingly, the Commission ordered that the two horses be disqualified, that the purses be redistributed, and that the trainers each be suspended for 15 days. As we observed, the Circuit Court for Prince George's County sustained the Commission's order; hence, this appeal.

The Regulations

At oral argument, appellants acknowledged that they had, indeed, administered phenylbutazone to their respective horses and that there was evidence before the Commission of that fact. Notwithstanding that concession, they make three attacks on the regulations applied in this case. They contend first that COMAR 09.10.01.11 B(7)—the provision declaring the trainer to be the "absolute insurer" of the condition of the horse—is unconstitutional on its face in that it creates an irrebuttable presumption. They argue second that, because of what they regard as sloppy Commission record-keeping and procedures and the likelihood that the samples taken from Smarterilla and Baca D'Or were also mishandled, that regulation is unconstitutional as applied. Finally, they assert that the standard of 2 (μg/ml), set forth in COMAR 90.10.01.11 B(2), has no rational relationship to any scientific or veterinary medical standard. None of these attacks has the slightest merit; indeed, in light of appellants' admission that they administered the drugs, their standing to mount the first two challenges is at least suspect.

The challenge to the facial validity of the "absolute insurer" regulation is based almost entirely on Mahoney v. Byers, 48 A.2d 600 (Md. 1946). The regulation under attack there, a precursor of the one at issue here, began by prohibiting anyone from administering or knowingly or carelessly permitting to be administered to a horse any drug within 48 hours before a race. It then provided that if the Commission found a violation of that proscription, the trainer would be subject to penalty "whether or not he administered the drug, or knowingly or carelessly permitted it to be administered." The presence of the drug, it continued, "shall be conclusive evidence either that there was knowledge of the fact on the part of the trainer or that he was guilty of carelessness in permitting it to be administered."

The Court regarded the latter part of the regulation as creating a conclusive or irrebuttable presumption which destroyed the right of the trainer to offer evidence of his innocence. It noted that there was no requirement that trainers actually guard their horses during the 48-hour period, that the actual practice in that regard varied from trainer to trainer, and that the Commission did not, therefore, apparently regard the failure to guard the horse as carelessness. In that circumstance, the Court declared the regulation invalid as "condemning a trainer for failure to do something that the rules never required him to do, and under the guise of carelessness, punishing him for something he failed to do, when he had no way in the world to know that it was required of him by the Commission to do."

The issue of a trainer's obligation was back before the Court in Maryland Racing Commission v. McGee, 128 A.2d 419 (Md. 1957). As in Mahoney v. Byers, a trainer had been disciplined because his horse had been found drugged, but, based on Byers, the circuit court had ordered the Commission to restore the license. The regulation at issue, however, was different from that dealt with in Byers. It still prohibited anyone from administering or conniving at the administration of drugs to a horse entered in a race, but, in place of the "conclusive evidence" language found deficient in Byers, it required a trainer to "guard, or cause to be guarded, each horse trained by him in such manner as to prevent any person or persons from administering to the horse, by any method, any drug prior to the time of the start of the race."

The Court recalled the concern expressed in Byers about an irrebuttable presumption that effectively precluded a trainer from presenting exculpatory evidence but concluded that the issue was really not evidentiary in nature but rather one of substantive law, "to be tested as to validity by the extent of legislative power as to substantive rights under the State and Federal Constitutions." In that regard, the Court noted cases holding that "a rule making the trainer of race horses an insurer of the fact that the horse has not been given a drug before a race, is a valid rule which the authorities in charge of regulation of racing can make without affront to the constitutional rights of the trainer." The decisions of those courts, the Maryland Court observed, "find support in many instances where responsibility or liability without fault has been held not to infringe constitutional rights," and thus it ultimately concluded that the Maryland regulation "that imposes the obligation on the trainer of a race horse to guard the horse against administration of drugs, is valid." Byers was distinguished on the ground that "the Commission at that time imposed no specific requirement to guard."

The "absolute insurer" provision of COMAR 09.10.01.11 B(7) is not a free-standing one. Also included in that regulation—indeed immediately following the "absolute insurer" provision—are the twin duties of the trainer not to allow a horse in his custody to be started if he has reason to believe that the horse has received a drug that could result in a positive test and to guard the horse "in such manner and for such period of time before racing the horse so as to prevent any person from administering a drug to the horse that could result in a positive test." The absolute insurer provision, therefore, does not really impose liability without fault; absent some extraordinary circumstance, of which there is no evidence in this case, the presence of a drug in a horse immediately following a race permits a fair inference either that the trainer administered the drug or allowed it to be administered or failed in his mandatory duty to guard the horse. That inference is especially appropriate in these cases, where, as we have indicated, the trainers have acknowledged administering the drug themselves.

Byers, we are convinced, does not govern this case and indeed is not really relevant to it. McGee, which reflects the nearly universal rule followed throughout the country, controls. Under that rule, COMAR 90.10.01.11 B(7) is a valid regulation.

The second challenge, as presented in appellants' brief, is that "appellants' evidence clearly indicated that the Commission laboratory mislabeling of the relevant samples more than likely led to sample 0829 being mistaken for sample 0133 by Commission employees." As so presented, this argument appears to relate only to Goldman; no such contention is made with respect to sample 0204, taken from Capuano's horse Smarterilla. It may be that "appellants' evidence" could lead to that conclusion. What appellants overlook, of course, is that there was other competent evidence, credited by the Commission, to the contrary. The Commission found as a fact that the chain of custody of the blood and urine samples of both Smarterilla and Baca D'Or was properly maintained and that there was no indication that any tampering or alteration of those samples took place. We find no basis upon which to disturb those findings.

Sufficiency of Evidence

As with the validity of the regulations, appellants present three complaints about the evidence. The first and third of these are essentially a repetition of appellants' assertion that the Commission mishandled at least sample 0133 and maybe sample 0204 as well and that the test results attributed to those samples were therefore unreliable. As we indicated, there was substantial evidence, credited by the Commission, that no such mishandling took place.

The second argument concerns a process known as hemolysis. The Commission laboratory, as we observed, ordinarily does not report findings of phenylbutazone less than 2.5 (μg/ml) , notwithstanding that the regulation precludes amounts greater than 2.0 (μg/ml) . The director of the laboratory explained that, at the time of the relevant events in these cases, there was neither a freezer nor a centrifuge at the Detention Barn and that the retained specimens were simply kept in a refrigerator. In that circumstance, the blood specimen was subject to hemolysis, a process in which the red blood cells break open and begin to permeate the clear plasma. Phenylbutazone collects in the plasma, and thus the effect of the hemolysis is to dilute the concentration of that substance. It is therefore expected that any testing of the retained specimens, which will occur later than the testing of the specimens by the Commission laboratory, will produce findings of lower concentrations. By reporting only concentrations of 2.6 or more, the Commission in effect gave a cushion to the trainer in order to preclude charges that could not be fairly verified by the independent testing to which the trainer was entitled.

In fact, the independent results obtained in these cases were lower than those reported by the Commission laboratory, although, as we noted, even they exceeded the allowable concentration of 2.0 (μg/ml).

Appellants' assertions to the contrary notwithstanding, the evidence fully explained the hemolysis process and its implications, and we find no error in the Commission's acceptance of that evidence.

BOATRIGHT v. KANSAS RACING COMMISSION
834 P.2d 368 (Kan. 1992)

HERD, Justice.

This is an appeal from the district court's judicial review of an administrative proceeding by the Kansas Racing Commission (Commission) to cancel the occupation racing licenses of William Don Boatright and Rodney L. Boatright. The Commission found the Boatrights used live lures to train racing greyhounds in violation of K.S.A. 74-8810(g) and canceled their licenses. On appeal, the district court consolidated the two cases and reversed the Commission's order. This appeal followed.

The facts are undisputed. William Boatright is Rodney Boatright's father. They each own and operate separate greyhound training businesses in Sumner County. William's racing kennel and training facility accommodate three to four hundred greyhounds. Rodney owns and operates a greyhound training farm. Both parties hold kennel owner occupation licenses issued by the Commission pursuant to K.S.A. 74-8816(a). Greyhounds owned by William compete at tracks in 10 states throughout the United States, including Wichita Greyhound Park and the Woodlands in Kansas City, Kansas.

Both parties use the same greyhound training procedure, which begins when the hounds are pups and continues until they arrive at the racetrack. The training starts with permitting the young greyhounds to chase live jackrabbits in a large field. Next, the greyhounds are allowed to chase live rabbits hooked to a mechanical arm which circulates around a small track called the "wheel." In the final training phase, the greyhounds are taught to run on a "schooling" or "training" track. This phase also involves the use of a live rabbit on a mechanical arm. The rabbits are used until killed by the greyhounds. When training is completed the greyhounds are shipped to the various racetracks.

The Commission instituted separate administrative actions against the Boatrights, alleging they had violated K.S.A. 74-8810(g) by using live lures in training racing greyhounds. The Boatrights argued the statute did not apply to their operations because the young dogs they trained were not yet racing greyhounds. In its initial orders the Commission found the statute applied to the training of all racing greyhounds whether they were currently racing at a track or would be racing at some future time. Pursuant to K.S.A. 74-8816(f), the Commission revoked both their licenses and fined William $2,500 and Rodney $1,000. After reviewing its initial orders, the Commission adopted them as final orders.

Each party petitioned the Sedgwick County District Court for review of the Commission's order. The cases were consolidated. The district court held K.S.A. 74-8810(g) applies only to greyhounds (1) registered with the National Greyhound Association; (2) at least 15 months of age at the time of training; and (3) registered at a racing greyhound track. None of the Boatright dogs met the court's definition of racing greyhounds. It thus reversed the orders of the Commission.

The district court also held in the alternative that the term racing greyhound is unconstitutionally vague under both the criminal and business standard of review and, therefore, does not apprise a reasonably prudent person of the act prohibited. This appeal followed.

The first issue for our consideration on appeal is whether K.S.A. 74-8810(g) is unconstitutionally vague. The statute provides: "It is a class B misdemeanor for any person to use any animal or fowl in the training or racing of racing greyhounds." We hold the language of K.S.A. 74-8810(g) conveys a sufficiently definite warning when measured by common understanding and practice to apprise the public of the prohibited activity. Hence, we hold the statute is not unconstitutionally vague.

We first note the term racing greyhound is not defined within the Act. Clearly the legislature meant to regulate the racing of greyhounds. K.S.A. 74-8802(i) states: " 'Greyhound' means any greyhound breed of dog properly registered with the national greyhound association of Abilene, Kansas." K.S.A. 74-8812(b) then provides the regulation: "Greyhounds shall not compete in any race meeting before reaching the age of 15 months." The district court took this regulation as a definition and held the meaning of racing greyhound within K.S.A. 74-8810(g) meant: (1) a greyhound registered with the National Greyhound Association; (2) a greyhound that is at least 15 months of age; and (3) a greyhound registered at a greyhound racing facility.

The Boatrights contend this interpretation is proper. The Commission, however, argues its interpretation of "racing greyhounds" should be given judicial deference under the doctrine of operative construction because the Commission is the agency charged with enforcing the Kansas Parimutuel Racing Act. Under the doctrine of operative construction, the court will give deference to the agency's interpretation of the law although the court may substitute its judgment for that of the agency's.

The Commission also argues legislative history supports its interpretation of the statute. Originally, H.B. 2044 did not contain a provision prohibiting the use of animals in the training of greyhounds for racing. After hearing testimony from animal rights groups, the House Committee on Federal and

State Affairs amended H.B. 2044 to include the following prohibition: "It is a class C felony for any person to use any animal or fowl in the training of racing greyhounds." Minutes of Senate Committee on Federal and State Affairs (February 16, 1987). The House Committee of the Whole then amended the section to prohibit the use of dogs, cats, or fowl in the training of racing greyhounds and the use of any animal or fowl in the training of a racing greyhound within the confines of a racetrack facility. House J. 1987, p. 284. This version of the bill would have allowed the use of rabbits at greyhound farms and training tracks. The Senate subsequently amended the section to read: "It is a class B misdemeanor for any person to use any animal or fowl in the training of racing greyhounds." Minutes of Senate Committee on Federal and State Affairs (April 8, 1987). According to the Commission, the Senate's first amendment to the provision would have allowed the use of animals or fowl in the actual racing of greyhounds at parimutuel tracks. The second amendment by the Senate, the statute's current language, extends the prohibition against using animals or fowl to the racing of racing greyhounds. Sen. J. 1987, p. 619. The Commission argues the Senate's final amendment "extended the prohibition to include racing as well as training activities."

The Commission cites Attorney General opinion No. 87-150 for support of its interpretation of K.S.A. 74-8810(g). A state representative asked the Attorney General whether the provision prohibited the use of live lures in the training of greyhounds that are being trained as racing greyhounds but have not yet raced. Concentrating upon the statute's term "training," the Attorney General found the ordinary meaning of the term training referred to "the instructing, drilling and teaching to obey commands." Therefore, the Attorney General concluded the prohibition extended to "the use of such lures in instructing, drilling and teaching greyhound dogs to be racing greyhounds regardless of racing experience."

We agree with the Attorney General's opinion and hold the legislative intent in enacting K.S.A. 74-8810(g) was to ban the use of live lures in the training of greyhounds for racing and in the actual racing of greyhounds. The use of the term "racing greyhounds" was to distinguish greyhounds used for racing from greyhounds used for hunting. Most of the training of greyhounds for racing occurs before the dog attains the age of 15 months. A statute applying only to older dogs already involved in racing on the track would do little to eliminate the use of live lures in the training and racing of greyhounds. Thus, we hold the use of live lures in the training of greyhounds for racing is prohibited.

We hold the Boatrights violated K.S.A. 74-8810(g). The judgment of the district court is reversed.

[The dissenting opinion of Justice Abbott is omitted.]

Notes

1. The "absolute insurer" rule applied in *Goldman* has been widely adopted. Because it imposes strict liability, no proof of intent is required. *See O'Daniel v. Ohio State Racing Commission*, 307 N.E.2d 529 (Ohio 1974). Likewise, it applies even where a third party may have administered the prohibited drug.

See Segura v. Louisiana State Racing Commission, 577 So. 2d 1031 (La. Ct. App. 1991). Nevertheless, the rule does not negate a defendant's right to question the circumstances under which samples have been collected or the results of any tests performed on them. *See further Barry v. Barchi*, 443 U.S. 55 (1979); *Monaci v. State Horse Racing Commission*, 717 A.2d 612 (Pa. Commw. Ct. 1998); *LaBorde v. Louisiana State Racing Commission*, 506 So. 2d 634 (La. Ct. App. 1987). For a useful discussion of the rule, *see* Luke P. Iovine, III & John E. Keefe, Jr., *Horse Drugging—The New Jersey Trainer Absolute Insurer Rule: Burning Down the House to Roast the Pig*, 1 Seton Hall J. Sport L. 61 (1991).

2. In certain instances, drug administration is permitted. Some horses, for example, are "bleeders" (meaning they are susceptible to exercise-induced pulmonary hemorrhaging). If a horse is certified as a bleeder, it may be allowed to take a drug (such as Lasix) on race day to control its condition. *See, e.g.*, Okla. Admin. Code § 325:45-1-12.

3. Disciplinary action sometimes requires determining whether a particular substance constitutes a prohibited drug. In *Plante v. Department of Business and Professional Regulation*, 685 So. 2d 886 (Fla. Dist. Ct. App. 1996), *review denied*, 695 So. 2d 701 (Fla. 1997), a mixture containing sodium bicarbonate, sucrose, and water was deemed illegal.

4. As one would expect, racing agencies generally have broad powers when it comes to protecting the health of animals. *See, e.g., Taunton Dog Track, Inc. v. State Racing Commission*, 674 N.E.2d 226 (Mass. 1997) (upholding the suspension of live horse racing at a track due to the outbreak of an equine virus).

5. In recent years, many people have come to the conclusion that racing greyhounds is inhumane and should be stopped. *See, e.g.*, Erin N. Jackson, Comment, *Dead Dog Running: The Cruelty of Greyhound Racing and the Bases for Its Abolition in Massachusetts*, 7 Animal L. Rev. 175 (2001). As a result, there now is a growing national movement to save greyhounds. *See further Greyhound Tales: True Stories of Rescue, Compassion and Love* (Nora Star ed. 1997). For a spirited defense of the sport, *see* Laura Thompson, *The Dogs: A Personal History of Greyhound Racing* (1994).

6. Because of their value (as well as the cost of maintaining them), some owners have had their race horses murdered so as to be able to collect on their insurance policies. *See generally* Lesley A. Hunter, Comment, *The Legal Prevention of Equine Insurance Fraud—How We Can Stop the Killing Game*, 22 Ohio N.U. L. Rev. 845 (1996). Indeed, the 1977 disappearance of candy heiress Helen Vorhees Brach eventually led to the discovery of a vast criminal conspiracy in which a hitman dubbed "The Sandman" eliminated horses on demand. For a gripping account of the affair, *see* Ken Englade, *Hot Blood: The Millionairess, the Money, and the Horse Murders* (1996). That same year, the television show *Law & Order* aired an episode based on the Sandman's killings (Episode 122, "Corpus Delicti"). In an interesting twist, Ralph Cifaretto's decision to kill Tony's beloved race horse Pie-O-My to collect a $200,000 insurance policy led to Ralph's untimely death during the 2002 season of *The Sopranos* (Episode 48, "Whoever Did This").

Problem 19

Article 26 of the Warsaw Convention, which governs international flights, requires any party whose goods are "damaged or delayed" to notify the carrier within seven days. Article 29 of the same treaty establishes a two year statute of limitation for the filing of lawsuits. Upon their arrival from overseas, the plaintiff discovered his champion greyhound racing dogs had suffocated to death during the flight. When he sued the carrier, it moved for summary judgment because the plaintiff had waited 20 days before giving notice. How should the court rule? *See Dalton v. Delta Airlines, Inc.*, 570 F.2d 1244 (5th Cir. 1978).

Chapter 5

SPORTS GAMING

A. OVERVIEW

Betting on sports is generally legal only in Nevada. Nevertheless, sports wagers are placed every day in offices, bars, and schools around the country. This fact presents enormous challenges for both law enforcement agencies and sports officials.

B. LEGAL WAGERS

NATIONAL FOOTBALL LEAGUE v. GOVERNOR OF THE STATE OF DELAWARE
435 F. Supp. 1372 (D. Del. 1977)

STAPLETON, District Judge.

In August 1976, the Office of the Delaware State Lottery announced a plan to institute a lottery game based on games of the National Football League ("NFL"). Immediately thereafter, the NFL and its twenty-eight member clubs filed suit in this Court against the Governor and the Director of the State Lottery seeking preliminary and permanent injunctive relief barring such a lottery scheme. The State of Delaware intervened, and the complaint was amended to add a request that the Court create a constructive trust on behalf of the NFL clubs of all revenues derived from such a lottery. Finding no threat of immediate irreparable injury to the NFL, the Court denied the prayer for a temporary restraining order.

During the week of September 12, 1976, the football lottery games commenced. Upon defendants' motion, the Court dismissed plaintiffs' claims that the games violated the Equal Protection Clause of the Fourteenth Amendment and the Commerce Clause of the Constitution. With respect to twelve other counts, defendants' motion to dismiss or for summary judgment was denied. The lottery games continued through the season.

In late Fall, a six day trial on the merits was held. That was followed by extended briefing. The matter is now ripe for disposition. This Opinion constitutes the Court's findings of fact and conclusions of law on the questions presented.

ACTUAL BACKGROUND

The Delaware football lottery is known as "Scoreboard" and it involves three different games, "Football Bonus," "Touchdown" and "Touchdown II." All are weekly games based on regularly scheduled NFL games. In Football Bonus, the fourteen games scheduled for a given weekend are divided into two pools of seven games each. A player must mark the lottery ticket with his or her

253

projections of the winners of the seven games in one or both of the two pools and place a bet of $1, $2, $3, $5 or $10. To win Football Bonus, the player must correctly select the winner of each of the games in a pool. If the player correctly selects the winners of all games in both pools, he or she wins an "All Game Bonus." The amounts of the prizes awarded are determined on a pari-mutuel basis, that is, as a function of the total amount of money bet by all players.

In Touchdown, the lottery card lists the fourteen games for a given week along with three ranges of possible point spreads. The player must select both the winning team and the winning margin in each of three, four or five games. The scale of possible bets is the same as in Bonus and prizes are likewise distributed on a pari-mutuel basis to those who make correct selections for each game on which they bet.

Touchdown II, the third Scoreboard game, was introduced in mid-season and replaced Touchdown for the remainder of the season. In Touchdown II, a "line" or predicted point spread on each of twelve games is published on the Wednesday prior to the games. The player considers the published point spread and selects a team to "beat the line," that is, to do better in the game than the stated point spread. To win, the player must choose correctly with respect to each of from four to twelve games. Depending upon the number of games bet on, there is a fixed payoff of from $10 to $1,200. There is also a consolation prize for those who beat the line on nine of out ten, ten out of eleven or eleven out of twelve games.

Scoreboard tickets are available from duly authorized agents of the Delaware State Lottery, usually merchants located throughout the State. The tickets list the teams by city names, e.g., Tampa or Cincinnati, rather than by nicknames such as Buccaneers or Bengals. Revenues are said to be distributed pursuant to a fixed apportionment schedule among the players of Scoreboard, the State, the sales agents and the Lottery Office for its administrative expenses.

THE PARTIES' CLAIMS

The core of plaintiffs' objections to Scoreboard is what they term a "forced association with gambling." They complain that the football lottery constitutes an unlawful interference with their property rights and they oppose its operation on a host of federal, state and common law grounds. Briefly stated, their complaint includes counts based on federal and state trademark laws, the common law doctrine of misappropriation, the federal anti-gambling laws, the Civil Rights Act of 1871 (42 U.S.C. § 1983), the Delaware Constitution and the Delaware lottery statute.

The defendants deny that the state-run revenue raising scheme violates any federal, state or common law doctrine. Further, they have filed a counterclaim for treble damages under the Sherman and Clayton Acts for federal antitrust law violations charging, inter alia, that the plaintiffs have brought this litigation for purposes of harassment and that they have conspired to monopolize property which is in the public domain.

For the reasons which follow, I have determined that the plaintiffs are entitled to limited injunctive relief, in the nature of a disclaimer on all

Scoreboard materials disseminated to the public. The Touchdown II game will also be invalidated. In all other respects, their claims for relief are denied. The defendants' claim for treble damages is likewise denied.

MISAPPROPRIATION

Plaintiffs have proven that they have invested time, effort, talent and vast sums of money in the organization, development and promotion of the National Football League. They have also convincingly demonstrated the success of that investment. The NFL is now a national institution which enjoys great popularity and a reputation for integrity. It generates substantial revenue from gate receipts, broadcasting rights, film rights, and the licensing of its trademarks.

There also can be no dispute that the NFL popularity and reputation played a major role in defendants' choice of NFL games as the subject matter of its lottery. Defendants concede that in making this election they expected to generate revenue which would not be generated from betting on a less popular pastime.

Based on these facts, plaintiffs assert that defendants are misappropriating the product of plaintiffs' efforts or in the words of the Supreme Court, that the State of Delaware is "endeavoring to reap where it has not sown." International News Service v. Associated Press, 248 U.S. 215, 239, 39 S.Ct. 68, 72, 63 L.Ed. 211 (1918) ("INS"). Thus, plaintiffs maintain the lottery must be halted and the ill-gotten gains disgorged.

This Court has no doubt about the continuing vitality of the INS case and the doctrine of misappropriation which it spawned. I conclude, however, that plaintiffs' argument paints with too broad a brush.

The only tangible product of plaintiffs' labor which defendants utilize in the Delaware Lottery are the schedule of NFL games and the scores. These are obtained from public sources and are utilized only after plaintiffs have disseminated them at large and no longer have any expectation of generating revenue from further dissemination. This fact distinguishes the situation in INS. In that case the Court recognized the right of INS to protection against misappropriation of the news it had collected for so long as that "product" still retained commercial value to AP. The court was careful to note that the injunction issued by the District Court limited the protection granted only until the time when "(the) commercial value as news to . . . (AP) and all of its . . . (customers had) passed away." 248 U.S. at 245, 39 S.Ct. at 75. I do not believe the INS case or any other case suggests use of information that another has voluntarily made available to the public at large is an actionable "misappropriation."

Plaintiffs insist, however, that defendants are using more than the schedules and scores to generate revenue for the State. They define their "product" as being the total "end result" of their labors, including the public interest which has been generated.

It is undoubtedly true that defendants seek to profit from the popularity of NFL football. The question, however, is whether this constitutes wrongful misappropriation. I think not.

We live in an age of economic and social interdependence. The NFL undoubtedly would not be in the position it is today if college football and the fan interest that it generated had not preceded the NFL's organization. To that degree it has benefited from the labor of others. The same, of course, can be said for the mass media networks which the labor of others have developed.

What the Delaware Lottery has done is to offer a service to that portion of plaintiffs' following who wish to bet on NFL games. It is true that Delaware is thus making profits it would not make but for the existence of the NFL, but I find this difficult to distinguish from the multitude of charter bus companies who generate profit from servicing those of plaintiffs' fans who want to go to the stadium or, indeed, the sidewalk popcorn salesman who services the crowd as it surges towards the gate.

While courts have recognized that one has a right to one's own harvest, this proposition has not been construed to preclude others from profiting from demands for collateral services generated by the success of one's business venture. General Motors' cars, for example, enjoy significant popularity and seat cover manufacturers profit from that popularity by making covers to fit General Motors' seats. The same relationship exists between hot dog producers and the bakers of hot dog rolls. But in neither instance, I believe, could it be successfully contended that an actionable misappropriation occurs.

The NFL plaintiffs, however, argue that this case is different because the evidence is said to show "misappropriation" of plaintiffs' "good will" and "reputation" as well as its "popularity." To a large extent, plaintiffs' references to "good will" and "reputation" are simply other ways of stating their complaint that defendants are profiting from a demand plaintiffs' games have generated. To the extent they relate to a claim that defendants' activities have damaged, as opposed to appropriated, plaintiff's good will and reputation, I believe one must look to other lines of authority to determine defendants' culpability. In response to plaintiffs' misappropriation argument, I hold only that defendants' use of the NFL schedules, scores and public popularity in the Delaware Lottery does not constitute a misappropriation of plaintiffs' property.

In the event a differing analysis is determined to be appropriate in the course of appellate review, I should add that the plaintiffs have not demonstrated that the existence of gambling on its games, per se, has or will damage its good will or reputation for integrity. By this, I do not suggest that an association of the NFL with a gambling enterprise in the minds of the public would not have a deleterious effect on its business. Such an association presupposes public perception of NFL sponsorship or approval of a gambling enterprise or at least confusion on this score, and I treat this subject hereafter. I do find, however, that the existence of gambling on NFL games, unaccompanied by any confusion with respect to sponsorship, has not injured the NFL and there is no reason to believe it will do so in the future. The record shows that extensive gambling on NFL games has existed for many years and that this fact of common public knowledge has not injured plaintiffs or their reputation.

The most prevalent form of such gambling is the illegal form—office polls and head-to-head bets with bookies. Virtually every witness testified that he was familiar with illegal football pools and knew they were available in schools, factories and offices around the country. John J. Danahy, Director of Security for the NFL and a former member of the Federal Bureau of Investigation, estimated that millions of dollars a week are spent for illegal betting on football games and that such gambling provides a major source of income to organized crime.

In addition to the illegal gambling, the evidence shows that there is a substantial volume of legalized sports betting. In Nevada, sports betting, including betting on NFL games, has been legal since 1949. The parties have stipulated that sports betting in Nevada in the fourth quarter of the year, when the betting is primarily on football games, has reached the following levels:

1972	$ 873,318
1973	$ 826,767
1974	$ 3,873,217
1975	$26,170,328

These figures represent both "by event" or "head-to-head" betting and parlay card betting. In addition, pool card gambling on professional football has been legal in Montana since 1974. The NFL has not shown that any of this gambling, legal or illegal, has injured the reputation of professional football or the member teams of the NFL.

Some comment on the plaintiffs' survey evidence on this subject is in order. A market survey was conducted at the direction of the plaintiffs for use in this litigation. One of the questions asked of those surveyed was:

> Suppose there would be legalized betting on National Football League games which was run by a state agency in each of the various states. Do you think that the reputation of the National Football League would be better, stay the same or be worse than before legalized betting?

Those who responded that they thought the NFL's reputation would decline were asked in a follow-up question to explain why they thought so. Fifty percent of those responding in the "National" portion of the survey said that they believed the NFL's reputation would be hurt. Those who conducted the survey broke down the reasons given for that belief into four separate categories:

26% Will mean more crime

29% Opposed to betting

19% Throwing or fixing game

30% Takes sportsmanship out of the game

While these results do suggest that gambling on NFL games would adversely affect the NFL, there are several reasons why I cannot credit the data. Most importantly, there is the overwhelming evidence already reviewed that, in actual experience, widespread gambling, both illegal and state-authorized, has not hurt the NFL. That evidence is far more persuasive than survey results based on hypothetical questions.

The survey itself bears out the conclusion that those with actual experience with state-run sports betting have far different views than those who are dealing with the question in the abstract. When Delawareans were asked whether the State's football lottery would injure the reputation of the NFL only 22% answered affirmatively.

In addition, there are a number of problems with the form of question used in the survey. It asks the person responding, not whether he or she would think less of the NFL, but rather whether he or she thinks others would have less regard for the NFL. The response is by nature speculation and it is quite conceivable that many who would have no objection to state-run sports betting would assume that others would hold a different view. The question as asked did not elicit relevant information.

Moreover, the question assumed that every state would institute such a program. While it has been suggested that a few other states are considering football lotteries, I have no reason to believe that the Delaware scheme will be imitated by forty-nine other states. In any event, the issue before this Court is whether Delaware's Scoreboard games will injure the NFL's reputation. The question asked in the "national" survey addressed a far broader subject which the plaintiffs have not shown to be relevant.

Finally, the phrasing of the question did not emphasize a proposed system run independently of the NFL. As will be seen, that may have influenced some responses.

TRADEMARK AND RELATED UNFAIR COMPETITION CLAIMS

The Delaware Lottery does not utilize the NFL name or any of plaintiffs' registered service marks for the purpose of identifying, as opposed to describing, the service which it offers. The name utilized for the football related betting games is "Scoreboard" and the individual games are identified as "Football Bonus," "Touchdown" and "Touchdown II." No NFL insignia or the like are utilized in the advertising. The cards on which the customers of the Delaware Lottery mark their betting choices, however, identify the next week's NFL football games by the names of the cities whose NFL teams are scheduled to compete against each other, e.g., Philadelphia v. Los Angeles, Washington v. Baltimore, etc. It is stipulated that, in the context in which they appear, these geographic names are intended to refer to, and are understood to refer to, plaintiffs' football teams. It is in this manner that defendants have made it known that the Delaware Lottery offers the opportunity to bet on NFL football.

Undoubtedly when defendants print "Philadelphia v. Los Angeles," the public reads "Philadelphia Eagles v. Los Angeles Rams," and, in this sense, the words utilized by defendants have a secondary meaning. But I do not understand this fact alone to constitute infringement of plaintiffs' registered marks or unfair competition. Defendants may truthfully tell the public what service they perform, just as a specialist in the repair of Volkswagen cars may tell the public of his specialty by using the word "Volkswagen," and just as the manufacturer of a razor blade may advertise the brand names of the razors they will fit. The same rule prevails in the area of comparative advertising which utilizes the tradenames of competing products.

What one may not do, however, is to advertise one's services in a manner which creates an impression in the mind of the relevant segment of the public that a connection exists between the services offered and the holder of the registered mark when no such connection exists. Moreover, this legal prohibition imposes a duty to take affirmative steps to avoid a mistaken impression which is likely to arise from a truthful description of the service even though it does not literally suggest a connection.

This case presents a novel situation for application of these well established principles. After carefully reading all of the materials disseminated in connection with the Delaware Lottery, I cannot point to any specific statement, symbol, or word usage which tends to suggest NFL sponsorship or approval. At the same time, however, plaintiffs have convinced me that a substantial portion of the present and potential audience for NFL games believes that the Delaware Lottery is sponsored or approved by the NFL.

In what is denominated the "Delaware Special" portion of the market survey referred to above, 19% of the Delaware residents surveyed and 21% of those designated as "fans" either said that, as far as they knew, the legalized betting on professional football was arranged by the State with the authorization of the teams or said that it was conducted by the teams alone. Before answering, some of those questioned were shown a sample lottery ticket and others were not. The results did not vary significantly between the two groups. These figures establish that there is substantial confusion on the part of the public about the source or sponsorship of the lottery.

This Court perceives only one way to reconcile these survey results with the absence of any affirmative suggestion of sponsorship or approval in the Delaware Lottery advertising and materials. Apparently, in this day and age when professional sports teams franchise pennants, teeshirts, helmets, drinking glasses and a wide range of other products, a substantial number of people believe, if not told otherwise, that one cannot conduct an enterprise of this kind without NFL approval.

While defendants are guilty of no affirmative statements suggesting affiliation and may well not have foreseen that a substantial number of people would infer an association with the NFL, the fact remains that the ultimate result of their promotion of the Delaware Lottery is significant public confusion and the loss to the NFL of control of its public image. I conclude that this fact entitles plaintiffs to some relief.

The only monetary relief sought by plaintiffs—a judgment directing transfer of the proceeds of the Lottery to NFL Charities Incorporated—is inappropriate. These proceeds are not funds that the NFL would have harvested for itself in the absence of the Lottery. Nor is there any reason to believe that the retention by the State of any of these proceeds would result in unjust enrichment. I have previously held that Delaware has a right to profit from a demand for gambling created by NFL games. Relief is appropriate only because of the failure of the defendants to avoid an impression of sponsorship, and this record does not suggest that the proceeds of the Lottery were in any way augmented by any public perception of affiliation. Given the nature of the service provided, I strongly suspect that this limited perception had no effect on revenue.

To eliminate the confusion as to sponsorship, an injunction will be entered requiring the Lottery Director to include on Scoreboard tickets, advertising and any other materials prepared for public distribution a clear and conspicuous statement that Scoreboard is not associated with or authorized by the National Football League.

Officials of the Delaware Lottery volunteered early in this litigation to employ such a disclaimer. The NFL was dissatisfied with the proposal and, as a result, the Lottery Office took no steps to adopt it. Scoreboard tickets were inscribed with the statement, "The 'Scoreboard' Lottery is sponsored solely by the Delaware State Lottery." However, this appeared at the very bottom of the back of the tickets and was not included in defendants' advertising and other promotional materials.

The survey indicates that this approach to the problem was not sufficient to dispel the idea that the NFL was somehow associated with the Lottery. That survey does not suggest to the Court, however, that a prominent statement on all Scoreboard materials disclaiming any affiliation would be insufficient to protect plaintiffs' legitimate interests.

DELAWARE TRADEMARK ACT

In a letter memorandum submitted after its initial post-trial brief, plaintiffs added for the first time the contention that Scoreboard violates the newly enacted Delaware Trademark Act, 6 Del.C. § 3301 (60 Del.Laws, Ch. 612). I have no occasion to consider the merits of that contention because the statute, by its very terms, does not apply to this case.

The Trademark Act, signed into law by the Governor on July 22, 1976, provides:

> This act shall be in force and take effect 1 month after its enactment but shall not affect any suit, proceeding or appeal then pending.

This lawsuit was filed on August 20, 1976, and thus, was pending when the Act became law. Despite the plain language of the new statute, plaintiffs attempt to bring themselves under its mantle in this lawsuit by arguing that, if they are not permitted to do so, they may institute a new lawsuit raising the same claim. That course of action may indeed be open to them but it does not further their cause in this suit. I cannot disregard the plain command of the statute.

DELAWARE LOTTERY LAW

The plaintiffs assert that the State Lottery Office is acting ultra vires in conducting the Scoreboard games. The NFL points to Article II, Section 17 of the Delaware Constitution which prohibits all forms of gambling in the State except lotteries under state control, pari-mutuel wagering on State licensed races, and Bingo. The heart of their contention based on Section 17 is that Scoreboard is not a lottery. The NFL further contends that, even if Scoreboard is a lottery within the meaning of the Constitution, the Lottery Office is operating it in a manner inconsistent with the requirements for state lotteries established by the General Assembly. The State's first line of defense is that the NFL lacks standing to raise these ultra vires arguments.

Standing

The question of standing with respect to claims based on the State Constitution and a State statute is governed by Delaware law. In the past, the Delaware Supreme Court has looked to and followed the rules of standing established in the federal courts on the law of standing as well as to its own precedents. I have done likewise here.

In Mills v. Trans-Caribbean Airways, Inc., 272 A.2d 702, 703 (Del. 1971), the court held that standing to attack the constitutionality of a statute or any action taken thereunder depends on a showing that "a right of the complainant is affected thereby." Association of Data Processing Services Organizations, Inc. v. Camp, 397 U.S. 150, 90 S.Ct. 827, 25 L.Ed.2d 184 (1970), sets forth a three-part analysis by which to determine whether such a litigable right exists. Camp held that a party must allege injury in fact; he must show that he is "arguably within the zone of interests to be protected or regulated by the statute or constitutional guarantee in question"; and finally, the complainant must establish that judicial review has not been precluded. 397 U.S. at 152-156, 90 S.Ct. at 830. Later cases have emphasized that the interest the plaintiff alleges must not be one which is held in common by all members of the public. Plaintiff must be suffering or threatened with a concrete, particularized injury. Schlesinger v. Reservists to Stop the War, 418 U.S. 208, 220, 94 S.Ct. 2925, 41 L.Ed.2d 706 (1974).

The original version of Section 17 contained a general prohibition of all forms of gambling in the State. It is fair to assume that it was based on some generalized belief that gambling was a corrupting, dangerous influence in society from which the people of the State should be protected.

Over the years, the constitutional provision has been amended in stages. Each amendment was designed to exempt from the general prohibition some particular form of gambling. Undoubtedly the amendments reflect a changing perception about the evils of gambling. Nevertheless, Section 17 continues to reflect a concern about the potentially deleterious influence of gambling on society.

A police power regulation of this kind is for the benefit of the society at large. As a component of that society, the NFL is within the zone of interests to be protected. In addition, the NFL has alleged a concrete injury in fact to itself. The NFL charges that the likelihood that games will be fixed or, more likely, that the public will imagine that the games have been fixed to produce a large payoff will hurt its reputation. In addition, it asserts that the same ill will toward gambling that prompted the legislature to enact the constitutional provisions will drive away those NFL fans who believe that the NFL has consented to or approved gambling on its games. This is a sufficient stake in the outcome to ensure that the matter has been presented in a true adversary context. Finally, the State does not contend that review has been precluded. Accordingly, the NFL has standing to make its constitutional claim.

The standing analysis with respect to NFL's contention that Scoreboard violates the lottery statute, 29 Del.C. § 4801, et seq., is much the same. The lottery statute embodies the same underlying mistrust for gambling qualified by the idea that State control will obviate the undesirable aspects of gambling while providing the State with a source of income. The zone of interests protected is the same and the same allegations of injury are sufficient.

Validity Of Scoreboard Under The Delaware Constitution

The 1974 Amendment to Article II, Section 17 of the Delaware Constitution authorizes lotteries under State control. It does not define the term "lottery." The NFL contends that the word lottery has a well established meaning in the law and that the Scoreboard games do not fall within that meaning because they entail an element of skill.

It is unquestioned that there are three elements necessary to a lottery: prize, consideration and chance. However, there is a split of authority as to whether a game that incorporates an element of skill as well can qualify as a lottery. Two approaches to the question have developed:

> Under the English rule, a lottery consists in the distribution of money or other property by chance, and nothing but chance, that is, by doing that which is equivalent to drawing lots. If merit or skill play any part in determining the distribution, there is no lottery . . . . In the United States, however, by what appears to be the weight of authority at the present day, it is not necessary that this element of chance be pure chance, but it may be accompanied by an element of calculation or even of certainty; it is sufficient if chance is the dominant or controlling factor. However, the rule that chance must be the dominant factor is to be taken in the qualitative or causative sense.

3 Wharton's Criminal Law and Procedure § 935 (Anderson ed. 1957).

The Delaware courts have not ruled on whether the "pure chance" or "dominant factor" rule applies in this State. Compare State v. Sedgwick, 2 Boyce's 453, 25 Del. 453, 81 A. 472, 473 (1911). The courts of two adjoining states considered this problem in the context of privately operated football pools and they concluded that the pools did fall within the meaning of lottery despite the presence of an element of skill. State v. Steever, 103 N.J.Super. 149, 246 A.2d 743 (1968); Commonwealth v. Laniewski, 173 Pa.Super. 245, 98 A.2d 215 (1953). In addition, over the last ten years the trend toward acceptance of the dominant factor rule described in Wharton has continued and expanded. See, e.g., Morrow v. State, 511 P.2d 127, 129 (Alaska 1973); Finster v. Keller, 18 Cal.App.3d 836, 96 Cal.Rptr. 241 (1971). Absent clear language in the Constitution supporting a contrary rule, I believe the Delaware Supreme Court would be inclined to adopt the majority, dominant factor rule.

Further support for the dominant factor rule can be found in the legislature's interpretation of the word lottery. The Delaware Constitution may be amended by a two-thirds vote of the General Assembly in two successive sessions with an intervening election. Del.Const., Art. XVI, § 1. The Amendment to Section 17 authorizing state lotteries was voted on favorably by the 126th General Assembly in 1972 and by the 127th General Assembly in 1973. The same Legislature that gave final approval to the constitutional amendment in its second session in 1974 established the State Lottery and State

Lottery Office. 29 Del.C. § 4801, et seq. In doing so, it construed the term lottery broadly:

> "Lottery" or "state lottery" or "system" shall mean the public gaming systems or games established and operated pursuant to this chapter and including all types of lotteries.

29 Del.C. § 4803(b). The Scoreboard games fall well within the accepted definitions of those terms. "Games" or "gaming" embrace a far wider range of activities than those based on pure chance. Moreover, the legislature contemplated that some lottery games would be related to or based on sporting events. 29 Del.C. § 4805(b)(4). (See also DX 7, a report prepared by Analytics, Inc., for the Delaware Lottery Study Committee. The study, which was distributed to the members of the General Assembly before they voted on the lottery bill, proposed a football lottery much like the one that has been adopted.)

This broad legislative definition is significant because the Delaware courts subscribe to the rule of construction that when terms of the Constitution are ambiguous, the interpretation of the legislature is entitled to deference . . . .

Given the near contemporaneous approval of the lottery amendment and the lottery statute, application of this rule of construction is particularly appropriate in this instance.

In sum then, I conclude that the legislative interpretation of the term lottery together with the weight of authority in other jurisdictions would persuade the Delaware Supreme Court that "lottery" should be interpreted to encompass not only games of pure chance but also games in which chance is the dominant determining factor. The question that remains is whether chance is the dominant factor in some or all of the Scoreboard games. Both the evidence and the case law suggest that it is.

The operation of Football Bonus, Touchdown and Touchdown II are described above. The winners of each are determined by the outcome of the NFL games. Plaintiffs acknowledge that the results of NFL games are a function of myriad factors such as the weather, the health and mood of the players and the condition of the playing field. Some educated predictions can be made about each of these but each is also subject to last minute changes and to an element of the unknowable, or to put it another way, to an element of chance.

In Scoreboard, the unknowable factors in each game are multiplied by the number of games on which the Scoreboard player bets. None of the games permits head-to-head or single game betting. Thus, the element of chance that enters each game is multiplied by a minimum of three and a maximum of fourteen games. In addition, in Touchdown II, the designated point spread or "line" is designed to equalize the odds on the two teams involved. This injects a further factor of chance.

The evidence tends to show that for the first nine weeks of the 1976 season chance was the dominant factor in the outcome of both the NFL games and the Delaware Football Lottery. "Jimmy the Greek" is a widely recognized oddsmaker, syndicated columnist and television personality who earns his living in part by predicting the outcome of NFL games. The record shows that, although he correctly predicted the winner of 101 out of 126 NFL games from

September 12 through November 8, if he had bet on both pools of games in Football Bonus each week, he would have won only three times. He would never have won the All-Game Bonus awarded to those who correctly choose the winners of all fourteen games in a single week. We cannot determine how he would have fared in Touchdown because we do not know which three, four or five games he would have placed wagers on each week. However, he successfully predicted the point spread in only 38 out of 126 games in nine weeks. This strongly suggests that expertise would not have carried the day in this game either.

We do not know anything about [the] football expertise of those who actually played Scoreboard. Nonetheless, over the first nine weeks, the average percentage of winners in each pool of Football Bonus and among the three-game Touchdown bettors hovered around 5%. Among those who bet on five games, the average percentage of winners was .22%. These results lend further support to the contention that chance rather than skill is the dominant factor in the games.

Other courts have likewise concluded that football betting pools and other similar betting schemes based on sporting events qualify as games of chance. In Commonwealth v. Laniewski, 173 Pa.Super. 245, supra, 98 A.2d at 217, responding to a claim that football pools are not games of chance, the court said:

> Past records, statistics and other data might be consulted and, by reasoning from them, a forecast might be made as to the outcome of any particular game or games. However, there are many unpredictable elements which can and do enter into the eventual outcome. These elements, including the fact that at least twenty-two men are concerned in playing the game, constitute the chance which makes this particular pool a lottery. No one knows what may happen once the game has begun.

Accord State v. Steever, 103 N.J.Super. 149, 246 A.2d 743 (App.Div.1968).

The plaintiffs make an alternate argument that the Scoreboard games do not fall within the definition of lottery based on the history of Section 17. They point to earlier versions of the constitutional provision which distinguished between lotteries and pool selling and prohibited both. They contend that this establishes that, under Delaware law, there is a distinction between the two types of gambling activity that survives the 1974 amendment and that pool selling continues to be a prohibited activity under the general interdiction of "all forms of gambling." I do not believe any clear inference as to legislative intent can be drawn from the failure to mention pool selling in the revised Section 17. However, if I were inclined to draw one, I find defendants' explanation, that the General Assembly intended to drop the distinction between lotteries and pool selling and to leave open the possibility that the State Lottery Office might adopt a pool selling type game as part of the State Lottery, the more plausible one.

Validity Of Scoreboard Under 29 Del.C. § 4801, et seq.

1. Duty to Affiliate

Plaintiffs assert next that, even if sports betting pools are permitted by the Delaware Constitution, the Lottery Director has violated the command of 29 Del.C. § 4805(b)(4) to enter into a contract of affiliation with the NFL before commencing a betting scheme based on its games. The NFL reads the relevant provision more narrowly than I believe is warranted. The statute provides:

(b) The Director shall also have the power and it shall be his duty to:

(4) Enter into contracts for the operation of any game or part thereof and into contracts for the promotion of the game or games. This authorization is to be construed to include, but not be limited to, contracting with any racing or other sporting association to conduct sporting events within any racetrack or sports field in the State the outcome of which shall determine the winners of a state game or, as an alternative, to affiliate the determination of the winners of a game with any racing or sporting event held within or without the State.

The NFL argues that this section requires the Lottery Director to obtain the contractual consent of any sporting association before basing a lottery game on its games. To arrive at this construction, it emphasizes the significance of the phrase "it shall be his duty . . . ." but ignores the context in which it appears. Subsection (b) of Section 4805 is the general enabling provision of the lottery statute enumerating in twelve separate subparagraphs a wide range of "powers and duties" of the Director designed to give him the authority required to conduct a lottery that "shall produce the maximum amount of net revenues consonant with the dignity of the State and the general welfare of the people." 29 Del.C. § 4805(a).

Fairly read, the statute gives the Director the power and the duty to engage in each of the specified activities as necessary to achieve the goals of the statute. Thus, under subparagraph (4), the Director is authorized to base lottery games on sport events or races and to enter into contracts to affiliate lottery games with sporting associations when that is necessary.

If one were to accept plaintiffs' interpretation of subparagraph (4) and be consistent, the provision would have to be read to impose an unqualified duty to base lottery games on sports events as well as to enter into contracts with the sporting associations conducting those events. I do not think plaintiffs would argue that the statute requires lottery games based on sports events. Rather, as the statute plainly reads, it is an "authorization," not a command.

One final comment is appropriate. If plaintiffs had the kind of property interest they argued for, then this section could be read to require a contract with the NFL. However, I have concluded that Delaware is not misappropriating any protectible property interest and, thus, no contract is necessary.

2. Revenue Apportionment

The lottery act requires that not less than 30% of the total revenues accruing from the sale of lottery tickets be paid into the General Fund of the State and that not less than 45% be distributed as prize money. Not more than 20% of the gross ticket sales may be devoted to administrative expenses. 29 Del.C. §§ 4805(a)(11) and 4815. As earlier noted, Touchdown II is a fixed payoff game unlike the other Scoreboard games in which prizes are determined on a pari-mutuel basis. The plaintiffs complain that this fixed payoff scheme violates the statutory mandate that not less than 45% of revenues be paid out in prizes and not less than 30% be paid into the State. I agree.

In Touchdown II, there is a prize scale ranging from $10 for four out of four correct selections to $1,200 for twelve out of twelve correct selections. In a given week, if those who play Touchdown II are extraordinarily successful, pay outs may run far over the 45% mark. Similarly, if the players fare very poorly, it is conceivable that there would be no prizes awarded at all. As an example of the former, during the week of December 5, 1976, bets totalling $95,929 were placed on Touchdown II. After an initial announcement that the game would be cancelled, the Lottery Office reinstated the bets and winning tickets totalled $67,330 or 70% of the amount wagered in the game that week.

On its face, the fixed payoff scheme does not comply with the revenue apportionment provisions of the statute. The Lottery Director contends that the probabilities are such that, over time, the payouts in Touchdown II would average 45% of revenues. In addition, he says that the 45% requirement refers to the total prize money awarded in all of the lottery games over an extended period, not on a game-by-game or week-by-week basis.

I have serious doubts that the statute authorizes the Lottery Office to average prize awards over several different games to maintain the 45% pay out level. As far as this Court is aware, the practice of the Office has been to adhere to the 45% standard game-by-game, week-by-week. Moreover, 29 Del.C. § 4815 requires that accumulated funds be turned over to the General Fund monthly. This severely restricts the ability to average prizes over time. But I need not resolve this issue of statutory interpretation because the State has not presented convincing evidence that the devices they propose to achieve the 45% prize structure would accomplish that purpose. The only evidence on this point is [a] declaration [by the Lottery Director] that, "(t)he probabilities we have studied indicate that on the average we would pay out what we are supposed to pay out, 45% or more." That testimony is not sufficient to rebut what the fixed payoff structure suggests, that the game was established and operated without regard to the 45% prize money requirement. It must be invalidated.

THE FEDERAL ANTI-GAMBLING LAW CLAIMS

Plaintiffs maintain that defendants are operating the Delaware Lottery in a manner which violates a number of sections of the federal anti-gambling laws, e.g., 18 U.S.C. §§ 1301, 1302, 1304 and 1084. I assume, without deciding, that this is true. Nevertheless, the relief sought cannot be granted on this ground.

Plaintiffs Have No Civil Claim Based Directly Upon The Federal Anti-Gambling Statutes

The Supreme Court recently observed in Piper v. Chris-Craft Industries, Inc., 430 U.S. 1, 97 S.Ct. 926, 51 L.Ed.2d 124 (1977), that "the reasoning of

. . . (the cases which have implied a private cause of action where none has been expressly provided by Congress) is that, where congressional purposes are likely to be undermined absent private enforcement, private remedies may be implied in favor of the particular class intended to be protected by the statute." 430 U.S. at 25, 97 S.Ct. at 941. The opinion in Piper also reaffirmed the court's position in Cort v. Ash, 422 U.S. 66, 95 S.Ct. 2080, 45 L.Ed.2d 26 (1975) that four factors are " 'relevant' in determining whether a private remedy is implicit in a statute not expressly providing one." 37 U.S. at 430, 97 S.Ct. at 947. They are: (1) whether plaintiff is one of the class for whose especial benefit the statute was enacted; (2) whether there is any indication of legislative intent, explicit or implicit, either to create such a remedy or deny one; (3) whether it is consistent under the underlying purposes of the legislative scheme to imply such a remedy for the plaintiff; and (4) whether the cause of action is one traditionally relegated to state law.

The anti-gambling laws upon which plaintiffs rely restrict the utilization of interstate commerce in aid of [a] gambling enterprise. They were enacted at the turn of the century "to protect the (private) citizen from the demoralizing (and) corrupting influence" of solicitations to gamble. United States v. Horner, 44 F. 677 (S.D.N.Y.1891), aff'd, 143 U.S. 207, 12 S.Ct. 407, 36 L.Ed. 126 (1892). I believe the suggestion that they were enacted for the "especial" benefit of sports entrepreneurs to be simply far fetched.

It is true that Congress in 1974 enacted 18 U.S.C. § 1307 for the purpose of exempting state sponsored lotteries from certain of the prohibitions of Sections 1301-1304 and defined "lottery" for this purpose as not including "the placing or accepting of bets or wagers on sporting events or contests." While this clearly exhibits an intent to exclude state sponsored sports betting from the exclusion, it does not alter the basic purpose of the statute or those who comprise its direct beneficiaries. Moreover, Section 1307 cannot be read to justify implication of a private right of action in favor of sports entrepreneurs without inferring a congressional intent to create a cause of action against state governments and the Supreme Court has cautioned that such an intent should not be inferred absent clear evidence in the legislative history. Employees of the Department of Public Health and Welfare of Missouri v. Department of Public Health and Welfare of Missouri, 411 U.S. 279, 285, 93 S.Ct. 1614, 36 L.Ed.2d 251 (1973).

No legislative history has been cited to the Court which indicates any congressional intent to create a private cause of action of any kind, much less a private cause of action by a commercial enterprise against a State. Nor is there any indication that private enforcement is necessary to effectuate the restrictions on interstate commerce which Congress sought to impose. For these reasons, I hold that plaintiffs have no private cause of action under the federal anti-gambling statutes.

Plaintiffs Have No Unfair Competition Claim Under Which Defendants' Duty Is Measured By The Federal Anti-Gambling Statutes

Plaintiffs have cited a number of cases which hold that a commercial enterprise has an unfair competition claim against a competitor who achieves a competitive advantage by conducting his business in an illegal manner. In

Featherstone v. Independent Service Stations Association, 10 S.W.2d 124 (Tex.Civ.App.1928), for example, the owner of a filling station was granted injunctive relief against a chain of competing stations which was promoting its own services and products by means of a lottery illegal under state law.

I do not question the reasoning of these cases. An entrepreneur who is willing to obey the law should not be put at a disadvantage by a competitor who is less scrupulous. This reasoning cannot be stretched to cover a situation like the one before this Court, however, without emasculating the settled principles discussed above which circumscribe judicial creation of private causes of action.

Moreover, the only potential injury to the NFL which this Court is able to perceive arises not from the aspects of defendants' activities which are alleged to violate the federal gambling statutes, but rather from those aspects of the Delaware Lottery which have produced confusion as to sponsorship. Stated another way, if such confusion is eliminated, this record does not support the view that the existence of the Delaware Lottery, whether legal in all respects or not, will cause injury to the NFL plaintiffs.

THE CIVIL RIGHTS ACT CLAIM

Plaintiffs maintain that the defendants, acting under color of state law, have taken their property without due process of law. I have previously concluded that the common law of unfair competition [as well as federal trademark law] entitled plaintiffs to protection against confusion as to source or affiliation and it is, therefore, unnecessary to consider whether they might be entitled to the same relief under 42 U.S.C. § 1983. I have also held that, with this exception, defendants have not deprived plaintiffs of any legally recognized property interest. Further relief under the Civil Rights Act would, accordingly, be inappropriate.

DEFENSES AND COUNTERCLAIMS

By way of affirmative defense, the defendants assert that the NFL is barred from obtaining any injunctive relief from this Court under the doctrines of acquiescence and unclean hands. I conclude that the defendants have established neither defense.

Acquiescence consists of conduct on the part of a trademark holder that amounts to "an assurance to the defendant, express or implied, that the plaintiff would not assert his trademark rights against the defendant." There was no acquiescence here. From the time the NFL learned that Delaware was considering a football lottery, it vigorously voiced its opposition and its belief that such a lottery was incompatible with the NFL's trademark rights.

The course of conduct of which the defendants complain is more consistent with an abandonment defense and it may be that that is the defense they intended to assert.

The defendant points to the NFL's failure to bring suit against other gambling related uses of NFL team names such as in the Nevada and Montana betting schemes, in tout sheets which publish predicted point spreads and in newspaper circulation contests.

It would appear that most of the examples the defendants cite are small scale and, in some cases, short lived uses of NFL registered marks. The NFL could reasonably have concluded that there was no risk that the public would be misled into believing that the NFL was involved in any way. And not every de minimis use must be pursued.

Football gambling in Nevada would appear to be the only large scale use of NFL names to which the defendants can point in support of their abandonment theory. Numerous representatives of the NFL testified that they considered the situation in Nevada unique and did not believe it posed the same kind of threat to their enterprise. Regardless of the validity of that judgment, an intent to abandon cannot be inferred from the mere failing to bring suit in Nevada. This is particularly true when one considers the number of instances in which the NFL has brought suit or taken other measures to protect its trademark rights in non-gambling contexts.

Defendants' unclean hands defense is based on what it characterizes as NFL's trademark misuse in its licensing program. Relying on a blank licensing agreement form for proof of its allegations, the defendants complain that the NFL is guilty of using its trademark in violation of the antitrust laws. In particular, defendants claim that all licenses are exclusive, that they are available only in a package deal for the marks of all twenty-eight clubs, that minimum royalty payments are required to pay royalties at a single fixed rate. I need not consider whether these practices alone or together would constitute antitrust violations. The blank form defendants proffer is simply insufficient proof of how the NFL trademark licensing program operates.

In addition to relying on these alleged antitrust violations as the basis of an unclean hands defense, the defendants raise the antitrust claims affirmatively as a counterclaim for treble damages. The failure of proof is quite obviously just as fatal to the counterclaim. Moreover, defendants have not shown that they were injured by the allegedly anti-competitive practices.

CONCLUSION

For all of the reasons discussed in the foregoing Opinion, the Court will enter an Order (1) enjoining the defendants to include in publicly disseminated Scoreboard materials a clear and conspicuous statement that Scoreboard is not associated with or authorized by the National Football League and (2) declaring Touchdown II in violation of 29 Del.C. §§ 4805(a)(11) and 4815. All other requests for relief are denied.

PETITION OF CASINO LICENSEES FOR APPROVAL OF A NEW GAME, RULEMAKING AND AUTHORIZATION OF A TEST

633 A.2d 1050 (N.J. Super. Ct. App. Div.),
aff'd mem., 647 A.2d 454 (N.J. 1993)

STEIN, Justice.

We accelerated this appeal, filed on November 18, 1993, permitted the professional major leagues to intervene and promptly heard oral argument.

We affirm the determination of the New Jersey Casino Control Commission that it has no constitutional or statutory authority to authorize sports betting in New Jersey's gambling casinos.

Appellants are the operators of all twelve licensed gambling casinos in Atlantic City. Intervenors are the leagues conducting major league professional sports in this country: the National Football League, the National Basketball Association, the National Hockey League and the Commissioner of Baseball. Earlier this year, the Legislature chose not to vote on a joint resolution to place a referendum on the ballot permitting a proposed constitutional amendment authorizing casino betting on sports events. The Leagues were among those who vigorously opposed submission of this proposed constitutional amendment to the voters.

Thereafter, on November 15, 1993, the Casinos filed a petition with the Commission seeking a determination that the 1976 state constitutional provision authorizing casino gambling and the regulatory legislation enacted pursuant to it authorized sports betting operated by casinos as a "gambling game" permissibly conducted in those establishments. N.J. Const. art. IV, § 7, ¶ 2D.

Attached to this petition was a comprehensive set of proposed regulations, modeled after those adopted in the state of Nevada where sports betting is legal. Sports betting, called "sports wagering" in the proposed regulations, is permitted on all sports events, professional and amateur, with the exception of sports contests in which there is participation by an educational institutional or non-professional organization principally located in New Jersey; high school sports events; the outcome of a public election held inside or outside of New Jersey; and any horse race not governed by the Simulcasting Racing Act, N.J.S.A. 5:5-110 to -126.

The Casinos required a speedy decision by the Commission. Under the Professional and Amateur Sports Protection Act, 28 U.S.C.A. § 3701 to 3704, governmentally-authorized betting on athletic events generally expired on January 1, 1993. However, the effective date of the prohibition is extended for New Jersey casinos to one year after the effective date of the Act, or January 1, 1994. 28 U.S.C.A. § 3704(a)(3)(A).

The Commission rejected the interpretation advanced by petitioners. So do we.

The constitutional amendment authorizing casino gambling provides:

> It shall be lawful for the Legislature to authorize by law the establishment and operation, under regulation and control by the State, of gambling houses or casinos within the boundaries, as heretofore established, of the city of Atlantic City, county of Atlantic, and to license and tax such operations and equipment used in connection therewith . . . .
>
> The type and number of such casinos or gambling houses and of the gambling games which may be conducted in such establishment shall be determined by or pursuant to the terms of the law authorizing the establishment and operation thereof. [N.J. Const. art. IV, § 7, ¶ 2D.]

The expression of legislative intent surrounding adoption of this constitutional amendment is so strong that we would be remiss if we were to decide that this constitutional amendment authorizes not only traditional in-house gambling games inside casinos but also permits sports betting therein. State v. Churchdale Leasing, Inc., 115 N.J. 83, 101, 557 A.2d 277 (1989) (examination of legislative history is relevant to determine legislative intent).

Gambling has been legalized in New Jersey very cautiously, one step at a time. The constitution of 1844 originally provided "no lottery shall be authorized by this state; and no ticket in any lottery not authorized by a law of this state shall be bought or sold within the state." N.J. Const. of 1844 art. IV, § 7, ¶ 2. That paragraph was amended on September 28, 1897, to a more restrictive provision, specifically prohibiting lotteries and all other forms of gambling:

> No lottery shall be authorized by the legislature or otherwise in this state, and no ticket in any lottery shall be bought or sold within this state, nor shall pool-selling, book-making or gambling of any kind be authorized or allowed within this state, nor shall any gambling device, practice or game of chance now prohibited by law be legalized, or the remedy, penalty or punishment now provided therefor be in any way diminished. [Id., as amended, September 28, 1897, proclamation October 26, 1897.]

No form of legalized betting was permitted in New Jersey until 1939, when the constitution was amended to permit pari-mutuel betting on horse races, but only at horse tracks:

> It shall be lawful to hold, carry on, and operate in this State race meetings whereat the trotting, running or steeplechase racing of horses only may be conducted between the hours of sunrise and sunset on week days only and in duly legalized race tracks, at which the pari-mutuel system of betting shall be permitted. [N.J. Const. of 1844 art. IV, § 7, ¶ 2, as amended June 20, 1939, proclamation July 11, 1939.]

The prohibition against any kind of gambling not specifically permitted by the constitution was carried over into our 1947 constitution:

> No gambling of any kind shall be authorized by the Legislature unless the specific kind, restrictions and control thereof have been heretofore submitted to, and authorized by a majority of the votes cast by, the people at a special election or shall hereafter be submitted to, and authorized by a majority of the votes cast thereon by, the legally qualified voters of the State voting at a general election . . . . [N.J. Const. art. IV, § 7, ¶ 2.]

The constitutional prohibition contained certain exceptions permitting the conduct of bingo and the selling of raffles by charitable, religious and other non-profit organizations. Id., art. IV, § 7, ¶ 2A and B.

The constitution was again amended in 1969 to specifically authorize the conduct of the state lotteries. Id., art. IV, § 7, ¶ 2C, amended general election November 4, 1969.

Following a rejection in 1974 by the voters of a proposed referendum authorizing state-wide casino gambling, the constitution was amended in 1976 to add the previously-cited provision authorizing in-house gambling in casinos located in Atlantic City. Id., art. IV, § 7, ¶ 2D.

When hearings on the proposed amendment were conducted before the Assembly State Government and Federal and Interstate Relations Committee, Steven P. Perskie, the Assembly sponsor of the proposed amendment, specifically stated that the amendment "would not authorize sports betting of any kind." Perskie is now chairman of the New Jersey Casino Control Commission. Its Senate sponsor, Joseph McGahn, stated:

> Gentlemen, I agree with you as far as all sports betting is concerned . . . . There is nothing in this bill which would permit casinos . . . to have all sports betting . . . .

When the Committee reported favorably on the proposed joint legislative resolution authorizing submission of Atlantic City casino gambling to the voters of this state, it issued the following statement:

> The committee is reporting this bill favorably with the expressed understanding that it is not the intention of the sponsors, the committee, or the Legislature that this constitutional amendment would authorize gambling legislation that would permit any form of gambling or betting on the outcome of any sports events or other activities that take place beyond the confines of the casino itself. [Senate Statement to Assembly Concurrent Resolution No. 126, May 19, 1976.]

The New Jersey Supreme Court has recognized this state's step-at-a-time approach to the introduction of legalized gambling within our borders. In Atlantic City Racing Ass'n v. Attorney General, 98 N.J. 535, 489 A.2d 165 (1985), the Court held that a specific constitutional amendment was required to authorize inter-track pari-mutuel betting on simulcast horse racing. Id. at 551-52, 489 A.2d 165. Its unanimous opinion authored by Judge Matthews, temporarily assigned, noted that:

> The evolution of legalized gambling in New Jersey has been grudging. Because of widespread abuses in various gambling activities and the attendant social and economic ills engendered, gambling has historically been viewed as an undesirable activity. [Id. at 539-40, 489 A.2d 165.]

> New Jersey's comprehensive policy against all forms of gambling (except where specifically authorized by the people) has been clear and long-standing . . . . This principle remains inviolate to this day. [Id. at 546, 489 A.2d 165.]

Elsewhere the Court noted:

> By adopting the Constitution of 1947, which contains Art. IV, § 7, par. 2, the people reaffirmed the sentiments implicitly expressed by the comprehensiveness of the 1939 amendment that any decisions as to the expansion of gambling in New Jersey were to be considered and resolved by its citizens at the polls and not by the Legislature. The adoption of the 1939 amendment in this historical context, following a forty-two year ban on all public gambling, suggests a cautious and restrictive approval of the circumstances under which the [then] sole

authorized activity, pari-mutuel wagering on horse races, would be allowed. [Id. at 544, 489 A.2d 165.]

The gambling provisions of the state constitution were later amended in 1990 by a provision authorizing the Legislature to permit casinos to accept bets on results of simulcast horse races conducted at tracks within or outside New Jersey:

> It shall be lawful for the Legislature to authorize, by law, (1) the simultaneous transmission by picture of running and harness horse races conducted at racetracks located within or outside of this State, or both, to gambling houses or casinos in the city of Atlantic City and (2) wagering at those gambling establishments on the results of those races. [N.J. Const. art. IV, § 7, ¶ 2E, amended November 6, 1990.]

The constitutional permission to authorize simulcast horse betting did not expand the definition of "gambling games" in subparagraph D. Instead, a specific provision was added, subparagraph E. Ibid.

The introduction of various forms of legalized gambling into this state has always been by specific constitutional amendment. Sports betting is not a constitutionally-authorized form of legalized gambling.

Moreover, the Commission lacks legislative as well as constitutional authority to authorize casino-operated sports betting. The Casino Control Act, N.J.S.A. 5:12-1 to -210, defines "game" or "gambling game" as

> [a]ny banking or percentage game located within the casino or simulcasting facility played with cards, dice, tiles, dominos, or any electronic, electrical, or mechanical device or machine for money, property, or any representative of value. [N.J.S.A. 5:12-21, as amended, L.1991, c. 182, § 9, eff. June 29, 1991; L.1992, c. 19, § 26, eff. June 12, 1992.]

Originally, the Legislature authorized only specified games as suitable for casino gambling, a list which was later expanded by statutory amendment so that it included roulette, baccarat, blackjack, craps, big six wheel, slot machines, minibaccarat, red dog, pai gow, and sic bo, and any variations or composites of those games found suitable by the Casino Control Commission for use after an appropriate test or experimental period. N.J.S.A. 5:12-5. Later, the statute was amended to permit any other game which is "determined by the commission to be compatible with the public interest and to be suitable for casino use after such appropriate test or experimental period as the commission may deem appropriate." L.1992, c. 9, § 1, eff. May 19, 1992.

Before this last amendment was adopted, its sponsors, Senator William L. Gormley and Assemblyman John F. Gaffney, sent a joint letter to the chairman of the Assembly Financial Institutions Committee:

> The question has been raised whether A-1233 and S-652 are intended to grant the Casino Control Commission power to authorize casinos to conduct wagering on sports events. As sponsors of these companion bills, we advise you that the bills have no such intent.
>
> The bills, even if so intended would not have that effect because a constitutional amendment approved by the voters is a prerequisite to

the commencement of sports wagering in any form in New Jersey. [Letter from Gormley and Gaffney to Penn of May 4, 1992.]

The Committee then released the bill with the following statement:

> The committee releases this bill after being informed by the sponsors, and with the understanding, that this bill is not intended to and does not grant the Casino Control Commission power to authorize casinos to conduct wagering of any kind on sports events.
>
> The committee, by the release of this bill, take no position with respect to sports wagering. The committee agrees with the sponsors that sports wagering can only be authorized by adoption of a constitutional amendment approved by the voters at a general election and by enactment of enabling legislation thereafter. [Assembly Financial Institutions Committee Statement to Assembly, No. 1233, May 4, 1992.]

Additionally, N.J.S.A. 5:12-194(e) provides that sports betting and casino simulcasting shall be conducted in the same area, and in accordance with regulations of the Casino Control Commission only "if wagering at casinos on sports events is authorized by the voters of this State and by enabling legislation enacted by the Legislature." Ibid.

The Commission's conclusion that sports betting is not a permitted form of gambling in Atlantic City's casinos is consistent with the constitutional and statutory scheme which, with one exception, permits only those games which take place completely within the confines of a casino. The conduct of in-house casino games is subject to the strict regulation of the Casino Control Commission, lessening the opportunity of a gambler, casino or third person to fix such games. Pari-mutuel horse betting is specifically permitted by our constitution, as is simulcast betting on horse races, whether the race is conducted inside or outside of this state. Horse racing is also a highly regulated activity stringently supervised by the New Jersey Racing Commission pursuant to N.J.S.A. 5:5-22 to -99. Betting on simulcast horse races is also controlled by the Simulcasting Racing Act, N.J.S.A. 5:5-110 to -126. Regulatory controls exist in every state where pari-mutuel betting is conducted.

Except for constitutionally-authorized simulcast horse race betting, gambling casinos may operate only those games conducted solely in-house. They may not offer betting on events which take place or where the result is determined at a location outside a casino's four walls.

Affirmed.

KENT v. MINDLIN
52 F.3d 333 (9th Cir. 1995)

PER CURIAM.

Plaintiffs Michael and John Kent agreed with Ivan Mindlin to pool their resources (skill and money) and place bets on sports events. After several profitable years, the Kents thought Mindlin was wrongfully withholding their share of wagering profits and brought this diversity action. The district court dismissed the action after taking enough testimony to decide that the action was basically a suit to enforce the terms of an illegal agreement. The Kents appeal. We affirm in part and vacate and remand in part.

I.

From 1981 until 1986, the Kents, Mindlin, and others were parties to a sports betting pool which placed bets at licensed sports books in Nevada, as well as with unlicensed bookies in states where sports betting is illegal.

In 1987, the Kents and Mindlin allegedly agreed that all bets would be placed with licensed Nevada bookmakers. The Kents claim that all bets placed in 1987 were therefore legal, and that they are owed approximately $200,000. The Kents also allege an additional 1987 sports betting agreement. Pursuant to this agreement, Michael Kent was to furnish Mindlin with odds for the college football season in exchange for a $700,000 fee. Mindlin was then free to lay bets on the games at licensed Nevada sports books and keep any gambling profits for himself. The agreement lasted one week, for which Michael Kent claims he is owed $35,650.

A. The 1984-1985 Agreement

In 1984 and 1985, the Kents knew that the pool was placing substantial bets with unlicensed bookmakers in states other than Nevada. Indeed, on one occasion Michael Kent himself travelled to New York City to pick up $100,000 that had been won on bets placed with New York bookmakers. Michael Kent explained that the pool placed bets with unlicensed bookmakers in addition to licensed Nevada sports books because unlicensed bookmakers would accept larger bets (Kent testified that Mindlin told him "you could bet more money with bookmakers in one square mile of Manhattan than you could in the entire state of Nevada."), and because bets placed with unlicensed bookmakers would not affect the "line" at the licensed Nevada sports books. Licensed sports books adjust their "lines" in response to wagering patterns. By placing bets with unlicensed bookmakers first, and with licensed Nevada sports books last, the pool could secure more favorable "lines," and, obviously, increase the pool's probability of success.

These facts have never been disputed. The dispute has been over which state's law should be applied to the enforceability of the 1984-1985 pool agreement.

1.

In contract cases, Nevada courts appear to follow the Restatement (Second) of Conflict of Laws (1971). See Laxalt v. McClatchy, 116 F.R.D. 438, 448-49 (D.Nev.1987). Applying Section 202 of the Restatement, the district court first looked to the laws of New York and Florida, two of many states where the pool placed bets with unlicensed bookmakers. Because sports gambling is illegal in those states, the district court concluded that the pool acted illegally. Applying Section 188 of the Restatement, the district court next applied Nevada law to determine whether the illegality of the pool's conduct affected the enforceability of the parties' agreement to share profits from the wagers. Because under Nevada law "contracts made in contravention of the law do not create a right of action," Vincent v. Santa Cruz, 98 Nev. 338, 381 (1982), the district court ruled that Nevada courts would not enforce the pool agreement.

Although the district court's choice of law analysis seems to be a straightforward application of Sections 202 and 188, and finds support in Florida Risk Planning Consultants, Inc. v. Transport Life Insurance Company, 732 F.2d 593, 595-96 (7th Cir.1984) and Don King Productions, Inc. v. Douglas, 742 F.Supp. 741, 753 n.13 (S.D.N.Y. 1990), the Kents argue that Nevada courts would approach the choice of law issue differently. They argue that because licensed sports-betting exists in Nevada, the courts of that state would apply Nevada law to determine the legality of the pool agreement; and would hold that it was legal. It is not necessary to spell out the details of the Kents' approach to the choice of law issue, because their premise—that under Nevada law the pool is legal—is wrong. In the end, it does not matter which state's law is used to analyze the legality of the pool: it is illegal in every state in the union, including Nevada.

2.

Nevada courts do enforce betting pool agreements to lay wagers at licensed casinos and share the profits. In Siegel v. McEvoy, 101 Nev. 623 (1985), the plaintiff agreed to pay the defendant's costs in entering a poker series sponsored by Las Vegas' Horseshoe Club, and the defendant agreed to pay the plaintiff twenty percent of any winnings he might receive. The defendant won a substantial sum, but refused to pay the plaintiff his twenty percent share. When the plaintiff sued for breach of contract, the defendant argued that the suit was premised on an unenforceable gaming debt. The Nevada Supreme Court held that the contract was not an unenforceable gambling contract, but a legally enforceable business arrangement:

> [Plaintiff] allegedly provided [defendant] with funds to cover [defendant's] costs in entering a lawful poker tournament sponsored by a duly licensed Las Vegas casino in which [plaintiff] did not participate. If his evidence prevails, their agreement was to divide between themselves the profits made in the tournament, and was not a situation in which one player was to lose to the other.

Id. at 626.

Had the parties' 1984-1985 pool agreement been limited to placing bets at licensed sports books, it would have been enforceable under Siegel. But the agreement was not so limited. The agreement was, in part, to place bets with unlicensed bookmakers, and unlicensed bookmaking is a crime in Nevada. See NRS 463.160.

Unlicensed gambling is obviously deleterious to Nevada's economy, because it goes untaxed. It is also deleterious to Nevada's public welfare, because it tends to attract crime. Over forty years ago the Nevada Supreme Court wrote:

> We note that while gambling, duly licensed, is a lawful enterprise in Nevada, it is unlawful elsewhere in this country; that unlawfully followed elsewhere it tends there to create as well as to attract a criminal element; that it is a pursuit which, unlawfully followed, is

conducive of corruption; that the criminal and corruptive elements engaged in unlawful gambling tend to organize and thus obtain widespread power and control over corruptive criminal enterprises throughout this country; that the existence of organized crime has long been recognized and has become a serious concern of the Federal government as well as the governments of the several states . . . . The risks to which the public is subjected by the legalizing of this otherwise unlawful activity are met solely by the manner in which licensing and control are carried out.

Nevada Tax Commission v. Hicks, 73 Nev. 115, 119-20 (1957). That the pool's unlicensed gambling occurred out of state does not change matters. Nevada's economy suffers just as much when gamblers place bets with unlicensed bookmakers out of state as it does when gamblers place bets with unlicensed bookmakers in state. It is the public policy of Nevada to refuse to allow its courts "to serve as paymaster of the wages of crime,'" Loomis v. Lange Financial Corporation, 109 Nev. 1121, 1165 (1993), quoting Stone v. Freeman, 298 N.Y. 268 (1948). The trial court correctly held that it was against the public policy of Nevada to enforce the parties' 1984-1985 pool agreement.

B. The 1987 Agreement

The Kents offered evidence that, in 1987, the parties concluded their earlier pool agreement and struck a new one. According to the Kents, in response to the "heat" of a federal investigation of the pool, the parties expressly agreed that their 1987 bets would be placed exclusively with licensed sports books in Nevada. The Kents also allege that Michael Kent reached an additional agreement with Mindlin, pursuant to which Michael Kent would provide Mindlin with odds on college football games in exchange for a $700,000 fee.

Both Michael Kent and Mindlin testified in depositions that, in 1987, bets were placed only in licensed Nevada sports books. At an evidentiary hearing, the Kents tried to present additional evidence to that effect, but were cut short when Mindlin's counsel notified the district court that he was unprepared to address the 1987 agreements.

At a later proceeding however, Mindlin's counsel brushed aside the parties' factual dispute. Applying the law of criminal conspiracy by analogy, Mindlin's counsel argued that because the 1987 agreements and the previous agreement were agreements to handicap and wager on sporting events, the 1987 agreements could not be considered distinct or untainted by the previous years' illegality. In its grant of summary judgment, the district court apparently agreed with this argument.

No valid reason appears in this record why the 1987 agreement, if proved at trial to have been a legal contract, could not be severed from its antecedents and enforced according to whatever terms the parties can prove.

The Kents say they will testify that, in 1987, "the Kents performed data collection and updating activities; that Mindlin performed wagering activities; that the parties agreed that all of the wagers were to be placed at licensed casinos in Nevada," and so forth. Under Siegel, that evidence could support the Kents' claims for sums accrued in 1987.

II.

We hold that the illegal agreement in effect between the parties prior to 1987 was unenforceable, and the court correctly left the parties where it found them. However, we vacate the summary judgment, and remand for trial to allow the Kents to present evidence pertaining to the 1987 wagering agreements. Each party shall bear its own costs.

AFFIRMED IN PART, VACATED AND REMANDED IN PART.

Notes

1. Despite prevailing in court, Delaware abandoned its NFL lottery at the end of the 1976-77 season. In April 1984, the Canadian Sports Pool Corporation, hoping to raise funds for the 1988 Winter Olympics in Calgary, began offering a similar lottery tied to Major League Baseball games (over the vehement protests of Commissioner Bowie Kuhn). The venture failed to catch on with consumers and retailers, however, and was terminated after just a few months.

In September 1989, Oregon started its own NFL-themed lottery known as "Sports Action," and in December 1989 added a basketball version (which it dropped after one year to settle a lawsuit that had been filed by the NBA). To date, Sports Action has raised $25 million for Oregon's colleges, of which 88% has been used to fund athletic scholarships. For the rules of Sports Action and a sample playing card, *see* www.oregonlottery.org/sports/index.shtml.

2. In 1992, due largely to the efforts of Senator Bill Bradley (D-N.J.), the one-time basketball star, Congress enacted the Professional and Amateur Sports Protection Act ("PASPA"), 28 U.S.C. §§ 3701-3704. The statute makes government-sanctioned betting on athletic contests illegal, but "grandfathers in" certain activities, including Delaware's and Oregon's NFL lotteries, pari-mutuel sports wagering in Montana, and licensed sports books in Nevada. *See* 28 U.S.C. § 3704. PAPSA also gave Atlantic City casinos one year to convince state officials to authorize sports bookmaking. As the *Petition of Casino Licensees* case explains, New Jersey declined this invitation. For a useful analysis of PASPA, *see* Bill Bradley, *The Professional and Amateur Sports Protection Act—Policy Concerns Behind Senate Bill 474*, 2 Seton Hall J. Sport L. 5 (1992).

3. Since 2000, a number of lawmakers have been seeking to amend PAPSA so as to ban all betting on collegiate games (due to a rash of "point shaving" scandals at such schools as Arizona State University, Northwestern University, and the University of Maryland). Because their bills, as a practical matter, would affect only Nevada's licensed sports books, the state's congressional delegation has resisted such efforts, calling instead for greater enforcement of existing laws. *See further* Jeffrey R. Rodefer & Daurean G. Sloan, *Nevada's Proposal to Strengthen Its Collegiate Sports Betting Regulations and the NCAA's Push for a Congressional Ban*, 9 Nev. Law. 10 (Mar. 2001), and Aaron J. Slavin, Comment, *The "Las Vegas" Loophole and the Current Push in Congress Towards a Blanket Prohibition on Collegiate Sports Gambling*, 10 U. Miami Bus. L. Rev. 715 (2002).

4. As the *Kent* case points out, far more bets are placed with illegal sports books than with legal ones. While Nevada's 150 licensed sports books annually handle $2.5 billion in bets, unlicensed sports books are estimated to do nearly $370 billion worth of business. For an inside look at Nevada's sports book industry, *see* Chad Millman, *The Odds: One Season, Three Gamblers, and the Death of Their Las Vegas* (2001).

5. Many Americans now participate in fantasy sports leagues, often betting on the results. At present, the lawfulness of such betting is unclear, although both the Florida and Louisiana attorneys general have issued opinions condemning it. *See* Michael J. Thompson, *Give Me $25 on Red and Derek Jeter for $26: Do Fantasy Sports Leagues Constitute Gambling?*, 8 Sports Law. J. 21 (2001), and Nicole Davidson, Comment, *Internet Gambling: Should Fantasy Sports Leagues be Prohibited?*, 39 San Diego L. Rev. 201 (2002).

6. The legal issues posed by sports betting are explored in further detail in Anthony N. Cabot & Robert D. Faiss, *Sports Gambling in the Cyberspace Era*, 5 Chap. L. Rev. 1 (2002), and Lori K. Miller & Cathryn L. Claussen, *Online Sports Gambling—Regulation or Prohibition?*, 11 J. Legal Aspects Sport 99 (2001). *See also* Richard O. Davies & Richard G. Abram, *Betting the Line: Sports Wagering in American Life* (2001); James Jeffries & Charles Oliver, *The Book on Bookies: An Inside Look at a Successful Sports Gambling Operation* (2000); Stanford Wong, *Sharp Sports Betting* (2001).

Problem 20

Each fall, a newspaper offers a weekly "forecasting game" that awards prizes to contestants who correctly predict the outcome of various football games selected by the paper's sports editor. No purchase is necessary to play, and there is no limit on the number of people who can win. Is the contest legal? *See Seattle Times Company v. Tielsch*, 495 P.2d 1366 (Wash. 1972).

C. ILLEGAL WAGERS

UNITED STATES v. BOX
530 F.2d 1258 (5th Cir. 1976)

GOLDBERG, Circuit Judge.

Henry Floyd 'Red' Box was convicted by a jury of violating 18 U.S.C. § 1955, the federal antigambling statute. On appeal, Box argues that the evidence was insufficient to support this verdict. We agree and therefore reverse the conviction.

Federal agents conducted an extensive investigation of several bookmaking operations in the Shreveport-Bossier City area during the 1973 football season, culminating in simultaneous raids on the last day of the season. A one-count indictment filed on April 25, 1974, charged appellant Box and ten other persons with the operation of an illegal gambling business in violation of 18 U.S.C. § 1955. The indictment named three unindicted principals as having been involved in the same illegal gambling business. One of the defendants was granted a continuance and severance, due to the death of his counsel. Six others entered pleas of nolo contendere or guilty prior to trial. Trial of the four remaining defendants began on September 30, 1974. The guilty plea of one of these was accepted on October 4, 1974. Later the same day the jury returned a verdict of guilty as to Box and the other two. Only Box has appealed.

18 U.S.C. § 1955 provides in part as follows:

(a) Whoever conducts, finances, manages, supervises, directs, or owns all or part of an illegal gambling business shall be fined not more than $20,000 or imprisoned not more than five years, or both.

(b) As used in this section—

(1) 'illegal gambling business' means a gambling business which—

(i) is a violation of the law of a State or political subdivision in which it is conducted;

(ii) involves five or more persons who conduct, finance, manage, supervise, direct, or own all or part of such business; and

(iii) has been or remains in substantially continuous operation for a period in excess of thirty days or has a gross revenue of $2,000 in any single day.

(2) 'gambling' includes but is not limited to pool-selling, bookmaking, maintaining slot machines, roulette wheels or dice tables, and conducting lotteries, policy, bolita or numbers games, or selling chances therein.

Louisiana Revised Statutes, § 14:90, provides as follows:

Gambling is the intentional conducting, or directly assisting in the conducting, as a business, of any game, contest, lottery, or contrivance whereby a person risks the loss of anything of value in order to realize a profit.

Whoever commits the crime of gambling shall be fined not more than five hundred dollars, or imprisoned for not more than six months, or both.

Our review of the evidence and application of the law in this case require an understanding of the general nature of a bookmaking operation, and so we preface our consideration of the issues here with a very brief summary on that subject.

THE NATURE OF A BOOKMAKING OPERATION

This section might be subtitled, 'How to Succeed in Gambling Without Really Gambling,' because a successful bookmaker makes his profit not from winning bets, but rather from collecting a certain percentage of the amount bet that losing bettors are required to pay for the privilege of betting. This percentage, 10% in the Shreveport area, is called 'juice' or 'viggerish,' and its effect is to require a bettor to risk $110 in an attempt to win $100. So that betting odds can remain even on each game, a bookmaker normally has a 'line'—on each game on which he is taking bets, one team will be favored by a certain number of points, called the 'point spread.' For further explanations of the concepts of 'line' and 'point spread,' see United States v. Joseph, 5 Cir. 1975, 519 F.2d 1068, 1070 n.2, cert. denied, 1976, _U.S._, 96 S.Ct. 1103, 47 L.Ed.2d 312 (44 U.S.L.W. 3471, 1976); United States v. Thomas, 8 Cir. 1975, 508 F.2d 1200, 1202 n.2, cert. denied, 1975, 421 U.S. 947, 95 S.Ct. 1677, 44 L.Ed.2d 100. See generally United States v. Pepe, 3 Cir. 1975, 512 F.2d 1129; United States v. Bobo, 4 Cir. 1973, 477 F.2d 974, cert. denied, 1975, 421 U.S. 909, 95 S.Ct. 1557, 43 L.Ed.2d 774.

In an ideal situation, a bookmaker would have bets from bettors exactly balanced on each contest, so that no matter which team 'wins' (read: beats the point spread), the bookmaker is assured a definite percentage of the amount bet. That is, he would collect 110% of the amount he would be required to pay. With a multitude of bets each week, this ideal of perfectly balanced books cannot be achieved. When the bets placed with a bookmaker on a certain contest become very unbalanced on one side, however, there are certain measures the bookmaker might take to lessen the incumbent risk. He can refuse to take further bets on that side, hoping enough bets will be placed on the other side to effect some rough balance. Alternatively, he can adjust his 'line' on the contest, thus making the underbet side more attractive. See United States v. Schaefer, 8 Cir. 1975, 510 F.2d 1312 n.7, cert. denied, 1975, 421 U.S. 978, 95 S.Ct. 1980, 44 L.Ed.2d 470; Thomas, supra, 508 F.2d at 1202 n.2. The adjustment of line is apparently disfavored as a solution, because it may result in two local bookmakers offering a significantly different point spread on an event. This would offer local bettors an opportunity for a 'middle'—two bets placed on different teams with two bookmakers which together could not lose more than 10% of one of the bets, and, if the actual point difference were in the middle, might both be won. See id.; United States v. Schullo, D.Minn.1973, 363 F.Supp. 246, 250, aff'd in Thomas, supra. Avoiding possibilities for 'middles' is one reason for the constant exchange of line information among bookmakers.

Another common solution to the bookmaker's problem of grossly unbalanced bets on a game is the 'lay off' bet. By this device, a bookmaker whose customers had bet $10,000 on Dallas $ 6 and only $6000 on Pittsburgh–6 would himself seek to make a $4000 bet on Dallas $ 6 with another individual. This bet would have the effect of 'laying off' $4000 of the $10,000 the bookmaker's customers had bet on Dallas, leaving the bookmaker in the net position of having $6000 bet with him on each side. Normally, the bookmaker would look to another bookmaker to make this bet, and would be required to give up the same favorable 11 to 10 odds which he had received from the Dallas bettors. Indeed, several cases dealing with § 1955 have in dicta defined a lay off bet as a 'bet between bookmakers.' See, e.g., United States v. Guzek, 8 Cir. 1975, 527 F.2d 552, 555 n.5; Thomas, supra, 508 F.2d at 1202 n.2; Schaefer, supra, 510 F.2d at 1311 n.5; United States v. Sacco, 9 Cir. 1974, 491 F.2d 995, 998 & n.1 (en banc). It seems clear, however, that the individual accepting a lay off bet from a bookmaker need not be another bookmaker. That individual could be part of a professional 'lay off' operation, an organization dealing only with book-makers rather than with retail customers, and having sufficient capital so that risk-taking at 11 to 10 odds posed little problem. On the other hand, the individual could be a mere bettor who wanted to bet $4000 on Dallas $ 6, but was told by his bookmaker that no more such bets were being taken and was invited by the bookmaker to accept instead a wager in which the bettor received 11 to 10 odds for agreeing to bet on Pittsburgh. The point of all this is that a 'lay off' bet should be defined solely in relation to the occupation and the purpose of the person making the bet—the occupation and motives of the person accepting the bet are irrelevant to the definition.

We do not warrant the foregoing as constituting all the structural information a lay person (as distinct from a lay off person) would need to organize his or her own business, but we think it sufficient for our purposes, and we turn now to the case before us.

THE EVIDENCE RELATING TO BOX

During this five day trial, twenty-one witnesses testified and several kilograms of evidence were introduced. The testimony of the only four witnesses who had any knowledge concerning Box may be summarized as follows.

F.B.I. Agent Beinner testified that Lombardino, a bookmaker, visited the Guys & Dolls Billiard Parlor, an establishment owned by Box, on three separate Tuesdays during the 1973 football season. Beinner believed Tuesday to be 'payoff day' in the bookmaking operations he had been investigating. Beinner had obtained and executed search warrants on the homes or places of business of eight of the defendants, but had been unsuccessful in his attempt to obtain a warrant on the home and place of business of Box. Beinner's principal informant, whose information was the basis for the search warrant affidavit, described the other defendants who were named in the affidavit as 'bookmakers' and described Box only as a 'bettor.' It was through the testimony of Agent Beinner that the government introduced the telephone toll records, discussed below.

Messina, a bookmaker who had been granted immunity by the government in return for his testimony, testified that he himself had never 'laid off' bets to Box, but that he had personal knowledge that Cook had done so.

Cook, a bookmaker also given immunity, testified that he had occasionally 'laid off' bets with Box and with several of the other defendants. Cook explained that when he lost such a bet to Box or one of the others, he would pay the winner an extra 10% in excess of the amount bet. Cook testified that Box, as a customer, also placed bets with Cook in which Cook received this 10% advantage. Cook did not consider Box a bookmaker and knew of no one who did. He related that Box had been free to take or reject bets offered by Cook, and he described Box only as a bettor.

Stewart, a bookmaker, testified that Box was one of his customers, i.e., a bettor. No one asked Stewart the direct question, 'Is Box a bookmaker?', but the prosecutor asked that question of Stewart concerning every other defendant remaining on trial when Stewart testified, and received an affirmative answer in each case. Stewart testified that Box placed bets with him, and that he (Stewart) placed bets for Box with other bookmakers. It was through Stewart that the betting slip testimony was introduced. Stewart testified that he made bets with two other bookmakers in which he gave the others 11 to 10 odds—some of these were 'lay off' bets, and some were bets Stewart made because he liked the team. Stewart did not testify that he ever made such bets with Box.

The two items of documentary evidence which related to Box were as follows.

The Telephone Toll Records. No wiretaps or pen registers were used in this case, but the Government introduced at trial several long distance telephone records, including those of the telephone at Box's house and the telephone at Guys & Dolls, Box's establishment. These records showed that during the period of the investigation (autumn, 1973), 20 calls were made from Box's home and 223 calls were made from Guys & Dolls to one Price, a Baton Rouge bookmaker.

The Betting Slips. The simultaneous raids conducted on the last day of the 1973 football season yielded, inter alia, large numbers of betting slips which had been used in the Stewart operation. Most of these slips were marked in a similar simple manner, e.g., G.B. $ 14 $ 200 (translated, the bettor had wagered $200 that the score of Green Bay plus fourteen points would be greater than that of Green Bay's opponent). In the lower right hand corner a name, a set of initials, or a number would appear, indicating the individual making the bet. Finally, an indication of the result was added, e.g., '$ 200' (the bettor won), or '-220' (the bettor lost and was required to pay the additional 10%).

A smaller number of these slips were marked in a second, distinct, fashion, e.g., G.B. $ 14 $ 330/300. On these, the results would be recorded as $ 330 or -300. The testimony of Stewart on this point was quite confused, but it could be inferred that the slips marked in this second fashion represented bets in which he was giving 11 to 10 odds to the person with whom he was betting. Of the five individuals whose names or initials appeared on Stewart's slips marked in this second fashion, four were clearly bookmakers. The fifth was Box. The seized slips represented about $230,000 of Stewart bets and approximately $3800 of this amount was comprised of slips labeled 'Box' and marked '330/300', '550/500', or the like.

STANDARDS FOR SUFFICIENCY

In reviewing the evidence upon which the jury based its verdict of guilty, we of course examine the evidence in the light most favorable to the government. Glasser v. United States, 1942, 315 U.S. 60, 62 S.Ct. 457, 86 L.Ed. 680; United States v. Warner, 5 Cir. 1971, 441 F.2d 821. When the conviction is based upon circumstantial evidence, our question becomes whether the jury could reasonably conclude that the evidence excluded all reasonable hypotheses of innocence. United States v. Gomez-Rojas, 5 Cir. 1975, 507 F.2d 1213, 1221; United States v. Squella-Avendano, 5 Cir. 1973, 478 F.2d 433, 436.

WAS BOX A BOOKMAKER?

If we were to find that the jury could reasonably conclude that Box was a bookmaker (engaged in a business with the other defendants), our analytical task would be at an end, for the statute in express terms covers bookmakers. See 18 U.S.C § 1955(b)(2). Even viewing the evidence most favorably to the

Government, however, we are convinced that the jury could not reasonably reach such a conclusion. This evidence must be regarded as consistent with the hypothesis that Box was not a bookmaker.

The only direct testimony on this matter clearly categorizes Box as a bettor rather than a bookmaker. Of course, the jury might not have credited this testimony, although we note that Cook and Stewart had no hesitation in labeling the other defendants as 'bookmakers.' The fact remains that there is no evidence in this record upon which an opposite conclusion, i.e., that Box was a bookmaker, could be based. Bookmakers have customers. The names of over 150 bettors were seized during the raids, numerous bettors were interviewed by the FBI, and bettors who were customers of each of the other defendants on trial testified, but no evidence was introduced relating to any 'customers' Box might have.

The testimony of Cook and the betting slips of Stewart indicate that Box on occasion accepted 'lay off' bets from two bookmakers. The Government argues that since a lay off bet must be defined as a bet between two bookmakers, Box was a bookmaker simply because he accepted lay off bets. As explained above, we reject the premise of this argument—a lay off bet is one placed by a bookmaker, but the individual accepting the bet need not be a bookmaker.

An additional characteristic of a bookmaker is that she distributes a 'line.' There is no testimony that Box ever distributed a line, either to customers or to bookmakers. Finally, we note the calls made from Box's telephones to Price. Assuming the jury could conclude that Box himself made all 223 calls to Price from the Guys & Dolls phone, it cannot be said that this number of calls in that direction is inconsistent with the hypothesis that Box was merely a heavy bettor, placing bets with Price.

§ 1955 AND NONBOOKMAKERS

Having established that Box cannot be labeled a bookmaker, we have not yet shown him to be within an unassailable hypothesis of innocence, because § 1955 clearly was meant to proscribe some bookmaking-related activities of individuals who were not themselves bookmakers. The legislative history indicates that § 1955

> applies generally to persons who participate in the ownership, management, or conduct of an illegal gambling business. The term 'conducts' refers both to high level bosses and street level employees.

See H.R.Rep. No. 1549, 91st Cong., 2d Sess. (1970), 1970 U.S.Code Cong. & Admin.News at p. 4029 ('House Report'). The language refers specifically to § 1911, but it has been held to apply as well to § 1955. See United States v. Becker, 2 Cir. 1972, 461 F.2d 230, 232, vacated and remanded on other grounds, 1974, 417 U.S. 903, 94 S.Ct. 2597, 41 L.Ed.2d 208.

[The foregoing] reflects an intent to reach employees of large bookmaking operations, and that intent has been followed in cases affirming § 1955 convictions of runners, telephone clerks, salesmen, and watchmen. See Becker, supra; United States v. Hunter, 7 Cir. 1973, 478 F.2d 1019. See also United States v. Harris, 5 Cir. 1972, 460 F.2d 1041, cert. denied, 1972, 409 U.S. 877,

93 S.Ct. 128, 34 L.Ed.2d 130; United States v. Ceraso, 3 Cir. 1972, 467 F.2d 653.

On the other hand, individuals who are only bettors or customers of bookmakers clearly are not within the scope of the statute. See House Report at p. 4029; S.Rep. No. 91-617, 91st Cong., 1st Sess. 70-75, 155-56 (1969) ('Senate Report'); United States v. Curry, 5 Cir. 1976, 530 F.2d 636; Thomas, supra, 508 F.2d at 1205 (explaining a change in the wording of the original bill made so that customers clearly would be excluded).

The case before us cannot be fit easily into either of these two categories. No evidence supports the theory that Box was an employee of other bookmakers; yet, Box's acceptance of lay off bets arguably makes him more important to the operation of a bookmaking business than would be a mere customer. Our question, then, is in what circumstances can an individual who accepted lay off bets from bookmakers be convicted under § 1955? The language of the statute does not resolve this, so we turn again to the legislative history.

Clearly, the dominant concern motivating Congress to enact § 1955 was that large-scale gambling operations in this country have been closely intertwined with large-scale organized crime, and indeed may have provided the bulk of the capital needed to finance the operations of organized crime. See House Report, supra; Senate Report, supra; 115 Cong.Rec. 5873 (1969) (remarks of Sen. McClellan); 116 Cong.Rec. 603 (remarks of Sen. Allot), and 35294-95 (remarks of Rep. Poff) (1970). The target of the statute was large-scale gambling operations—local 'mom and pop' bookmaking operations were to be left to state law. See Hearings on S. 30 and related proposals before Subcomm. No. 5 of the House Comm. on the Judiciary, 91st Cong., 2d Sess., ser. 27 at 325-26 ('House Hearings') (Report of Committee on Federal legislation of New York City Bar Association); 116 Cong.Rec. 589-91 (1970) (remarks of Sen. McClellan); Thomas, supra, 508 F.2d at 1205. In this connection, the requirements of dollar volume ($2000 gross on any day) or duration (30 days or more), and number of participants (5), were drafted into the legislation. See 18 U.S.C. § 1955(b)(1); 116 Cong.Rec. 603 (1970) (remarks of Sen. Allot); House Hearings at 84 (testimony of Sen. McClellan); United States v. Bridges, 5 Cir. 1974, 493 F.2d 918. These requirements are such that relative small-fry can conceivably be ensnared in the statutory strictures, see House Hearings at 325-26, but apparently Congress was of the opinion that the size of gambling operations was often much larger than could be proved, and that law enforcement officials needed some flexibility in order effectively to combat the largescale operations. See Senate Report at 73; 116 Cong.Rec. 603 (1970) (remarks of Sen. Allot); Sacco, supra, 491 F.2d at 1000.

For our purposes, of course, the question is whether Box falls within the statutory terms. If he does, the absence of a showing that he was connected with a truly large-scale gambling operation or with organized crime avails him not. Our review of the general purposes of the Act as expressed in the legislative history is intended only to provide guidance in this situation for which the application of the statutory terms is not immediately apparent.

There are indications in the legislative history of a concern that one way in which large-scale organized crime profited from bookmaking operations was to act as a regular market for lay off bets from local bookmakers. See Thomas, supra, 508 F.2d at 1205, quoting testimony of Attorney General Mitchell at House Hearings and The President's Commission Report on The Challenge of Crime in a Free Society at 189 (1967). Remarks of supporters of the bill demonstrate that the Congress was aware of the general function of lay off betting. For example, Senator McClellan stated:

> (A bookmaker) has at least the virtue of exploiting primarily those who can afford it. Yet he seldom gambles either. He gives track odds or less without track expenses, pays no taxes, is invariably better capitalized or 'lays off' a certain percentage of his bets with other gamblers . . . .

115 Cong.Rec. 5873 (1969).

Nothing in the legislative history, however, deals with the question of whether the recipient of a lay off bet, on that basis alone, should be convicted under the statute.

The silence of the statute and the legislative history on this matter can be contrasted with § 1831(a)(2) of President Nixon's proposed Revised Criminal Code, not accepted by Congress, under which one who received a lay off bet would be in violation of an express statutory provision. See 13 Crim.L.Rep. 3015 (1973).

The phenomenon of lay off betting has been a factor in a large number of cases which have construed § 1955. See, e.g., Guzek, supra; Joseph, supra; Schaefer, supra; Thomas, supra; United States v. Bohn, 8 Cir. 1975, 508 F.2d 1145, cert. denied, 1975, 421 U.S. 947, 95 S.Ct. 1676, 44 L.Ed.2d 100; United States v. DeCesaro, 7 Cir. 1974, 502 F.2d 604; United States v. McHale, 7 Cir. 1974, 495 F.2d 15; Sacco, supra; Schullo, supra; United States v. Ciamacco, W.D.Pa.1973, 362 F.Supp. 107, aff'd 3 Cir., 491 F.2d 751. In almost every case, the question has been whether the exchange of lay off bets, usually in addition to the exchange of line information, could be enough to link two separate bookmaking operations into one business for the purposes of meeting the § 1955 jurisdictional requirement of five participants in one business. The answer has in every case been affirmative—the regular direct exchange of lay off bets and line information can connect otherwise independent gambling operations, which alone would be illegal under state but not federal law (because less than five participants were involved), into one business. Further, the case law supported by legislative history establishes that an individual who is in the business of providing a regular market for a large volume of lay off bets should also be considered to be part of the gambling operation he services. Finally, it seems clear that, at least in this circuit, a professional gambler who accepts bets in the nature of lay off bets and, additionally, provides line information to the same bookmaking operation can be convicted as part of that operation under § 1955.

The cases establish, then, that one who accepts lay off bets can be convicted if any of the following factors is also present: evidence that the individual provided a regular market for a high volume of such bets, or held himself out to be available for such bets whenever bookmakers needed to make them; evidence that the individual performed any other substantial service for the bookmaker's operation, as, for example, in the supply of line information; or evidence that the individual was conducting his own illegal gambling operation and was regularly exchanging lay off bets with the other bookmakers. Our review of the legislative history, and our adherence to the doctrine that statutes mandating penal sanctions are to be strictly construed, convinces us that one of the listed factors, or other evidence that the defendant was an integral part of the bookmaking business, is necessary before an individual who accepts lay off bets can be convicted under the statute. See Iannelli v. United States, 1975, 420 U.S. 770, 798, 95 S.Ct. 1284, 1300, 43 L.Ed.2d 616, 635 (Brennan, J., dissenting). Evidence establishing only that a person received occasional lay off bets from bookmakers cannot be considered inconsistent with the possibility that the individual was for all practical purposes only a bettor. Cf. Joseph, supra, 519 F.2d at 1071 ("A person who performs a necessary function other than as a mere customer or bettor in the operation of illegal gambling 'conducts an illegal gambling business.' United States v. Jones, 9 Cir. 1974, 491 F.2d 1382, 1384.")

In these circumstances, we do not feel that the cases finding 'lay off bettors' within the scope of § 1955 are dispositive. Cf. Joseph, supra, 519 F.2d at 1068; DeCesaro, supra, 502 F.2d at 611; McHale, supra, 495 F.2d at 18; Sacco, supra, 491 F.2d at 998, 1004. If dicta in these cases can be read to indicate that a 'lay off bettor,' as the recipient of a lay off bet, is on that basis alone a part of an illegal gambling operation, we reject such dicta as being based on an erroneous assumption regarding the nature of lay off betting. We stress again that the recipient of a lay off bet need not be a bookmaker, but rather might be any individual willing to accept a single bet.

Section 1955 was directed at the professionals—the persons who avoided gambling themselves, but profited from the gambling of others. Assistant Attorney General Mark Wilson, who was primarily responsible for drafting the section of the bill which became § 1955, testified before the House Subcommittee as follows:

> The whole intent and purpose of this bill is aimed at the proprietor, the professional, and not the bettors.

House Hearings at 191. Although a heavy bettor might be a crucial source of revenue for a bookmaking operation, the statute was meant to exclude bettors. Gambling becomes a federal case only when a person is charged with more than betting, and evidence that a person accepted lay off bets, without more, is insufficient to expel that person from § 1955's sanctuary of bettordom.

The question remaining, then, is whether the evidence relating to Box, viewed most favorably to the Government, could sustain a jury finding that one of the additional factors noted above was present in this case. Such a jury finding would in effect be a conclusion that the evidence was inconsistent with any hypothesis of innocence. In reaching this conclusion, of course, the jury is limited to evidence in the record and supportable inferences therefrom. If a conclusion that all hypotheses of innocence have been excluded by the evidence could be reached only as a result of speculation or assumptions about matters not in evidence, then the jury verdict must be overturned.

The evidence against Box shows that he accepted lay off bets of undetermined amounts from Cook on a number of occasions, and that in one week he may have accepted $3800 in lay off bets from Stewart. These are the only two pieces of evidence which distinguish Box in any way from the 'mere bettor' so clearly excluded from the statute's scope. We do not find any reasonable basis in the evidence upon which the jury could conclude that Box was an integral part of these bookmaking operations. While the volume of bets with Stewart was substantial, no evidence indicates that Box regularly accepted lay off bets from Stewart. There is no evidence on amounts from Cook, and while Cook's testimony could support a conclusion that Box accepted lay off bets on several occasions, that testimony flatly contradicts any suggestion that Box held himself out to be a regular market for such bets upon which local bookmakers could depend. As we have already noted, no evidence supports the suggestion that Box was himself a bookmaker, or that he provided line or other gambling information to bookmakers.

The only evidence on this point is the testimony of Cook, who indicated that when he bet with Box, it was a 'free and voluntary thing' and that Box was 'free to take the bet or not take the bet' (the phrases are from questions posed by defense counsel.) Again, the jury need not have credited Cook on this issue, but there was no evidence on which to base an opposite conclusion.

Box may have gamboled with the gamblers, but he has not been shown to be a gaming entrepreneur. Nothing indicates that he solicited the lay off bets that he accepted. Box was a customer of bookmakers and was perhaps a bargain-seeking bettor, but the record does not permit him to be cast in a role as a necessary or integral part of a gambling operation. The testimony of admitted bookmakers, the multiplicity of phone calls and the shower of betting slips suggest only that Box bet with continuity and in magnitude, and on occasion received a discount when the professionals with whom he dealt needed to lay off a bet. We conclude, then, that the jury could not reasonably find the evidence inconsistent with the hypothesis that Box was simply a heavy bettor who on occasion received favorable odds in bets with bookmakers. For purposes of § 1955, this hypothesis is one of innocence.

Since we thus have concluded that the evidence in this case was insufficient to support a verdict of guilty, we need not reach any of the other eleven points argued by appellant. The conviction of Box is reversed, the sentence is vacated, and the case is remanded to the district court for entry of a judgment of acquittal.

STATE v. GREENFIELD
622 N.W.2d 403 (Minn. Ct. App. 2001)

RANDALL, Judge.

Appellant Gerald J. Greenfield appeals his conviction for felony sports bookmaking, arguing that the evidence is insufficient to prove that he accepted a bet, as statutorily defined, because he did not stand to gain or lose anything by the transactions and did not charge the caller for more than the amount of the wager. Appellant also argues that the district court erred in allowing the state to introduce into evidence a false identity card seized from appellant's home when appellant offered to stipulate to identity. We affirm.

FACTS

Appellant was charged with felony sports bookmaking in violation of Minn.Stat. § 609.76, subd. 2 (1994). Following a jury trial, Greenfield was found guilty of felony sports bookmaking; gross misdemeanor receiving, recording or forwarding a bet; and misdemeanor making a bet. Greenfield filed a motion for judgment of acquittal or for a new trial. The district court denied Greenfield's motion, entered judgment, and sentenced him for felony sports bookmaking.

In April 1996, the Minnesota Department of Safety's Alcohol and Gambling Enforcement Division (the Department) was contacted by the New York State Police with information acquired through legal wiretaps and pen registers regarding an illegal bookmaking operation in New York connected to Minnesota. New York provided the Department with two Minnesota phone numbers and copies of the Minnesota conversations from their investigation.

Investigation of the Minnesota phone numbers revealed Greenfield set up an elaborate phone system using landlines and cell phones registered to two different addresses of adjoining townhouses. Greenfield owned one townhouse, and the other townhouse, although actually owned by a couple who lived out of state during the winter, had a post office box registered to that address by a J.P. Field for purposes of setting up a cell phone. Surveillance of the two properties revealed a high probability that Greenfield and J.P. Field was the same person.

Investigators executed a search warrant for Greenfield's townhouse. They noticed, before entering, Greenfield sitting at a desk where they later found betting sheets, a cellular phone directory, phone bills for J.P. Field, a cellular phone registered to J.P. Field, tout service books, and various other items commonly used in gambling. In a floor safe in Greenfield's bedroom closet, police found approximately $87,000 cash in marked envelopes, an envelope with J.P. Field written on it, and two I 94 identification cards under the name of John Patrick Field with Greenfield's picture. Possession of false I 94 identification cards is not illegal.

The cellular phone directory contained coded names and numbers that coincided with column headings on the betting sheets. The initials MA and the corresponding coded phone number in the phone directory coincided with Melvin Amiel's New York phone number. Amiel was the subject of the New York investigation. Further, the recorded conversations between Amiel and Greenfield corresponded closely with the data in the column marked MA on the betting sheets. The March 31, 1996, betting sheet showed that Greenfield received $18,300 in wagers, "passed off" a bet of $10,000 to a bookie in Ohio, and retained $8,300 for himself.

ISSUES

1. Was there sufficient evidence to sustain appellant's conviction?

2. Did the district court err in admitting the false identification cards into evidence?

ANALYSIS

I. Sufficient Evidence

In considering a claim of insufficiency of the evidence, this court's review is limited to a painstaking analysis of the record to determine whether the evidence, when viewed in the light most favorable to the conviction, is sufficient to allow a jury to reach its verdict. State v. Webb, 440 N.W.2d 426, 430 (Minn.1989). The reviewing court must assume the jury believed the state's witnesses and disbelieved any evidence to the contrary. State v. Moore, 438 N.W.2d 101, 108 (Minn.1989). The reviewing court will not disturb the jury's verdict if, acting with due regard for the presumption of innocence and the requirement of proof beyond a reasonable doubt, the jury could reasonably conclude the defendant was guilty of the charged offense. State v. Alton, 432 N.W.2d 754, 756 (Minn.1988).

Greenfield argues the evidence was legally insufficient to support his conviction for sports bookmaking, and therefore he is entitled to have his conviction vacated. He argues that he did not actually participate in any bets, except on one occasion, but was rather a "beard," which falls outside the scope of the sports bookmaking statute. A beard is someone who places wagers for other individuals without revealing the true identity of the person responsible for the wager.

Greenfield focuses his argument on what constitutes a bet, and stresses that to have betting, which is part of the statutory language for sports bookmaking, there must be self-defeating wagers. He claims he never stood to gain or lose anything from the bets placed on behalf of others. He argues that passing bets on behalf of other bettors as a beard does not constitute bookmaking. Greenfield asserts he cannot be both a beard and a bookie. Greenfield concedes that the taped telephone conversations appear to show Amiel placing bets with Greenfield; however, he argues that careful analysis of the contents of the conversations in conjunction with inspection of the betting sheets demonstrates that he had no risk of loss with Amiel.

The interpretation of a statute is a question of law, and thus this court reviews it de novo. Lolling v. Midwest Patrol, 545 N.W.2d 372, 375 (Minn.1996). The purpose of statutory interpretation is to ascertain the effective legislative intent. Minn.Stat. § 645.16 (2000). If statutory language is plain and unambiguous, the court must give it its plain meaning. Tuma v. Commissioner of Econ. Sec., 386 N.W.2d 702, 706 (Minn.1986). The rule of strict construction of criminal statutes guards against creating additional criminal offenses not intended by the legislature to be part of the statute. State v. Soto, 378 N.W.2d 625, 628 (Minn.1985).

Sports bookmaking is defined as

> the activity of intentionally receiving, recording or forwarding within any 30-day period more than five bets, or offers to bet, that total more than $2,500 on any one or more sporting events.

Minn.Stat. § 609.75, subd. 7 (1994). A "bet" or "offer to bet" is part of an element of sports bookmaking; therefore, the meaning of a bet is at issue. A "bet" under Minn.Stat. § 609.75, subd. 2, is

a bargain whereby the parties mutually agree to a gain or loss by one
to the other of specified money, property or benefit dependent upon
chance although the chance is accompanied by some element of skill.

Greenfield argues that the definition for "bet" states that a gain or loss is
experienced by one of the parties by mutual agreement. But "forwarding" a
bet, by definition, means that someone else, even if not the forwarder himself,
will have a gain or a loss. Greenfield argues that there is nothing in the record
to prove he took "vigorish" or "vig," the bettor's/bookie's term for a fee to bet
that is often paid by the loser in a sports bookmaking situation, over and above
the amount of the wager. There is, however, nothing in the definition of a bet
or sports bookmaking requiring a showing of the bettor's fee, or vigorish, to
constitute a bet within the meaning of bookmaking.

Applying the plain meaning of a bet to the facts of this case, the people in
the telephone conversations with Greenfield and on the betting sheets stood
to lose money they placed on various sports games through Greenfield. If the
bettor were to lose the bet, he would lose his money either to Greenfield or
the person to whom Greenfield forwarded the bet for final determination (final
determination simply meaning the ultimate person who accepted the bet, and,
thus, stood to collect if the bettor lost or had to pay up if the bettor won). In
every instance, either Greenfield or a bookie down the road would gain money
or lose money.

It is apparent from the definition of sports bookmaking that the intent of
the statute is to encompass a broad range of transactions dealing with bets.
Sports bookmaking does contain the word "bet"; however, the definition of
sports bookmaking also includes "receiving, recording, or forwarding" a bet
or an offer to bet. Thus, anyone receiving, recording, or forwarding a bet or
offer to bet can be convicted of sports bookmaking under the statute (assuming
the other elements are present; i.e., 30 day period, six or more bets or offers
to bet, $2,501 total or more) whether they choose to call themselves a bookie,
a beard, or just a bettor. The offense of forwarding bets would have no teeth
and the statute would be worthless for that activity if a complete defense was,
as Greenfield argues, that he merely bet for someone else and personally did
not stand to gain or lose. A beard, even one claiming that he does not stand
to gain or lose anything from the deal, acts as an intermediary by forwarding
the bet to a bookmaker. The language of the statute shows the legislature
intended that statute to cover transactions involving persons who receive,
record, or forward bets.

Greenfield conceded that he was at least a beard. In addition, he agreed
that if MA won a bet Greenfield placed as a beard, MA would look to Greenfield
for his winnings, and if MA lost, Greenfield would receive the lost bet from
MA and forward it to the person with whom Greenfield placed the bet. On
March 31, 1996, Greenfield forwarded $10,000 to a bookmaker in Ohio.
Whether this was laying off bets as a bookie or placing the bet as a beard
so that another bettor could remain anonymous, both come under the statute.
Both transactions are acts of forwarding. The recorded telephone conversa-
tions between Amiel and Greenfield establish that Greenfield committed an
offense outlined in sports bookmaking. The record bolsters this conclusion.
He had tout service books; coded names and phone numbers, a common

practice in gambling for bookies; dozens of betting sheets; $87,000 cash, along with false identification cards and an envelope marked for J.P. Field in a floor safe; and phone records and bills for both Greenfield and J.P. Field. In addition, the record shows Greenfield took complicated steps to set up a post office box so he could register a cell phone to J.P. Field in order to conceal his operation.

Reading the definition of sports bookmaking in Minn.Stat. § 608.75, subd. 7, and giving it a plain meaning, sports bookmaking includes the actions of beards, bookies, and bettors involving both bets and offers to bet, providing all other essential elements of the statute have been established by proof beyond a reasonable doubt. Viewing the evidence in the light most favorable to the state, we conclude the evidence sufficiently supported Greenfield's conviction of felony sports bookmaking.

II. Admissibility of Evidence

Greenfield argues, under Minn.R.Evid. 403 and 404(b), that the district court committed prejudicial error by admitting the false identification cards into evidence. Greenfield was willing to stipulate that he and J.P. Field was the same person, arguing that the false identification cards would imply other wrongdoing and unfairly prejudice Greenfield if admitted into evidence. He asks that this court reverse his conviction and remand for a new trial without introduction of the false identification cards.

Greenfield, in trying to show why this evidence was prejudicial, draws analogies to cases involving admitting evidence of prior bad acts, such as a felon charged with possession of a weapon. Greenfield argue[s] that introduction of the false identification cards implies criminal activity above and beyond the crime that is charged. Greenfield argues that granting the stipulation in his case would have been the correct ruling. Finally, Greenfield asserts that the false identification cards created a substantial risk that the jury convicted Greenfield "based not on the relevant evidence in the record, but rather on [Greenfield's] perceived bad character," inferred from his possessing the false identification cards.

The State offered the false identification cards for two purposes: first, to show that Greenfield and J.P. Field was the same person; and second, to use as part of its chain of proof to show the extent to which Greenfield used the false identification cards to conceal his operation. If the parties had agreed to the stipulation that J.P. Field was Greenfield and the identity cards were not admitted, the state would not have been able to show that the false identity cards were an integral part of Greenfield's efforts to obtain telephone service used for the sole purpose of the bookmaking operation.

The false identification cards show that Greenfield created a false identity and that he did it in order to apply for a post office box so he could register for a cell phone and regular phone line to use in his bookmaking operation. The identification cards were part of the sequence of steps Greenfield took to conceal his operation. Because the false identification cards were part of Greenfield's concealment of identity, it could be inferred by a jury that, from their use, in combination with the other evidence, Greenfield had the intent to and did receive, record, or forward bets or offers to bet. We cannot conclude that the district court erred in admitting the false identification cards.

DECISION

There was sufficient evidence to sustain appellant's conviction under the sports bookmaking statute. The district court did not err in admitting the false identification cards into evidence.

Affirmed.

LEICHLITER v. STATE LIQUOR LICENSING AUTHORITY, DEPARTMENT OF REVENUE, STATE OF COLORADO
9 P.3d 1153 (Colo. Ct. App. 2000)

DAVIDSON, Judge.

This is an appeal from the judgment entered in a C.R.C.P. 106(a)(4) proceeding reversing the action of the Colorado Department of Revenue Liquor Licensing Authority (Liquor Authority) in suspending the liquor license of plaintiff, Robert Leichliter, d/b/a Top Hat Lounge, for permitting gambling on its premises. The primary issue is whether the National Collegiate Athletic Association (NCAA) basketball pool held on the premises was incidental to a bona fide social relationship. We agree with the trial court that it was and therefore affirm.

The relevant facts as set forth in the trial court's order are not in dispute. On March 25, 1998, two investigators from the Liquor Authority went to the Lounge on an unrelated complaint. While there, the investigators noticed a grid for an NCAA basketball pool on a shelf on the back bar and, at their request, were allowed to participate in the pool. Based upon this, the Liquor Authority issued an order to show cause to plaintiff alleging a violation of the Colorado Liquor Code relating to the prohibition of gambling at an establishment licensed to serve alcoholic beverages.

Under the Colorado Liquor Code, § 12-47-901(5), C.R.S.1999, with exceptions not relevant here, a licensed retailer may not authorize or permit gambling on its premises. "Gambling," as used in this statute has the same meaning as "gambling" in the criminal code, see Brownlee v. State, 686 P.2d 1372 (Colo.App.1984), and includes, inter alia, risking money or other things of value for gain contingent, in whole or part, upon the happening of a sporting event over which the person taking a risk has no control. See § 18-10-102(2), C.R.S.1999. However, any game, wager, or transaction which is incidental to a bona fide social relationship, is participated in only by natural persons, and in which no person is participating, directly or indirectly, in professional gambling, is excluded from the definition of gambling. See § 18-10-102(2)(d), C.R.S.1999.

After a hearing on the alleged violation, the hearing officer determined that the basketball pool was not incidental to a bona fide social relationship and, therefore, constituted illegal gambling in violation of § 12-47-901(5), C.R.S.1999, and regulation 47-922 A 1., 1 Code Colo. Reg. 203-2 (prohibiting licensee from authorizing or permitting gambling on the premises). Plaintiff's liquor license was suspended for ten days, but six days of the suspension were deferred for one year pending proof of any future violation.

Plaintiff then instituted this C.R.C.P. 106(a)(4) action for review of the Liquor Authority's decision. The trial court reversed after determining that the hearing officer's finding that the basketball pool was not a game, wager, or transaction which was incidental to a bona fide social relationship was clearly erroneous, unsupported by substantial evidence, and contrary to law. On appeal, the Liquor Authority argues that this was error. We agree with the trial court.

In order for a reviewing court to set aside a decision by an administrative agency, the decision must be clearly erroneous, without evidentiary support in the record, or contrary to law. Brownlee v. State, supra. Under C.R.C.P. 106(a)(4), the appropriate consideration for an appellate court is whether there is sufficient evidentiary support for the decision rendered by the administrative tribunal. The appellate court is not bound by any determination made by the trial court, but reviews the issues presented to that court de novo. See City of Colorado Springs v. Givan, 897 P.2d 753 (Colo.1995).

Here, the hearing officer based his determination that the activity did not constitute social gambling on his finding that there was no bona fide social relationship among the participants in the transaction because, although "the establishment was characterized as a friendly neighborhood bar, it is apparent that anyone could walk in and participate in the gambling activity." Indeed, argues the Liquor Authority, there could be no bona fide social relationship among the participants here because this was an "open" pool in which the individuals who participated did not necessarily know one another. We disagree.

The phrase, "incident to a bona fide social relationship" is not defined in the statute or Liquor Code regulations. However, it has been addressed in prior decisions of the supreme court.

In People v. Wheatridge Poker Club, 194 Colo. 15, 569 P.2d 324 (1977), the court held that poker playing for money in a social club that derived its profits solely from yearly membership dues, a set "per chair" fee, and in which members were brought together through advertisements and promotions for the sole purpose of gambling was not incidental to a bona fide social relationship. In Houston v. Younghans, 196 Colo. 53, 580 P.2d 801 (1978), however, the court determined that poker playing for money among friends at the home of one of the players was incidental to a bona fide social relationship. More recently, in Charnes v. Central City Opera House Ass'n, 773 P.2d 546 (Colo.1989), the court held that a fundraising event which featured gambling was incidental to a bona fide social relationship based on the fact that the event was limited to participants who, although not necessarily friends, were brought together for the common purpose of raising money and not solely for the purpose of gambling.

Although each of these decisions necessarily is fact-specific, from them we can conclude nevertheless that the phrase, "incidental to a bona fide social relationship," refers to a game or wager which is made available to participants who have some legitimate common relationship to one another other than to engage in gambling. For example, a typical office sports pool, although all participants usually are not friends, would likely fall into this category by virtue of the shared business purposes of the office employees.

Hence, the critical inquiry is whether the participants here came together for any shared purpose other than gambling. See Charnes v. Central City Opera House Ass'n, supra (raising money for the Opera House Association); Houston v. Younghans, supra (existing social friendship); People v. Wheatridge Poker Club, supra (no shared purpose except gambling).

Were it not for the participation of the two Liquor Authority investigators, the answer to this inquiry would not be difficult. Indeed, as set forth in the trial court's order, it was undisputed that this particular bar was a neighborhood gathering place with a regular and devoted clientele where "just all the different walks of life came in to have a drink and have conversation with friends." The patrons of the Lounge did not go there to gamble and would continue to patronize the establishment regardless of the availability of a basketball pool. There was no advertising of any sort outside the Lounge of the availability of a sports pool; patrons were not even told about the pool or encouraged to participate in it. The pool was a once-a-year event and the cost was $2 a square. With such small cost of participation and maximum winnings of $200, it was provided simply as entertainment for persons who otherwise came into the Lounge for a drink and camaraderie. The pool grid itself contained mostly first names, initials, or nicknames, and, except for the two investigators, plaintiff knew every person who had participated in the pool. In fact, in his testimony before the Liquor Authority, plaintiff gave lengthy and detailed facts about the background, family history, and relationships of numerous patrons whose names were on the grid.

Based on this, we would agree with the trial court that the determination that, under the circumstances here, the sports pool was not incident to a bona fide social relationship, would be clearly erroneous.

The question then becomes whether the participation of the two investigators, who by appearances were simply patronizing the Lounge, and, apparently in a gesture of western hospitality, were permitted to participate in the pool, render illegal that which otherwise was incidental to a bona fide social relationship among the other participants? The Liquor Authority maintains that it does. We do not agree.

Regardless whether occasional strangers were allowed to participate in the pool, the undisputed facts show that this particular bar provided a social gathering place for a close-knit portion of the local community. We cannot agree that this limited participation by the Liquor Authority investigators, whose purpose at the Lounge was unrelated to the existence of a sports pool— they were there to investigate the possibility of the Lounge serving alcohol to intoxicated persons—could of itself change the fact that this once-a-year, $200 pool was available as incidental amusement to the regular patrons whose legitimate common relationship was to come to the Lounge "for a drink and conversation with friends."

Similarly, we also disagree with the Liquor Authority that the Lounge itself participated in the pool, in contravention of § 18-10-102(2)(d) (precluding participation by other than natural persons). The hearing officer found that any profit to the Lounge was "incidental" to the existence of the basketball pool. Moreover, even though the grid was drawn on paper which contained the Lounge logo, there was no evidence that the Lounge did anything more than safekeep the participants' money and have the grid available to bar patrons who wanted to participate in it. Cf. Charnes v. Central City Opera House Ass'n, supra (Association's conduct in running the game constituted a "significant level of participation" by a non-natural person, thereby taking case out of permissible social gambling exception). The grid in the pool was filled in only by individuals, and there was no soliciting or advertising outside the Lounge to encourage people to participate.

Accordingly, the judgment of the trial court is affirmed.

Notes

1. In *Box*, the defendant was indicted for violating 18 U.S.C. § 1955 (commonly referred to as the "Federal Antigambling Statute"), which makes it a crime for five or more persons to carry on large-scale bookmaking operations. In addition to § 1955, there are a number of other federal statutes that, directly or indirectly, make sports betting illegal. Among the more important ones are 18 U.S.C. § 224 (sports bribery), 18 U.S.C. § 1084 ("Wire Act") (placing sports bets through wire communications, such as telephones or telegraphs), 18 U.S.C. § 1952 ("Travel Act") (travel or use of the mails to carry on unlawful activities), and 18 U.S.C. § 1953 ("Paraphernalia Act") (distribution of illegal gambling aids). Of course, where sufficient facts exist, a single enterprise can lead to a charge of multiple violations. *See, e.g., United State v. Segal*, 867 F.2d 1173 (8th Cir. 1989) (18 U.S.C. §§ 1084, 1952, and 1955, as well as 26 U.S.C. § 7203—failure to file tax return), and *United States v. Kaczowski*, 114 F. Supp. 2d 143 (W.D.N.Y. 2000) (18 U.S.C. §§ 1084, 1952, 1953, and 1955).

2. The *Greenfield* case is an example of a prosecution for illegal sports bookmaking under state law. For other state prosecutions, *see, e.g., Sacco v. State*, 784 P.2d 947 (Nev. 1989) (no double jeopardy where bookmaker who conducted illegal operations in two states was charged and convicted in both); *Papuchis v. Commonwealth*, 422 S.E.2d 419 (Va. Ct. App. 1992) (sports publications could not be used to prove defendant's papers were betting sheets); *People v. Nadel*, 100 Cal. Rptr. 444 (Ct. App. 1972) (affiant's subjective belief that defendant was running illegal bookmaking operation insufficient for search warrant); *State v. Allen*, 525 N.E.2d 1267 (Ind. Ct. App. 1988) (no error where informant had personally placed bets using phone numbers immediately before search warrant was issued); *People v. Decker*, 613 N.Y.S.2d 531 (Sup. Ct. 1994) (observing that the "majority of sports bookmaking is conducted between the hours of 4:00 p.m. and 8:00 p.m.").

3. As the court in *Leichliter* explains, many people participate in office pools. Although the practice is widespread, it is illegal in most states (prosecutions, however, are rare) and some employers have issued written guidelines specifically prohibiting the practice. *See further* Joseph Giordono, *One Big Pool Party: Office Betting Thrives*, L.A. Daily News, Mar. 11, 2001, at N1; Ritz Mary

Kaye, *Wanna Bet?*, Honolulu Advertiser, Nov. 19, 2002, at E1; Dan Sheehan, *March Madness? You Bet!*, Harrisburg Patriot, Mar. 12, 2002, at A1.

Problem 21

A criminal indictment charged the defendant, who lived in a state that did not permit sports betting, with using the telephone to place wagers with licensed operators in Nevada. If the defendant appeals, arguing that his conduct falls outside the scope of the Wire Act, how should the court rule? *See Martin v. United States*, 389 F.2d 895 (5th Cir.), *cert. denied*, 391 U.S. 919 (1968).

D.　LEAGUE RESTRICTIONS

MOLINAS v. PODOLOFF
133 N.Y.S.2d 743 (Sup. Ct. 1954)

JOSEPH, Justice.

Plaintiff brings this action for a permanent injunction to set aside his suspension as a player in the National Basketball Association, to maintain his rights to be a player member in the association and for other relief. The defendant, an unincorporated association, conducts and supervises a professional basketball league consisting of teams owned by nine clubs. The owners of the said clubs comprising the membership of the National Basketball Association (hereinafter designated as N. B. A.) employed professional basketball players known as player members of the association.

A duly-adopted constitution and bylaws regulated the rights, privileges and duties of the members and player members.

The Zollner Machine Works, Inc., of Fort Wayne, Indiana, was the owner of the club known as Fort Wayne Zollner Pistons, a member of the N. B. A.; it entered into a written contract on the form prescribed by the N. B. A. with the plaintiff to play professional basketball in the said league for its club, whereby the club and the plaintiff became bound by the terms of the said agreement, and the constitution and bylaws of the N. B. A.

It is undisputed that on January 9, 1954, the police of Fort Wayne, Indiana, conducted an inquiry as to the Zollner Piston Basketball Team, and the plaintiff, by reason of such investigation, in the late evening of that day, or in the early morning of January 10, 1954, signed a written statement of his having wagered on his team. Specifically the plaintiff admitted:

> 'I have been a member of the Zollner Piston Basketball Team since October 1953. After being on the team for approximately a month I called a man in New York by the name of Mr. X, knowing this man for a long period of time I called him on the telephone and asked him if he could place a bet for me. He said that he could and he would tell me the odds on the game either for or against the Pistons. After hearing the odds or points on the game I either placed a bet on the Pistons or else told him that the odds were too great and I did not

want to place the bet. Several times I talked to him over the phone and odds or points were not mentioned and I told him that I thought on some occasions that we could win a particular game and I placed a bet. I did this about ten times. At no time was there a pay off to throw any games made to me by Mr. X. Nor was there any mention of the fact; however, the only reimbursement I received was for my phone calls which I made to him. Also I received approximately $400 for the total times that I have been betting with him. This included the phone bill also.'

The plaintiff has admitted, and so testified at the trial, that the statement was a voluntary, free and truthful statement of fact.

Maurice Podoloff, President of the N. B. A., and Mr. Zollner, President of the Fort Wayne Zollner Pistons, arrived at the police station about midnight, and subsequent to being shown plaintiff's statement Mr. Podoloff sent for him. In the conversation that ensued, relating to the wagering situation, and the plaintiff's participation therein, Mr. Podoloff informed the plaintiff that he was 'through' as a player, and Mr. Podoloff indefinitely suspended the plaintiff.

The plaintiff predicates his action upon two contentions: (1) that no notice of hearing and charges were given the plaintiff as provided by the contract and the constitution; (2) there was no authority to indefinitely suspend the plaintiff. The defendant contends: (1) that there was due notice and hearing; (2) plaintiff's admissions of wagering constituted a waiver of his rights; (3) plaintiff comes into equity with unclean hands.

The pertinent provisions of the contract and the constitution of the N. B. A. applicable to this matter are as follows. Section 15 of the contract provides:

'It is severally and mutually agreed that any player of a Club, who directly or indirectly bets money or anything of value on the outcome of any game played for any National Basketball Association Club, shall be expelled from the National Basketball Association by the President after due notice and hearing and the President's decision shall be final, binding, conclusive and unappealable; and the Player hereby releases the President and waives every claim he may have against the President and/or the National Basketball Association, and against every Club in the National Basketball Association, and against every director, officer and stockholder of every Club in the National Basketball Association, for damages and for all claims and demands whatsoever arising out of or in connection with the decision of the President of the National Basketball Association.'

Section 43 of the constitution of the N. B. A. provides:

'* * * He shall have the power to suspend for a definite or indefinite period or to impose a fine not exceeding $1,000 or inflict both upon any manager, coach, player or officer who in his opinion shall be guilty of conduct prejudicial or detrimental to the association regardless whether the same occurred in or outside of the playing building. * * *'

Section 79 of the constitution of the N. B. A. provides:

'79. Any officer, director, coach or employee of a club, team, corporation or organization operating a franchise in the N. B. A. who or which directly or indirectly wagers money or anything of value on the outcome of any game played by a team of the N. B. A. shall on being charged with such wagering be given a hearing by the President of the Association after due notice, and the decision given by the President shall be final, binding and conclusive and unappealable, and anyone so charged and found guilty shall have no claim against the President and/or N. B. A. or its members or against any club or organization operating a franchise of the N. B. A.'

After the plaintiff made his statement to the police, he was peremptorily sent for by Mr. Podoloff and Mr. Zollner. Assuming, but not conceding, that there was no due notice and hearing, as provided by the contract and the constitution of the N. B. A., this court finds that elaboration on plaintiff's contentions is rendered unnecessary because of the conclusions reached by this court in the determination of this matter.

Certain amateur and professional sports, and the athletes participating in such sports, have recently occupied the spotlight of unfavorable public attention. The radio and television have been contributing causes for creating industries out of certain sports. America is sport-minded; we admire the accomplishment of our athletes; we are pleased with the success of our favorite teams and we spend a considerable part of our time rooting, but relaxing nevertheless, with our favorite sports. We inherit from the Greeks and Romans a love for stadia and sport competition.

When the breath of scandal hits one sport, it casts suspicion on all other sports. It does irreparable injury to the great majority of the players, destroys the confidence of the public in athletic competition, and lets down the morale of our youth. When the standards of fair play, good sportsmanship and honesty are abandoned, sporting events become the property of the gamblers and racketeers.

Much has happened in basketball to displease the public. Bribing, fixing and wagering, especially when associated with gamblers and racketeers, are matters of serious nature. This court need not review the sordid details. It is necessary to recall them to realize the importance of the situations existing in this case.

Courts take cognizance of public interests and public problems; they reflect the spirit of the times and the sentiment and thoughts of the citizens. Laws are promulgated and contracts are made to protect the public and are abreast with the demands, interest and protection of the people. The wagering by player members of N. B. A. and the contract calling for expulsion is an aftermath of the abuses with which we are concerned. To maintain basketball competition in the N. B. A., to have open competitive sport, the public confidence and attendance, every effort had to be made to eliminate the slightest suspicion that competition was not on an honest, competitive basis.

The player that wagers on games does much to destroy the sport. Unfortunately, in wagering on a basketball game, it is not merely the bet that the team wins, but it is a wager on points, and the wager on the point spread in the manner which this plaintiff made such wagers is censurable. In the light of his knowledge of the basketball scandals, the express prohibitions in wagering and the manner of his betting, I am constrained to say plaintiff's conduct was reprehensible.

This plaintiff wagered, and admitted it, as I have hereinbefore set forth. If there was the slightest suggestion that the statement was involuntary or untrue, or a single suggestion offered to question it, if there was a triable issue, this court would have relegated the defendant to his contractual obligations and ordered a hearing. However, the testimony of the plaintiff before the court that the statement was free, voluntary and true eliminates any question as to the plaintiff's admissions.

The position of the plaintiff, in reality, seems to be one of asserting that he wagered on games, he breached his contract, he violated the constitution of the N. B. A. and was morally dishonest. Nevertheless, he now requests this court to order the defendant to cross all its t's and dot all its i's, and award damages for defendant's suspension without due notice and hearing.

To adjudge the suspension null and void, to bring about a hearing for this plaintiff, that must unquestionably and inevitably result in his expulsion or suspension, would be a mere futile gesture.

It is only by looking at the intent, rather than at the form, that equity is able to treat that as done which in good conscience ought to be done. Camp v. Boyd, 229 U.S. 530, 33 S.Ct. 785, 57 L.Ed. 1317.

There is no doubt that the matter now before this court has evoked a considerable amount of public interest and discussion. While the interest of the public at large in a given case, as an abstract proposition, can never be allowed to influence the court or become determinative, nevertheless, situations arise wherein the decision of the court is made against a background of public interest which is based on public morality. That morality is one which concerns the public desire of honest sport and clean sportsmanship. It necessarily follows, as the day follows the night, that one who has offended against this concept of good morals, and who admits such offense in open court, does not by that very fact, satisfy the equitable maxim, that he who comes into equity must come with clean hands.

This plaintiff seeks the aid of the chancellor to compel a hearing on charges admitted by him to be true. Such an attitude must constitute its own refutation and condemnation. To compel a hearing, and on that decision, to seek damages in salary for the period of time elapsing between plaintiff's suspension and the said hearing is an affront to the conscience of the chancellor. That equity will not decree such a ludicrous position or the performance of such a useless act is too well-established to require extended argument. See Gueutal v. Gueutal, 113 App.Div. 310, 98 N.Y.S. 1002; Morse v. Miller, Sup., 39 N.Y.S.2d 815, affirmed 267 App.Div. 801, 47 N.Y.S.2d 288, leave to appeal denied 293 N.Y. 936, 56 N.E.2d 311; 30 C.J.S., Equity, § 16.

The maxim of 'clean hands' is also expressed in the form 'He that hath committed iniquity shall not have equity' (2 Pomeroy Eq.Jur. 5th ed., sec. 397). It applies to unconscientious acts or inequitable conduct. Its application is confined to misconduct in regard to or at all events connected with, the matter in litigation. Rice v. Rockefeller, 134 N.Y. 174, 186, 31 N.E. 907, 910, 17 L.R.A. 237. Here the admitted misconduct of the plaintiff is most certainly connected with the matter in litigation. An act which would be pronounced wrongful by honest and fair-minded men renders the hands of a moving party unclean.

In the application of this doctrine, whenever a party seeks to set the judicial machinery in motion to obtain some remedy, and has violated conscience or good faith, or other equitable principle in his prior conduct, then the doors of the court will be shut against him; the court will refuse to interfere on his behalf, to acknowledge his right or to award him any remedy (Pomeroy's 5th ed., sec. 397 cases cited).

Accordingly, the complaint is dismissed on the merits and judgment is directed in favor of the defendant.

ROSE v. GIAMATTI
721 F. Supp. 906 (S.D. Ohio 1989)

HOLSCHUH, District Judge.

INTRODUCTION

This action by Peter Edward Rose against A. Bartlett Giamatti and others, initially filed in the Court of Common Pleas of Hamilton County, Ohio at Cincinnati, and removed to the United States District Court for the Southern District of Ohio on July 3, 1989, was transferred forthwith to the Eastern Division of this Court by an order issued by Judge Carl B. Rubin and Judge Herman J. Weber, Judges of this Court sitting in the Western Division at Cincinnati. In that transfer order, Judges Rubin and Weber stated:

> Plaintiff is not just another litigant. He is instead a baseball figure of national reputation closely identified with the Cincinnati Reds and the City of Cincinnati. Under such circumstances, it would appear advisable that [this case] be transferred to a city of the Southern District of Ohio other than Cincinnati.

Although in that same order Judges Rubin and Weber expressed doubt whether this action is removable to federal court, that doubt was expressed, of course, without the benefit of the extensive briefs, voluminous exhibits and oral argument presented to the undersigned judge subsequent to removal. Within the expedited time schedule set by the Court and the parties, I have resolved those issues based upon the record now before me.

The Court emphasizes that the issues decided by this Memorandum and Order are solely questions of law concerning the jurisdiction of a United States district court when a case is removed from a state court based upon diversity of citizenship of the parties to the controversy. The essential facts relative to these jurisdictional issues are not in dispute, and the merits of the controversy between plaintiff Rose and defendant Giamatti are not before the Court at this time. The fact that a judge of the Court of Common Pleas of Hamilton County, Ohio, where this action was commenced, issued a temporary restraining order against the defendants, while a relevant factor among all the circumstances, is clearly not dispositive of any of the jurisdictional issues confronting this Court. The sole question raised by the notice of removal and the motion to remand is whether, under applicable law, the federal court has jurisdiction over the subject matter of this action. For the reasons stated hereafter, I conclude that the action was properly removed to this Court, and that this Court does have jurisdiction over the action which I have a duty to recognize and to enforce.

PROCEDURAL HISTORY

Plaintiff, Peter Edward Rose, is the Field Manager of the Cincinnati Reds baseball team. In February of this year, then Commissioner of Baseball Peter V. Ueberroth and then Commissioner of Baseball-elect A. Bartlett Giamatti initiated an investigation regarding allegations that Rose wagered on major league baseball games. On February 23, 1989 Giamatti retained John M. Dowd as Special Counsel for the purpose of conducting the investigation. On May 9, 1989 Dowd submitted a report to Giamatti summarizing the evidence obtained during the investigation. Commissioner Giamatti ultimately scheduled a hearing concerning the allegations for June 26, 1989.

In an effort to prevent Commissioner Giamatti from conducting the June 26 hearing, Rose filed an action in the Court of Common Pleas of Hamilton County, Ohio, on June 19, 1989, seeking a temporary restraining order and preliminary injunction against the pending disciplinary proceedings. Named as defendants in that action were A. Bartlett Giamatti, Major League Baseball, and the Cincinnati Reds. The crux of the complaint is Rose's contention that he is being denied the right to a fair hearing on the gambling allegations by an unbiased decisionmaker. The complaint requests permanent injunctive relief, which, if granted, would prevent Commissioner Giamatti from ever conducting a hearing to determine whether Rose has engaged in gambling activities in violation of the Rules of Major League Baseball. Rose asks that the Court of Common Pleas of Hamilton County, Ohio determine whether he has wagered on major league baseball games, including those of the Cincinnati Reds.

Subsequent to a two-day evidentiary hearing, Common Pleas Court Judge Norbert Nadel issued a temporary restraining order on June 25, 1989. The order enjoined all defendants (1) from any involvement in deciding whether Rose should be disciplined or suspended from participation in baseball and (2) from terminating Rose's employment as Field Manager of the Cincinnati Reds, or interfering with his employment in response to any action taken by Giamatti, or in retaliation for Rose having filed the action. Judge Nadel set July 6, 1989 as the date for a hearing on plaintiff Rose's motion for a preliminary injunction. Commissioner Giamatti and Major League Baseball unsuccessfully sought review of the temporary restraining order in the Ohio Court of Appeals, First Judicial District, in Hamilton County, Ohio; the Court of Appeals held on June 28, 1989 that the temporary restraining order was not an appealable order.

On July 3, 1989, defendant Giamatti filed a notice of removal of the action from the state court to the United States District Court for the Southern District of Ohio, Western Division at Cincinnati, contending that the federal court has diversity jurisdiction over this action. Defendants Cincinnati Reds and Major League Baseball consented to the removal of the action. As previously noted, when the notice of removal was filed Judges Rubin and Weber issued an order transferring the case from the Western Division of this District to the Eastern Division for a random draw among the resident judges. The case was randomly drawn and assigned to the undersigned judge.

On July 5, 1989, Rose filed a motion to remand this action to the Court of Common Pleas of Hamilton County, Ohio, asserting that there is a lack of complete diversity of citizenship between himself and the defendants, and that even if complete diversity exists, defendant Giamatti waived his right of removal by participating in the above-described proceedings in the state courts. At a conference of counsel held on July 5, 1989, the parties agreed and stipulated that the defendants would take no action against Rose until three days after the determination of the pending motion to remand. On July 10, 1989 the Cincinnati Reds filed a memorandum regarding the motion to remand, stating that the Reds take no position concerning the propriety of removal and have assumed an "entirely neutral" position in the litigation. The Commissioner filed a memorandum opposing the motion to remand on July 12, 1989, and Rose filed a reply memorandum on July 17, 1989. Oral argument was heard on July 20, 1989, and the Court, in order to decide the jurisdictional questions promptly, agreed to render its decision on July 31, 1989.

DIVERSITY JURISDICTION

The United States district courts are courts of limited jurisdiction, and the federal statute permitting removal of cases filed in state court restricts the types of cases which may be removed from state court to federal court. The removal statute provides in pertinent part that "any civil action brought in a State court of which the district courts of the United States have original jurisdiction, may be removed by the defendant or the defendants to the district court of the United States for the district and division embracing the place where such action is pending." 28 U.S.C. § 1441(a). The statute also provides that except for a civil action founded on a claim arising under federal law, "[a]ny other such action shall be removable only if none of the parties in interest properly joined and served as defendants is a citizen of the State in which such action is brought." 28 U.S.C. § 1441(b).

Defendant Giamatti contends in his notice of removal that the district court has original jurisdiction of this action by virtue of 28 U.S.C. § 1332(a), which grants original jurisdiction to the district courts in civil actions where the amount in controversy exceeds $50,000 and the action is between citizens of different states. This jurisdiction of federal courts is commonly known as "diversity" jurisdiction.

The diversity statute has historically been interpreted to require complete diversity of citizenship: "diversity jurisdiction does not exist unless each defendant is a citizen of a different State from each plaintiff." Owen Equipment & Erection Co. v. Kroger, 437 U.S. 365, 373, 98 S.Ct. 2396, 2402, 57 L.Ed.2d 274 (1978). If diversity of citizenship is found to exist among the parties to this action and none of the defendants in interest properly joined and served is a citizen of Ohio, then the action is properly removable from the state court. If the required diversity of citizenship does not exist, then the action is not properly removable and must be remanded to the state court.

With regard to the citizenship of the parties to this controversy, the complaint contains the following allegations concerning their identity and citizenship. Rose is alleged to be a resident of Hamilton County, Ohio. Commissioner Giamatti's residence is not stated in the complaint; in the notice of removal, however, he is alleged to be a citizen of the State of New York. Defendant Major League Baseball is alleged in the complaint to be an unincorporated association headquartered in New York and consisting of the two principal professional baseball leagues (National and American) and their twenty-six professional baseball clubs. The Cincinnati Reds, dba the Cincinnati Reds Baseball Club, is identified in the complaint as an Ohio limited partnership (hereinafter referred to in the singular as the "Cincinnati Reds").

The Court will accept as true for purposes of ruling on the motion to remand that plaintiff Rose is a citizen of the State of Ohio, that defendant Giamatti is a citizen of the State of New York, that defendant Cincinnati Reds is a citizen of the State of Ohio, and that defendant Major League Baseball, assuming it exists as a legal entity, is comprised of the two major professional baseball leagues and their constituent twenty-six major league baseball clubs, at least one of which, the Cincinnati Reds, is a citizen of the State of Ohio.

In the present case, it appears from the allegations of the complaint that defendant Cincinnati Reds and defendant Major League Baseball are citizens of the same state as plaintiff Rose. Recognizing that diversity jurisdiction is not demonstrated on the face of the complaint, defendant Giamatti includes in his notice of removal a number of allegations in support of his contention that this Court has diversity jurisdiction over this action such that it is properly removable. First, with respect to the defendant identified as Major League Baseball, the notice asserts that defendant Major League Baseball is not a "juridical entity," but is only a trade name utilized by the professional baseball clubs of the American and National Leagues and thus has no citizenship for diversity purposes. Notice of Removal, ¶ 7. Second, the notice asserts that any citizenship ascribed to Major League Baseball should be disregarded for purposes of removal, "since Major League Baseball is not a proper party to this action and is at most a nominal party against which no claim or cause of action has been asserted." Id. Finally, the notice asserts that Major League Baseball was "fraudulently joined" as a defendant for the purpose of attempting to defeat the removal jurisdiction of this Court. In a similar vein, the notice asserts that the defendant Cincinnati Reds is not a proper party to this action, is only a nominal party, and was fraudulently joined for the same purpose of defeating this Court's removal jurisdiction. Id., at ¶ 8.

The issues framed by the notice of removal, the motion to remand, and the briefs of the parties are, accordingly, as follows:

1. Is the named defendant, Major League Baseball, a legal entity which has a state of citizenship for diversity purposes?

2. Can the citizenship of either Major League Baseball or the Cincinnati Reds be disregarded for diversity purposes?

3. If diversity of citizenship among the parties properly joined in this action is found to exist, has defendant Giamatti nevertheless waived his right to remove this action to federal court?

The Court will address each of these issues in turn.

THE CITIZENSHIP OF DEFENDANT MAJOR LEAGUE BASEBALL

The Cincinnati Reds Baseball Club, a citizen of Ohio, is one of the twenty-six major league baseball clubs which are members of the association doing business as Major League Baseball. Therefore, Major League Baseball is deemed to be a citizen of Ohio for diversity purposes. Because plaintiff Rose and the defendants Major League Baseball and the Cincinnati Reds are all citizens of Ohio, if either Major League Baseball or the Cincinnati Reds is a party properly joined in this action and whose citizenship, for diversity purposes, cannot be ignored, the lack of diversity of citizenship between plaintiff and all defendants would require the Court to conclude that the removal of the case to this Court was improper. Consequently, the Court must determine whether, as the Commissioner contends, the citizenship of these defendants should be ignored for the purpose of determining whether the removal of this case to this Court was proper.

DETERMINATION OF PROPER PARTIES TO THIS ACTION FROM "THE PRINCIPAL PURPOSE OF THE SUIT"

It is apparent from the complaint that the actual controversy in this case is between Rose and Commissioner Giamatti. The complaint is replete with allegations of wrongdoing on the part of Giamatti. For example, Rose asserts that Giamatti and investigators hired by him attempted to bolster the credibility of witnesses against Rose, prejudged the truthfulness of certain testimony given as a part of the investigation, acted unreasonably in demanding information from Rose, improperly threatened him with refusing to cooperate in the investigation, requested that Rose step aside as the Reds' Field Manager without revealing to him the evidence which had been compiled concerning his alleged gambling activities, and otherwise acted improperly in violation of Giamatti's alleged duty to provide Rose with a fair and impartial hearing with respect to the allegations against him. The ultimate purpose of the action is to prevent Giamatti from conducting any hearing because of his alleged improper conduct and bias against Rose. The crux of the controversy is contained in ¶ 61 of the complaint:

> In light of Giamatti's actual displayed bias and outrageous conduct in this cause, his service as an investigator, a prosecutor and a prospective judge, his written prejudgment on the case before even hearing from Pete Rose and all of the evidence to be offered, and his denial of the procedural rights guaranteed to Pete Rose under the Rules of Procedure and the various contracts herein involved, Pete Rose will suffer irreparable injury if Giamatti is allowed to conduct the hearing. To submit to such a fatally flawed process would guarantee that Pete Rose would not receive a fair hearing, and he would be irrevocably tainted by Giamatti's continuing to pursue his various roles in this proceeding and his prejudging of the case.

The critical question now before the Court is whether, in this controversy between Rose and Giamatti, there is "the necessary collision of interests" between Rose on the one hand and the Cincinnati Reds and Major League Baseball on the other hand so that the citizenship of these defendants may not be disregarded by the Court. If the necessary collision of interests exists, then the action was improvidently removed and must be remanded to the state court. If, however, the Cincinnati Reds and Major League Baseball were fraudulently joined as parties or are only nominal parties in the controversy, then diversity of citizenship is not defeated and Rose's motion to remand this case to the Court of Common Pleas of Hamilton County, Ohio must be denied.

Just as it is clear that the crux of the present controversy is between Rose and Giamatti, it is equally clear that, in reality, there is no controversy between Rose and the Cincinnati Reds. The complaint explicitly asserts that Rose "alleges no wrongful conduct on the part of the Reds." Complaint at ¶ 4. Despite this explicit assertion, Rose contends that "all defendants herein owe Pete Rose the contractual duty to ensure that the Commissioner adheres to the Major League Agreement and discharges his duties in accordance with [baseball's] Rules of Procedure . . . ." Complaint at ¶ 57. In essence, Rose asserts that the Commissioner's rules of procedure concerning fair disciplinary hearings are incorporated as a part of his employment contract with the Cincinnati Reds, and that any action by Commissioner Giamatti in violation of his own rules of procedure would constitute a breach of Rose's contract with the Cincinnati Reds. It is Rose's position that the Cincinnati Reds owes him a contractual duty to see that the procedural rules are not violated, and that if Giamatti violates these rules by holding an unfair hearing and, as a result, sanctions Rose, the Reds will have failed in its duty and will have breached his contract. Rose's claim against the Cincinnati Reds, involving no present wrongful conduct on the part of the Reds, is for "anticipatory breach" of his contract.

The Major League Agreement, which unquestionably is incorporated as a part of Rose's contract with the Cincinnati Reds, creates the office of Commissioner of Baseball and vests extraordinary power in the Commissioner. The Commissioner has unlimited authority to investigate any act, transaction or practice that is even suspected to be "not in the best interests" of baseball. In connection with this authority, the Commissioner may (1) summon persons and order the production of documents, and, in case of refusal to appear or produce, impose penalties; (2) determine after investigation what preventative, remedial or punitive action is appropriate, and (3) take such action against the leagues, the clubs or individuals. Major League Agreement, Art. 1, Sec. 2. The Commissioner is given virtually unlimited authority to formulate his own rules of procedure for conducting those investigations, the only limitations being that whatever rules he adopts must recognize the right of any party in interest to appear before him and be heard, and the right of the presidents of the two major leagues to appear and be heard on any matter affecting the interests of the leagues. Id. at Sec. 2(e). These rules of procedure are not rules adopted by the members of Major League Baseball; they are rules promulgated solely by the Commissioner of Baseball.

In contrast to the Commissioner's own rules of procedure, the members of Major League Baseball have formally adopted extensive rules governing relations between clubs and their employees, misconduct of players and other persons, and many other matters. These rules are known as the "Major League Rules." These detailed rules governing major league professional baseball have been accepted by the twenty-six major league professional baseball clubs and are recognized as binding upon them.

Rose's contract with the Cincinnati Reds provides in relevant part:

> The National League Constitution, Regulations and/or Rules and the Major League and Professional Baseball Agreements and Rules, and all amendments thereto hereafter adopted, are hereby made a part of this contract.

Notice of Removal, Exhibit 2, Exhibit Q to Complaint at ¶ 5(a).

Considering the Major League Agreement, with its provisions vesting in the Commissioner the authority to promulgate his own procedural rules governing his investigation of matters not in the best interests of baseball, and its provisions for the adoption of Major League Rules binding upon every league, club, and player in major league professional baseball, it is apparent that "the Major League . . . Rules" which are expressly incorporated into Rose's contract with the Cincinnati Reds are the extensive rules of conduct formally adopted by the members of Major League Baseball and not the procedural rules independently promulgated by the Commissioner which govern only his own proceedings. Furthermore, and of greater importance, there is nothing in the Major League Agreement, the Major League Rules, or in Rose's contract with the Cincinnati Reds which gives the Reds any right to prevent the Commissioner from holding a disciplinary hearing or to interfere with proceedings within the jurisdiction of the Commissioner. In fact, the parties are in agreement that the Cincinnati Reds has no such right.

Rose concedes that the Cincinnati Reds has done nothing that would be considered a breach of his contract at this time, nor does he allege that the Cincinnati Reds has taken any action that indicates an intention to refuse to perform its contract with him in the future so as to constitute an anticipatory breach of his contract under Ohio law. Rose's argument that any violation by Giamatti of the Commissioner's own procedural rules would somehow constitute an automatic breach of Rose's contract with the Cincinnati Reds is without legal basis.

It is undeniable that the Cincinnati Reds has, as a practical matter, an interest in the outcome of these proceedings, but not in the legal sense that requires its joinder as a defendant in this action. Rose's complaint specifically alleges that there has been no wrongdoing on the part of the Cincinnati Reds, and the Reds specifically states that it will comply with the terms and conditions of its contract with Rose; there is no real controversy between these parties. The Court concludes that, for the purpose of determining diversity of citizenship, the defendant Cincinnati Reds was, in a legal sense, fraudulently joined as a defendant and that it is, at best, a nominal party in this action. Consequently, the citizenship of the Cincinnati Reds as a defendant may be disregarded for the purpose of determining whether there is complete diversity of citizenship among the parties to this action.

In addition to being sued individually as a defendant, the Cincinnati Reds, for the purpose of this analysis of diversity of citizenship, is also a member of Major League Baseball, and the Court turns next to the consideration of that named defendant.

If Major League Baseball were a typical unincorporated association, its jurisdictional status would be more easily determined. The reality, however, is that Major League Baseball is a unique organization. A brief history of the background of the Major League Agreement and the extraordinary powers vested in the Commissioner by the association is set forth in Charles O. Finley & Co., Inc. v. Kuhn, 569 F.2d 527 (7th Cir.), cert. denied, 439 U.S. 876, 99 S.Ct. 214, 58 L.Ed.2d 190 (1978).

Prior to 1921, professional baseball was governed by a three-man National Commission formed in 1903 which consisted of the presidents of the National and American Leagues and a third member, usually one of the club owners, selected by the presidents of the two leagues. Between 1915 and 1921, a series of events and controversies contributed to a growing dissatisfaction with the National Commission on the part of players, owners and the public, and a demand developed for the establishment of a single, independent Commissioner of baseball.

On September 28, 1920, an indictment issued charging that an effort had been made to 'fix' the 1919 World Series by several Chicago White Sox players. Popularly known as the 'Black Sox Scandal,' this event rocked the game of professional baseball and proved the catalyst that brought about the establishment of a single, neutral Commissioner of baseball.

In November, 1920, the major league club owners unanimously elected federal Judge Kenesaw Mountain Landis as the sole Commissioner of baseball and appointed a committee of owners to draft a charter setting forth the Commissioner's authority. In one of the drafting sessions an attempt was made to place limitations on the Commissioner's authority. Judge Landis responded by refusing to accept the office of Commissioner.

On January 12, 1921, Landis told a meeting of club owners that he had agreed to accept the position upon the clear understanding that the owners had sought

> 'an authority . . . outside of your own business, and that a part of that authority would be a control over whatever and whoever had to do with baseball.' Thereupon, the owners voted unanimously to reject the proposed limitation upon the Commissioner's authority, they all signed what they called the Major League Agreement, and Judge Landis assumed the position of Commissioner . . . .

> The agreement, a contract between the constituent clubs of the National and American Leagues, is the basic charter under which major league baseball operates. The Major League Agreement provides that '[t]he functions of the Commissioner shall be . . . to investigate . . . any act, transaction or practice . . . not in the best interests of the national game of Baseball' and 'to determine . . . what preventive, remedial or punitive action is appropriate in the premises, and to take such action . . . .' Art. I, Sec. 2(a) and (b). The Major League Rules, which govern many aspects of the game of baseball, are promulgated by vote of major league club owners . . . .

The Major Leagues and their constituent clubs severally agreed to
be bound by the decisions of the Commissioner and by the discipline
imposed by him. They further agreed to 'waive such right of recourse
to the courts as would otherwise have existed in their favor.' Major
League Agreement, Art. VII, Sec. 2.

Id. at 532-33 (footnotes omitted).

Given the background of the Major League Agreement and the unique manner in which the twenty-six major league baseball clubs have agreed to govern
the conduct of players and others by a completely independent Commissioner,
it is clear that Major League Baseball cannot be compared or equated with
a typical unincorporated association engaged in any other business. The
Commissioner's jurisdiction under the Major League Agreement to investigate
violations of Major League Rules, or any activity he believes is "not in the
best interests" of baseball, is exclusive. The major leagues and the twenty-six
major league clubs have absolutely no control over such an investigation or
the manner in which the Commissioner conducts it. Rose does not challenge
any provision of the Major League Agreement or the Major League Rules,
including the rule prohibiting wagering on major league baseball games, nor
does he challenge the Commissioner's authority under Article I, Section 2(e)
of the Major League Agreement to promulgate his own rules of procedure
dealing with investigations of suspected violations of the Major League Rules.
What Rose challenges is Commissioner Giamatti's conduct of the investigation
and disciplinary proceedings in his particular case. In short, Rose's controversy is not with Major League Baseball, but is with the office of the
Commissioner of Baseball for the Commissioner's alleged failure to follow his
own procedural rules in conducting the investigation of Rose's alleged gambling activities. Clearly, complete relief can be afforded with regard to the
primary relief sought in the complaint—preventing Commissioner Giamatti
from conducting a disciplinary hearing—without the need for any order against
Major League Baseball or its constituent major league professional baseball
clubs.

Rose argues that, "[m]ost important to the present case is the fact that it
is the members of [Major League Baseball] who must act if any action is to
be taken against Pete Rose." Reply Memorandum at 20. However, it is only
if the Commissioner is allowed to proceed with a hearing, finds Rose has
violated the Major League Rules concerning wagering on major league
baseball games, and places him on the ineligible list does any obligation to
take any action arise on the part of the major league baseball clubs. In the
meantime, the member clubs of Major League Baseball occupy a necessarily
neutral role in the dispute between Rose and the Commissioner. As neutral
bystanders to the battle between Rose and the Commissioner which is the
subject of this action, the member clubs of Major League Baseball have no
legal interest in the controversy, and at most would be considered to be
nominal parties for the purpose of determining diversity of citizenship. Pesch
v. First City Bank of Dallas, 637 F.Supp. 1530 (N.D.Tex.1986).

WAIVER OF RIGHT TO REMOVE

Rose contends that even if the Court should find that it has diversity
jurisdiction in this case, the Commissioner has nevertheless waived any right

to remove this action to federal court by virtue of his actions in the state courts.

The law is clear that a defendant may, by making affirmative use of the processes of the state court, waive the right to remove the action to federal court. California Republican Party v. Mercier, 652 F.Supp. 928, 931 (C.D.Cal.1986). The basis for this rule of law is that it is unfair to permit a defendant to experiment with his case in state court, and, upon adverse decision, remove the case for another try in federal court. Bolivar Sand Co., Inc. v. Allied Equipment, Inc., 631 F.Supp. 171, 172 (W.D.Tenn.1986). Any intent to waive the right to remove, however, must be evidenced by "clear and unequivocal" action. Bedell v. H.R.C. Ltd., 522 F.Supp. 732, 738 (E.D.Ky.1981) (footnote omitted).

Rose acknowledges these principles and admits that, as a general rule, merely defending against a temporary restraining order does not constitute a waiver of the right to remove. It is Rose's position that

> by seeking to appeal the temporary restraining order ("TRO") to the State Court of Appeals, by taking discovery, and by requesting an evidentiary hearing, Defendants have foresworn their usual policy of litigating baseball cases in federal court and have taken a stand to fight 'tooth and nail' against the State Court TRO.

Rose cites Rothner v. City of Chicago, 692 F.Supp. 916 (N.D.Ill.1988), for the proposition that vigorous defense of a temporary restraining order waives the right to seek removal.

The Rothner case, cited by plaintiff, was reversed by the Seventh Circuit Court of Appeals on July 5, 1989. While questioning whether the concept of waiver applies to removal cases subsequent to 1948 Congressional amendments to the removal statute setting specific time limits for filing petitions for removal, the court nevertheless held that waiver of the right to remove occurs only where the parties have fully litigated the merits of the dispute. Rothner v. City of Chicago, 879 F.2d 1402, 1416-17 (7th Cir.1989). The decision is in accord with the majority of cases which have held that taking defensive action in the state court in any preliminary proceedings short of an adjudication on the merits of an action will not constitute a waiver of the statutory right of removal. Bolivar Sand, 631 F.Supp. at 173; Bedell, 522 F.Supp. at 738; Universal Steel & Metal Co. (1975) Ltd. v. Railco, Inc., 465 F.Supp. 7, 10 (D.Vt.1978); Haun v. Retail Credit Co., 420 F.Supp. 859, 863 (W.D.Pa.1976).

In this case, the defendants did appear and contest Rose's entitlement to a temporary restraining order and, after the order was issued, sought appellate review of the issuance of that order. That activity is not materially different from the activity engaged in by the defendant in Atlanta, K. & N. Ry. Co. v. Southern Ry. Co., 131 F. 657 (6th Cir.), cert. denied, 195 U.S. 634, 25 S.Ct. 791, 49 L.Ed. 354 (1904), because it related to the propriety of the issuance of relief designed to preserve the status quo pending an adjudication of the merits of the underlying claims. The discovery that was conducted was taken for purposes of the preliminary injunction hearing. There is no indication in the record of bad faith, or that any of the defendants ever made a clear and unequivocal statement that removal would not be sought. Defendants did not utilize any remedy available in state court for purposes unrelated to the preliminary relief sought by Rose, nor unduly delay filing the removal petition. The petition for removal was clearly timely. Under these circumstances, and giving deference to the principle that a court should be reluctant to imply a waiver, see Hildreth v. General Instrument, Inc., 258 F.Supp. 29, 30 (D.S.C.1966), the Court concludes that no waiver of the right of removal has occurred.

CONCLUSION

In light of the foregoing analysis, the Court holds that the controversy in this case is between plaintiff Rose and defendant Giamatti; that they are the real parties in interest in this case; that the Cincinnati Reds and Major League Baseball, are, at best, nominal parties in this controversy; and that, consequently, the citizenship of the Cincinnati Reds and Major League Baseball may be disregarded for diversity purposes. The Court determines that diversity of citizenship exists between Rose, a citizen of Ohio, and Commissioner Giamatti, a citizen of New York, and that the Court has diversity subject matter jurisdiction over this action. Defendant Giamatti is not a citizen of the State of Ohio and has not waived his right to remove this action, therefore, the action was properly removable from the Court of Common Pleas of Hamilton County, Ohio. Plaintiff Rose's motion to remand is DENIED.

GOTTLOB v. CONNECTICUT STATE UNIVERSITY
1996 Conn. Super. LEXIS 231 (Conn. Super. Ct. 1996)

CORRADINO, Judge.

Dr. Gottlob was hired by Connecticut State University to set up and direct an academic center. The center was to provide help for students with academic problems; it provided tutoring services and counselling and its primary purposes was to aid student athletes in their course work.

Dr. Gottlob reported to university officials that on or about December 2, 1991 one of her assistants found a notebook at the center which might indicate one or more students were involved in gambling on professional sports. The assistant said the notebook appeared to contain nicknames and dollar amounts bet on games; it also appeared to belong to a student athlete on the football team. Dr. Gottlob told officials she no longer had the notebook. It was apparently returned to the student by someone, not Dr. Gottlob, at the center.

She also told university officials at the same time that prior to the discovery of the notebook a student from the football team had approached her and told her about a personal gambling problem that he had and she referred him for special counselling.

The university has an extensive athletic program in which many students are involved. It is important that it be in full compliance with NCAA regulations in order that its participation in that organization be maintained and so that the integrity of the athletic programs be guaranteed. In fact one of the very purposes for the setting up of the academic center was to ensure that NCAA rules and regulations be complied with as to academic requirements.

NCAA regulations require that student athletes should comport themselves with honor and dignity. It is a violation of NCAA rules if gambling activity goes on regarding college sports and it is a violation of NCAA rules to refuse to furnish information concerning possible violation of NCAA regulations when requested. Apparently those regulations require an immediate investigation into alleged gambling activity—failure to do so could result in the loss of the school's ability to compete in NCAA games.

The general importance of compliance with these regulations is obvious; for many students an important part of their college experience depends on their ability to participate in and compete in athletic events. The school, its administration and faculty have an important responsibility to make sure that NCAA regulations are complied with.

The danger to particular students involved in gambling activities surrounding athletic events should even be clearer. Widespread activity of this sort would compromise the integrity of athletic competition and thus destroy its enjoyment for students participating in these programs. A major concern is also the possibility that students engaging in such activity would be participating in crime that in certain circumstances could endanger their educational career and, depending on the elements they were involved with, even their safety. The morally corrupting influence on 18 and 19 year olds of such conduct should be a concern to all school officials charged with their welfare.

Dr. Beyard was the plaintiff's immediate supervisor. She requested that Dr. Gottlob reveal the name of the student to police authorities. Dr. Gottlob refused. She claimed that an important part of her function was to counsel students. It was of the utmost importance that students could talk to her in confidence. The student involved asked for confidentiality and Dr. Gottlob said she would honor that request. Dr. Gottlob got the student involved in counselling. Dr. Beyard insisted, however, that Dr. Gottlob must reveal the student's name. Dr. Gottlob requested time to speak to a lawyer regarding this matter which Dr. Beyard gave her. The lawyer told her she should cooperate with the police but that she was not obligated to reveal the student's name.

Dr. Beyard sent the plaintiff a memo indicating she should talk to [Chief Powell,] the university chief of police. She met with the chief. [According to Chief Powell's testimony, he] expressed his concern with gambling activities and said if organized crime figures were involved a concern would be how far people would go to collect their debt. The Chief corroborated Dr. Gottlob's testimony that at their meeting he did not request the name of the student who came for counselling on his gambling problem. He said too much time had passed and without the notebook the student's individual name wouldn't be of interest to him.

That Dr. Gottlob was not prepared to reveal the name and thought as a matter of principle the name of the student coming for counselling over a matter such as gambling shouldn't be revealed is consistent with her testimony as to when she felt a student's name should be disclosed to authorities. She reserved to herself the right to determine the ambit of confidentiality and said there are limits to confidentiality—she would not feel bound to confidentiality if a life-threatening situation presented itself, if someone was in physical danger were the examples she gave.

Dr. Shumaker, the university president, received Dr. Beyard's recommendation that the plaintiff's contract not be renewed on December 21, 1991. By a letter dated December 27, 1991 he informed the plaintiff that her contract would not be renewed for the 1993-94 calendar year. Dr. Shumaker had the ultimate responsibility of deciding whether the contract would be renewed.

Merits

The plaintiff bases her action [for reinstatement] on § 31-51q of the General Statutes. That statute provides that an employer is liable for the discipline and discharge of an employee on account of the employee's exercise of certain constitutional rights including the first amendment to the federal constitution. The parties have imported the 42 USC § 1983 analysis of cases involving discharge for alleged exercise of First Amendment rights into their analysis of how § 31-51q should apply. This certainly seems appropriate although our statutory language granting a cause of action only where the allegedly protected activity is found not to "substantially or materially interfere with the employee's bona fide job performance or the working relationship between the employee and the employee" reads somewhat differently from federal case law. In any event at this point I will adopt the federal § 1983 analysis for a First Amendment claim under our statute . . . .

[T]he fact that Dr. Gottlob didn't give her concerns a more public airing— contact with media or nonuniversity officials—does not preclude a court from finding that her statements were a matter of public concern. In this case the content of the statements and the context in which they were made is more determinative of this issue. The content of Dr. Gottlob's communications to Dr. Beyard and Chief Powell revolved around the issue of confidentiality. Dr. Gottlob informed these individuals that a notebook had been found at the student center she ran containing what might be gambling notations and that a student athlete came to her for counselling and revealed he had a gambling problem. However, she refused to reveal the identity of the student because she felt that this would violate his request for confidentiality. Dr. Gottlob believed that request had to be honored because, if it was not, her ability to perform her job at the student center would be seriously compromised. Although the center was set up to help students with academic problems it is obvious that such problems often arise because youngsters are having serious personal problems related to school and nonschool activities. If students couldn't be assured that what they said in counselling sessions at the center were kept confidential then they would not seek counselling in situations where they need it and where failure to get such counselling might seriously affect their ability to perform well academically and as participants in even nonacademic college activities.

First it should be said that Dr. Gottlob in her testimony and through the testimony she presented and even that presented by the defendant impressed the court as a person of great integrity. The very way in which she communicated the information she had underlines that. She did not hide what she knew to protect herself or even the position she had arrived at. Neither does the court find that she acted out of narrow personal financial or job condition or job security interests. She acted on the basis of what she felt was a commitment she made to an individual student and on what she felt was in the best interests of a proper running of her student center. The student center performed an important role in the university's life and the devotion this individual had to accomplishing its goals was well established by the testimony, not the least of which being the enormous amount of hours she put into her work.

All of this having been said, however, doesn't mean that the communications Dr. Gottlob made were a matter of public concern. The plaintiff quite forcefully argues in one of its briefs that it defies logic and common sense to conclude that an issue of public concern wasn't involved here—Dr. Gottlob was trying to protect the confidentiality interests of a student not advance her own personal interests. But such an argument merely sets forth a conclusion as to the propriety of finding a public concern here rather than providing a reason.

From reading the cases there are [several] broad categories of fact patterns. One type of case involves situations where an employee is dissatisfied with an employer's decision concerning his or her job condition or placement. The employee then makes complaints or sends memos to fellow workers complaining about the employer's actions and might even embellish the complaint by saying for example that the morale at the office was poor and job supervisors were incompetent. Courts have had no problem with finding that communications on such matters do not raise issues of public concern.

Another category of cases involves those employee statements that [go] to the heart of the First Amendment interest sought to be advanced. Thus, [for example, if] the employee was a district attorney a matter of public concern would be raised if the employee sought to inform the public that the district attorney's office was not discharging its public duties in prosecuting criminals, or where there were instances of breach of public trust or wrongdoing involved. If such allegations are made the courts have been quick to find the employee statements and allegations raised issues of public concern . . . .

A third type of case involves perhaps a situation where the employee responds to limitations put on his or her job conditions but the public itself by recent public debate over the issue or legislation enacted to cover the matter has itself defined the matter as one of public concern. Thus there is the interesting case of Caron v. Silvia, 588 NE 2d 711, 714 (Mass.1992) where an employee spoke out [about] an alleged interference with her rights as a smoker. The court noted, in finding the matter one of public concern, that the issue had been one of considerable public debate and state legislation.

This case appears to be a special category to itself. The employee plaintiff does not speak out for her own selfish or immediate personal interests. However, although her position is framed in the guise of protecting the confidentiality rights of a student it can be said that what is really involved here is a dispute over the internal operations of the university when it confronts an issue of student confidentiality. Should senior university officials decide whether confidentiality should be extended to student communications involving possible criminal activity or should individual faculty or university employees entrusted with a counselling role make that determinate? If there is to be confidentiality should it only apply to nonuniversity parties but not operate as to prevent disclosure to university officials or university police investigators? From one perspective what transpired here is purely a matter of internal university policy over spheres of authority. Dr. Gottlob headed a student center which did counselling. She honestly believed the effective accomplishment of the goals of the center—improving academic performance and adjustment to university life—required confidentiality as to student disclosures made to her. A university official disagreed with her based on what she perceived as broader university interest—compliance with regulations which would determine school participation in athletic events and ensuring that students didn't become involved in criminal activity.

Are such questions matters of public concern? Dr. Gottlob made a personal commitment of confidentiality to a student. She would have had to break that commitment if she disclosed his name. Certainly a principled person like Dr. Gottlob would have been deeply upset if she had to break her promise to this individual student. But that hardly makes the issue now before the court and the communications Dr. Gottlob made relative to this matter ones of public concern. As [other courts have] said the communication must be examined in the context and under the circumstances in which it was made.

Dr. Gottlob's concern beyond the fact that she made a personal commitment to this student, in fact her major concern, was that failure to grant counsellors like her the right to determine the ambit of confidentiality would mean that students wouldn't be open in disclosing problems that caused them academic difficulties.

But even she put some limits on the right of a student to expect confidentiality. She indicated that she would disclose information where a person's physical safety was threatened. Can the courts safely intervene in this area or do they even have the competency to resolve these issues that arise in an academic setting?

A Fourth Circuit case, Daniels v. Quinn, 801 F.2d 687 (CA 4, 1986) makes an interesting comment. There a teacher complained to a public official that she hadn't received materials for a remedial reading course. She claimed the decision not to rehire her was made because of these comments and this violated her First Amendment rights. The court recognized that the threshold question was to determine if the plaintiff's remarks were about a matter of public concern. The court at page 690 said the following:

> She contends, however, that the late arrival of remedial reading materials is a matter of public concern because it affects her ability, and that of others, to teach. The identical point can be made about innumerable conditions at a school, including, for example, the number of teacher aides, the tightness of class scheduling, the size of blackboards, or the adequacy of laboratory equipment. Questions of this sort do not belong in federal court. They are best resolved by local school boards and individual school administrators. To accord to all such grievances the status of protected speech is to invite a measure of educational involvement that federal tribunals are ill equipped to undertake.

This is a close case and a difficult one but I would have to say that the matter does not raise an issue of public concern.

If the plaintiff had established that the matter she raised was one of public concern the court would still have to consider whether "her interest in 'commenting upon matters of public concern' was greater than the defendants' interest in 'promoting the efficiency of the public services (they) perform,' " Frazier v. King, 873 F.2d 800, 825 (CA 5, 1989); White Plains Touring Corp. v. Patterson, 991 F.2d 1049, 1058-59 (1993). The language of Rankin v. McPherson, 483 U.S. 378, 388 (1987) sets forth the pertinent considerations:

> statements will not be considered in a vacuum; the manner, time and place of (the employee's) expression are relevant, as is the context in which the dispute arose . . . . Pertinent considerations are whether the statement impairs discipline by superiors or harmony among co-workers, has a detrimental impact on close working relationships for which personal loyalty and confidence are necessary, or impeded the performance of the speaker's duties or interferes with the regular operation of the enterprise.

I believe the dispute in this matter should be set in context in order for the court to address this issue. It won't do to parcel out the issue of the notebook from the refusal to disclose the student's name. Both occurred close in time and both incidents considered together presented to the administration a serious concern that student athletes were involved in gambling activities. The notebook contained notations concerning gambling activities. A student came to the center seeking counselling because of such activities. The court won't repeat the danger such a matter presents to the life of the university, its continued involvement in athletic activity and the welfare and perhaps even physical safety of students.

University officials when they heard of these matters met, regarded the issue at one of great seriousness and determined that Dr. Gottlob should be contacted. Dr. Beyard and Chief Powell asked Dr. Gottlob for the notebook and that the name of the student who came for counselling be revealed to police authorities at the university. The notebook was apparently already turned back by another person at the student center and Dr. Gottlob refused to reveal the student's name claiming she had an obligation to protect the student's confidentiality. Dr. Gottlob was very open and honest about her position; she did not assert it in an unpleasant or abrasive way. She asked to speak to a lawyer. Up to two weeks passed and she was then directed to go to a meeting with the Chief. At least on the court's view of the record it doesn't entirely ring true for the plaintiff to now say she cooperated fully with university authorities. It is true that at her last meeting with the Chief he did not ask her for the name of the student but he did not do so since in his opinion too much time had passed and the notebook had been returned. As the court previously noted there is no reason to think that Dr. Gottlob would have revealed the name if asked or would ever consider doing so in the future if a similar situation were to arise.

In any event given the firm stance taken by Dr. Gottlob over the course of this matter, her failure to reveal the name despite being told to and every indication that she would act similarly in the future if the same problem arose, it is difficult to conclude how her stance would not have caused divisive relations regarding this incident and any like future incident. In fact in a phone conversation with Chief Powell he told her that by not revealing the name she might be violating the law and subjecting herself to prosecution. At her actual meeting with Powell her suggestion was that she would contact the student and try to get him to come forward. Given her position of not having to reveal the name without the student's consent, he would have realized that there was a diversion of opinion as to university policy on a very important matter. The reverberations on community life that this would have caused don't have to be exaggerated to be appreciated.

Another point should be mentioned although it is not meant as a personal criticism of the plaintiff. She acted out of the best of motives but her activity during the period when the matter was open did amount to insubordination. Since she would have been head of the student center in the future if her contract had been renewed, it is difficult to see how it could be said that her speech in the context in which it was made and given its content, wouldn't have disrupted working relationships between herself and her immediate assistants on the one hand and supervising university officials and police and investigatory authorities on the other hand.

[Thus], in light of my ruling on whether First Amendment protection applies to this speech in the first instance (public concern issue) and my ruling on the university's defense of interference with efficient operations, I will grant judgment to the defendant.

Notes

1. After being banned by the NBA, Jack Molinas attended Brooklyn Law School, became a member of the New York State bar, played in the Eastern Basketball League, continually pressed Maurice Podoloff for reinstatement, and eventually filed a federal anti-trust action against the NBA, which was dismissed. *See Molinas v. National Basketball Association*, 190 F. Supp. 241 (S.D.N.Y. 1961). Until his death in Los Angeles in 1975 (in what may have been a gangland slaying), rumors persisted that Molinas was involved with gamblers, and at one point the NBA went so far as to preemptively ban two college freshmen—Roger Brown and Connie Hawkins—for associating with Molinas while playing high school basketball in Brooklyn. For a detailed account of Molinas's life, *see* Charley Rosen, *The Wizard of Odds: How Jack Molinas Almost Destroyed the Game of Basketball* (2001).

2. Shortly after Judge Holschuh refused to send his case back to state court, Pete Rose voluntarily agreed to a lifetime ban from baseball. *See* Ronald J. Rychlak, *Pete Rose, Bart Giamatti, and the Dowd Report*, 68 Miss. L.J. 889 (1999). Recently, however, Rose has sought to have the ban rescinded so that he can enter the Hall of Fame, and Commissioner Bug Selig has indicated a willingness to consider the matter. A similar effort is underway on behalf of Shoeless Joe Jackson, the most famous member of the 1919 "Black Sox," so that he too can enter the Hall of Fame. For a closer look at the Rose and Jackson affairs, *see, e.g.*, Thomas J. Ostertag, *From Shoeless Joe to Charley Hustle: Major League Baseball's Continuing Crusade Against Sports Gambling*, 2 Seton Hall J. Sport L. 19 (1992); Michael W. Klein, Comment, *Rose*

is in Red, Black Sox are Blue: A Comparison of Rose v. Giamatti and the 1921 Black Sox Trial, 13 Hastings Comm. & Ent. L.J. 551 (1991); Matthew B. Pachman, Note, *Limits on the Discretionary Powers of Professional Sports Commissioners: A Historical and Legal Analysis of Issues Raised by the Pete Rose Controversy*, 76 Va. L. Rev. 1409 (1990).

3. Molinas, Rose, and Jackson are not the only sports figures to have run afoul of their sport's gambling prohibitions. Other notables include Charles Barkley (basketball), Albert Belle (baseball), Mike Ditka (football), Leo Durocher (baseball), Lenny Dykstra (baseball), Don Gallinger (hockey), Paul Hornung (football), Michael Jordan (basketball), Alex Karras (football), Sonny Liston (boxing), Mickey Mantle (baseball), Willie Mays (baseball), Denny McLain (baseball), Joe Namath (football), Art Schlichter (football), Billy Taylor (hockey), and Johnny Unitas (football). *See further* Bob Oates, *Rose in Long Line of Betting Ballplayers*, Seattle Times, Aug. 20, 1989, at C10; Jim O'Donnell, *Safe Bet We've Seen This Before*, Chi. Sun-Times, Feb. 13, 1997, at 108; *Black Sox to Rose: The Shades of Scandal*, USA Today, June 25, 1991, at 9C.

4. As the *Gottlob* decision makes clear, gambling by college athletes (and their classmates) is a serious problem. Nowhere has this been more true than in basketball, which has suffered from periodic point-shaving scandals since the early 1950s, when New York City, then the center of the college basketball world, found itself mired in a vast scandal. *See* Charley Rosen, *Scandals of '51: How the Gamblers Almost Killed College Basketball* (1978).

One of the most famous college basketball scandals occurred during the 1978-79 season, when gamblers were able to convince several Boston College players to fix games. Their operation came to light when mobster Henry Hill was arrested on an unrelated robbery charge and, as part of a plea agreement, spilled the beans. *See United States v. Burke*, 700 F.2d 70 (2d Cir.), *cert. denied*, 464 U.S. 816 (1983). Hill's life was later made into the 1990 movie "Goodfellas," starring Ray Liotta and Joe Pesci, and the scandal is now the subject of an engrossing book by that name. *See* David Porter, *Fixed: How Goodfellas Bought Boston College Basketball* (2001).

5. In addition to their player rules, many leagues refuse to do business with gaming venues. In January 2003, the NFL barred the Las Vegas Convention and Visitors Authority from airing commercials during the Super Bowl, even though they contained no mention of gambling. *See* Christina Binkley, *Long Odds for Las Vegas Ads in Super Bowl*, Wall St. J., Jan. 14, 2003, at B1. Nevertheless, as the need to find new ways to attract fans and generate revenue becomes more of a challenge, some cracks are beginning to appear. In February 2000, the Sycuan Band of Kumeyaay Indians, which runs a highly profitable casino in El Cajon, California, paid $1.5 million to sponsor the San Diego Padres' upcoming season (using the carefully-worded slogan "Padres 2000 Presented by Sycuan" so as not to violate baseball's consorting rules); in September 2002, the Phoenix Coyotes became the first professional sports team to have a tie-in with a state lottery (Arizona's daily "Pick 3" game); and in January 2003, the WNBA began holding talks with the Mohegan Indians to place a team in the tribe's entertainment complex in Connecticut, which includes both a basketball arena and a casino. Even the NCAA, which

regularly asks newspapers not to publish betting lines, has allowed its corporate partners (such as Pepsi) to link March Madness to scratch games and bracket contests. *See further* Bill Finley, *W.N.B.A. and Casino in Talks for a Team*, N.Y. Times, Jan. 17, 2003, at C22; Greg Johnson, *Baseball Allows Gambling Industry to Make Its Pitch*, L.A. Times, Apr. 6, 2000, at A1; Michael O'Keefee, *Jocks Are Wild*, N.Y. Daily News, Apr. 14, 2002, at 92; Phil Stukenborg, *Casinos Have Strong Ties to City's Sporting Scene*, Comm. Appeal, May 22, 2002, at D1 (describing the numerous links between northern Mississippi casinos and Memphis's various sports franchises).

6. For a further discussion of college sports gambling, *see, e.g.*, Benje Bailey, *Gambling on College Sports*, 4 Gaming L. Rev. 339 (2000); John Warren Kindt & Thomas Asmar, *College and Amateur Sports Gambling: Gambling Our Youth Away?*, 8 Vill. Sports & Ent. L.J. 221 (2002); Ante Z. Udovicic, Comment, *Sports and Gambling: A Good Mix? I Wouldn't Bet on It*, 8 Marq. Sports L.J. 401 (1998).

Problem 22

To boost sales, a trading card company decided to print on the back of each pack the odds of getting one of its highly-prized "limited edition" cards. Has it, or the sports leagues that have licensed it, violated any laws? *See Price v. Pinnacle Brands, Inc.*, 138 F.3d 602 (5th Cir. 1998).

Chapter 6

CASINO GAMING

A. OVERVIEW

Nevada was the first state to legalize land-based casinos, doing so in 1931 to make up for falling tax receipts during the Great Depression. In 1976, New Jersey, hoping to revitalize Atlantic City (a once fabled beach resort), became the second state to approve such gaming. In recent years, four other states have allowed casinos to begin operating, chiefly to spur tourism: Colorado (in three historic mining towns), Louisiana (New Orleans), Michigan (Detroit), and South Dakota (Deadwood).

B. EXTERNAL CONTROLS

ROSENTHAL v. STATE ex rel. NEVADA GAMING COMMISSION
620 P.2d 874 (Nev. 1980)

THOMPSON, Justice.

This case is sequel to State of Nevada v. Rosenthal, 93 Nev. 36, 559 P.2d 830 (1977), where we noted the distinction between the status of one who seeks to acquire a gaming license and the status of one who possesses a work permit as a gaming employee. The former does not have existing privileges, but is attempting to acquire them. The latter does have an existing privilege and is entitled to receive notice and a hearing before his privilege to work as a gaming employee can be nullified. In that case we found it permissible for the Gaming Commission to deny Rosenthal's application to be licensed as a key employee of Argent Corporation, but impermissible automatically to revoke his work permit as a gaming employee without prior notice and an opportunity to be heard. The statutes and regulations then in effect which would allow such automatic revocation could not stand for want of fairness.

Because of that decision, Rosenthal could no longer direct the Nevada operations of Argent Corporation since he had been denied a state gaming license. He became Food and Beverage Director for the Stardust Hotel and later its Entertainment Director for a salary of $65,000 a year. Believing that Rosenthal, in the mentioned positions, continued to significantly influence gaming, the Commission deemed Rosenthal still to be a key employee and once again directed him to submit an application for a gaming license.

The Gaming Control Board and the Gaming Commission, meeting in joint session, denied Rosenthal a license. In reviewing that decision, the district court found that there was evidence to support a determination that Rosenthal was a key employee, and not suitable to be licensed. The court also found that Rosenthal's work permit had expired.

The finding that Rosenthal's work permit had expired appears to have been a gratuitous act on the part of the district court. His work permit could only expire if he failed to work as a gaming employee for a period of 90 days. NRS 463-335(10). The finding is inconsistent with and contradicts the fundamental holding of the court that Rosenthal was so involved in gaming that he qualified as a key employee.

On this appeal it is Rosenthal's primary contention that he has the right to work in the gaming industry, and that this right has been denied without due process of law.

1. Following the Rosenthal decision by this court the 1977 legislature amended the Gaming Control Act. (The legislature also amended the Act in 1979. All references herein are to the 1977 enactments.) A portion of the reworded Act, NRS 463.165 and 463.560, provides that if an employee required to be licensed is denied a license because of lack of good character, honesty or integrity, the gaming licensee by whom he is employed shall terminate his employment upon notification by registered or certified mail to the licensee of that action.

Such an automatic revocation of one's privilege to work as a gaming employee in a capacity other than that of a key employee was condemned by this court in the first Rosenthal case under statutes and regulations then in effect. In our view NRS 463.165 and 463.560 are equally infirm for want of procedural due process.

Here, as in the first Rosenthal case, the hearing before the Board and Commission was focused upon the suitability of Rosenthal to be licensed as a key employee. His right to work in a capacity other than that of a key employee was not in issue at all. We therefore conclude that Rosenthal may continue to enjoy a work permit as a gaming employee. As in the first case, our conclusion shall not be construed to preclude further action by the gaming authorities to revoke his work permit should they deem such action advisable.

2. Rosenthal interposed objection to the hearing before the Gaming Control Board and the Gaming Commission in joint session. The statutory procedures do not appear to contemplate a hearing before the two bodies in joint session.

The Gaming Control Board performs an investigatory function, and makes recommendations to the Gaming Commission. NRS 463.210. If the Board recommends denial, it should file written reasons for its recommendation with the Commission. NRS 463.210(2). The Commission may deny the application, remand the matter back to the Board for further investigation or grant approval. NRS 463.220(4). If the Gaming Commission is not satisfied that the applicant is qualified for licensing, the Gaming Commission may conduct a hearing. NRS 463.220(5).

The regulatory scheme appears to contemplate that proceedings before the Commission shall be subsequent to and separate from proceedings before the Board. However, this record does not disclose prejudice to Rosenthal by reason of the joint meeting of the two bodies. Each body deliberated and voted separately. Consequently, we conclude that the fact of a joint hearing provides no basis for this court to annul the administrative determination.

3. We need not consider other assigned errors.

The judgment of the district court is affirmed in so far as it upholds the decision of the Nevada Gaming Commission that Rosenthal, as a key employee, is not suitable to be licensed. That part of the judgment which affirms an automatic revocation of Rosenthal's work permit is reversed and set aside.

MANOUKIAN, Justice, concurring.

I am in accord with the views expressed in the majority opinion. However, I wish to add a note regarding our affirmance of that part of the trial court's grant of declaratory relief to respondents, which upheld the Nevada Gaming Commission's denial of appellant's application for a gaming license and our reversal of the determination concerning the work permit.

The gaming industry is one which is subject to complete and careful control by the state due to criminal elements commonly involved in the industry. Nevada Tax Comm'n v. Hicks, 73 Nev. 115, 119, 310 P.2d 852, 854 (1957). Thus, individuals desiring to be employed by or to operate a business in the industry are necessarily required to submit to rigid investigation and regulation. That degree of scrutiny increases when an individual occupies a key position in the industry.

Here, the record shows inter alia that Rosenthal appeared at the payoff window of the racebook when a gaming official questioned the racebook's refusal to pay a wager; that Rosenthal questioned gaming officials' authority to examine work permits; that he was observed standing in the casino pit; and that he telephoned gaming officials to complain about gaming agents and accompanied Stardust employees to United Coin to view a new type of electronic scoreboard. I agree with the Gaming Commission's determination, as characterized by the majority, that Rosenthal "continued to significantly influence gaming." I too believe that there was cause for the Commission's summoning of Rosenthal to submit an application for a gaming license and that there existed evidence to support a determination that Rosenthal was a key employee and was unsuitable for licensing.

Moreover, in my view, the legislature could properly conclude that a person who cannot meet the requirements to occupy a key position with an employer, cannot be employed in any position by that employer and remain divorced from the decisions made in running the gaming business of that employer. As such, our statutes can be read to prohibit further employment in any capacity of a person whose application for a license to be employed in a key position is denied. Nevertheless, although it is convincingly argued that the statutes themselves provide sufficient notice of the result of a denial of an application and the hearing for the license is a sufficient hearing for the work permit revocation, I also concur with the majority that specific notice and an opportunity to be heard are preconditions to revocation of this existing right. State v. Rosenthal, 93 Nev. at 46, 559 P.2d at 837. See NRS 463.337.

[The concurring opinion of Justice Gunderson is omitted.]

APPLICATION OF BOARDWALK REGENCY CORPORATION FOR CASINO LICENSE

447 A.2d 1335 (N.J.),
appeal dismissed, 459 U.S. 1081 (1982)

CLIFFORD, Judge.

Boardwalk Regency Corporation (BRC) applied for a plenary license pursuant to the Casino Control Act, N.J.S.A. 5:12-1 to -152 (Act). After conducting investigations and hearings on the application, the Casino Control Commission (Commission) found that two of the directors of BRC, Clifford S. and Stuart Z. Perlman, had failed to satisfy the standards set forth in the Act regarding "casino key employees." The Commission ruled that if the Perlmans were not removed from positions of control in the extensive corporate hierarchy of which BRC and its corporate parents, Caesars New Jersey, Inc. (CNJ) and Caesars World, Inc. (CWI), were a part, BRC's application would be denied. The Commission further required BRC to choose, by November 26, 1980, either (1) to sever the Perlmans permanently from any ownership or employment connection with BRC, any of its parent companies, and any subsidiary of CWI in this or any other jurisdiction, or (2) withdraw as a casino licensee from New Jersey. BRC was also directed to submit a plan for Commission approval to implement whichever alternative it chose. Following the Appellate Division's denial of a stay of these conditions this Court granted a stay pending appeal.

On consolidated appeals of the Perlmans and the corporations the Appellate Division affirmed the Commission's decision as to the non-qualification of the Perlmans, but reversed to the extent that it required the Perlmans to divest their personal interests from non-New Jersey subsidiaries of CWI having no "gaming" activities. It remanded to the Commission to recast its order consistent with the Appellate Division opinion and for "reasonable revision of the timetable." The stay imposed by this Court remains in effect.

The Perlmans and the corporations then filed notices of appeal to this Court, asserting "a substantial question arising under the Constitution of the United States," R. 2:2-1(a); and we granted the petitions for certification of the Attorney General and the Commission regarding the Appellate Division's modification of the Commission's order, 89 N.J. 405 (1982). In addition, the Attorney General filed a notice of cross-appeal directed to the same issue raised in his petition, namely, the Appellate Division's invalidation of the Commission's requirement that the Perlmans disconnect themselves from all non-New Jersey non-gaming activities.

Specifically, the Commission required that as one of the conditions of BRC's casino licensure, the Perlmans must dispose of any interest whatsoever in subsidiaries of CWI that are situated outside of New Jersey and are not engaged in casino gaming activities; must be removed from any position as an officer, director or employee of such subsidiaries; and must not receive any remuneration in any form from such subsidiaries. It is this condition that the court below struck down. Today we reinstate that condition of licensure. With the exception of that single modification, we affirm the judgment of the Appellate Division substantially on the basis of Judge Fritz's comprehensive and perceptive opinion for that court.

I

While the Appellate Division's discussion of the facts suffices for our purposes today, several features nonetheless bear repeating. Initially, it is noteworthy that CWI, aptly described below as "[a] creature of humble beginnings," is today a multifaceted corporate giant, which, through its various nationwide subsidiaries, owns and operates businesses in both the gaming and non-gaming industries. Of particular import to this case, however, is CWI's relationship to BRC: BRC is a wholly owned subsidiary of CNJ in which CWI owns an 85% stock interest.

Moreover, since the Appellate Division decision, there have been several developments regarding the Perlmans' relationship with CWI and its subsidiaries. By way of background, when the matter first came before the Commission in September 1978, both Perlmans owned an extensive interest in CWI, CNJ, and thereby BRC. Clifford Perlman was Chairman of the Board of Directors and chief executive officer of CWI and CNJ, in addition to holding a 10% stock interest in CWI, and a 1.4% interest in CNJ. Stuart Perlman was Vice-Chairman of the Board of Directors of CWI and CNJ. His stock ownership in CWI, about 8%, was second only to that of Clifford Perlman. He also held approximately a 1% interest in CNJ.

In contrast to the facts as they appeared when the case was before the Commission and the Appellate Division, the Perlmans' relationship to BRC through their extensive interest in CWI and CNJ has since changed. On October 30, 1981, CWI and the Perlmans entered into an agreement that provided that (1) the Perlmans would sell, and CWI would purchase, the Perlmans' shares of CWI and CNJ stock; (2) the Perlmans would acquire promissory notes for part of the purchase price of their CWI and CNJ stock; and (3) the Perlmans would resign from all of their positions as officers and directors of CWI and its subsidiaries, save for the fact that Clifford Perlman would enter into an agreement to continue as Chairman of the Board and chief executive of Desert Palace, Inc., a CWI subsidiary responsible for operating CWI's Nevada based casino-hotels. On December 15, 1981, the Commission, upon application by CWI, approved of the arrangement except for Clifford Perlman's continued relationship with Desert Palace, Inc. A shareholder's suit challenging the arrangement was settled before we heard argument on the case.

II

We turn to the merits of the case. Judge Fritz's exhaustive opinion below rejected a vigorous attack mounted by the Perlmans and the corporations regarding the Commission's determination that neither Clifford nor Stuart Perlman had met the statutory requirement of demonstrating by clear and convincing evidence their good character, honesty and integrity.

That attack has been renewed before this Court. The Appellate Division initially rejected the argument that the Commission failed to discuss adequately the relevant evidence in reaching its ultimate conclusions and that its conclusions were not based on sufficient credible evidence in the record. The Appellate Division also found "ingenious" but "unpersuasive" the contentions of the Perlmans and the corporations that the Act requires only a demonstration of the putative casino key employee's reputation for good character. In this regard the court below found that the Act requires a demonstration of good character in fact, given the Legislature's explicit statements of public policy and of the "evils" it sought to address through the imposition of exacting and rigorous licensing procedures.

The Appellate Division also considered a barrage of constitutional challenges to the statutory "good character" criterion. It rejected the contention that this criterion violated the Perlmans' due process rights, because it was unduly vague, stating that "the potential key employee is reasonably apprised by the statute, as a matter of common knowledge, in light of ordinary human experience, as to the kind of conduct necessary to satisfy the statute." Similarly lacking in merit, in the court's view, was the contention that the good character criterion "allow[ed] the Commission to rely on guilt by association."

We have reviewed the legal principles that underlie each of these arguments and the record developed below upon which the Commission based its findings. As to the arguments raised by the Perlmans and the corporations, set forth above, we repeat our endorsement of Judge Fritz's painstaking analysis and of the conclusions achieved in his opinion for the Appellate Division . . . .

IV

There remains one further area of discussion. As a final point of contention the Perlmans and the corporations maintain that the Commission's Order unconstitutionally conditions BRC's licensure on the Perlmans' divestiture of their interests in non-New Jersey subsidiaries of CWI. Their challenge in this regard is mounted on the basis of the Commerce Clause and the Due Process Clause.

As matters stand today, BRC is operating a New Jersey casino and Clifford Perlman is acting as chairman of the board of CWI's subsidiary Desert Palace, Inc., operator of CWI's Nevada gaming casino, Caesars Palace. Caesars Palace's position in the scheme of things is only partially illustrated by the fact that it is CWI's principal and most profitable asset, having generated for the year ending April 30, 1980 about 43% of CWI's total gross revenues.

In addition, it is the model after which CWI's hotel casino facilities, including BRC, are patterned, and it provides BRC with consultant services and management counseling. BRC and Caesars Palace share some directors in common. In his current position as Desert Palace's chairman Clifford Perlman has a direct relationship with Caesars Palace's management, and BRC has a direct relationship with the Nevada casino. The circumstances of Clifford Perlman's ability to influence BRC policy, too apparent to require further belabored explication, prompt our agreement with the Appellate Division's disposition of the Commerce Clause argument: The fallacy in this argument is that the order is said to purport "to regulate the management of substantial non-New Jersey operations * * * and to limit the Perlmans' business activities outside of New Jersey," when in fact it does no such thing. It neither regulates CWI nor any of its subsidiaries except BRC or the Perlmans, nor tells them what they must do. It only tells BRC, in terms completely in line with the statute and its purposes, the condition which must exist in view of its corporate connections, before it can enjoy the privilege of a casino license. No one will argue that New Jersey does not have a legitimate local public interest in determining who shall be thus licensed in New Jersey and under what conditions. We are satisfied this issue has no merit and warrants no further discussion.

With the same dispatch, and on the same basis, can we address the Due Process argument, it being manifest that the Commission's divestiture order bears a rational relationship to a legitimate state interest. Insofar as the Due Process Clause is concerned, since no fundamental right is affected by the Commission's order, that ends the matter.

The Commission's order also required the disassociation of the Perlmans' personal interest in the non-New Jersey subsidiaries of CWI that had and have no connection with the gaming industry. As to this aspect of the Order, the Appellate Division was not convinced that traditional notions of due process had been satisfied. Essentially, the court seemed uncertain that requiring divestiture to this extent would serve any "legitimate state interest." We harbor no doubts on the issue, and we fail to see why, in the context of this case, any distinction should be made between gaming and non-gaming subsidiaries. The question remains, in either instance, whether the presence of either Perlman in the CWI corporate structure carries with it the opportunity for them to exert their personal influence in the operation of BRC. In the non-gaming as well as the gaming setting that question must be answered in the affirmative.

The record demonstrates that for many years the Perlmans have wielded enormous power and influence throughout CWI, which, it should be recalled, is simply a holding company with operating subsidiaries. Permitting the Perlmans to remain in or assume a structured, formal relationship of ownership, employment or management in one of those subsidiaries, albeit a non-gaming enterprise, would encourage—or at the very least allow—the exertion of power and influence within the corporate structure. Indeed, the court below appears to have recognized this possibility by its reservation unto the Commission of the right to act should a "Perlman effect" become "manifest."

What the Commission sought to do was prevent the Perlmans from influencing gaming policy, rather than react to that influence after it has been exerted. This is a reasonable aim, particularly inasmuch as the evidence demonstrated a substantial likelihood that the Perlmans would leave their mark on BRC policy were they to obtain or continue to occupy official positions within the corporate family. This perception of the Perlmans' presence within the corporate structure is borne out by the corporation's assertion that "the loss of the Perlmans' services has been, and continues to be, a substantial detriment" to CWI.

Moreover, the corporations call attention to the "substantial and uncontradicted" evidence as to the importance of the Perlmans' functions in CWI and as to "the harm which has resulted to the company since the Perlmans have been isolated from its affairs."

Given the degree of importance that the corporations themselves attach to Clifford and Stuart Perlman, we cannot say that the Commission's apprehension of their influence on CWI and BRC, even from a non-gaming subsidiary position, is ill-founded; nor can we conclude that there is insufficient evidence to support the conclusion that divestiture of the Perlmans' interests in CWI's non-gaming subsidiaries bears a rational relationship to the state's legitimate interest in preventing them from exercising corporate power and influence over BRC.

V

Except as modified herein the judgment below is affirmed. All provisions of the Commission's order are reinstated, and the Commission is directed to establish a new timetable for submission of BRC's plans. The stay heretofore entered is vacated, effective ten days after release of this opinion.

PETITION OF NIGRIS
577 A.2d 1292 (N.J. Super. Ct. App. Div. 1990)

SKILLMAN, Justice.

The primary issue presented by this appeal is whether § 74(e) of the Casino Control Act (the Act), N.J.S.A. 5:12-1 et seq., requires the Casino Control Commission (the Commission) to seal any exhibit admitted into evidence at a public hearing which contains "information and data pertaining to an applicant's criminal record, family and background."

The issue arose in the context of an application for a casino license filed by Griffin Company following its acquisition of and merger with Resorts International, Inc. In August 1988, Mervyn Griffin (Griffin), who holds a substantial interest in Griffin Company, was informed by an investment banker involved in financing the Resorts acquisition that he had learned that Michael J. Nigris (Nigris), the then President, Treasurer and Chief Executive Officer of Griffin Company, had questionable business associations which could have a negative impact upon the Commission's consideration of Griffin Company's pending casino application. Mr. Griffin then retained a private investigating firm, which provided an oral report to him confirming the adverse information about Nigris. Upon receipt of this oral report in August 1988, Griffin removed Nigris from any involvement in his casino operations but continued to employ him until late May or early June 1989 in connection with his non-casino businesses. On October 25, 1988, Mr. Griffin received a written summary prepared by the private investigating firm which contained more detailed information relating to Nigris' questionable business associations.

Prior to the commencement of the hearing on Griffin Company's application, Nigris became aware that the Division of Gaming Enforcement (the Division) intended to introduce evidence relating to his background and business relationships. This evidence included the memorandum submitted to Griffin in October 1988 summarizing the results of the private investigation of Nigris, a report prepared by the Division regarding Nigris' qualifications, a summary of an interview of Nigris conducted by the Division's investigators and a transcript of a sworn interview of Nigris. The primary import of these exhibits was that Nigris had close business associations with Ernest Barbella (reputed to be "a member of La Cosa Nostra"), Herbert S. Cannon (a disbarred lawyer with two bank fraud convictions and numerous securities laws convictions), and Peter Aiello ("a frequent securities law violator"). This information was pertinent to whether Mr. Griffin's continued employment of Nigris from August 1988 until late May or early June 1989 reflected adversely upon Griffin's "good character, honesty and integrity" and thus was grounds under N.J.S.A. 5:12-84(c) for denial of a casino license.

Nigris' counsel sent two letters to the Commission requesting it to seal these exhibits in order to prevent their public disclosure. After reviewing the documents and hearing arguments of counsel, the Commission denied Nigris' application.

Nigris then appealed to this court. A single judge temporarily stayed the unsealing of the documents but permitted reference to the documents in counsel's summations and in the Commission's final decision.

The Commission issued a final decision on September 27, 1989 granting Griffin Company's application for a plenary casino license. A full panel of this court entered an order on October 10, 1989, staying the unsealing of the documents pending a final decision on Nigris' appeal. The Supreme Court subsequently denied the Division's motion to vacate the stay.

This appeal turns primarily on the interpretation of § 74(e) (N.J.S.A. 5:12-74(e)), which provides:

> All information and data pertaining to an applicant's criminal record, family, and background furnished to or obtained by the commission from any source shall be considered confidential and shall be withheld in whole or in part, except that any information shall be released upon the lawful order of a court of competent jurisdiction or, with the approval of the Attorney General, to a duly authorized law enforcement agency.

Nigris' basic argument is that § 74(e) requires the Commission to seal and thus prevent public disclosure of any exhibit admitted into evidence at a public hearing which contains information pertaining to an applicant's criminal record, family or background unless a court enters an order permitting release of the document.

To determine whether this was the intent of § 74(e), it is appropriate to consider not only the particular statute in question, but also the entire legislative scheme of which it is a part. Moreover, § 74(e) must be read in a reasonable manner to include only those situations legitimately contemplated by the Legislature. Therefore, a court will not "permit the intent of the Legislature to be subverted by language which, read literally, appears to contravene that which the Legislature actually intended."

One of the basic objectives of the Act, as declared in N.J.S.A. 5:12-1(b)(6), is to promote "public confidence and trust in the credibility and integrity of the regulatory process and of casino operations." To the same effect, N.J.S.A. 5:12-1(b)(13) states that the provisions of the Act are "designed to engender and maintain public confidence and trust in the regulation of the licensed enterprises." The Supreme Court of New Jersey also has taken note of the fact that one of the essential objectives of the Act is to sustain "public confidence and trust in the honesty and integrity of the State's regulatory machinery." Knight v. Margate, 86 N.J. 374, 392, 431 A.2d 833 (1981). Thus, the question is whether Nigris' interpretation of § 74(e) can be reconciled with the underlying legislative goal of promoting public confidence in the casino industry and the state's regulation of that industry.

At the outset, it is important to note the full ramifications of Nigris' interpretation of § 74(e). The confidentiality requirement of § 74(e) is not limited to documents but rather applies to all "information and data" furnished to or obtained by the Commission regardless of its form. Thus, Nigris' interpretation of § 74(e) would require not only the sealing of documents introduced into evidence but also the closing of any hearing in which testimony regarding "confidential information" is presented, the impounding of transcripts of such testimony and, indeed, even the impounding of any final decision of the Commission which refers to such confidential information. Moreover, it is extremely common for evidence regarding the "background" of applicants, including their alleged business relationships with members of organized crime or other unsavory persons, to be presented at casino licensing hearings. In fact, such evidence has been the primary focus of several of the Commission's most significant hearings involving the licensing of casinos and their officers, directors and employees. Therefore, the acceptance of Nigris' interpretation of § 74(e) would compel the sealing of exhibits and the closing of hearings to the public in some of the most significant casino licensing proceedings conducted by the Commission.

We also note that § 74(e) does not expressly deal with the conduct of contested cases. Instead, this subject is addressed in §§ 107 through 110 of the Act, N.J.S.A. 5:12-107 to 110. N.J.S.A. 5:12-107(a) indicates that hearings before the Commission are subject to the provisions of the Administrative Procedure Act (APA), N.J.S.A. 52:14B-1 et seq., and N.J.S.A. 5:12-107(a)(4) states that "[e]ach party to a hearing shall have the right to call and examine witnesses" and "to introduce exhibits relevant to the issue of the case, including the transcript of testimony at any investigative hearing conducted by or on behalf of the commission." However, the sections of the Act dealing with hearings in contested cases are silent as to the sealing of exhibits and closing of hearings to the public. Therefore, the Legislature undoubtedly intended casino licensing hearings to be subject in this regard to the same rules as govern other hearings in contested cases.

Pursuant to N.J.S.A. 52:14F-5(e) and (f), the Director of the Office of Administrative Law has adopted a rule which provides that:

> In considering whether to close a hearing and/or seal a record, the judge shall consider the requirements of due process of law, other constitutional and statutory standards and matters of public policy. The judge shall consider the need to protect against unwarranted disclosure of sensitive financial information or trade secrets, to protect parties or witnesses from undue embarrassment or deprivations of privacy, or to promote or protect other equally important rights or interests. [N.J.A.C. 1:1-14.1(b)].

Since licensing hearings before the Commission are "contested cases," and thus subject to the rules which govern quasi-judicial hearings under the APA,

N.J.A.C. 1:1-14.1(b) would govern any application to seal exhibits or close a licensing hearing before the Commission.

Viewing § 74(e) within this overall statutory framework, we are persuaded that the Legislature did not intend to require the closing of the Commission's hearings in contested cases or the sealing of exhibits admitted into evidence. The Legislature was undoubtedly aware that the Commission would receive and routinely process thousands of applications for various licenses without conducting hearings. Such applications frequently contain highly personal information concerning an applicant's family and background, the revelation of which could embarrass or harm the applicant without serving any overriding public interest. Thus, the Legislature included § 74(e) in the Act in order to prevent the Commission from revealing information relating to an applicant's criminal record, family and background in the course of the ordinary administration of the Act. However, the balancing of private and public interests is significantly different in contested adjudicative hearings relating to the issuance of casino licenses. While the privacy interests of applicants are dominant in the routine administrative processing of applications for employee and other licenses required by the Act, the public interest in preserving public confidence in the integrity of the regulatory process by allowing public access to the evidence on which the Commission bases its decisions is paramount in contested adjudicatory hearings.

The licensing of casinos and casino employees is similar in this respect to the administration of various other laws which require the submission of reports and other documents containing personal information which administrators are directed to keep confidential. For example, the Director of the Division of Taxation is required to keep tax returns and other tax records confidential pursuant to N.J.S.A. 54:50-8. However, this does not mean that a tax court judge hearing a case relating to a question of tax liability must close the trial or seal a tax return which is admitted into evidence.

Although the Commission is not compelled by § 74(e) to automatically grant an application to seal an exhibit or close a hearing where information is presented relating to an applicant's criminal record, family or background, it is required in passing on such an application under N.J.A.C. 1:1-14.1(b) to conscientiously balance the privacy interests of the applicant and the public interest in full public disclosure of evidence pertinent to casino licensure. In fact, the Commission's opinion in this case expressly acknowledges that it has a responsibility to "strike a proper balance" between the "fundamental interests" in protecting "the confidentiality of the vast amount of highly personal information it receives" and fostering "public confidence in the casino industry and the regulatory process."

Moreover, we are satisfied that the Commission did not abuse its discretion in denying Nigris' motion to seal the exhibits relating to his background and business relationships. This information, especially the report summarizing the results of the private investigation of Nigris submitted to Griffin in October 1988, was highly relevant to one of the Commission's primary concerns as to Griffin Company's suitability for licensure: that is, whether Mr. Griffin should have immediately severed all ties with Nigris when he first received information that Nigris had business relationships with a reputed member of organized crime and others who were convicted fraud artists and securities swindlers. Since the protection of New Jersey's gaming industry against infiltration by organized crime and other undesirable persons is one of the fundamental objectives of the Act, the Commission properly concluded that public confidence in the integrity of the regulatory process would be undermined if it withheld evidence relating to this subject from public scrutiny.

Finally, we reject Nigris' argument that the sealing of exhibits relating to his background and business relationships is compelled because public disclosure would violate the constitutional right of privacy recognized in In re Martin, 90 N.J. 295, at 316-325, 447 A.2d 1290 (N.J. 1982). In Martin the Court rejected a constitutional challenge to the statutory and regulatory provisions requiring applicants for casino employee licenses to answer various personal questions relating to subjects such as business interests, criminal records and marital status and to authorize release of confidential records held by institutions such as banks, employers, and educational institutions. The Court also held that "in order for the release authorization to pass constitutional muster, the State must undertake adequate precautions to safeguard the material against disclosure to the public once it is in government hands." Id. at 322, 447 A.2d 1290. However, Martin involved solely the routine processing and retention of uncontested applications for casino employee licenses rather than the conduct of public hearings relating to contested applications for casino licenses. Thus, the Court specifically pointed to "the absence of any substantial government interest in public disclosure of the information" as a primary basis for requiring the State to take precautions against disclosure. Id. at 323, 447 A.2d 1290. In contrast, there is a substantial governmental interest in preserving public confidence in the integrity of the regulatory process by allowing public access to information on which the Commission decides contested cases which clearly outweighs whatever privacy interests a party in the position of Nigris may have in preventing disclosure. Indeed, the right of public access to evidence presented in an adjudicatory hearing may be of constitutional dimension. Therefore, we conclude that public disclosure of the information introduced into evidence at the hearing on Griffin Company's application for a casino license relating to Nigris' questionable business associations will not violate his constitutional right of privacy.

Affirmed.

Notes

1. Almost every aspect of a casino's existence is regulated by the government. (As the industry matures, however, certain responsibilities tend to be shifted to internal compliance officers.) Closely related to the goal of keeping organized crime out is ensuring that an owner has the financial means needed to properly conduct its business.

2. Frank Rosenthal's lengthy (and ultimately unsuccessful) battle with the Nevada Gaming Commission over whether he was "suitable" (i.e., fit to work in the gaming industry) was dramatically brought to the big screen in the 1995 movie *Casino*, which starred Robert De Niro as Sam "Ace" Rothstein. The film

suggests that Rosenthal lost his license not so much because of his mob ties but because of his decision to not give a job to the local sheriff's nephew.

3. Singer Frank Sinatra was denied a casino license by the Nevada Gaming Commission because of his suspected association with such figures as Joseph Fischetti, James "Jimmy the Weasel" Fratianno, Carlo Gambino, Sam Giancana, Charles "Lucky" Luciano, and Willie Moretti. It was reported that Sinatra flew to Havana to pay tribute to Luciano (who had been deported from the United States), and that he introduced Judith Campbell Exner to Giancana and John F. Kennedy (both of whom allegedly ended up having affairs with the California socialite). But the most damning piece of evidence was a photograph of Sinatra with several known gangsters, including Gambino, at the Westchester Premium Theater (Sinatra claimed they were uninvited guests). Whether Sinatra really was connected to the Mafia remains an open question.

4. As the *Boardwalk* case makes clear, gaming commissions can require applicants to make wholesale changes in their business operations. However, in *Gulch Gaming, Inc. v. State of South Dakota*, 781 F. Supp. 621 (D.S.D. 1991), a South Dakota rule requiring corporations, partnerships, and associations applying for gaming licenses to be majority-owned by state residents was deemed unconstitutional.

5. The holding of *Nigris* was reaffirmed in *Petition of Atlantic City Press Requesting Certain Files of Casino Control Commission*, 649 A.2d 1302 (N.J. Super. Ct. App. Div. 1994). A newspaper reporter investigating possible ties between Atlantic City casinos and Asian gangsters sought copies of various investigatory reports compiled by the Casino Control Commission. Although the Commission was willing to provide the information, the court again drew a distinction between contested hearings and the "routine processing of applications."

6. There is considerable variability among states as to who is subject to licensure. Some jurisdictions focus only on persons engaged in gaming-related activities, while others require all employees, regardless of duties or work location, to be licensed.

Licensure for rank-and-file gaming personnel usually entails a standardized criminal background check. This may include a review of an applicant's credit, driving, employment, and medical history. Individuals who have a criminal past or negative work record usually are prohibited from holding positions on the casino floor but may qualify for hotel or restaurant jobs. Typically, any felony conviction will disqualify an applicant (as will denial or revocation of a license in another gaming jurisdiction). Some states go further and include misdemeanor convictions for crimes involving dishonesty or moral turpitude.

7. Entities that provide gaming devices and equipment to casinos—such as cards, chips, dice, roulette wheels, slot machines, table layouts, and tokens— also must be licensed. Prospective suppliers are subjected to investigations similar to those conducted on prospective casino operators. Many states also require regular reporting on sales activity and financial status. In most instances, businesses that deal in non-gaming services and supplies (such as food, furnishings, laundry, and linens) do not need to be licensed.

8. Licensing authority normally is vested in a statewide casino regulatory entity. The primary exception is Nevada, where county government is responsible for the issuance of work permits for lower-level casino personnel. Nevertheless, the Nevada Gaming Commission can object to the granting of a work permit for various "good cause" reasons.

9. With the exception of Nevada, every state that has authorized casino gambling has placed limits on the number or location of casino licensees, or both. For a look at the pros and cons of doing so, *see* Jennifer S. Graham, *Limited Versus Unlimited Casino Licenses: The Benefits and Consequences of Restricting the Number of Casinos in a Jurisdiction*, 6 Gaming L. Rev. 319 (2002).

10. For a further discussion of casino regulation, *see, e.g.*, Tim Basting, *Regulators, Industry Representatives Air Their Pet Peeves*, 4 Gaming L. Rev. 349 (2000); Max Goldstein, *A Look into Nevada's List of Excluded Persons*, 4 Gaming L. Rev. 19 (2000); Gerald M. Gordon & Scott D. Fleming, *Bankruptcy Trends in the Gaming Field*, 4 Gaming L. Rev. 1 (2000); David F. Maron, Comment, *The Mississippi Gaming Commission: An Analysis of the Structure, Duties and Regulatory Role of the Agency in Light of the Growing Mississippi Gaming Industry*, 64 Miss. L.J. 635 (1995).

Problem 23

When the federal government informed a group of television and radio stations that they could not accept advertising from casinos in their state because of the possibility that the commercials might be heard in neighboring jurisdictions, where casinos are illegal, the broadcasters sued to have the rule enjoined. Is the prohibition unconstitutional? *See Greater New Orleans Broadcasting Association, Inc. v. United States*, 527 U.S. 173 (1999).

C. INTERNAL CONTROLS

APPLICATION OF PLAYBOY-ELSINORE ASSOCIATES
497 A.2d 526 (N.J. Super. Ct. App. Div. 1985)

COHEN, Justice.

Elsinore Shore Associates (ESA) is a New Jersey partnership. It owns and operates a casino hotel in Atlantic City, known as Elsinore Atlantis, which opened in 1981 under the authority of a temporary casino permit issued by the Casino Control Commission. N.J.S.A. 5:12-95.1 et seq. (repealed). In April 1982, the Commission issued it an annual casino license and renewed it in April 1983. In March 1984, the Commission heard ESA's application for renewal and granted it, effective April 14, 1984.

Like its predecessors, the resolution granting the application contained a number of conditions. One of them, # 135, read as follows:

That the Licensee continue its support for and make a meaningful contribution by November 14, 1984 to the construction training program administered by Atlantic Community College designed to improve minority and female participation in the Atlantic County construction workforce.

Another of the conditions, # 142, read as follows:

> That to ensure the independence of the Licensee's internal audit and surveillance departments pursuant to N.J.A.C. 19:45-1.11(c), both the Director of Internal Audit and the Director of Surveillance shall report directly to Elsinore Corporation's Board of Directors' Audit Committee and that appropriate documentation defining the authority and responsibility of these two departments be provided to the Commission.

On appeal to this court, ESA challenges both of these conditions on the grounds that they are unauthorized by statute or regulation and are arbitrary and unlawful. We agree that Condition # 135 is improper and order it set aside. We disagree with ESA, however, on Condition # 142, and confirm its validity.

Condition # 142 arose out of ESA's unusual business organization. When formed in 1979, ESA was a partnership of Playboy of Atlantic City, also a partnership, and Elsub Corporation, a subsidiary of Elsinore Corporation, which is publicly owned. In 1984, Elsub bought most of the interest of ESA owned by Playboy of Atlantic City, as a result of which Elsub now owns 91.5% of ESA. ESA, as a partnership, has no board of directors, but only a two-person executive committee, consisting of the president and vice president of Elsub and Elsinore.

Part of the Commission's statutory responsibilities is to see to it that a system of internal controls is established by each casino. The Commission adopted N.J.A.C. 19:45-1.11 to create standards for those controls. The various operations of a casino are to be divided into at least seven departments: surveillance, internal audit, casino, slot, credit, security and casino accounting. The regulation provides that the surveillance and internal audit departments should "report directly to the Board of Directors, or its audit committee or equivalent regarding matters of policy, purpose, responsibilities and authority." The idea is to establish lines of reporting that will guarantee independence of the various departments from one another, independence for the more sensitive functions from operating management and clear responsibility at the highest level for internal audit and surveillance responsibilities.

If ESA's surveillance and internal audit departments reported to its two-person executive committee, the result would frustrate the Commission's valid goal of assigning and insulating responsibility, institutionalizing oversight over operating management and creating checks and balances within the casino operation. Therefore, it required the two departments to report directly to the audit committee of the board of directors of the publicly traded parent, Elsinore. ESA complains here, as it did to the Commission, that the regulation does not permit the Commission to impose responsibilities on the directors of unregulated parent corporations and that imposing surveillance and internal audit responsibilities on Elsinore's corporate directors is burdensome, inconvenient and unnecessary. We disagree.

We will not rehearse the sound and frequently repeated reasons for the detailed, intensive and pervasive regulation of casino operations in New

Jersey. It is a legitimate part of the regulatory fabric to require corporate structures that will create highest level responsibility and independence from operating management for such sensitive casino functions as surveillance and internal audit. A publicly traded company can not isolate itself from responsibility by operating a casino through a subsidiary corporation and a partnership with only two managers. Faced with such an operation, the Commission has sufficient flexibility under N.J.A.C. 19:45-1.11 to impose the kind of responsibilities on the parent corporation that are involved here.

It is of no consequence that the operations of the license applicant may be relatively free of violations. The Commission's reasonable role includes requiring business structures that will keep them that way. It does not matter that the parent's board of directors is not prepared to undertake the responsibilities which the Commission imposed on it. The Commission's response to its legitimate concerns is a reasonable one, and the board of directors will have to accommodate to it. The Commission need not accept the relationship between the casino licensee and its parent, if, as here, alteration is necessary to meet significant regulatory interests. Condition # 142 will stand.

Condition # 135, however, is invalid. It arises out of the statutory duty of every applicant to provide equal employment opportunities in the construction and renovation of casino and hotel premises. We were advised at oral argument that every casino has been unable to meet its obligations in that regard, that the reason was the small number of minority workers available in the construction industry and that the casinos were all required to make a "meaningful contribution" to the construction training program administered by the Atlantic County College.

We have no difficulty with the Commission's general approach. Where compliance with statutory employment standards is blocked by unavailability of minority workers, it is reasonable to require casino contributions to a program designed to create a pool of qualified minority workers. One of ESA's objections to Condition # 135 is that it appears to be a penalty for noncompliance imposed without a hearing. That objection is dissipated by recognizing that the requirement is imposed on all casinos, not as a penalty but as a reasonable substitute for compliance.

ESA's other objections, however, are well founded. The first is addressed to the vagueness of the phrase "meaningful contribution." It is impossible to tell how or by whom "meaningfulness" is intended to be measured. Without a standard, the condition is subject to arbitrary and inconsistent enforcement. Behind the quoted phrase is a quantitative thought which deserves expression. As it is now worded, Condition # 135 is too vague to enforce and must be invalidated.

ESA's other valid objection is that Condition # 135 is a de facto rule because it is imposed as a matter of policy on all casinos. Since the condition is imposed on the entire industry according to some yet unspoken standard and meets, generally, the test of Metromedia, Inc. v. Director, Div. of Taxation, 97 N.J. 313, 334-335 (1984), it is a subject which can be dealt with only by the rulemaking power. Thus Condition # 135 is invalid.

The imposition of Condition # 135 is set aside. The imposition of Condition # 142 is confirmed as valid.

PETITION OF ADAMAR OF NEW JERSEY, INC.
537 A.2d 704 (N.J. Super. Ct. App. Div. 1988)

HAVEY, Justice.

In these consolidated appeals, five casino licensees challenge the Casino Control Commission's (Commission) denial of the casinos' application to collect outstanding counter checks "in the field" or at branch offices. We now affirm.

In 1980, several casino licensees sought to implement passive collection activities for accepting payments from patrons on outstanding patron counter checks at casino branch offices located within and outside New Jersey. "Outstanding counter checks" are patron gaming checks which have not yet been deposited in the bank for collection. "Passive collection" is a procedure whereby a licensed casino employee is sent at the patron's request to a location other than the cashiers' cage for receipt of payment of a patron's gaming checks. The Commission notified the casino licensees that in order to implement branch office procedures for passive collection, the casinos would have to seek formal Commission approval. In response, the casinos submitted internal control procedures for branch office collection and were granted approvals, ratified by the Commission, on a case-by-case basis from 1983 to 1985. The casinos receiving approval were Atlantis, Sands, Golden Nugget, Resorts and Boardwalk.

In 1985, Adamar of New Jersey, Inc. (Adamar), doing business as the Tropicana Hotel and Casino, submitted procedures for "field" collections of outstanding counter checks at unspecified locations, including a patron's home or place of business. After the Division of Gaming Enforcement interposed an objection, Adamar petitioned the Commission seeking a declaratory ruling that off-site acceptance of payments on outstanding counter checks did not violate the Casino Control Act or its attendant regulations. Under Adamar's proposed collection procedure, the patron would be given a receipt by the collecting employee but the original counter check would not be released from the cashiers' cage until the funds were received and accepted at the cage. It was stressed that the proposed collection activity would be instigated only on the initiative of the patron.

During the pre-hearing conferences, the present appellants intervened and joined Adamar's petition. After the hearing, the Commission denied the casinos' request to receive payments on outstanding counter checks either in the field or in branch offices. In denying the request, the Commission noted that under N.J.S.A. 5:12-101, the act's credit provision, there can be no "collection" on an outstanding counter check other than bank deposit for payment, except for redemption or consolidation of the check by the patron, and that the statute permits collection efforts only on returned counter checks. "Returned counter checks" are checks which are issued by a patron to a casino for gaming credit and which have been returned by a depository bank unpaid for insufficient funds. The Commission also reviewed the comprehensive regulations pertaining to receipt of cash or cash equivalents and redemption of outstanding counter checks, and concluded that such receipt and redemption must occur within the well-monitored casino cashiers' cage. Also, while acknowledging that the Commission and Division staff had approved collection procedures at branch offices and that it had ratified these procedures, the Commission determined it was empowered to reopen and vacate the approvals to protect the public interest and integrity of the casino industry. Finally, it granted the casinos' request to collect returned counter checks both in the field and at branch offices.

Appellants contend that disapproval of off-site collection of counter checks was over-broad and incorrect as a matter of law because: (1) neither the act nor the regulations prohibit passive collection on outstanding counter checks in the field; (2) such collection does not constitute "redemption" in violation of the act or regulations; (3) the prior case law relied on by the Commission is inapposite and unpersuasive, and (4) there is no logical distinction between collection of returned counter checks and outstanding counter checks. Appellants also challenge the Commission's revocation of prior approvals to collect outstanding counter checks at branch offices as being unfair and unreasonable.

Generally, we are not bound by an agency's determination of a strictly legal issue. However, we accord substantial deference to an interpretation of a statute or regulation by the agency responsible for enforcing it. Further, we must defer to the administrative agency's expertise in relation to technical matters.

Moreover, statutes and regulations promulgated thereunder must be read so as to implement the legislative intent permitted by statute. In that regard, our Supreme Court has recognized "the strong state interest in promoting scrupulous conduct by the casino industry and regulatory officials." Greenberg v. Kimmelman, 99 N.J. 552, 560 (1985). Further, the Law Division in Playboy-Elsinore Assocs. v. Strauss, 189 N.J. Super. 185, 191 (Law Div.1983), noted that "practices and procedures involved with the extension of credit by the casinos are among the most sensitive aspects of casino operations."

Prior to the passage of the act, there was strong resistance to allowing credit to patrons at all. See Report and Recommendations of Casino Gambling by the Commission of Investigation of the State of New Jersey (April 1977). The Commission of Investigation was concerned with the potential for illegal diversion of funds and "strong arm" methods of debt collection. The particularized sections of the act governing credit obviously responded to this opposition and must be read as intending to accomplish several purposes: to provide for a traceable, efficient "paper trail" of credit transactions; to prevent "skimming"; and to require prompt deposits of credit checks thereby allowing regulators to monitor the collection of debts.

Thus, the act's credit provision narrowly circumscribes the manner by which credit shall be offered to patrons. Section 101(c) provides for the time and manner by which counter checks shall be deposited in the bank. The only exception to the check deposit obligation is redemption, partial redemption or consolidation by the patron. There is no provision for the collection of counter checks by casino personnel; "collection" activities are expressly limited to checks returned by banks without full or final payment. Considering the legislative intent to carefully limit and control credit transactions, we agree with the Commission that it would be an abuse of the interpretative process to read § 101 as intending to allow collection of outstanding counter checks except as expressly provided therein.

We also agree with the Commission that the comprehensive attendant regulations require collection on outstanding counter checks to take place at the cashiers' cage. Appellants contend that N.J.A.C. 19:45-1.15(b)(1)(i) provides only that the duties of the cage personnel include receipt of payments for redemption but does not mandate receipt of payments at the cage. It notes the contrasting language under N.J.A.C. 19:45-1.25(e) which states that "[c]ash equivalents and casino checks . . . shall only be accepted at the cashiers' cage by general cashiers" and argues that it was not the drafters' intent to restrict receipt of payments as they restricted acceptance of payment.

Appellants' argument ignores the overall regulatory scheme. The cashiers' cage has the responsibility for "the exchange, redemption and consolidation of patron checks received for the purposes of gaming," as well as of maintaining custody of patron checks, documents and records normally associated with the operation of the gaming cage. N.J.A.C. 19:45-1.11(c)(9)(i) and (ii). All consolidations, redemptions or substitutions of checks by gaming patrons shall be made at the general cashiers' cage. N.J.A.C. 19:45-1.26(d). Further, cashiers shall perform their functions within the physical confines of the cashiers' cage. N.J.A.C. 19:45-1.15. The cashier's function shall be, but not limited to, the following:

> Receive cash, cash equivalents, checks, gaming chips and plaques from patrons for check consolidations, total or partial redemptions or substitutions[.] [N.J.A.C. 19:45-1.15(b)(1)(i)].

The unmistakable thrust of these regulations is that the sensitive function of receiving cash or cash equivalents for the payment and redemption of outstanding counter checks is given exclusively to the cashier and must occur within the well-fortified and highly monitored confines of the cashiers' cage. The regulatory scheme recognizes the overriding need to provide security during cash transactions, to centralize the place for sensitive credit transactions and to facilitate monitoring by casino and Commission officials. Collection of outstanding counter checks at off-site locations does not carry with it these protections and thus runs counter to the spirit of the act and its attendant regulations.

Appellants next contend that while "redemption" must occur at the general cashiers' cage, receipt of payment by casino personnel at an off-site location does not constitute redemption. Citing N.J.A.C. 19:45-1.25(e), appellants argue that if payment is received in the form of a cash equivalent, "redemption" does not occur until the casino has accepted the cash equivalent and physically returned the counter check. If payment is received in cash, appellants claim that "redemption" occurs when the cashier voids the original counter check and returns it to the patron. Under the procedure proposed by appellants, the patron would be given a receipt by the collecting employee, but the counter check would not be released until the funds were received at the cage.

This type of bifurcated transaction conflicts with the plain language of N.J.A.C. 19:45-1.15(b)(1)(i) which requires cashiers to receive cash or cash equivalents "from patrons . . . for total or partial redemption." Thus, receipt of cash or cash equivalents at the cashiers' cage must be from the patron, not from a casino employee who has collected the cash or cash equivalents in the field or some other location.

Further, appellants' argument contradicts the evident statutory and regulatory intent to create a well-documented, traceable and efficient "paper trail" to allow internal casino control and efficient access by regulators to all information respecting credit transactions. See Playboy-Elsinore Assocs., 189 N.J. Super. at 189-192. As the court in Playboy observed, "[i]t is clear that the thrust of the regulatory scheme is to require all credit transactions to be administered through the cashiers' cage . . . ." Id. at 193. Finally, N.J.S.A. 5:12-101(c) allows redemption of a counter check "by exchanging cash or chips in an amount equal to the amount for which the check is drawn," and N.J.A.C. 19:45-1.26(a) provides that a counter check may be redeemed by "exchanging cash, cash equivalents, gaming chips" or any combination thereof. As the Division persuasively argues, a sensible reading of both § 101(c) and the regulation requires a contemporaneous exchange of funds and surrender of the patron's counter check to effect a redemption. A bifurcated collection procedure may spawn litigation resulting from claims that the funds were lost or converted before they reached the cashiers' cage. The regulations governing receipt of funds and redemption transactions must be read together in order to ensure that the most sensitive part of the transaction, receipt of funds, occurs in the well-monitored cage.

For the foregoing reasons we are persuaded that the Commission's prohibition of the practice of collecting outstanding counter checks at locations other than the casino cashiers' cage is consistent with the act and the pertinent regulations.

CITIBANK v. TRUMP TAJ MAHAL ASSOCIATES
1996 U.S. Dist. LEXIS 16480 (S.D.N.Y. 1996)

PATTERSON, District Judge.

Plaintiff's claims arise out of a series of embezzlements of approximately $2.5 million between April 1988 and April 1993 by Yota Kalikas ("Kalikas"), an operations manager at a Citibank branch. In March 1993, during a routine random audit of cash equivalents received at Trump Taj Mahal Associates ("TTMA"), Agent Thomas Havey ("Havey") of the New Jersey Division of Gaming Enforcement ("DGE") discovered that Kalikas was the authorized signatory of two official Citibank checks dated February 26, 1993, totaling $100,000, and that she presented these two checks to TTMA in payment of or as credit toward gambling debts. Upon a review of Kalikas' TTMA credit application, Havey confirmed Kalikas' employment at Citibank, and noticed that Kalikas' signature on the credit application matched the authorized signature on the Citibank official checks. Havey then contacted Citibank's Investigation and Potential Loss Department and spoke with Citibank investigator John Rogan ("Rogan"), who informed Havey that it would be "irregular" under Citibank policy for a Citibank employee to be listed both as remitter and authorized signatory of an official check. As a result of Havey's finding, the DGE investigated Kalikas' activity at the TTMA to determine whether any TTMA employee had knowledge of Kalikas' embezzlement. Neither the DGE nor the New Jersey Casino Control Commission (the "Casino Control Commission") filed charges or took any other action against TTMA regarding Kalikas' play there.

In this diversity action, Citibank seeks to recover nine cashier's checks each in the amount of $50,000, one cashier's check in the amount of $75,000, and one cashier's check for $40,000, all drawn on Citibank to the order of TTMA and signed by Kalikas as the issuing officer, with either her name or her initials as remitter. Two of the checks also bore Kalikas' endorsement and her driver's license number on the reverse side. All the checks were presented to and accepted by TTMA on weekends between October 1992 and March 1993. Citibank honored all eleven cashier's checks which totalled $565,000.

It is not in dispute that Kalikas came to the casinos on Friday evenings or on weekends, outside of banking hours, so that the sufficiency of the funds in the pertinent Citibank account could only be verified on the following business day. It is also not in dispute that cashiers at TTMA accepted the checks and when banking hours resumed they verified that each of Kalikas' cashier's checks would be honored by Citibank by calling a 1-800 telephone number listed on the back of the check to determine if there were sufficient funds in the account to pay the check. It is also undisputed that TTMA did not call the bank to confirm that Kalikas, the bank officer who authorized the checks, had the right to present the check for her own use.

According to David Walker ("Walker"), TTMA's casino shift manager from 1992-1993, TTMA's "rules, policies and practices" called for verification of cashier's checks by placing a telephone call to the issuing bank to determine whether funds were available for every cashier's check received; if the check, like these checks, was not presented during banking hours, the check would be verified "by other means", and the call would be placed to the issuing bank when banking hours resumed. As stated by Walker, under TTMA policy "other means" included a visual inspection of the check or a comparison of the check with previously verified checks from the same institution and/or the same patron.

While Kalikas used some of the checks to pay off her credit line, she used others to make "front money deposits" for vouchers against which she could draw chips at the blackjack table. TTMA also had internal regulations governing front money deposits, which required TTMA's cashiers to have the customer sign a Customer Deposit Form in the presence of a casino cage cashier simultaneously with each front money deposit, and required the cashiers to maintain a computerized record of those customers using front money deposits. The cashiers were required to examine a computerized facsimile of the customer's signature and other personal signature identification.

Defendant moves for summary judgment asserting that the checks in question were negotiable instruments, and TTMA was a holder in due course under N.Y.U.C.C. § 3-302(1). Plaintiff does not dispute that the checks were negotiable instruments, but claims TTMA was not a holder in due course because the evidence does not show that TTMA accepted the bad checks in good faith. Plaintiff's cross-motion is based on the evidence adduced of TTMA's negligence and its position that TTMA is not a holder in due course. Defendant counters that under New Jersey law there is no common law right of private action for negligence against casinos. The holder in due course issue is dispositive of both motions for summary judgment because holder in due course status precludes liability for common law negligence.

DISCUSSION

A party is entitled to summary judgment if the pleadings, depositions, answers to interrogatories, and admissions on file, together with the affidavits, if any, show that there is no genuine issue as to any material fact and that the party is entitled to judgment as a matter of law. "Summary judgment will not lie if the dispute about a material fact is 'genuine,' that is, if the evidence is such that a reasonable jury could return a verdict for the nonmoving party."

A holder in due course is one who is (1) a holder (2) of a negotiable instrument (3) who took it for value (4) in good faith, and (5) without notice of any defense or claim to it on the part of another. Payment or acceptance of any instrument is final in favor of a holder in due course.

There is no question that TTMA is a holder who took the notes for value. TTMA either used the checks to reduce Kalikas' debt to TTMA or to provide her with gambling chips. Plaintiff contends, however, that TTMA is not a holder in due course because it had notice that the cashier's checks were irregular and did not take the checks in good faith.

The holder's initial burden on the issues of notice and good faith, in response to a defense that a check is facially irregular, is "a slight one" that may be satisfied by [its] affidavit disclaiming any knowledge of the maker's defense when the notes were negotiated . . . . The holder will be entitled to summary judgment based on such an affidavit unless the maker proffers evidence of facts that, if accepted, would establish the holder's notice of a valid defense.

Generally, the issue of whether a holder of a negotiable instrument gave value for the checks in good faith is a subjective one that requires proof of what the holder actually knew, not speculation as to what it had reason to know or what would have aroused suspicion of a reasonable person in the holder's circumstances.

In order to deny defendant holder in due course status, plaintiff must show defendant had actual notice of irregularity, not just the opportunity to have noticed it. Plaintiff need not, however, show "actual notice" to defeat a motion for summary judgment; plaintiff need only show there is a genuine issue of fact from which a reasonable jury could infer notice and bad faith. Gross carelessness may also be sufficient to refute a claim to holder in due course status. "Gross carelessness . . . or willful ignorance . . . may constitute evidence of bad faith."

New Jersey statutory law governing casinos, and the case law interpreting it, sheds further light on the requirements of good faith for transactions involving cash equivalents at gambling casinos. There is no dispute that TTMA was aware of the special requirements for the acceptance of negotiable instruments by casinos under New Jersey law, which provides that, prior to the acceptance of any cash equivalent from a patron, the general cashier shall determine the validity of such cash equivalent by performing the necessary verification for each type of cash equivalent and such other procedures as may be required by the issuer of such cash equivalent. According to the Casino Control Commission, "the phrase 'necessary verification' in this regulation has been construed to require whatever action is 'reasonable under the circumstances.' Casinos and their employees are obliged to exercise reasonable care in the conduct of their business, and thereby assure that they are neither conduits for nor victims of criminal enterprise . . . ."

TTMA argues that its phone call to the bank on the first business day subsequent to acceptance should be sufficient to satisfy this standard. A jury could regard this verification procedure, however, as only designed to ensure that sufficient funds were available for payment of the check, and not designed to help ascertain whether TTMA was being used as a "conduit for criminal enterprise" by the check's presenter. A trier of fact could find that TTMA had knowledge, based on its own records, that Kalikas was a heavy and habitual gambler, and that, as compulsive gamblers often resort to crime in order to obtain money to continue gambling, TTMA's practices deliberately avoided inquiry into the customer's right to present the cash equivalent.

TTMA's internal regulations, relating to the front money vouchers, could be regarded by the trier of fact as designed to verify the customer's identity and gambling history for Trump Taj Mahal's internal use, and not designed to ensure that the presenter of a cashier's check placed on deposit has a legitimate right to use the cash equivalent in question. The law, as interpreted by the Casino Control Commission, the agency with the responsibility for its administration, places a responsibility on casinos to do more than merely to protect themselves by ensuring that the funds presented are available, but rather to also protect the public through policies that take reasonable care to prevent gamblers from using cash equivalents which do not belong to them.

TTMA claims that on each occasion that Kalikas presented a faulty check the cashiers did not notice that the signature of the bank officer who authorized the cashier's check was identical with that on Kalikas' customer deposit form and the computerized facsimile signature the cashiers were often required to examine; that the cashiers had no obligation to notice the similarities of the signatures; that plaintiff has presented no evidence that the cashiers did notice the similarities; and that plaintiff has thus failed to establish notice. Joyce Clegg ("Clegg"), one of the cashiers whose signature appeared on customer deposit slips and redemption vouchers relating to the cashier's checks Kalikas presented on December 19, 1992 and February 27, 1993, testified that she had no recollection of the transactions involving Kalikas. She also added she did not notice the authorized signature was similar to Kalikas' signature, but if she had, she would have called it to the attention of her supervisor. A trier of fact could determine that such testimony, far from exonerating TTMA, merely shows that the procedures adopted by TTMA did not meet its duty to train its cashiers to exercise reasonable care in scrutinizing the instrument before honoring a cash equivalent.

The facts here permit Citibank to attempt to persuade a jury that TTMA has not implemented internal procedures designed to elicit the "sound judgment" of its cashiers, and ensure that the cashiers are trained to inspect closely and scrutinize effectively the instruments that are presented to them. If such heightened procedures had been in place, it could be found that TTMA's cashiers would have noticed, like Agent Havey, the suspicious fact that the signature of the bank's issuing officer, on the face of the check, was the same as the signature presented on the patron's identification; and that they would also have noticed, in turn, that the patron's identification had the same name as that of the check remitter, printed on the face of the check. A reasonable juror could determine that TTMA's failure to institute appropriate training and oversight procedures, that would ensure adequate verification and careful scrutiny, constituted a deliberate avoidance of the casino's responsibility to ensure that it was not used as a criminal conduit by gamblers, and amounted to bad faith. Summary judgment is thus inappropriate on the issue of whether TTMA is a holder in due course.

IT IS SO ORDERED.

Notes

1. In most jurisdictions, the state gaming board has promulgated internal control system requirements that casinos must implement. Typical subjects include the conduct of games, the movement and handling of cash and cash equivalents, the creation and maintenance of accounting records, and the deployment and use of surveillance equipment.

2. Besides checking for internal controls, regulatory agencies direct and review audits of casino operations. In some states, private firms are engaged by the regulatory body (at the casino's cost) to conduct compliance audits to measure operator conformance with internal control system requirements (in such instances, the audit protocols are prescribed by the regulatory agency).

Many states require compliance audits to be conducted on a quarterly basis. Most state regulatory bodies also conduct compliance audits and special or focused audits with state agency audit personnel.

In addition to the foregoing, casinos are required to have an internal audit staff to conduct regular, on-going compliance audits and reviews. These are on top of the required annual financial audits conducted by accounting firms that are typically selected by casino operators, subject to regulatory authorization.

3. To prevent money laundering, banks and other financial institutions must file a "Currency Transaction Report" whenever a customer engages in a cash transaction of more than $10,000. In *Ratzlaf v. United States*, 510 U.S. 135 (1994), a casino patron was charged with attempting to get around this requirement after he obtained multiple cashier's checks from different banks to settle his account. The idea for doing so had come from the casino:

> On the evening of October 20, 1988, defendant-petitioner Waldemar Ratzlaf ran up a debt of $160,000 playing blackjack at the High Sierra Casino in Reno, Nevada. The casino gave him one week to pay. On the due date, Ratzlaf returned to the casino with cash of $100,000 in hand. A casino official informed Ratzlaf that all transactions involving more than $10,000 in cash had to be reported to state and federal authorities. The official added that the casino could accept a cashier's check for the full amount due without triggering any reporting

requirement. The casino helpfully placed a limousine at Ratzlaf's disposal, and assigned an employee to accompany him to banks in the vicinity. Informed that banks, too, are required to report cash transactions in excess of $10,000, Ratzlaf purchased cashier's checks, each for less than $10,000 and each from a different bank. He delivered these checks to the High Sierra Casino.

Id. at 137.

4. It has been suggested that casinos should have to file "Suspicious Activity Reports" whenever a customer behaves in an unusual manner, even if the cash involved is less than $10,000. Federal efforts in this direction have stalled, but some states do require such reports.

Problem 24

When a company discovered that one of its employees had used embezzled funds to gamble, it sued the casino and demanded to see its internal control procedures. The casino refused, claiming the information constituted proprietary trade secrets and also was shielded by the confidentiality provisions of the state gaming code. If the company brings a motion to compel disclosure, how should the court rule? *See Canadian Imperial Bank of Commerce v. Boardwalk Regency Corp.*, 108 F.R.D. 737 (D.N.J. 1986).

D. BETS

ERICKSON v. DESERT PALACE, INC.
942 F.2d 694 (9th Cir. 1991),
cert. denied, 503 U.S. 937 (1992)

BRUNETTI, Circuit Judge.

Appellants Russell, Beth, and Kirk Erickson appeal the district court's order dismissing their complaint for lack of subject matter jurisdiction and for failure to state a claim. The Ericksons brought this action against corporate defendants operating Caesar's Palace Casino in Las Vegas, Nevada, seeking to recover a $1,061,812.00 slot machine jackpot won by Kirk, a minor. The Ericksons alleged breach of contract, quasi-contract, fraud and cheating, and interference with contract, and sought declaratory judgment regarding the unconstitutional implementation and enforcement of a Nevada statute. The Ericksons appeal only the dismissal of their third cause of action alleging fraud and cheating. We have jurisdiction pursuant to 28 U.S.C. § 1291 and affirm.

The Ericksons assert diversity jurisdiction. Therefore state law applies to this action and we are bound by Nevada's Supreme Court case law. Erie Railroad v. Tompkins, 304 U.S. 64, 58 S.Ct. 817, 82 L.Ed. 1188 (1938); Olympic Sports Prod., Inc. v. Universal Athletic Sales Co., 760 F.2d 910, 912-13 (9th Cir.1985), cert. denied sub nom Whitaker Corp. v. Olympic Sports Prod., Inc., 474 U.S. 1060, 106 S.Ct. 804, 88 L.Ed.2d 780 (1986).

I.

On August 5, 1987, the Ericksons visited Caesar's Palace Casino in Las Vegas, Nevada. Kirk, then 19, purchased tokens and won a jackpot of $1,061,812.00. Because Kirk was under 21, the legal gambling age in Nevada, the casino refused to pay him the jackpot. See NRS 463.350.

Under Nevada law, an unpaid slot machine jackpot is a gaming debt not evidenced by a credit instrument. Harrah's Club v. State Gaming Control Bd., 104 Nev. 762, 766 P.2d 900 (1988) (casino patron's claim to an unpaid slot machine jackpot considered "disputed gaming debt"); State Gaming Control Bd. v. Breen, 99 Nev. 320, 323, 661 P.2d 1309, 1311 (1983) (patron seeking recovery of unpaid keno winnings found to have "no claim other than a gambling debt").

NRS 463.361, enacted in 1983, states: "Except as provided in NRS 463.361 to 463.366, inclusive, gaming debts not evidenced by a credit instrument are void and unenforceable and do not give rise to any administrative or civil cause of action." NRS 463.362 to 463.366 provide for review of a casino's refusal to pay alleged winnings to a patron by the State Gaming Control Board (the "Board"). NRS 463.3662 to 463.3668 provide for review of the Board's decision by a Nevada District Court and by the State Supreme Court. NRS 463.3668(2) provides that judicial review by the state courts is the exclusive method for review of the Board's actions.

The Ericksons filed a formal complaint under NRS 463.363 with the Board on August 7, 1987. When the Board's Enforcement Division denied the Ericksons' claims on November 9, 1988, they filed a petition seeking reconsideration which was also denied. Specifically, the Board found that NRS 463.350 prohibited Kirk Erickson from collecting the slot machine jackpot and that any contract that may have existed between the defendant casino and Erickson was inoperative because it violated NRS 463.350. The Board also held that Erickson had not properly stated a claim for restitution, quasi contract or unjust enrichment, because he sought payment of the jackpot rather than return of the three $1 tokens he had used, and those theories permit only damages to the extent of the benefit to the defendant. Finally, the Board held because the Casino had properly warned Erickson that the legal gambling age is twenty-one and had made no misrepresentations of gambling rules, defendant was not guilty of fraud.

Pursuant to NRS 463.3662, the Ericksons petitioned the Eighth Judicial District Court of Nevada for Clark County to review the Board's ruling. The district court affirmed the denial of the claim, whereupon the Ericksons petitioned the Nevada Supreme Court for judicial review. The Nevada Supreme Court dismissed the appeal on May 21, 1990. The Court agreed with the Board that NRS 463.350 prohibited Erickson from collecting the jackpot, and that there was no evidence the casino "knowingly allowed Kirk Erickson to gamble while underage," which might support a claim of fraud.

II.

The Ericksons filed a complaint in federal district court on August 11, 1988, before the decision of the Board. Defendants State of Nevada, Nevada Gaming

Control Board, and Caesars filed motions to dismiss the action. The district court granted the motions dismissing the complaint for lack of subject matter jurisdiction due to the Ericksons' failure to exhaust the administrative remedies provided by Nevada law. Because the Nevada Supreme Court has issued its decision, the Ericksons now have exhausted their administrative remedies.

We decline to remand this case to the district court, however, because that court provided an alternative ground for dismissing the complaint. The court found that NRS 463.361 limits a plaintiff to an administrative proceeding followed by judicial review in state court. The court therefore determined the Ericksons could not state a claim upon which relief could be granted. Fed.R.Civ.P. 12(b)(6). The district court held because "plaintiffs claim can most accurately be characterized as an attempt to recover a gaming debt not evidenced by a credit instrument . . . plaintiffs cannot maintain a civil action to recover a jackpot, but instead are limited to an administrative proceeding followed by judicial review."

We therefore affirm the decision of the district court.

DECKER v. BALLY'S GRAND HOTEL CASINO
655 A.2d 73 (N.J. Super. Ct. App. Div. 1994)

KLEINER, Justice.

On January 8, 1992, the Casino Control Commission ("the Commission") adopted amendments to N.J.A.C. 19:45-1.37 and N.J.A.C. 19:45-1.39. Prior to the adoption of these amendments, casino licensees were precluded from removing or reducing a jackpot in a progressive slot machine until a jackpot was won by a patron. The amendments, which became effective February 3, 1992, changed this regulatory scheme to allow casinos to establish time limits of not less than thirty days for the offering of progressive jackpots. Thus, the amended regulations permit casino licensees to remove progressive slot machines from the casino floor or to reduce the progressive jackpot after thirty days notice to the public and with prior Commission approval.

On October 23, 1992, plaintiff filed a complaint which named eight Atlantic City casino licensees as defendants. The complaint alleged breach of express and implied contract in that defendants had closed and removed progressive slot machines from their casino floors and sought an undefined amount of damages. In his complaint, plaintiff alleged that he had gambled in every Atlantic City casino since gambling was legalized in 1978. Due to the amount of his gambling losses since 1978, plaintiff decided that the only way to recoup his losses was to play progressive slot machines. He maintains that he has lost substantial amounts of money playing the progressive slot machines. Plaintiff further alleged that on or after February 1992, defendants closed and removed certain progressive slot machines with jackpot prizes totaling over $20 million. Plaintiff maintained that as a result of defendants removing the progressive slot machines, they breached an express and implied contract with the public that the progressive jackpot amount would be awarded to the winning player.

On December 4, 1992, the court granted the Sands' motion and ordered plaintiff's complaint dismissed as to all defendants. In its memorandum of decision, the trial court found that the casino licensees had complied with the regulation's notice requirement by posting the applicable notices on all of their progressive slot machines and had received approval of all changes from the Commission in accordance with the procedures set out in the regulations. The trial court also concluded that plaintiff had no standing to sue since his complaint did not state that he had played and won the jackpot on a progressive slot machine on which the amount of the progressive meter had been reduced.

The defendants here did not take away the opportunity to win a progressive jackpot before plaintiff pulled the handle on the progressive slot machine. Since he did not win any jackpot, plaintiff has no personal stake in the outcome of the proceedings. Cf. Patrolmen's Benev. Ass'n v. East Brunswick Tp., 180 N.J.Super. 68, 72, 433 A.2d 813 (App.Div.1981).

Plaintiff has no basis to assert a claim for breach of contract, express or implied, resulting from the removal of a progressive slot machine or the reduction in a prospective jackpot after the plaintiff discontinues his play on a particular machine. The plaintiff's only contract with any defendant is the obligation of the defendants to pay the posted machine jackpot to the plaintiff immediately after the plaintiff has inserted the requisite coinage if the deposit of coinage registers a jackpot on the particular machine then in use. Plaintiff therefore lacks standing and fails to assert a cognizable claim.

The judgment dismissing plaintiff's complaint is affirmed.

CAMPIONE v. ADAMAR OF NEW JERSEY, INC.
714 A.2d 299 (N.J. 1998)

POLLOCK, Judge.

This appeal presents several issues. The first is whether the Casino Control Commission (CCC) has exclusive jurisdiction over claims by patrons against casinos for discrimination and breach of contract. A related issue is whether patrons may maintain such claims as common-law causes of action. The final issue questions the award of damages of $1,000,213.50 for malicious prosecution in favor of plaintiff Anthony Campione.

Campione was a blackjack player and professional card counter who frequented casinos in Atlantic City. The defendants are Adamar of New Jersey, which operates the TropWorld Casino; Michael Imperatrice, a floor supervisor and a member of TropWorld's card counting team; and Patrick Scully, TropWorld's Sergeant of Security.

On February 14, 1991, plaintiff sued defendants for discrimination, breach of contract, and malicious prosecution. He alleged that defendants selectively enforced gaming regulations against him because he was a card counter. The jury found that defendants were liable for discrimination and malicious prosecution and returned a verdict totaling $1,519,873.43.

The Appellate Division reversed and remanded the matter to the Law Division. It found that the CCC had exclusive jurisdiction over plaintiff's claims and that plaintiff could not maintain a private cause of action against defendants. The court also reversed the malicious prosecution award.

We granted plaintiff's petition for certification. 152 N.J. 9, 702 A.2d 348 (1997). We granted motions of the Casino Control Commission and the

Division of Gaming Enforcement (DGE) to intervene and the CCC's petition for certification. 152 N.J. 9, 702 A.2d 348 (1997). The petition for certification of Doug Grant, Inc., which conducts a school to train card counters, was denied. 151 N.J. 472, 700 A.2d 883 (1997). We now modify the judgment of the Appellate Division and remand the matter to the Law Division.

I.

The purpose of blackjack is to obtain cards having a higher count than those of the dealer without exceeding a total count of twenty-one. In blackjack, unlike in other games of chance, players' skill can increase the odds in their favor. Card counting is a method of playing blackjack that involves keeping track of the number of "high value" cards. This technique allows a blackjack player to identify a favorable count, which occurs when an unusually high percentage of the cards remaining in the "dealing shoe" are high value cards. At that time, the chances increase that the dealer will "bust," or deal cards that exceed 21 points, thereby permitting the card counter to win. A favorable count occurs infrequently, and almost exclusively after most of the cards have been dealt. Consequently, card counters must maximize their play at such times. To do so, card counters may increase their bet, play two hands at once, or both.

Neither the Casino Control Act, N.J.S.A. 5:12-1 to -142 (Act), nor the CCC prohibits card counting. The CCC, however, authorizes casinos to use various "countermeasures" to discourage card counting. For example, CCC regulations give casinos the discretion to shuffle the cards at will, N.J.A.C. 19:47-2.5a, or to lower the betting limit at any time, N.J.A.C. 19:47-8.3c. In addition to issuing its own regulations, the CCC allows, subject to its approval, casinos to adopt "Section 99 internal controls." N.J.S.A. 5:12-99.

To identify card counters, TropWorld employed a "Card Counting Team." After identifying plaintiff as a card counter, TropWorld's team applied countermeasures against him. Although TropWorld admitted to treating card counters differently from other patrons, it asserted that the treatment complied with CCC regulations and its Section 99 internal controls.

Plaintiff's action against TropWorld arises from two incidents. According to plaintiff, on April 27, 1989, TropWorld allowed other blackjack players, but not him, to play two hands during one deal. When plaintiff put his chips in the betting circle, the casino floor person instructed the dealer to deal past plaintiff. As a result, plaintiff filed a patron complaint with the CCC. By letter dated May 15, 1989, the CCC informed plaintiff that TropWorld's actions did not constitute a violation of the Act or the regulations. The CCC also explained:

> Be advised that the Commission does not conduct hearings on individual patron complaints. Rather, efforts are made to resolve such matters informally where possible. In addition, all patron complaints are reconsidered in connection with the annual renewal of each casino's license to determine whether it is providing the type of entertainment and services envisioned by the Legislature when it adopted the Casino Control Act.

The second incident took place on November 10, 1989, when plaintiff was playing blackjack at a TropWorld table with a minimum bet of $25 and a maximum bet of $1000. When the card count became favorable, plaintiff placed several unsuccessful bets of $300 and $350. The parties disagree over the ensuing facts.

According to plaintiff, after he placed a $350 bet, Imperatrice placed a sign on the table lowering the betting limit to $100. Imperatrice, however, maintained that plaintiff's initial bet was not in the betting circle before he lowered the limit. Otherwise, according to Imperatrice, he would have honored the bet.

Imperatrice informed plaintiff that he could not bet more than $100. According to plaintiff, Imperatrice then told the other player at the table that he could wager up to $1000. Without responding, that player left the table.

When Imperatrice pushed plaintiff's $350 bet out of the circle, plaintiff pushed it back. Plaintiff testified that Imperatrice then instructed the dealer to deal, but to pay plaintiff, if he won, based on a $100 bet. The dealer dealt a hand that qualified for a "double down," which entitled plaintiff to double his bet. N.J.A.C. 19:47-2.10. Plaintiff then placed another $350 in the betting circle and won. Imperatrice instructed the dealer to pay plaintiff $200—for an initial $100 bet and a $100 "double down" bet. Plaintiff claimed that he was entitled to $700—for the initial $350 bet and the $350 "double down" bet.

Plaintiff stated that he then placed his hand on top of the cards, pulled the cards toward him, and advised the dealer that she had not paid him the proper amount of money. Although plaintiff knew he was not permitted to touch the cards, N.J.A.C. 19:47-2.6n, he wanted to preserve the cards as evidence. According to Imperatrice, however, plaintiff grabbed the cards. When Imperatrice informed plaintiff that he had been paid the proper amount, plaintiff asked to see a CCC representative. Imperatrice told plaintiff that to complain he must go to the CCC booth. He also informed plaintiff that if he did not relinquish his cards, Imperatrice would call security.

Shortly thereafter, Imperatrice called David Duffield, a lieutenant of security. Duffield called Scully, who told plaintiff to remove his hands from the cards. Plaintiff refused. Plaintiff's version is that he explained that he had been paid improperly and that he wanted to keep the cards as evidence. Scully, however, testified that he told plaintiff two or three times that if he did not take his hands off the cards and leave the game, Scully would arrest him. According to plaintiff, when he relinquished the cards, Duffield and Scully arrested him.

On February 4, 1991, plaintiff filed this action in the Law Division against TropWorld, Imperatrice, and Scully. Initially, plaintiff sued several other TropWorld employees, who obtained a dismissal of the action. Seeking both compensatory and punitive damages, plaintiff alleged malicious prosecution, denial of equal access, discrimination, and breach of implied contract.

In April 1993, TropWorld moved for partial summary judgment. TropWorld claimed that CCC regulations authorized it to treat card counters differently; that plaintiff had failed to exhaust his administrative remedies; that the CCC had exclusive jurisdiction over the claims regarding application of CCC regulations; and that no cause of action existed for damages for a violation of or improper application of CCC regulations.

The Law Division rejected the argument that plaintiff had failed to exhaust his administrative remedies. 274 N.J.Super. 63, 643 A.2d 42 (Law Div.1993). Noting that it already had jurisdiction over plaintiff's breach of contract and malicious prosecution claims, the Law Division ruled that it could also hear his claim for discrimination. Ibid.

Concerning plaintiff's allegations of discrimination, the Law Division recognized that casinos must treat patrons fairly. Id. at 75, 643 A.2d 42. The court reasoned that the selective enforcement of card counting countermeasures against patrons at the same table constituted discrimination. Id. at 76, 643 A.2d 42. Hence, "it is discriminatory to allow others at the same table to play two hands, while limiting [plaintiff] to one." Ibid. The court, however, rejected plaintiff's complaints about TropWorld's right to "shuffle-at-will." Id. at 79, 643 A.2d 42. Because shuffling the cards affects all players at the table evenly, "it is not discrimination." Ibid.

The jury returned a $1,519,873.43 verdict in plaintiff's favor: $300,625.87 against TropWorld and Imperatrice on the discrimination claim; $219,034.06 in compensatory damages against TropWorld and Scully for malicious prosecution; and $1,000,213.50 in punitive damages against TropWorld for malicious prosecution.

All parties appealed. The Appellate Division reversed the judgment and remanded the matter to the Law Division. Initially, the Appellate Division stated that it had "grave reservations" about the Law Division's ruling that a casino must apply countermeasures uniformly to all players, including non-card counters. 302 N.J.Super. at 110, 694 A.2d 1045. According to the court, the CCC adopted countermeasures precisely to authorize the disparate treatment of card counters. Ibid.

The court held that the Law Division should not have entertained plaintiff's complaint. Ibid. The Appellate Division concluded that "the Act compels the concentration in the Commission of the power to define and regulate the manner in which games are played, and that this power extends to resolution of controversies regarding application and interpretation of the Commission's rules of play." Id. at 114, 694 A.2d 1045. Therefore, the Appellate Division found no private cause of action against a casino for the alleged violation of CCC regulations governing the manner in which games are played. Instead, the CCC has exclusive jurisdiction over such claims. Id. at 118, 694 A.2d 1045. Rejecting the Law Division's conclusion that plaintiff lacked an adequate administrative remedy, the Appellate Division found that the CCC had responded to each of plaintiff's complaints. In addition, the court noted that the CCC has the power to make a patron whole by ordering a casino to make restitution of unlawfully retained money. Id. at 117, 694 A.2d 1045. Consequently, the court reversed the judgment awarding plaintiff damages for the casino's discriminatory treatment, but allowed plaintiff to submit his complaints to the CCC within sixty days. Id. at 118, 694 A.2d 1045 . . . .

III.

In Uston v. Resorts Int'l Hotel, Inc., 89 N.J. 163, 166, 445 A.2d 370 (1982), this Court addressed the right of a casino to exclude patrons solely because they were card counters. Although we recognized that the CCC has the exclusive authority to exclude patrons, we ruled that it had not adopted regulations authorizing any such exclusion. Consequently, we concluded that casinos were not authorized to exclude card counters. Ibid. We explained:

> The exhaustive statutes and regulations make clear that the Commission's control over the rules and conduct of licensed casino games is intended to be comprehensive. The ability of casino operators to determine how the games will be played would undermine this control and subvert the important policy of ensuring the "credibility and integrity of the regulatory process and of casino operations." [Id. at 169, 445 A.2d 370 (quoting N.J.S.A. 5:12-1b).]

We also addressed the effect of the Act on the casino's common-law right of exclusion and the public's corresponding right of reasonable access. Id. at 170-74, 445 A.2d 370. Noting that casino property was dedicated to use by the public, we held that casinos should not act in an arbitrary and discriminatory manner toward their patrons. Id. at 173, 445 A.2d 370. In the absence of a regulation authorizing casinos to exclude card counters, Uston's common-law right to reasonable access survived. Although we declined to decide whether the Act empowered the CCC to exclude card counters, we gave the CCC ninety days to adopt regulations permitting countermeasures. Id. at 175, 445 A.2d 370.

Although the CCC declined to authorize the exclusion of card counters, it adopted specific countermeasures. 14 N.J.R. 841(b) (Aug. 2, 1982); 14 N.J.R. 991(a) (Sept. 7, 1982). According to the CCC, the countermeasures, as opposed to exclusion, "would result in one player segment having the opportunity to play blackjack who has thus far been excluded from enjoying this game." 14 N.J.R. 559(b) (June 7, 1982). Nevertheless, the CCC intended these countermeasures to minimize the perceived threat of card counters to the statistical advantage that casinos need to remain profitable. See 14 N.J.R. 467-70 (May 17, 1982); 14 N.J.R. 559-69 (June 7, 1982); 14 N.J.R. 841(b) (Aug. 2, 1982); 14 N.J.R. 991(a) (Sept. 7, 1982).

The countermeasures promulgated by the CCC in 1982 included: (1) the "Bart Carter Shuffle," which is a special shuffling procedure, N.J.A.C. 19:47-2.5d; (2) the continuous shuffling shoe, N.J.A.C. 18:47-2.20; (3) shuffling-at-will, which allows casinos to shuffle after any round of play, N.J.A.C. 19:47-2.5a; and (4) increasing the number of decks from which the cards are dealt, N.J.A.C. 19:47-2.2.

In 1978, before our decision in Uston, the CCC had adopted a regulation providing that "[a] casino licensee may permit a player to wager on more than one box at a Blackjack table provided however that the Commission and its agents shall have the authority and discretion to prohibit this during hours when there are insufficient seats in a casino to accommodate patron demand." N.J.A.C. 19:47-2.14 (subsequently amended); 23 N.J.R. 1784(a) (June 3, 1991); 23 N.J.R. 2869(b) (Sept. 16, 1991). The CCC did not intend this rule to serve as a countermeasure, but as a means of permitting casinos, through approval of Section 99 internal controls, to prevent card counters from betting on more than one box. Doug Grant, Inc. v. Greate Bay Casino Corp., 3 F.Supp.2d 518, 526 (D.N.J.1998).

During the pendency of this action, the CCC adopted two additional regulations that authorize card-counting countermeasures. One regulation states that a casino, on posting a notice, "may at any time change the permissible minimum or maximum wager at a game table . . . ." N.J.A.C. 19:47-8.3(c); see 23 N.J.R. 1784(b) (June 3, 1991); 23 N.J.R. 2613(a) (Sept. 3, 1991); 23 N.J.R. 3350(a), 3354(c) (Nov. 4, 1991). A 1993 regulation permits a casino to offer "different maximum wagers" at the same or different gaming tables. N.J.A.C. 19:47-8.2(b)-(d); see 25 N.J.R. 3953(a) (Sept. 7, 1993); 25 N.J.R. 5521(a) (Dec. 6, 1993).

At the time of the incidents that provide the basis for this action, TropWorld had adopted Section 99 internal controls. Those internal controls recognized that TropWorld had the discretion to shuffle at will, to permit a player to make more than one wager at a table, and to permit known "high limit players" to exceed the table's betting limit. Plaintiff claims that TropWorld discriminated against him by applying the CCC regulations and its Section 99 internal controls selectively against him, but not against other players seated at the same table.

IV.

The lower courts disagreed on the issue whether the CCC has authorized casinos to apply CCC regulations in a discriminatory manner. As the Law Division saw it, a casino discriminates by allowing non-card counters to play multiple hands while limiting card counters at the same table to one hand. 274 N.J.Super. at 76, 643 A.2d 42. The Appellate Division, however, had "grave reservations" whether a casino must uniformly apply such a countermeasure against all players at one table. 302 N.J.Super. at 110, 694 A.2d 1045.

Within its delegated authority, the CCC may adopt regulations that require the uniform application of countermeasures to all players at a blackjack table or that permit the selective application of such countermeasures against card counters only. Regulations in effect in 1989 failed to state expressly whether casinos could selectively apply countermeasures against players at one table. The CCC suggests that casinos could so apply countermeasures, but at oral argument it was uncertain whether a casino could lower the limit for card counters and simultaneously allow other players to bet at the former limit or higher. Absent a regulation, a patron may not be on notice of the rules of the game.

V.

We next turn to the question whether the Superior Court may entertain a casino patron's private damage claim. The Act does not address whether a casino patron may maintain a civil action for damages based on violations of statutory or administrative provisions.

In the absence of a common-law basis, courts have been reluctant to imply a private right of action for money damages in favor of casino patrons. See, e.g., Marcangelo v. Boardwalk Regency Corp., 847 F.Supp. 1222, 1228 (D.N.J.1994) (holding no implied private cause of action under Act for casino patron for inadequate or defective slot machine signage when casino complied with applicable statutory and regulatory requirements), aff'd, 47 F.3d 88 (3rd Cir.1995); Decker v. Bally's Grand Hotel Casino, 280 N.J.Super. 217, 222, 655 A.2d 73 (App.Div.1994) (holding CCC has exclusive jurisdiction over claims that casino violated regulations regarding gaming equipment signage); Miller v. Zoby, 250 N.J. Super. 568, 576–77, 595 A.2d 1104 (App. Div.), certif. denied, 127 N.J. 553, 606 A.2d 366 (1991) (holding no implied private action for money damages for violation of Act's credit provisions). Given the elaborate regulatory scheme, we likewise decline to imply a cause of action when no such cause of action exists at common law.

Plaintiff's claim of discriminatory treatment, however, has a common-law basis. Even without statutory or regulatory support, a casino has a common-law duty to treat patrons fairly. Uston, supra, 89 N.J. at 173, 445 A.2d 370. Remaining is the issue whether the CCC permits casinos to discriminate among patrons by lowering the betting limit for a card counter while retaining or raising it for other patrons. The impact of such discrete treatment is less drastic than that of the exclusion of card counters in Uston. Although the CCC has not adopted an express regulation, by other regulations, the CCC may have implicitly permitted casinos to apply a separate set of rules to card counters seated at the same table as other patrons. An issue of this kind is especially suited for consideration by the CCC in the exercise of its primary jurisdiction. Accordingly, the Law Division should remand the matter to the CCC so that agency may interpret its own regulations . . . .

VII.

As modified, the judgment of the Appellate Division is affirmed.

Notes

1. As the *Erickson* court explains, the Nevada Gaming Act vests the state's Gaming Control Board with exclusive jurisdiction over disputes between casinos and patrons regarding the conduct of games. If the dispute involves at least $500, the casino must immediately notify the Board; otherwise, the casino need only inform the patron of his right to a Board investigation. Nev. Rev. Stat. § 463.362(1). An agent of the Board must conduct an investigation and determine within 30 days whether payment should be made. A party aggrieved by the agent's decision may request a hearing before the Board, Nev. Rev. Stat. § 463.363, and ultimately obtain judicial review of the Board's decision.

2. Every state that has legalized gaming restricts it to persons of "legal age," which in most jurisdictions is 21. Casinos have been fined substantial amounts for failing to keep out or remove underage persons from their gaming areas. No operator has challenged the right of regulators to impose such penalties. *See further* Frank Catania & Gary Ehrlich, *When Crime Pays: A Gaming Regulatory Perspective on What to Do When a Minor or Other Prohibited Person Wins or Loses Money in a Casino*, 3 Gaming L. Rev. 129 (1999), and Kimberly A. Courtney, *Unattended Children in Casinos—Whose Responsibility?*, 6 Gaming L. Rev. 101 (2002).

3. Aware that his son was too young to have been betting, Mr. Erickson immediately sat down at the machine to make it appear that he had won the

jackpot. A security camera had caught the entire incident on tape, however, making it easy to disprove his claim.

4. In *Vinson v. Casino Queen, Inc.*, 123 F.3d 655 (7th Cir. 1997), the mother of a teenage gambler who had lost $77,000 playing blackjack sued to recover his losses, claiming that because her son was underage the casino should not have let him in (he had presented a fake ID card). The Seventh Circuit rejected her argument because

> [If Illinois law] could be interpreted to create a cause of action in this type of case, it would signal to potential plaintiffs that it is profitable to encourage minors to forge identification cards or otherwise partici-pate in gambling games they are not permitted to play . . . . That is an absurd result, which cannot be countenanced.

Id. at 658.

5. As *Decker* and *Campione* illustrate, just about any aspect of a casino's operations can lead to a patron lawsuit. In one particularly notable case, a guest named Heather Devon had a $1 slot machine she had been playing for 12 straight hours "locked up" so she could go get breakfast. While she was eating, the machine was released to another player, who proceeded to hit a $97,000 jackpot. When Devon returned and learned what had happened, she sued the casino for breach of promise.

At trial, Devon asserted that a worker had been bribed $20 by the other player to release the machine; the casino countered that Devon had taken too long to return, and claimed its normal policy was to hold machines for no more than 45 minutes (Devon had been gone for just under two hours). The parties also disagreed as to whether Devon had asked for a break or been persuaded to take one by a casino employee. After several days of deliberations, the jury unanimously found in favor of the house. *See* Phil Willon, *Gambler Loses Lawsuit Over Jackpot*, L.A. Times, Sept. 8, 1999, at B1.

6. For a further look at player disputes, *see, e.g., Grand Casino Biloxi v. Hallmark*, 823 So. 2d 1185 (Miss. 2002) (machine malfunction); *Chen v. Nevada State Gaming Control Board*, 994 P.2d 1151 (Nev. 2000) (card counter); *Harrison v. Boyd Mississippi, Inc.*, 700 So. 2d 247 (Miss. 1997) (em-ployee ejected from premises while playing during his off-hours). *See also* Ronald J. Rychlak, *Videotape and Casino Lawsuits*, 3 Gaming L. Rev. 241 (1999) (discussing the use of casino surveillance videotapes in patron slip-and-fall cases), and Michelle Smith, *The Gaming Industry in Mississippi: Proce-dural Requirements for Patron Disputes—Who Will Protect the Patron When the Law Won't?*, 4 Gaming L. Rev. 225 (2000) (reporting that 50% of disputes in Mississippi's casinos involve machines, 20% table games, 20% promotions, and 10% "other").

Problem 25

A sign over a slot machine advertised that a "sequential royal flush" carried a jackpot of $250,000. When a player achieved such a hand, the casino refused to pay, claiming the sign meant the cards had to be in ascending order (Ten, Jack, Queen, King, Ace). The player's cards were in descending order (Ace,

King, Queen, Jack, Ten). If the player sues, arguing the sign is ambiguous, how should the court rule? *See IGT v. Kelly*, 778 So. 2d 773 (Miss. 2001).

E. DEBT COLLECTION

WEST INDIES, INC. v. FIRST NATIONAL BANK OF NEVADA
214 P.2d 144 (Nev. 1950)

PRIEST, District Judge.

The complaint alleges that on October 23, 1948, decedent Leonard H. Wolff, drew three checks upon respondent in the respective amounts of $7,000.00; $29,000.00; and $50,000.00, and sets out the checks in haec verba, and alleges that same were presented to respondent for payment on October 24, 1948, and dishonored; that Leonard H. Wolff died testate on October 23, 1948; that on November 22, 1948, the respondent was appointed by the Second Judicial District Court, administrator, cum testamento annexo, and on said date qualified, and is now qualified and acting as such administrator of the estate of the said Leonard H. Wolff; that on February 15, 1949, the appellant duly presented its claim to said administrator for the sums set out in said checks totaling $86,000.00, which claim was rejected and refused on February 16, 1949, by an instrument in writing. Plaintiff prayed for judgment against the defendant as administrator of the estate of Leonard H. Wolff, in the sum of $86,000.00 and for costs of suit, payable out of said estate in due course of administration.

Respondent answered and set up as an affirmative defense that the said checks had been given by decedent to plaintiff in payment of money theretofore won by plaintiff from defendant at the gambling game of 'twenty one' and for no other purpose and that the sole consideration for the execution and delivery thereof was money theretofore won by plaintiff from decedent at said gambling game.

Plaintiff's reply admitted the allegations of the affirmative defense heretofore set out. Subsequent to the filing of its reply the plaintiff moved the court for an order permitting an amendment to the reply in such a manner as to show that at all times material to the action, appellant was regularly licensed by state authorities as by law provided and required, to operate the said game referred to. Without objection this proposed amendment was allowed.

Defendant then moved the court for the entry of judgment on the pleadings dismissing the action, upon the ground that if said checks were so executed and delivered, they were executed upon the sole consideration of money won at gambling. Upon stipulation of counsel the motion to dismiss was heard by Hon. Merwyn H. Brown, Judge of the Sixth Judicial District Court. Upon presentation and argument the court entered an order granting the motion for judgment on the pleadings and accordingly entered judgment for defendant. From the judgment of dismissal plaintiff appeals.

At the argument herein counsel for the respective sides mentioned possible distinctions between actions based upon the checks or based upon the alleged indebtness or otherwise founded, but upon being asked by the court whether or not it was the desire of counsel that the opinion should pass squarely upon the point of collectibility by the gambling establishment of money won at a duly licensed game, each replied that he would like the opinion to determine squarely such question. There is therefore the one question presented here to this court, viz: May a gambling house or the proprietor thereof maintain an action at law for the collection of money won at a duly licensed game?

Appellant contends: That the earlier decisions of this court are not controlling being decided under other statutes declaratory of a different public policy; that the English common law, if adopted by Nevada, has been altered by statute; that since 1909 the public policy of this state has been substantially altered with reference to gambling; that licensed gambling is no longer a public nuisance or contrary to public policy; and that our gambling enactments are repugnant to the English statutes.

Respondent contends: That a portion of the common law known as the Statute of Anne, 9 Anne, c. 14, 4 Bac.Abr. 456, relevant to gambling has been effectually adopted by this state; that if not effectually adopted heretofore it is nevertheless an integral part of the law of this state; that the statute is severable and the adoption of a pertinent part is not dependent upon the adoption of the whole; that the law does distinguish in its regulatory power between useful callings and those that do not contribute to the economic good; that the statute is prohibitive rather than permissive; that an express clause in the act making such accounts collectible would have been ineffectual in the absence of a change of title; and that the social consequences of a change in the recognized law are great and that an intent to repeal by implication should not be imputed to the legislature in the absence of a clear showing.

The first pronouncement of this court upon this question was in Scott v. Courtney, 1872, 7 Nev. 419, in which case the court construed the statute of 1869, p. 119.

In Scott v. Courtney, supra, suit was brought by the proprietor of a duly licensed game to collect money lost at such game. Without a declaration that Nevada had adopted any portion of the common law of England known as the Statute of Anne, heretofore referred to, for it appears that the question was never raised, the court nevertheless concluded, in reliance principally upon decisions of the state courts under similar statutes, that the so-called indebtedness was not collectible and that the action could not be maintained. The court said:

> 'In the United States, wagering and gaming contracts seem to have met with no countenance from the courts, and consequently in nearly every state they are held illegal, as being inconsistent with the interests of the community and at variance with the laws of morality. 2 Smith's Leading Cases, 343.'

Section 9021 N.C.L. of 1929, provides as follows:

> 'The common law of England, so far as it is not repugnant to, or in conflict with the constitution and laws of the United States, or the constitution and laws of this state, shall be the rule of decision in all the courts in this state.'

This has been held to include the English statutes in force at the time of the American Declaration of Independence. Ex parte Blanchard, 9 Nev. 101.

In Evans v. Cook, 11 Nev. 69, decided in 1876, and hence decided under the statute of 1869, defendant was sued under his statutory undertaking, posted to prevent levy of attachment upon one Hanley. Cook having been deceived by Hanley, who had represented to Cook that he would defend and set up the defense that the entire consideration was a gambling debt, allowed default to be taken against him. Before judgment Cook then moved the court for an order to set aside the default and for leave to defend on the merits, the motion being based upon the theory of excusable neglect. The trial court denied the motion to set aside the default and subsequently entered judgment for plaintiff. Upon appeal defendant Cook contended among other things that the court erred in refusing to set aside the default and permit a defense in the action on the merits.

The court then having concluded that there was excusable neglect, proceeded to a consideration of whether the proposed defense was meritorious, i.e. it proceeded to determine whether the proprietor of an establishment could maintain an action for money won by it at one of its duly licensed games. The court then held that there had been an adoption of the applicable portions of the Statute of Anne.

In Burke & Co. v. Buck, 1909, 31 Nev. 74, 99 P. 1078, 22 L.R.A., N.S., 627, 21 Ann.Cas. 625, decided under the statute of 1879, the uncontroverted evidence showed that Buck while playing roulette at a Goldfield saloon, endorsed and delivered a negotiable certificate of deposit of $500.00 back to the house. Buck then notified John S. Cook and Co., the issuing corporation, that he had lost possession of same, without consideration and requested said company to refuse payment of said certificate. Judgment was for plaintiff, the gambling house proprietor, in the trial court and upon appeal reversed. The opinion refers approvingly to Evans v. Cook, supra, and approves the adoption of all parts not inconsistent, of the English Statute of Anne. Again there is a declaration as in Scott v. Courtney, supra, that the licensing of gambling is merely permissive, and serves to give immunity from criminal prosecution and nothing more.

In Menardi v. Wacker, 32 Nev. 169, 105 P. 287, 288, Ann.Cas.1912C, 710, it was held that

> 'A check given for a gambling debt is void under the law of this state, and, there being no valid obligation, there could be no lawful consideration for the security as a pledge.'

Citing Burke & Co. v. Buck, 31 Nev. 74, 99 P. 1078, 22 L.R.A., N.S., 627, 21 Ann.Cas. 625.

Looking at the matter historically and by way of throwing light upon the question of legislative intent, it is deemed fitting to show that in or about the year 1909, the pendulum of public opinion had reached the extreme right, and from 1909 through 1915 a series of anti-gambling statutes were enacted. Sufficient to conclude without going into great detail that this was a period of extreme conservatism in the public policy of the state with reference to gambling. This attitude was first manifested by a statute of 1909, p. 307, entitled; 'An Act prohibiting gambling, providing for the destruction of gambling property and other matters relating thereto.'

Public opinion having changed again toward liberality the legislature enacted the so-called open gambling law in 1931. The statute is entitled:

'An Act concerning slot machines, gambling games, and gambling devices; providing for the operation thereof under license; providing for certain license fees and the use of the money obtained therefrom; prohibiting minors from playing and loitering about such games; designating the penalties for violations of the provisions thereof; and other matters properly relating thereto.'

Statutes of 1931, 165-169, Secs. 3302-3302.16, N.C.L. Supplement 1931-1941.

Appellant as a result of tireless and exhaustive research shows to the court that a great deal of the gambling law of England in force at the time of the American Declaration of Independence, is peculiarly applicable to that country because of the structure of their government. From this he argues that under our form of government and particularly in view of the liberality of our statutory enactments pertaining to this subject, from the year 1931, no part of the said Statute of Anne can now have any controlling force. In support of this position appellant shows:

That by Statute 33, Henry VIII c. 9, enacted A.D. 1541, in England, it was made unlawful to maintain a house or place of dicing, table or carding, or other gambling;

That by Section 12 of said Act all other gambling statutes were repealed;

That by Statute 10 and 11, Will. 3 C 17(c), enacted 1710, lotteries were declared common nuisances;

That under Statute 8, George 1, c. 22 S.S. 36, 37 enacted 1721, further penalties for conducting lotteries were provided and certain other enforcement provisions were provided;

That under Statute 9, George 1, c. 19, enacted 1722, certain prohibitions against foreign lotteries were provided;

That the said Statute of Anne was enacted for the purpose of implementing and enforcing the previous anti-gambling statutes;

That said statute contained a limitation or exception to its operation by express terms by provision that it should have no force or effect within His Majesties Royal Palaces, etc., and otherwise excepting the sovereigns;

That by Statute 4, George IV, c. 60, Secs., 1-18, a treasury lottery was authorized;

That by Section 2 of the Statute of Anne, any person who had lost at gaming, could within three months maintain an action of debt, and recover said sum with costs, and in the event the loser failed to commence such an action same might be maintained by any one for treble the amount lost plus costs;

That section 5 of said act provided for corporal punishment to a person winning by fraud;

That the Statute of Anne does not, as do the Nevada statutes, license gambling;

That said statute expressly permits unlicensed gambling in the royal palaces under certain conditions;

That said Statute of Anne permits unlicensed gambling by the royal family 'for ready money only,' while the Nevada statutes permit gambling not only for money but for 'property, checks, credit, or any representative of value.'

We understand that certain of the statutes of England, not here under investigation, but which cast light upon the gambling status and public policy of England at that particular time, are discussed only for these purposes.

Certain portions of the Statute of Anne that are at hopeless variance with the structure of government in America, were equally at hopeless variance at the time of the admission of Nevada to statehood [in 1864]. Admittedly, without attempting to define just which portions, certain portions of the Statute of Anne are not in harmony with the structure of government here, either national or state. But from this fact we cannot conclude that no part of the statute has been adopted unless the statute itself is totally inseparable, or non-severable. Apparently this question of severability has not been raised or urged in any of the gambling cases heretofore decided by this court. Such contention therefore merits careful consideration. 34 L.R.A. 341, footnote 'n'.

The determination of Evans v. Cook, supra, and Burke v. Buck, supra, elicited the declaration that the first section of the Statute of Anne had been adopted. The wording of the first section alone was required to sustain the conclusion reached. The first section of said statute reads as follows:

'That all notes, bills, bonds, judgments, mortgages, or other securities or conveyances whatsoever given, granted, drawn, or entered into, or executed by any person or persons whatsoever, where the whole, or any part of the consideration of such conveyances or securities shall be for any money, or other valuable thing whatsoever, won by gaming or playing at cards, dice, tables, tennis, bowls, or other game or games whatsoever, or by betting on the sides or hands of such as do game at any of the games aforesaid, or for the reimbursing or repaying any money knowingly lent or advanced at the time and place of such play, to any person or persons so gaming or betting as aforesaid, or that shall, during such play, so play or bet, shall be utterly void, frustrate, and of none effect, to all intents and purposes whatsoever.'

The first section heretofore quoted, provides that gambling debts may not be collected at law; the second section that money lost at gambling and paid over may be recovered by the loser and the ninth section is a proviso declaring that nothing in the act shall prevent gambling at the palaces of St. James, or Whitehall when the sovereign is in residence and that such gaming shall be for ready money only.

The general law on the subject of statutes void or ineffectual in part, is clear:

'* * * the adjudging of a certain portion of a statute to be unconstitutional does not affect any other portion, save and except so much thereof as is dependent upon that portion which is declared null and void.'

Ex parte Arascada, 44 Nev. 30, 189 P. 619, 621; Ex parte Goddard, 44 Nev. 128, 190 P. 916.

The first and second sections of the statute are entirely independent and severable. The first provides a shield for one who has lost at gambling but has not paid his losses, while the second provides a sword by which he may recover back what he has paid over. The first provides a defense and the second a remedy. It is difficult or impossible to conceive of a single transaction in which both sections could be invoked. The first section cannot be invoked if the gambling debt has been paid. The second section cannot be invoked if the gambling debt has not been paid. The first section is not dependent upon the ninth section. As heretofore stated the ninth section is a proviso to the effect that nothing in the act shall prevent gambling at certain palaces for ready money. The first section does not prohibit gambling at these palaces or elsewhere nor does it prohibit or require play for ready money only. On the other hand, the ninth section does not purport to legalize gambling debts but by its express terms requires that gambling at Whitehall and St. James palaces shall be for cash only. What has heretofore been stated as to the effect and severability of the first and second sections applies with equal force to the first and ninth. There could be no single transaction under which both sections could be invoked and either section can be dropped from the act without affecting the rights or defenses conferred by the other.

Only such portions of the common law as are applicable to our conditions, have been adopted as the law of this state. In Esden v. May, 36 Nev. 611, 135 P. 1185, the court held that only those portions of the Statute of Anne are in force which are applicable to our conditions and not in conflict with our statutory law, and that particularly the Nevada statutes governing matters of practice control when in conflict with portions of the Statute of Anne. This court having held that not all of the sections of the Statute of Anne have been adopted, Esden v. May, supra, and having held on three occasions, Evans v. Cook, supra, Burke v. Buck, supra, and Menardi v. Wacker, supra, that the first section of said statute is the law of this state, under the rule of stare decisis, the contention of appellant that the statute is non-severable can hardly meet with serious consideration. 21 C.J.S., Courts, § 187, p. 302. We are satisfied that there has been an effectual declaration of adoption of the first section of the Statute of Anne. We are not required to decide if more was adopted and without limiting such possibility we pass the matter for future determination in a proper case.

We are now confronted with the question of whether any of the gambling statutes enacted from the date 1931, have in legal effect repealed by implication the first section of the Statute of Anne. Such repeal would necessarily be by implication for there is nothing in any of the statutes repealing it directly, i.e. there is no provision in any of the statutes to the effect that money won by the establishment at a licensed game may be collected by suit at law.

We have quoted the statutes rather fully and particularly to show that the present law was modeled after the earlier acts of 1869 and 1879, the principal changes being the imposition of a tax upon gross receipts, a grant to the state tax commission of certain regulatory powers, and the legal effect of operating with license. As heretofore mentioned a license under the act of 1869 'shall protect the licensee and his employer or employers (employee or employees) against any criminal prosecution for dealing or carrying on the game mentioned * * *.' The statute of 1879, p. 114 is of the same wording in this respect. Under the statute of 1931 p. 165, 'Said license shall entitle the holder or holders, or his or their employee or employees, to carry on, conduct, and operate the specific slot machine, game or device for which said license is issued * * *'.

Appellant's contention for a repeal by implication is based particularly upon three points, viz;

> 1. That the use of the word 'checks' in the statute of 1931 impliedly authorizes suit to collect same.

> 2. That the statute of 1931 in omitting the immunity clause contained in the earlier statute did so with the intent of giving authority to the licensee to maintain an action for winnings of licensed games.

> 3. That if the repeal of the first section of the Statute of Anne was not effected by the act of 1931 it nevertheless was effected by the act of 1945, p. 492, under the terms and provisions of which it is urged 'the state became a partner'.

In all of the statutes under scrutiny, 1869, 1879, 1931, in which gambling under license is authorized, the word 'checks' appears. It is not new to the statute of 1931, which statute is clearly modeled from the other statutes. The first section deals with the unlawful and is prohibitive rather than permissive. In effect it declares that it is unlawful for all persons, natural or artificial, to carry on certain games of chance, enumerating them, for property of all kinds unless properly licensed. It cannot be legally inferred from this wording of the statute that the statute is a grant of authority to take checks in properly licensed games, and that there is a corollary power granted to maintain an action at law for the collection of such checks.

What is the legal significance of the omission of the immunity clause, that is, the clause in regard to immunity from criminal prosecution? The inclusion of the immunity clause in the earlier statutes was entirely unnecessary to protect a licensed gambling operator from criminal prosecution, for when a license tax is imposed upon a particular form of gambling or gambling device, one who pays the tax cannot be prosecuted for gambling, i.e. that which is contemplated by the license. State v. Moseley, 14 Ala. 390; State v. Allaire, 14 Ala. 435; Rodgers v. State, 26 Ala. 76; Hawkins v. State, 33 Ala. 433; Overby v. State, 18 Fla. 178; Berry v. People, 36 Ill. 423; State v. Duncan, 84 Tenn. 79; Houghton v. State, 41 Tex. 136; Miller & Co. v. Stropshire, 124 Ga. 829, 53 S.E. 335, 4 Ann.Cas. 574, 575, and note; 27 C.J. p. 1014, § 179, notes 59-50, 38 C.J.S., Gaming, § 82; 24 Am.Jur. p. 405, sec. 10, note 19.

It has been urged that the purpose of including such clause in the statutes of 1869 and 1879, was, as held in Scott v. Courtney, supra, to limit and restrict the effect of the license to simple protection of the persons so engaged in gambling against criminal punishment, and that [by omitting] such immunity clause from the statute of 1931, is in legal effect to remove the disability enunciated in Scott v. Courtney, supra. This could have been the intent but this possibility is surely discounted or discredited when one reflects that the effect of the license is still limited under the statute. Under the earlier statutes the license protected the licensee from criminal prosecution. Under the present statute the license 'shall entitle the holder or holders, or his or their employee or employees, to carry on, conduct and operate the specific slot machine, game or device for which said license is issued * * *'. It is the opinion of the court that the substitution of another limiting clause for the former immunity clause cannot have the effect urged by counsel. Who can say but that the omission of the immunity clause was for the purpose of removing surplusage.

But to resolve this question of repeal by implication, we are not required to indulge in speculation, we can reach it very directly. We quote from 15 C.J.S., Commerce, § 12, p. 620, as follows:

'Although the common law may be impliedly repealed by a statute which is inconsistent therewith, or which undertakes to revise and cover the whole subject matter, repeal by implication is not favored, and this result will be reached only where there is a fair repugnance between the common law and the statute, and both cannot be carried into effect.'

The statute of 1931 did not attempt to 'revise and cover the whole subject matter', as evidenced by the fact that section 10201 N.C.L. of 1929, which was a law with reference to gambling effective January 1, 1912, was amended in 1941 p. 64: Sec. 10201, 1931-1941 N.C.L. Supplement.

In Cunningham v. Washoe County, 66 Nev.__, 203 P.2d 611, 613, in which appellant contended for repeal of the common law by implication, Mr. Justice Badt stated the law applicable to this action at bar in these words:

'Nevada has by statute adopted the principles of the common law and has in a number of instances modified the common law by statutory enactment. That this may be done by way of constructive repeal of the common law (as in cases where a statute has revised the whole subject) or that it may be the result of "the clear and unquestionable implication from legislative acts," as maintained by appellant, we may concede to be true where such situations sufficiently appear. However to sustain a justification of the particular acts under this theory, where such acts are not authorized by the express terms of the statute under which the justification is made, we should have to find the plainest and most necessary implication in the statute itself. This rule appears to be frankly admitted even in the authorities submitted by appellant.'

We now approach the question of liberal and strict construction.

The law makes a distinction between liquor and gambling industries and useful trades. In State ex rel. Grimes v. Board of Commissioners, 53 Nev. 364, 1 P.2d 570, 572, the court said:

'We think the distinction drawn between a business of the latter character and useful trades, occupations, or businesses is substantial and necessary for the proper exercise of the police power of the state. Gaming as a calling or business is in the same class as the selling of intoxicating liquors in respect to deleterious tendency. The state may regulate or suppress it without interfering with any of those inherent rights of citizenship which it is the object of government to protect and secure.'

Considering the limitations placed by law upon the license, the special class of industry licensed and its deleterious effect, the fact that it is in contravention of the common law, the fact that it is a statute granting special privileges, we entertain no doubt but that the statute is one meriting strict construction against the licensee, and must therefore conclude from the application of the rule of strict construction, that the omission of the immunity clause in the statute of 1931, does not in legal effect grant the right to maintain an action for winnings at a duly licensed game. There is no such 'clear and unquestionable implication from legislative acts.' In Ex parte Pierotti, 43 Nev. 243, 184 P. 209, 211, Mr. Justice Sanders speaking in opposition to judicial construction to nullify the obvious meaning of a statute said: 'It is not the province of courts to confound by construction what the legislature has made clear.'

For the reasons heretofore given it is ordered that the judgment of the District Court be, and the same is hereby affirmed, with costs.

FLEEGER v. BELL
95 F. Supp. 2d 1126 (D. Nev. 2000),
aff'd mem., 23 Fed. App. 741 (9th Cir. 2001)

PRO, District Judge.

BACKGROUND

Defendant Desert Palace, Inc., dba Caesars Palace (hereinafter referred to as "Desert Palace") is a well-known provider of resort hotel and casino amenities. In order to better serve its gaming patrons, Desert Palace extends lines of gambling credit to those who fill out a pre-printed application form. This form requires specific information, such as a patron's name, home address, business address, telephone numbers, social security number, bank and bank account number. Upon approval of this credit application by Desert Palace, a patron may request the issuance of certain instruments commonly known as casino "markers."

The markers, if signed by the patron, may in turn be used to obtain casino chips with which to gamble at a Desert Palace establishment. Each marker identifies its value in United States dollars and bears the instruction "PAY TO THE ORDER OF." The markers also bear the following stipulation:

> I authorize the payee to complete any of the following items on this negotiable instrument: (1) any missing amounts; (2) a date; (3) the name, account number and/or address and branch of any bank or financial institution; and (4) any electronic encoding of the above items. This information can be for any account from which I may in the future have the right to withdraw funds, regardless of whether that account now exists or whether I provided the information on the account to the payee. I acknowledge that I incurred the debt evidenced by this instrument in Nevada. I agree that any dispute regarding or

involving this instrument, the debt, or the payee shall be brought only in a court, state or federal, in Nevada. I hereby submit to the jurisdiction of any court, state or federal, in Nevada.

According to Plaintiff Matthew Fleeger ("Fleeger"), spaces for information such as account number, bank address and bank branch are left blank on the marker at the time of execution. When a patron is finished gambling, he either cashes out the markers (i.e., pays them off) or leaves the casino with the markers outstanding as a debt owed to Desert Palace.

On at least two occasions in November 1997 and January 1998, Fleeger executed several such markers with Desert Palace. By April 1998, Fleeger had accumulated a debt of approximately $183,856.00 as reflected in unpaid markers owed to Desert Palace. When Desert Palace attempted to deposit some of the markers reflecting this outstanding debt, however, they were returned by Fleeger's banks with the notations "NSF" and "Returned Not Paid." After sending a payment demand letter to Fleeger, Desert Palace requested Clark County District Attorney Stewart L. Bell and Douglas County District Attorney Scott Doyle ("the District Attorneys") to collect the debt as a "bad check" under Nev.Rev.Stat. § 205.130. The District Attorneys each filed criminal charges against Fleeger. Arrest warrants were issued therefrom in both Nevada and Texas, leading to Fleeger's eventual arrest and detention in both Dallas, Texas and Colin, Texas.

On November 4, 1999, Fleeger filed a Class Action Complaint on behalf of himself and other similarly situated plaintiffs. Desert Palace filed a Motion to Dismiss the Class Action Complaint for failure to state a claim on December 13, 1999. Instead of opposing this motion, Fleeger filed the extant Amended Class Action Complaint on January 5, 2000.

In his Amended Complaint, Fleeger contends that the markers were not negotiable "checks" or "drafts" for purposes of Nevada gaming and commercial law, but rather IOU's or promissory notes. He therefore argues that Desert Palace's request to the District Attorneys to collect the unpaid markers and prosecute him and other debtors for passing bad checks lacked proper foundation in either Nevada or federal law. To this end, Fleeger has alleged that Desert Palace directly violated and/or conspired with the District Attorneys to violate: (1) the Fair Debt Collection Practices Act ("FDCPA"), 15 U.S.C. §§ 1692-1692o; (2) Nevada false arrest and false imprisonment laws; (3) substantive due process rights guaranteed by the Fourteenth Amendment of the United States Constitution; (4) 42 U.S.C. § 1983; and (5) Regulation 5.140 of the Nevada Gaming Commission and State Gaming Control Board. Desert Palace has moved to dismiss these allegations with prejudice for failure to state claims upon which relief can be granted. See Fed.R.Civ.Pro. 12(b)(6).

DISCUSSION

In his First Amended Complaint, Fleeger has asserted claims individually and on behalf of other similarly situated plaintiffs. However, since the proposed class has not yet been certified, it is appropriate to consider only Fleeger's claims against Desert Palace at this time.

A. First Cause of Action: Alleged Violation of FDCPA

At the outset, Desert Palace requests the dismissal of Fleeger's allegations that it violated the FDCPA both through (1) its individual acts and (2) its unlawful "conspiracy" with the District Attorneys. The FDCPA prevents "debt collector[s]" from using "any false, deceptive, or misleading representation or means in connection with the collection of any debt." 15 U.S.C. § 1692e. Fleeger contends, in essence, that Desert Palace violated these provisions by demanding repayment of its markers under Nevada's bad check statute and referencing the matter to the local District Attorneys. Neither allegation, however, is sustainable.

1. Direct FDCPA Liability

In order to assert direct liability under the FDCPA, a plaintiff must show that the defendant's actions or status rendered it a "debt collector" for purposes of the Act. See Heintz v. Jenkins, 514 U.S. 291, 292, 115 S.Ct. 1489, 131 L.Ed.2d 395 (1995); Fox v. Citicorp Credit Servs., Inc., 15 F.3d 1507, 1513 (9th Cir.1994). Ordinarily, the FDCPA protects consumers against only those entities that collect debts for third parties. See Romine v. Diversified Collection Servs., Inc., 155 F.3d 1142, 1146 (9th Cir.1998). The FDCPA does provide, however, that "any creditor who, in the process of collecting his own debts, uses any name other than his own which would indicate that a third person is collecting or attempting to collect such debts" may also fall within the ambit of the term "debt collector." 15 U.S.C. § 1692a(6)(A). Nevertheless, examination of Fleeger's Complaint fails to unearth any allegations lying in conformity with these standards.

Here, Fleeger has conceded that the sums pursued by Desert Palace were for those monies owed to it as a result of gambling losses. While it is true that Desert Palace conducts business under the name "Caesars Palace," nowhere does the Amended Complaint allege that it presented itself under any identity other than the "Caesars" moniker during the period of alleged malfeasance. Indeed, the dishonored checks forming the basis of this suit are made payable to "Caesars Palace." Similarly, Desert Palace's payment demand letters and credit application form bear the "Caesars" name. Thus, this Court finds a complete absence of the necessary false suggestion of third-party debt collection required by § 1692a(6)(A) to bar the self-help efforts of a creditor. The identical conclusion has been reached by at least one other district court. See Friedman v. Rubinstein, No. 97 C 6610, 1997 WL 757875, at *3 (N.D.Ill.Dec.1, 1997) ("In the [FDCPA] case at bar, the use of the name 'Caesars Palace' would not indicate that a third person was collecting or attempting to collect the gambling debt. Plaintiff incurred the debt with an entity using the name 'Caesars Palace,' so the use of that name by Desert Palace, Inc., would indicate that the original creditor, not some third party, was collecting or attempting to collect the debt."). Fleeger's allegations of direct liability against Desert Palace are therefore dismissed.

2. Conspiracy Liability Under the FDCPA

Similarly misplaced is any allegation of FDCPA conspiracy liability. Conspiracy liability can arise only when there is the commission of a wrongful, actionable tort. See Harrell v. 20th Century Ins. Co., 934 F.2d 203, 208 (9th Cir.1991); Eikelberger v. Tolotti, 96 Nev. 525, 611 P.2d 1086, 1088 n.1 (1980). In his Amended Complaint, Fleeger accuses Desert Palace of unlawfully conspiring with the District Attorneys to violate the FDCPA by "unfairly and unconscionably using the legal process" in order to force repayment of Desert Palace's markers. However, the FDCPA specifically exempts from its field of regulated "debt collectors" any officer or employee of any state or its political subdivisions "to the extent that collecting or attempting to collect any debt is in the performance of his official duties." 15 U.S.C. § 1692a(6)(C); see also Brannan v. United Student Aid Funds, Inc., 94 F.3d 1260, 1263 (9th Cir.1996). Thus, FDCPA conspiracy liability may fall upon Desert Palace only insofar as the District Attorneys acted in contravention of their statutory or official duties.

Nevada's bad check legislation prohibits an individual from drawing or passing "a check or draft" to obtain services, money or use of property "when the person has insufficient money, property or credit with the drawee of the instrument to pay it in full upon its presentation." Nev.Rev.Stat. § 205.130(1). While the Nevada criminal codes are silent as to what instruments may constitute a "check," this Court may reference sections of Nevada's commercial law code for interpretive aid. See 2B Norman J. Singer, Sutherland Stat. Const. §§ 53.02-53.04 (5th ed.1992) (outlining theory of interpretive harmony in statutory systems). Under the Nevada Uniform Commercial Code, a "check" is defined as "[a] draft, other than a documentary draft, payable on demand and drawn on a bank." Nev.Rev.Stat. § 104.3104(6). A draft is "payable on demand" when no time for payment is otherwise stated. See Nev.Rev.Stat. § 104.3108.

Here, the markers referenced within Fleeger's Amended Complaint specifically state that the payor empowers Desert Palace to fill in the amount, name, account number and address of any financial institution in which the payor holds funds. The markers also do not delineate any explicit dates for repayment, thereby subjecting the payor to a repayment obligation at the will of the payee. Thus, this Court finds the disputed casino markers to be negotiable "checks" for purposes of Nev.Rev.Stat. §§ 104.3104(6) and 205.130. Any nonpayment of casino markers of the type provided by Desert Palace would therefore fall within the prosecutorial purview of the Nevada District Attorneys. Accordingly, Fleeger's FDCPA conspiracy claim will also be dismissed.

B. Second Cause of Action: False Imprisonment and False Arrest

Desert Palace next requests dismissal of Fleeger's unauthorized detention allegations. In his second cause of action, Fleeger alleges that while Desert Palace did not itself detain his person, it did cause his unlawful arrest and jailing in Texas. According to Fleeger, these acts violated state false imprisonment and false arrest laws. In Nevada, a false imprisonment is effected where there is a "confinement or detention [of another] without sufficient legal authority." Nev.Rev.Stat. § 200.460. An integral part of the proof of this tort is the commission or instigation of a false arrest (i.e., an unlawful arrest or restraint of personal liberty). See Garton v. City of Reno, 102 Nev. 313, 720 P.2d 1227, 1228 (1986) (quotation and citation omitted). As mentioned, supra,

Fleeger's arrest and detention in Texas for the nonpayment of casino markers lay within the legal bounds of Nevada's bad check statute. The Court will therefore dismiss Fleeger's second cause of action insofar as it relates to Desert Palace.

C. Third Cause of Action: Alleged Violation of the Fourteenth Amendment

Fleeger's third cause of action alleges that Desert Palace both directly violated and conspired to violate Fleeger's Fourteenth Amendment right to substantive due process. A litigant, however, may not directly pursue a cause of action under the United States Constitution. See Azul-Pacifico, Inc. v. City of Los Angeles, 973 F.2d 704, 705 (9th Cir.1992). Accordingly, this Court will also dismiss Fleeger's third cause of action.

D. Fourth Cause of Action: 42 U.S.C. § 1983

In his fourth cause of action, Fleeger restates his due process allegation within the statutory vehicle of a 42 U.S.C. § 1983 claim. To maintain a § 1983 action, a plaintiff must show (1) that the conduct complained of was committed under color of state law and (2) that the conduct deprived the plaintiff of a constitutional right. See Balistreri v. Pacifica Police Dept., 901 F.2d 696, 699 (9th Cir.1988) (citations omitted). Fleeger alleges that Desert Palace "acted under the color of [Nev.Rev.Stat.] § 205.130 in filing criminal charges against Plaintiff" and conspired to "caus[e] [his] arrest for 'passing bad checks,' even though the markers [were] not 'checks' or 'drafts.'" Desert Palace correctly argues, however, that such allegations fail to state a violation of the federal civil rights laws.

As a general rule, conduct by private parties such as Desert Palace will not constitute governmental action under color of law for purposes of § 1983. See Sutton v. Providence St. Joseph Medical Ctr., 192 F.3d 826, 835 (9th Cir.1999); Aasum v. Good Samaritan Hospital, 542 F.2d 792, 794 (9th Cir.1976). Nevertheless, it is true that liability may arise in the special instance in which the private party willfully participates in joint action with state officials. See Franklin v. Terr, 201 F.3d 1098, 1100 (9th Cir.2000); United Steelworkers of America v. Phelps Dodge Corp., 865 F.2d 1539, 1540 (9th Cir.1989). However, contrary to the suggestion extended in Fleeger's submissions, the mere reporting of suspected criminal activity to law enforcement officials does not constitute the type of joint action capable of transforming a private party into a state actor for purposes of § 1983. See Lee v. Town of Estes Park, Colo., 820 F.2d 1112, 1115-16 (10th Cir.1987); see also Sims v. Jefferson Downs Racing Ass'n, Inc., 778 F.2d 1068, 1079 (5th Cir.1985) (finding no joint action liability where police officer made independent determination of probable cause to arrest on complaint sworn by private entity's general manager).

Nor is Fleeger's Amended Complaint saved by its conclusory allegations that Desert Palace "entered into a conspiracy and concert of action" with the District Attorneys to unlawfully collect unpaid markers as checks under Nev.Rev.Stat. § 205.130. Allegations of constitutional injury that are unsupported by specific facts may be properly disposed of through motions to dismiss. See Burns v. County of King, 883 F.2d 819, 821 (9th Cir.1989). Here, the Amended Complaint is bereft of the focused, requisite allegations of constitutional wrongdoing. Indeed, as mentioned, supra, the District Attorneys prosecution of the makers' nonpayment was completely proper under a facial reading of Nevada's bad check statute. Accordingly, Fleeger's fourth cause of action will be dismissed.

E. Fifth Cause of Action: Regulation 5.140

In his fifth cause of action, Fleeger asserts that Desert Palace's reporting of marker nonpayment to the District Attorneys also violated Nevada Gaming Commission Regulation 5.140. This regulation states, in pertinent part, that:

> 1. Only bonded, duly licensed collection agencies, or a licensee's employees, junket representatives, attorneys, or affiliated or wholly-owned corporation and their employees, may collect, on the licensee's behalf and for any consideration, gaming credit extended by the licensee.

Nev. Gaming Comm'n Reg. 5.140(1). In order to best maintain the "strict and uniform regulation of all aspects of the gaming industry," courts should be loath to infer private causes of action under Nevada's gaming regulatory regime barring "express language to the contrary." Sports Form, Inc. v. Leroy's Horse and Sports Place, 108 Nev. 37, 823 P.2d 901, 903 (1992). Here, perusal of the debt collection regulations does not reveal the faintest suggestion of the presence of a judicial remedy. See, e.g., Nev. Gaming Comm'n Reg. 5.140(3) (requiring debt collection licensees to maintain records for state gaming board inspection). Accordingly, Fleeger's request for judicial relief from an alleged violation of Regulation 5.140 is also dismissed.

CONCLUSION

IT IS THEREFORE ORDERED that Defendant Desert Palace, Inc.'s Motion to Dismiss is GRANTED. All causes of action asserted against Desert Palace, Inc. are DISMISSED.

INTERNATIONAL RECOVERY SYSTEMS, INC. v. GABLER
527 N.W.2d 20 (Mich. Ct. App. 1994)

PER CURIAM.

Plaintiff, International Recovery Systems, Inc., appeals as of right from dismissal of its action seeking enforcement of a foreign judgment based upon an underlying gambling debt. We affirm.

I

Defendant, John Gabler, issued four checks to the Las Vegas Sands Hotel for $5,000. He used the sum to purchase gambling chips and ultimately dishonored the checks. The hotel assigned defendant's debt to plaintiff, which obtained a default judgment against defendant in a state court of Nevada on November 20, 1991. The judgment awarded plaintiff the amount of the debt plus interest and costs.

Plaintiff sought to enforce the judgment in the courts of our state under the Full Faith and Credit Clauses of the United States Constitution and the

Uniform Foreign Money-Judgments Recognition Act. U.S. Const. art. IV, § 1; M.C.L. § 691.1151 et seq.; M.S.A. § 27.955(1) et seq.

Plaintiff moved for summary disposition pursuant to MCR 2.116(C)(9) and (10), and the trial judge found no cause of action against defendant. He reasoned that contracts made in furtherance of gambling are unenforceable as contrary to Michigan public policy.

Later, the judge agreed to reconsider his ruling if plaintiff could present a Michigan appellate court case supporting enforcement of a foreign judgment based upon an underlying gambling debt. Plaintiff conceded that no such case law existed. The judge then denied the motion for reconsideration.

On appeal, plaintiff argues that the trial court erred in failing to render full faith and credit to the Nevada judgment.

II

We review a trial court's grant of summary disposition de novo, examining the record to determine whether the prevailing party was entitled to judgment as a matter of law. G & A Inc. v. Nahra, 204 Mich.App. 329, 330, 514 N.W.2d 255 (1994). M.C.L. § 691.1154(2); M.S.A. § 27.955(4)(2) provides:

> A foreign judgment need not be recognized if:
>
> (c) The cause of action on which the judgment is based is repugnant to the public policy of this state.

Courts in our state have long held that, as a matter of public policy, contracts made in furtherance of gambling are unenforceable, and loans made for gambling purposes cannot be recovered. Gibson v. Martin, 308 Mich. 178, 13 N.W.2d 252 (1944); Raymond v. Leavitt, 46 Mich. 447, 9 N.W. 525 (1881). The conclusion is amply supported by the language of M.C.L. § 600.2939(3); M.S.A. § 27A.2939(3), which provides:

> All notes, bills, bonds, mortgages, or other securities or conveyances whatever, in which the whole or any part of the consideration, shall be for any money or goods won by playing at cards, dice, or any other game whatever, or by betting on the sides or hands of such as are gaming, or by any betting or gaming whatever, or for reimbursing or repaying any moneys knowingly lent or advanced for any gaming or betting, shall be void and of no effect, as between the parties to the same, and as to all persons, except such as shall hold or claim under them in good faith, and without notice of the illegality of such contract or conveyance.

The viability of similar default judgments has been considered in the federal District Court for the Eastern District of Michigan on two separate occasions, in 1987 and 1990 respectively. Nat'l Recovery System v. Kasle, 662 F.Supp. 139 (E.D.Mich., 1987); Boardwalk Regency Corp. v. Travelers Express Co., 745 F.Supp. 1266 (E.D.Mich., 1990).

In Kasle, the judge concluded that enforcement of a judgment based on a gambling debt did not violate Michigan public policy because: 1) otherwise the Michigan statute voiding gambling debts would be given an extraterritorial effect beyond that anticipated by the Legislature; 2) Michigan's interest in prohibiting a competent adult Michigan resident from voluntarily choosing to leave the state and wager in another state is minimal; 3) the facts did not indicate that Kasle was the victim of an illicit activity. The judge also reasoned that, as bingo and the state-run lottery are acceptable enterprises within the state, he could not conclude that gambling is morally and socially unacceptable here.

However, in Boardwalk, decided some three years later, a different judge again applied Michigan law and came to the opposite conclusion: the courts of our state have long held that contracts made in furtherance of gambling were unenforceable, and loans made for gambling cannot be recovered. Gibson, supra; Raymond, supra. He denied plaintiff's request to honor stolen money orders that defendant signed in order to discharge a prior gambling debt and obtain gambling chips.

The Boardwalk court reasoned that M.C.L. § 600.2939(3); M.S.A. § 27A.2939(3) is the conclusive statement of Michigan public policy regarding the validity of gambling contracts or conveyances. Furthermore, it explicitly rejected the reasoning of Kasle, concluding that our Legislature has made limited exceptions to M.C.L. § 600.2939(3); M.S.A. § 27A.2939(3). Thus, Michigan does not prohibit "legal" gambling here or "legal" gambling in other states. However, that fact does not alter the explicit public policy statement against the enforcement of gambling debts set forth in the statute. Boardwalk, supra, at p. 1271.

Conclusions of the federal district court are not binding upon this Court. By contrast, public policy pronouncements of the Michigan Legislature enacted as statutes certainly do bind us. Lieberthal v. Glens Falls Indemnity Co., 316 Mich. 37, 40, 24 N.W.2d 547 (1946). M.C.L. § 600.2939(3); M.S.A. § 27A.2939(3) renders gambling debts unenforceable as against public policy. Moreover, M.C.L. § 691.1154(2); M.S.A. § 27.955(4)(2) authorizes the court to refuse to enforce a foreign judgment which is repugnant to public policy.

Since enforcement of gambling debts is repugnant to Michigan public policy, the trial court correctly entered a judgment of no cause of action for defendant.

Affirmed.

ON REHEARING

PER CURIAM.

This case is before us on rehearing. Plaintiff, International Recovery Systems, Inc., appeals from dismissal of its action seeking enforcement of a foreign judgment based upon an underlying gambling debt. We reverse.

It is clear that gambling is contrary to public policy in Michigan, aside from those narrowly circumscribed exceptions created by the Legislature. It is also clear that the enforcement of gambling debts is contrary to the public policy of our state. Such debts are unenforceable in our courts. Gibson v. Martin, 308 Mich. 178, 13 N.W.2d 252 (1944), Raymond v. Leavitt, 46 Mich. 447, 9 N.W. 525 (1881). The conclusion is amply supported by the language of MCL 600.2939(3); MSA 27A.2939 which provides:

> All notes, bills, bonds, mortgages, or other securities or conveyances, whatever, in which the whole or any part of the consideration shall

be for any money or goods won by playing at cards, dice, or any other game whatever, or by betting on the sides or hands of such as are gaming, or by any betting or gaming whatever, or for reimbursing or repaying any moneys knowingly lent or advanced for any gaming or betting, shall be void and of no effect, as between the parties to the same, and as to all persons, except such as shall hold or claim under them in good faith, and without notice of the illegality of such contract or conveyance.

In the case before us, further briefing has convinced us that we must treat as irrelevant our state's public policy and our courts' long-standing refusal to enforce gambling debts. We are dealing with a fait accompli, a foreign judgment. We are compelled to enforce Nevada's judgment against this defendant due to accepted construction of the Full Faith and Credit Clause of the federal Constitution. U.S. Const., Art. IV, § 1; Fauntleroy v. Lum, 210 U.S. 230, 28 S.Ct. 641, 52 L.Ed. 1039 (1908). We note that when the U.S. Supreme Court issued Fauntleroy four justices were sufficiently troubled by it to dissent, raising issues not unlike those considered in our earlier opinion.

We reflect, in passing, that in times of intense financial stress for the individual states, some have embraced gambling to relieve their financial woes. It is possible to imagine a time in the not-so-distant future when, under the Full Faith and Credit Clause, our courts could be used to enforce similar foreign judgments. Unfortunately, the underlying debts could arise from no-longer-illegal sales of street drugs, prostitution and like goods or services. Some would argue that they, too, hold a promise of quick revenue and prosperity for the individual states.

Reversed.

Notes

1. As the *West Indies* case shows, the question of whether the Statute of Anne applies to gaming debts in the United States (and if so, with what consequences), is a source of considerable confusion. For an illuminating article that describes how the statute currently is viewed in different jurisdictions, *see* Joseph Kelly, *Caught in the Intersection Between Public Policy and Practicality: A Survey of the Legal Treatment of Gambling-Related Obligations in the United States*, 5 Chap. L. Rev. 87 (2002) (explaining that Nevada did not affirmatively repudiate the Statute of Anne until 1983, when it passed what is now Nev. Rev. Stat. § 463.368).

2. In *Nguyen v. State*, 14 P.3d 515 (Nev. 2000), the Nevada Supreme Court agreed with Judge Pro's decision in *Fleeger*; a similar result was reached in *TeleRecovery of Louisiana, Inc. v. Gaulon*, 738 So. 2d 662 (La. Ct. App.), *writ denied*, 751 So. 2d 224 (La. 1999). Why do casinos file criminal charges for unpaid gaming debts? Is it to collect the debt, punish the defendant, or send a warning to others?

3. The court in *Gabler* realized it had made a mistake, and had no choice but to enforce the Nevada judgment, because of the "full faith and credit" clause of the United States Constitution. As a result, casinos typically first obtain a judgment in their home state and then seek to enforce it in the

debtor's home state. Of course, the clause does not apply to judgments rendered by foreign country courts, which are enforceable only to the extent required (or permitted) by comity. *See further Intercontinental Hotels Corp. (Puerto Rico) v. Golden*, 203 N.E.2d 210 (N.Y. 1964).

4. In *Froug v. Carnival Leisure Industries, Ltd.*, 627 So. 2d 538 (Fla. Dist. Ct. App. 1993), a Bahamian casino sued a Florida resident over a gambling debt. In refusing to permit collection, the court rejected the casino's contention that the introduction of a state lottery had abrogated Florida's longstanding prohibition against the enforcement of gaming debts. The court also found it significant that Bahamian law makes it illegal for Bahamian citizens to enter a Bahamian casino (except as employees). The Fifth Circuit, applying Texas law, came to a similar conclusion in *Carnival Leisure Industries, Ltd. v. Aubin*, 53 F.3d 716 (5th Cir. 1995).

5. For a further look at casino credit and collection policies, *see* Anthony N. Cabot, *Casino Collection Lawsuits: The Basics*, 4 Gaming L. Rev. 319 (2000), and Robert D. Faiss, *Nevada Gaming Industry Credit Practices and Procedures*, 3 Gaming L. Rev. 145 (1999).

Problem 26

A casino accepted three $500 checks from a customer in return for $1,500 in chips. Due to an oversight, the casino failed to deposit the checks within seven days, as required by the rules of the state's gaming commission. Is the casino now barred from enforcing the debt? *See Resorts International Hotel, Inc. v. Salomone*, 429 A.2d 1078 (N.J. Super. Ct. App. Div. 1981).

F. CHEATING

SHERIFF v. ANDERSON
746 P.2d 643 (Nev. 1987)

PER CURIAM.

Anderson was charged with possession of a cheating device and entering a building with intent to use a cheating device (burglary). He was arrested in the Westward Ho Casino after he was observed using "computer shoes" while playing Blackjack. A casino surveillance technician observed that Anderson exerted unusual toe movements while playing. He observed that the toe movements corresponded with the appearance of certain cards on the table.

Casino personnel confronted Anderson and explained that they suspected him of wearing "computer shoes." Anderson admitted using a hidden micro-computer to assist him in the game.

Anderson wore shoes and socks. The socks were cut away in order that the bare toes could input data into the computer. Switches were attached in the shoes with velcro. Anderson would push up with his toes for one, down for two, up for eight, down for four. These combinations permitted Anderson to add up to any number. Wires extended up Anderson's legs to a battery pack located in his left rear pocket. The main portion of the computer was strapped to his left calf. Inflated balloons kept the apparatus away from the skin in order to prevent burns. The computer sent vibratory signals to a special receiver located inside an athletic supporter. The signal told Anderson whether to hit, stand, double down, or split. The computer calculated Anderson's advantage or disadvantage with the house and advised him of the remaining cards in the deck.

Anderson was arrested and indicted. His pre-trial petition for a writ of habeas corpus was granted. The writ was issued and deemed permanent. On appeal, it is argued that the district court erred in finding that NRS 465.075 was unconstitutional.

The statute prohibits the use of a "device" for various gaming purposes. Anderson argues, and the district court found, that this term was unconstitutionally vague. We disagree. In Hoffman Estates v. Flipside, Hoffman Estates, 455 U.S. 489, 102 S.Ct. 1186, 71 L.Ed.2d 362 (1982), the Supreme Court established standards for evaluating vagueness. A person of ordinary intelligence must have a reasonable opportunity to know what conduct is prohibited. Laws must also provide standards for law enforcement personnel. 455 U.S. at 498, 102 S.Ct. at 1193. However, one who engages in clearly proscribed conduct cannot complain of the vagueness of the law as applied to others. 455 U.S. at 495, 102 S.Ct. at 1191.

We hold that NRS 465.075 is not vague, at least as applied to Anderson. Use of a hidden computer is precisely the type of conduct envisioned by the statute. While there may be circumstances when the term "device" is vague, we are not confronted with such a case. Whatever else it may include, the term certainly includes computers. No person of ordinary intelligence could believe otherwise. If one did have some question as to whether or not the statute prohibited the use of computers, then reference to any standard dictionary would provide the answer.

Reversed and remanded.

SKIPPER v. STATE
879 P.2d 732 (Nev. 1994)

PER CURIAM.

FACTS

The facts of record are brief and uncontested on appeal. While playing craps at two different gaming establishments in Reno, Skipper was videotaped throwing the dice in a manner that is colloquially referred to as "dice sliding." As the term implies, dice sliding occurs when one or both of the dice slides down the table without tumbling or otherwise altering the number(s) preselected by the gambler to face upward. Dice sliding is a difficult manipulation because it requires both dexterity of the ring and pinkie fingers and the aid of an inattentive or collaborating craps dealer or, as here, an accomplice who is able to obscure the dealer's view of play. The surveillance tapes admitted into evidence show that Skipper's occasional attempts to slide a die (some of which were successful) were preceded by changes in his betting pattern and manner of throw. Additionally, Skipper refrained from such attempts whenever the floor boss was watching the game. More importantly, the tapes show that Skipper's method of play was aided by a confederate who sought to block the dealer's view of the sliding die.

Skipper presented no defense to the charges brought against him, choosing instead to challenge the constitutionality of the criminal statutes under which he was charged. The jury convicted Skipper of two counts of cheating at gaming and this appeal followed.

DISCUSSION

Skipper's sole argument on appeal is that NRS 465.070(7) and NRS 465.083 are unconstitutionally vague because they fail to alert persons of ordinary intelligence that dice sliding constitutes criminal conduct. The Due Process Clause contained in the Fourteenth Amendment to the United States Constitution prohibits states from holding an individual " 'criminally responsible for conduct which he could not reasonably understand to be proscribed.' " Sheriff v. Martin, 99 Nev. 336, 339, 662 P.2d 634, 636 (1983) (quoting United States v. Harris, 347 U.S. 612, 617-18, 74 S.Ct. 808, 812, 98 L.Ed. 989 (1954)). However, the Due Process Clause does not require an impossible standard of specificity in our penal statutes, and we have earlier held that a statute will not be void for vagueness "if there are well settled and ordinarily understood meanings for the words employed when viewed in the context of the entire statutory provision." Woofter v. O'Donnell, 91 Nev. 756, 762, 542 P.2d 1396, 1400 (1975); see also Sheriff v. Martin, 99 Nev. 336, 339, 662 P.2d 634, 636 (1983). Finally, legislation is presumptively constitutional and Skipper bears the burden of clearly demonstrating that the challenged statutes are invalid. Id. NRS 465.083 makes it unlawful for any person to "cheat" at any gambling game. NRS 465.015 defines "cheat" as "alter[ing] the selection of criteria" that determines either the "result of a game" or "the amount or frequency of payment in a game." We have previously concluded that NRS 465.083 and NRS 465.015 are constitutionally certain as they relate to card crimping, but unconstitutionally vague as they relate to slot machine handle manipulation ("handle popping"). Sheriff v. Martin, 99 Nev. 336, 662 P.2d 634 (1983); Lyons v. State, 105 Nev. 317, 775 P.2d 219 (1989); see also Childs v. State, 107 Nev. 584, 816 P.2d 1079 (1991); Childs v. State, 109 Nev. 1050, 864 P.2d 277 (1993).

In Sheriff v. Martin, 99 Nev. 336, 662 P.2d 634 (1983), Jesse Martin and an accomplice were playing blackjack at the same table when the accomplice was observed crimping cards and aiding Martin's play. The two players were arrested and charged by criminal information with violating NRS 465.083. Id. at 338, 662 P.2d at 636. The district court dismissed the charges against Martin on grounds that the definition of cheating provided by NRS 465.015, on which NRS 465.083 rests, was unconstitutionally vague. After fully discussing the "void for vagueness" doctrine, we concluded that the statute was not vague as applied to Martin's conduct:

> In light of the statutory purpose, we interpret the current cheating statutes to proscribe the alteration of the group of characteristics which identify and define the game in question. The attributes of the game— its established physical characteristics and basic rules—determine the

probabilities of the game's various possible outcomes. Changing those attributes to affect those probabilities is a criminal act . . . .

Thus, if a player or dealer deceitfully alters the identifying characteristics or attributes of a game with the intent to deprive another of money or property by affecting the otherwise established probabilities of the game's various outcomes, he or she is guilty of cheating within the meaning of NRS 465.015 and NRS 465.083.

Id. at 341, 662 P.2d at 637-38.

In Lyons, the defendant was arrested for manipulating the handles of vulnerable slot machines. We noted that NRS 465.015 extends to "knowing, purposeful, unlawful conduct designed to alter the criteria that determines the outcome of any lawful gambling activity," and thus proscribes, in addition to card crimping, the use of "mirrors, confederates, electronic equipment, magnets, tools or other devices." We also concluded that gifted patrons who simply exploit their skills or play of the game (e.g., card counting or serendipitously observing the dealer's cards) in hopes of altering the usual criteria of play do not run afoul of the statute. 105 Nev. at 321, 775 P.2d at 221. We then held that handle popping, which neither damages nor mechanically alters a slot machine, and which is discoverable by an innocent novice, is within the latter category.

Skipper assumes, without meaningful discussion, that Lyons and its progeny limit our holding in Martin and control the disposition of this case. We are constrained to disagree because of the expressly narrow application of Lyons and the distinct differences between handle popping and die sliding. A "handle popper" alters no mechanism in the machine, and merely adopts a handle pulling methodology that summons the best advantages to the player that the mechanical conditions of the slot machine will provide. On the other hand, a dice slider uses a methodology of play that is based upon a purposefully orchestrated combination of factors designed to change the nature of play through affirmative acts of cheating and deception. For example, as noted above, Skipper utilized an accomplice to obscure the dealer's vision of the table while Skipper purposely engaged in sliding the dice.

The game of craps understandably involves players who throw the dice in accordance with the rules of play. The rules of play require the "roll" of the dice, thus resulting in the dice either tumbling or bouncing off the end of the table as a result of the player's throw. The evidence adduced at trial indicated that craps dealers are trained to call a "no roll" unless the dice are thrown in the manner described. Thus players who may accidently slide the dice simply have their play nullified by the dealer's call. Skipper, however, sought to prevent the dealer from detecting and invalidating his method of play by utilizing a confederate to obscure the dealer's vision. In effect, Skipper was blindfolding the dealer while placing the dice on the table in a winning combination. This method of altering the elements of chance clearly constitutes cheating. Innocent players would not engage in this type of deceptive, manipulated play.

NRS 465.083 and NRS 465.015 have clear and certain application to those who attempt to supplant elements of chance with surreptitious conduct that alters both the nature of the game and the criteria for winning. A skilled dice slider such as Skipper, surreptitiously and contrary to the rules of the game, alters the probable outcome of a throw and drastically increases the chances of winning certain types of bets on the craps table.

According to the standard of law enunciated in Martin, Skipper is guilty of cheating within the meaning of NRS 465.015 and NRS 465.083. Skipper deceitfully altered an integral attribute of the game in affecting the otherwise established probabilities of its various outcomes. However, unlike the dice slider, a "handle popper" does not alter the physical characteristics of the game (slot machine) or violate any established or defined rule of play. See Lyons, 105 Nev. at 322, 775 P.2d at 222.

Finally, we conclude that persons of average intelligence who play the game of craps in Nevada will have no difficulty understanding that a surreptitious manipulation of the dice contrary to the rules of the game, in order to alter its outcome, constitutes an act of cheating as defined in NRS 465.015 and proscribed as a criminal act under NRS 465.083. In light of our ruling, it is unnecessary to discuss the application of NRS 465.070(7) to the instant case.

For the reasons discussed above, the judgments of conviction entered by the district court are affirmed.

VAN v. GRAND CASINOS OF MISSISSIPPI, INC.
767 So. 2d 1014 (Miss. 2000)

SMITH, Justice.

STATEMENT OF THE CASE

This case comes on appeal from the Circuit Court of Harrison County, First Judicial District, where Circuit Judge John H. Whitfield granted summary judgment in favor of defendants Grand Casinos of Mississippi, Inc. and Bruce Loprete in this action for malicious prosecution.

STATEMENT OF FACTS

On March 19, 1997, Cong Vo Van ("Cong"), Ut Thi Nguyen ("Ut"), Lan Thi Tran ("Lan"), and Minh Hoang Van ("Minh") collectively the plaintiffs filed an action for malicious prosecution against Grand Casinos of Mississippi, Inc. ("Grand Casinos") and Bruce Loprete ("Loprete") in the Harrison County Circuit Court. Minh and Lan, his wife, were arrested on July 24, 1993, and August 2, 1993, respectively, on charges of cheating at a gambling game in violation of Miss.Code Ann. § 75-76-301(b) and § 75-76-307 (1993). Minh and Lan were employed as card dealers at Grand Casinos located in Gulfport, Mississippi. Both administered playing cards at the mini baccarat tables. Cong and Ut, the parents of Minh, were arrested on August 18, 1993, on charges of participating in a common plan or scheme to cheat at a gambling game in violation of Miss.Code Ann. § 75-76-301 and § 75-76-307 (1993).

On July 13, 1993, video surveillance recorded Cong and Ut sitting at a mini baccarat table at which Lan was dealing. The cameras recorded Lan allegedly deviate from the established card-shuffling policy enforced by Grand Casinos.

During this time, the mini baccarat players seated at Lan's table, including Cong and Ut, won eleven consecutive games. Prior to Lan's deviation in shuffling, video surveillance revealed sporadic betting patterns by the players. However, during the winning span, the players' wagers greatly increased resulting in a loss to Grand Casinos in excess of $40,000. Lan was later filmed on July 20, 1993, allegedly utilizing a similar "false shuffling" technique.

On July 19, 1993, video surveillance captured Minh allegedly digress from the established card-shuffling policy at a mini baccarat table. As a result, the mini baccarat players seated at Minh's table, including Cong and Ut, won seven consecutive games. Again, the players' wagers greatly increased during this time in relation to the wagers placed prior to the unusual shuffling technique exhibited by Minh. As a result of these seven wins, Grand Casinos paid the players over $15,000.

A preliminary hearing was conducted, and indictments were returned against all plaintiffs by a Harrison County grand jury. However, on March 26, 1996, the Harrison County Circuit Court dismissed with prejudice the indictments for failure of the State to provide a speedy trial. Cong, Ut, Lan, and Minh subsequently filed this malicious prosecution action against Grand Casinos and Loprete, director of surveillance at Grand Casinos. Grand Casinos and Loprete filed a motion for summary judgment, which was granted by order of the circuit court on the ground that the dismissal of the prior criminal charges against Cong, Ut, Lan, and Minh on speedy trial grounds was not a "favorable termination" necessary to support a civil action for malicious prosecution. Cong, Ut, Lan, and Minh appealed this determination, and this Court reversed the order of the circuit court, holding that a dismissal of criminal charges on constitutional grounds is a "favorable termination" which would support a subsequent action for malicious prosecution. Van v. Grand Casinos of Miss., Inc., 724 So.2d 889, 893 (Miss.1998) ("Van I"). The case was remanded to the trial court for proceedings consistent with the Court's opinion. Id.

On February 24, 1999, Grand Casinos and Loprete filed a second motion for summary judgment, arguing that there was no issue of fact regarding whether Grand Casinos and Loprete lacked probable cause for instigating the criminal proceedings. The plaintiffs filed a Motion to Dismiss the Defendants' Motion for Summary Judgment. On June 7, 1999, subsequent to a hearing on the matter, the trial court again granted summary judgment in favor of Grand Casinos and Loprete. After the trial court granted the plaintiffs' Motion to Reopen Time for Appeal pursuant to M.R.A.P. 4(h) on August 10, 1999, the plaintiffs filed a notice of appeal on August 13, 1999 . . . .

DISCUSSION OF LAW

The plaintiffs argue that the trial court improperly granted summary judgment on the probable cause issue because there is an issue of fact as to whether the defendants lacked probable cause to instigate criminal proceedings against the plaintiffs. The tort of malicious prosecution must fail where a party has probable cause to institute an action. Allstate Ins. Co. v. Moulton, 464 So.2d 507, 510 (Miss.1985). To establish probable cause there must be a concurrence of (1) an honest belief in the guilt of the person accused and

(2) reasonable grounds for such belief. C & C Trucking Co. v. Smith, 612 So.2d at 1100 (citing Strong v. Nicholson, 580 So.2d at 1294). "Probable cause is determined from the facts apparent to the observer when prosecution is initiated. When the facts are undisputed, it is the function of the court to determine whether or not probable cause existed." Moon v. Condere Corp., 690 So.2d at 1195 (quoting Owens v. Kroger Co., 430 So.2d at 846). "So long as the instigator of the action 'reasonably believed he [had] a good chance of establishing [his case] to the satisfaction of the court or the jury[,]' he is said to have had probable cause." Id. at 1195 (quoting Presley v. South Cent. Bell Tel. Co., 684 F.Supp. 1397, 1399 (S.D.Miss.1988)).

The defendants argue that they had probable cause to institute the proceedings against the plaintiffs. The evidence submitted by the defendants in support of their motion for summary judgment consisted of the affidavit of Bruce Loprete, who was employed in the surveillance department at the Gulfport Grand Casino at the time the alleged incidents occurred. The affidavit states that Loprete based his belief that he had probable cause to suspect that the plaintiffs were involved in a "shuffling scam" on the following factors: (1) On July 13, 1993, surveillance cameras recorded Lan "breaking the established card shuffling policy and procedure at the mini baccarat table." Prior to the "false shuffle" performed by Lan, the betting pattern of the players was sporadic. After the "false shuffle," the players won eleven consecutive times, resulting in a loss to the casino in excess of $40,000. (2) Two of the players at the table during this time were Cong and Ut, parents of Minh. (3) Lan was also filmed on July 20, 1993, utilizing a similar "false shuffle." (4) On July 19, 1993, the surveillance cameras recorded Minh breaking the established card shuffling procedure, after which the players won seven consecutive times, resulting in a loss to the casino in excess of $15,000. (5) Again, Cong and Ut were two of the players at the table during this time. (6) On July 24, 1993, officials from the Gulfport Police Department and Mississippi Gaming Commission viewed the surveillance tapes. (7) Loprete also met with Jim Slade, an investigator with the Isle of Capri Casino in Biloxi, Mississippi, to discuss mini-baccarat false shuffles which occurred at the Isle of Capri. Loprete states that after reviewing the surveillance tape from the Isle of Capri, Lan and Minh were identified as being players during the "false shuffle scam" at the Isle of Capri. (8) On August 17, 1993, affidavits against the plaintiffs were signed by members of the Gulfport Police Department, and warrants for the arrest of the plaintiffs were subsequently issued. The affidavit of Detective Lt. Steve Barnes is included as support for the defendants' motion for summary judgment. (9) On November 18, 1993, a preliminary hearing was conducted, and the plaintiffs were bound over to the grand jury. On July 24, 1994, indictments were returned against the plaintiffs by the grand jury.

The plaintiffs argue that the defendants should have investigated further prior to instigating criminal action. This Court has stated that "where a reasonable person would investigate further before instituting a proceeding, the failure to do so is an absence of probable cause." Junior Food Stores, Inc. v. Rice, 671 So.2d 67, 74 (Miss.1996) (citing Benjamin v. Hooper Elec. Supply Co., Inc., 568 So.2d 1182, 1191 (Miss.1990)). To determine whether a reasonable person would have investigated further before instituting criminal proceedings against the plaintiffs, this Court need only look at the facts available to the defendants at the time they caused the arrest of the plaintiffs. See id. at 74.

In support of their claim that the defendants failed to investigate properly prior to initiating criminal proceedings, the plaintiffs urge this Court to consider its opinions in Junior Food Stores, Inc. v. Rice, 671 So.2d 67 (Miss.1996), and Nassar v. Concordia Rod & Gun Club, Inc., 682 So.2d 1035 (Miss.1996). In Junior Food Stores, Rice filed a complaint against Junior Food Stores (hereinafter "Super Stop") alleging malicious prosecution by Super Stop for causing an affidavit to be issued charging him with grand larceny. The district manager of Super Stop had Rice, an employee of the store, arrested after money from the store was stolen subsequent to Rice's locking up the store for the night. Super Stop argued it had probable cause to institute proceedings against Rice because Rice failed a polygraph test and because Rice worked the last shift prior to the disappearance of the money. 671 So.2d at 75. However, the evidence showed that other employees, who were not given polygraph tests, possessed keys to the store as well. The grand jury found insufficient evidence to indict Rice. In Rice's action for malicious prosecution, the jury returned a verdict for Rice, and Super Stop appealed. This Court found that the jury reasonably could have believed that Rice had done no wrong and that there was no reasonable basis for a belief to the contrary. Id. at 75.

Junior Food Stores is distinguishable from the case at hand. The sole piece of evidence against Rice was the polygraph test, which was admittedly subject to erroneous conclusions and inadmissible as evidence. Id. at 74-75. The Court noted that there was no witness produced who could implicate Rice in the theft and that Super Stop had not sought the advice of an attorney before instituting criminal proceedings. Id. at 74. Even the grand jury found insufficient evidence to issue an indictment against Rice. In the case at hand, the grand jury found sufficient evidence to indict the plaintiffs. Also, though Loprete's conclusions regarding the plaintiffs' "shuffling scam" are not based on the testimony of an eye witness, they are based on something perhaps even more reliable than an eye witness—that is, a video surveillance camera. Furthermore, Loprete did not immediately institute criminal proceedings against the plaintiffs. Rather, he viewed the tapes, [and then] viewed them again with members of the Gulfport Police Department and the Mississippi Gaming Commission. Also, he met with an investigator with the Isle of Capri Casino in Biloxi, Mississippi, to discuss mini-baccarat false shuffles that occurred at the Isle of Capri. After reviewing the surveillance tape from the Isle of Capri, Loprete identified Lan and Minh as players during the "false shuffle scam" at the Isle of Capri. Clearly, Loprete based his suspicions on much more than the store manager in Junior Food Stores, and his investigation was certainly more extensive.

The plaintiffs also cite to Nassar v. Concordia Rod & Gun Club, Inc., 682 So.2d 1035 (Miss.1996), for the assertion that the defendants should have investigated further before instigating criminal proceedings. In Nassar, Canady, after hearing a gunshot come from the levee near his home, proceeded to investigate the shot and found a vehicle on the levee containing two white males. Though Canady asked for the names of the occupants of the vehicle, only the driver disclosed his identity. In an effort to determine the identity of the passenger in the vehicle, Canady spoke with the caretaker of a neighboring hunting club who told Canady that Nassar often "road around" with the driver of the vehicle and that he "bet that it was them." On this information alone, Canady filed an affidavit against Nassar. After filing the affidavit, Canady discovered that Nassar was not the occupant of the vehicle. When Canady attempted to have the charges dismissed, he found that they had already been dismissed.

In Nassar's subsequent malicious prosecution action, Nassar offered, in order to refute Canady's claim that he had probable cause to institute the criminal proceedings, the testimony of two persons questioned by Canady regarding the identity of the second occupant of the vehicle. Those persons testified that they told Canady that though they thought the occupant might have been Nassar, but, at the same time, expressed reservations regarding the identity of the occupant. This Court held that Canady did not have an objectively reasonable basis to have probable cause to file the charges against Nassar. Id. at 1046. The Court noted that prior to filing the charges, Canady and the others knew where Nassar resided and could be located, but Canady did not attempt to "eye-ball" Nassar to verify his suspicions. Id. at 1037. The Court stated that, given this knowledge, Canady should have tried to locate Nassar to confirm his identity prior to filing the charges. Id. at 1046.

The plaintiffs' reliance on Nassar is misplaced. In the case at hand, Loprete viewed the tape from a video surveillance camera, from which he concluded that Minh and Lan had shuffled the cards in an irregular fashion resulting in large losses to the casino. At the time Loprete's affidavit was filed, the tape was viewed by members of the Gulfport Police Department prior to the officers' filing affidavits against the plaintiffs. Loprete also viewed the tape with members of the Mississippi Gaming Commission and met with an investigator from the Isle of Capri to discuss mini-baccarat false shuffles at the Isle of Capri. After reviewing the surveillance tape from the Isle of Capri, Loprete identified Lan and Minh as players during the "false shuffle scam" at the Isle of Capri. Again, Loprete's investigation was certainly more extensive and based on more reliable information than that of Canady in Nassar.

The plaintiffs complain that the case against them was not supported by the affidavits of more eye witnesses to the irregular shuffling and argue that there was nothing irregular about their shuffling of the cards. It is difficult to imagine a more thorough investigation of the plaintiffs' activities. Not only did Loprete base his suspicions on a video surveillance tape of the "false shuffling" tactics of Minh and Lan, Minh's parents were identified as players at the table. Loprete talked to members of the Gulfport Police Department as well as members of the Gaming Commission and an investigator at another casino where Minh and Lan had allegedly participated in a similar scam. In fact, while the case against Nassar was immediately dismissed, a grand jury ultimately found sufficient evidence to indict the plaintiffs in the case at hand.

The plaintiffs complain that the affidavit of Loprete is insufficient, standing alone, to demonstrate probable cause, and argue rather that the casino should have included affidavits of other witnesses to the incidents. They contend that the shuffling of the cards was overseen by floor supervisors and argue that the Casino should have obtained the affidavits of the floor supervisors as well as Loprete. The plaintiffs, however, have offered no testimony of a floor supervisor that they were not shuffling the cards irregularly. The plaintiffs also complain that though members of the Gaming Commission and Gulfport Police Department viewed the surveillance tapes, none filed affidavits verifying Loprete's interpretation of the tapes. The plaintiffs, however, offer no evidence that the members of the Gaming Commission and the Gulfport Police Department did not agree with Loprete's interpretation of the tapes. In fact, members of the Gulfport Police Department, after viewing the tapes, issued affidavits against the plaintiffs charging them with willfully, unlawfully and feloniously conspiring to alter and manipulate associated gaming equipment.

The evidence offered by the defendants was sufficient to show that the investigation conducted led to the honest and reasonable conclusion that the plaintiffs were guilty of the crime charged. Again, this Court has explained that once the absence of genuine material issues has been shown by the movant, the burden of rebuttal falls upon the non-moving party. Wilbourn v. Stennett, Wilkinson & Ward, 687 So.2d at 1213. The plaintiffs thus must produce specific facts showing that there is a genuine material issue for trial. Id. (citing M.R.C.P. 56(e); Fruchter v. Lynch Oil Co., 522 So.2d at 199). Specifically, the plaintiffs must support their claim that the defendants lacked probable cause in instituting criminal proceedings by more than a mere scintilla of colorable evidence. Id. at 1214 (citing Anderson v. Liberty Lobby, Inc., 477 U.S. at 248, 106 S.Ct. at 2510). Rather, they must produce evidence upon which a fair-minded jury could find that probable cause did not exist. Id. The plaintiffs did not produce such evidence.

The only evidence offered by the plaintiffs to rebut the defendants' claim that Grand Casino and Loprete had probable cause to institute criminal proceedings are the affidavits of Minh, Lan, and Cong in which they state that the casino was required to file criminal charges against someone in order to collect for their losses from the insurance company and that they, as Vietnamese, were mere scapegoats for the casino. The plaintiffs do not, however, attach a copy of the alleged insurance policy as required by Rule 56(e). They also assert that there were other witnesses, such as floor managers, who witnessed the fact that they did not shuffle the cards irregularly. However, they do not identify these floor managers or include affidavits or any indication that they have been interviewed. The plaintiffs assert that Loprete's interpretation of the surveillance tapes is merely subjective and incorrect. They offer, however, no evidence that Loprete's interpretation was incorrect. They argue that the jury should be allowed to view the video surveillance tape to determine whether the plaintiffs were in fact shuffling the cards irregularly. They urge this Court to view the video. They have failed, however, to offer into evidence a copy of the video at any point since the inception of their action.

It is not the duty of this Court to determine the guilt or innocence of the plaintiffs of the crime charged. It is only to look at the information available to the defendants at the time criminal proceedings were instigated to determine whether the defendants honestly and reasonably believed in the guilt of the plaintiffs. C & C Trucking Co. v. Smith, 612 So.2d at 1100 (citing Strong

v. Nicholson, 580 So.2d at 1294). The evidence offered reveals no dispute regarding the information available to the defendants at the time criminal proceedings were initiated. The question of probable cause was thus properly a determination of law for the trial judge. The plaintiffs offered no evidence, save unsubstantiated assertions, to rebut the defendants' evidence as to their honest and reasonable beliefs at the time they initiated criminal proceedings. The defendants investigated the matter in a reasonable, complete and diligent manner.

CONCLUSION

Based on the evidence put forth by the parties, a fair minded jury could not conclude that the criminal proceedings were instigated without probable cause. The trial court did not err in granting summary judgment in favor of the defendants. Therefore, the judgment of the trial court is affirmed.

BANKS, Presiding Justice, dissenting.

I respectfully dissent because there is a material factual dispute as to the "false shuffle" allegedly made by Lan Thi Tran.

Here the trial court judge was ultimately presented with an affidavit of a Grand Casino employee and some casino videotapes. Bruce Loprete, the employee of the Grand Casino, stated in his affidavit that Lan Thi Tran broke established shuffling policy and procedure when she performed a "false shuffle." However, Loprete's affidavit did not identify when this "false shuffle" occurred. Moreover, Grand Casino did not enter the established card shuffling policy into evidence. A close look at the videotape does not reveal anything out of the ordinary.

Lan Thi Tran stated in her affidavit that she did not shuffle the cards in a "false" manner. Likewise, Minh Hoang Van stated that he did not "false" shuffle the cards. Lan Thi Tran noted that her supervisor and several others could see her every move. She further stated that she dealt the cards as directed by her supervisor.

Cong Vo Van also stated via affidavit that he saw the videotape of Lan shuffling the cards. Cong Vo Van stated that he was an experienced baccarat player, and Lan did nothing wrong.

With these conflicting affidavits and a videotape that does not clearly show an improper shuffle, the trial court granted a summary judgment. This was error. The affidavits alone establish genuine issues of material fact. Was there a false shuffle? Was there sufficient cause to believe that a false shuffle occurred to the extent that such a belief amounted to probable cause to institute a criminal prosecution? These are questions which may not be resolved on this record to pretermit jury consideration.

The majority holds that there was no dispute as to a genuine issue of material fact here. I disagree and would reverse and remand for a trial.

Notes

1. The reference in *Skipper* to "crimping" one's cards refers to situations in which two people are playing at a table and one of them slightly bends,

or "crimps," her cards so that both players can see them. As *Skipper* explains, this practice was held to be illegal in *Sheriff v. Martin*, 662 P.2d 634 (Nev. 1983).

2. In *City of Las Vegas v. Eighth Judicial District Court of the State*, 59 P.3d 477 (Nev. 2002), the Nevada Supreme Court struck down as unduly vague a municipal ordinance that made it a misdemeanor for any person to "annoy or molest" a minor. In its decision, the court specifically abrogated *Anderson*, as well as all "other decisions of this court [that] indicate that a facial vagueness challenge may only be appropriate where First Amendment concerns are implicated . . . ." How is this development likely to affect Nevada's casinos?

3. As *Van* makes clear, it is possible to find cheating by specific casino employees. As entities, however, licensed casinos are quite honest, for two reasons: (a) the odds give them a sufficient natural advantage, and (b) the potential loss of their licenses acts as a powerful deterrent. For a rare example of an entire casino being sued for cheating, *see Kelly v. First Astri Corp.*, 84 Cal. Rptr. 2d 810 (Ct. App. 1999) (alleged use of marked cards at blackjack tables).

4. For a further looking at swindling in casinos, *see, e.g.*, Donna Pinion, *Cheating at Blackjack: The Case of the Barthelme Brothers*, 4 Gaming L. Rev. 127 (2000) (describing the life and times of Frederick and Steven Barthelme, a flamboyant pair of card players who were indicted for cheating a Mississippi casino; the charges were later dropped for lack of evidence).

Problem 27

To prove the defendant had cheated while playing blackjack, the state introduced the casino's surveillance videotapes. Because the images were hard to see, the judge allowed the jury to watch them a second time using a magnifying glass. By doing so, did she commit reversible error? *See Dumas v. State*, 806 So. 2d 1009 (Miss. 2000).

G. COMPULSIVE GAMBLERS

RAHMANI v. RESORTS INTERNATIONAL HOTEL, INC.
20 F. Supp. 2d 932 (E.D. Va. 1998),
aff'd mem., 182 F.3d 909 (4th Cir. 1999)

ELLIS, District Judge.

In this unusual diversity case, a Virginia plaintiff hopes to use her home state's laws against gambling to help her recover from New Jersey casinos the large gambling losses she incurred there. Plaintiff Najia Rahmani alleges that defendants Boardwalk Regency Corporation ("Boardwalk") and Resorts International Hotel, Inc. ("Resorts") induced her to travel to New Jersey and squander her money in their casinos. She further alleges that her acceptance of such inducements created a contract between the parties, but that these contracts were void as a matter of Virginia law. She therefore seeks restitution of all monies she has lost gambling in defendants' New Jersey casinos over the past thirteen years. For the reasons that follow, plaintiff's effort fails; the law sensibly affords no remedy in these circumstances.

I.

Rahmani is a Virginia citizen, while defendants Resorts and Boardwalk are New Jersey corporations that own and operate gambling casinos. Resorts owns and operates Resorts International Casino, in Atlantic City, New Jersey, while Boardwalk owns and operates Caesars, another gambling establishment in Atlantic City, New Jersey.

Rahmani's first experience with casino gambling occurred in 1984 when she visited Resorts. During that visit, Resorts employees noticed that Rahmani lost a considerable sum of money, and that she appeared to be a wealthy woman. As a result of these observations, Resorts repeatedly contacted Rahmani in Virginia over the course of the next thirteen years and induced her to return to Atlantic City to gamble. Boardwalk became aware of Rahmani's gambling habits in 1990, and it, too, began to encourage her to visit Atlantic City. Specifically, Resorts and Boardwalk called Rahmani and sent her letters, promising that if she agreed to come to the casino to gamble, Resorts or Boardwalk would send limousines to transport her and her friends and family to New Jersey, where she would be provided free hotel accommodations, meals and entertainment. These solicitations, which continued through November 1997, largely succeeded, for according to Rahmani, soon after her introduction to casino gambling in 1984, she became addicted to the activity, i.e., she became a compulsive gambler. Over approximately a thirteen year period, Rahmani claims to have lost over $3.8 million while gambling at Resorts and Caesars.

Rahmani filed suit on February 11, 1998, arguing that her agreements with Resorts and Boardwalk were void under Virginia law and seeking rescission of the contracts and restitution of the money she gambled and lost at the casinos over the thirteen-year period. She alleged other state law claims as well, including negligence and "unlawful harassment." On April 4, 1998, Boardwalk's Motion to Dismiss was granted; on July 17, 1998, Resorts' Motion to Dismiss was granted, and Counts I, II, III, V, and VI were dismissed with prejudice in their entirety. Count IV, a forgery claim, was dismissed without prejudice to allow Rahmani leave to amend her Complaint solely on this count, as requested by Rahmani's counsel. This memorandum opinion sets forth the reasons for the dismissals.

II.

As this is a diversity case, Virginia's choice-of-law rules govern. In this regard, Virginia adheres to the traditional First Restatement rule for contracts cases, namely that the laws of the place of contracting govern the validity of a contract. Under the traditional First Restatement rule, the place of contracting is determined by the location of the last act necessary to complete the contract. The threshold inquiry, therefore, is where the last act necessary to complete the contracts occurred, and thus where the contracts between Rahmani and the defendants were formed.

To determine where the last act necessary to complete the contracts occurred, it is important to identify with some precision just what the contracts were. In this regard, Rahmani alleges that the contracts consisted of the defendants' promise of limousines and free accommodations (the offer) and her agreement to travel to Atlantic City to enjoy these amenities and gamble (the acceptance). Accordingly, under Rahmani's theory, the last act necessary to form the contracts, namely Rahmani's acceptance of the offers, occurred in Virginia. Thus, Rahmani argues, Virginia law should apply.

Boardwalk and Resorts counter by arguing that common sense suggests that the contracts were formed not in Virginia, but in New Jersey when Rahmani placed her bets at the casino gambling table. Resorts attacks Rahmani's characterization of the contracts on the ground that such contracts could not have been enforced under Virginia law for they would lack the mutuality required for formation of a valid contract in Virginia. Thus, if after arriving in Atlantic City and enjoying Resorts' hospitality, Rahmani had decided not to gamble, Resorts would not have been able to enforce such a contract under Virginia law. Both defendants argue that the only contracts between the casinos and Rahmani arose when Rahmani placed her bets at the casino gambling tables in New Jersey, and thus New Jersey law governs.

Although not free from doubt, the argument for application of New Jersey law is more persuasive. No mutually enforceable obligations were created until Rahmani placed a bet at a New Jersey gambling table.

Given that New Jersey law governs, Rahmani's claims for rescission and restitution plainly fail. In New Jersey, "[c]asino gambling has been legal . . . since 1977, and the casino industry is purely a creature of statute." Hakimoglu v. Trump Taj Mahal Assoc., 876 F.Supp. 625, 633 (D.N.J.1994), aff'd 70 F.3d 291 (3d Cir.1995). New Jersey's casino industry is governed exclusively by New Jersey's Casino Control Act, N.J.S.A. §§ 5:12-1 to -210 (1997) ("CCA"), which provides a "regulatory scheme [that] is both comprehensive and minutely elaborate." Knight v. City of Margate, 86 N.J. 374, 431 A.2d 833 (1981); Hakimoglu, 876 F.Supp. at 631. The Casino Control Commission establishes the rules governing the operation of casinos, including setting the odds for each game, odds that always favor the casino. See Tose v. Greate Bay Hotel & Casino Inc., 819 F.Supp. 1312, 1319 (D.N.J.1993). More importantly, the CCA specifically "permits casinos to offer free food, lodging, transportation and other inducements to potential customers" as part of "junkets" that casinos may offer to their patrons. See Tose, 819 F.Supp. at 1320 n.11 (describing a junket as the provision of "complimentary transportation, food, lodging and entertainment based on [a] person's propensity to gamble").

Under New Jersey law, therefore, the casino gambling contracts are valid. Not only does the CCA legalize casino gambling generally, it specifically recognizes and authorizes the very activity Rahmani complains of, namely the practice of offering junkets to people with a propensity to gamble for the purpose of encouraging them to travel to New Jersey to do so. See N.J.S.A. 5:12-29 and 5:12-102 (defining junkets and setting forth conditions for junkets). Accordingly, under New Jersey law, the contracts are valid and enforceable, and thus Rahmani cannot sue for their rescission or for restitution.

III.

Given the closeness of the choice of law issue, it is worth noting that Rahmani fares no better under Virginia law. To begin with, it is readily apparent that Virginia affords Rahmani no contract remedies. If, as Rahmani asserts, the last act necessary to the contract occurred in Virginia, the contract created, putting aside the absence of mutuality, would be deemed a gambling contract under Virginia law. Such a contract, of course, is void under Virginia law; it is "a complete nullity, one that has no legal force or binding effect." Kennedy v. Annandale Boys Club, Inc., 221 Va. 504, 272 S.E.2d 38, 39 (Va. 1980). Further, "[i]t is one which never had any legal existence or effect, and one which cannot in any manner have life breathed into it." Id. As gambling contracts are illegal or immoral contracts in Virginia, "[Virginia] law simply leaves the litigants in the plight in which they have seen fit to place themselves without undertaking to balance benefits or burdens." Phillip Levy & Co. v. Davis, 115 Va. 814, 80 S.E. 791, 792 (Va.1914) ("[T]he law . . . will neither lend its aid to enforce [the illegal or immoral] contract while executory nor to rescind it and recover the consideration parted with when executed."). See also Higgins v. McCrea, 116 U.S. 671, 6 S.Ct. 557, 29 L.Ed. 764 (1886) (" 'No court will lend its aid to a man who founds his cause of action upon an immoral or illegal act.' "). Given that the contracts defined by Rahmani are a nullity under Virginia law, it follows that she cannot sue for rescission or restitution; under Virginia law, she is simply left "in the plight in which [she has] seen fit to place [herself]." Phillip Levy, 80 S.E. at

Nor does Virginia law afford Rahmani any statutory remedies for the losses she incurred at casino gambling tables in New Jersey. To be sure, Virginia's statutes reflect an unambiguous hostility to gambling. Thus, § 11-15 of the Virginia Code provides for the return of gambling losses sought within the three month statutory limit. But § 11-15 cannot be applied to gambling losses that occur lawfully outside Virginia. A state cannot invalidate the lawful statutes of another state or penalize activity that lawfully occurs in another state. Put another way, the Virginia General Assembly has no power to invalidate lawful gambling taking place wholly outside of Virginia. See, e.g., Edgar v. MITE Corp., 457 U.S. 624, 642-43, 102 S.Ct. 2629, 73 L.Ed.2d 269 (1982) (noting that the Commerce Clause precludes application of state statutes to commerce taking place wholly outside of the state's borders). Were this not so, absurd results would follow. If this statute could provide a basis for relief from a gaming contract entered into and fully performed in another state, then it would wreak havoc on the established—and legal—gambling industries across the country. Any gambling loser from Virginia could simply invoke § 11-15 and thereby absolve herself of any losses she suffered in Atlantic City, Las Vegas, or any other city where gambling is legal. Indeed, were § 11-15 to permit this, it would have the perverse effect of encouraging Virginians to gamble, albeit out-of-state. Therefore, even under Virginia law, Rahmani has neither a common law contractual basis nor a statutory basis for her claims for the return of her gambling losses.

For the foregoing reasons, Count I (rescission and restitution) and Count II (equitable accounting) must be dismissed.

IV.

Rahmani also asserted a number of other claims. In Count III, Rahmani alleged that the defendants "negligently permitted and encouraged [her to] continue to gamble even though they knew, or should have known, that she was a compulsive gambler." Under Virginia's choice of law rules, tort claims are governed by the law of the place of the wrong. The place of the wrong or injury is the place where the injury was suffered, not where the tortious act took place. Here, the alleged injuries are gambling losses that occurred in New Jersey, and hence New Jersey law governs this tort claim.

Rahmani has adduced no New Jersey law to support her suggestion that Boardwalk and Resorts had a legal duty to stop her from gambling. To the contrary, there is New Jersey case authority suggesting that no such duty exists. See Hakimoglu, 876 F.Supp. at 625 (holding that casino has no legal duty to prevent intoxicated gambler from continuing to gamble). Nor is it arguable that such a duty is a "predictable extension of common law tort principles" under New Jersey law. See Hakimoglu, 876 F.Supp. at 633. Nothing in the CCA, which is manifestly comprehensive, suggests that the New Jersey legislature intended to create such a duty. See id.; see also Miller v. Zoby, 250 N.J.Super. 568, 595 A.2d 1104, 1110 (N.J.Super.Ct.App.Div.) (holding that breadth of issues covered under CCA precluded creation of tort cause of action for violation of the Act), cert. denied, 127 N.J. 553, 606 A.2d 366 (1991). Instead, the CCA specifically permits casinos to rely on individuals' propensity to gamble. See Tose, 819 F.Supp. at 1320 n.11; N.J.S.A. 5:12-29.

Count V alleges that defendants harassed Rahmani "by persistently and continuously soliciting" her business. Rahmani does not provide any relevant authority holding that either New Jersey or Virginia recognizes such a tort. Thus, this count must be dismissed.

Finally, in Count VI Rahmani alleges that Boardwalk violated two criminal fraud statutes, 18 U.S.C. §§ 1028 and 1546. These statutes do not provide for any private cause of action, and Rahmani suggests no basis for implying a private cause of action under these statutes. Accordingly, this count also must be dismissed.

UNITED STATES v. SCHOLL
166 F.3d 964 (9th Cir. 1998),
cert. denied, 528 U.S. 873 (1999)

RYMER, Circuit Judge.

William L. Scholl appeals his conviction in the district court on four counts of filing false tax returns in violation of 26 U.S.C. § 7206(1) and three counts of structuring currency transactions in violation of 31 U.S.C. § 5324. The government cross-appeals the district court's imposition of sentence. We affirm in each instance.

I

Scholl was a Superior Court Judge in Tucson, Arizona, from 1984 until he was indicted. He was a compulsive gambler who took numerous trips to Las

Vegas to gamble. Throughout the 1980s, he gambled on credit lines established at various casinos. In 1989, he had outstanding balances on credit lines from six different casinos totaling $163,000. In the latter part of 1989 and the beginning of 1990, Scholl settled his outstanding credit line balances, paying a total of $50,000. From that point through 1994, he continued to gamble as a cash player.

Once he became a cash player, Scholl would purchase a cashier's check from his checking account or bank credit line payable to the casino where he was staying. He would deposit the cashier's check in the cage of that casino upon his arrival and draw against his deposit to gamble at various casinos during the trip. After the end of the trip, he would withdraw his deposit in the form of cash and transport the cash back to Tucson. Records were not kept of these withdrawals.

Upon returning to Tucson, Scholl would put the currency into the gun safe at his house. When he went to work, he would take one bundle of $5,000 in his pocket. At lunch time, he would deposit the money into a bank. He was aware that currency forms may be generated when a person deposits more than $10,000 in currency at a bank, and part of the reason he broke up deposits into amounts less than $10,000 in currency was to avoid the preparation of those reports. Scholl made numerous deposits in various accounts that avoided the reporting requirements and, in addition, made sub-$10,000 deposits into a personal credit line that was his main account for gambling.

Scholl's accountant, Ken Silva, had a conversation with Scholl in 1987 in which he told Scholl that both gambling winnings and gambling losses must be reported separately on Scholl's tax return. Scholl's 1987 return reflected "gambling winnings" of $128,680 and an itemized deduction for "gambling losses" of $128,680. In connection with preparation of Scholl's 1988 tax return, Silva asked Scholl if he had any gambling winnings. Scholl responded that he did not have any, or that he had "lost his ass there." Scholl's tax returns for 1990 and 1993 do not reflect any gambling income or losses, and his returns for 1991, 1992, and 1994 reflect only small amounts. In each of those years, the only gambling income reported was gambling income of the type reflected on a Form W-2G, which he was required to file with the IRS.

Scholl testified to his belief that he could "net out" his gambling wins and losses in any particular year and, if losses exceeded wins, nothing needed to be reported on the return. He did not, however, "net out" gambling winnings that were reflected on Forms W-2G.

On December 5, 1995, a grand jury in Tucson, Arizona, returned an indictment charging Scholl with filing false tax returns for the years 1989 through 1994, in violation of 26 U.S.C. § 7206(1) (Counts 1 through 6), and five counts of structuring currency transactions to avoid the Treasury reporting requirements, in violation of 31 U.S.C. § 5324 (Counts 7 through 11). Trial to a jury began September 24, 1996. The court granted Scholl's motion for judgment of acquittal on Count 8. On November 19, the jury found Scholl guilty of counts 2, 3, 4, 6, 7, 9, and 10, but acquitted him on counts 1, 5, and 11. On February 27, 1997, the court sentenced Scholl to five years probation on each count, to run concurrently. Although Casino Market Analysis Center Reports and eyewitnesses indicated that Scholl had substantial unreported winnings, the district court did not find them a sufficiently reliable indicator of tax loss to make a reasonable estimate for purposes of determining Scholl's offense level under the Guidelines.

Scholl timely appeals his conviction. The government cross-appeals from sentence, challenging the district court's failure to calculate Scholl's offense level based on a reasonable estimate of tax loss . . . .

III

Scholl sought to have Dr. Robert Hunter, his expert on compulsive gambling, testify that pathological gamblers have distortions in thinking and "denial," which impact their ability and emotional wherewithal to keep records. He would have testified that compulsive gamblers do not want to keep records because that would force them to confront the reality of losses, which creates too much upheaval. Hunter also would have opined that a pathological gambler is not motivated by money, but believes that the next "big win" will fix their lives.

In a published opinion the district court applied the two-part analysis set out in Daubert v. Merrell Dow Pharmaceuticals, Inc., 509 U.S. 579, 113 S.Ct. 2786, 125 L.Ed.2d 469 (1993). See United States v. Scholl, 959 F.Supp. 1189, 1194 (D.Ariz.1997). The court concluded that a diagnosis of compulsive gambling disorder satisfied the validity prong of Daubert, and ruled that Hunter could testify that Scholl was a compulsive gambler at the time the alleged crimes occurred. However, the court limited Hunter's testimony to the ten diagnostic criteria for pathological gambling set forth on page 618 of the Diagnostic and Statistical Manual of Mental Disorders, Fourth Edition (DSM-IV), and excluded proffered evidence regarding distortion in thinking and denial of the existence of a gambling problem. Distortion and denial are "Associated Descriptive Features" but are not regarded as sufficiently sensitive or specific to be recognized as diagnostic criteria.

The district court also excluded the proffered testimony under Federal Rules of Evidence 402 and 403, noting among other things that Hunter said it was not his opinion that gamblers could not truthfully report on their income tax returns. Hunter did not state that compulsive gamblers have no memory of what occurred when they prepare their tax returns. Accordingly the court ruled that Hunter's opinion on denial was not relevant and could be confusing, inconsistent, and misleading to the jury.

At best, Hunter's opinion would have been that compulsive gambling disorder makes one believe that he has lost more money than he has won—not that it renders one unable to remember what occurred, or unable to enter both winnings and losses on a Form 1040. While Hunter was prepared to testify that Scholl could have misevaluated his winnings and losses and believed he was telling the truth, Hunter also acknowledged that there was no support in the literature for this opinion or for the idea that pathological gamblers cannot truthfully report gambling income. Indeed, Hunter made it clear that it was not his opinion that compulsive gamblers cannot truthfully report income on their tax returns. Thus, evidence that compulsive gamblers are in denial, or that their thinking about gambling in relation to their life is distorted, would not tend to show that Scholl did not believe his tax return to be correct in reporting winnings and losses, or that he did not falsely subscribe to it specifically intending not to report gambling wins and losses.

Thus, as the district court concluded, the proffered opinion on denial is not relevant. In any event, had Hunter been allowed to testify as proffered, his opinion may have been mistaken to mean that Scholl lacked intent to report wins or losses because of his disorder. This conclusion would have been without support either in the scientific community or Hunter's own experience. It would therefore have been misleading and confusing. For these reasons, the district court had discretion under Rules 402 and 403 to limit Hunter's testimony to well-recognized characteristics of compulsive gamblers, and to exclude that portion of his proffered opinion which had slight (if any) relevance, and was both speculative and misleading.

IV

Scholl argues that asking character witnesses whether they had heard that Scholl believed himself to be a compulsive gambler was improper because it had nothing to do with his character and the government had no good faith basis to believe that any of this had been discussed in the relevant community. However, Scholl could not have been prejudiced by this line of questioning because he himself invoked his compulsive gambling disorder in his defense, and his counsel said in opening statement that Scholl never concealed the disorder.

Scholl makes a number of loosely-connected misconduct charges about his own cross-examination. We treat these most summarily, because neither singly nor cumulatively do they constitute misconduct. Scholl opened the door to questions about how compulsive gambling affected his ability to follow the Canon of Judicial Ethics and act as a judge by contending that his gambling had not interfered with his work. Questions regarding when he disclosed his compulsive gambling problems were properly responsive to Scholl's position that he was "open as far as discussing [his] gambling activity." And questions about loans that he failed to disclose on his state financial form were relevant to credibility . . . .

VI

Scholl contends that the court improperly admitted Market Analysis Center (MAC) reports prepared by casinos to establish amounts allegedly won or lost by Scholl and the source of money he allegedly structured. The MAC reports were received under the business records exception to the hearsay rule, Fed.R.Evid. 803(6).

MAC reports are prepared by a floor worker at the casino that serve as estimates of particular gamblers' winnings or losses. Generally, the floor worker keeps track of cash or chips that the gambler has when he arrives at the table, records the average bet made by the gambler, and, to the extent possible, keeps track of how much money the gambler is winning or losing. Typically, this information is used by the casino to determine the amount of complimentary services to give the gambler.

Scholl argues that these reports should be inadmissible under Rule 803(6) because they are rough estimates and insufficiently trustworthy. However, a party need not prove that business records are accurate before they are admitted.

In this case, the government established that the records were made at or near the time of the activity reflected in the records, made by a person with knowledge based on their observations, kept in the ordinary course of business, and made as part of the regular practice of the casinos' operations. Hence, the Rule 803(6) requirements were fulfilled.

The jury was informed that the reports were mere estimates. Given that the records are trustworthy for what they are—estimates—and that Scholl was permitted to elicit testimony going to their questionable accuracy, we conclude that the MAC reports were properly admitted into evidence.

[The remainder of the court's opinion is omitted.]

REISS v. REISS
566 N.Y.S.2d 365 (App. Div.),
appeal dismissed, 577 N.E.2d 1061 (N.Y. 1991),
leave to appeal denied, 594 N.E.2d 940 (N.Y. 1992)

MEMORANDUM BY THE COURT.

In an action for a divorce and ancillary relief, the defendant husband appeals, as limited by his brief, from so much of a judgment of the Supreme Court, Nassau County (DiNoto, J.), entered May 18, 1990, as, after a nonjury trial, (1) dismissed his counterclaim for a divorce on ground of cruel and inhuman treatment, (2) awarded custody of the parties' child to the plaintiff wife, (3) awarded the plaintiff child support in the amount of $634.10 per week, and (4) awarded the plaintiff $7,720.25 in counsel fees and disbursements.

ORDERED that the judgment is modified, on the law and the facts, by (1) deleting so much of the first decretal paragraph thereof as dismissed the defendant's counterclaim for a divorce and substituting therefor a provision awarding him a divorce on the ground of cruel and inhuman treatment, and (2) deleting the third decretal paragraph thereof; as so modified, the judgment is affirmed insofar as appealed from, without costs or disbursements, and the matter is remitted to the Supreme Court, Nassau County, before a different Justice, for a new determination with respect to child support, a determination with respect to the defendant's visitation, and a determination as to equitable distribution of the parties' assets and any other financial issues; and it is further,

ORDERED that, in the interim, the defendant shall pay the plaintiff child support in the sum of $270 per week.

Contrary to the determination of the trial court, we conclude that, in this marriage of short duration, the defendant sufficiently demonstrated a course of conduct by the plaintiff which is harmful to his physical and mental health, rendering cohabitation with the plaintiff unsafe and improper (see, Domestic Relations Law § 170[1]; Brady v. Brady, 64 N.Y.2d 339, 486 N.Y.S.2d 891, 476 N.E.2d 290; Spinelli v. Spinelli, 160 A.D.2d 992, 554 N.Y.S.2d 713; Rieger v. Rieger, 161 A.D.2d 227, 554 N.Y.S.2d 613; McKilligan v. McKilligan, 156

A.D.2d 904, 550 N.Y.S.2d 121; Weilert v. Weilert, 115 A.D.2d 473, 495 N.Y.S.2d 707). Specifically, the record supports the defendant's assertion that the plaintiff's compulsive gambling and its deleterious impact upon the parties' relationship, and, together with certain other acts committed by the plaintiff, created an oppressive and unsafe marital environment, causing the defendant to suffer from, and seek professional treatment for, stress, depression, and certain physical ailments, including chest pains and boils. Since the proof adduced at the trial established that the plaintiff's conduct rendered it impossible and unsafe for the defendant to continue cohabitation with the plaintiff, the Supreme Court erred in denying the defendant a judgment of divorce (cf., McKilligan v. McKilligan, supra).

We are in accord, however, with that portion of the court's order which awarded custody of the parties' 4 1/2 year old son to the plaintiff. It is well settled that the trial court's determination with respect to the issue of child custody is accorded great respect and is not to be lightly set aside, involving as it does, an assessment of the parties' credibility, character and temperament (see, Eschbach v. Eschbach, 56 N.Y.2d 167, 451 N.Y.S.2d 658, 436 N.E.2d 1260; Lenczycki v. Lenczycki, 152 A.D.2d 621, 622-623, 543 N.Y.S.2d 724; Lohmiller v. Lohmiller, 140 A.D.2d 497, 498, 528 N.Y.S.2d 586). At bar, the trial court was in the best position to assess the parties' conflicting assertions, as well as those of their retained experts, in reaching its determination with regard to the best interests of the child. Upon our review of the record, we are unable to say that the court improvidently exercised its discretion in examining the evidence before it and concluding that, under the circumstances presented, the best interests of the child would be served by awarding custody to the plaintiff.

In light of our determination, the matter should be remitted to the Supreme Court, Nassau County, for further proceedings for a new determination as to child support, and determinations with respect to the defendant's visitation, equitable distribution of the parties' assets, and any other financial issues.

Notes

1. The court in *Rahmani* makes several references to *Hakimoglu v. Trump Taj Mahal Associates*, 70 F.3d 291 (3d Cir. 1995). In that case, the plaintiff sought to recover his losses on the ground that the casino had intentionally plied him with free liquor, both to keep him playing and to disorient him. The Third Circuit rejected the argument. Nevertheless, as a matter of social policy, the question remains whether casinos should be allowed to target individuals who, like Hakimoglu and Rahmani, lack the ability to control their spending. *See further* Jeffrey C. Hallam, Comment, *Rolling the Dice: Should Intoxicated Gamblers Recover Their Losses?*, 85 Nw. U. L. Rev. 240 (1990); Jessica L. Krentzman, Note, *Dram Shop Law—Gambling While Intoxicated: The Winner Takes It All?*, 41 Vill. L. Rev. 1255 (1996); Joy Wolfe, Comment, *Casinos and the Compulsive Gambler: Is There a Duty to Monitor the Gambler's Wagers?*, 64 Miss. L.J. 687 (1995). Nevada law deals with the issue as follows:

   A patron's claim of having a mental or behavioral disorder involving gambling:

(a) Is not a defense in an action by a licensee or a person acting on behalf of a licensee to enforce a credit instrument or the debt that the credit instrument represents.

(b) Is not a valid counterclaim to such an action.

Nev. Rev. Stat. § 463.368(6).

2. In addition to free trips and complimentary alcohol, casinos use a variety of other methods to keep patrons playing, including placing ATMs in or close to gaming areas. In 1999 (and again in 2001), Representative John J. LaFalce (D-N.Y.) introduced legislation ("The Gambling ATM and Credit/Debit Card Reform Act") to prohibit this practice, leading to protests by both the banking and casino industries. *See further* Tony Batt, *Legislation Targets ATMs in Casinos*, Las Vegas Rev.-J., Sept. 9, 1999, at 1D, and Marie Harf, *LaFalce Revives Casino ATM Bill*, Am. Banker, July 24, 2001, at 5.

3. As *Scholl* briefly explains, a gambler is permitted to deduct losses on his or her income tax return, but only to the extent of winnings. *See* Stephen A. Zorn, *The Federal Income Tax Treatment of Gambling: Fairness or Obsolete Moralism?*, 49 Tax Law. 1 (1995). Under the bankruptcy code, gambling debts generally are non-dischargeable. *See* Derek A. Wu, *Dischargeability of Credit Card Debt Incurred for Gambling: How to Determine if a Debtor Committed Actionable Fraud Under § 523(a)(2)(A) in Light of* Field v. Mans *and Other Recent Court Pronouncements*, 4 Gaming L. Rev. 13 (2000).

4. Compulsive gamblers like Scholl often try to raise novel criminal defenses. In *United States v. LiButti*, 1994 U.S. Dist. LEXIS 19913 (D.N.J. 1994), for example, the defendant, who was charged with tax evasion, sought to raise a "pathological gambling lifestyle" defense. According to the defendant's experts, he could not pay his taxes because of his need to acquire and surround himself with the trappings of an opulent lifestyle. The judge refused to allow the defense to be heard by the jury. For a further discussion, *see* Ronald J. Rychlak & Julie M. Jarrell, *Compuslive Gambling as a Criminal Defense*, 4 Gaming L. Rev. 333 (2000), and Michael J. Davidson, *"Aces Over Eights"— Pathological Gambling as a Criminal Defense*, Army Law., Nov. 1989, at 11.

5. Although most compulsive gamblers are men (67%), women are not immune from the disease (as *Reiss* illustrates). Whatever their gender, compulsive gamblers destroy both their own lives and those of their loved ones. As a result, every gaming jurisdiction now devotes considerable resources to the prevention and treatment of the condition. In addition, casinos regularly declare that they do not want compulsive gamblers as customers. For a further discussion, *see* Sandra D. Buchanan, *Not Knowing When to Walk Away: Mississippi Identifies and Addresses Compulsive Gambling*, 6 Gaming L. Rev. 325 (2002); Christian Marfels, *Visitor Suicides and Problem Gambling in the Las Vegas Market: A Phenomenon in Search of Evidence*, 2 Gaming L. Rev. 465 (1998); Rachel A. Volberg et al., *Unaffordable Losses: Estimating the Proportion of Gambling Revenues Derived from Problem Gamblers*, 2 Gaming L. Rev. 349 (1998).

Problem 28

An individual was found guilty of computer fraud. At sentencing, he asked for leniency, claiming that as a result of his compulsive gambling, he was suffering from a "reduced mental capacity" at the time he committed his crimes. To what extent should the court take his request into account? *See United States v. Sadolsky*, 234 F.3d 938 (6th Cir. 2000).

Chapter 7

SHIPBOARD GAMING

A. OVERVIEW

At present, shipboard gaming takes place aboard three distinct types of vessels: foreign-flagged cruise ships engaged in extended voyages on the high seas; smaller crafts offering what are known as "day cruises" or "cruises-to-nowhere"; and inland riverboats, which may or may not leave their docks. Although all three types of gaming implicate maritime law, in many instances shore law provides the governing rule.

B. REGIMES

UNITED STATES v. BLACK
291 F. Supp. 262 (S.D.N.Y. 1968)

WEINFELD, District Judge.

The indictment in this case centers about the alleged operation of a gambling ship. Counts 1 and 2 charge all the defendants with the operation of a gambling establishment on such a ship in violation of 18 U.S.C., section 1082; count 3 charges the defendants Snow and Halpern with the use of a facility of interstate commerce to promote a gambling activity illegal under New York state law, in violation of 18 U.S.C., section 1952; and count 4 charges all defendants with conspiracy to violate the foregoing statutes.

THE MOTION TO DISMISS THE INDICTMENT

The indictment is challenged upon statutory and constitutional grounds. In support of the motion, defendants' attorneys submit their own affidavits, based upon information and belief, setting forth factual details as to the ship's sailing, the nature of the cruise, passenger activities and other matters relating to the indictment charges. In further support of the dismissal motion, the defendants seek an inspection of the grand jury minutes, which it is alleged will reveal the following: that T.S.S. Olympia, a vessel of the Greek Line, Inc., sailed from New York harbor on a nonstop weekend voyage, described by counsel as a cruise 'to nowhere'; that it departed on Friday evening, November 4, 1966 and returned to the port of origin on Monday morning, November 7; and that while the ship was beyond twelve miles from the United States coast line, a fraternal group known as 'The Sons of Italy' engaged in gambling activities for eleemosynary purposes in a common area set aside by the ship's master.

A. Arguments with Respect to Section 1082

1. Statutory arguments.

The defendants deny both that the activities described above constituted 'gambling' and that the ship was 'used principally for the operation of one or more gambling establishments' within the meaning of section 1082, [which] provides:

> 'It shall be unlawful for any citizen or resident of the United States, or any other person who is on an American vessel or is otherwise under or within the jurisdiction of the United States, directly or indirectly—
>
> (1) to set up, operate, or own or hold any interest in any gambling ship or any gambling establishment on any gambling ship; or
>
> (2) in pursuance of the operation of any gambling establishment on any gambling ship, to conduct or deal any gambling game, or to conduct or operate any gambling device, or to induce, entice, solicit, or permit any person to bet or play at any such establishment, if such gambling ship is on the high seas, or is an American vessel or otherwise under or within the jurisdiction of the United States, and is not within the jurisdiction of any State.'

This contention is premature. It may well be that section 1082 applies only to 'large-scale commercial gambling,' and that Olympia harbored so little gambling activity that it was not used 'principally' for gambling within the statute. But these are fact issues not before the Court on this motion. The validity of the indictment is to be tested by its allegations, not by defense counsel's forecast of the ultimate trial evidence. The indictment is sufficient upon its face, and is not subject to dismissal on the basis of factual questions, the resolution of which must await trial. This branch of the motion fails, and the accompanying motion for inspection of grand jury minutes is denied.

The defendants' next statutory challenge to the sufficiency of the indictment rests upon the assertion that the alleged proscribed gambling activities occurred aboard Olympia when it was beyond the twelve-mile limit. The contention is that the statute applies to a gambling ship on the high seas only when it is 'otherwise under or within the jurisdiction of the United States'; that the quoted phrase limits the Act to vessels on the high seas, and only when they are within the territorial waters of the United States, i.e., within the three-mile limit but in no event beyond the twelve-mile limit. The argument proceeds upon a claim that section 1082 was enacted to prevent the establishment of floating gambling casinos on ships anchored just off the coast of the United States, and that Congress, in effect, chose to overlook the few instances where such ships anchored beyond the three-mile limit.

Defendants have misread the statute. It is true that it was enacted to outlaw the gambling ship, a device employed to evade state gambling laws. But they overlook its component elements. First, the Act applies to American citizens, American residents, and other persons either on an American vessel or otherwise subject to the jurisdiction of the United States. Second, it prohibits both operating a gambling establishment on a gambling ship and either running a gambling game or inducing any person to bet or play at such a gambling establishment. Third, it requires that the ship be either on the high seas, or an American vessel, or otherwise under or within the jurisdiction of the United States. Finally, it excludes from its coverage ships within the jurisdiction of any State.

The interpretation urged by defendants would, in large measure, nullify the objective of the Act to reach conduct occurring on the high seas and beyond the territorial waters of the United States. Indeed, to accept their narrow interpretation would require the insertion of the word 'territorial' before 'jurisdiction' in the phrase 'or otherwise under or within the jurisdiction of the United States.' Under section 7 of Title 18, the special maritime and territorial jurisdiction of the United States extends to the high seas and any other water within the admiralty and maritime jurisdiction of the United States and out of the jurisdiction of any particular State. Nothing has been presented to suggest that Congress intended section 1082 to be of lesser reach.

The very language of section 1082(a) rebuts defendants' interpretation. The comma after 'if such gambling ship is on the high seas,' followed by 'or is an American vessel,' indicates that the phrase 'or (is) otherwise under or within the jurisdiction of the United States' enlarges rather than restricts the jurisdictional scope of the statute. One obvious purpose of the 'otherwise' phrase is to ensure jurisdiction over violations not involving American citizens or residents, as, for example, in the case of a foreign ship or foreign citizen's conducting gambling operations within the three-mile limit. This aspect of defendants' motion must also fail.

2. Constitutional arguments.

Defendants advance two constitutional claims, but these, too, are without substance. First, they assert that since the vessel was not an American ship and the gambling activity occurred beyond the twelve-mile limit, the United States was without jurisdiction to declare criminal the acts of those aboard. However, the indictment charges that the defendants were American citizens and residents. It is settled that citizenship alone, apart from locus, suffices to confer upon the United States jurisdiction over extraterritorial acts. Whether based on concepts of personal jurisdiction or otherwise, the power of Congress to enact statutes in the national interest extending to all its citizens—even those upon the high seas—cannot be doubted.

Defendants also claim constitutional infirmity of the statute for vagueness. Here the argument centers about the definition of a gambling ship in section 1081 as one used 'principally' for the operation of a gambling establishment. The basic question is whether the statute fails to give fair notice to a person of ordinary intelligence that the Act proscribes given conduct. 'Principally' is a word of ordinary usage, readily understood; a well-intentioned individual should have no difficulty in grasping its meaning. There is authority that use of the word 'principally' will not necessarily invalidate a statute. Moreover, where a statute plainly reaches the general class of cases to which it is directed, the statute will not be struck down as vague, 'even though marginal cases could be put where doubts might arise.' In advance of trial the Court will not seek to determine whether the nature and extent of the gambling aboard Olympia—questions of fact intertwined with the issues on the merits—were such as to preclude the constitutional application of the statute to defendants' conduct.

The motion to dismiss upon constitutional grounds is denied.

[The remainder of the court's opinion is omitted.]

STARDANCER CASINO, INC. v. STEWART
556 S.E.2d 357 (S.C. 2001)

PLEICONES, Justice.

This is an appeal from a circuit court order declaring that respondent's operation of a gambling "day cruise to nowhere" (day cruise) is not in violation of any of nine existing state criminal statutes. S.C.Code Ann. §§ 16-19-10; 16-19-20; 16-19-30; 16-19-40; 16-19-50; 16-19-120; 16-19-130; 12-21-2710; and 12-21-2712. We affirm.

Facts

Respondent brought this declaratory judgment action to determine whether any of its activities are unlawful, and to obtain a permanent injunction against appellants (the State). From a circuit court order declaring respondent's actions not unlawful but denying the injunction, the State appeals.

Respondent's day cruises begin and end at an Horry County port, and make no intervening stops. The United States flag vessel is equipped with gambling devices, including slot machines, blackjack tables, a roulette table, craps tables, and poker tables. Once the ship is beyond South Carolina's three mile territorial waters, gambling is permitted. Before the vessel reenters the territorial waters, the equipment is secured and unavailable for use. The equipment remains on the vessel at all times.

At least one other cruise line operates "day cruises" out of Charleston County. No prosecution has been made or threatened against the cruise line(s) operating out of Charleston, while respondent has been threatened with criminal prosecution and seizure of its gambling devices.

The issue in this case is whether respondent's operations violate any existing state criminal statute.

Federal Law

In order to explain our decision, we find it necessary to briefly review federal law in this area. Prior to 1992, federal law prohibited gambling on any United States flag ship. See 18 U.S.C § 1081 (2000) [part of the Gambling Ship Act, 18 U.S.C. §§ 1081-1084]; 15 U.S.C. § 1175(a) [part of the Johnson Act, 15 U.S.C. §§ 1171-1178]. The effect of these federal statutes was to put U.S. flag vessels at a competitive disadvantage in the passenger cruise industry, since the statutes did not prevent foreign flag vessels from offering gambling once the ship was beyond state territorial waters. See Casino Ventures v. Stewart, 183 F.3d 307 (4th Cir.1999), cert. denied, 120 S.Ct. 793 (2000); United States v. One Big Six Wheel, 987 F.Supp. 169 (E.D.N.Y.1997), aff'd, 166 F.3d 498 (2d Cir.1999).

In 1992, Congress amended § 1175 of the Johnson Act and created several exceptions to its general prohibition on the use or possession of any gambling device on a U.S. flag vessel. 15 U.S.C. § 1175(b). Pursuant to the amendment, the possession or transport of a gambling device within state territorial waters is not a violation of § 1175(a) if the device remains on board the vessel and is used only outside those territorial waters. § 1175(b)(1). Although the effect of this subsection was to permit the operation of "day cruises," another section provided states with a method for having "day cruises" remain a federal offense. § 1175(b)(2)(A). Thus, "day cruises" such as that operated by respondent may be subject to federal criminal prosecution under § 1175(a) if they begin and end in a state that "has enacted a statute the terms of which prohibit that use . . . ." Id.

As noted above, the issue in this case is whether respondent's operations violate any existing state criminal statute. The amendments to the Johnson Act do not preempt state laws prohibiting gambling and gambling devices, Casino Ventures, supra, and thus the Act has no direct bearing on the issues before the Court. However, while federal litigation pertaining to the meaning of the 1992 amendments was pending, the General Assembly amended several of the relevant state statutes. As explained below, the legislature's expression of intent in amending these statutes is relevant to the issue we decide today.

State Statutes

This declaratory judgment action determined the applicability to respondent's activities of nine criminal statutes. The circuit court held four of the statutes were inapplicable to respondent's operations, and the State concedes that the three lottery statutes, S.C.Code Ann. §§ 16-19-10; -20; and -30 (1985 and Supp.2000), and the bookmaking statute, S.C.Code Ann. § 16-19-130 (1985), are not implicated here. Two of the challenged statutes, S.C.Code Ann. § 12-21-2712 (Supp.2000) and § 16-19-120 (1985), provide for the seizure and destruction of unlawful gambling and gaming devices. Since we agree with the circuit court that respondent's possession and use of the devices on board its vessel are not unlawful under our substantive state statutes, we need not discuss these two seizure statutes.

We will explain below why respondent's operations do not violate the remaining statutes, S.C.Code Ann. §§ 16-19-40; 16-19-50; and § 12-21-2710.

§ 16-19-40

Section 16-19-40 provides:

> [From and after July 1, 2000, this section reads as follows:] If any person shall play at any tavern, inn, store for the retailing of spirituous liquors or in any house used as a place of gaming, barn, kitchen, stable or other outhouse, street, highway, open wood, race field or open place at (a) any game with cards or dice, (b) any gaming table, commonly called A, B, C, or E, O, or any gaming table known or distinguished by any other letters or by any figures, (c) any roley-poley table, (d) rouge et noir, (e) any faro bank (f) any other table or bank of the same or the like kind under any denomination whatsoever or (g) any

machine or device licensed pursuant to Section 12-21-2720 and used for gambling purposes, except the games of billiards, bowls, backgammon, chess, draughts, or whist when there is no betting on any such game of billiards, bowls, backgammon, chess, draughts, or whist or shall bet on the sides or hands of such as do game, upon being convicted thereof, before any magistrate, shall be imprisoned for a period of not over thirty days or fined not over one hundred dollars, and every person so keeping such tavern, inn, retail store, public place, or house used as a place for gaming or such other house shall, upon being convicted thereof, upon indictment, be imprisoned for a period not exceeding twelve months and forfeit a sum not exceeding two thousand dollars, for each and every offense.

Section 16-19-40 has two clauses; the first prohibits the playing of games in certain locations and the second provides for punishment of the person "keeping" that location. Since it is a criminal statute, it must be construed strictly against the State and in favor of the defendant. State v. Blackmon, 304 S.C. 270, 403 S.E.2d 660 (1991) (strict construction of §§ 16-19-40 and -60). Ironically, the current statute does not cover respondent's video poker machines. The 1999 amendment added clause (g), which prohibits gambling on a machine licensed pursuant to § 12-21-2720. Video poker machines can no longer be licensed, and consequently are not covered by this statute. As explained later in this opinion, this statute does not apply to the machines located on respondent's ship. State v. Blackmon, supra. At most, then, § 16-19-40 may apply to respondent's gaming tables. For the reasons given below, however, we conclude that it does not.

We first consider the portion of the statute that criminalizes the playing of certain games. The statute lists numerous specific locations at which the playing of games are prohibited. Since the list of prohibited locations does not include any term such as 'vessel,' 'ship,' or 'boat,' we hold that the "playing" clause does not apply to respondent's operations. See Brown v. State, 343 S.C. 342, 540 S.E.2d 846 (2001) (where criminal statute very specifically lists locations covered, those not mentioned are excluded, applying maxim expressio unius est exclusio alterius).

Further, because a 'vessel or float' is not a prohibited location under the "playing" clause of § 16-19-40, but is a named location under the bookmaking statute, § 16-19-130, and because both statutes are part of the anti-gambling criminal statutes, we hold that the circuit court properly concluded this portion of the statute was inapplicable to respondent's operations. See, e.g., Great Games, Inc. v. South Carolina Dep't of Revenue, 339 S.C. 79, 529 S.E.2d 6 (2000) (statutes which are part of the same legislative scheme should be construed together).

The portion of § 16-19-40 criminalizing the "keeping" of a gaming location uses slightly different language and arguably could be read to cover respondent's gaming table activities. While the "playing clause" lists specific locations, the "keeping clause" punishes "every person so keeping such tavern, inn, retail store, public place, or house used as a place for gaming . . . ." Respondent's vessel is a public place, and therefore seemingly covered under the literal language of this clause. Reading the statute as a whole, however, we conclude this 'public place' language is a reference back to the locations listed in the "playing" part of the statute. The "keeping" clause does not literally track the language of the "playing" clause, but does refer to "keeping such" a location. To read the "keeping" clause otherwise would result in "playing" being a criminal act in more and different locations than would "keeping." This, in turn, would lead to the absurd result that the person running the game could not be prosecuted if, for example, he was operating in a private street, field, or open wood while a person playing there would be prosecuted. The absurdity of this result is heightened by the fact the General Assembly has chosen to punish a "keeper" more harshly than a "player." See Broadhurst v. City of Myrtle Beach Elec. Comm'n, 342 S.C. 373, 537 S.E.2d 543 (2000) (no matter how plain statutory language is, it will be construed to avoid absurd result). Respondent's vessel is not a "public place" within the meaning of § 16-19-40.

We affirm the circuit court's conclusion that respondent's operations do not violate § 16-19-40.

§ 16-19-50 and § 12-21-2710

These two code sections criminalize actions of a "person who shall set up, keep, or use [games used for gambling purposes]" (§ 16-19-50) and make it unlawful "to keep on your premises" any devices used for gambling (§ 12-21-2710). In determining the applicability of these two statutes, we look at the General Assembly's expression of its legislative intent, as reflected in 1999 Act No. 125.

As noted above, in 1999 the Fourth Circuit held the Johnson Act did not preempt existing state gambling statutes. Casino Ventures, supra. This appellate decision reversed a district court opinion which had held that under the 1992 amendments to the Johnson Act, a state could only ban "day cruises" by enacting a statute which "opted out" of the Act by prohibiting the repair or use of gambling equipment on voyages. Casino Ventures v. Stewart, 23 F.Supp.2d 647 (D.S.C.1998).

While the appeal from that district court decision was pending before the Fourth Circuit, the General Assembly enacted comprehensive video poker legislation which, among other things, amended § 16-19-50 and § 12-21-2710. 1999 Act No. 125. Act No. 125 contains an intent clause, Section 22(B), which states in part:

> The General Assembly by enactment of this act has no intent to enact any provision allowed by 15 U.S.C. 1175, commonly referred to as the Johnson Act, or to create any state enactment authorized by the Johnson Act.

The intent of the legislature is determined in light of "the overall climate in which the legislation was amended." State v. Thrift, 312 S.C. 282, 440 S.E.2d 341 (1994). At the time the legislature enacted Act No. 125, a federal district court had ruled "day cruises," like those operated by respondent, were permissible unless and until the legislature "opted out" of the Johnson Act. While this ruling was later found to be erroneous by the Fourth Circuit, we agree with the circuit court that "in light of the overall climate" then existing, this intent clause in Act No. 125 must be read to evince a legislative intent not to make the cruises unlawful.

The State offers no alternative construction of this intent clause, but instead argues "[w]hatever may have prompted the insertion of [this intent language in Act No. 125], the Fourth Circuit's subsequent decision made its purpose clear." We do not agree that subsequent action by a separate entity can either alter or elucidate legislative intent.

In light of this language in the act amending §§ 12-21-2710 and 16-19-50, we conclude the legislature did not intend them to prohibit "day cruises." Our conclusion that the General Assembly does not intend that any current statute be construed to ban "day cruises" is reinforced by its subsequent rejection of legislation which would have enacted new gaming statutes explicitly criminalizing them in 1999 and 2000. See House Bill 3002 (1999); Senate Bill 0002 (2000).

Accordingly, we affirm the circuit court's conclusion that neither of these two "possession" statutes apply to respondent's conduct. As explained below, § 12-21-2710 is also inapplicable for a separate reason.

§ 12-21-2710

Section 12-21-2710 makes it a misdemeanor for a person to keep a slot machine or video gambling machine "on his premises." Mere possession, even of an inoperable machine, is a violation of this statute. State v. 192 Coin-Operated Video Game Machines, 338 S.C. 176, 525 S.E.2d 872 (2000). On its face, then, respondent is in violation of this statute. This section is part of the Video Game Machines Act, pursuant to which the Department of Revenue has promulgated regulations which define "premises" as:

> A single place or premises must be a fixed location. It does not include moving property such as a boat or train, unless such property is permanently affixed to a specific location.

27 S.C. Regs. 117-190 (Supp.2000).

Since this regulatory definition was submitted to, and acquiesced in, by the General Assembly, it is entitled "most respectful consideration," Faile v. South Carolina Employment Sec. Comm'n, 267 S.C. 536, 230 S.E.2d 219 (1976), and "should be given great weight." Stone Mfg. Co. v. South Carolina Employment Sec. Comm'n, 219 S.C. 239, 64 S.E.2d 644 (1951). While we are not bound to accept this definition, Stone Mfg. Co., supra, giving this regulation the deference it is due, we hold that there is no cogent reason to overturn it. Faile, supra. Accordingly, respondent is not in violation of § 12-21-2710 because it is not storing gaming equipment on a "premises" within the meaning of that statute.

Conclusion

We affirm the circuit court's ruling that respondent is not in violation of any state criminal statute. As noted above, the applicability of the three lottery statutes (§§ 16-19-10; -20; -30) and the bookmaking statute (§ 16-19-130) are not at issue here. Further, § 16-19-40 is inapplicable because respondent's vessel is not a prohibited location nor a public place as described therein, and § 12-21-2710 does not apply since the vessel is not a proscribed "premise." In light of the intent clause of 1999 Act No. 125, we agree with the circuit court that the legislature did not intend that either § 12-21-2710 or § 16-19-50 apply to "day cruise" operations. Further, we conclude that the General Assembly's rejection of statutes which would explicitly criminalize day cruises is evidence of its understanding that none of our existing statutes apply to such operations. Since the devices are not unlawful, they are not subject to seizure under either § 12-21-2712 or § 16-19-120.

Respondent is not subject to criminal prosecution under any existing criminal statute, and therefore we need not address its "selective enforcement" argument. Further, we emphasize that the General Assembly is free to enact legislation which effectively bans or makes a state crime "day cruise" operations such as that operated by respondent.

For the reasons given above, the order of the circuit court is

AFFIRMED.

BURNETT, Justice, dissenting.

I respectfully dissent from the majority's conclusion [that] respondent is not subject to criminal prosecution under any existing state statute. Respondent admits it possesses slot machines, blackjack tables, roulette tables, craps tables, and poker tables. In my opinion, possession of these items within the territorial waters of the State of South Carolina subjects respondent to the criminal laws of this state.

S.C.Code Ann. § 16-19-50 (Supp.2000) makes it

> unlawful to set up, keep, or use any (a) gaming table, commonly called A, B, C, or E, O, or any gaming table known or distinguished by any other letters or by any figures, (b) roley-poley table, (c) table to play at rouge et noir, (d) faro bank (e) any other gaming table or bank of the like kind or of any other kind for the purpose of gaming . . . .

Violators of this section are subject to fines and possible imprisonment. Id.; see also S.C.Code Ann. § 16-19-100 (1985).

S.C.Code Ann. § 12-21-2710 (Supp.2000) makes it unlawful for any person

> to keep on his premises or operate or permit to be kept on his premises or operated within this State any vending or slot machine, or any video game machine with a free play feature operated by a slot in which is deposited a coin or thing of value, or other device operated by a slot in which is deposited a coin or thing of value for the play of poker, blackjack, keno, lotto, bingo, or craps, or any machine or device licensed pursuant to Section 12-21-2720 and used for gambling or any punch board, pull board, or other device pertaining to games of chance of whatever name or kind, including those machines, boards, or other devices that display different pictures, words, or symbols, at different plays or different numbers, whether in words or figures or, which deposit tokens or coins at regular intervals or in varying numbers to the player or in the machine, but the provisions of this section do not extend to coin-operated nonpayout pin tables, in-line pin games, or

to automatic weighing, measuring, musical, and vending machines which are constructed as to give a certain uniform and fair return in value for each coin deposited and in which there is no element of chance.

Respondent's gambling devices which are prohibited by § 12-21-2710 are subject to seizure, and, if a magistrate determines they violate § 12-21-2710 after a hearing, destruction. S.C.Code Ann. § 12-21-2712; State v. 192 Coin-Operated Video Game Machines, 338 S.C. 176, 525 S.E.2d 872 (2000).

Nowhere do these statutes provide exceptions for gambling devices or tables located on boats. Yet despite the plain language of these statutes, the majority concludes the General Assembly did not intend them to apply to the gambling devices aboard vessels such as respondent's. The majority bases this conclusion on the "intent" clause contained in Act 125, which stated in part:

> The General Assembly by enactment of this act has no intent to enact any provision allowed by 15 U.S.C. 1175, commonly referred to as the Johnson Act, or to create any state enactment authorized by the Johnson Act.

The majority acknowledges the Fourth Circuit Court of Appeals has explicitly held the Johnson Act does not preempt state gambling laws: "That federal enactment does not even apply to South Carolina's territorial waters—it leaves regulation of those waters to the state." Casino Ventures v. Stewart, 183 F.3d 307, 312 (4th Cir.1999), rev'g 23 F.Supp.2d 647 (D.S.C.1998), cert. denied 528 U.S. 1077, 120 S.Ct. 793, 145 L.Ed.2d 669 (2000). In fact, as the majority correctly explains, the Fourth Circuit held that any state enactment pursuant to the Johnson Act would determine whether gambling day cruises violate federal law, not state law. Thus, under Casino Ventures, the legislature's intent statement in Act 125 has no impact on state law whatsoever. Nevertheless, the majority concludes that, because the Fourth Circuit's opinion in Casino Ventures was not filed until four days after Act 125 was signed into law—Act 125 was signed into law on July 2, 1999, [while] Casino Ventures was filed on July 6, 1999—the General Assembly must have intended to exempt gambling day cruises from the general prohibition on possession of gambling tables or devices. In essence, the majority would have us infer this startling intent, in clear contravention of the plain language of these statutes, solely on the basis of an earlier erroneous construction of federal law by the District Court of South Carolina.

South Carolina's authority over gambling activity extends to the State's territorial waters. See Casino Ventures, 183 F.3d at 308. The criminal statutes of this state unequivocally make it unlawful to keep gambling tables or devices in this state. See §§ 16-19-50 and 12-21-2710. We have held mere possession of gambling devices in this state—operational or inoperational, in storage or in use—violates state law. State v. 192 Coin-Operated Video Game Machines, supra. If the General Assembly had intended to exempt vessels conducting day cruises from this prohibition, it would have done so in plain terms. See Tilley v. Pacesetter, 333 S.C. 33, 508 S.E.2d 16 (1998) (if legislature had intended certain result in statute it would have said so). The majority's ruling exempts casino day cruises from the general criminal laws of this state, without any clear expression of legislative intent to do so.

The majority also concludes § 12-21-2710 is inapplicable for an additional reason. Although the majority acknowledges respondent is in violation of the statute on its face, it nevertheless finds the statute inapplicable because, according to the majority, the word "premises" in § 12-21-2710 does not include a boat. In support of this reading, the majority quotes the following language of 27 S.C. Regs. 117-190:

> A single place or premises must be a fixed location. It does not include moving property such as a boat or a train, unless such property is permanently affixed to a specific location.

This regulation is both inapplicable and defunct. The regulation, by its own terms, defines "single place or premises" in the now-repealed statute which limited the number of machines which may be located in a "single place or premises." Id.; see S.C.Code Ann. § 12-21-2804 (repealed, effective July 1, 2000) (limiting number of video poker machines which could be licensed in a "single place or premises."). The regulation's definition of "single place or premises" under a now-defunct statute is in no way applicable to the definition of the word "premises" in § 12-21-2710. On the contrary, in the absence of a statutory definition, the word "premises" should receive its plain and ordinary meaning. As the majority acknowledges, § 12-21-2710, on its face, criminalizes respondent's possession of gambling devices within the State of South Carolina.

I would reverse the order of the circuit court and hold boats located within South Carolina and its territorial waters are subject to the same laws concerning gambling as any other premises in this state. Furthermore, I would decline to address respondent's selective enforcement argument since the record reflects no enforcement of these statutes has taken place as of this time.

MAYS v. TRUMP INDIANA, INC.
255 F.3d 351 (7th Cir. 2001)

EVANS, Circuit Judge.

It was extremely controversial, and it passed over the veto of then-Governor Evan Bayh, but Indiana enacted legislation in 1993 permitting, for the first time, riverboat gambling in several Hoosier counties contiguous to Lake Michigan, the Ohio River, and Patoka Lake. Two of several possible gambling licenses were earmarked for Gary, a troubled city in the shadow of a megatropolis—Chicago.

Promoters of gambling argued that it would bring loads of cash into communities like Gary and spark an economic renaissance. This was welcome news for a smokestack-shrouded, rust-belt city like Gary, a city devastated by the loss of thousands of steel industry jobs and left with block after block of decaying houses and empty storefronts. Things had gotten so bad in Gary that in 1993, when the gambling measure passed, its homicide rate (91 slayings per 100,000 residents) left it with the nasty moniker of "Murder Capitol" of the United States.

This case is a saga about the gambling-license-snaring process and its fallout. The cast of characters includes two folks from Indianapolis: William Mays and Louis Buddy Yosha. Mays is a successful businessman, the owner (with his wife) of the Mays Chemical Company and two radio stations (KISS 106.7 and WIRED 100.9 FM), an investor in many other enterprises, a philanthropist, and a multimillionaire. Yosha is a very successful plaintiff's personal injury attorney. In the other corner is Donald Trump, known to some as The Donald and to others as the former husband of Ivana. Trump's activities here were through several of his companies, particularly a new one called Trump Indiana, but we'll refer to all of them simply as "Trump" (and we'll use "he" and "it" interchangeably) as we slug our way through this opinion.

In a nutshell, Mays and Yosha (and several trusts Yosha created for the benefit of his children, another detail we can ignore) claim Trump breached a contract (1) to make them minority (1 percent each) partners in his Indiana gambling enterprise and (2) to create a foundation—with the two of them on its board of directors and little control from Trump—to benefit various charitable causes in Indiana. A jury found for Mays and Yosha and awarded them $1.4 million in damages. After a court trial, the district judge denied Mays and Yosha's request for specific performance, finding that a different charitable organization—the Trump Indiana Foundation—was an acceptable novation-inspired substitute for what Mays and Yosha wanted. The judge did, however, order that Mays and Yosha get seats on the board of the new foundation. Mays and Yosha appeal on the specific performance question and Trump cross-appeals, saying no contract was ever formed and Mays and Yosha are entitled to nothing.

To best understand this case, and to support why we resolve it as we do, a lengthy review of the facts, sprinkled with several observations as we go along, is necessary.

Normally, when someone wants to start a business, one simply starts it. But everything's different in a regulated industry, and it's even more different in a super-regulated, explosively charged business like legal gambling. There's a lot of politics involved in this sort of undertaking and a lot of minefields to traverse before the prize—a license to engage in legal gambling—is won. And under the 1993 law, the Indiana Gaming Commission decided who would win that prize.

The two Gary licenses were to be issued first, and applicants were required "to provide assurances that economic development will occur in [Gary] and that adequate infrastructure and site preparation will be provided to the riverboat operation." Ind.Code § 4-33-6-7(b). Consequently, Gary applicants had to build an "approved hotel" or "cause economic development that [would] have an economic impact on the city [exceeding] the economic impact that the construction of an approved hotel would have." Ind.Code § 4-33-6-7(b).

This was a State of Indiana operation, yet the City of Gary was, quite understandably, very interested in the license-awarding process. It wanted a voice, and one can easily understand why. So Gary requested proposals from potential applicants even before they made contact with the state commission. Gary's request outlined several demands to be met before the city would endorse (though its endorsement wasn't legally required) an application to the commission. One of Gary's requirements was that an applicant have 15 percent local ownership.

Most people can smell money when they hear the phrase "riverboat gambling." That was especially true when it was "riverboat gambling" within sight of a place like Chicago. Trump—and Mays and Yosha, for that matter—had nothing wrong with their noses. They could sniff the smell of money. Trump, as most everyone knows (judicial notice is usually confined to undisputable facts like Greenwich mean time, but we feel safe here), controls an empire that includes a gambling casino in Atlantic City, New Jersey. Mays was active in politics and a member of the Indiana State Lottery Commission. He testified during the trial that "gaming was a really profitable activity" and a "printing press for money." As things were playing out, it looked like the road to that money ran through Gary, and Trump—along with his competitors—took steps to secure a favorable nod from the city.

As the process unfolded it became apparent that, as far as Gary was concerned, there were four horses in this race but only two would finish in the winner's circle. Trump was one of the four, and it was trying hard to enhance its standing with the city as 1993 came to a close.

Fifteen percent local ownership in the riverboat casino came to be seen as a nonnegotiable demand for winning Gary's endorsement. Trump did not need nor want local investment, yet it gave in. According to a Trump executive:

> It [15% local ownership] was not something that we wanted to do. As indicated on that first line in the first page [of Exhibit 200, a December 30, 1993, letter to Trump from the Gary mayor's office], we were at this time negotiating with the City to get their endorsement of [Trump Indiana's] application when we did go before the Gaming Commission. And the City had indicated that they were not under any circumstance going to give us that endorsement absent our agreement to do this. So we did agree to make 15% of the equity available to Gary residents essentially in exchange for the City's endorsement.

The city memorialized its understanding of Trump's commitment (the same December 30, 1993, letter just mentioned) to be: (1) spending at least $153.35 million on the riverboat and accompanying facilities; (2) creating 1,675 new permanent jobs; (3) filling 67 percent of those jobs with Gary residents and 90 percent with Lake County residents; (4) using best efforts to maintain 70 percent racial minority and 52% female employment; and (5) making at least 15 percent of the equity in the company available to Gary residents. If Trump was selected by the state gaming commission, a binding development agreement was required to memorialize these commitments. Trump was not alone here, as all other applicants for licenses made similar commitments to the city. Competition for Gary's endorsement, and a license from the state, was obviously fierce.

Trump then turned his attention to identifying local investors before February 14, 1994, the date another step in the application process was due before the state commission. But bad news arrived when Trump learned Gary would not endorse its application, but would instead endorse two other applicants. Undaunted, Trump continued its efforts to identify local investors because it believed a third license might be awarded to Gary, and if the commission gave it to Trump, a development agreement with the city, which would require local ownership, would still be necessary. As a Trump executive put it, "We wanted to be sure that on a going-forward basis if we were fortunate enough to be awarded the license that our relationship with the City of Gary was on very amicable terms."

By early 1994, seven individuals from the Gary area and two from Indianapolis—Mays and Yosha—were tapped to be Trump's "local investors." The entree to Mays was through a Trump attorney (Greg Hahn), Mays' friend since the days when both were living and apparently going to school in Evansville, Indiana. Mays (and Yosha, for that matter) had no connection with Gary, but because this was still a State of Indiana license, it was thought that someone of statewide prominence would gussy up Trump's application.

At this point it is helpful to step back and view the lawsuit claims of these parties. Mays and Yosha claim they entered into a binding contract with Trump and that they held up their part of the bargain, while Trump did nothing he was contractually obligated to do. Mays and Yosha find "the contract" by cobbling together several documents, notably letters of February 26, 1994 (trial exhibit 5), April 6, 1994 (trial exhibit 10), and September 16, 1994 (trial exhibit 35). Trump says no binding deal was reached: there were negotiations, there were ideas, there were proposals, and there were plans, but there was no finished contract upon which Mays and Yosha could seek damages or specific performance in court. While the jury, in a simple general verdict, found for Mays and Yosha on their claim that a contract was breached, whether as a matter of law (Indiana law applies) a contract was formed is a different question, one committed to a judge or, at this stage of the case, a panel of judges.

Back to the facts. Mays and Yosha (and the seven folks—later reduced to six—from Gary, including a doctor, an optometrist, a steel worker, a union president, and a school administrator) were listed as "proposed local minority participants" on Trump's license application filed with the state gaming commission. The February 26 letter (we'll have something to add from this letter in the penultimate paragraph of our opinion), sent to Mays and Yosha by Trump's attorneys, said "nine (9) investors . . . will own, collectively, 7.5 percent of the project being developed in Gary." The letter also stated that "7.5 percent will be owned by a trust, which will make contributions to charitable organizations throughout the Gary area."

On April 6, 1994, Trump attorney Hahn sent letters to Mays and Yosha which included the following statements regarding the terms of the proposed deal:

● The investors will be holders of Class "B" stock which "will not have the full voting privileges of Class 'A' stock but will have the same per share economic rights with respect to dividends."

● The Class "B" stock will be owned equally by a charitable trust (7.5%) and the identified group of eight (8) individual investors (7.5%), of which you are one.

● Trump has agreed to "loan" each investor an amount equal to their investment. By executing the nonrecourse promissory note, you, as an investor, agree to pay Trump the principal sum of $1,434,750.00.

• [T]he principal amount is to be paid solely from cash distributions or dividends declared by Trump Hotels & Casino Resorts, Inc.

• Trump will have the first right of refusal to purchase your stock if you decide to sell said stock in the future.

The finality of these terms is qualified in the letter by the following statements:

• [I]t is reasonable to assume that the accompanying financial information will also be fluctuating as the proposal is revamped.

• Presently, it is anticipated that 85% of the total number of stock issued will be Class "A" and the remaining 15% will be Class "B."

• Again, the total development cost figure ($153 million) and the ultimate amount that your investment represents is subject to change.

• We have not completed all the terms of this transaction. We hope to have all the documents finished for your review within the next 2-3 weeks.

On May 24, 1994, Hahn wrote Mays and Yosha regarding the charitable foundation project mentioned in the April 6 letter:

> In order to give the [Indiana Gaming] commission an idea of what we are striving for, we would like to go ahead and designate ten local charities as part of the foundation. In that vein, please give us an indication as to whether or not you would be willing to serve on the foundation, and a list of charities you believe should be included.

> * * *

> We will be contacting you on or about June 1, 1994, with the date and times of the investment meetings to be held in Gary and we would appreciate having received your input with respect to the charitable organizations and/or your willingness to serve on the foundation by that time.

Enclosed with the letter was a copy of a document entitled "The Trump-Indiana Charitable Foundation," identifying Trump Marina Resorts, Inc. d/b/a Trump Princess Indiana, Inc. as the "Donor" but with an open space for the names of the "Trustees."

In August and September 1994, the Indiana Gaming Commission conducted hearings regarding the license selection process. At those hearings, commissioners raised questions about Trump's application centering on the "local investors." In answer to a question from one of the commissioners (Sundwick), a Trump representative explained:

> A: Can I address one part of your question with respect to why we did this because I was the decision-maker. It was strongly suggested during the approval process. This was one of the major criteria in determining the acceptability of a proposal from the City of Gary, that local participation was mandatory and that was what was carried back to me by our representatives. If you're asking me, Does this make economic sense? Does it make business sense? Absolutely not. I have to finance this project. I have to put in real dollars and real equity.

* * *

But as for investors, in all candor, there is no economic basis to do that. It became part of the process.

Q: It wasn't the policy that was actually just required.

A: No, no, it certainly wasn't. Mr. Trump and I discussed it in some great deal [sic] because we had a lot of problems understanding why and on what basis we would do something like this.

Another commissioner, Bochnowski, then commented:

I mean the intent is to have local involvement. This is not local involvement. This is like buying names so that you can look like you have local involvement, and you're no different than anybody else in this regard, and that's why we have these so-called local investors from Indianapolis. Hopefully this experience will not be carried out in other states.

During the hearing process, in answer to a commission letter asking for responses to six questions, Hahn (with another member of his law firm) sent a letter to the gaming commission on September 16. This letter, which we noted earlier is relied on (along with the letters of February 26 and April 6) by Mays and Yosha to prove the existence of their contractual rights, listed the eight investors, their net worth, and a range of details about the investors' involvement and the structure and workings of the proposed charitable foundation.

We are now at the critical point in time in the case. Trump says he decided that the whole "local investors" thing was not helping the quest for a license, so he jettisoned the idea and proceeded on a different track. This move, says Mays and Yosha, was a breach of contract for which they are entitled to damages representing the value of the equity interest in the casino that did not come their way plus the establishment of a foundation over which they would exercise substantial power.

After the Trump/Mays-Yosha divorce, Trump moved stock around several of his companies and eventually offered new stock in a public sale. This was happening at a time of uncertainty because Trump did not yet have a license to operate the casino. In addition, there were concerns about whether operating a riverboat casino on Lake Michigan would be permissible under federal law. And Trump also was fighting a rearguard action against Mays and Yosha who tried to convince the gaming commission that Trump should not get a license for several reasons, including his breach of contract with them and his involvement in inappropriate financing and public stock offerings. Ultimately, the commission issued a license, the project went forward, and Trump established a different charitable foundation that was acceptable to the City of Gary.

The pivotal issue is whether the alleged contractual agreement Mays and Yosha say they had with Trump was sufficiently certain to create the two enforceable obligations they seek to establish. The first obligation would require Trump to cut Mays and Yosha in on the final deal to the extent of a 1 percent ownership (a .9375 percent share, to be exact) interest for each.

The second obligation would be to create a charitable foundation exactly as described in the letters of February 26, April 6, and September 16 of 1994.

Before the trial of this case, both sides moved for summary judgment, arguing that the facts were not in dispute and that a contract existed (Mays and Yosha) or didn't exist (Trump), as a matter of law. The motions were denied. After Mays and Yosha presented their case, and again before the jury spoke, Trump moved for judgment in his favor as a matter of law. Both motions were denied. For the reasons we are about to note, we think no binding contractual agreement was reached.

Under Indiana law, and in fact the law of every jurisdiction, a meeting of the minds on all essential terms must exist in order to form a binding contract. See Eastern Natural Gas Corp. v. Aluminum Co. of America, 126 F.3d 996, 1002 (7th Cir.1997) (applying Indiana law). And a mere agreement to agree does not a binding contract make. As the Indiana Supreme Court observed in Wolvos v. Meyer, 668 N.E.2d 671 (Ind.1996),

> [i]t is quite possible for parties to make an enforceable contract binding them to prepare and execute a subsequent final agreement. In order that such may be the effect, it is necessary that agreement shall have been expressed on all essential terms that are to be incorporated in the document. That document is understood to be a mere memorial of the agreement already reached. If the document or contract that the parties agree to make is to contain any material term that is not already agreed on, no contract has yet been made; the so-called "contract to contract" is not a contract at all.

Id. at 674-75 (quoting Corbin on Contracts § 2.8, p. 131 (rev. ed. 1993)). The Wolvos court clarified this statement by noting, "The question of whether an agreement is an enforceable . . . contract or merely an agreement to agree involves two interrelated areas: 'intent to be bound and definiteness of terms.' " Id. at 675. Without an express statement of intent, the focus is on whether the contract is too indefinite to enforce. Thus, the existence or nonexistence of a contract turns on whether material terms are missing. And here, material terms are absent in spades.

Mays and Yosha, unlike the six Gary "local investors," (who, by the way, settled their disputes with Trump before trial) were savvy in the ways of business deals and law. While we have no reason to doubt that both were interested in the proposed charitable aspects of the arrangement, the fact remains that this was a financial deal for them that was almost too good to be true. For essentially doing little more than adding their names to the Trump license application—which would demonstrate that the Trump team was "Hoosierized"—they were to receive a financial windfall. They would get a million or so dollars with no risk because, for most of the time, the proposed "loan" to them for the purchase price of their "investment" was without recourse and the "loan" was to be repaid with Trump's money. Anyone in his right mind would jump at the chance to get on a gravy train like this.

As a general proposition, common sense dictates that as an agreement becomes more complex, the need for clarity and formality increases. An agreement to sell a sofa at a rummage sale requires a lot less than an agreement to sell a house. And this was a very complex, multimillion-dollar venture. Early in the process, Trump thought adding "locals" like Mays and Yosha to his team would have value when the city and/or the state gaming commission considered his license application. But the details of how they were to participate, although sketched in broad outline, were never cemented. Would the Mays/Yosha "notes" be recourse or nonrecourse? What if any interest rate would attach to the "loan"? Neither Mays nor Yosha ever saw a finalized promissory note. What was the duration of the loan? What were its terms of repayment? Would security for the loan (if it was recourse) be required? And a particularly key element in the deal—also undefined—was Trump's right to repurchase the proposed investors' stock. If that right was exercised, how would the price and terms of repurchase be established? None of these details, it seems, were even discussed, much less finalized. In short, what we have here is best characterized as an agreement to agree, and that is unenforceable under Indiana law. Wolvos, at 674-75.

Further support for finding that essential terms were still to be nailed down can be found, ironically, in two of the three letters Mays and Yosha point to as evidence of the existence of a finished contract. The February 26 letter, while opening with a confusing statement that (Mays or Yosha) is "an investor in the Trump application" (whatever that means), concludes with this state-ment: "Our office looks forward to working with you and we will be communi-cating with you in the next few days to arrange a meeting wherein you can meet with us . . . to discuss, in further detail, the Gary project and your specific participation." The letter of April 6, while noting the Trump right-of-first refusal if an investor decides to sell the stock, says, "We have not completed all the terms of this transaction. We hope to have all the documents finished for your review within the next 2-3 weeks." These statements demonstrate that further clarifications and modifications on material points were anticipated.

In their suit, Mays and Yosha were essentially seeking millions for almost nothing because for a time they thought they were going to get exactly that, millions for almost nothing. For lending their names to the Trump team during the license application process, but without actually investing any money or putting any of their assets at risk, Mays and Yosha hoped to hit a jackpot once the casino boat was launched. The desire to put one's self in that position is completely understandable. But this complicated deal was never reduced to the kind of solid contract that could be comfortably enforced in a court of law. The judgment of the district court is REVERSED and the case REMANDED to the district court for the entry of judgment in favor of the defendants.

Notes

1. Since the late 1980s, shipboard gaming has experienced spectacular growth. Casinos now are a standard amenity (as well as a significant source of revenue) on most large cruise ships; cruises-to-nowhere have sprouted up in a number of jurisdictions, including Florida, Georgia, Massachusetts, New York, South Carolina, and Texas; and riverboat gaming has been authorized in six states (Illinois, Indiana, Iowa, Louisiana, Mississippi, and Missouri).

For a recent novel that uses shipboard gaming as its backdrop, *see* Dave Barry, *Tricky Business* (2002).

2. The recent surge in riverboat gaming marks the second time in our nation's history that such wagering has been popular. The first such period occurred in the early 19th century:

> American history shows a rich tradition of gaming aboard ships. The riverboats of the nineteenth century were infamous as havens for the American gambler. In 1840, there were approximately 2,000 gamblers plying their trade on the Mississippi River between Louisville and New Orleans. The riverboat gambler was described as "perhaps the grandest and most picturesque dresser of his day . . . ."
>
> The early gamblers on the steamboats were generally honest and relied upon superior skills to earn their livings. By the 1850's, however, the lure of easy money resulted in the prevalence of the "sharpie," or dishonest gambler. One historian noted that if an honest gambler did exist, he was suspected of being a crook.
>
> River gambling was curtailed during the Civil War as the Mississippi became the battlefield for Union and Confederate gunboats and, therefore, the navigation of passenger steamboats virtually ceased. After the war, attempts were made to revitalize the gaming trade on the steamboats. Changing economic conditions and attitudes toward the gamblers, however, spelled doom to the industry. The plantation owners who were the favorite mark of the sharpies disappeared, fewer ships were plying their trade on the river, and states on both sides of the river began passing laws calculated to suppress gaming. By 1870, river gambling was rare and most of the old-time riverboat gamblers left for the city or the western frontier.

Robert D. Faiss & Anthony N. Cabot, *Gaming on the High Seas*, 8 N.Y.L. Sch. J. Int'l & Comp. L. 105, 107-08 (1986) (footnotes omitted). For a more detailed look at the history of riverboat gaming, *see* Scott Faragher, *The Complete Guide to Riverboat Gambling: Its History, and How to Play, Win, and Have Fun* (1994).

3. As is obvious, getting a handle on the legal framework surrounding shipboard gaming is difficult because of how many statutes are involved. The following commentary, however, may help clear up some of the confusion:

> Although casino gaming is only one of a myriad of activities offered aboard cruise ships, it nevertheless constitutes an intrinsic part of the cruise experience for many passengers. It is also a significant source of revenue for cruise ship operators. At the same time, federal and state regulations have created a complex and often uncertain situation as to the viability of casino gambling for both U.S. and foreign-flagged vessels sailing on various itineraries.
>
> The Gambling Devices Act, more commonly referred to as the Johnson Act, states the general federal rule that the use of any gambling device is prohibited on waters "within the special maritime and territorial jurisdiction of the United States as defined in section

7 of Title 18 . . . ." However, a broad exception allows the use of gambling devices on all vessels when they are not within the territorial waters of any state or possession of the U.S. (i.e., anywhere outside the three-mile limit). It also allows cruise operators to offer gambling on cruises to foreign destinations from U.S. ports.

As a consequence of these rules, foreign-flagged cruise ships sailing international itineraries have always been able to offer gambling as one of their shipboard activities. By the same token, gambling historically was prohibited aboard U.S.-flagged cruise ships. To eliminate this competitive disadvantage, Congress amended the Johnson Act in 1992 to allow gambling on U.S.-flagged cruise ships. The amendment did not signal a complete end to the ban, however, for it also provided that individual states could prohibit gambling, even on the high seas, if the voyage or any segment of a voyage began or ended in that state.

In response, some states passed legislation regulating shipboard gambling, ostensibly to thwart efforts to establish a "cruise to no-where" market. For example, California banned gaming on all intra-state voyages or voyage segments. The California Attorney General justified the ban by arguing it was necessary to avoid problems under the federal Indian Gaming Regulatory Act, which requires that a state permitting any form of gambling must extend the same right to that state's Indian reservations. As a result, the majority of cruise lines either eliminated or significantly reduced calls at California ports, thereby gravely affecting the state's tourism revenue.

Concerned by such developments, in 1996 Congress further amended the Johnson Act by exempting certain cruises from state regulation. Thus, the Johnson Act today only allows states to regulate gambling outside state waters if the voyage begins and ends in the same state *and* the ship does not visit any other state or nation within three days.

Lawrence W. Kaye, *Gaming Regulations, in* 10 Benedict on Admiralty § 2.05 (Robert M. Jarvis ed., 2000) (footnotes omitted). It should be pointed out that in December 2000, Congress amended the Johnson Act to prohibit casinos on any "voyage or a segment of a voyage that begins and ends in the State of Hawaii." *See* Edwin McDowell, *Hawaii Still Resists Cruise Ship Gambling*, N.Y. Times, May 6, 2001, § 5, at 3.

Accordingly, the key to understanding shipboard gaming laws is to keep in mind the distinction between "United States waters" and the "high seas." Waters that are within three miles of the coastline are United States waters and, as such, are subject to federal control (three miles was once the distance a cannon could shoot and, thus, a sovereign could defend). Waters beyond three miles constitute the high seas and are governed by international law (as a practical matter, however, this means the law of the country in which the ship is registered, often referred to as "the law of the flag"). *See generally United States v. One Big Six Wheel*, 166 F.3d 498 (2d Cir. 1999) (holding that although the United States has in recent times asserted control of waters up to 12 miles from its coastline, the relevant limit for gaming remains three miles).

The federal government has made it clear that no gaming shall take place within its waters. Thus, cruise ships that travel between foreign ports and the United States are free to conduct gaming on the high seas but must lock up their casinos upon entering United States waters. In contrast, riverboats, which operate on inland waters, are left to the dictates of state law (as in *Mays*).

Cruises-to-nowhere, of course, are the anomaly. Although they leave the coastline and venture onto the high seas, they do not "touch foreign" (i.e., they do not embark or disembark passengers overseas). At one time, Congress made these ships illegal (hence the result in *Black*). Today, however, it has turned the matter over to the states. Accordingly, as is explained in the *Stardancer* case, such vessels are legal unless the state from which they sail passes legislation affirmatively banning them.

For further commentary on the regulation of shipboard gaming, *see* William Blake Bennett, *Waterborne Woes: Legal Difficulties of Riverboat Gaming in Emerging Jurisdictions*, 3 Nev. Law. 19 (Feb. 1995); Joseph Z. Fleming, *The Gaming Industry: River Boats and Cruise Ships: Calm Waters and High Rollers*, SF89 ALI-ABA 93 (Mar. 29, 2001); Trudy D. Fountain, *Rolling Down the Mississippi from Minnesota to Louisiana and Out Into the High Seas—Riverboat Gambling and Cruise Ship Gambling*, SF89 ALI-ABA 79 (Mar. 29, 2001); Joseph R. Marbach, *Riverboat Gambling in Illinois: A Policy Assessment*, 3 Gaming L. Rev. 151 (1999); Robert M. Jarvis, Note, *United States v. One Big Six Wheel*, 29 J. Mar. L. & Com. 449 (1998); Jeremy Robert Kriegel, Note, *Place Your Bets on the Constitutionality of Riverboat Gambling Acts: Do They Violate the Commerce Clause?*, 47 Wash. U. J. Urb. & Contemp. L. 123 (1995); Christopher T. O'Connor, Comment, *A Return to the Wild West: The Rapid Deregulation of the Riverboat Casino Gambling Industry in Missouri*, 19 St. Louis U. Pub. L. Rev. 155 (2000); Shanna L. Peterson, Note, *High Stakes and Low Tides: The Fourth Circuit Gambles by Forbidding Casinos in Casino Ventures v. Stewart*, 7 Vill. Sports & Ent. L.J. 397 (2000).

4. Even with the vast number of laws that pertain to shipboard gaming, a serious loophole exists:

> The statement that legalized casino gaming is one of the most highly regulated industries in the United States will find little dispute . . . . In stark contrast, the gaming industry on the high seas is generally not operated under direct government control. There are no regulations controlling these floating casinos and any person can operate the casinos regardless of suitability. More importantly, the casino owner is not required to implement internal controls and pays no gaming taxes. Thus, a player has no governmental assurance that the games are conducted honestly.

> Despite the general absence of governmental controls, most cruise lines claim their casinos are operated honestly with restricted betting limits. The cruise ship lines assert that the casino is a small part of the leisure package offered on a cruise. Consistent with this philosophy, cruise lines have an individual company policy addressing areas such as internal controls, hiring practices, and conduct of the game.

Additionally, the game rules are adjusted and implemented to account for the location of the ship on a moving body of water.

Robert D. Faiss & Anthony N. Cabot, *Gaming on the High Seas*, 8 N.Y.L. Sch. J. Int'l & Comp. L. 105, 105-07 (1986). *See also* Fran W. Golden, *The Complete Idiot's Travel Guide to Cruise Vacations 2000* 255 (1999) (noting that "[m]any of the onboard casinos are, in fact, operated by major land-based gaming companies that are bound by the rules and regulations of the Nevada State Gaming Commission"); Edmund Mander, *Day Cruise Gaming: Ships Sail an Unsure Course*, Int'l Gaming & Wagering Bus., Dec. 2000, at 13; Bill Ordine, *You Can Bet Money that Shipboard Gambling Differs from Vegas*, Pitt. Post-Gazette, Dec. 3, 2000, at F6.

5. State legislators are particularly incensed at not being allowed to tax shipboard gaming. *See, e.g., New Sea Escape Cruises, Ltd. v. Florida Department of Revenue*, 823 So. 2d 161 (Fla. Dist. Ct. App. 2002). To counter this situation, they have called for amendments to the Johnson Act that would give them a broad array of fiscal and regulatory powers over such operations. *See Final Report of the Public Sector Gaming Study Commission* (Mar. 31, 2000), available at www.fsu.edu/~iog/psgcs.html.

6. Perhaps not surprisingly, the legal battles that have engulfed gaming aboard ships also are taking place with respect to airplanes:

> On August 23, 1994, the United States Congress passed the Federal Aviation Administration Authorization Act. Section 41311 of the law (the Gorton Amendment) prohibits any air carrier from installing, transporting, operating or permitting the use of any gambling device on an aircraft. This law applies to foreign airlines as well as to airlines based in the United States. As a result, gambling is banned on all international aircraft flying into or out of the United States.

> The Gorton Amendment has had a significant impact on air carriers worldwide. Several foreign airlines have been planning to offer gambling to their passengers. Recent technological advances have made it possible for airlines to install entertainment video systems with gambling software. However, the Gorton Amendment prevents foreign airlines from allowing gambling on planes serving the U.S., even when foreign aircraft fly over the high seas or their own airspace. Foreign airlines around the world have united to protest this law.

Brian C. O'Donnell, Comment, *Gambling to be Competitive: The Gorton Amendment and International Law*, 16 Dick. J. Int'l L. 251, 251 (1997) (footnotes omitted). For a further look at in-flight gaming, *see* Andrew W. McCune & Alexis Andrews, *The Legality of Inflight Gaming: It's Up in the Air*, 2 Gaming L. Rev. 361 (1998), and Jesse Witt, Note, *Aces & Boats: As the Popularity of Cruise Ship Gambling Soars, Why Do the Airlines Remain Grounded?*, 28 Transp. L.J. 353 (2001).

Problem 29

A recently-passed state constitutional amendment authorizes riverboat gaming (all other forms of wagering remain prohibited). In the months leading up to the referendum, the proponents made it clear their goal was to "recreate and foster interest in this state's riverboat history, which dates from the early 19th century and is an important part of our collective cultural heritage." Will a casino built to resemble a riverboat but placed in the middle of an artificial lake be deemed legal under the amendment? *See Akin v. Missouri Gaming Comm'n*, 956 S.W.2d 261 (Mo. 1997).

C. MARITIME LAW

HORAK v. ARGOSY GAMING COMPANY
648 N.W.2d 137 (Iowa 2002)

NEUMAN, Justice.

This is an appeal of the jury's verdict for the plaintiffs in an action brought under our state's dram shop act, Iowa Code section 123.92 (1999). Because the dram shop at issue is a riverboat casino, the principal question on appeal is whether the district court erred when it refused to apply federal admiralty law instead of Iowa statutory law. We conclude that because there is no federal maritime dram shop law, federal preemption principles do not apply and the district court properly instructed the jury to consider the casino's civil liability in accordance with section 123.92.

Although many other errors are cited in the trial of the case, none warrant reversal. We therefore affirm the judgment entered upon the jury's verdict.

I. Background

A jury could have found the following facts. Leticia Morales, a thirty-one year old mother of three children, dropped her daughter off at a birthday party. There she met Juan Jurado and Gerardo Graciano. After socializing briefly with the young people, Morales and the two men left the party and headed to the Belle of Sioux City riverboat and gambling casino. The casino is owned by defendant, Argosy Gaming Company.

The record reveals that Morales may have drunk some beer before arriving at the casino, but she was by no means intoxicated. That situation soon changed. While Jurado and Graciano played blackjack, Morales began ordering cocktails and playing the slot machines. Estimates of how many drinks Morales consumed over the next three or four hours varied widely, but witnesses described her as becoming very inebriated. Her loud and obnoxious behavior eventually led security officers to forcibly remove her from the boat. When she attempted to start her car, police were called to the scene. Jurado and Graciano, who had not been drinking, convinced officers to let them get her home. The trio left with Graciano behind the wheel of Morales' car.

What happened in the next hour is the subject of some dispute. Graciano, unfamiliar with operating a manual transmission, quickly stalled Morales' car. He testified that this angered Morales, who demanded that she be allowed to drive and literally kicked him out of the vehicle. He said that Jurado got out of the car as well, and the two walked to his house and then to a nearby convenience store. Jurado, on the other hand, testified that he asked to be dropped off first because he was tired. He said that Graciano joined him within half an hour or so, explaining that Morales had kicked him out of the car and suggesting that they walk to the house where they had first met her to see if she had returned to retrieve her daughter. On the way they stopped at the convenience store.

Upon leaving the convenience store, Jurado and Graciano saw emergency vehicles and Morales' car sitting on its top in the yard of a nearby duplex. An off-duty officer who witnessed the one-car collision testified that he saw the vehicle careening down the street at a high rate of speed. It then missed the turn and flipped over several times, landing against the house. The car's only passenger—Morales—was thrown from the vehicle. She suffered severe injuries in the collision, including a fatal blow to her head.

A forensic toxicologist reported that, at the time of the accident, Morales' blood alcohol count was .250, more than twice the legal limit. She was found some distance from the car, partially wrapped in a blanket. A police investigation determined that the blanket came from a motel room rented that night by Juan Jurado. The motel was located roughly a mile from the scene of the collision.

Suit was brought on behalf of Morales' three minor children by Shelley A. Horak, administrator of the decedent's estate. Plaintiffs brought their petition under Iowa Code section 123.92, alleging that the defendant, Argosy Gaming, sold and served intoxicants to plaintiffs' decedent while she was a patron on defendant's riverboat casino. The defendant answered with a general denial and asserted the affirmative defense that the injuries and damages claimed neither resulted from, nor were proximately caused by, the alleged intoxication of Leticia Morales.

Following trial, the jury returned verdicts finding the defendant liable for the losses sustained by Morales' children, assessing damages for past and future loss of parental consortium as follows: $250,000 for Antonia, $500,000 for Francisco, and $500,000 for Marc. Further facts and procedural events will be detailed as they pertain to the issues urged by the defendant on appeal.

II. Issues on Appeal

State law versus maritime law

In advance of trial, Argosy filed an application to adjudicate law points which asserted that federal admiralty law applied, preempting the plaintiffs' state dram shop claim. The district court rejected the defendant's assertion, ruling that any decision concerning the applicable law would depend on the facts proved at trial and, even if maritime principles were implicated, Iowa's statutory dram shop act would not be preempted by federal law. The court reaffirmed its conclusion in response to Argosy's motions for directed verdict and judgment notwithstanding the verdict urged on the same ground at trial. We review these rulings for correction of errors at law. Iowa R.App. P. 6.4.

Our analysis begins with the fundamental observation that plaintiffs' suit rests solely on a statutory cause of action. Iowa's Dramshop Act, section 123.92, provides that anyone injured "in person or property or means of support" as a result of the intoxication of another has a right of action for all damages actually sustained, severally or jointly, against any licensee or permittee . . . who sold and served any beer, wine, or intoxicating liquor to the intoxicated person when the licensee or permittee knew or should have known the person was intoxicated, or who sold to and served the person to a point where the licensee or permittee knew or should have known the person would become intoxicated.

This court has long recognized that the dram shop statute was enacted because, at common law, no cause of action for negligence could be maintained against one who merely sold alcoholic beverages; as a matter of law, only the drinking of liquor—not the furnishing of it—satisfied the proximate cause element in an action by a third party for damages. Snyder v. Davenport, 323 N.W.2d 225, 226 (Iowa 1982); accord Haafke v. Mitchell, 347 N.W.2d 381, 384 (Iowa 1984), overruled on other grounds by Gail v. Clark, 410 N.W.2d 662 (Iowa 1987). In other words, the statute was "[c]onceived as a means to create liability where none existed at common law." Slager v. HWA Corp., 435 N.W.2d 349, 354 (Iowa 1989). Because the statute's benefits are plainly reserved to "innocent parties," comparative fault principles play no part in the trial of a dramshop case. Id. at 356, 358; accord Jamieson v. Harrison, 532 N.W.2d 779, 781 (Iowa 1995). And despite subsequent statutory changes and corresponding interpretive commentary by this court, it has remained the rule that "Iowa Code section 123.92 provides the exclusive remedy against liquor licensees and permittees for losses related to the furnishing of alcohol to an intoxicated adult." Summerhays v. Clark, 509 N.W.2d 748, 750 (Iowa 1993).

Against this backdrop, we consider Argosy's preemption claim. It is undisputed that the casino derives its authority to sell and serve alcoholic beverages from a license issued by the state of Iowa; it is a licensee as that term is used in section 123.92. Yet Argosy contends that the suit between the parties involves a "maritime tort." So, the argument continues, the suit is governed by admiralty law, not Iowa's dramshop statute. For the reasons that follow, we find the argument unpersuasive.

Maritime law

Any attempt to articulate a cogent explanation of the relationship between federal maritime law and state substantive law is a daunting task, at best. As even the Supreme Court has observed, "[i]t would be idle to pretend that the line separating permissible from impermissible state regulation is readily discernible in our admiralty jurisprudence, or indeed is even entirely consistent within our admiralty jurisprudence." Am. Dredging Co. v. Miller, 510 U.S. 443, 452, 114 S.Ct. 981, 987, 127 L.Ed.2d 285, 296 (1994). We begin, then, with the basics.

Consistent with Article III of the United States Constitution, Congress has vested federal district courts with "original jurisdiction, exclusive of the courts of the States" in matters of admiralty or maritime jurisdiction, "saving to suitors in all cases all other remedies to which they are otherwise entitled." 28 U.S.C. § 1333(1) (2001). This "saving to suitors" clause effectively grants state courts concurrent jurisdiction in cases grounded in admiralty law. Keefe

v. Bahama Cruise Line, Inc., 867 F.2d 1318, 1321 n.1 (1989), aff'd, 902 F.2d 959 (11th Cir.1990); 2 Am.Jur.2d Admiralty § 9, at 656 (1996).

General "admiralty" or "maritime" law is not codified. It exists as "a species of judge-made federal common law." Yamaha Motor Corp. v. Calhoun, 516 U.S. 199, 206, 116 S.Ct. 619, 624, 133 L.Ed.2d 578, 586 (1996). Whether a particular controversy "sounds" in admiralty depends on factors most often discussed in cases where one of the disputants seeks removal from state to federal court or, conversely, dismissal for lack of admiralty jurisdiction. See, e.g., Jerome B. Grubart, Inc. v. Great Lakes Dredge & Dock Co., 513 U.S. 527, 529-32, 115 S.Ct. 1043, 1046-47, 130 L.Ed.2d 1024, 1032-33 (1995) (admiralty jurisdiction properly invoked to permit dredging company protection under Limitation of Vessel Owner's Liability Act (LVOLA) in action for damages sustained by business owners due to flooding of Chicago River); Duluth Superior Excursions, Inc. v. Makela, 623 F.2d 1251, 1251-52, 1254 (8th Cir.1980) (reversing dismissal of federal court action brought by excursion boat to limit potential liability under LVOLA for injuries sustained by passenger following "booze cruise" on Lake Superior). But to meet the test of admiralty jurisdiction, whether invoked in state or federal court,

> a party . . . must satisfy conditions both of location and of connection with maritime activity. A court applying the location test must determine whether the tort occurred on navigable water or whether injury suffered on land was caused by a vessel on navigable water. The connection test raises two issues. A court, first, must "assess the general features of the type of incident involved" to determine whether the incident has "a potentially disruptive impact on maritime commerce." Second, a court must determine whether "the general character" of the "activity giving rise to the incident" shows a "substantial relationship to traditional maritime activity."

Grubart, 513 U.S. at 534, 115 S.Ct. at 1048, 130 L.Ed.2d at 1035 (citations omitted).

"The exercise of admiralty jurisdiction, however, 'does not result in automatic displacement of state law.'" Yamaha Motor, 516 U.S. at 206, 116 S.Ct. at 623, 133 L.Ed.2d at 585 (citation omitted). When exercising concurrent admiralty jurisdiction, state courts are free to adopt remedies fitting the case, so long as the state law does not undermine general maritime principles or unduly interfere with the harmonious and uniform application of maritime law. Am. Dredging Co., 510 U.S. at 447, 114 S.Ct. at 985, 127 L.Ed.2d at 293; accord Clements v. Gamblers Supply Mgmt. Co., 610 N.W.2d 847, 849 (Iowa), cert. denied, Gamblers Supply Mgmt. Co. v. Clements, 531 U.S. 873, 121 S.Ct. 175, 148 L.Ed.2d 120 (2000); see generally Grant Gilmore & Charles L. Black, Jr., The Law of Admiralty 48 (2d ed.1975) [hereinafter Gilmore & Black]. Put another way, "where there is a gap in federal maritime law, a state may apply its own law where not inconsistent with federal maritime law." 2 Am.Jur.2d Admiralty § 142, at 762; see Yamaha Motor, 516 U.S. at 202, 116 S.Ct. at 621-22, 133 L.Ed.2d at 583 (affirming tradition that state remedies apply in maritime wrongful-death cases "in which no federal statute specifies the appropriate remedy and the decedent was not a seaman, longshore worker, or person otherwise engaged in a maritime trade").

Plainly the line marking the contours of this concurrent jurisdiction is not well defined. State court remedies have enjoyed a broad scope, extending to admiralty cases involving state-created liens, remedies for wrongful death and survival actions, the partition and sale of ships, specific performance of arbitration agreements and breach of warranty for maritime insurance. Am. Dredging Co., 510 U.S. at 452, 114 S.Ct. at 987, 127 L.Ed.2d at 296. Yet not all actions grounded in state law have survived federal scrutiny. Notable within this classification are cases sounding in premises liability. In Kermarec v. Compagnie Generale Transatlantique, 358 U.S. 625, 626, 631-32, 79 S.Ct. 406, 407, 410, 3 L.Ed.2d 550, 552, 555 (1959), for example, where the guest of a cruise ship passenger sued the cruise line for injuries sustained in a fall on a stairway of the vessel, the Supreme Court emphatically rejected New York's premises liability law (with its distinctions between licensee and invitee) in favor of the "settled principle of maritime law" that a ship owner owes a duty of reasonable care under the circumstances toward anyone lawfully aboard the vessel. Kermarec's "reasonable care under the circumstances" rule appears to have been consistently followed in other negligence actions tried in admiralty. See, e.g., Keefe, 867 F.2d at 1322; Smith v. S. Gulf Marine Co. No. 2, 791 F.2d 416, 421 (5th Cir.1986); Rainey v. Paquet Cruises, Inc., 709 F.2d 169, 172 (2d Cir.1983).

A review of cases where the federal courts have applied state law in an admiralty context is illuminating. In Sun Ship, Inc. v. Pennsylvania, 447 U.S. 715, 100 S.Ct. 2432, 65 L.Ed.2d 458 (1980), the Supreme Court upheld a state supreme court decision applying state workers' compensation laws to claims of shipbuilding laborers whose land-based injuries fell within the coverage of the federal Longshoremen's and Harbor Workers' Compensation Act (LHWCA). Rejecting the employer's claim that the LHWCA preempted state law, the Court observed that Congress intended the federal law to supplement, rather than supplant, remedies for workers, particularly where the injury— although maritime in nature—occurred ashore. Sun Ship, 447 U.S. at 720, 100 S.Ct. at 2436, 65 L.Ed.2d at 463. More recently, in a negligence case stemming from a fatal jet ski accident off the coast of Puerto Rico, the Court considered the jet ski manufacturer's claim that federal maritime law preempted available state law remedies because the death occurred in navigable waters, thereby limiting the recoverable damages to funeral expenses. Yamaha Motor, 516 U.S. at 201-02, 116 S.Ct. at 621-22, 133 L.Ed.2d at 583. The Supreme Court rejected this assertion, observing that Congress "has not prescribed remedies for the wrongful deaths of nonseafarers in territorial waters," so damages available for the jet ski death of plaintiffs' decedent were properly governed by state law. Id. at 215-16, 116 S.Ct. at 628-29, 133 L.Ed.2d at 592. The Court expressly limited its decision, however, to the remedy available under the saving to suitors clause. It specifically left open the "source— federal or state—of the standards governing liability, as distinguished from the rules on remedies." Id. at 216 n.14, 116 S.Ct. at 629 n.14, 133 L.Ed.2d at 592 n.14.

Pertinent to the case before us, two noted commentators have observed that one consistent theme seems to emerge from these otherwise murky waters:

> Maritime law clearly prevails over inconsistent state law in actions
> brought under the saving to suitors clause, at least where the

maritime law rule is more favorable to plaintiff's recovery than the state law rule; it is possible that plaintiff may have the best of both worlds and claim the benefit of a state law rule that is more favorable to him than the maritime rule would be.

Gilmore & Black at 279. This observation is echoed in Yamaha Motor, where the Court acknowledged that its 1970 decision in Moragne v. States Marine Lines, Inc.—which recognized a maritime cause of action for wrongful death caused by breach of the duty of seaworthiness but left undisturbed a state law claim of negligence—centered on the humanitarian extension of relief, not the contraction of it. Yamaha Motor, 516 U.S. at 213, 116 S.Ct. at 627, 133 L.Ed.2d at 590 (citing Moragne v. States Marine Lines, Inc., 398 U.S. 375, 387, 90 S.Ct. 1772, 1781, 26 L.Ed.2d 339, 349 (1970)). Indeed the Court's most recent pronouncement—which extended Moragne's reach to a maritime cause of action for wrongful death stemming from negligence as well as unseaworthiness—clarified its view that congressional intent with respect to maritime law tends to preserve state law claims rather than preempt them, at least insofar as nonseamen are concerned. See Norfolk Shipbuilding & Drydock Corp. v. Garris, 532 U.S. 811, 819, 121 S.Ct. 1927, 1932-33, 150 L.Ed.2d 34, 42 (2001).

Applying maritime law in the dram shop context

That brings us back to the question at issue: whether this suit on behalf of Morales' children constitutes a "maritime tort," as Argosy contends, in which admiralty law preempts Iowa's dram shop law. Argosy theorizes that because the plaintiffs could have maintained a maritime negligence action against the casino for Morales' death, they are thereby prevented from grounding their cause of action in a state statute. The plaintiffs counter that, assuming their suit invokes admiralty at all, the lack of a maritime dram shop law necessarily means that application of state law neither undermines general maritime principles nor unduly interferes with the harmonious application of maritime law.

Turning first to the question of admiralty jurisdiction, we conclude that because the statutory harm complained of—the sale and service of alcohol to an intoxicated adult—occurred on a vessel capable of transporting passengers on a navigable waterway, the Grubart "location" test for concurrent admiralty jurisdiction is satisfied. See Iowa Code § 99F.1(6)-(8), .1(7) (1999) (defining "excursion gambling boat" to mean self-propelled vessel required to cruise away from dock for minimum number of days during excursion season); cf. Ketzel v. Mississippi Riverboat Amusement Ltd., 867 F.Supp. 1260, 1268 (S.D.Miss.1994), aff'd, Pavone v. Mississippi Riverboat Amusement Corp., 52 F.3d 560 (5th Cir.1995) ("floating casino" incapable of serving any transportation function held not a vessel for purposes of invoking admiralty jurisdiction). Moreover, the incident arguably satisfies the two prongs of Grubart's "connection" test: the alleged wrong has a "potentially disruptive impact on maritime commerce" and "shows 'a substantial relationship to traditional maritime activity.'" Grubart, 513 U.S. at 534, 115 S.Ct. at 1048, 130 L.Ed.2d at 1035 (citation omitted); see Duluth Superior Excursions, 623 F.2d at 1252-53 (carrying passengers for hire, supervising their alcohol consumption and providing safe means of disembarking all "related to" traditional maritime activity); Quinn v. St. Charles Gaming Co., 815 So.2d 963, 966 (La.Ct.App.2002) (vessel's alleged failure to supervise passengers' on-board alcohol consumption meets Grubart's connection test). But see Davis v. Players Lake Charles Riverboat, Inc., 74 F.Supp.2d 675, 676 (W.D.La.1999) (short trips by riverboat casino over navigable water not substantially related to traditional maritime activity but merely incidental to primary function as gambling facility and "activity which gave rise to the plaintiffs' injury, gaming").

Acknowledging the admiralty character of the case does not resolve the controversy before us, however. The question remains whether, as Argosy contends, maritime law preempts Iowa statutory law. Argosy correctly asserts that ordinary negligence principles have been applied in maritime cases involving intoxicated passengers or crewmembers. See Reyes v. Vantage Steamship Co., 609 F.2d 140, 141-42, 146 (5th Cir.1980) (suit brought by widow of crewman who drowned after unsupervised consumption of large quantity of alcohol aboard "floating dram shop" remanded for comparison of fault between crew member and ship owner); Guinn v. Commodore Cruise Line, Ltd., No. 94 Civ. 5890(TPG), 1997 WL 164290, at *1 (S.D.N.Y. Apr.7, 1997) (court denied summary judgment to cruise ship in negligence action involving passenger's fall in a stairwell, identifying actionable claims for "negligent service of alcoholic beverages, negligent failure to assist [the passenger] when intoxicated, and negligent maintenance of a stairwell"); Thier v. Lykes Bros., Inc., 900 F.Supp. 864, 866, 879 (S.D.Texas 1995) (in action by cadet/crewman for injuries sustained in car crash, ship owner found negligent for "failing to monitor alcohol consumption onboard, fostering a party atmosphere, and failing to prohibit drunk officers from driving"); see also Bay Casino, L.L.C. v. M/V Royal Empress, 199 F.R.D. 464, 465, 467 (E.D.N.Y.1999) (permitting intervention in action to limit gambling boat's liability, where interveners asserted boat's negligence in serving alcohol to underage patron who was later involved in auto accident).

We deem it significant, however, that plaintiffs rest their claims, not on ordinary negligence, but on Iowa Code section 123.92, a statutory remedy preserved to innocent third parties who are allegedly injured by the dram shop's sale and service of alcohol to an intoxicated adult. Slager, 435 N.W.2d at 351. In comparable cases, federal trial courts have disagreed over whether the foregoing decisions constitute a "maritime dram shop law" that trumps state dram shop laws that either permit, or disallow, actions against purveyors of alcohol. Compare Meyer v. Carnival Cruise Lines, Inc., No. C-93-2383 MHP, 1994 WL 832006, at *4 (N.D.Cal. Dec.29, 1994) (finding no authority supporting claimed federal maritime dram shop law and therefore applying California's dram shop law), with Young v. Players Lake Charles, L.L.C., 47 F.Supp.2d 832, 837 (S.D.Texas 1999) (existing maritime negligence standards govern issue of dram shop liability to exclusion of Louisiana anti-dram shop legislation).

In wrestling with this decision, we are guided by the fundamental tenet of preemption doctrine that federal law will not preempt state law "absent a clear statement of congressional intent to occupy an entire field" or unless applying state law would conflict with or otherwise frustrate a federal regulatory scheme. Barske v. Rockwell Int'l Corp., 514 N.W.2d 917, 925 (Iowa 1994).

Plainly there is no federal maritime statute comparable to Iowa Code section 123.92 governing the rights and liabilities of dram shops or third parties victimized by their patrons. And as the federal trial court in Meyer observed, neither is there a consistent or uniform body of maritime common law imposing tort liability on sellers of alcohol for injuries resulting from their sales. Meyer, 1994 WL 832006, at *4. As the federal trial court in Young rightly observed (while characterizing the maritime common law of negligence as a maritime dram shop law), the problem is that application of some state laws—like the Louisiana anti-dram shop law at issue in Young—would leave innocent parties without a remedy for wrongs committed by navigable dram shops. Young, 47 F.Supp.2d at 837. But, in Iowa, where the state law remedy available to plaintiffs such as Morales' children proves more generous than relief under general maritime negligence law would be, we are convinced that the "humane and liberal character" of admiralty law described in Yamaha Motor compels the application of the more beneficent state law. Yamaha Motor, 516 U.S. at 213, 116 S.Ct. at 627, 133 L.Ed.2d at 590. In other words, in the absence of a comprehensive federal scheme with which Iowa's law would conflict, we are convinced plaintiffs were entitled to pursue their state law claim against Argosy under Iowa Code section 123.92.

In truth it would be absurd to hold that Argosy, carrying dram shop insurance and having secured its gaming license as well as its authorization to sell alcoholic beverages on the condition that it comply with Iowa's liquor laws, could circumvent the reach of those laws by claiming federal preemption. Just as in Clements, where we wrestled with the preemption question in the context of gambling boat crewmen's claims of wrongful discharge, we perceive no "fundamental tenet of substantive maritime law" frustrated by the application of section 123.92 to the case before us. Clements, 610 N.W.2d at 850. The district court was correct in so ruling and, accordingly, we affirm its decision on this point.

[The remainder of the court's opinion, as well as Justice Cady's dissent, is omitted.]

WIORA v. HARRAH'S ILLINOIS CORPORATION
68 F. Supp. 2d 988 (N.D. Ill. 1999)

WILLIAMS, District Judge.

Plaintiff Susan Wiora ("Wiora") filed a three count complaint in federal court against her former employer Defendant Harrah's Illinois Corporation ("Harrah's"). In Count I, Wiora alleges that Harrah's invaded her right to privacy. In Count II, she sets forth a claim for intentional infliction of emotional distress, and in Count III, she presents a Title VII sexual discrimination claim under the Civil Rights Act, 42 U.S.C. § 2000e-3. Defendant now asks the court to grant partial summary judgment in its favor and dismiss Counts I and II. For reasons set forth below, this court grants Defendant's motion.

Background

Plaintiff Susan Wiora, an Illinois resident, worked as a waitress on Defendant Harrah's Joliet Casino. (Def.'s 12(M) Stmt. ¶ 2.) Harrah's

Entertainment, Inc. is a holding company of Harrah's Illinois Corporation. Incorporated in Nevada, the Harrah's Illinois Corporation has its principal place of business in Illinois, the only place it is licensed to operate its casino-style gambling boat, the M/V Northern Star. (Def.'s 12(M) Stmt. ¶ 10-11.)

On December 15, 1996, a customer of Harrah's accidentally spilled hot coffee on Wiora's chest. (Compl. ¶ 3.) Immediately following the accident, Wiora received medical care from a paramedic, also an employee of Harrah's, in the first aid room on Harrah's Joliet Casino boat. (Compl. ¶ 4.) Wiora alleges that when she asked the paramedic if the surveillance cameras were filming, he assured her that they were off and instructed her to disrobe and apply certain medication to her chest. (Compl. ¶¶ 5-7.) After Wiora applied the medication, the paramedic instructed her to lay down in the first aid room after applying the aforementioned medication. (Compl. ¶ 8.) Before being transported to the hospital, an agent or servant of Harrah's gave Wiora a sweatshirt to wear. (Def.'s 12(M) Stmt. ¶ 4.)

Wiora claims that on or about February 1, 1998, she discovered that on the date of her accident, Harrah's did indeed film her as she was applying medication to her chest. (Compl. ¶¶ 12-14.) Defendant admits that there does exist a videotape that portrays Wiora applying medication to her chest. (Def.'s 12(M) Stmt. ¶ 5.) Wiora asserts that at least four agents and servants of Harrah's were present in the surveillance room at the time of the taping and saw the video tape from the cameras and/or photographs. (Compl. ¶ 17.) Wiora further contends that agents or servants of Harrah's showed the videotape and/or photographs to third persons. (Compl. ¶ 16.)

On July 30, 1998, Wiora filed a two count complaint against Defendant Harrah's claiming invasion of privacy and intentional infliction of emotional distress. She brought this original complaint on the basis of diversity jurisdiction under 28 U.S.C. § 1332. About a month later, Wiora amended her complaint to include a third count, a Title VII sexual harassment claim. Rather than filing an amended complaint, Wiora filed an amendment to the complaint, only adding Count III, the Title VII claim. In her amendment, Wiora states the court has federal question jurisdiction under 28 U.S.C. § 1331. Defendants now ask the court to grant partial summary judgment in its favor for Counts I and II.

Analysis

Harrah's argues that since Wiora can be considered a seaman by law, the Jones Act is her sole means to recover for personal injuries sustained while working on the casino boat. Harrah's further contends that under the Jones Act, employees may not recover for purely emotional injuries such as those resulting from invasion of privacy and intentional infliction of emotional distress. Since Harrah's maintains that Wiora has no remedy for her claims under the Jones Act, Harrah's asks this court to grant summary judgment on Counts I and II.

In the alternative, Harrah's argues that even if the Jones Act does not apply, the court lacks jurisdiction over Counts I and II. Defendant claims that the parties are not diverse and therefore, the court does not have diversity jurisdiction. Additionally, Harrah's urges the court not to exercise supplemental jurisdiction by virtue of Title VII. In response, Wiora claims that the Jones Act does not apply, given the facts of this case. In addition, Wiora contends that even if the Jones Act applies in this case, the court may not exercise admiralty jurisdiction, either under general admiralty law or the Jones Act. Furthermore, she argues, Title VII provides a means for the court to exercise supplemental jurisdiction over Counts I and II.

Therefore before the court can make its decision, it must resolve three questions: (1) does the Jones Act apply in this case, in other words, can Wiora be considered a seaman under the Jones Act and may the court exercise admiralty jurisdiction over this case; (2) if she is a seaman, does the Jones Act preclude her from bringing tort claims designed to compensate for emotional injury; and (3) if these claims are not precluded by the Jones Act, does the court have an independent basis upon which to exercise jurisdiction?

I. Applicability of the Jones Act

A. Is Wiora a seaman under the Jones Act?

A review of the case law suggests that Wiora does satisfy the criteria set out to determine seaman status under the Jones Act. The Jones Act sets forth a scheme of recovery for personal injury incurred by seamen while working on a vessel in navigable waters. 46 U.S.C.App. § 688. The Jones Act provides, in relevant part:

> Any seaman who shall suffer personal injury in the course of his employment may, at his election, maintain an action for damages at law, with the right of trial by jury, and in such action all statutes of the United States modifying or extending the common law right or remedy in cases of personal injury to railway employees shall apply.

A central question is whether Wiora was a seaman. To be a seaman, the employee: (1) must have duties which contribute to the function of the vessel or to accomplishment of its mission, and (2) must have a connection to the vessel in navigation or to an identifiable group of such vessels that is substantial in terms of both duration and its nature. See Harbor Tug & Barge Co. v. Papai, 520 U.S. 548, 117 S.Ct. 1535, 137 L.Ed.2d 800 (1997). In McDermott International, Inc. v. Wilander, 498 U.S. 337, 111 S.Ct. 807, 112 L.Ed.2d 866 (1991), the United States Supreme Court held that an employee on board a vessel in navigation need not aid in navigation of the vessel in order to qualify as a seaman under the Jones Act. Rather, the Court emphasized that the term "seaman" should be defined in terms of an employee's connection to the vessel in navigation, and a necessary element of this connection is that the employee's duties contribute to the function of the vessel or the accomplishment of its mission. Wilander, 498 U.S. at 337-38, 111 S.Ct. 807.

"The inquiry into seaman status is of necessity fact specific; it will depend on the nature of the vessel and the employee's precise relation to it." Wilander, 498 U.S. at 356, 111 S.Ct. 807. While the court found no case in which a waitress was deemed a seaman, other courts have conferred seaman status upon individuals engaged in "non-traditional" maritime activities who were injured on board passenger vessels. See e.g., Mahramas v. American Export Isbrandtsen Lines, 475 F.2d 165, 170 (2nd Cir.1973) (holding that a hairdresser employed on board passenger vessel was a seaman); Lunsford v. Fireman's Fund Insurance Co., 635 F.Supp. 72 (E.D.La.1986) (finding that a part time cleaning lady aboard a docked pleasure yacht was a "seaperson" for purposes of the Jones Act); and Dick v. United States Lines, 38 F.Supp. 685, 686 (S.D.N.Y.1941) (holding that musician employed on board vessel was a seaman). Wiora worked for Harrah's as a waitress on one of its riverboat casinos. A review of the case law as well as Wiora's duties suggest that she satisfies the first prong of the test.

To meet the criteria of the second prong, plaintiff must show "an employment-related connection to a vessel in navigation." Southwest Marine, Inc. v. Gizoni, 502 U.S. 81, 88, 112 S.Ct. 486, 116 L.Ed.2d 405 (1991). Wiora had a clear employment-related connection to the riverboat casino. Her connection with the vessel was substantial in both duration and nature. Wiora was a full-time employee on Harrah's riverboat casino and she played an integral role in the service of customers on the boat. A number of courts have considered the question of whether a riverboat casino can be considered a "vessel in navigation." A review of those cases suggests that the M/V Northern Star was indeed a vessel in navigation.

"Where the vessel status of an unconventional craft is unsettled, it is necessary to focus upon the purpose for which the craft is constructed and the business in which it is engaged." Gremillion v. Gulf Coast Catering Co., 904 F.2d 290, 293 (5th Cir.1990). The Fifth Circuit has engaged in this inquiry on more than one occasion. That circuit considers three factors when determining the applicability of the Jones Act to the region's harborside, floating casinos. The factors to be considered are whether "(1) the structure was constructed to be used as a work platform; (2) the structure is moored or otherwise secured at the time of the accident; and (3) although the platform is capable of movement, and is sometimes moved across navigable waters in the course of normal operations, any transportation function is merely incidental to the platform's primary purpose." Pavone v. Mississippi Riverboat Amusement Corporation, et al., 52 F.3d 560, 570 (5th Cir.1995).

There are a number of similarities between the Biloxi Belle, the vessel at issue in Pavone and other cases, and the M/V Northern Star in this case. Both possess bilge pumps, raked bows and both are authorized to travel on United States waterways. The similarities end there however. While the Biloxi Belle was towed to its current home, the M/V Northern Star was constructed in New Orleans and traveled to Illinois on its own power up the Mississippi River. (Def.'s 12(M) Stmt. ¶ 22, 25.) Unlike the Biloxi Belle, the M/V Northern Star has an engine, a captain, lifesaving equipment, crew quarters and full-time marine operations department employees. (Def.'s 12(M) Stmt. ¶ 25.) As such, the court finds that the only reasonable conclusion is that the M/V Northern Star does qualify as a vessel in navigation. Having found that Wiora satisfies both prongs of the tests established for determining seaman status, the court concludes that Wiora is a seaman under the Jones Act.

Wiora makes the argument that the court need not even reach the question of whether she qualifies as a seaman. Wiora contends that the court may not exercise admiralty jurisdiction, general or under the Jones Act, because under Executive Jet Aviation, Inc. et al. v. City of Cleveland, Ohio, et al., 409 U.S. 249, 251, 93 S.Ct. 493, 34 L.Ed.2d 454 (1972), the tortious wrongs at issue in this case occurred on land, not water. In Executive Jet, the plaintiffs brought suit invoking federal admiralty jurisdiction for damages resulting from the crash-landing and sinking in the navigable waters of Lake Erie of their jet aircraft. The Supreme Court held that claims arising from airplane accidents are not cognizable in admiralty unless the wrong bears a significant relationship to traditional maritime activities. Executive Jet, 409 U.S. at 249, 93 S.Ct. 493. More notably, the court expounded upon the limits of admiralty jurisdiction. "The mere fact that the alleged wrong 'occurs' or 'is located' on or over navigable waters . . . is not of itself sufficient to turn an airplane negligence case into a 'maritime tort'. It is far more consistent with the history and purpose of admiralty to require also that the wrong bear a significant relationship to traditional maritime activity." Id. at 268, 93 S.Ct. 493.

Wiora first urges the court to find that both of the torts alleged in this case did not occur on the riverboat, but occurred on land, when her image was published to third parties. Furthermore, she claims that no nexus exists between the torts alleged and traditional maritime service, navigation or commerce on navigable waters. However, in other cases involving a seaperson alleging the same or similar torts, courts have exercised admiralty jurisdiction. See Williams v. Treasure Chest Casino, L.C.C., et al., Nos. 95-3968, 97-0947, 1998 WL 42586, *4-8 (E.D.La. Feb. 3, 1998) (considering viability of two casino boat emergency medical technicians' claims of sexual harassment and discrimination and intentional infliction of emotional distress under the Jones Act and for unseaworthiness and maintenance and cure); Johnston v. M/V Dieu Si Bon, No. C96-1050R, 1996 WL 866112, *2 (W.D.Wash. Oct. 19, 1996) (examining plaintiff crew member's claims for intentional and negligent infliction of emotional distress under the Jones Act and emotional distress under the unseaworthiness doctrine); Yballa v. Sea-Land Services, Inc., 919 F.Supp. 1428, 1433 (D.Haw.1995) (ruling on crew member's claims of negligent and intentional infliction of emotional distress under Jones Act and claims of unseaworthiness).

Additionally, the case Wiora relies upon, Lamontagne v. Craig, 632 F.Supp. 706 (N.D.Ca.1986), as well as other Ninth Circuit cases with similar holdings, can be distinguished. See Clinton v. Joshua Hendy, 285 F.2d 199 (9th Cir.1960) (finding that plaintiff who was terminated due to a libelous letter sent to someone on land did not state a claim in admiralty); Clinton v. Int'l Org. of Masters, Mates, & Pilots, 254 F.2d 370 (9th Cir.1958) (holding that defendant's alleged violation of union by-laws was not committed on navigable waters because labor contract was entered into, performed and breached on land).

In Lamontagne, a seaman brought a defamation suit against, not his employer, but the ship's chief engineer, for publishing a defamatory letter in Hong Kong. The court dismissed plaintiff's claim and held that the court lacked admiralty jurisdiction. The court noted that while the letter was written on the boat, the tort was committed "only upon publication of the . . . letter an event which occurred only upon its reception and consideration . . . in Hong Kong, on land." Lamontagne, 632 F.Supp. at 708.

In contrast, much of Wiora's injury appears to have occurred on the riverboat. Publication first took place when individuals watched Wiora on surveillance cameras as she disrobed and applied medication to her chest and when others viewed the video and/or photos while on board. Wiora has presented no facts to the court to support her claim that publication of the video and/or photos occurred on land. Without evidentiary support for such a claim, the court must find that admiralty jurisdiction exists. See Guidry v. Durkin, 834 F.2d 1465, 1470 (9th Cir.1987) (finding that all prima facie requirements of tortious libel were met at sea on board ship and that plaintiff's defamation claim sounded in admiralty).

Under the facts available to the court at this time, plaintiff's case satisfies both the locality and nexus test established under Executive Jet. Because she is a seaperson seeking to sue her employer for an injury that, at the very least, began while she was working on a vessel in navigable waters, she cannot escape admiralty jurisdiction.

Plaintiff's concern that in exercising admiralty jurisdiction, the court lets Harrah's off the hook is unfounded. In fact, it is the rule of law set forth in Executive Jet which prevents vessel owners from getting a " 'free pass' to commit torts on land so long as the wrongful conduct commences on the water." (Pl.'s Mem. at 5.) A seaperson, injured by her employer in the course of duty may recover regardless of the location. See O'Donnell v. Great Lakes Dredge & Dock Co., 318 U.S. 36, 41-42, 63 S.Ct. 488, 87 L.Ed. 596 (1943) (finding that "maritime law has recognized the seaman's right to maintenance and cure for injuries suffered in the course of his service to his vessel, whether occurring on sea or on land").

B. Preclusion of Counts I and II

Harrah's argues that since Wiora is a seaperson, the Jones Act stands as the only avenue she can pursue to obtain relief for the injuries claimed in Counts I and II. However, under the Jones Act, recovery for pure emotional injury is not available. Therefore, under defendant's interpretation of the law, the Jones Act effectively precludes Wiora from seeking a remedy for defendant's alleged privacy invasion and intentional infliction of emotional distress. Lacking any legal means to recover, Harrah's asks the court to dismiss Count I and II entirely and grant its motion for partial summary judgment.

1. Intentional Infliction of Emotional Distress

While circuit court decisions on this issue vary, it is well-settled in the Seventh Circuit that a FELA or Jones Act claim for infliction of emotional distress requires a showing of offensive physical contact or a threat of physical harm. See Ray v. Consolidated Rail Corp., 938 F.2d 704, 705 (7th Cir.1991).

We may look to the Federal Employers' Liability Act for guidance in determining the applicability of the Jones Act to emotional injury torts. The Jones Act incorporates the Federal Employer's Liability Act (FELA) by reference, 46 U.S.C.App. § 688(a), and extends to seamen the same remedies and liability standards afforded to railroad workers under FELA. See Ferguson v. Moore-McCormack Lines, 352 U.S. 521, 77 S.Ct. 457, 1 L.Ed.2d 511

(1957). As such, FELA is a good point of reference for courts considering Jones Act issues.

A number of courts have dismissed plaintiff's claims of negligent and intentional infliction of emotional distress where plaintiff pleads no facts to suggest that she suffered physical injury or at the very least, was a bystander in the "zone of physical danger." See Benvenuto v. Action Marine, Inc., No. 91 C 7365, 1992 WL 194649, *3-4 (N.D.Ill. Aug. 6, 1992). See also, Lancaster v. Norfolk and Western Railway Co., 773 F.2d 807, 812 (7th Cir.1985) (finding no cognizable FELA claim where alleged supervisory misconduct led to his "descent into madness"); Thomas v. Burlington Northern Railroad Co., No. 90 C 2453, 1991 WL 249720 (N.D. Ill. Nov. 15, 1991) (dismissing plaintiff's FELA claim for intentional infliction of emotional distress based on allegations of harassment).

Here, Wiora makes no claim of physical harm or injury. In her complaint, she merely asserts that she "suffered severe emotional and psychological damage." (Compl. ¶ 22.) As such, being bound by the law set forth in Ray, this court must hold that her claim for intentional infliction of emotional distress is not cognizable under the Jones Act. The Supreme Court has held that the Jones Act provides the exclusive recovery for personal injury claims by seamen against their employer. See Miles v. Apex Marine, 498 U.S. 19, 29, 111 S.Ct. 317, 112 L.Ed.2d 275 (1990). Since Wiora is a seamen seeking recovery from her employer, the court must therefore grant defendant's motion for summary judgment as it relates to Count II.

2. Invasion of Privacy

The question of whether invasion of privacy is cognizable under the Jones Act is one of first impression in this circuit. To fully understand whether the Jones Act was meant to preclude Wiora's invasion of privacy claim, the court must look at the statute's legislative history and how it has evolved. At its inception, the Jones Act was created to provide seamen with the option to sue his or her employer at law, rather than under general admiralty and maritime law. See 14A Wright & Miller: Federal Prac. & Proc. § 3677, Jurisdiction Under the Jones Act (1996). When Congress enacted the Jones Act it sought to remedy what it recognized as a defect in the law. "Seaman are the wards of the admiralty whose traditional policy it has been to avoid, within reasonable limits, the application of rules of the common law which would affect them harshly because of the special circumstances attending their calling and hence remedial legislation for benefit and protection of seaman must be liberally construed, to attain the end." Socony-Vacuum Oil Co. v. Smith, 305 U.S. 424, 59 S.Ct. 262, 83 L.Ed. 265 (1939).

Originally, Congress constructed the Jones Act to award seaman damages for a bodily injury caused by the negligence of any of the officers, agents, or employees of such carrier. See McAllister v. Magnolia Petroleum Company, 357 U.S. 221, 232, 78 S.Ct. 1201, 2 L.Ed.2d 1272 (1958). While the scope of the Jones Act was decidedly narrow at the time it was enacted, over time it has expanded to provide relief for a variety of personal injuries suffered by seapersons. See Lunsford, 635 F.Supp. at 74 ("the Congress which passed the

Jones Act would doubtless be amazed to learn that Mary Lunsford, a shore-based part time cleaning lady, has now become a 'seaperson' with all the rights and privileges attendant to that status"). The court derives guidance from the seminal case of Atchison, Topeka and Santa Fe Railway Co. v. Buell, 480 U.S. 557, 107 S.Ct. 1410, 94 L.Ed.2d 563 (1987), in which the Supreme Court indicated that under FELA an individual may, under certain circumstances, recover for wholly emotional injury:

> Assuming, as we have, that FELA [and Jones Act] jurisprudence gleans guidance from common law developments, whether one can recover for emotional injury might rest on a variety of subtle and intricate distinctions related to the nature of the injury and the character of the tortious activity . . . . In short, the question whether one can recover for emotional injury may not be susceptible to an all-inclusive 'yes' or 'no' answer. As in other areas of law, broad pronouncements in this area may have to bow to precise application of developing legal principles to the particular facts at hand.

Id. at 568, 107 S.Ct. 1410. Subsequent to Buell, several courts have allowed recovery for wholly emotional injury, e.g., Taylor v. Burlington Northern R.R. Co., 787 F.2d 1309, 1313 (9th Cir.1986), Carroll v. Consolidated Rail Corp., 1991 WL 32859 (E.D.Pa.1991).

The Seventh Circuit however, is not one of those courts. In her complaint, Wiora does not evince any traditional, physical harm resulting from defendant's alleged privacy invasion. The rule set forth in Ray, requiring some physical injury or threat of physical injury for a tort to be cognizable under FELA, suggests that Wiora's claim for invasion of privacy would not be cognizable under the Jones Act in this circuit. See Ray, 938 F.2d at 705. Upon a closer examination of the reasoning set forth in Lancaster, 773 F.2d at 807, which first articulated the rule at issue, this court finds that without some showing of an injury of the type complained of in traditional torts such as assault and battery, Wiora may not maintain an invasion of privacy claim under the Jones Act either.

In Lancaster, a railroad worker claimed that his working conditions brought about the complete deterioration of his mental condition. Id. at 811. The court noted that because the Railway Labor Act provides a "swift and adequate remedy" for "tortious harms brought about by acts that lack any physical contact or threat of physical contact," there is no need to make recovery under FELA for these torts available. Id. at 813. The court opined that complaints of too much work, rather than too dangerous work, were not appropriately addressed by FELA. "That is not our idea of a FELA claim; it has nothing to do with the security of the person from physical invasions or menaces." Id. The court indicated that while a false arrest claim might be allowed under FELA, "limiting a person's freedom of movement by arrest or imprisonment is a form of physical interference and firing a person is not." Id.

Using the Seventh Circuit's language as a guide, the court does not believe that the invasion of someone's privacy can be considered a physical invasion or menace compensable by FELA or the Jones Act. Nor can the court conclude that a privacy invasion amounts to a form of physical interference. Admittedly, if the facts are as Wiora claims, such an invasion of privacy would certainly threaten the stability of one's psyche and emotional security. However, this court is bound by the laws of the Seventh Circuit and the court finds no authority permitting it to find that Wiora's invasion of privacy claim speaks to anything but a purely psychological or emotional injury. Therefore, the court must grant defendant's motion for partial summary judgment on Count I as well.

Defendant Harrah's relies upon Lindgren v. United States, 281 U.S. 38, 46, 50 S.Ct. 207, 74 L.Ed. 686 (1930), in arguing that Wiora's claim for invasion of privacy is subject solely to the remedial provisions of the Jones Act. Lindgren states that "the Jones Act is the sole remedial scheme by which a seaman can seek redress against his employer for personal injuries." (Def.'s Mem. at 5.) However, other avenues of relief may exist for plaintiff. First, as a seaperson, Wiora may opt to sue at admiralty law rather than under the Jones Act. An action for unseaworthiness or maintenance and cure might be available under general maritime law. See Wingerter v. Chester Quarry Co., 98-3069, No. 185 F.3d 657, 664-66 (7th Cir.1999). The language of the Act is instructive: "any seaman who shall suffer personal injury in the course of his employment, may, at his election, maintain an action for damages at law." 46 U.S.C.App. § 688. Wiora maintains the option to bring her claims under general admiralty law.

Furthermore, Wiora may initiate state law actions of intentional infliction of emotional distress and invasion of privacy against individual defendants. There is nothing in the statute which bars Wiora from suing the individual persons who distributed the photos and/or surveillance video of her (assuming she can meet any statute of limitation requirements). Any reading of the Jones Act that would require this court to preclude Wiora from bringing her tort claim entirely would thwart the statute's original purpose. For it is clear from a number of Supreme Court holdings that the Jones Act is to be interpreted broadly, so as to enable seapersons to recover for personal injury caused while on his employer's watch. The Jones Act "created new rights in seamen for damages arising from maritime torts and is entitled to a liberal construction to accomplish its beneficent purposes." Cosmopolitan Shipping Co. v. McAllister, 338 U.S. 839, 70 S.Ct. 32, 94 L.Ed. 513 (1949). See also Garrett v. Moore-McCormack Co., 317 U.S. 239, 63 S.Ct. 246, 87 L.Ed. 239 (1942) (holding that the statute must be liberally construed to carry out its full purpose, which was to enlarge admiralty's protection to its wards).

Having found that the court may exercise admiralty jurisdiction over Wiora's claims in Counts I and II, the court need not engage in a protracted discussion of arguments concerning alternative bases for subject matter jurisdiction. Defendant is correct in asserting that the parties are not diverse, therefore no diversity jurisdiction exists. While Harrah's is a Nevada corporation, its principal place of business is in Illinois. (Def.'s 12(M) Stmt. ¶ 9-11.) Since Wiora is also an Illinois citizen, the parties are not completely diverse and the court may not exercise diversity jurisdiction over this case. See 28 U.S.C. § 1332(c)(1). As noted earlier, the Jones Act preempts plaintiff's putative state law claims of intentional infliction of emotional distress and privacy invasion. See Lancaster, 773 F.2d at 812. As such, no supplemental jurisdiction of state law claims by virtue of Title VII exists either.

Conclusion

Thus, for the reasons set forth above, the court finds that the Jones Act provides Wiora, a seaman, with the exclusive remedy for her claims in Counts I and II. Since the Seventh Circuit has held that non-physical injury torts are not cognizable under the Jones Act, the court must dismiss Counts I and II against Harrah's. The court therefore grants defendant's motion for partial summary judgment on Counts I and II. The court instructs parties to discuss settlement prior to the next scheduled court date.

BAY CASINO, LLC v. M/V ROYAL EMPRESS
20 F. Supp. 2d 440 (E.D.N.Y. 1998)

JOHNSON, District Judge.

Introduction

This matter is currently before the Court on Defendants' application, pursuant to Rule E(4)(f) of the Supplemental Rules for Certain Admiralty and Maritime Claims ("Supplemental Rules"), to vacate the arrest and attachment of the M/V ROYAL EMPRESS, and to allow Defendants to post a $200,000 bond instead. Defendants have also moved this Court pursuant to Supplemental Rule E(7) to require Plaintiff to post a $1,069,000 bond as security for their proposed counter-and cross-claims. On April 2, 1998, the Court conducted an evidentiary hearing and directed the parties to submit proposed findings of fact and conclusions of law. The following constitutes the Court's findings of fact and conclusions of law. For the reasons discussed below, the warrant of arrest and process of maritime attachment and garnishment are upheld and Defendants' motion to vacate is DENIED.

FINDINGS OF FACT

A. The Parties

1. Plaintiff Bay Casino, LLC ("Bay Casino" or "Plaintiff" or "Charterer") is a limited liability company organized under the laws of the State of Delaware with its office and principal place of business located at 3202 Emmons Avenue, Brooklyn, New York 11235. Verified Complaint at ¶ 2. Bay Casino has been granted a shipboard gambling license by the New York City Gambling Control Commission.

2. Defendant CGG Ltd. # 1 ("CGG") is a Florida limited partnership having its principal place of business at Tampa, Florida. Joint Venture Agreement between CGG and Belair Financial Services, Inc. ("Joint Venture Agreement"); Plaintiff's Hearing Ex. 1.

3. Defendant Belair ("Belair") is a Delaware corporation having its principal place of business located at Fort Lauderdale, Florida. Joint Venture Agreement at p. 1.

4. Defendant SeaCo Ltd ("SeaCo" or "Defendant" or "Owner") is a joint venture and unincorporated business association with its office and principal place of business located at Tampa, Florida. SeaCo is comprised of CGG and

Belair ("Defendants"). Joint Venture Agreement at p. 1; Hearing at 21-22. The Joint Venture Agreement is dated January 15, 1998, is signed by Buddy Levy, and one of its general purposes was to acquire the M/V Royal Empress—the vessel at issue in the instant case. Id.

5. The M/V ROYAL EMPRESS (the "Vessel") is a passenger vessel owned by SeaCo and registered under the laws of St. Vincent and the Grenadines currently within the jurisdiction of this Court and subject to a warrant of arrest and process of maritime attachment and garnishment pursuant to the Supplemental Rules. Verified Complaint ¶ 3; Warrant of Arrest filed 3/27/98; Process of Maritime Attachment and Garnishment filed 3/27/98; Joint Venture Agreement at p. 1; Claim of Owner filed by Seaco April 3, 1998.

SeaCo purchased the Vessel in January of 1998 for five million dollars with the purpose of placing it at Sheepshead Bay with Bay Casino in order to operate it as a gaming ship. Hearing at 23-24. The Vessel was certified by the Florida office of the United States Coast Guard to carry 896 passengers. Hearing at 46. The Vessel is not certified in New York. Hearing at 47, 51.

6. At all relevant times, Buddy Levy was the Manager of Defendant SeaCo and at the same time, until his termination on March 27, 1998, the Chief Executive Officer of Plaintiff Bay Casino. Levy is also the President of Coastal Gaming Group, Inc. ("CGGI")—a general partner of CGG. Levy testified before the Court at the Hearing and also submitted an affidavit sworn to April 1, 1998. ("Levy Aff."). In connection with the charter, Levy made six trips to New York from Tampa, Florida between January and April of 1998. Hearing at 37.

7. Joseph Kelleher is Executive Vice President of Plaintiff Bay Casino. He also testified at the Hearing and he submitted two affidavits sworn to April 1, 1998 and April 9, 1998, respectively. ("Kelleher Affs.").

8. Gold Star Casinos Inc. ("Gold Star") is a Florida company that is involved in the shipboard management of casinos. Hearing at 33. On December 17, 1996, Bay Casino had entered into an exclusive contract with Gold Star at the inception of the Liberty I cruises. Kornblum Aff. ¶ 13.

B. Background

9. Commencing in or about December, 1996, Plaintiff Bay Casino began operation of shipboard gambling cruises on board the vessel Liberty I departing from a pier leased by Plaintiff in Sheepshead Bay, Brooklyn. Hearing at 7. The pier facility is zoned at two hundred passengers pursuant to a New York City zoning ordinance. Id. Originally, the Liberty I sailed with two hundred passengers. However, between July 2, 1997 and November 3, 1997 when its operations were suspended, the boat sailed with four hundred passengers per cruise. Id. at 7-8. The Liberty I was able to increase its passenger capacity after a permanent floatable barge was employed by Plaintiff. This barge brought the vessel outside the pier headline and excluded it from being covered by the zoning ordinance. Id.

10. On or about June 26, 1997, in response to "cruises to nowhere" that operate from New York City locations, the Council of the City of New York passed a Local Law amending the administrative code of the City of New York

which, in part, established the New York City Gambling Control Commission and established licensing procedures and regulations for applicants seeking to conduct shipboard gambling businesses. Defendants' Ex. 4 to Proposed Findings.

11. On January 8, 1998, Bay Casino filed a Shipboard Gambling Business License Application ("Shipboard Gambling Application") with the New York City Gambling Control Commission. The Shipboard Gambling Application was signed by Levy as Chief Executive Officer of Bay Casino. Hearing at 23 and Defendants' Ex. 5 to Proposed Findings.

12. On or about February 11, 1998, SeaCo filed a Key Vendor Application for License ("Key Vendor Application") with the New York City Gambling Control Commission. The Key Vendor Application was signed by Levy as General Manager of SeaCo. Defendants' Ex. 6 to Proposed Findings.

13. SeaCo's Key Vendor Application, signed by Levy, lists "Applicant's [defendant SeaCo] business address within New York City" as 3202 Emmons Avenue, Brooklyn, N.Y. 11235, which is Bay Casino's address, and also lists two Brooklyn telephone numbers for SeaCo. One of the Brooklyn telephone numbers listed on SeaCo's Key Vendor Application (718-368-9000) is identical to a telephone number listed on the Shipboard Gambling Application filed by Bay Casino. Defendants' Ex. 5 to Proposed Findings at 2; Defendants' Ex. 6 to Proposed Findings at 2.

14. SeaCo's Key Vendor Application, signed by Levy, lists Levy as the designated agent for service of process and his address for service of process as 7439 E. Hillsborough Avenue, Tampa, Florida, 33610. Defendants' Ex. 6 to Proposed Findings at 4.

C. The Bare Boat Agreement

15. Pursuant to an agreement entitled "Bare Boat Charter Party" dated January 29, 1998 (hereinafter "Bare Boat Agreement"), SeaCo as Vessel "Owner agrees to let and demise and Charterer agrees to hire the passenger vessel Royal Empress . . . to be renamed Liberty II" for an initial term of 3 years. Bare Boat Agreement ¶ 1; 5.1. The Bare Boat Agreement was signed by Levy, Manager of SeaCo, as "Owner" on February 10, 1998 and by Joseph Kelleher, COO of Bay Casino, as "Charterer" on February 8, 1998. Id. at p. 15.

16. Pursuant to the Bare Boat Agreement, Levy was appointed Chief Executive Officer of Bay Casino while at the same time continuing in his role as the "exclusive" Manager of defendant SeaCo. Hearing at 23.

17. The Vessel was to be delivered to and accepted by the Charterer no later than February 17, 1998—in which event Charterer could terminate Charter at its option. Id. ¶ 2. The Vessel was to be complete with mechanical and cosmetic upgrades, fully operable in class, and Coast Guard Certified for New York City use. Id. ¶¶ 3, 7.1. Acceptance of the Vessel by Charterer was to be conclusive proof as to the Vessel's compliance with the Charter, subject to latent defects. Id. ¶ 3.

18. Charterer was to have posted in a conspicuous place on the Vessel a notice reading in relevant part: THIS VESSEL IS OWNED BY SEACO, LTD. AND IS UNDER DEMISE CHARTER TO BAY CASINO, LLC. Id. ¶ 9.

19. Charterer was to have "full use and exclusive possession and control of the vessel . . . ." Id. ¶ 4. Charterer was to man, supply, equip, upkeep, navigate, and operate the Vessel at its own expense. Id.

20. The provision for "charter hire" required that Bay Casino as Charterer pay the sum of $5,500 per day to SeaCo commencing "on and from the day and hour of her initial revenue voyage . . . ." Id. ¶ 3; Hearing at 18. Bay Casino's failure to pay "charter hire" would not be deemed a default under the Bare Boat Agreement until only after the first 12 months that charter hire was due. Bare Boat Agreement ¶ 3; Hearing at 41-42.

21. The Vessel never undertook any "revenue voyages" as defined under the Bare Boat Agreement and no charter hire was ever earned or paid. Hearing at 19.

22. Under the Agreement, Charterer would have been paid a monthly "Dock Fee" of $7.50 for each revenue passenger. Bare Boat Agreement ¶¶ 16.3; 17(b).

23. The Bare Boat Agreement required SeaCo to "advance certain funds and credits for the benefit of Charterer" as follows:

A "bank" for casino operations in the amount of $250,000 (¶ 15.8(a)(1)); A cash advance "sufficient to cover all working capital requirements of the Charterer's operations, including the Casino operation, Charter Hire and dock fee . . . in the amount of $100,000 as an advance of initial working capital and in the amount of $150,000 as an additional advance due February 13, 1998." (¶ 15.8(a)(2)); As "Special Advances" against dock fees, $150,000 in cash, and upon execution of the Bare Boat Agreement, an additional $150,000 cash advance, and on February 13, 1998, a further $200,000 advance, totaling $500,000. (¶ 15.8(a)(3)). These Special Advances were to be repaid to owner in 36 monthly installments, provided the vessel was on hire. (¶ 17).

24. The Bare Boat Agreement also provided that SeaCo would share in the profits by being paid a "Consulting Fee" based on 75% of the Net Operating Revenue, calculated by subtracting Operating Expenses and Dock Fees from Gross Revenues. "Gross Revenues" were defined to include revenue from shoreside operations, such as cash machines, and a possible gift shop. Bare Boat Agreement ¶¶ 16.1-16.2, 16.4; Hearing at 19, 41-42.

25. Additionally, the Bare Boat Agreement required that Plaintiff, as Charterer, at its sole cost and expense, obtain and pay for all insurance on the Vessel. Bare Boat Agreement ¶¶ 10.1; 11.

26. SeaCo was to provide casino consulting services by designating two of the four Casino Management Committee members. Id. ¶ 15.2(b)(1). However, Bay Casino was to nominate the Casino Manager and all other Casino personnel. Id. ¶ 15.2(a). SeaCo was to make available to Bay Casino certain services relating to the recruiting and recommendation for hiring suitable employees for food and beverage services, or alternatively, at Bay Casino's request, was to identify and recruit a suitable concessionaire to provide those services. SeaCo was also permitted to negotiate a food and beverage concession agreement. Id. ¶ 15.4.

27. SeaCo also was to "recruit and recommend for hiring suitable employees for all terminal operations and other shoreside services," was empowered to

"identify and recruit" a suitable contractor to provide such services, and was authorized to "negotiate a services agreement on behalf of Charterer" for provision of such services. Id. ¶ 15.4.

28. Finally, Owner was obligated to "make available and provide consulting services to Charterer with respect to all purchasing of fuel, lubricants, other consumables, materials, supplies, food and beverages, furniture and equipment and all other articles of any nature whatsoever for use by or on [sic] onboard the Vessel." Bay Casino was allowed to appoint SeaCo "as its limited purpose agent to effect purchases of such materials, supplies and equipment." Id. ¶ 15.6.

29. The Charter stated that the Charter Party shall be governed by New York law and that the parties submit to the exclusive jurisdiction and venue of the courts of the United States and the State of New York. Id. ¶ 23.4

30. Levy testified at the hearing that he believed he had a joint venture agreement with Bay Casino when he signed the Charter. Hearing at 24. On February 2, 1998, Levy, acting in his capacity as Manager of SeaCo, sent a letter to Michael Kornblum, principal of Bay Casino, wherein Levy described the Bare Boat Agreement as follows:

> Of a more serious nature are some changes which are probably necessary [to the Bare Boat Agreement] because of the unusual relationship which exists between Bay Casinos and SeaCo. Clearly, this is not the normal charter agreement and upon further review it appears to me that certain amendments should be considered to properly reflect the type of relationship which actually exists. What has been created by this Charter Agreement is not only a charter for hire, but also a joint venture arrangement whereby operational control and profit divisions are provided.

Ex. 8 to Defendants' Proposed Findings at 2; Hearing at 24-25.

31. Levy never received a response to his letter. Hearing at 25-26.

32. The Bare Boat Agreement was terminated by a telefaxed letter dated March 27, 1998 from Kornblum at Bay Casino to Levy at SeaCo. Defendants' Ex. 9 to Proposed Findings. The reasons given for the termination were "the various defaults and prior writings to date." Id.

33. Levy was terminated "for cause" as CEO of Bay Casino via a telefaxed letter dated March 27, 1998. Ex. 4 to Levy Aff.

D. Defendants' Alleged Breach and Plaintiff's Termination of the Bare Boat Agreement

34. Pursuant to the terms of the Bare Boat Agreement, the Vessel was required to be "delivered to and accepted by [Bay Casino] as soon as possible, but in no event later than February 17, 1998 at the Port of New York . . . ." Additionally, the Bare Boat Agreement gave Plaintiff the right to terminate the Charter "[i]n the event of non-delivery of the Vessel on or before February 17, 1998." Bare Boat Agreement ¶¶ 2, 5.2(a)(10).

35. The Bare Boat Agreement also gave Bay Casino the right to terminate the Charter if (1) the operation of the Vessel or casino did not conform to any

applicable laws or regulations; (2) non-payment of the monthly dock fee in a timely manner; (3) owner failed to provide sufficient working capital required in a timely manner; (4) Coastal Gaming ceased to own at least 50 percent of owner; (5) Levy was no longer exclusive manager of owner; (6) owner breached its obligations to provide cash advances for working capital and advance dock fees in a timely manner; (7) owner materially breaches any warranties and representations of the charter; and (8) Levy was terminated with cause from CEO position of Bay Casino. Id. ¶ 5.2(a)(1)-(8).

36. The Vessel was not delivered in New York until on or about February 26, 1998. It was "conditionally delivered" to Plaintiff on February 26, 1998 but was not in the condition required by the charter. Verified Complaint at ¶ 7.

37. When delivered in New York on February 26, 1998, the Vessel was not Coast Guard Certified for operations in New York. Hearing at 47. At the hearing, Kelleher testified that she was still uncertified and therefore could not carry any passengers. Id. at 6.

38. Before the Coast Guard will certify the Vessel, it requires that two lifeboats be repaired, that a telephone be repaired, and that it undergo a sea trial of her maneuverability. Kelleher Aff. ¶¶ 17; 21; Hearing at 9.

39. The owner, SeaCo, is responsible for the Coast Guard certification. Id. at 9.

CONCLUSIONS OF LAW

A. Jurisdiction

1. This Court has subject matter jurisdiction of this matter based upon the admiralty and maritime jurisdiction of the United States. 28 U.S.C. § 1333; U.S. Const. Art. III., § 2, cl. 1; California and State Lands Comm. v. Deep Sea Research, 523 U.S. 491, __, 118 S.Ct. 1464, 1469, 149 L.Ed.2d 626 (1998) (judicial power of federal courts extends to all cases of admiralty and maritime jurisdiction).

B. Overview of In Rem and In Personam Proceedings in Admiralty

2. Under the admiralty law of the United States, in personam and in rem actions may arise from the same claim, and may be brought separately or in the same suit. Supplemental Rule C(1)(b). As its name implies, the in personam action is filed against the owner personally, whereas the in rem action is filed against the res, the vessel—a maritime lien on the vessel being a prerequisite to an action in rem. Belcher Co. of Alabama, Inc. v. M/V Maratha Mariner, 724 F.2d 1161, 1163 (5th Cir.1984), citing G. Gilmore & C. Black, The Law of Admiralty 685 (2d ed.1975), § 1-12 at 35. Quasi in rem actions are based on a claim for money and initiated by an attachment or other seizure of property when the court has no jurisdiction over the person of the defendant, but has jurisdiction over a thing belonging to him. Supplemental Rule E; Belcher, 724 F.2d at 1163-1164.

3. The distinction between these types of proceedings is explained by the Supplemental Rules. Attachment issues "with respect to any admiralty or

maritime claim in personam and its purpose is to attach the defendant's goods or chattels or other assets if the defendant shall not be found in the jurisdiction." Belcher, 724 F.2d at 1164; Supplemental Rule B. In contrast, an action in rem is available only to enforce a maritime lien and the arrest warrant extends only to the vessel. Id.; Supplemental Rule C. In the instant case, Plaintiff has filed an in rem action against the vessel and an in personam action against SeaCo, CGG, and Belair. Verified Complaint.

4. In both in rem and in personam proceedings involving seized vessels, the vessel is seized, may be released and substituted for security, and may later be sold to satisfy a judgment. Belcher, 724 F.2d at 1165.

5. However, in the in rem proceeding, the owner of the vessel bears no personal liability. The vessel is sold to satisfy the lien. If the proceeds of the sale of the vessel are inadequate to cover the lien, the owner is not liable for the balance. Id. In contrast, in the in personam proceeding (the attachment action), the vessel is seized only to compel the owner's appearance and if the proceeds of the sale of the vessel do not satisfy the judgment, the owner remains liable for the balance of the amount. Id.

6. Rule C allows in rem and in personam causes of action to be tried in the same proceeding, where appropriate. Dowell Division of the Dow Chemical Co. v. Franconia Sea Transport, Ltd., 504 F.Supp. 579, 582 (S.D.N.Y.1980), aff'd. 659 F.2d 1058 (2d Cir.), cert. denied, 454 U.S. 941, 102 S.Ct. 478, 70 L.Ed.2d 249 (1981). When a maritime lien attaches, the plaintiff may pursue an in rem action against the vessel and the plaintiff may also bring an in personam action against the defendant who is allegedly liable in contract, tort, etc. Id. The two rules may be invoked simultaneously, as they are here. Amstar Corp. v. S/S Alexandros T., 664 F.2d 904, 906 (4th Cir.1981); Navieros Inter-Americanos, S.A., v. M/V Vasilia Express, 120 F.3d 304 (1st Cir.1997).

C. Rule C Arrest of the Vessel

7. Supplemental Rule C allows an action in rem to "enforce any maritime lien."

8. It is well-settled that although arrest of maritime property is a remedy available within the maritime jurisdiction, it requires an underlying maritime cause of action supporting a maritime lien in the property arrested. Thus, the only basis for the arrest of a vessel in rem is the enforcement of a maritime lien in favor of the party suing the vessel and seeking the arrest. Rainbow Line, Inc. v. M/V Tequila, 480 F.2d 1024, 1027-28 (2d Cir.1973); Marubeni America Corp. v. M/V Unity, 802 F.Supp. 1353, 1355 (D.Md.1992) (citing Gilmore and Black, The Law of Admiralty § 9-19).

9. In order to avail itself of the device of maritime arrest, a plaintiff has the burden of showing that it is entitled to a maritime lien; if it cannot do so, the arrest fails and must be dissolved. See Supplemental Rule E(4)(f) (stating that the plaintiff "shall be required to show why the arrest or attachment should not be vacated").

I. Joint Ventures and Maritime Liens

10. Under well-established maritime law, one who is a joint venturer does not have a maritime lien, and cannot enforce one against his co-venturer.

Sasportes v. M/V Sol de Copacabana, 581 F.2d 1204, 1208 (5th Cir.1978). A co-venturer may only entertain an in personam action against the vessel owner for claims arising out of their mutual joint venture. A co-venturer may not lawfully have a maritime lien against the ship itself. Sasportes, 581 F.2d at 1208-09.

11. The rationale for this established doctrine is that a co-venturer is not a "stranger to the vessel," and therefore relies not upon the credit of the ship, but rather upon the credit of the owner for payments, claims and reimbursement. Vera, Inc. v. The Tug Dakota, 769 F.Supp. 451, 457 (E.D.N.Y.1991).

12. In New York, in order to form a joint venture, all of the following elements must be met: (1) two or more persons must enter into a specific agreement to carry on an enterprise for profit; (2) their agreement must evidence their intent to be joint venturers; (3) each must make a contribution of property, financing, skill, knowledge, or effort; (4) each must have some degree of joint control over the venture; and (5) there must be a provision for the sharing of both profits and losses. Itel Containers International Corp. v. Atlanttrafik Express Service Ltd., 909 F.2d 698, 701 (2d Cir.1990); Independent Energy Corp. v. Trigen Energy Corp., 944 F.Supp. 1184, 1201 (S.D.N.Y.1996).

13. "The ultimate inquiry [in determining whether a joint venture exists] is whether the parties have so joined their property, interest, skills and risks that for the purposes of the particular adventure their respective contributions have become as one and the commingled property and interests of the parties have thereby been made subject to each of the associates on the trust and inducement that each would act for their joint benefit." Independent Energy Corp. v. Trigen Energy Corp., 944 F.Supp. 1184 (S.D.N.Y.1996).

14. The finding of a joint venture is predicated on an examination of the entire relationship between the parties; no one factor is considered decisive. Fulcher's Point Pride Seafood v. M/V "Theodora Maria", 935 F.2d 208, 211-12 (11th Cir. 1991); Sasportes, 581 F.2d at 1207.

15. In this case, the Court finds that the parties had a owner-charterer relationship under the Bare Boat Agreement, and not a joint-venture as Defendants argue. First, all five elements required to be in existence under New York law in order to find a joint venture have not been shown to exist in the parties' Charter. First, although there was sharing of profits under the Agreement, there was no sharing of losses. Second, although under the agreement SeaCo was to contribute skills, knowledge, and financing, the Bare Boat Agreement did not evidence a mutual intent to be joint venturers as the second element requires. The Agreement is entitled "Bare Boat Charter Party" and in numerous places refers to SeaCo as "Owner" and to Bay Casino as "Charterer."

Notwithstanding Levy's claims in his February 2 letter to Kornblum that the Agreement was "not only a charter for hire, but also a joint venture arrangement," Levy signed the Agreement on February 10, 1998 without the changes he had requested to reflect a joint venture arrangement. In addition, just approximately one month earlier Levy had signed an agreement between CGG and Belair which established SeaCo as a joint venture with its purpose as the purchase of the M/V Royal Empress. Plaintiff's Hearing Ex. 1. In comparing the two documents, many differences are apparent.

Unlike the Bare Boat Charter Agreement, the agreement between CGG and Belair is entitled and referenced throughout as a "Joint Venture Agreement." Furthermore, it refers to the parties throughout the document as the "parties" and as "joint venturers," and not as "owner" or "charterer" as SeaCo and Bay Casino are described in the Bare Boat Charter. Furthermore, there is an explicit provision for the sharing of both profits and losses. Id. at ¶ 2.2. Finally, the Bare Boat Charter required Bay Casino to post a visible notice stating that the Vessel was owned by SeaCo and was under a demise charter to Bay Casino. For these reasons, the Court holds that Plaintiff and Defendants did not have a joint venture agreement.

II. Maritime Liens Arising from Breach of Charter Party

16. The term "charter party" refers to the document setting forth the terms of a contract when one person (the "charterer") takes over the use of the whole ship belonging to another ("the owner"). G. Gilmore & C. Black, supra, at 193, cited in Int'l Marine Towing, Inc. v. Southern Leasing Partners, Ltd., 722 F.2d 126, 130 (5th Cir.1983), cert. denied sub nom, First Miss. Nat'l Bank v. Int'l Marine Towing Inc., 469 U.S. 821, 105 S.Ct. 94, 83 L.Ed.2d 40 (1984).

17. There are three types of charter parties: the first two, the "voyage charter" and the "time charter," occur when the vessel is manned and navigated by the owner. Id. The third charter, the "bareboat" or "demise charter," occurs when the charterer operates the ship and is regarded as the owner of the ship pro hac vice. Id. The charter in the instant case belongs to this third category.

18. Under the executory contract doctrine, a charterer has a maritime lien against an owner once performance of the charter contract begins. In other words, there can be no maritime lien for breach of an executory contract. Rainbow Line, Inc. v. M/V Tequila, 480 F.2d 1024, 1027 n. 6 (2d Cir.1973).

19. With respect to time charters, courts are in agreement that delivery of the vessel to a time charterer commences the performance of a time charter and removes it from executory status. Rainbow Line, 480 F.2d 1024, Int'l Marine Towing, 722 F.2d at 126.

20. However, in the case of the bareboat charter, there is a "dearth of case law" and discussions in treatises are "equally oblique." Int'l Marine Towing, 722 F.2d at 130 n. 7.

21. In Int'l Marine Towing, the Court explained in a footnote the differences between when performance begins in a time charter as opposed to a bareboat charter: "Delivery of the vessel commences the performance of a time charter and removes it from executory status. Delivery of the vessel to the charterer and its use by the same also commences the performance of a bareboat charter as so to remove its executory status." 722 F.2d at 131 n. 8. However, in a later case, the Court stated in dictum that in relying on the Second Circuit's reasoning in Rainbow Line, Inc. v. M/V Tequila, 480 F.2d at 1027 n. 6, it noted that a bareboat charter "ceases to be executory when the vessel is delivered

to the charterer." E.A.S.T., Inc. of Stamford, Conn. v. M/V Alaia, 876 F.2d 1168, 1175 (5th Cir.1989), rehearing and rehearing en banc denied.

22. In an earlier Eastern District of New York case involving a bareboat charter arrangement for a tug boat, the Court held that a maritime lien existed and the bareboat charter was no longer executory "since it was delivered to the charterer . . . ." Petersen Towing Corp. v. Capt. Abrams, Inc., 388 F.Supp. 1166, 1169-1170 (E.D.N.Y.1975), cited as persuasive authority in Int'l Marine Towing, 722 F.2d at 131. See also Florida Yacht Brokers, Inc. v. Yacht Huckster, 249 F.Supp. 371 (S.D.Fla.1965) (finding that breach of bareboat charter by owner gave rise to maritime lien), also cited as persuasive authority by the Fifth Circuit in Int'l Marine Towing.

23. The Court finds that in the case at bar, the charter was no longer executory because the boat had been delivered to and accepted by Bay Casino. In addition, between February 4th and March 6th, SeaCo had made advances and payments to Bay Casino for working capital. See § E, "Damages," below. Therefore, because the charter was no longer executory, SeaCo's alleged breach of the demise charter gave rise to maritime liens by unpaid vendors. Thus, Defendants' motion to vacate the Rule C arrest of the vessel is denied.

D. Process of Maritime Attachment and Garnishment

24. Supplemental Rule B authorizes, in admiralty and maritime cases, attachment of a defendant's assets as a means of obtaining jurisdiction over a defendant when he cannot be "found" within the federal district in which the attachment is sought. The purpose of Rule B is to enable the plaintiff both to acquire jurisdiction over the defendant and obtain security for any resulting judgment. Swift & Co. Packers v. Compania Colombiana Del Caribe, S.A., 339 U.S. 684, 70 S.Ct. 861, 94 L.Ed. 1206 (1950). Attachment may not be utilized solely for the purpose of acquiring security. Chilean Line Inc. v. United States, 344 F.2d 757, 760 (2d Cir.1965); Seawind Compania, S.A. v. Crescent Line, Inc., 320 F.2d 580, 582 (2d Cir.1963).

25. Rule B provides:

Rule B. Attachment and Garnishment: Special Provisions

(1) When Available; Complaint, Affidavit, Judicial Authorization, and Process. With respect to any admiralty or maritime claim in personam a verified complaint may contain a prayer for process to attach the defendant's goods and chattels, or credits and effects in the hands of garnishees to be named in the process to the amount sued for, if the defendant shall not be found within the district. Such a complaint shall be accompanied by an affidavit signed by the plaintiff or the plaintiff's attorney that, to the affiant's knowledge, or to the best of the affiant's information and belief, the defendant cannot be found within the district.

26. Because jurisdiction over the person is gained only through the attached property, Rule B jurisdiction is quasi in rem in nature. Limonium Maritime, S.A. v. Mizushima Marinera, S.A., 961 F.Supp. 600, 605 (S.D.N.Y.1997), citing Maryland Tuna Corp. v. M/S Benares, 429 F.2d 307, 311 (2d Cir.1970) (Rule B attachment is quasi in rem proceeding).

27. Courts have enunciated a two-prong test to determine whether a defendant is "found within the district" for purposes of a Supplemental Rule B attachment: (1) can the foreign defendant be found within the district in terms of jurisdiction, and (2) can the defendant be found for service of process. Seawind Compania, S.A. v. Crescent Line, Inc., 320 F.2d 580, 582 (2d Cir.1963); Navieros Inter-Americanos v. M/V Vasilia Express, 120 F.3d 304, 314-15 (1st Cir.1997). In other words, the defendant must be able to accept process as well as being " 'engaged in sufficient activity in the district to subject it to jurisdiction even in the absence of a resident agent expressly authorized to accept process.' " VTT Vulcan Petroleum v. Langham-Hill Petroleum, Inc., 684 F.Supp. 389 (S.D.N.Y.1988), quoting Seawind, 320 F.2d at 583.

28. The party that has obtained the attachment bears the burden of showing its validity. See Supplemental Rule E(4)(f).

I. First Prong: Found Within District in the Jurisdictional Sense

29. A defendant corporation is found within jurisdiction of a federal district court if in the recent past it has conducted substantial commercial activities in the district and will probably continue to do so in the future. United States v. Cia Naviera, 178 F.Supp. 561 (S.D.N.Y.1959); International Shoe Co. v. Washington, 326 U.S. 310, 66 S.Ct. 154, 90 L.Ed. 95 (1945). Such substantial business includes sending a vessel into the district. Navieros Inter-Americanos, S.A. v. M/V Vasilia Express, 120 F.3d 304, 315 (1st Cir.1997).

30. The Second Circuit has held that when a contract that is at issue in a lawsuit had been made and breached in a State, personal jurisdiction exists over the foreign defendant in that particular State. See Seawind, 320 F.2d at 583 (corporation's activities in making contract in New York and allegedly breaching it in New York made the corporation subject to suit in New York). See also VTT Vulcan, 684 F.Supp. at 392 ("Seawind stands for the proposition that where a contract, which is the subject of a lawsuit, has been made and allegedly breached in the jurisdiction where attachment is sought, the contract can provide continued 'jurisdictional presence' even after the defendant has physically terminated other contacts with the jurisdiction").

31. In addition, a forum selection clause provides a basis for exercise of in personam jurisdiction. See M/S Bremen v. Zapata Off-Shore, 407 U.S. 1, 9-10, 92 S.Ct. 1907, 32 L.Ed.2d 513 (1972) (a forum-selection clause is tantamount to consent to jurisdiction in a particular forum); Maritime Ventures Int'l Inc. v. Caribbean Trading & Fidelity, Ltd., 689 F.Supp. 1340, 1348 (S.D.N.Y.1988), recons. denied, 722 F.Supp. 1032 (S.D.N.Y.1989) ("The Supreme Court has held that a federal court sitting in admiralty should give full effect to forum-selection clauses").

32. The Court finds in the case at bar that SeaCo was found within the district in the jurisdictional sense because it had conducted substantial commercial activities in the district by sending the Vessel into the district, by sending payments to Plaintiff, and by executing and breaching the charter in New York. In addition, the Charter contained a forum selection clause whereby the parties consented to suit in New York. However, even if a foreign defendant "is found to be within the district in the jurisdictional sense, its

property is not immune from attachment." Navieros, 120 F.3d at 315, quoting United States v. Cia. Naviera Continental S.A., 178 F.Supp. 561, 563-64 (S.D.N.Y.1959). The fact that the defendant is present in the jurisdictional sense will not suffice, if he cannot be found for service of process within the district (the second prong of the test). Integrated Container Service, Inc. v. Starlines Container Shipping, Ltd., 476 F.Supp. 119, 122 (S.D.N.Y.1979). This is because Rule B's purpose is two-fold: (1) to assure defendant's appearance and (2) to assure satisfaction in case the suit is successful. A post-attachment appearance may later moot the first purpose, but it does not address the second. Id., citing Swift v. Compania Colombiana, 339 U.S. 684, 693-95, 70 S.Ct. 861, 94 L.Ed. 1206 (1950).

II. Second Prong: Found Within District for Service of Process

33. A party seeking a Rule B attachment must make a bona fide effort to find its adversary in the district. Seawind, 320 F.2d at 583, but it is not necessary that an exhaustive search be conducted. Royal Swan Navigation Co. v. Global Container Lines, Ltd., 868 F.Supp. 599, 603 (S.D.N.Y.1994).

34. The presence of a transient individual almost once a week at a certain office within the district has been held to be insufficient to satisfy the second prong of the test. Royal Swan, 868 F.Supp. at 603.

35. In addition, the mere known presence of an agent authorized to accept process does not, by itself, preclude foreign attachment. Antco Shipping Co. v. Yukon Compania Naviera, 318 F.Supp. 626, 628 (S.D.N.Y.1970), citing Seawind, 320 F.2d at 583.

36. This Court finds that Plaintiff made reasonable efforts to find Defendants in the district, but that Defendants' presence in the district was not sufficient to satisfy the second prong of the test. Levy had only been within the district six times over the course of approximately three months. Furthermore, his designated address for service of process on behalf of SeaCo was in Florida. Finally, Kelleher of Bay Casino was unable to reach Levy after March 20th. Kelleher Supplemental Aff. ¶ 3. Levy did not return any of Kelleher's phone calls during the week of March 23rd. Id.

37. Therefore, because Defendants could not be found in this district for service of process, Defendant's motion to vacate the attachment is denied.

E. Damages

38. It is well-settled that in an attachment proceeding, the plaintiff need not prove its damages with exactitude but the court must be satisfied that the plaintiff's claims are not frivolous. Dongbu Express Co. v. Navios Corp., 944 F.Supp. 235 (S.D.N.Y.1996).

39. Bay Casino is seeking to recover damages under three categories: unpaid working capital, indemnity for maritime liens, and lost revenues.

40. Defendant failed to provide working capital to Plaintiff. Kornblum Aff. ¶ 30.

(a) On February 4, 1998, SeaCo made an initial advance of $100,000 that was due on the signing of the Bare Boat Agreement. Kelleher Aff. ¶ 9.

(b) On February 11, Bay Casino requested an additional $300,000 advance. Kelleher Aff. ¶ 9 & Ex. 2.

(c) On February 13, SeaCo made a partial payment of $60,000 and on February 20 and 25, SeaCo made further partial payments of $100,000 and $50,000. Kelleher Aff. ¶ 9.

(d) On February 27, 1998, Bay Casino demanded an additional $400,000 for working capital. On March 5 and 6, Plaintiff received partial advances of $100,000 and $60,000. Kelleher Aff. ¶ 11.

(e) On March 18, Plaintiff demanded a working capital advance of $200,000, which was allegedly never made and as a result, Bay Casino failed to meet its payroll obligations. Kelleher Aff. ¶ 9.

(f) As alleged by Plaintiff, at the time of the Hearing the amount allegedly owed for working capital was $724,893. Kelleher Aff. ¶¶ 13, 23 and Ex. 6.

41. As alleged by Plaintiff, the amount for unpaid vendors with maritime liens is $639,457. Kelleher Aff. ¶¶ 14, 15, 24 and Exs. 8 and 9; Hearing at 17.

42. The amount of lost revenue claimed by Bay Casino is $12,177,584—which is comprised of dock fees and twenty-five percent of casino profits. Hearing at 17; Kelleher Aff. ¶ 25 and Ex. 10. This number is derived from the pro forma attached to the Bare Boat Agreement as an exhibit and initialed on every page by both Levy and Kelleher on February 10, 1998. Kelleher Aff. Ex. 1; Hearing at 28. The pro forma represented the parties' joint projections as to the level of net revenue to be derived from the charter and was arrived at with input from both Bay Casino and SeaCo. Kornblum Aff. ¶¶ 23-24; Hearing at 45. Levy testified at the hearing that the "pro forma was crucial to the operation of the agreement because it set the parameters under which the parties would have to operate in terms of expenses and funding requirements." Hearing at 28.

43. For the year 1998, the pro forma lists total revenue as $34,472,483 and net revenue as $33,527,034 after total cost of sales of $945,449 is deducted. Total payroll is $9,185,624, total other expenses is $16,735,539, adding up to a total operating expense of $25,921,163. Pro forma at 1; Hearing at 44. After the expenses are deducted from the net revenue, the EBITDA (earnings before interest, taxes, depreciation and amortization) is $7,605,871. Id. Twenty-five percent of this number is $1,901,467.75.

44. Dock fees of $7.50 per passenger for a three-year period in accordance with the Charter ¶ 16.3 and the pro forma passenger projection add up to $6,473.181. Kelleher Aff. Ex. 10. The pro forma projects that for the Year 1998, the average number of passengers per cruise would be 363 and the total number of passengers 314,364. Pro forma at 2. Although the pro forma indicates that the Vessel's passenger capacity is 800, the projection indicates that each cruise would contain between 252 and 440 passengers. Id.; Hearing at 29-30.

45. On February 8, 1998, two days before Levy initialed the pro forma, he sent a fax to Kornblum at Bay Casino questioning why the Vessel was limited to 200 passengers at its inception. Defendants' Hearing Ex. A; Hearing at 30.

In the fax, Levy states that it was his understanding that they could start at 400 passengers and increase to 800 almost immediately. Id. In a letter dated March 17, 1998, Kornblum responded to Levy's assertions as follows: "You and I agreed that, although we believe that New York City zoning does not apply, Bay Casino was to resume its casino cruise service 'softly' at an initial capacity of 200 and increase such capacity to 400, 600, and 800 over a 90 day period . . . . To this end, Bay Casino has consistently indicated to SeaCo that the initial capacity was to be 200, as discussed in our meeting of Wednesday, March 4, 1998, which you were in agreement." Defendants' Hearing Ex. B; Hearing at 31-32.

46. This Court finds that the numbers in the pro forma to be a reasonable basis for calculating damages. The pro forma was composed by both parties, initialed by both parties, and attached to the Bare Boat Charter Agreement as an exhibit. In addition, because Bay Casino's Liberty I had sailed with 400 passengers during its run, it is reasonable to conclude that the Liberty II would sail with between 252 and 440 passengers as the pro forma estimated.

47. At this early stage of the litigation, the attachment of the Vessel is reasonable given the extent of the amount of damages claimed by Plaintiff. This Court reminds Plaintiff, however, that it has a continuing duty to mitigate damages.

CONCLUSION

For the reasons stated above, Defendants' motion to vacate the Rule C arrest of the Vessel and the Rule B attachment of the Vessel is DENIED.

Defendants' request for counter-security in the amount of $1,069,000 related to its proposed counter-and cross-claims will be addressed in a separate opinion. Based on the record currently before it, the Court cannot reasonably determine how much counter-security, if any, Defendants are entitled to obtain from Plaintiff. Therefore, Plaintiff is directed to respond in brief to Defendants' request for counter-security on or before May 22, 1998 and Defendants' reply is to be filed no later than two weeks after receipt of Plaintiff's response.

SO ORDERED.

Notes

1. As *Horak* and *Wiora* explain, claims involving shipboard gaming enterprises are subject to maritime law if the structure is a "vessel" operating on "navigable waters" and the potential exists to disrupt "maritime commerce." *See further Soloman v. Blue Chip Casino, Inc.*, 772 N.E.2d 515 (Ind. Ct. App. 2002) (dismissing Jones Act lawsuits filed by slot representative and table games specialist because vessel was docked on man-made lake that could not be used by commercial shipping).

2. After the court upheld the arrest and attachment in *Bay Casino*, the parties agreed to go their separate ways, all of the claims were dropped, and the case was dismissed. Bay Casino subsequently lost its New York gaming license, while SeaCo's principals briefly operated the ship in Jacksonville, Florida, before putting her up for sale.

3. A particularly notable example of maritime law affecting a gaming operation arose in February 2000 when the federal government ordered Konstantinos "Gus" Boulis, the owner of SunCruz Casinos, the country's largest cruises-to-nowhere fleet, to sell his ships because he had concealed his initial involvement in their operation. Boulis had done so because at the time he was a Greek national and federal maritime law permits only United States citizens to hold a majority interest in American-flagged vessels.

To comply with the government's demand, Boulis in September 2000 sold SunCruz to Adam Kidan, a disbarred New York lawyer, and others for $147.5 million. The two men soon had a falling out over the terms of the deal, but just as matters were coming to a head Boulis was killed in a gangland slaying. Pressured by creditors, overwhelmed by lawsuits, and with the company in bankruptcy, Kidan in July 2001 agreed to transfer his 35% interest in SunCruz to Boulis's estate for a mere $200,000. *See* Jeff Shields, *Boulis Estate Wins SunCruz; Federal Court Resolves Bankruptcy*, S. Fla. Sun-Sentinel, July 31, 2001, at 1A.

4. For a further look at the interplay between admiralty law and shipboard gaming, *see* Steve B. Belgrade, *The Riverboat Casino Employee Who Primarily Works on Land: An Accidental Seaman?*, 2 Gaming L. Rev. 57 (1998); Michael DiDomenico, *Injured Riverboat Casino Employees: Jones Act Juries or State Workers' Compensation Remedies?*, 6 Gaming L. Rev. 97 (2002); Nancy L. Hengen, *Riverboat Gaming and the Jones Act*, SC91 ALI-ABA 211 (June 25, 1998); Richard J. McLaughlin, *Floating Casinos, Personal Injury and Death Claims, and Admiralty Jurisdiction*, 64 Miss. L.J. 439 (1995); Steven E. Psarellis et al., *Bet Your Lien and Roll the Dice: Maritime Liens and Riverboat Gambling*, 6 U.S.F. Mar. L.J. 49 (1993); Leland S. Smith, III & John D. Brady, *A Case for the Exercise of Federal Court Jurisdiction Over Certain Personal Injury Claims Against Riverboat Casinos*, 64 Miss. L.J. 555 (1995); Daniel A. Tadros, Note, *Pavone v. Mississippi Riverboat Amusement Corp.*, 26 J. Mar. L. & Com. 630 (1995); Brian P. Brancato, Comment, *Blackjack or Bust: Personal Injury Suits on Riverboat Casinos*, 19 Tul. Mar. L.J. 133 (1994); Alice K. Mulvaney, Note, *King v. Grand Casinos of Mississippi, Inc.—Gulfport: Is Vessel Status More than a Roll of the Dice?*, 73 Tul. L. Rev. 365 (1998).

Problem 30

While on a foreign-flagged ship on the high seas, two passengers made a bet. If the loser ultimately refuses to pay and the winner sues, what role, if any, will federal maritime law play in the dispute? *See Wells v. Liddy*, 186 F.3d 505 (4th Cir. 1999), *cert. denied*, 528 U.S. 1118 (2000).

D. SHORE LAW

LEISURE TIME CRUISE CORPORATION v. TOWN OF BARNSTABLE
62 F. Supp. 2d 202 (D. Mass. 1999)

SARIS, District Judge.

This case involves a high-stakes struggle over gambling off the coast of Cape Cod in the waters of Nantucket Sound. Plaintiff Leisure Time Cruise Corporation ("Leisure Time") has moved for a preliminary injunction enjoining the defendants from interfering with its operation of a gambling boat, a so-called "cruise to nowhere," out of Hyannis Harbor. Because state regulation of gambling is not federally preempted and no due process rights have been violated, gambling is not in the cards this summer for Cape Cod. After hearing, the motion for preliminary relief is DENIED.

BACKGROUND

Site Plan Approval

In April 1999, Leisure Time obtained a lease for a parcel of property in Hyannis, Massachusetts, containing a restaurant, docking, and parking facilities. As it was required to do by local law, on May 11, 1999, Leisure Time made Site Plan Application to the Town of Barnstable and provided specific information to the Town's building commissioner regarding its intention to operate a twice-daily gambling cruise out of the harbor on the MV Leisure Lady, a United States flag vessel. Known as a "cruise to nowhere," the trip would entail carrying 500 passengers daily into international waters in Nantucket Sound for several hours of gambling, dining, drinking, and entertainment. The ship would then return to the dock without making any intervening stops. After a lengthy public hearing on May 18, 1999, at which several Town Councilors objected to the proposed gaming activities, the building commissioner requested and received supplemental information from Leisure Time concerning these activities. The Site Plan Review hearing concluded on June 1, 1999.

Despite the opposition to the project, the building commissioner issued a Site Plan approval, which Leisure Time agreed to and signed in draft form on June 8, 1999, and in final form on June 10, 1999. Successful completion of a Site Plan Review does not allow the applicant to bypass local or regional requirements. Therefore, the approval (and hence operation of the gambling boat) was explicitly conditioned on Leisure Time's procurement of a number of local permits and on the performance of a long list of improvements to the waterfront and parking areas. To date, plaintiff has not fulfilled many of these conditions.

The Conservation Commission

On June 9, 1999, the Town of Barnstable Conservation Commission (the "Conservation Commission") issued a cease and desist order requiring Leisure Time to remove permanently the gambling boat from its berth, in part on the ground that the pilings did not comply with the conditions to Site Plan approval.

After a hearing on June 15, 1999, a second cease and desist order issued. The Conservation Commission has the authority to regulate public trust rights, recreation, and navigation under the Wetlands Protection Ordinance, Chapter III, Article 27. See Fafard v. Strauss, No. 97-771 (Barnstable Sup.Ct. Apr. 22, 1999).

The Cape Cod Commission

In the meantime, on May 27, 1999, the Conservation Commission referred the project to the Cape Cod Commission, a regional planning and land use commission created by an Act of the Massachusetts General Court and possessing broad authority to regulate developments of regional impact ("DRI"s), see 1990 Mass.Acts ch. 716, § 1(b). A DRI is generally defined as "a development which, because of its magnitude or the magnitude of its impact on the natural or built environment, is likely to present development issues significant to or affecting more than one municipality." Id. § 2(h). The Barnstable County Assembly of Delegates has the authority to adopt "standards and criteria" for determining what constitutes a DRI. Id. at § 12(a); see also Flynn v. Burman, 30 F.Supp.2d 68, 71 (D.Mass.1998) (discussing the Cape Cod Commission's jurisdiction). Municipal agencies must refer any proposed development that meets the pertinent criteria to the Cape Cod Commission for review as a DRI before they can take any action to grant approval for the project. See 1990 Mass.Acts ch. 716, § 12(h); Flynn, 30 F.Supp.2d at 71. While the Cape Cod Commission is considering the mandatory referral, the local authorities' review of the matter is suspended, as are the statutory time periods governing such review. See 1990 Mass.Acts ch. 716, § 12(h); Flynn, 30 F.Supp.2d at 71.

In addition, the Cape Cod Commission has the discretion to consider proposed developments that do not fall within the criteria warranting mandatory referral. See 1990 Mass.Acts ch. 716, § 12(e); Flynn, 30 F.Supp.2d at 71. The standards and criteria to be used in determining whether a project should be reviewed include, among other things, the impact on environmental and natural resources, the impact on existing capital facilities, the physical size of the development, the amount of pedestrian and vehicular traffic the development would produce, the location of the development near a waterway, and the importance of the development to economic development in the region. See 1990 Mass.Acts ch. 716, § 12(b).

If the Cape Cod Commission ultimately approves the proposed DRI, the municipality may issue the appropriate permits. See id. § 13(d), (e); Flynn, 30 F.Supp.2d at 71. If the Cape Cod Commission disapproves the DRI, "no further work may be done on the development." 1990 Mass.Acts ch. 716, § 13(e).

The Cape Cod Commission accepted the Conservation Commission's referral under its discretionary referral power at a hearing on June 17, 1999. Prior to the hearing, plaintiff had the opportunity to respond in writing to the Cape Cod Commission's staff report discussing the potential impact on Cape Cod resources. The Cape Cod Commission also voted to take jurisdiction of the proposed project as a mandatory referral on the ground that the project constituted a DRI. It has not yet received a DRI application from Leisure Time or taken any further steps in its review process. In accordance with regulations, all review by municipal agencies of local permit applications has been suspended pending the outcome of the Cape Cod Commission's review.

The Lawsuit

Plaintiff filed this lawsuit on June 11, 1999, seeking a declaratory judgment that federal law prevents defendants from asserting jurisdiction over, regulating, or taking any action that has the effect of regulating the operation of its gambling cruise. Plaintiff also seeks damages pursuant to 42 U.S.C. § 1983 for alleged violations of its due process and equal protection rights.

While still at its berth, the Leisure Lady vows to fight state regulation "to the death."

DISCUSSION

In determining whether a preliminary injunction is warranted, this Court must consider "(1) the likelihood of success on the merits, (2) the potential for irreparable harm to the movant, (3) the balance of the movant's hardship if relief is denied versus the nonmovant's hardship if relief is granted, and (4) the effect of the decision on the public interest." Philip Morris, Inc. v. Harshbarger, 159 F.3d 670, 673 (1st Cir.1998). "Likelihood of success is the touchstone of the preliminary injunction inquiry." Id. at 674.

I. Likelihood of Success

A. Johnson Act Preemption

Plaintiff's primary claim is that the Johnson Act, 15 U.S.C. §§ 1171-1178, which governs the transportation, possession, and use of gambling devices, preempts any effort by the state of Massachusetts, the Cape Cod Commission, or the Town of Barnstable to regulate, directly or indirectly, Leisure Time's gambling boat operation.

Section 1175 of the Act generally prohibits the "manufacture, recondition[-ing], repair, s[ale], transport, possess[ion], or use [of] any gambling device" within the special maritime jurisdiction of the United States. 15 U.S.C. § 1175(a). However, the statute creates the following exception:

(b) Exception

(1) In general

Except as provided in paragraph (2), this section does not prohibit—

(A) the repair, transport, possession, or use of a gambling device on a vessel that is not within the boundaries of any State or possession of the United States;

(B) the transport or possession, on a voyage, of a gambling device on a vessel that is within the boundaries of any State or possession of the United States, if—

. . . .

(ii) the gambling device remains on board that vessel while the vessel is within the boundaries of that State or possession;

. . . .

(2) Application to certain voyages

(A) General rule

Paragraph (1)(A) does not apply to the repair or use of a gambling device on a vessel that is on a voyage or segment of a voyage described in subparagraph (B) of this paragraph if the State or possession of the United States in which the voyage or segment begins and ends has enacted a statute the terms of which prohibit that repair or use on that voyage or segment.

(B) Voyage and segment described

A voyage or segment of a voyage referred to in subparagraph (A) is a voyage or segment, respectively—

(i) that begins and ends in the same State or possession of the United States, and

(ii) during which the vessel does not make an intervening stop within the boundaries of another State or possession of the United States or a foreign country.

Id. § 1175(b).

The Town of Barnstable argues that, under a two-hundred-year-old Massachusetts statute outlawing gaming houses, gambling "cruises to nowhere" are illegal in the state. See Mass.Gen.L. ch. 271, § 5 ("Whoever keeps or assists in keeping a common gaming house, or building or place occupied, used or kept for [gaming purposes], . . . shall be punished by a fine of not more than fifty dollars or by imprisonment for not more than three months."); id. § 1A (specifying that "[t]he words 'house', 'building' and 'place' used severally or together in this chapter shall mean and include a ship or vessel when it is within the territorial limits of the commonwealth"); see also, e.g., id. § 5A (prohibiting, inter alia, the "manufacture[], transport[], s[ale], . . . stor[age], display[], repair[], . . . possess[ion] or use[][of] any gambling device or parts for use therein"). According to the Town, § 1175(b)(2)(A) applies, and any state regulation is lawful.

Leisure Cruise responds that § 1175(b)(2)(A) does not authorize state regulation because Massachusetts has not specifically prohibited "cruises to nowhere" as described in § 1175(b)(2)(B). In a well-reasoned opinion, the Fourth Circuit has held that the Johnson Act does not preempt existing pre-Act state criminal prohibitions against gambling and gambling devices and that states "remain free to regulate gambling within their territorial waters." Casino Ventures v. Stewart, No. 98-2653, 1999 WL 455357, at *1, *6 (4th Cir. July 6, 1999) (concluding that state authorities are "free to enforce state criminal prohibitions against illicit gambling cruise activity"); see also Butterworth v. Chances Casino Cruises, Inc., No. 97-846-CIV-J-20, 1997 WL 1068628, at *4 (M.D.Fla. July 14, 1997) (rejecting the contention that the

Johnson Act completely preempts pre-Act state laws regulating the possession and use of gambling devices). Because it was ruling on preemption grounds, the court did not reach the question of whether a state must reenact its laws against gambling in order to make it a federal crime to operate a gambling cruise to nowhere under § 1175(b)(2)(A). See Casino Ventures, 1999 WL 455357, at *6 n.1.

This Court need not reach the issue of whether the cruise to nowhere is illegal under state and/or federal law, because all that is contemplated here is regulation by local and regional authorities of the land, wetland, and pier uses ancillary to Leisure Time's operation of its gambling cruise. The Johnson Act does not explicitly preempt such regulation. Courts imply preemption if the law in question " 'actually conflicts' with federal law," Philip Morris, Inc. v. Harshbarger, 122 F.3d 58, 68 (1st Cir.1997) (quoting Cipollone v. Liggett Group, Inc., 505 U.S. 504, 516, 112 S.Ct. 2608, 120 L.Ed.2d 407 (1992)), such that "compliance with both [local] and federal law is a 'physical impossibility,' " id. (quoting Florida Lime & Avocado Growers, Inc. v. Paul, 373 U.S. 132, 143, 83 S.Ct. 1210, 10 L.Ed.2d 248 (1963)), or the "[local] law 'stands as an obstacle to the accomplishment and execution of the full purposes and objectives of Congress,' " id. (quoting Hines v. Davidowitz, 312 U.S. 52, 67, 61 S.Ct. 399, 85 L.Ed. 581 (1941)). In addition, "the pervasiveness of a federal scheme, the dominance of the federal interest, or the federal goals and obligations" may indicate that Congress intended the federal law to occupy the field and preclude state and local supplemen

Compliance with both the Johnson Act and local and regional regulation would by no means be impossible in this case. As Leisure Cruise agrees, the Town of Barnstable's permitting laws and Site Plan approval process do not cut off plaintiff's ability to run its business, but only impose certain prerequisites to its operation. Nothing in the present record suggests that undergoing regulation by the Conservation Commission or the Cape Cod Commission would impede Leisure Time's ability to comply with any federal statutory requirements.

Additionally, defendants' regulation of the project presents no obstacle to achieving Congress's purposes in the Johnson Act—to ensure that United States flag vessels are not at a competitive disadvantage with foreign flag vessels, see Casino Ventures, 1999 WL 455357, at *1 (discussing legislative history).

The 1992 amendments to the Johnson Act altered the Act's general ban on maritime gambling, which had prevented American flag vessels, but not foreign flag vessels, from offering gambling to their passengers. See id. To remedy this competitive disadvantage, the amendments to the Johnson Act make the Act applicable to both foreign and American vessels and forge exceptions to the categorical ban on gambling within the maritime jurisdiction of the United States. See id.

There is also no indication that Congress intended the Act to occupy the gaming field. In fact, the statute was designed to extend states' police power to control gambling. See id. at *3-*4 (noting that § 1175 "does not even apply" to states' territorial waters and that it "permits states to change the content of federal law" with respect to gambling on the high seas); see also id. at *4 (finding "the plain language, structure, and purpose of section 1175" of the Act to be "completely at odds with preemption"). The statute's effect on local regulation of gambling is no different. See Padavan v. City of New York, 685 N.Y.S.2d 35, 35-36 (N.Y.App.Div.1999) (holding that § 1175 "cannot be understood to deprive . . . municipalities of the prerogative, in the exercise of their police powers, to reasonably regulate the conduct of shipboard gambling businesses operating from within their jurisdictional bounds").

If § 1175 permits state and municipal efforts to regulate gambling directly, then it cannot be interpreted to preempt local zoning or other laws regulating Leisure Time's restaurant, parking, or docking facilities—laws at the very heart of local governance—even if they indirectly impact the operation of plaintiff's gambling cruise. Cf. Morales v. Trans World Airlines, Inc., 504 U.S. 374, 390, 112 S.Ct. 2031, 119 L.Ed.2d 157 (1992) (cautioning that, even in the context of an expressly preemptive federal statute, " '[s]ome state actions may affect [the subject of the federal regulation] in too tenuous, remote, or peripheral a manner' " to be preempted (quoting Shaw v. Delta Air Lines, Inc., 463 U.S. 85, 100 n. 21, 103 S.Ct. 2890, 77 L.Ed.2d 490 (1983))).

This Court concludes that Leisure Time has failed to demonstrate a likelihood of success on its federal preemption claim.

B. Substantive Due Process

Plaintiff also claims that defendants have deprived it of property without due process of law by manipulating their own regulatory and jurisdictional schemes in order to control its gambling activities. According to Leisure Time, defendants' efforts to enforce local zoning and other laws and to subject plaintiff's project to the Conservation Commission and Cape Cod Commission review are a "regulatory piling on" or a "smokescreen" set up for the purpose of regulating gambling through the backdoor. As part of its evidence, plaintiff points to a recent article in The Boston Globe in which Robert Gatewood, an official with the Conservation Commission, indicated that the gambling issue was the Conservation Commission's primary concern in reviewing the project.

Leisure Time's allegations do not rise to the level of a substantive due process violation. The First Circuit has adopted an extremely high threshold for such claims, especially in the permitting context. See, e.g., Nestor Colon Medina & Sucesores, Inc. v. Custodio, 964 F.2d 32, 45 (1st Cir.1992) ("[W]e have consistently held that the due process clause may not ordinarily be used to involve federal courts in the rights and wrongs of local planning disputes."); PFZ Properties, Inc. v. Rodriguez, 928 F.2d 28, 31 (1st Cir.1991) (same). In order to show a violation, the plaintiff must set forth an " 'abuse of government power that shocks the conscience,' or 'action that is legally irrational in that it is not sufficiently keyed to any legitimate state interests.' " Id. at 31-32 (quoting Committee of U.S. Citizens Living in Nicaragua v. Reagan, 859 F.2d 929, 943 (D.C.Cir.1988)).

Plaintiff's allegations do not meet this standard. The Cape Cod Commission in particular has extremely broad authority to further environmental protection and conservation and the "preservation of historical, cultural, . . . and recreational values." 1990 Mass.Acts ch. 716, § 1(c). Concerns such as zoning compliance and increased traffic congestion on Cape Cod are matters well within the jurisdiction of the Cape Cod Commission to address. This sweeping authority embraces an evaluation of the impact of gambling on Cape Cod's tourist industry and the economy of the region. However, even if defendants' regulatory enforcement actions are an illegitimate smokescreen or "outside of the normal channels," plaintiff has not demonstrated a likelihood of success on its due process claim. It would be difficult to do so, because the Cape Cod Commission proceedings have not even commenced. Generally, in the absence of matters that implicate the Constitution, such as racial animus, violations of state law or administrative procedures have not been held to constitute a substantive due process deprivation. See, e.g., Custodio, 964 F.2d at 45 (citing cases); PFZ Properties, 928 F.2d at 31 (same). Although plaintiff claims that some officials are motivated by an anti-gambling animus, plaintiff has presented no evidence of a First Amendment retaliation claim.

C. Procedural Due Process

Plaintiff also asserts a procedural due process claim. Though not particularly well-articulated, the thrust of this complaint appears to be Leisure Time's allegation that it never received notice of or an opportunity to be heard in connection with the Conservation Commission's vote to refer the project to the Cape Cod Commission. Although the Cape Cod Commission's regulations entitle affected parties to notice and a hearing once its review process is underway, see, e.g., 1990 Mass.Acts ch. 716, § 5(h), plaintiff has pointed to no such regulatory requirement concerning initial decisions by municipal agencies to refer projects to the Cape Cod Commission. In any event, plaintiff was given an opportunity to be heard at the Cape Cod Commission prior to its decision to accept the referral.

On a more troubling note, plaintiff complains of the enforcement order under the Massachusetts Wetlands Protection Act, Mass.Gen.L. ch. 131, § 40, issued by the Conservation Commission without advance notice on June 9, 1999. This ordered, among other things, that the "MV Leisure Lady . . . be permanently removed from the slip it occupies by June 16, 1999 at noon" and that "[c]luster piling" be removed by the same deadline. This dispute apparently arises from a disagreement over the configuration of the pilings and the allegation of improper dredging. The order noted that any appeal had to be directed to the Superior Court and that the enforcement would be discussed at a hearing on June 15. Plaintiff contends that the Conservation Commission's abrupt ex post facto action ordering the boat to leave the pier and alleged sudden about-face on the permissibility of the plaintiff's pilings and pier raise procedural due process concerns. Gatewood retorts that he informed plaintiff at the May 20, 1999, Site Plan Review hearing of his concern that it needed to get authority to convert a recreational slip to a commercial one. Although the actions of the Conservation Commission are hotly disputed, a hearing was held and the state provides an adequate review process. Cf. PFZ Properties, 928 F.2d at 31 (finding adequate process where the developer, through a "combination of administrative and judicial remedies," had the right to petition the state agency for reconsideration of its adverse decision and to petition the Superior Court for review). In any event, any procedural irregularities in the issuance of the enforcement order are without consequence here, because once the Cape Cod Commission accepted the referral, all permitting had to stop.

D. Equal Protection

Finally, Leisure Time has not demonstrated a likelihood of success on its discrimination claim. In order to make out an equal protection claim outside the context of invidious classifications like race and sex, a plaintiff must show "egregious procedural irregularities or abuse of power." Id. at 32; see also Custodio, 964 F.2d at 44-45 (expressing reluctance to "open [] up local permitting decisions to detailed federal judicial scrutiny under equal protection rubric" for fear of creating a flood of litigation).

Leisure Time has not met this difficult standard. It has presented no evidence of differential treatment of similar projects by the defendants, as required to substantiate an equal protection violation. See, e.g., id. at 43 (rejecting an equal protection claim because the plaintiff had "point[ed] to no allegations of fact in the complaint, nor to anything in the record, bearing out the conclusory assertion that others similarly situated were treated differently from himself").

II. Irreparable Harm

In any event, the Court further finds that Leisure Time has not shown that it will suffer irreparable harm if it is prevented from running its cruise while its claims are being litigated. To demonstrate a risk of irreparable harm, a plaintiff must show that it has experienced "a substantial injury that is not accurately measurable or adequately compensable by money damages." Ross-Simons of Warwick, Inc. v. Baccarat, Inc., 102 F.3d 12, 19 (1st Cir.1996).

Leisure Time has not lost the sort of "unique or fleeting business opportunity" that the First Circuit has held may be sufficiently immeasurable to constitute irreparable harm. See Starlight Sugar, Inc. v. Soto, 114 F.3d 330, 332 (1st Cir.1997). Leisure Time runs a similar gambling boat out of Gloucester, Massachusetts, and thus has a solid basis for calculating its lost profits on the Hyannis cruise. In addition, as a new business, plaintiff has not yet established goodwill or a customer base in the area and is not likely to be affected by any "restricted access" to its property or by "less commodious parking." K-Mart Corp. v. Oriental Plaza, Inc., 875 F.2d 907, 915 (1st Cir.1989) (identifying loss of goodwill, "diminished visibility," and restricted access and parking as injuries that may "defy precise dollar quantification").

III. Balance of Hardships and Public Interest

"[A] trial court need not make findings concerning the third and fourth factors [of the preliminary injunction analysis] if the moving party fails to establish either of the first two factors." Abbott Labs. v. Selfcare, Inc., 17 F.Supp.2d 43, 50 (D.Mass.1998) (quoting Polymer Techs. v. Bridwell, 103 F.3d 970, 973-74 (Fed.Cir.1996)). Nevertheless, the Court notes that the public interest would not be served by an order allowing a gambling cruise owner, in a hurry to capture the benefits of the Cape Cod tourist season, to bypass state and local efforts to assess the regional impact of gambling.

ORDER

Plaintiff's motion for a preliminary injunction (Docket No. 3) is DENIED.

CARNIVAL CORPORATION v. SEAESCAPE CASINO CRUISES, INC.

74 F. Supp. 2d 1261 (S.D. Fla. 1999)

MORENO, District Judge.

The Plaintiff, Carnival Corporation ("Carnival"), is suing the Defendant, SeaEscape Casino Cruises, Inc. ("SeaEscape"), for federal trademark infringement and dilution, as well as various state law claims. Carnival argues that SeaEscape's slogan, "SeaEscape to a Ship Full of Fun!" infringes and dilutes Carnival's "Fun Ship" mark. Because the Court finds that the SeaEscape slogan is not likely to cause confusion among consumers as to the source of the service or affiliation between the companies, Carnival's infringement claim fails. Carnival's trademark dilution claim likewise fails because the Court finds that the "Fun Ship" mark is not sufficiently famous to warrant protection from dilution.

PROCEDURAL HISTORY

The Complaint, filed on June 18, 1999, seeks damages, as well as injunctive relief, for trademark infringement, trademark dilution, and false designation of origin and false description of goods under the Lanham Act, 15 U.S.C. §§ 1114 and 1125(a), (c). Carnival also states claims under Florida common law for unfair competition and trademark infringement, as well as for trademark dilution under Florida Statute section 495.151.

The parties agreed on an expedited discovery schedule and to proceed in a non-jury trial on liability as to all claims. The trial was conducted on August 27, 30, and September 1, 1999. Pursuant to Rule 52 of the Federal Rules of Civil Procedure, the Court makes findings of fact and separate conclusions of law as more fully detailed in this Order.

FINDINGS OF FACT

I. The Parties

Carnival has a fleet of fourteen ships in Miami, Florida, and elsewhere, which cruise for up to fourteen days to foreign ports. Carnival services up to 1.8 million passengers per year on these vacation cruises. For the last fifteen years, Carnival has spent approximately $1 billion promoting its registered trademarks, which include various uses of the "Fun Ship" mark attached to the well-known "Carnival" mark.

SeaEscape operates one ship from Fort Lauderdale, Florida offering six-hour casino cruises, often called "cruises to nowhere." Recently, SeaEscape expanded its entertainment program to promote non-gambling activities, as well. In order to promote this expanded format, SeaEscape's advertising agent, James Lobel of GNL Group, suggested that the Defendant use the slogan "SeaEscape to a Ship Full of Fun!" The Chief Operating Officer of SeaEscape, Bruce

Yasukochi, approved the $1 million advertising campaign, despite expressing concern of probable trademark litigation from Carnival. The use of this phrase by SeaEscape forms the basis of Carnival's lawsuit, claiming violation of its registered trademark "the Fun Ships."

II. The Marks

Both "Carnival" and "SeaEscape" are federally registered trademarks. The "Fun Ship" marks, in both singular and plural forms, are separately registered marks. Carnival began using the "Fun Ship" mark in the early 1970s and first registered its mark in 1975. However, rather than use the "Fun Ship" mark alone in advertisements, Carnival uses the "Fun Ship" mark in conjunction with the "Carnival" mark 95% of the time.

On the other hand, SeaEscape's tagline "to a ship Full of Fun!" is not a registered mark, although the symbol "SM" (signifying "service mark") is clearly visible next to all of the SeaEscape advertisements submitted in evidence. SeaEscape began its "SeaEscape to a Ship Full of Fun!" advertising campaign in March of 1999.

At the trial, Carnival witnesses Christine Arnholt, Vice President of Marketing Services; Ellen Levenson, Trademark Administrator; and Robert Dickinson, President, credibly testified that Carnival vigorously protects all of its trademarks, including the "Fun Ship" mark.

Mr. Yasukochi testified that he was well aware of Carnival's "Fun Ship" mark during his tenure as a private auditor of Carnival's account. Although Yasukochi testified that he did not participate in the creation of the alleged infringing slogan, he admitted that he approved the slogan. Yasukochi's experience as a private accounting auditor at Carnival prior to assuming his duties at SeaEscape led him to conclude that Carnival would vigorously prosecute any alleged infringement. This resulting litigation bears out that Yasuknochi was correct in his prediction that litigation would ensue.

CONCLUSIONS OF LAW

To prevail on a trademark infringement claim under 15 U.S.C. § 1114, the plaintiff must show that it owns a valid trademark, that its mark has priority, that the defendant used such mark in commerce without the plaintiff's consent, and that the defendant's use is likely to cause consumer confusion as to the source, affiliation or sponsorship of its goods or services. See Frehling Enter., Inc. v. International Select Group, Inc., 192 F.3d 1330, 1334 (11th Cir.1999); McDonald's Corp. v. Robertson, 147 F.3d 1301, 1307 (11th Cir.1998); Lone Star Steakhouse & Saloon, Inc. v. Longhorn Steaks, Inc., 122 F.3d 1379, 1382 (11th Cir.1997); Dieter v. B & H Indus. of Southwest Florida, Inc., 880 F.2d 322, 326 (11th Cir.1989), cert. denied, 498 U.S. 950, 111 S.Ct. 369, 112 L.Ed.2d 332 (1990).

There is no question, and the Court finds, that both "Carnival" and "Fun Ship" are registered marks entitled to protection. It is undisputed that Carnival's "Fun Ship" mark has priority over the Defendant's "SeaEscape to a Ship Full of Fun" mark. The Court also finds that SeaEscape used the alleged infringing mark without Carnival's consent. However, the conclusion as to whether the Defendant's use of its slogan "SeaEscape to a Ship Full of Fun" would likely cause confusion with Carnival's "Fun Ship" mark is not as easily reached.

"Likelihood of confusion" means probable confusion rather than mere possible confusion. See Michael Caruso & Co., Inc. v. Estefan Enter., Inc., 994 F.Supp. 1454, 1458 (S.D.Fla.1998) (citing Shatel Corp. v. Mao Ta Lumber and Yacht Corp., 697 F.2d 1352, 1356 n. 2 (11th Cir.1983) (discussing "substantial likelihood of success on the merits" and stating that "likelihood" is synonymous with "probability"), aff'd, 166 F.3d 353 (11th Cir.1998). In determining the likelihood of confusion, the court must analyze the following seven factors: (1) the type of trademark; (2) the similarity of the marks; (3) the similarity of the products the marks represent; (4) the similarity of the parties' retail outlets and purchasers; (5) the similarity of the advertising media used; (6) the defendant's intent; and (7) actual confusion. See Lone Star, 122 F.3d at 1382; Dieter, 880 F.2d at 326. Of the seven factors, the Eleventh Circuit considers the type of mark and the evidence of actual confusion to be the two most important factors. See id.

A. Type of Mark

The type of mark is important because it dictates the level of protection that the trademark is accorded. See John H. Harland Co. v. Clarke Checks, Inc., 711 F.2d 966, 973 (11th Cir.1983). The four categories of trademarks, from strongest to weakest, are: 1) arbitrary or fanciful; 2) suggestive; 3) descriptive; or 4) generic. See Dieter, 880 F.2d at 327. The categories are based on the relationship between the name and the service or good it describes. See Frehling, 192 F.3d 1330, 1332.

The "Fun Ship" mark falls into the descriptive category, as it describes a characteristic or quality of the product or service, such as its desirable features. See John H. Harland Co., 711 F.2d at 974. Generally, a descriptive mark is considered weak and is given a narrow range of protection. See id. However, because the "Fun Ship" marks are "incontestable," their strength is enhanced. See Frehling, 192 F.3d 1330, 1332. Once a mark has achieved incontestable status, the Defendant may not argue that the mark is "merely descriptive." Dieter, 880 F.2d at 328. Moreover, an incontestable mark is presumed to be at least descriptive with secondary meaning, and therefore a "relatively strong mark." See id. at 329 (holding that incontestable status affects the strength of the mark for purposes of determining whether there is a likelihood of confusion).

However, the Court must also take into account third-party use in assessing the strength of a mark. See Frehling, 192 F.3d 1330, 1332; John H. Harland Co., 711 F.2d at 973-75; Michael Caruso & Co., 994 F.Supp. at 1459 (stating that incontestable status alone does not render a mark strong). The less that third parties use the mark, the stronger it is, and the more protection it deserves. See Frehling, 192 F.3d 1330, 1332. As the Eleventh Circuit explained in Frehling, "[w]here there is lack of third-party use, the mark's strength is enhanced, as it is distinctive, and therefore more easily recognized by consumers." See id.

Conversely, a mark is weakened by extensive third party use of the mark or a term used in the trademark. See Michael Caruso & Co., 994 F.Supp. at 1459 (finding that defendant's evidence of extensive third-party use of the term "bongo" renders it unlikely that the mark will have strong trademark significance). In Sun Banks of Florida, Inc. v. Sun Federal Savings and Loan Ass'n, 651 F.2d 311 (5th Cir. July 20, 1981), the court found that although the term "sun" may be arbitrary as applied to a bank, extensive third-party use of the word "sun" was "impressive evidence that there would be no likelihood of confusion between Sun Banks and Sun Federal." Id. at 316.

SeaEscape's evidence reveals numerous third-party registrations for marks including the term "fun" in the travel, gaming, and entertainment industries. This evidence weakens the strength of the "Fun Ship" mark. Taking into account the mark's descriptive quality, incontestable status, and third-party use, the Court concludes that the "Fun Ship" mark is not very strong and is entitled to a low level of trademark protection. Therefore, this factor weighs in favor of SeaEscape.

B. Similarity of the Marks

The similarity of the marks is determined by considering the overall impression created by the marks as a whole rather than comparing individual features of the marks. John H. Harland Co., 711 F.2d at 975; Michael Caruso & Co., 994 F.Supp. at 1459. Some factors to consider are the appearance, sound, and meaning of the marks, as well as the way in which the marks are used. John H. Harland Co., 711 F.2d at 975.

The most obvious similarity between the "Fun Ship" mark and the "SeaEscape to a Ship Full of Fun!" mark is the use of the words "fun" and "ship" in both slogans. However, as the Defendant points out, its slogan is a full sentence, beginning with a play on the word "SeaEscape." Another distinguishing feature between the two marks is that the SeaEscape slogan does not use the words "fun" and "ship" next to each other.

As for appearance, the "Fun Ships" mark is typically written in cursive and is surrounded by quotation marks. Also, the slogan is used in conjunction with the "Carnival" mark and Carnival's Reverse-C design 95% of the time. The SeaEscape slogan, on the other hand, typically appears in print letters, always begins with the word "SeaEscape" in larger font, and ends with an exclamation mark. In addition, above the word "SeaEscape" is a distinctive fantail design.

The meaning of the marks is similar in that both companies are trying to represent their on-board services as being "fun" and an experience consumers would enjoy.

C. Similarity of Products

The greater the similarity between the products and services, the greater the likelihood of confusion. See John H. Harland Co., 711 F.2d at 976. The Court finds that while both companies offer entertainment on board a ship, the similarities end there.

As discussed above, Carnival has a number of ships that cruise out of Miami to various ports of call, primarily in the Caribbean and Mexico. Carnival cruises are seldom shorter than three days and typically last seven days and sometimes last as long as fourteen days. Prices for the Carnival cruises are typically in the hundreds, if not thousands, of dollars per person.

The SeaEscape cruises, which cost $39 per person, last six hours, depart from and return to Fort Lauderdale, and are mainly, although not exclusively, gambling trips, are distinct from the vacation cruises offered by Carnival. Christine Arnholt, Carnival's Vice President of Marketing Services, offered further support for this position when she testified that Carnival was in a "vacation" market while SeaEscape was in a different market—the "day cruise" market. Moreover, the Court finds persuasive the Defendant's argument that its service is more of a "night on the town" rather than the vacation experience that Carnival offers.

D. Identity of Retail Outlets and Purchasers

Dissimilarities between the retail outlets for and the predominant customers of plaintiff's and defendant's goods lessen the possibility of confusion, mistake, or deception. See John H. Harland Co., 711 F.2d at 975.

According to Robert Dickinson, Carnival's President, 96% of Carnival's bookings are made through travel agents, and bookings are generally made at least two months in advance. He acknowledged that in his experience, casino cruises are not booked through travel agents. He also testified that the average person who books a cruise with Carnival does so with a good deal of forethought. While the applicable standard in assessing likelihood of confusion is "the typical buyer exercising ordinary caution," when the goods are expensive, the buyer can be expected to exercise greater care in his purchases. See AMF Inc. v. Sleekcraft Boats, 599 F.2d 341, 353 (9th Cir.1979).

The Defendant points out that about half of SeaEscape's passengers are members of its VIP Club for frequent gamblers. SeaEscape argues its VIP Club members are sophisticated consumers who are not likely to be confused regarding the source of the goods or any affiliation between Carnival and SeaEscape. Aside from its VIP Club members, SeaEscape relies on direct bookings by South Florida residents and tourists.

E. Similarity of Advertising Media Used

The greater the similarity in advertising campaigns the greater the likelihood of confusion. See Ross Bicycles, Inc. v. Cycles USA, Inc., 765 F.2d 1502, 1508 (11th Cir.1985), cert. denied, 475 U.S. 1013, 106 S.Ct. 1190, 89 L.Ed.2d 306 (1986). Both Carnival and SeaEscape advertise through print media, as well as through radio and Internet advertisements. However, Carnival engages in national advertising, while casino cruises such as SeaEscape traditionally advertise locally.

F. Defendant's Intent

Although objective factors are most important in assessing the likelihood of confusion between two marks, courts also examine the defendant's subjective intent. See John H. Harland Co., 711 F.2d at 977; see also Sun Banks of Florida, Inc., 651 F.2d at 318-19 ("That a latecomer adopts another's name or mark, deliberately seeking to capitalize on the other's reputation and benefit from the confusion, is an important factor for any court").

The Court finds that SeaEscape did intend to benefit from Carnival's "Fun Ship" mark to some extent. Bruce Yasukochi, SeaEscape's Chief Executive, testified that he was well aware of Carnival's "Fun Ship" mark as he had previously worked as a private auditor of Carnival's account. Yasukochi wanted to reinvent SeaEscape's image from a gambling cruise to one offering a more fully balanced assortment of on-board activities and entertainment. Yasukochi admits that he approved the SeaEscape slogan despite strongly suspecting that Carnival would vigorously prosecute any use of the word "fun." Based on the evidence, the Court finds that SeaEscape, in selecting its new slogan, did intend to benefit to some degree from the "Fun Ship" mark.

The law states that if it can be shown that the defendant adopted the plaintiff's mark with the intention of deriving a benefit from the plaintiff's business reputation, this fact alone may be sufficient to justify the inference that there is confusing similarity. See Frehling, 192 F.3d 1330, 1336; John H. Harland Co., 711 F.2d at 977. Although this factor weighs in Carnival's favor, the Court does not deem that it is sufficient to find a likelihood of confusion in light of the other factors which favor the Defendant—namely the strength of the mark and actual confusion.

G. Actual Confusion

The Plaintiff concedes that there is no evidence of actual confusion. Proof of actual confusion is not a prerequisite to a finding of likelihood of confusion. See United States v. Torkington, 812 F.2d 1347, 1352-53 (11th Cir.1987); E. Remy Martin & Co., S.A. v. Shaw-Ross Int'l Imports, Inc., 756 F.2d 1525, 1530 (11th Cir.1985). Nevertheless, actual evidence is the best evidence of likelihood of confusion. See Ross Bicycles, Inc., 765 F.2d at 1508.

In the absence of actual confusion, Carnival relies, as plaintiffs often do, upon surveys. The Court overruled SeaEscape's objection to the introduction of the surveys, finding that the surveys' weaknesses in methodology went to the weight of the evidence and not to their admissibility.

The conclusion of the survey was that 41% of those surveyed thought the two slogans—"Fun Ships" and "Ship Full of Fun"—were from cruise lines owned and managed by the same company. Forty-two percent of the respondents thought the slogans were from two different companies.

H. Summary

Even taking into account the survey results, the Court concludes that the average consumer is not likely to become confused or deceived as to the source of the product or into thinking that Carnival and SeaEscape are affiliated after seeing or hearing the slogan "SeaEscape to a Ship Full of Fun!"

Following Eleventh Circuit guidance, the Court must give substantial weight to the fact that the Plaintiff is unable, at this time, to prove actual confusion. See Dieter, 880 F.2d at 326. Moreover, the lack of similarity between the services offered by Carnival and SeaEscape—namely the distinction between an expensive vacation trip versus a six-hour gambling trip—supports a finding of no likelihood of confusion.

In addition, while the marks are similar to the extent that they both use the words "fun" and "ship," considering the marks as a whole leads the Court to conclude that they are not similar enough to create a likelihood of confusion. Especially persuasive is the fact that the "Fun Ship" mark is used in conjunction with the "Carnival" mark 95% of the time and that the SeaEscape slogan always features the "SeaEscape" name prominently.

Despite the Court's finding that SeaEscape did intend to benefit to some degree from the "Fun Ship" mark, the Court concludes that the Plaintiff has not shown a likelihood of confusion. Therefore, judgment is entered in favor of the Defendant on all trademark infringement claims.

[The remainder of the court's opinion is omitted.]

LYONS v. STATE
711 So. 2d 71 (Fla. Dist. Ct. App.),
review denied, 719 So. 2d 287 (Fla. 1998)

BLUE, Acting Chief Judge.

Terry Lyons appeals his conviction for grand theft from a casino ship that embarked from Florida shores. Although the majority of Lyons' thievery occurred outside of Florida's territorial waters, we conclude that the State had jurisdiction to prosecute him for his criminal conduct. We reject Lyons' legal challenges to his conviction and therefore affirm.

Lyons boarded a casino ship in Treasure Island, Florida. The ship left Treasure Island and when it was outside of Florida's territorial waters, the gambling machines were turned on. In less than five minutes, Lyons was confronted by the casino staff for his use of a cheating device. Lyons had been using the device on a $1 slot machine and had obtained between $100 and $150 in tokens from the machine. He was detained by the ship's captain and subsequently turned over to the Treasure Island police. The State of Florida thereafter charged Lyons with grand theft of $300 or more from the casino ship.

Lyons filed three motions to dismiss the charge: a motion challenging the jurisdiction of the State of Florida over the subject matter; a motion challenging the constitutionality of section 910.006, Florida Statutes (1993); and a motion pursuant to Florida Rule of Criminal Procedure 3.190(c)(4). Following hearings, the trial court denied the motions. Lyons entered a plea of no contest to the grand theft charge, specifically reserving his right to appeal the denial of the motions.

Florida has state criminal jurisdiction over "[a]n offense that is committed partly within this state if either the conduct that is an element of the offense or the result that is an element, occurs within the state." § 910.005(2), Fla. Stat. (1993). By boarding the ship armed with the "cheating device," Lyons obviously boarded the ship having formed his plan to steal from the casino. The element of intent having occurred in Florida, the State had jurisdiction. See Keen v. State, 504 So.2d 396 (Fla.1987), overruled on other grounds, Owen

v. State, 596 So.2d 985, 990 (Fla.1992). Because the State had jurisdiction under section 910.005(2), there is no need to reach the question challenging the constitutionality of section 910.006 in this case.

Additionally, the court correctly denied Lyons' rule 3.190(c)(4) motion. In the motion, Lyons swore that he had taken less than 300 tokens with a value of one dollar each. Lyons contended that the undisputed facts supported a charge of petit, not grand, theft. The State filed a traverse to the motion to dismiss in which it specifically alleged facts to support the greater charge. A material fact was therefore in dispute and the court properly denied the motion. See Fla. R.Crim. Pro. 3.190(d).

The State of Florida properly exercised its jurisdiction under section 910.005 over Lyons' criminal conduct. We affirm his conviction and sentence.

Affirmed.

Notes

1. As the *Leisure Time* case makes clear, many people do not want a water-borne casino in their backyards. As a result, siting disputes are fairly common. For two notable examples, *see Hoosier Environmental Council, Inc. v. U.S. Army Corps of Engineers*, 105 F. Supp. 2d 953 (S.D. Ind. 2000), and *St. Charles Gaming Co. v. Riverboat Gaming Commission*, 648 So. 2d 1310 (La. 1995). For a further discussion, *see* M. Jackson Akers, *The Big Black River Question: Suitable Site or Suited for Trouble?*, 4 Gaming L. Rev. 147 (2000); Robert S. Little, Jr., *The Public Trust Doctrine and Casino Development Along the Mississippi Gulf Coast*, 6 Gaming L. Rev. 439 (2002); Jeffrey P. Reynolds & Daniel L. Singletary, *Environmental Concerns and the Impact of Wetlands Regulations on Mississippi's Gaming Industry*, 64 Miss. L.J. 517 (1995); Richard F. Russell, *Casino Development and Environmental Protection on the Mississippi Gulf Coast: Where Will All the Good Times Go?*, 2 Gaming L. Rev. 387 (1998); Allan B. Solomon & Gregory D. Guida, *Riverboat Gaming: Legislation, Licensing, Site Selection, and Caselaw*, 29 J. Mar. L. & Com. 215 (1998); Ben H. Stone et al., *Site Approval of Casinos in Mississippi—A Matter of Statutory Construction, or a Roll of the Dice?*, 64 Miss. L.J. 363 (1995); Frank Aiello, Note, *Gambling with Condemnation: An Examination of Detroit's Use of Eminent Domain for Riverfront Casinos*, 46 Wayne L. Rev. 1639 (2000).

2. The differences between SeaEscape and Carnival can be most readily seen by viewing their respective web sites (www.seaescape.com and www.carnivalcruises.com). If you had been general counsel to either company, would you have pursued (or defended) the suit? Why or why not?

3. Although the question of whether Florida could extend its criminal laws to the high seas was not reached in *Lyons*, the question was considered in a subsequent non-gaming case and answered in the affirmative. *See State v. Stepansky*, 761 So. 2d 1027 (Fla.), *cert. denied*, 531 U.S. 959 (2000), analyzed in Bernard H. Oxman & Mary Coombs, *Case Note*, 95 Am. J. Int'l L. 438 (2001).

4. In *Association for Disabled Americans, Inc. v. Concorde Gaming Corporation*, 158 F. Supp. 2d 1353 (S.D. Fla. 2001), a disabled patron filed a lawsuit

claiming that a casino ship and terminal did not comply with various provisions of the Americans with Disabilities Act of 1990, 42 U.S.C. §§ 12101-12213. Although the court ordered certain changes to be made, it refused the plaintiff's requested modifications to the craps tables:

At trial, Plaintiffs' counsel stated that the only issue with respect to the gaming activities concerned the accessibility of the craps tables. Therefore, the Court will not address the accessibility of the other casino games or the slot machines.

Plaintiffs maintain that the craps tables are inaccessible because the areas designated for players to roll the dice, place wagers, and observe the game are too high to allow individuals in wheelchairs to participate. Plaintiffs proposed two modifications to cure this problem. First, Plaintiffs contend that wheelchair players could be permitted to play at the areas on the craps table designated for the game's attendants, the two croupiers and the stickman, where the railing is lowered. Second, Plaintiffs aver that the table's railing could be lowered at other spots or the entire table could be lowered.

Neither of Plaintiffs' proposed modifications of the craps tables is viable, because both would fundamentally alter the nature of the game. In PGA Tour, Inc. v. Martin, 531 U.S. 1049, 121 S.Ct. 1879, 149 L.Ed.2d 904 (2001), the Supreme Court recently explained, in the context of golf, what constitutes a fundamental alteration of a game for purposes of Title III. See 121 S.Ct. at 1893-97. Although the Supreme Court held that waving the PGA tour's walking requirement would not fundamentally alter the game of professional golf, it explained that there are two ways in which a modification could fundamentally alter a game: "In theory, a modification of petitioner's golf tournaments might constitute a fundamental alteration in two different ways. It might alter such an essential aspect of the game of golf that it would be unacceptable even if it affected all competitors equally; changing the diameter of the hole from three to six inches might be such a modification. Alternatively, a less significant change that has only a peripheral impact on the game itself might nevertheless give a disabled player, in addition to access to the competition as required by Title III, an advantage over others, and for that reason, fundamentally alter the character of the competition . . . ." Id. at 1893 (footnote omitted).

Thus, a modification alters the fundamental nature of a game if it either (a) changes an essential aspect of the game that affects all competitors or (b) provides the disabled player with an advantage over the non-disabled players.

In the present case, both of Plaintiffs' proposed modifications would alter a fundamental aspect of craps—the dimensions by which the game is played. Craps is a common casino game, and it is played under common conditions, including the positioning of the players and the boundaries of the playing surface. Lowering the rail of a craps table or lowering the entire table would alter the playing surface in a manner that is the equivalent of changing the dimensions of a playing field or the size of the diameter of a golf hole. Similarly, moving one of the croupiers or the stickman from his designated spot on the table to another spot would change the dimensions of where competitors play. Moving a croupier or the stickman would also require lowering the railing of the table on the spot that he is moved to, further distorting the playing surface. Moreover, allowing disabled players to play from a spot on the table that other players cannot play from may provide the disabled players with an advantage not enjoyed by the other players. As Plaintiffs' proposed modifications of the craps tables would fundamentally alter the nature of the game, Plaintiffs are entitled to no relief with respect to the craps tables.

Id. at 1366-67.

Problem 31

When its application for a berth was rejected, the owner of a gaming ship filed a federal lawsuit. If the state port authority, which has a firm policy against leasing piers to gaming ships, argues the Eleventh Amendment requires the complaint to be dismissed, how should the court rule? *See Federal Maritime Commission v. South Carolina State Ports Authority*, 535 U.S. 743 (2002).

Chapter 8

INDIAN GAMING

A. OVERVIEW

In the 1970s, Indian tribes began establishing gaming operations as a means of providing their members with much-needed jobs and benefits. But when they claimed their ventures were not subject to state law, clashes quickly arose. In 1988, after years of controversy, Congress finally entered the fray by passing the Indian Gaming Regulatory Act ("IGRA"), 25 U.S.C. §§ 2701-2721.

Rather than bringing order to the subject, however, IGRA has spawned a host of complex issues, including the extent to which states can prevent Indian gaming and whether federal, state, or tribal law is to be used in the event of disputes. Indeed, even the constitutionality of IGRA has been questioned.

B. PRE-STATUTORY LAW

LAC DU FLAMBEAU BAND OF LAKE SUPERIOR CHIPPEWA INDIANS v. WILLIQUETTE
629 F. Supp. 689 (W.D. Wis. 1986)

CRABB, Chief Judge.

This is a civil action for declaratory and injunctive relief from defendants' threatened enforcement of state criminal law against plaintiff for the sale of "pulltabs" at its bingo games. It is before the court on cross-motions for summary judgment.

FACTS

Plaintiff Lac du Flambeau Band of Lake Superior Chippewa Indians is a federally recognized Indian tribe operating with a constitutional form of government. Defendant James Williquette is the Vilas County Sheriff responsible for state law enforcement in Vilas County.

Plaintiff is a functioning government that regulates the conduct of its members on the reservation through codes and ordinances enforced by plaintiff's court system. Pursuant to plaintiff's Bingo and Raffle Control Ordinance, as revised July 23, 1984, games known as "pulltabs" or "Vegas tickets" are being conducted on the reservation.

Pulltabs share certain common characteristics. Each pulltab ticket in a box is identical on its front, displaying the winning combinations, the prize for each, and the number of winning tickets in each box. The reverse contains three to five tabs that the buyer pulls back to reveal the symbols printed beneath the tabs, which may be feathers, tepees, and moccasins, or cherries, bells, and gold bars. If any of the rows of symbols under the tabs match the winning combinations shown on the front, the ticket is a winning one.

Distributors sell pulltabs to plaintiff in boxes containing between a few hundred to over two thousand tickets. Each box has a fixed number of winners of different cash prizes, ranging from $1.00 or $2.00 to $100.00 or more. The top prize has the fewest number of winners, and the number of winners gradually increase with the decreasing value of the prize. Tickets are sold for either fifty cents or one dollar.

Pulltabs are sold under the auspices of the tribe through the Tribal Bingo Manager. Pulltabs are sold only by tribal bingo workers, only at the tribal bingo hall located on the reservation within Vilas County, and only during bingo games, which occur on Wednesday, Thursday, and Saturday evenings, and on Sunday afternoons.

Two employees sell tickets, and one pays out the prizes. The tickets are drawn from a tub in the amount purchased by the player, who is required to claim his or her prize by returning the winning ticket that same night. Tribal employees keep records on each lot.

The percentage of gross profit (take minus price pay off) on each box of pulltabs is generally between 18% and 33%, excluding the cost of the box, salary, overhead, and other expenses of sale.

Plaintiff has 2,138 members, two-thirds of whom live on the reservation. Of those who are eligible for employment, two-thirds are unemployed. One-fourth of those who are employed earn less than $7000.00 a year. In addition to program-specific funds which it receives from federal or state sources, plaintiff receives revenues from several sources which are unrestricted in use, and which comprise plaintiff's general fund. The largest single source of the general fund, accounting for well over half its revenues, is the net profit from plaintiff's bingo and raffle operations.

The general fund is appropriated by the Tribal Council annually to fund a variety of tribal programs and services, including various general governmental expenses, the President's salary, the Enrollment Department, the Realty and Natural Resources Department, the library and museum, water and sewer service, a youth alcohol and drug program, the elderly nutrition program, tourism promotion, the tribal attorneys, and the Ojibway Cultural Association.

In addition to the annually budgeted amounts, during the fiscal year the Tribal Council appropriates by resolution general fund monies for a variety of purposes of a charitable, educational, spiritual, or governmental nature.

By letter of February 15, 1985, defendant Hoyt, the Vilas County District Attorney, informed the tribal chairman, Michael Aller, that the State of Wisconsin intended to prosecute plaintiff's sale of pulltabs.

OPINION

The question before the court is whether the State of Wisconsin can prohibit the sale of pulltabs by the plaintiff tribe on its own reservation. Pursuant to Public Law 280 (18 U.S.C. § 1162, 28 U.S.C. § 1360), Wisconsin and certain other states have been granted limited civil and general criminal jurisdiction over the Indian lands within their states, with some specific exceptions. This grant of criminal jurisdiction has been held to permit states to enforce criminal laws that are essentially prohibitory in nature, designed to protect the health, safety, and general well-being of its citizens; it does not authorize the states to enforce criminal laws that are intended merely to regulate specific conduct and generate revenue.

Historically, the State of Wisconsin has prohibited all forms of gambling, including lotteries, and has imposed criminal sanctions upon violators of the gambling laws. In 1973, however, the state's voters approved an amendment to the constitution, excepting bingo games played under certain circumstances from the general prohibition of "lotteries," which are defined as enterprises

> wherein for a consideration the participants are given an opportunity to win a prize, the award of which is determined by chance, even though accompanied by some skill.

Wis.Stat. § 945.01(5)(a). In 1977, the voters amended the constitution again to except certain raffles from the criminal prohibition. Pursuant to these changes in the state's constitution, the Wisconsin legislature enacted Wis.Stat. Chapter 163, which governs the conduct of bingo and raffles in the state, and amended Wis.Stat. § 945.01, which contains definitions relating to gambling, to provide: " 'Lottery' does not include bingo or a raffle as defined in s. 163.03 if conducted under ch. 163." Wis.Stat. § 945.01(2)(am). With the exception of bingo games and raffles conducted in accordance with the provisions of Wis.Stat. Chapter 163, the state continues to treat other forms of gambling, including any other version of a lottery, as criminal, with operators and players subject to prosecution.

In an opinion entered in Oneida Tribe of Indians of Wisconsin v. Wisconsin, 518 F. Supp. 712, 719 (W.D.Wis. 1981), I held that under the jurisdictional scheme of Public Law 280, Wisconsin could not enforce its laws governing bingo games on the reservations because these laws do not prohibit the playing of bingo by the general public on health and safety grounds, but merely regulate the manner in which the bingo games are operated and for what purposes the profits are used. The state did not appeal that decision, and it does not argue in this case that it has any authority to prohibit the operation of bingo games or ordinary raffles on the reservations. It bases its claim in this case on its contention that plaintiff's pulltabs games are not raffles under the statute. For its part, plaintiff makes two arguments: first, that pulltabs are raffles and, alternatively, even if they are not, the state statutes governing lotteries are so riddled with exceptions as to evidence a legislative change of mind about the need to protect the state's citizens from lotteries.

The statutes defining raffles read as follows:

> 163.03(12m) "Raffle" means a game of chance in which tickets are sold and a drawing for prizes is held . . . .

> (14m) "Regular raffle" means a raffle for which a single drawing for prizes is held on a specified date after the sale of tickets has been completed . . . .

(17) "Special raffle" means a raffle for which one or more drawings are held and prizes awarded on the same day as the tickets are sold.

The parties do not dispute that, as operated by plaintiff, the game of pulltabs involves chance, the pulltabs are tickets which are sold, the pulltabs are drawn from a tub, and prizes are awarded to the winning ticket holders. It would seem that having made these concessions, defendants have left little room for their argument that plaintiff's pulltabs games are not raffles. However, defendants contend that because the pulltabs game is not operated in the way raffles are ordinarily conducted, that is, with a lapse of time between the purchase of ticket and the drawing of the prize, it is a prohibited lottery, rather than a raffle. As plaintiff points out, however, the question is not whether pulltabs fit the defendants' idea of the ordinary meaning of the word raffle, but whether they fit the specific definition of a raffle as enacted by the state legislature. Since the legislature did not make the lapse of time a specific element of a raffle and indeed even made special provision for raffles that have drawings on the same day, it is difficult to accept defendants' argument that plaintiff's pulltabs game is not a raffle simply because the prizes can be determined immediately after the ticket is sold and drawn.

Defendants make the additional argument that pulltabs cannot constitute a statutorily excepted raffle because the odds change every time a pulltab ticket is pulled, whereas in an "ordinary" raffle, the odds remain the same for every ticket sale. However, there is nothing in the statutory definition of raffle that makes constant odds an essential element. It would have been easy enough for the legislature to have written such a requirement into the legislation had it believed it to be a critical characteristic of a legal raffle.

I conclude that defendants have failed to show that plaintiff is conducting a prohibited lottery not excepted from the statutes prohibiting lotteries in general. Therefore, defendants may not enforce the state's criminal laws regulating lotteries against plaintiff or its members who conduct pulltab games on plaintiff's reservation. Having reached this conclusion, I decline to address plaintiff's broader contention that Wisconsin's gambling laws are so riddled with exceptions that the state is no longer in a position to characterize them as prohibitory in nature, rather than regulatory.

I hold only that the state has no authority to enforce the state law governing raffles against plaintiff for the conduct of pulltabs games operated as described herein. I imply no opinion about the legality of any other kinds of games that might be encompassed by the definition of raffle in plaintiff's ordinance.

CALIFORNIA v. CABAZON BAND OF MISSION INDIANS
480 U.S. 202 (1987)

Justice WHITE delivered the opinion of the Court.

The Cabazon and Morongo Bands of Mission Indians, federally recognized Indian Tribes, occupy reservations in Riverside County, California. Each Band, pursuant to an ordinance approved by the Secretary of the Interior, conducts bingo games on its reservation. The Cabazon Band has also opened a card club at which draw poker and other card games are played. The games are open to the public and are played predominantly by non-Indians coming onto the reservations. The games are a major source of employment for tribal members, and the profits are the Tribes' sole source of income. The State of California seeks to apply to the two Tribes Cal.Penal Code § 326.5. That statute does not entirely prohibit the playing of bingo but permits it when the games are operated and staffed by members of designated charitable organizations who may not be paid for their services. Profits must be kept in special accounts and used only for charitable purposes; prizes may not exceed $250 per game. Asserting that the bingo games on the two reservations violated each of these restrictions, California insisted that the Tribes comply with state law. Riverside County also sought to apply its local Ordinance No. 558, regulating bingo, as well as its Ordinance No. 331, prohibiting the playing of draw poker and the other card games.

The Tribes sued the county in Federal District Court seeking a declaratory judgment that the county had no authority to apply its ordinances inside the reservations and an injunction against their enforcement. The State intervened, the facts were stipulated, and the District Court granted the Tribes' motion for summary judgment, holding that neither the State nor the county had any authority to enforce its gambling laws within the reservations. The Court of Appeals for the Ninth Circuit affirmed.

I

The Court has consistently recognized that Indian tribes retain "attributes of sovereignty over both their members and their territory," and that "tribal sovereignty is dependent on, and subordinate to, only the Federal Government, not the States." It is clear, however, that state laws may be applied to tribal Indians on their reservations if Congress has expressly so provided. Here, the State insists that Congress has twice given its express consent: first in Public Law 280 (Pub. L. 280) in 1953 [codified at 18 U.S.C. § 1162 and 28 U.S.C. § 1360] and second in the Organized Crime Control Act in 1970. We disagree in both respects.

In Pub.L. 280, Congress expressly granted six States, including California, jurisdiction over specified areas of Indian country within the States and provided for the assumption of jurisdiction by other States. In § 2, California was granted broad criminal jurisdiction over offenses committed by or against Indians within all Indian country within the State. Section 4's grant of civil jurisdiction was more limited. In Bryan v. Itasca County, 426 U.S. 373 (1976), we interpreted § 4 to grant States jurisdiction over private civil litigation involving reservation Indians in state court, but not to grant general civil regulatory authority. We held, therefore, that Minnesota could not apply its personal property tax within the reservation. Congress' primary concern in enacting Pub.L. 280 was combating lawlessness on reservations. The Act plainly was not intended to effect total assimilation of Indian tribes into mainstream American society. We recognized that a grant to States of general civil regulatory power over Indian reservations would result in the destruction of tribal institutions and values. Accordingly, when a State seeks to enforce a law within an Indian reservation under the authority of Pub.L. 280, it must be determined whether the law is criminal in nature, and thus fully applicable to the reservation under § 2, or civil in nature, and applicable only as it may be relevant to private civil litigation in state court.

The Minnesota personal property tax at issue in Bryan was unquestionably civil in nature. The California bingo statute is not so easily categorized. California law permits bingo games to be conducted only by charitable and other specified organizations, and then only by their members who may not receive any wage or profit for doing so; prizes are limited and receipts are to be segregated and used only for charitable purposes. Violation of any of these provisions is a misdemeanor. California insists that these are criminal laws which Pub.L. 280 permits it to enforce on the reservations.

Following its earlier decision in Barona Group of Capitan Grande Band of Mission Indians, San Diego County, Cal. v. Duffy, 694 F.2d 1185 (9th Cir. 1983), which also involved the applicability of § 326.5 of the California Penal Code to Indian reservations, the Court of Appeals rejected this submission. In Barona, applying what it thought to be the civil/criminal dichotomy drawn in Bryan v. Itasca County, the Court of Appeals drew a distinction between state "criminal/prohibitory" laws and state "civil/regulatory" laws: if the intent of a state law is generally to prohibit certain conduct, it falls within Pub.L. 280's grant of criminal jurisdiction, but if the state law generally permits the conduct at issue, subject to regulation, it must be classified as civil/regulatory and Pub.L. 280 does not authorize its enforcement on an Indian reservation. The shorthand test is whether the conduct at issue violates the State's public policy. Inquiring into the nature of § 326.5, the Court of Appeals held that it was regulatory rather than prohibitory. This was the analysis employed, with similar results, by the Court of Appeals for the Fifth Circuit in Seminole Tribe of Florida v. Butterworth, 658 F.2d 310 (1981), which the Ninth Circuit found persuasive.

We are persuaded that the prohibitory/regulatory distinction is consistent with Bryan's construction of Pub.L. 280. It is not a bright-line rule, however; and as the Ninth Circuit itself observed, an argument of some weight may be made that the bingo statute is prohibitory rather than regulatory. But in the present case, the court reexamined the state law and reaffirmed its holding in Barona, and we are reluctant to disagree with that court's view of the nature and intent of the state law at issue here.

There is surely a fair basis for its conclusion. California does not prohibit all forms of gambling. California itself operates a state lottery, and daily encourages its citizens to participate in this state-run gambling. California also permits parimutuel horse-race betting. Although certain enumerated gambling games are prohibited under Cal.Penal Code § 330, games not enumerated, including the card games played in the Cabazon card club, are permissible. The Tribes assert that more than 400 card rooms similar to the Cabazon card club flourish in California, and the State does not dispute this fact. Also, as the Court of Appeals noted, bingo is legally sponsored by many different organizations and is widely played in California. There is no effort to forbid the playing of bingo by any member of the public over the age of 18. Indeed, the permitted bingo games must be open to the general public. Nor is there any limit on the number of games which eligible organizations may operate, the receipts which they may obtain from the games, the number of games which a participant may play, or the amount of money which a participant may spend, either per game or in total. In light of the fact that

California permits a substantial amount of gambling activity, including bingo, and actually promotes gambling through its state lottery, we must conclude that California regulates rather than prohibits gambling in general and bingo in particular.

California argues, however, that high stakes, unregulated bingo, the conduct which attracts organized crime, is a misdemeanor in California and may be prohibited on Indian reservations. But that an otherwise regulatory law is enforceable by criminal as well as civil means does not necessarily convert it into a criminal law within the meaning of Pub.L. 280. Otherwise, the distinction between § 2 and § 4 of that law could easily be avoided and total assimilation permitted. This view, adopted here and by the Fifth Circuit in the Butterworth case, we find persuasive. Accordingly, we conclude that Pub.L. 280 does not authorize California to enforce Cal.Penal Code § 326.5 within the Cabazon and Morongo Reservations.

California and Riverside County also argue that the Organized Crime Control Act (OCCA) authorizes the application of their gambling laws to the tribal bingo enterprises. The OCCA makes certain violations of state and local gambling laws violations of federal law. The Court of Appeals rejected appellants' argument. The court explained that whether a tribal activity is "a violation of the law of a state" within the meaning of OCCA depends on whether it violates the "public policy" of the State, the same test for application of state law under Pub.L. 280, and similarly concluded that bingo is not contrary to the public policy of California.

There is nothing in OCCA indicating that the States are to have any part in enforcing federal criminal laws or are authorized to make arrests on Indian reservations that in the absence of OCCA they could not effect. We are not informed of any federal efforts to employ OCCA to prosecute the playing of bingo on Indian reservations, although there are more than 100 such enterprises currently in operation, many of which have been in existence for several years, for the most part with the encouragement of the Federal Government. [T]here is no warrant for California to make arrests on reservations and thus, through OCCA, enforce its gambling laws against Indian tribes.

II

Because the state and county laws at issue here are imposed directly on the Tribes that operate the games, and are not expressly permitted by Congress, the Tribes argue that the judgment below should be affirmed without more. They rely on the statement in McClanahan v. Arizona State Tax Comm'n., 411 U.S. 164 (1973), that "State laws generally are not applicable to tribal Indians on an Indian reservation except where Congress has expressly provided that State laws shall apply." Our cases, however, have not established an inflexible per se rule precluding state jurisdiction over tribes and tribal members in the absence of express congressional consent. "[U]nder certain circumstances a State may validly assert authority over the activities of nonmembers on a reservation, and . . . in exceptional circumstances a State may assert jurisdiction over the on-reservation activities of tribal members." New Mexico v. Mescalero Apache Tribe, 462 U.S. 324, 331-332 (1983). [W]e held that, in the absence of express congressional permission, a State could require tribal smokeshops on Indian reservations to collect state sales tax from their non-Indian customers. Both McClanahan and Mescalero involved nonmembers entering and purchasing tobacco products on the reservations involved. The State's interest in assuring the collection of sales taxes from non-Indians enjoying the off-reservation services of the State was sufficient to warrant the minimal burden imposed on the tribal smokeshop operators.

This case also involves a state burden on tribal Indians in the context of their dealings with non-Indians since the question is whether the State may prevent the Tribes from making available high stakes bingo games to non-Indians coming from outside the reservations. Decision in this case turns on whether state authority is pre-empted by the operation of federal law; and "[s]tate jurisdiction is pre-empted . . . if it interferes or is incompatible with federal and tribal interests reflected in federal law, unless the state interests at stake are sufficient to justify the assertion of state authority." The inquiry is to proceed in light of traditional notions of Indian sovereignty and the congressional goal of Indian self-government, including its "overriding goal" of encouraging tribal self-sufficiency and economic development.

These are important federal interests. They were reaffirmed by the President's 1983 Statement on Indian Policy. More specifically, the Department of the Interior, which has the primary responsibility for carrying out the Federal Government's trust obligations to Indian tribes, has sought to implement these policies by promoting tribal bingo enterprises. Under the Indian Financing Act of 1974, 25 U.S.C. § 1451 et seq., the Secretary of the Interior has made grants and has guaranteed loans for the purpose of constructing bingo facilities. The Department of Housing and Urban Development and the Department of Health and Human Services have also provided financial assistance to develop tribal gaming enterprises. Here, the Secretary of the Interior has approved tribal ordinances establishing and regulating the gaming activities involved. The Secretary has also exercised his authority to review tribal bingo management contracts under 25 U.S.C. § 81, and has issued detailed guidelines governing that review.

These policies and actions, which demonstrate the Government's approval and active promotion of tribal bingo enterprises, are of particular relevance in this case. The Cabazon and Morongo Reservations contain no natural resources which can be exploited. The tribal games at present provide the sole source of revenues for the operation of the tribal governments and the provision of tribal services. They are also the major sources of employment on the reservations. Self-determination and economic development are not within reach if the Tribes cannot raise revenues and provide employment for their members. The Tribes' interests obviously parallel the federal interests.

California seeks to diminish the weight of these seemingly important tribal interests by asserting that the Tribes are merely marketing an exemption from state gambling laws. We held that the State could tax cigarettes sold by tribal smokeshops to non-Indians, even though it would eliminate their competitive advantage and substantially reduce revenues used to provide tribal services, because the Tribes had no right "to market an exemption from state taxation to persons who would normally do their business elsewhere." We stated that "[i]t is painfully apparent that the value marketed by the smokeshops to persons coming from outside is not generated on the reservations by activities in which the Tribes have a significant interest." Here, however, the Tribes are not merely importing a product onto the reservations for immediate resale to non-Indians. They have built modern facilities which provide recreational opportunities and ancillary services to their patrons, who do not simply drive onto the reservations, make purchases and depart, but spend extended periods of time there enjoying the services the Tribes provide. The Tribes have a strong incentive to provide comfortable, clean, and attractive facilities and well-run games in order to increase attendance at the games.

The State also relies on Rice v. Rehner, 463 U.S. 713 (1983), in which we held that California could require a tribal member and a federally licensed Indian trader operating a general store on a reservation to obtain a state license in order to sell liquor for off-premises consumption. But our decision there rested on the grounds that Congress had never recognized any sovereign tribal interest in regulating liquor traffic and that Congress, historically, had plainly anticipated that the States would exercise concurrent authority to regulate the use and distribution of liquor on Indian reservations. There is no such traditional federal view governing the outcome of this case, since, as we have explained, the current federal policy is to promote precisely what California seeks to prevent.

The sole interest asserted by the State to justify the imposition of its bingo laws on the Tribes is in preventing the infiltration of the tribal games by organized crime. To the extent that the State seeks to prevent any and all bingo games from being played on tribal lands while permitting regulated, off-reservation games, this asserted interest is irrelevant and the state and county laws are pre-empted. Even to the extent that the State and county seek to regulate short of prohibition, the laws are pre-empted. The State insists that the high stakes offered at tribal games are attractive to organized crime, whereas the controlled games authorized under California law are not. This is surely a legitimate concern, but we are unconvinced that it is sufficient to escape the pre-emptive force of federal and tribal interests apparent in this case. California does not allege any present criminal involvement in the Cabazon and Morongo enterprises, and the Ninth Circuit discerned none. An official of the Department of Justice has expressed some concern about tribal bingo operations, but far from any action being taken evidencing this concern—and surely the Federal Government has the authority to forbid Indian gambling enterprises—the prevailing federal policy continues to support these tribal enterprises, including those of the Tribes involved in this case.

We conclude that the State's interest in preventing the infiltration of the tribal bingo enterprises by organized crime does not justify state regulation of the tribal bingo enterprises in light of the compelling federal and tribal interests supporting them. State regulation would impermissibly infringe on tribal government, and this conclusion applies equally to the county's attempted regulation of the Cabazon card club. We therefore affirm the judgment of the Court of Appeals and remand the case for further proceedings consistent with this opinion.

It is so ordered.

Justice STEVENS, with whom Justice O'CONNOR and Justice SCALIA join, dissenting.

Unless and until Congress exempts Indian-managed gambling from state law and subjects it to federal supervision, I believe that a State may enforce its laws prohibiting high-stakes gambling on Indian reservations within its borders. Congress has not pre-empted California's prohibition against high-stakes bingo games and the Secretary of the Interior plainly has no authority to do so. While gambling provides needed employment and income for Indian tribes, these benefits do not, in my opinion, justify tribal operation of currently unlawful commercial activities. Accepting the majority's reasoning would require exemptions for cockfighting, tattoo parlors, nude dancing, houses of prostitution, and other illegal but profitable enterprises.

In my opinion the plain language of Pub.L. 280 authorizes California to enforce its prohibition against commercial gambling on Indian reservations. The State prohibits bingo games that are not operated by members of designated charitable organizations or which offer prizes in excess of $250 per game. In § 2 of Pub.L. 280, Congress expressly provided that the criminal laws of the State of California "shall have the same force and effect within such Indian country as they have elsewhere within the State." Moreover, it provided in § 4(a) that the civil laws of California "that are of general application to private persons or private property shall have the same force and effect within such Indian country as they have elsewhere within the State."

Today the Court seems prepared to acknowledge that an Indian tribe's commercial transactions with non-Indians may violate "the State's public policy." The Court reasons, however, that the operation of high-stakes bingo games does not run afoul of California's public policy because the State permits some forms of gambling and, specifically, some forms of bingo. I find this approach to "public policy" curious, to say the least. The State's policy concerning gambling is to authorize certain specific gambling activities that comply with carefully defined regulation and that provide revenues either for the State itself or for certain charitable purposes, and to prohibit all unregulated commercial lotteries that are operated for private profit. To argue that the tribal bingo games comply with the public policy of California because the State permits some other gambling is tantamount to arguing that driving over 60 miles an hour is consistent with public policy because the State allows driving at speeds of up to 55 miles an hour.

In my view, Congress has permitted the State to apply its prohibitions against commercial gambling to Indian tribes. Even if Congress had not done so, however, the State has the authority to assert jurisdiction over appellees' gambling activities.

[I]t is painfully obvious that the value of the Tribe's asserted exemption from California's gambling laws is the primary attraction to customers who would normally do their gambling elsewhere. The Cabazon Band of Mission Indians has no tradition or special expertise in the operation of large bingo parlors. Indeed, the entire membership of the Cabazon Tribe—it has only 25 enrolled members—is barely adequate to operate a bingo game that is patronized by hundreds of non-Indians nightly. How this small and formerly impoverished

Band of Indians could have attracted the investment capital for its enterprise without benefit of the claimed exemption is certainly a mystery to me.

I am entirely unpersuaded by the Court's view that the State of California has no legitimate interest in requiring appellees' gambling business to comply with the same standards that the operators of other bingo games must observe. The State's interest is both economic and protective. Presumably the State has determined that its interest in generating revenues for the public fisc and for certain charities outweighs the benefits from a total prohibition against publicly sponsored games of chance. Whatever revenues the Tribes receive from their unregulated bingo games drain funds from the state-approved recipients of lottery revenues—just as the tax-free cigarette sales in the Confederated Tribes case diminished the receipts that the tax collector would otherwise have received.

Moreover, I am unwilling to dismiss as readily as the Court does the State's concern that these unregulated high-stakes bingo games may attract organized criminal infiltration.

Appellants and the Secretary of the Interior may well be correct, in the abstract, that gambling facilities are a sensible way to generate revenues that are badly needed by reservation Indians. But the decision to adopt, to reject, or to define the precise contours of such a course of action, and thereby to set aside the substantial public policy concerns of a sovereign State, should be made by the Congress of the United States. It should not be made by this Court, by the temporary occupant of the Office of the Secretary of the Interior, or by non-Indian entrepreneurs who are experts in gambling management but not necessarily dedicated to serving the future well-being of Indian tribes.

I respectfully dissent.

Notes

1. Because federal law traditionally has used the term "Indian," one normally speaks of "Indian gaming." The more modern (and less offensive) "Native American" is beginning to catch on, however, and there is a growing tendency to refer to "tribal casinos" rather than "Indian casinos."

2. Native American governments are known as "tribes," although the terms "band," "pueblo," and "rancheria" can be found in a number of federal statutes. In addition, some tribes have "Nation" as part of their official name. In Canada, tribes typically are "bands," or, more recently, "First Nations." "Aboriginal" also frequently appears in Canadian law, as in the phrase "aboriginal rights." The word "aboriginal" almost never appears in United States Indian gaming law.

3. Until 1988, federal law almost always described land held in trust for tribes as "Indian Country." IGRA introduced a new term, "Indian lands," with a complex definition that differs only slightly from "Indian Country." *Compare* 25 U.S.C. § 2703 *with* 18 U.S.C. § 1151. But even IGRA uses the more traditional nomenclature when making it a federal crime to violate state anti-gaming laws in "Indian Country." *See* 18 U.S.C. § 1166. Tribal land is usually called a "reservation," but is sometimes referred to as "dependent Indian communities" or "Indian allotments." *See, e.g.,* 15 U.S.C. § 1175.

4. To support its conclusion in *Cabazon* that "Tribes have a strong incentive to provide comfortable, clean, and attractive facilities and well-run games," the majority quoted the testimony of an agent of the California Bureau of Investigation, who had visited the Cabazon bingo parlor:

> In attendance for the Monday evening bingo session were about 300 players . . . . On row 5, on the front left side were a middle-aged latin couple, who were later joined by two young latin males. These men had to have the game explained to them. The middle table was shared with a senior citizen couple. The aisle table had 2 elderly women, 1 in a wheelchair, and a middle-aged woman . . . . A goodly portion of the crowd were retired age to senior citizens.

480 U.S. at 220 n.23. Based on the foregoing, the Court concluded: "We are unwilling to assume that these patrons would be indifferent to the services offered by the Tribes." *Id*.

5. In a footnote, Justice White responded to Justice Stevens's slippery slope argument by writing: "Nothing in this opinion suggests that cock-fighting, tattoo parlors, nude dancing, and prostitution are permissible on Indian reservations within California. The applicable state laws governing an activity must be examined in detail before they can be characterized as regulatory or prohibitory." *Id*. at 211 n.10. Nevada does have legal prostitution. Can tribes in that state open brothels? *See Moapa Band of Paiute Indians v. United States Department of the Interior*, 747 F.2d 563 (9th Cir. 1984).

6. The Supreme Court's decision in *Cabazon* was both unexpected and viewed by many as a devastating blow to state governments. Others, however, considered it to be little more than an exercise in statutory construction whose effect would be largely limited to Public Law 280 states. In either event, *Cabazon* made the acceptance of Indian gaming complete by all three branches of the federal government. Beginning with President Nixon, the executive branch had endorsed Indian bingo as a way of reducing Indian dependence on federal funds. *See President's 1983 Statement on Indian Policy*, 19 Weekly Comp. Pres. Doc. 99 (1983). Conservatives in Congress agreed, while liberal members supported Indian bingo as a way of strengthening tribal self-government.

Problem 32

An Indian tribe gave one of its members permission to hold bingo games on reservation land. The member subsequently entered into an agreement with a non-Indian operator. Is the latter subject to the tribe's authority? *See United States ex rel. Morongo Band of Mission Indians v. Rose*, 34 F.3d 901 (9th Cir. 1994).

C. STATUTORY FRAMEWORK

SYCUAN BAND OF MISSION INDIANS v. ROACHE
54 F.3d 535 (9th Cir. 1994),
cert. denied, 516 U.S. 912 (1995)

CANBY, Circuit Judge.

This appeal presents a conflict over the power of state authorities to prohibit certain forms of Indian gaming. Edwin L. Miller, the District Attorney of San Diego County, California (the State), appeals the district court's injunction forbidding the State's prosecution of certain individuals employed in Indian gaming operations on the reservations of the Barona, Sycuan and Viejas Bands of Mission Indians. On cross-appeal, the Sycuan Band challenges the district court's finding that its video "pull-tab" machines offer Class III games that were operated in violation of the Indian Gaming Regulatory Act (IGRA), 25 U.S.C. §§ 2701-2721. We affirm the district court's judgment in all respects.

Background

After obtaining search warrants in the San Diego Municipal Court, sheriff's deputies raided gaming centers operated by the Barona, Sycuan, and Viejas Bands of Mission Indians on their reservations. The deputies seized gaming machines, cash and records. A short time later, District Attorney Miller commenced prosecutions of four persons employed in the Bands' respective gaming centers. The Bands brought actions in the district court for declaratory relief and injunctions against the state prosecutions.

The district court granted declaratory and injunctive relief in favor of the Bands. See 788 F.Supp. 1498 (S.D.Cal.1992). It declared that the county officials were precluded by the Indian Gaming Regulatory Act (IGRA) from jurisdiction to execute the warrants and prosecute the tribal gaming officials. Accordingly, it enjoined the pending prosecutions of these individuals.

The district court denied, however, the Sycuan Band's motion to return the seized gaming devices. The district court found that the Band's video pull-tab machines were Class III gaming devices that could be lawfully operated only if authorized by a Tribal-State compact. Because there was no such compact, the district court eventually ordered the San Diego County Sheriff, pursuant to a stipulation, to return the gaming devices to Video Autotab, Inc., the owner and lessor of the gaming devices.

The State appeals from the district court's injunction, contending that 42 U.S.C. § 1983 failed to authorize the court to issue an injunction; that the injunction violated the Anti-Injunction Act, 28 U.S.C. § 2283; and that the injunction violated the Younger abstention doctrine. Finally, the State appeals the ruling that it has no criminal jurisdiction over the gambling offenses at issue.

On cross-appeal, the Sycuan Band contends that the district court erred in finding that the Band's video "pull-tab" machines are Class III gaming devices. Before reaching that issue, we address the State's appeal.

On the merits, the district court had strong authority for its conclusion that the State lacked jurisdiction to enforce its criminal laws against electronic machine gambling. IGRA extends state laws punishing certain types of gambling into Indian country, 18 U.S.C. § 1166(a), (b), (c), but it also contains a highly explicit limitation on jurisdiction to enforce those laws:

> The United States shall have exclusive jurisdiction over criminal prosecutions of violations of State gambling laws that are made applicable under this section to Indian country, unless an Indian tribe pursuant to a Tribal-State compact . . . has consented to the transfer to the State of criminal jurisdiction with respect to the gambling on the lands of the Indian tribe.

18 U.S.C. § 1166(d). The Bands have not consented to the transfer of criminal jurisdiction to the State. As far as IGRA is concerned, therefore, the State had no authority to prosecute the Bands' employees for conducting the Bands' gaming. Having correctly so concluded, the district court was well within its equitable power to enjoin the prosecutions, unless some federal statute or decisional law affirmatively bars the injunction. We discuss those questions below, but first we deal with a final substantive contention of the State.

IGRA, Public Law 280 and State Criminal Jurisdiction

The State points out that section 1166(d) provides for exclusive federal enforcement of state criminal laws "made applicable under this section to Indian country." 18 U.S.C. § 1166(d). It argues that California had preexisting authority to enforce its criminal laws in Indian country under Public Law 280, 18 U.S.C. § 1162. Accordingly, the State contends that the prosecutions were lawfully maintained under the State's Public Law 280 jurisdiction.

We reject the State's arguments for two reasons. First, we do not agree that the State had jurisdiction over the Bands' gaming activities under Public Law 280. That statute granted California and certain other states jurisdiction over criminal violations and civil causes of action on Indian reservations. It left civil regulatory jurisdiction in the hands of the Tribes. Bryan v. Itasca County, 426 U.S. 373, 385, 388-90, 96 S.Ct. 2102, 2109, 2110-12, 48 L.Ed.2d 710 (1976) (construing § 4 of Public Law 280, 28 U.S.C. § 1360).

In California v. Cabazon Band of Mission Indians, 480 U.S. 202, 208-11, 107 S.Ct. 1083, 1088-89 (1987), the Supreme Court made it clear that state law in a Public Law 280 state may be excluded from Indian country as "regulatory" even though the regulatory aspects of the law are enforced by criminal penalties. The key is "whether the conduct at issue violates the State's public policy." Id. at 209, 107 S.Ct. at 1088. In Cabazon Band, the Supreme Court undertook this inquiry in regard to California's attempt to ban high-stakes bingo and certain card games in Indian country, and concluded that the State had no public policy against the gambling: it simply regulated it. Id. at 211, 107 S.Ct. at 1089. Accordingly, California could not prohibit the games in issue, carried on by the Bands in Indian country.

The State here points, however, to the Supreme Court's statement in Cabazon that "applicable state laws governing an activity must be examined in detail before they can be characterized as regulatory or prohibitory." Id. at 211 n.10, 107 S.Ct. at 1089 n.10. The State argues that Cabazon Band does not control this case, because the issue here is not bingo or card games, but electronic machine gambling that California permits nowhere. We conclude, however, that the State's argument is useful only when applied to the distinctions between classes of gambling set up by IGRA. We express no opinion concerning Class III, but at least insofar as the State's argument is directed at Class II-type gaming, of the sort engaged in by the Tribes in Cabazon Band, the state cannot regulate and prohibit, alternately, game by game and device by device, turning its public policy off and on by minute degrees. Cabazon Band addressed the problem at a higher level of generality than that. The State has shown us no determinative changes in California public policy since Cabazon Band, and that decision controls. Its import is clear. California had no Public Law 280 jurisdiction to enforce its gambling laws against the gaming operations of the Barona, Sycuan, or Viejas Indian Reservations, at least insofar as the Bands were engaged in the type of gaming that would fall within Class II of IGRA.

If, on the other hand, the state prosecutions are directed solely at gaming devices that IGRA would classify under Class III (as we hold below the electronic pull-tab games to be), then the effect of IGRA itself is to preclude the state prosecution. IGRA provides that "[t]he United States shall have exclusive jurisdiction over criminal prosecutions of violations of State gambling laws that are made applicable under this section to Indian country" in the absence of a compact providing for state jurisdiction. 18 U.S.C. § 1166(d). The State emphasizes "made applicable under this section" and draws an implication that, if it can find another source (Public Law 280) making its laws applicable in Indian country, then it can prosecute violations. But that conclusion does not follow, nor is it a sensible application of section 1166(d). If, as we hold below, the Bands' electronic pull-tab machines are Class III gaming devices, then section 1166(d) makes the State's law against such machines applicable in Indian country. Section 1166(d) also grants the federal government exclusive power to enforce that law. Even if there were some other route making that same state law applicable in Indian country, the Federal government's right to enforce that law is still exclusive. If that exclusivity is incompatible with any provision of Public Law 280, then the Public Law 280 provision has been impliedly repealed by section 1166(d). See United Keetoowah Band of Cherokee Indians v. Oklahoma ex rel. Moss, 927 F.2d 1170, 1176-81 (10th Cir.1991) (IGRA § 1166(d) occupies Indian gaming field to exclusion of Assimilative Crimes Act, 18 U.S.C. § 13, and its incorporation of state law). Whether IGRA has made broader inroads on Public Law 280 we need not decide; it has clearly made criminal enforcement of the State's laws prohibiting "slot machines" the exclusive province of the federal government.

The district court accordingly did not err in rejecting the State's argument that Public Law 280 authorized the state prosecutions of the Bands' gaming officials.

[The remainder of the court's opinion is omitted.]

SEMINOLE TRIBE OF FLORIDA v. FLORIDA
517 U.S. 44 (1996)

Chief Justice REHNQUIST delivered the opinion of the Court.

The Indian Gaming Regulatory Act provides that an Indian tribe may conduct certain gaming activities only in conformance with a valid compact between the tribe and the State in which the gaming activities are located. 25 U.S.C. § 2710(d). The Act, passed by Congress under the Indian Commerce Clause, U.S. Const., Art. I, § 10, cl. 3, imposes upon the States a duty to negotiate in good faith with an Indian tribe toward the formation of a compact, and authorizes a tribe to bring suit in federal court against a State in order to compel performance of that duty. We hold that notwithstanding Congress' clear intent to abrogate the States' sovereign immunity, the Indian Commerce Clause does not grant Congress that power, and therefore § 2710(d)(7) cannot grant jurisdiction over a State that does not consent to be sued. We further hold that the doctrine of Ex parte Young, 209 U.S. 123 (1908), may not be used to enforce § 2710(d)(3) against a state official.

I

Congress passed the Indian Gaming Regulatory Act in 1988 in order to provide a statutory basis for the operation and regulation of gaming by Indian tribes. The Act divides gaming on Indian lands into three classes—I, II, and III—and provides a different regulatory scheme for each class. Class III gaming—the type with which we are here concerned—is defined as "all forms of gaming that are not class I gaming or class II gaming," and includes such things as slot machines, casino games, banking card games, dog racing, and lotteries. It is the most heavily regulated of the three classes. The Act provides that class III gaming is lawful only where it is "conducted in conformance with a Tribal-State compact entered into by the Indian tribe and the State under paragraph (3) that is in effect." § 2710(d)(1).

The "paragraph (3)" to which the last prerequisite of § 2710(d)(1) refers is § 2710(d)(3), [which] describes the process by which a State and an Indian tribe begin negotiations toward a Tribal-State compact: "(A) Any Indian tribe having jurisdiction over the Indian lands upon which a class III gaming activity is being conducted, or is to be conducted, shall request the State in which such lands are located to enter into negotiations for the purpose of entering into a Tribal-State compact governing the conduct of gaming activities. Upon receiving such a request, the State shall negotiate with the Indian tribe in good faith to enter into such a compact."

The State's obligation to "negotiate with the Indian tribe in good faith," is made judicially enforceable by §§ 2710(d)(7)(A)(i) and (B)(i): "(A) The United States district courts shall have jurisdiction over (i) any cause of action initiated by an Indian tribe arising from the failure of a State to enter into negotiations with the Indian tribe for the purpose of entering into a Tribal-State compact under paragraph (3) or to conduct such negotiations in good faith." "(B)(i) An Indian tribe may initiate a cause of action described in subparagraph (A)(i) only after the close of the 180-day period beginning on the date on which the Indian tribe requested the State to enter into negotiations under paragraph (3)(A)." Sections 2710(d)(7)(B)(ii)-(vii) describe an elaborate remedial scheme designed to ensure the formation of a Tribal-State compact. A tribe that brings an action under § 2710(d)(7)(A)(i) must show that no Tribal-State compact has been entered and that the State failed to respond in good faith to the tribe's request to negotiate; at that point, the burden then shifts to the State to prove that it did in fact negotiate in good faith. If the district court concludes that the State has failed to negotiate in good faith toward the formation of a Tribal-State compact, then it "shall order the State and Indian tribe to conclude such a compact within a 60-day period." If no compact has been concluded 60 days after the court's order, then "the Indian tribe and the State shall each submit to a mediator appointed by the court a proposed compact that represents their last best offer for a compact." The mediator chooses from between the two proposed compacts the one "which best comports with the terms of [the Act] and any other applicable Federal law and with the findings and order of the court," and submits it to the State and the Indian tribe. If the State consents to the proposed compact within 60 days of its submission by the mediator, then the proposed compact is "treated as a Tribal-State compact entered into under paragraph (3)." If, however, the State does not consent within that 60-day period, then the Act provides that the mediator "shall notify the Secretary [of the Interior]" and that the Secretary "shall prescribe procedures under which class III gaming may be conducted on the Indian lands over which the Indian tribe has jurisdiction."

In September 1991, the Seminole Tribe of Indians, petitioner, sued the State of Florida and its Governor, Lawton Chiles, respondents. [P]etitioner alleged that respondents had "refused to enter into any negotiation for inclusion of [certain gaming activities] in a tribal-state compact," thereby violating the "requirement of good faith negotiation" contained in § 2710(d)(3). Respondents moved to dismiss the complaint, arguing that the suit violated the State's sovereign immunity from suit in federal court. The District Court denied respondents' motion, 801 F. Supp. 655 (S.D.Fla. 1992), and the respondents took an interlocutory appeal of that decision.

The Court of Appeals for the Eleventh Circuit reversed the decision of the District Court, holding that the Eleventh Amendment barred petitioner's suit against respondents. 11 F.3d 1016 (1994). The court agreed with the District Court that Congress in § 2710(d)(7) intended to abrogate the States' sovereign immunity, and also agreed that the Act had been passed pursuant to Congress' power under the Indian Commerce Clause, U.S. Const., Art. I, § 8, cl. 3. The court disagreed with the District Court, however, that the Indian Commerce Clause grants Congress the power to abrogate a State's Eleventh Amendment immunity from suit, and concluded therefore that it had no jurisdiction over petitioner's suit against Florida. The court further held that Ex parte Young, 209 U.S. 123 (1908), does not permit an Indian tribe to force good faith negotiations by suing the Governor of a State. Finding that it lacked subject-matter jurisdiction, the Eleventh Circuit remanded to the District Court with directions to dismiss petitioner's suit.

Petitioner sought our review of the Eleventh Circuit's decision, and we granted certiorari, in order to consider two questions: (1) Does the Eleventh

Amendment prevent Congress from authorizing suits by Indian tribes against States for prospective injunctive relief to enforce legislation enacted pursuant to the Indian Commerce Clause?; and, (2) Does the doctrine of Ex parte Young permit suits against a State's governor for prospective injunctive relief to enforce the good faith bargaining requirement of the Act? We answer the first question in the affirmative, the second in the negative, and we therefore affirm the Eleventh Circuit's dismissal of petitioner's suit.

The Eleventh Amendment provides: "The Judicial power of the United States shall not be construed to extend to any suit in law or equity, commenced or prosecuted against one of the United States by Citizens of another State, or by Citizens or Subjects of any Foreign State." Although the text of the Amendment would appear to restrict only the Article III diversity jurisdiction of the federal courts, "we have understood the Eleventh Amendment to stand not so much for what it says, but for the presupposition . . . which it confirms." Blatchford v. Native Village of Noatak, 501 U.S. 775, 779 (1991). That presupposition, first observed over a century ago in Hans v. Louisiana, 134 U.S. 1 (1890), has two parts: first, that each State is a sovereign entity in our federal system; and second, that "'[i]t is inherent in the nature of sovereignty not to be amenable to the suit of an individual without its consent.' quoting The Federalist No. 81, p. 487 (C. Rossiter ed. 1961) (A. Hamilton)." For over a century we have reaffirmed that federal jurisdiction over suits against unconsenting States "was not contemplated by the Constitution when establishing the judicial power of the United States." Here, petitioner has sued the State of Florida and it is undisputed that Florida has not consented to the suit. Petitioner nevertheless contends that its suit is not barred by state sovereign immunity. First, it argues that Congress through the Act abrogated the States' sovereign immunity. Alternatively, petitioner maintains that its suit against the Governor may go forward under Ex parte Young, supra.

II

Petitioner argues that Congress through the Act abrogated the States' immunity from suit. In order to determine whether Congress has abrogated the States' sovereign immunity, we ask two questions: first, whether Congress has "unequivocally expresse[d] its intent to abrogate the immunity," and second, whether Congress has acted "pursuant to a valid exercise of power."

A

Congress' intent to abrogate the States' immunity from suit must be obvious from "a clear legislative statement." Here, we agree with the parties, with the Eleventh Circuit in the decision below and with virtually every other court that has confronted the question that Congress has in § 2710(d)(7) provided an "unmistakably clear" statement of its intent to abrogate. Section 2710(d)(7)(A)(i) vests jurisdiction in "[t]he United States district courts . . . over any cause of action . . . arising from the failure of a State to enter into negotiations . . . or to conduct such negotiations in good faith." Any conceivable doubt as to the identity of the defendant in an action under § 2710(d)(7)(A)(i) is dispelled when one looks to the various provisions of § 2710(d)(7)(B), which describe the remedial scheme available to a tribe that files suit under § 2710(d)(7)(A)(i). [I]f a suing tribe meets its burden of proof, then the "burden of proof shall be upon the State"; if the court "finds that the State has failed to negotiate in good faith, the court shall order the State"; "the State shall submit to a mediator appointed by the court" and the mediator "shall submit to the State." In sum, we think that the numerous references to the "State" in the text of § 2710(d)(7)(B) make it indubitable that Congress intended through the Act to abrogate the States' sovereign immunity from suit.

B

Having concluded that Congress clearly intended to abrogate the States' sovereign immunity through § 2710(d)(7), we turn now to consider whether the Act was passed "pursuant to a valid exercise of power." Petitioner suggests that one consideration weighing in favor of finding the power to abrogate here is that the Act authorizes only prospective injunctive relief rather than retroactive monetary relief. But we have often made it clear that the relief sought by a plaintiff suing a State is irrelevant to the question whether the suit is barred by the Eleventh Amendment. The Eleventh Amendment does not exist solely in order to "preven[t] federal court judgments that must be paid out of a State's treasury;" it also serves to avoid "the indignity of subjecting a State to the coercive process of judicial tribunals at the instance of private parties."

Similarly, petitioner argues that the abrogation power is validly exercised here because the Act grants the States a power that they would not otherwise have, viz., some measure of authority over gaming on Indian lands. It is true enough that the Act extends to the States a power withheld from them by the Constitution. See California v. Cabazon Band of Mission Indians, 480 U.S. 202 (1987). Nevertheless, we do not see how that consideration is relevant to the question whether Congress may abrogate state sovereign immunity. The Eleventh Amendment immunity may not be lifted by Congress unilaterally deciding that it will be replaced by grant of some other authority.

Thus our inquiry into whether Congress has the power to abrogate unilaterally the States' immunity from suit is narrowly focused on one question: Was the Act in question passed pursuant to a constitutional provision granting Congress the power to abrogate? Previously, in conducting that inquiry, we have found authority to abrogate under only two provisions of the Constitution. [W]e recognized that the Fourteenth Amendment, by expanding federal power at the expense of state autonomy, had fundamentally altered the balance of state and federal power struck by the Constitution. We noted that § 1 of the Fourteenth Amendment contained prohibitions expressly directed at the States and that § 5 of the Amendment expressly provided that "The Congress shall have the power to enforce, by appropriate legislation, the provisions of this article."

In only one other case has congressional abrogation of the States' Eleventh Amendment immunity been upheld. In Pennsylvania v. Union Gas Co., 491 U.S. 1 (1989), a plurality of the Court found that the Interstate Commerce Clause, Art. I, § 8, cl. 3, granted Congress the power to abrogate state sovereign immunity, stating that the power to regulate interstate commerce would be "incomplete without the authority to render States liable in damages."

In arguing that Congress through the Act abrogated the States' sovereign immunity, petitioner does not challenge the Eleventh Circuit's conclusion that the Act was passed pursuant to neither the Fourteenth Amendment nor the Interstate Commerce Clause. Instead, accepting the lower court's conclusion that the Act was passed pursuant to Congress' power under the Indian Commerce Clause, petitioner now asks us to consider whether that clause grants Congress the power to abrogate the States' sovereign immunity.

Following the rationale of the Union Gas plurality, our inquiry is limited to determining whether the Indian Commerce Clause, like the Interstate Commerce Clause, is a grant of authority to the Federal Government at the expense of the States. The answer to that question is obvious. If anything, the Indian Commerce Clause accomplishes a greater transfer of power from the States to the Federal Government than does the Interstate Commerce Clause. This is clear enough from the fact that the States still exercise some authority over interstate trade but have been divested of virtually all authority over Indian commerce and Indian tribes. Under the rationale of Union Gas, if the States' partial cession of authority over a particular area includes cession of the immunity from suit, then their virtually total cession of authority over a different area must also include cession of the immunity from suit. We agree with the petitioner that the plurality opinion in Union Gas allows no principled distinction in favor of the States to be drawn between the Indian Commerce Clause and the Interstate Commerce Clause.

The Court in Union Gas reached a result without an expressed rationale agreed upon by a majority of the Court. [J]ustice Brennan's opinion received the support of only three other Justices. Of the other five, Justice White, who provided the fifth vote for the result, wrote separately in order to indicate his disagreement with the majority's rationale and four Justices joined together in a dissent that rejected the plurality's rationale.

Never before the decision in Union Gas had we suggested that the bounds of Article III could be expanded by Congress operating pursuant to any constitutional provision other than the Fourteenth Amendment. Indeed, it had seemed fundamental that Congress could not expand the jurisdiction of the federal courts beyond the bounds of Article III. Marbury v. Madison, 1 Cranch 137 (1803). The plurality claimed support for its decision from a case holding the unremarkable, and completely unrelated, proposition that the States may waive their sovereign immunity, and cited as precedent propositions that had been merely assumed for the sake of argument in earlier cases.

Reconsidering the decision in Union Gas, we conclude that none of the policies underlying stare decisis require our continuing adherence to its holding. The decision has, since its issuance, been of questionable precedential value, largely because a majority of the Court expressly disagreed with the rationale of the plurality. The case involved the interpretation of the Constitution and therefore may be altered only by constitutional amendment or revision by this Court. Finally, both the result in Union Gas and the plurality's rationale depart from our established understanding of the Eleventh Amendment and undermine the accepted function of Article III. We feel bound to conclude that Union Gas was wrongly decided and that it should be, and now is, overruled.

For over a century, we have grounded our decisions in the oft-repeated understanding of state sovereign immunity as an essential part of the Eleventh Amendment. It is true that we have not had occasion previously to apply established Eleventh Amendment principles to the question whether Congress has the power to abrogate state sovereign immunity (save in Union Gas). But consideration of that question must proceed with fidelity to this century-old doctrine.

The dissent, to the contrary, disregards our case law in favor of a theory cobbled together from law review articles and its own version of historical events.

In overruling Union Gas today, we reconfirm that the background principle of state sovereign immunity embodied in the Eleventh Amendment is not so ephemeral as to dissipate when the subject of the suit is an area, like the regulation of Indian commerce, that is under the exclusive control of the Federal Government. Even when the Constitution vests in Congress complete law-making authority over a particular area, the Eleventh Amendment prevents congressional authorization of suits by private parties against unconsenting States. The Eleventh Amendment restricts the judicial power under Article III, and Article I cannot be used to circumvent the constitutional limitations placed upon federal jurisdiction. Petitioner's suit against the State of Florida must be dismissed for a lack of jurisdiction.

III

Petitioner argues that we may exercise jurisdiction over its suit to enforce § 2710(d)(3) against the Governor notwithstanding the jurisdictional bar of the Eleventh Amendment. Petitioner notes that since our decision in Ex parte Young, 209 U.S. 123 (1908), we often have found federal jurisdiction over a suit against a state official when that suit seeks only prospective injunctive relief in order to "end a continuing violation of federal law." The situation presented here, however, is sufficiently different from that giving rise to the traditional Ex parte Young action so as to preclude the availability of that doctrine.

Here, the "continuing violation of federal law" alleged by petitioner is the Governor's failure to bring the State into compliance with § 2710(d)(3). But the duty to negotiate imposed upon the State by that statutory provision does not stand alone. Rather, as we have seen, Congress passed § 2710(d)(3) in conjunction with the carefully crafted and intricate remedial scheme set forth in § 2710(d)(7).

Where Congress has created a remedial scheme for the enforcement of a particular federal right, we have, in suits against federal officers, refused to supplement that scheme with one created by the judiciary. Here, of course, the question is not whether a remedy should be created, but instead is whether the Eleventh Amendment bar should be lifted, as it was in Ex parte Young, in order to allow a suit against a state officer. Nevertheless, we think that the same general principle applies: therefore, where Congress has prescribed a detailed remedial scheme for the enforcement against a State of a statutorily created right, a court should hesitate before casting aside those limitations and permitting an action against a state officer based upon Ex parte Young.

Here, Congress intended § 2710(d)(3) to be enforced against the State in an action brought under § 2710(d)(7); the intricate procedures set forth in that provision show that Congress intended therein not only to define, but also significantly to limit, the duty imposed by § 2710(d)(3). For example, where the court finds that the State has failed to negotiate in good faith, the only remedy prescribed is an order directing the State and the Indian tribe to conclude a compact within 60 days. And if the parties disregard the court's order and fail to conclude a compact within the 60-day period, the only sanction is that each party then must submit a proposed compact to a mediator who selects the one which best embodies the terms of the Act. Finally, if the State fails to accept the compact selected by the mediator, the only sanction against it is that the mediator shall notify the Secretary of the Interior who then must prescribe regulations governing Class III gaming on the tribal lands at issue. By contrast with this quite modest set of sanctions, an action brought against a state official under Ex parte Young would expose that official to the full remedial powers of a federal court, including, presumably, contempt sanctions. If § 2710(d)(3) could be enforced in a suit under Ex parte Young, § 2710(d)(7) would have been superfluous; it is difficult to see why an Indian tribe would suffer through the intricate scheme of § 2710(d)(7) when more complete and more immediate relief would be available under Ex parte Young.

Here, of course, we have found that Congress does not have authority under the Constitution to make the State suable in federal court under § 2710(d)(7). Nevertheless, the fact that Congress chose to impose upon the State a liability which is significantly more limited than would be the liability imposed upon the state officer under Ex parte Young strongly indicates that Congress had no wish to create the latter under § 2710(d)(3). Nor are we free to rewrite the statutory scheme in order to approximate what we think Congress might have wanted had it known that § 2710(d)(7) was beyond its authority. If that effort is to be made, it should be made by Congress, and not by the federal courts. We hold that Ex parte Young is inapplicable to petitioner's suit against the Governor of Florida, and therefore that suit is barred by the Eleventh Amendment and must be dismissed for a lack of jurisdiction.

IV

The Eleventh Amendment prohibits Congress from making the State of Florida capable of being sued in federal court. The narrow exception to the Eleventh Amendment provided by the Ex parte Young doctrine cannot be used to enforce § 2710(d)(3) because Congress enacted a remedial scheme, § 2710(d)(7), specifically designed for the enforcement of that right. The Eleventh Circuit's dismissal of petitioner's suit is hereby affirmed.

It is so ordered.

JUSTICE STEVENS, dissenting.

This case is about power—the power of the Congress of the United States to create a private federal cause of action against a State, or its Governor, for the violation of a federal right. [I]n a sharp break with the past, today the Court holds that with the narrow and illogical exception of statutes enacted pursuant to the Enforcement Clause of the Fourteenth Amendment, Congress has no such power.

The importance of the majority's decision to overrule the Court's holding in Pennsylvania v. Union Gas Co. cannot be overstated. The majority's opinion does not simply preclude Congress from establishing the rather curious statutory scheme under which Indian tribes may seek the aid of a federal court to secure a State's good faith negotiations over gaming regulations. Rather, it prevents Congress from providing a federal forum for a broad range of actions against States, from those sounding in copyright and patent law, to those concerning bankruptcy, environmental law, and the regulation of our vast national economy.

The fundamental error that continues to lead the Court astray is its failure to acknowledge that its modern embodiment of the ancient doctrine of sovereign immunity "has absolutely nothing to do with the limit on judicial power contained in the Eleventh Amendment." It rests rather on concerns of federalism and comity that merit respect but are nevertheless, in cases such as the one before us, subordinate to the plenary power of Congress.

Fortunately, and somewhat fortuitously, a jurisdictional problem that is unmentioned by the Court may deprive its opinion of precedential significance. The Indian Gaming Regulatory Act establishes a unique set of procedures for resolving the dispute between the Tribe and the State. If each adversary adamantly adheres to its understanding of the law, if the District Court determines that the State's inflexibility constitutes a failure to negotiate in good faith, and if the State thereafter continues to insist that it is acting within its rights, the maximum sanction that the Court can impose is an order that refers the controversy to a member of the Executive Branch of the Government for resolution. 25 U.S.C. § 2710(d)(7)(B). As the Court of Appeals interpreted the Act, this final disposition is available even though the action against the State and its Governor may not be maintained. 11 F.3d 1016, 1029 (11th Cir. 1994) (The [Supreme] Court does not tell us whether it agrees or disagrees with that disposition.) In my judgment, it is extremely doubtful that the obviously dispensable involvement of the judiciary in the intermediate stages of a procedure that begins and ends in the Executive Branch is a proper exercise of judicial power. It may well follow that the misguided opinion of today's majority has nothing more than an advisory character. Whether or not that be so, the better reasoning in JUSTICE SOUTER's far wiser and far more scholarly opinion will surely be the law one day.

For these reasons, as well as those set forth in JUSTICE SOUTER's opinion, I respectfully dissent.

JUSTICE SOUTER, with whom JUSTICE GINSBURG and JUSTICE BREYER join, dissenting.

In holding the State of Florida immune to suit under the Indian Gaming Regulatory Act, the Court today holds for the first time since the founding of the Republic that Congress has no authority to subject a State to the jurisdiction of a federal court at the behest of an individual asserting a federal right.

The fault I find with the majority today is not in its decision to reexamine Union Gas, for the Court in that case produced no majority for a single rationale supporting congressional authority. Instead, I part company from the Court because I am convinced that its decision is fundamentally mistaken, and for that reason I respectfully dissent.

[T]he power to regulate commerce with Indian Tribes has been interpreted as making "Indian relations . . . the exclusive province of federal law." We have accordingly recognized that "[s]tate laws generally are not applicable to tribal Indians on an Indian reservation except where Congress has expressly provided that State laws shall apply." We have specifically held, moreover, that the states have no power to regulate gambling on Indian lands. California v. Cabazon Band of Mission Indians, 480 U.S. 202, 221-222 (1987). In sum, since the States have no sovereignty in the regulation of commerce with the tribes there is no source of sovereign immunity to assert in a suit based on congressional regulation of that commerce.

An order requiring a "State" to comply with federal law can, of course, take the form of an order directed to the State in its sovereign capacity. But as Ex parte Young and innumerable other cases show, there is nothing incongruous about a duty imposed on a "State" that Congress intended to be effectuated by an order directed to an appropriate state official. If, then, IGRA's references to "a State's" duty were not enforceable by order to a state official, it would have to be for some other reason than the placement of the statutory duty on "the State."

It may be that even the Court agrees, for it falls back to the position that only a State, not a state officer, can enter into a compact. This is true but wholly beside the point. The issue is whether negotiation should take place as required by IGRA and an officer (indeed, only an officer) can negotiate.

Finally, one must judge the Court's purported inference by stepping back to ask why Congress could possibly have intended to jeopardize the enforcement of the statute by excluding application of Young's traditional jurisdictional rule, when that rule would make the difference between success or failure in the federal court if state sovereign immunity was recognized. Why would Congress have wanted to go for broke on the issue of state immunity in the event the State pleaded immunity as a jurisdictional bar? Why would Congress not have wanted IGRA to be enforced by means of a traditional doctrine giving federal courts jurisdiction over state officers, in an effort to harmonize state sovereign immunity with federal law that is paramount under the Supremacy Clause? There are no plausible answers to these questions.

Construing the statute to harmonize with Young, as it readily does, would have saved an act of Congress and rendered a discussion on constitutional grounds wholly unnecessary. This case should be decided on this basis alone.

Because neither text, precedent, nor history supports the majority's abdication of our responsibility to exercise the jurisdiction entrusted to us in Article III, I would reverse the judgment of the Court of Appeals.

Notes

1. Most players did not like the electronic pull-tab dispensers that were at issue in *Roache* (in part because they used a video screen and in part because they "paid off" in paper chits). Nevertheless, they proved highly profitable in locations where real slot machines were not legal. The Sycuan casino, for example, had 30 units, and each one netted about $900 a day, more than eight times what a typical slot machine makes in Las Vegas.

2. As *Roache* makes clear, unless a tribe and a state have agreed in a compact that the latter has criminal jurisdiction, only the federal government can enforce state gaming laws in Indian country. Nevertheless, courts are split on what should happen to illegal devices that have been wrongfully seized. Some, like the Ninth Circuit, place significant weight on the fact the machines are contraband, while others focus more on the state agents' failure to respect the tribe's sovereign land.

3. In *Seminole*, the Supreme Court declared part of IGRA unconstitutional. So what is left? One possibility is that there is a right but no remedy: a tribe can seek a compact, but cannot sue the state if it refuses to negotiate.

The Eleventh Circuit found a way out of the dilemma by authorizing tribes to go to the Secretary of the Interior if a state refused to negotiate. *See Seminole Tribe of Florida v. Florida*, 11 F.3d 1016 (11th Cir. 1994). The Supreme Court declined to discuss this ruling: "We do not here consider, and express no opinion upon, that portion of the decision below that provides a substitute remedy for a tribe bringing suit." 517 U.S. at 76 n.18. In *Spokane Tribe of Indians v. Washington State*, 28 F.3d 991 (9th Cir. 1994), *vacated on other grounds*, 517 U.S. 1129 (1996), the Ninth Circuit rejected the notion that tribes could bypass the states and turn "the Secretary of the Interior into a federal czar [of Indian gaming]."

If IGRA is unconstitutional, it would seem that the pre-statutory law, particularly *Cabazon*, again becomes controlling, but no one knows for certain. For more on IGRA's prospects, *see, e.g.*, William Bennett Cooper, III, Comment, *What's in the Cards for the Future of Indian Gaming Law?*, 5 Vill. Sports & Ent. L.J. 129 (1998); Nicholas S. Goldin, Note, *Casting a New Light on Tribal Casino Gaming: Why Congress Should Curtail the Scope of High Stakes Indian Gaming*, 84 Cornell L. Rev. 798 (1999); Rebecca S. Lindner-Cornelius, Comment, *The Secretary of the Interior as Referee: The States, the Indian Nations, and How Gambling Led to the Illegality of the Secretary of the Interior's Regulations in 25 C.F.R. § 291*, 84 Marq. L. Rev. 685 (2001); Daniel Twetten, Comment, *Public Law 280 and the Indian Gaming Regulatory Act: Could Two Wrongs Ever Be Made Into a Right?*, 90 J. Crim. L. & Criminology 1317 (2000).

4. It also has been suggested that IGRA is unconstitutional because it forces states to enter into compacts authorizing Indian gaming, thereby violating the Tenth Amendment. Tribal advocates reject this characterization, contending that IGRA merely allows states to participate in the decision-making process. In *Seminole*, the Tenth Amendment was not considered by the Supreme Court because the issue had not been preserved for review. For a further discussion, *see* Neil Scott Cohen, Note, *In What Often Appears to be*

a Crapshoot Legislative Process, Congress Throws Snake Eyes When It Enacts the Indian Gaming Regulatory Act, 29 Hofstra L. Rev. 277 (2000).

5. It should be pointed out that IGRA applies only to tribes that have been formally recognized by the federal government. Thus, tribes that have achieved only state-recognition, or have not been recognized at all, are not presently permitted to offer gaming. *See generally* Kathryn R.L. Rand, *There Are No Pequots on the Plains: Assessing the Success of Indian Gaming*, 5 Chap. L. Rev. 47 (2002). *See also* David M. Herszenhorn, *Indian Bureau Rejects Bid for Status as a Tribe*, N.Y. Times, Jan. 22, 2003, at C14 (reporting on the failed effort of the Golden Hill Tribe of the Paugussett Indian Nation to win federal recognition as a first step to opening a casino in Bridgeport, Connecticut).

Problem 33

A state and a tribe entered into a compact permitting the latter to offer simulcast wagering on tribal lands. When the state later sought to renege on the compact, the tribe took it to federal court. If the state raises the Eleventh Amendment as a defense, how should the court rule? *See Cabazon Band of Mission Indians v. Wilson*, 124 F.3d 1050 (9th Cir. 1997), *cert. denied*, 524 U.S. 926 (1998).

D. CLASSIFICATION

CABAZON BAND OF MISSION INDIANS v. NATIONAL INDIAN GAMING COMMISSION
14 F.3d 633 (D.C. Cir.),
cert. denied, 512 U.S. 1221 (1994)

RANDOLPH, Circuit Judge.

This is an appeal from the order of the district court, Lamberth, J., granting summary judgment in favor of the defendants National Indian Gaming Commission and its Chairman, the Department of the Interior and its Secretary, and the Department of Justice and the Attorney General; and in favor of the fifteen States listed in the caption as intervenors. Cabazon Band of Mission Indians v. National Indian Gaming Comm'n, 827 F.Supp. 26 (D.D.C. 1993). Seven federally recognized Indian Tribes, each alleging that it conducted gaming activities on Indian lands within the Tribe's jurisdiction, sued the original defendants for an injunction and a declaratory judgment, claiming that new regulations of the Indian Gaming Commission, promulgated under the Indian Gaming Regulatory Act of 1988, 25 U.S.C. §§ 2701-2721, were invalid and that the Commission improperly considered certain computerized games to be in a different regulatory category than their non-computerized counterparts. An eighth federally recognized Tribe, the Delaware Tribe of Western Oklahoma, later joined in the action. On September 23, 1993, a panel of this court, over Judge Henderson's dissent, granted the Tribes' motion for an injunction, pending appeal, forbidding the defendants from interfering with the Tribes' use and operation of certain gaming devices. In this expedited appeal, we vacate the injunction and affirm the judgment of the district court.

Congress enacted the Indian Gaming Regulatory Act in the wake of the Supreme Court's decision in California v. Cabazon Band of Mission Indians, 480 U.S. 202, 107 S.Ct. 1083, 94 L.Ed.2d 244 (1987), holding that State gaming laws could not be enforced on Indian reservations within States otherwise permitting such gaming. With the objective of regulating tribal gaming operations on Indian lands, the Act established the Indian Gaming Commission as an agency within the Department of the Interior, 25 U.S.C. § 2704(a), and conferred upon the Commission the power and duty to monitor Indian gaming activities, to investigate and audit certain types of Indian gaming, to enforce the collection of civil fines, and to "promulgate such regulations and guidelines as it deems appropriate to implement the provisions of" the Act. 25 U.S.C. § 2706.

The Commission's principal responsibilities relate to what the Act designates as "class II gaming." See 25 U.S.C. § 2706(b). The Act divides all forms of gaming into three categories. "Class I gaming" consists of social games for prizes of minimal value and traditional forms of Indian gaming. These are considered within a Tribe's exclusive jurisdiction. "Class II gaming" is "the game of chance commonly known as bingo (whether or not electronic, computer, or other technologic aids are used in connection therewith) including (if played in the same location) pull-tabs, lotto, punch boards, tip jars, instant bingo, and other games similar to bingo." 25 U.S.C. § 2703(7)(A). Class II gaming does not include "electronic or electromechanical facsimiles of any game of chance or slot machines of any kind." 25 U.S.C. § 2703(7)(B)(ii). Tribes may engage in class II gaming on Indian lands in any State where such gaming is permitted for any purpose, so long as the particular form of gaming is not otherwise prohibited on Indian lands by federal law. The Tribe must be the sole owner of the class II gaming enterprise. The Act restricts the Tribe's use of the revenues from class II gaming and requires the Tribe to maintain a system of controls to ensure the integrity of the gaming and the personnel operating it. "Class III gaming" encompasses "all forms of gaming that are not class I gaming or class II gaming." 25 U.S.C. § 2703(8). Class III gaming on Indian lands is permitted only if "such gaming is not otherwise specifically prohibited on Indian lands by federal law"; the Tribe enters into a compact governing gaming with the State in which the Indian lands are located; and the Secretary of the Interior approves the Tribal-State compact. 25 U.S.C. § 2710(b)(1)(A), (d)(1) and (d)(8).

The game at issue in this case is "pull-tabs," one of the games included in the definition of class II gaming. The most common form of pull-tabs is the paper version. Gamblers purchase a card from a deck. The set of cards ("the deal") contains a predetermined number of winners. Upon purchasing the card, the gambler pulls the paper tab open to find out if he is a winner. In the paper version each gambler competes against all other gamblers in the hall playing the game. There is now a computerized version of pull-tabs. The computer randomly selects a card for the gambler, pulls the tab at the gambler's direction, and displays the result on the screen. The computer version, like the paper version, has a fixed number of winning cards in each deal. The computers may be interconnected so that each gambler simultaneously plays against other gamblers in "pods" or "banks" of as many as forty machines.

The focus on computer or video pull-tabs reflects a considerable narrowing of the case since the parties appeared before Judge Lamberth. Invoking the Administrative Procedure Act, 5 U.S.C. § 701 et seq., the Tribes then had challenged Commission regulations, promulgated in April 1992 (57 Fed.Reg. 12,382), defining class II gaming (25 C.F.R. § 502.3); class III gaming (25 C.F.R. § 502.4); "electronic, computer, or other technologic aid" (25 C.F.R. § 502.7); and "electronic or electromechanical facsimile" (25 C.F.R. § 502.8). Judge Lamberth's cogent opinion rejected each of the Tribes' arguments against these regulations as "either moot or meritless." 827 F.Supp. at 32.

In this appeal, the Tribes have devoted their arguments to a different question, the only one set forth in their Statement of Issues: "Did the district court err in finding that the video pull-tab games at issue in this case are class III 'electronic facsimiles' rather than class II pull-tab games which utilize 'electronic, computer or technologic aids' under §§ 2703(7)(A) and 2703(7)(B)(ii) of the Indian Gaming Regulatory Act and under §§ 502.7 and 502.8 of the Commission's regulations?" Tribes' Brief at 2. This is the question raised by the final count of the Tribes' complaint, which asks for a declaratory judgment. In ruling on it, we follow Judge Lamberth's carefully reasoned opinion and agree with him that the decision is "a simple one that may be accomplished solely by examining the statute itself (that is, without looking to the Commission's rules)." 827 F.Supp. at 32. There is no need to consider the Tribes' general point that 25 C.F.R. §§ 502.7 and 502.8 sweep too many games otherwise within class II gaming into the category of class III gaming. For whatever might be said about the breadth of the regulations with respect to other games, "without any doubt" computerized pull-tab games of the type involved here "clearly are facsimiles of games of chance and therefore are class III gaming." 827 F.Supp. at 32.

Here, as in the district court, the Tribes concede that the video version of pull-tabs is the same game as the paper version. Tribes' Brief at 24; 827 F.Supp. at 28 n.2, 32. Because class II gaming does not include "electronic or electromechanical facsimiles of any game of chance" (25 U.S.C. § 2703(7)(B)(ii)), this concession alone demonstrates that the video game is not in the class II category. "By definition, a device that preserves the fundamental characteristics of a game is a facsimile of the game." Sycuan Band of Mission Indians v. Roache, 788 F. Supp. 1498 (S.D.Cal. 1992). As commonly understood, facsimiles are exact copies, or duplicates. Although there may be room for a broader interpretation of "facsimile," the video version of pull-tabs falls within the core meaning of electronic facsimile. It exactly replicates the paper version of the game, and if that is not sufficient to make it a facsimile, we doubt, as did Judge Lamberth (827 F.Supp. at 32), that anything could qualify.

The Tribes' contrary position is this: "the only point at which the use of electronics or other technology could fall into the class III category is where a different game—a copy, or imitation, something other than the genuine article; in plain English, a 'facsimile'—is created by such technology." All other uses of technology, according to the Tribes, should be considered "aids" within the meaning of § 2703(7)(A). We view it as something other than "plain English" to say that only electronic versions of games different from the originals are exact duplicates. The meanings of words in a statute do not necessarily correspond with dictionary definitions. Context matters. So often does history. Yet there are limits to how far language, written in the formal style of a statute, may be wrenched. We would no sooner take "yes" to signify "no" than we would take "same" to denote only "different." One might stretch "facsimiles" to cover inexact copies, but the possibility of such a construction does not assist the Tribes. Even if the stretch were justified, the consequence would be to expand the category of games defined as facsimiles, not to constrict it. Exact duplicates—such as the video pull-tab games the Tribes wish to operate—would remain covered by § 2703(7)(B)(ii). In short, we agree with Judge Lamberth that, at the least, the Act's exclusion of electronic facsimiles removes games from the class II category when those games are wholly incorporated into an electronic or electromechanical version.

The sentences in the Senate Committee report to which the Tribes refer do not alter our judgment. Near the end of a lengthy paragraph discussing how separate Tribes might coordinate their gaming businesses, the following appears: "Simultaneous games participation between and among reservations can be made practical by use of computers and telecommunications technology as long as the use of such technology does not change the fundamental characteristics of the bingo or lotto games . . . . In other words, such technology would merely broaden the potential participation levels and is readily distinguishable from the use of electronic facsimiles in which a single participant plays a game with or against a machine rather than with or against other players." S.REP. NO. 446, 100th Cong., 2d Sess. 9 (1988), U.S.Code Cong. & Admin.News 1988 pp. 3071, 3079.

Pointing to the Report's caution about not using technology to change the "fundamental characteristics" of the games, the Tribes argue that an electronic version of a game cannot be a "facsimile" unless it fundamentally changes the game. While the Report is less than clear about the distinction between electronic aids and electronic facsimiles, Judge Lamberth's response is conclusive when it comes to the Tribes' video pull-tab game. As he wrote, this portion of the Report focuses not on how using technology might create an electronic facsimile, but on "communications technology that might be used to link bingo players in several remote locations." 827 F.Supp. at 33. That sort of technology is, as the Report itself recognizes, distinguishable from electronic facsimiles of the game itself. See Spokane Indian Tribe v. United States, 972 F.2d 1090, 1093 (9th Cir. 1992). To be sure, the only supposed electronic "facsimiles" mentioned in this paragraph of the Report are those in which "a single participant plays a game with or against a machine rather than with or against other players." Although in video pull-tabs the gambler is playing the game "with . . . a machine," the Tribes are right that, as in paper pull-tabs, the gambler is playing against other gamblers. But the Tribes are wrong to suppose that the example mentioned in this passage must be the only type of electronic copies Congress meant to include under § 2703(7)(B)(ii). The Report says nothing of the sort and neither does the statute. An illustration given in one sentence of a committee report scarcely excludes the possibility of other examples. Still less does it, rather than the language of the statute, express the will of Congress.

Ambiguous statutes, the Tribes tell us, should be construed in favor of the Indians. See Montana v. Blackfeet Tribe of Indians, 471 U.S. 759, 766, 105 S.Ct. 2399, 2403, 85 L.Ed.2d 753 (1985). Congress believed the Indian Gaming Regulatory Act would benefit Indians in several ways. The Tribes focus on the Act's objective of advancing tribal economic interests. The Act has another objective, however: protecting tribes and their members from the dangers associated with large-scale gaming operations. Which construction of the Act favors the Indians, the one including electronic pull-tab games under class II gaming or the one placing this version of the game under the more restrictive category of class III? In this case there is no need to choose. When the statutory language is clear, as it is here, the canon may not be employed. See South Carolina v. Catawba Indian Tribe, Inc., 476 U.S. 498, 506, 106 S.Ct. 2039, 2044, 90 L.Ed.2d 490 (1986).

The injunction pending appeal is vacated and the judgment of the district court is affirmed.

UNITED STATES v. 103 ELECTRONIC GAMBLING DEVICES
223 F.3d 1091 (9th Cir. 2000)

BERZON, Circuit Judge.

This case poses the question, what is bingo? In particular, we determine whether an electronic game called MegaMania, manufactured and sold by Appellee Multimedia Games, Inc. ("Multimedia"), is "bingo" as that term is defined in the Indian Gaming Regulatory Act ("IGRA"), 25 U.S.C. §§ 2701-2721.

Appellant the United States thinks not. The Government claims that the terminals on which MegaMania is played are "gambling devices" within the meaning of the Johnson Act, 15 U.S.C. §§ 1171-1178. The Johnson Act prohibits the possession and operation of any "gambling device", as defined in the Act, on Indian land unless authorized by a tribal-state compact. Invoking the Johnson Act, the Government brought this forfeiture action against, inter alia, some twenty-odd MegaMania game terminals located at the Red Fox Casino, an Indian gaming facility in Northern California.

Under IGRA, however, bingo and electronic aids thereto are generally permissible in Indian country. Multimedia asserts that MegaMania is a bingo game, and that the use of the games at the casino was therefore legal.

In MegaMania, players compete against each other in a single, interlinked electronic game via a network of individual computer terminals located at tribal gaming facilities throughout the country. At their respective terminals, players may make an initial purchase at 25 cents per card of up to four electronic game "cards," displayed on the video screens of each terminal. A participant may play up to four cards at a time.

MegaMania does not commence until at least twelve people begin playing a minimum of 48 cards collectively. Once the game begins the players start receiving a series of three-number draws displayed on-screen and announced through audio channels. For each three number draw a player must pay 25 cents per card that he or she is playing (e.g., if a player has three cards on her screen, she must pay 75 cents per draw). This pay-per-draw style of play is called "ante up" bingo. After a set of numbers is drawn players must press a "Daub Cards" button ("daub button") to "cover" the called numbers on the cards. When a player presses the daub button, the computer automatically covers corresponding numbers on the player's cards. After each three-number draw is displayed a player has eight seconds to decide whether to continue playing the card(s) for another draw.

When a player covers a straight line either horizontally, vertically or diagonally and declares "bingo" (by pressing the daub button) on one or more cards, every player in every facility nationwide is notified of the bingo. Once a player (or players) get(s) bingo, this straight-line game ends. Each player with bingo wins a monetary prize, the amount of which is based on the total number of cards being played in the game, the number of balls drawn since the game began, and the number of players reaching bingo simultaneously. The top jackpot on the straight-line game is $5000, awarded for a bingo achieved after the first four numbers are drawn, the earliest point at which a player can get bingo.

In addition to the traditional straight-line game, there is a "corners game" (dubbed "CornerMania"). In the corners game, each player who covers two, three, or four corners of a card gets a prize. The corners game is played continuously until the straight-line game ends, so there can be one or more CornerMania winners on each draw after the first. If no corners game prize has been awarded before the straight-line game ends, additional numbers are drawn three at a time until at least one corner prize is given out.

In 1988, Congress adopted IGRA. Only if a tribe has negotiated a tribal-state compact may it run class III games on its land. At the time the Government brought this forfeiture action, no such compact was in place between the Cahto Tribe and the State of California. Thus, for our purposes the critical question is whether MegaMania and the MegaMania terminals are class II gaming under IGRA.

IGRA defines class II gaming in relevant part as follows:

> (i) the game of chance commonly known as bingo (whether or not electronic, computer, or other technologic aids are used in connection therewith)—
>
> (I) which is played for prizes, including monetary prizes, with cards bearing numbers or other designations,
>
> (II) in which the holder of the card covers such numbers or designations when objects, similarly numbered or designated, are drawn or electronically determined, and
>
> (III) in which the game is won by the first person covering a previously designated arrangement of numbers or designations on such cards,
>
> including (if played in the same location) pull-tabs, lotto, punch boards, tip jars, instant bingo, and other games similar to bingo . . . .

Id. § 2703(7)(A). IGRA, however, explicitly excludes from Class II gaming "electronic or electromechanical facsimiles of any game of chance or slot machines of any kind."

As part of its initiative to deal with tribal gaming, Congress created the National Indian Gaming Commission ("NIGC") to regulate tribal gaming. The NIGC's broad powers include inspecting tribes' books and records, approving tribal-state pacts, levying and collecting civil fines, monitoring and even shutting down games, and promulgating regulations and guidelines it deems appropriate to implement IGRA. The NIGC has developed regulations to refine the scope of class II gaming.

Before considering whether MegaMania satisfies the three criteria for a class II bingo game set forth in 25 U.S.C. § 2703(7)(A)(i)(I)-(III), we turn to the Government's argument that these three factors are not the only criteria a game must meet to be an IGRA class II bingo game: The Government maintains that because IGRA uses the phrase "the game of chance commonly known as bingo" before spelling out the three criteria, other features that have traditionally characterized bingo games are also pertinent in determining whether or not a game is a class II bingo game. The Government contends, specifically, that (i) traditional bingo games lack the ante-up feature Mega-Mania possesses, (ii) in a traditional bingo game, unlike CornerMania, earnings depend on those of other players, and (iii) MegaMania's "manic pace" and potentially high stakes are markedly different than the placid tranquility and token rewards and losses associated with a traditional bingo game, see Appellant's Opening Brief ("AOB") at 23 (citing Alice Andrews, Hooked on Bingo 11 (1988) ("There is a calm and peacefulness in playing Bingo. There is a get-away-from-it-all feeling, kind of like bamboo fishing.")).

The Government's efforts to capture more completely the Platonic "essence" of traditional bingo are not helpful. Whatever a nostalgic inquiry into the vital characteristics of the game as it was played in our childhoods or home towns might discover, IGRA's three explicit criteria, we hold, constitute the sole legal requirements for a game to count as class II bingo.

There would have been no point to Congress's putting the three very specific factors in the statute if there were also other, implicit criteria. The three included in the statute are in no way arcane if one knows anything about bingo, so why would Congress have included them if they were not meant to be exclusive?

Further, IGRA includes within its definition of bingo "pull-tabs, . . . punch boards, tip jars, [and] instant bingo . . . ," none of which are similar to the traditional numbered ball, multi-player, card-based game we played as children. Cf. Merriam-Webster's Collegiate Dictionary 114 (10th ed. 1999) (defining bingo as "a game of chance played with cards having numbered squares corresponding with numbered balls drawn at random and won by covering five such squares in a row"). Instant bingo, for example, is as the Fifth Circuit explained in Julius M. Israel Lodge of B'nai B'rith No. 2113 v. Commissioner, 98 F.3d 190 (5th Cir. 1996), a completely different creature from the classic straight-line game. Instead, instant bingo is a self-contained instant-win game that does not depend at all on balls drawn or numbers called by an external source.

Moreover, § 2703(7)(A)(i)'s definition of class II bingo includes "other games similar to bingo," explicitly precluding any reliance on the exact attributes of the children's pastime.

Finally, and critically, the NIGC's interpretation of both IGRA and the NIGC's primary IGRA implementing regulation, 25 C.F.R. § 502, rests on the proposition that neither Congress nor the Commission intended to "limit bingo to its classic form." Action for Final Rule 25 C.F.R. § 502 ("§ 502 Action"), 57 Fed.Reg. 12382, 12382. The NIGC's conception of what counts as bingo under IGRA, as articulated in the agency's Final Action on § 502 a few years after IGRA was enacted, is entitled to substantial deference, for "[administrative] practice has peculiar weight when it involves a contemporaneous construction of a statute by the men charged with the responsibility of setting its machinery in motion, of making the parts work as efficiently and smoothly while they are yet untried and new." Norwegian Nitrogen Co. v. United States, 288 U.S. 294, 315, 53 S.Ct. 350, 77 L.Ed. 796 (1933) (Cardozo, J.).

The Government contends that the "ante-up" feature of MegaMania "distinguishes [it] from the game commonly known as bingo, as historically played throughout this country and indeed even today in tribal bingo facilities," AOB at 18-19, observing that in a traditional (presumably church-hall style) bingo game, players pay a fixed price for a "session pack" of cards, which lets them play for an evening. But the Government invokes nothing other than tradition to explain precisely why the ante-up pricing method is proscribed by IGRA. As the district court noted, "there is nothing in the statute or the regulations that requires a player to pay one price up front to play the entire game."

All told, § 2703(7)(A)(i)'s definition of "the game of chance commonly known as bingo" is broader than the Government would have us read it. We decline the invitation to impose restrictions on its meaning besides those Congress explicitly set forth in the statute. Class II bingo under IGRA is not limited to the game we played as children.

The Government contends the "continuous-win" feature (or "interim win", as Multimedia puts it) of CornerMania does not comply with IGRA's third requirement because (i) CornerMania can result in multiple payouts before the straight-line game ends; and (ii) each CornerMania payout does not depend on the number of other players receiving CornerMania prize money but rather on the number of corners covered on each draw and on the number of balls drawn since the game began. For these two reasons, maintains the Government, MegaMania is not "won by the first person covering a previously designated arrangement of numbers or designations on such cards," 25 U.S.C. § 2703(7)(A)(i)(III).

The question before us, though, is whether MegaMania, not one of its constituent components, satisfies IGRA's statutory criteria for class II gaming. Thus, MegaMania as a whole is "the game" to which § 2703(7)(A)(i)(III) pertains.

Turning to the question of whether MegaMania satisfies § 2703(7)(A)(i)(III), as an initial matter, there is no reason that the "previously designated arrangement" to which the statute refers must be a straight line. Indeed, the statutory description just quoted quite clearly permits any pattern to yield a prize, as long as the pattern is "previously designated." Moreover, even if we were to resort for this purpose to the inquiry into "essential" bingo we have already rejected, we would not rule otherwise. As an affidavit submitted to the district court by an FBI racketeering investigator attests, "[i]n the game commonly known as bingo . . . [e]xamples of pre-designated winning patterns include the traditional straight line, four corners, letters X or L, or covering the full card."

As for the ultimate question of whether MegaMania is "won" by the first person covering a previously designated arrangement, assuming that in a given game of MegaMania players win several rounds of CornerMania before the straight-line game ends, it would appear that each such player has "won" by "covering a previously designated arrangement." The first focus of this issue is nothing less than the meaning of the word "win": Can someone "win" a game even though the other players may also "win"? That is, does "win" necessarily mean "beat"?

The answer, according to Webster's II New College Dictionary, is that "win" can mean "beat" but need not: That dictionary's first definition of "win" is " '[t]o achieve victory over others in a competition or contest,' " Webster's II New College Dictionary 1264 (1995), while the second is " '[t]o receive [money] as a prize or a reward for performance.' " So, for example, in an instant lottery game, everyone whose scratch card entitles them to ten dollars "wins" a prize, with no effect on how many others may win or in what amount.

Because "winning" does not necessarily entail vanquishing one's opponents, the meaning of "win" in the statute is at worst ambiguous. In light of that ambiguity, we look for indications that Congress intended to preclude the award of multiple prizes in a single game of bingo.

The record in this case establishes that, in addition to the usual straight-line prize, some traditional live bingo games also make interim payouts to players who cover the corners of their cards; we presume those players believe that they have "won" prizes, even though the game has not ended and others may "win" as much or more. Additionally, as already stated, IGRA explicitly designates instant bingo as a class II game if it is played "in the same location" as a bingo game. 25 U.S.C. § 2703(7)(A)(i). That Congress would permit this variant of bingo, yielding interim prizes while the main game is ongoing, indicates it did not intend to forbid interim prizes like those CornerMania awards during a game of MegaMania.

In light of the foregoing considerations, it is telling that IGRA does not state the game has to end when the first person wins anything. Had Congress intended to proscribe interim prizes, the statute could have been drafted to say that "the game ends" instead of "the game is won," or could have included an express restriction that only one prize be given during the game.

IGRA's implementing regulations designate any house banking game as class III gaming. Recall that a house banking game is "any game of chance that is played with the house as a participant in the game, where the house takes on all players, collects from all losers, and pays all winners, and the house can win." 25 C.F.R. § 502.11. The Government reasons that MegaMania fits within this definition because CornerMania's payouts do not hinge on the success of other players but are instead based on a mathematical formula that ensures that over time the house will net fifteen percent of players' antes.

In MegaMania, however, the house is not a participant in the game the way it is in blackjack, for example, where the house plays a hand, and the success of the players depends on the success of the house. And the mere fact that the house nets a percentage of the players' fees for playing certainly cannot define a "house banking" game. In any church-hall bingo game, the "house" regularly nets some portion of the money it takes in, or there would be no point in sponsoring the game. Just because the house turns a profit on players' deposits doesn't make the house "a participant in the game" that "takes on all players" and that "can win."

The Government claims the MegaMania terminal is an "electronic facsimile", Multimedia, an "electronic, computer, or other technologic aid." The distinction under IGRA between an electronic "aid" and an electronic "facsimile" is one that has been litigated and decided before. When the issue arose in Spokane Indian Tribe v. United States, the court looked to the Senate Report on IGRA to distinguish between the two. See 972 F.2d 1090, 1093 (9th Cir. 1992). The Senate Report states:

> [T]ribes should be given the opportunity to take advantage of modern methods of conducting class II games and the language regarding technology is designed to provide maximum flexibility. In this regard, the Committee recognizes that tribes may wish to join with other tribes to coordinate their class II operations and thereby enhance the potential of increasing revenues. For example, linking participant players at various reservations whether in the same or different States, by means of telephone, cable, television or satellite may be a reasonable approach for the tribes to take. Simultaneous games participation between and among reservations can be made practical by use of computers and telecommunications technology as long as the use of such technology does not change the fundamental characteristics of the bingo or lotto games . . . . In other words, such technology would merely broaden the potential participation levels and is readily distinguishable from the use of electronic facsimiles in which a single participant plays a game with or against a machine rather than with or against other players.

Senate Report at 9. Relying on the Senate Report, Spokane Indian Tribe noted that an "electronic aid" "enhance[s] the participation of more than one person in . . . Class II gaming activities." 972 F.2d at 1093. Because the Pick 6 game at issue in the case involved only "a single participant play[ing] against the machine," the court held that it was an electronic facsimile rather than an electronic aid.

The MegaMania terminal, in contrast, does "link[] participant players at various reservations whether in the same or different States [thereby] broaden[ing] the potential participation levels." Senate Report at 9. As such, the MegaMania terminal is not a "facsimile of any game of chance," 25 U.S.C. § 2703(7)(A)(ii), or, indeed, a facsimile of anything. Rather, the terminal is merely an electronic aid to human players of bingo, something like electronic mail with a graphic user interface. And, while the government has argued that MegaMania resembles a slot machine in certain limited respects, there has been no argument that the terminal is a "slot machine", id., which it plainly is not. Unlike a slot machine, MegaMania is in truth being played outside the terminal; the terminal merely permits a person to connect to a network of players comprising each MegaMania game, and without a network of at least 12 other players playing at other terminals, an individual terminal is useless.

The Government urges that in CornerMania players effectively do play against the machine because their winnings do not depend on those of other players. First, in CornerMania players are competing against each other either to be the first to get a corners prize (if the straight-line game has ended), or (if a corners prize has already been awarded) to get a corners prize before another player gets straight-line bingo. Second, while the Government's argument could have relevance were CornerMania a free-standing game, one cannot play CornerMania without playing the whole game—MegaMania—and MegaMania requires twelve players to play.

The Government maintains that the MegaMania terminal, although specifically authorized under IGRA, is nonetheless an illegal "gambling device" under the Johnson Act. The Johnson Act's definition of "gambling device" includes slot machines (statutorily defined in painstaking detail, see 15 U.S.C. § 1171(a)(1)), and also any other "machine or mechanical device" designed "primarily" for gambling that, when operated, either delivers money or property or entitles a player to receive the same "as the result of the application of an element of chance," id. § 1171(a)(1) & (2). The definition also includes "essential part[s] intended to be used in connection with any such machine . . . but which is not attached." Id. § 1171(a)(3). In most circumstances, the Johnson Act prohibits the possession or operation of any gambling device on federal land and in Indian country. IGRA explicitly repealed the application of the Johnson Act to class III gaming devices used pursuant to tribal-state compacts, but did not explicitly address the relationship between IGRA and the Johnson Act as applied to class II gaming.

We are not aware of any authority pre-dating IGRA that addresses how the Johnson Act applied to bingo aids. In any event, there is little point at this juncture in engaging in time travel to determine how the Johnson Act would have applied to bingo in Indian country in the absence of IGRA. What matters now is how the two are to be read together—that is, how two enactments by Congress over thirty-five years apart most comfortably coexist, giving each enacting Congress's legislation the greatest continuing effect.

The text of IGRA quite explicitly indicates that Congress did not intend to allow the Johnson Act to reach bingo aids. The statute provides that bingo using "electronic, computer, or other technologic aids" is class II gaming, and therefore permitted in Indian country. Reading the Johnson Act to forbid such aids would render the quoted language a nullity. Why would Congress carefully protect such technologic aids through the text of § 2703(7)(A)(i), yet leave them to the wolves of a Johnson Act forfeiture action?

In short, while complete, self-contained electronic or mechanical facsimiles of a game of chance, including bingo, may indeed be forbidden by the Johnson Act after the enactment of IGRA, cf. 25 C.F.R. § 502.8 (defining "electronic facsimile" under IGRA as "any gambling device as defined in 15 U.S.C. § 1171(a)(2) or (3) [i.e., the Johnson Act]"); Cabazon Band, 827 F.Supp. at 31 ("[I]t is plainly evident that IGRA's 'facsimiles' are the Johnson Act's 'gambling devices.'"), we hold that mere technologic aids to bingo, such as the Mega-Mania terminal, are not.

By so holding, we maintain fidelity to two entrenched canons of statutory construction: (i) courts should give effect to both of two statutes covering related or overlapping subjects, and (ii) a specific statute governs a general one.

Congress's most recent relevant word on gaming is that aids to bingo are legal in Indian country. Section 2703 of IGRA is a "specific provision applying to a very specific situation," Morton v. Mancari, 417 U.S. 535, 550, 94 S.Ct. 2474, 41 L.Ed.2d 290 (1974), and we must accordingly give it effect here.

Finally, our decision carries out Congress's goal—expressed in the text of IGRA—of providing "a statutory basis for the operation of gaming by Indian tribes as a means of promoting tribal economic development, self-sufficiency, and strong tribal governments." 25 U.S.C. § 2702(1).

MegaMania is class II bingo. Because the MegaMania terminal is a class II aid to bingo, we conclude that it is not an illicit gambling device under the Johnson Act.

For the foregoing reasons, Multimedia scores bingo; the judgment is AFFIRMED.

Notes

1. For another case concerning how a particular game should be classified under IGRA, see Diamond Game Enterprises, Inc. v. Reno, 230 F.3d 365 (D.C. Cir. 2001) (machine that took money and had a video screen but produced a paper pull-tab held to be a Class II device).

2. Even where the nature of a game is clear, other issues regarding its operation can arise. In Chickasaw Nation v. United States, 534 U.S. 84 (2001), for example, the Supreme Court held that tribes are required to pay federal wagering and occupational excise taxes on Class II pull-tab devices. The tribes had argued that no taxes were due given IGRA's text. In rejecting this argument, the majority concluded that Congress had made an obvious drafting error. In a dissent, Justice O'Connor chided the Court for not resolving the ambiguity in the tribes' favor.

Problem 34

When it was asked for an advisory opinion under IGRA, the federal government opined that a new type of machine constituted Class III gaming. Your client, who did not ask for the opinion, believes the device should have been designated Class II gaming. To date, the government has taken no further action on the matter. Can you client sue to have the advisory opinion withdrawn or changed? See Cheyenne-Arapaho Gaming Commission v. National Indian Gaming Commission, 214 F. Supp. 2d 1155 (N.D. Okla. 2002).

E. COMPACTS

LAC DU FLAMBEAU BAND OF LAKE SUPERIOR CHIPPEWA INDIANS v. STATE OF WISCONSIN

770 F. Supp. 480 (W.D. Wis. 1991),
appeal dismissed, 957 F.2d 515 (7th Cir.),
cert. denied, 506 U.S. 829 (1992)

CRABB, Chief Judge.

This is a civil action brought under the Indian Gaming Regulatory Act, 25 U.S.C. § 2701 et seq., arising out of defendants' alleged failure to bargain in good faith with plaintiffs on the terms of a tribal-state Indian gaming compact. Defendants concede that the state has refused to bargain over certain gaming activities that it believes are not proper subjects of negotiation. They represent, however, that the state is prepared to return to negotiations once the court has determined whether the disputed activities are proper subjects for a compact.

The Indian Gaming Regulatory Act is the product of years of legislative effort to devise a comprehensive scheme for regulating gaming activities on Indian lands. It reflects congressional concerns about the increasing reliance of Indian tribes on gaming revenues for the provision of governmental services to tribal communities and the lack of mechanisms for regulating gaming activity. The essential feature of the Act is the tribal-state compact process, the means Congress devised to balance the states' interest in regulating high stakes gambling within their borders and the Indians' resistance to state intrusions on their sovereignty. The structure of the Act conforms to the basic principle that the states and tribes negotiate as sovereigns. See S.Rep. No. 100-446, 100th Cong., 2d Sess. at 13:

> After lengthy hearings, negotiations and discussions, the Committee concluded that the use of compacts between tribes and states is the best mechanism to assure that the interests of both sovereign entities are met with respect to the regulation of complex gaming enterprises such as pari-mutuel horse and dog racing, casino gaming, jai alai and so forth. The Committee notes the strong concerns of states that state laws and regulations relating to sophisticated forms of class III gaming be respected on Indian lands where, with few exceptions, such laws and regulations do not now apply. The Committee balanced these concerns against the strong tribal opposition to any imposition of State jurisdiction over activities on Indian lands. The Committee concluded that the compact process is a viable mechanism for setting [sic] various matters between two equal sovereigns.

The Act divides gaming activities into three classes. Class I includes social games played solely for prizes of minimal value and traditional forms of Indian gaming engaged in as part of a tribal celebration or ceremony. These activities are within the exclusive jurisdiction of the tribe. Class II games include bingo and related games and non-banking card games, as well as certain "grandfathered" card games that were operated by Indian tribes in four named states before May 1, 1988. Specifically excepted from Class II are non-grandfathered banking games such as baccarat, chemin de fer or blackjack, and video games of chance and slot machines. Class II gaming is within the jurisdiction of the tribes, subject to the requirements of the Act, with some oversight by the National Indian Gaming Commission.

Class III includes all other forms of gaming. Class III gaming activities are lawful on Indian lands only if the activities are (1) authorized by an ordinance or resolution adopted by the governing body of the tribe that meets the requirements of the statute and is approved by the commission chairman; (2) located in a state that permits such gaming for any purpose by any person, organization or entity; and (3) conducted in conformance with a tribal-state compact entered into by the tribe and the state.

The parties dispute whether the state is required to include casino games, video games and slot machines in its negotiations with the tribes. I conclude that it is required to negotiate those activities because they are permitted under Wisconsin law within the meaning of 25 U.S.C. § 2710(d)(1)(B). Accordingly, I will deny defendants' motion for summary judgment.

For the purpose only of deciding defendants' motion for summary judgment, I find that there is no genuine issue with respect to any of the following material facts set forth under the heading "Facts." It is irrelevant whether the state bargained in good faith because it concedes it has not bargained on the disputed activities and is prepared to conclude a compact once it has been determined which activities must be included in the negotiations. It is irrelevant also what the negotiators thought the statute requires; the requirements of the statute raise an issue of law and not of fact.

FACTS

Plaintiffs Lac du Flambeau Tribe of Lake Superior Chippewa Indians and Sokaogon Chippewa Community are federally-acknowledged Indian tribes with reservations in the State of Wisconsin. Defendant State of Wisconsin is a sovereign state of the United States. Defendant Tommy G. Thompson is Governor of the State of Wisconsin. Defendant David Penn is the District Attorney for Vilas County, Wisconsin. At all times relevant to this suit, defendant Donald J. Hanaway was the Attorney General of the State of Wisconsin, and defendant Janet Marvin was the District Attorney for Forest County, Wisconsin.

The Indian Gaming Regulatory Act, 25 U.S.C. § 2701 et seq., became effective October 17, 1988. On November 16, 1988, plaintiff Lac du Flambeau submitted a written request for tribal-state compact negotiations.

On July 19, 1989, plaintiff Lac du Flambeau proposed as class III gaming activities the following games: "Black Jack21—cards, Cards, Video/Slots, games such as Black-Jack and Poker, Craps, Roulette, Keno, off track betting parlor, Sports book."

When bill drafts of the tribal-state gaming compacts were requested, legislative lawyers raised questions about the scope of the games that had been negotiated, particularly about the inclusion of activities not conducted by anyone else in Wisconsin. On October 24, 1989, the Wisconsin Lottery

Board requested an attorney general's opinion on the scope of gaming permitted in Wisconsin. On February 5, 1990, defendant Hanaway issued an opinion to the effect that class III games were prohibited in Wisconsin with the exception of lotteries and on-track parimutuel wagering. Since then, the State of Wisconsin has refused to negotiate on any class III activities other than lotteries and on-track betting.

At the present time, the Wisconsin Lottery conducts three types of lotteries in which prizes are distributed among persons who purchase tickets: instant scratch games, pull-tab or break-open games, and on-line games. Instant scratch games are lotteries that use preprinted tickets with a latex covering that is scratched off to reveal the play symbols underneath. A player wins when a winning combination of play symbols is printed on the ticket. The lottery also offers additional methods of play such as secondary drawings for persons who hold winning instant scratch tickets.

Pull-tab or break-open games utilize preprinted tickets made of laminated paper that is partially perforated to allow a strip to be torn to reveal the symbols underneath. As in instant scratch games, the player wins if there is a winning combination of symbols on the ticket.

In on-line games, the player chooses (or the computer selects) a subset of six numbers from a larger set of numbers. The winning numbers are determined by a drawing, and prizes are paid for matching, in any order, six, five or four of the numbers drawn. Tickets are issued by a computer terminal connected electronically to a central computer that records and confirms the play. The ticket is the evidence of the player's entry numbers and is the only basis on which a prize may be claimed. Wisconsin's MEGABUCKS, Lotto*America, is an on-line game in which the player chooses (or the computer selects) six different numbers between 1 and 54, and prizes are awarded for matching four, five or six of the numbers drawn. It is offered simultaneously by sixteen governmental jurisdictions within the United States through a commonly administered drawing and prize pool. SuperCash is an on-line game with a set top prize of $250,000 for matching correctly, in any order, six, five or four of the numbers drawn. A third type of on-line game adds a secondary method of playing an on-line game. For example, a person may win a small cash prize if he or she happens to be the 99th person to purchase a ticket, as determined by the central computer.

The Wisconsin Racing Board is an agency of the State of Wisconsin. It regulates racing and on-track parimutuel wagering in the state, and issues licenses to applicants who wish to own and operate racetracks at which on-track parimutuel wagering is conducted. It has licensed five dog racetracks since it began operating.

OPINION

The issue between the parties centers on the provision in 25 U.S.C. § 2710(d)(1) that "Class III gaming activities shall be lawful on Indian lands only if such activities are . . . (B) located in a State that permits such gaming for any purpose by any person, organization, or entity . . . ." Defendants argue that casino games, video games and slot machines are not permitted for any purpose by any person, organization or entity within Wisconsin;

because they are not, the state is not required to bargain over these games. Defendants' position is that Congress meant "permits" to be given its usual dictionary meaning of formally or expressly granting leave; therefore, unless a state grants leave expressly for the playing of a particular type of gaming activity within the state, that activity cannot be lawful on Indian lands. Under this approach, the state is required to bargain only over gaming activities that are operating legally within the state.

Defendants' reading of "permits" ignores the other meanings assigned to the word, such as "[t]o suffer, allow, consent, let; to give leave or license; to acquiesce by failure to prevent, or to expressly assent or agree to the doing of an act." Black's Law Dictionary (5th ed.). More important, it ignores the Supreme Court's opinion in California v. Cabazon Band of Mission Indians, 480 U.S. 202, 107 S.Ct. 1083, 94 L.Ed.2d 244 (1987), on which Congress relied in drafting the Indian Regulatory Gaming Act. In Cabazon, the Supreme Court held that in determining whether a state's criminal laws would apply to gambling on Indian lands under Public Law 83-280, a court must analyze the state's policy toward gambling. If the policy is to prohibit all forms of gambling by anyone, then the policy is characterized as criminal-prohibitory and the state's criminal laws apply to tribal gaming activity. On the other hand, if the state allows some forms of gambling, even subject to extensive regulation, its policy is deemed to be civil-regulatory and it is barred from enforcing its gambling laws on the reservation.

The Senate Report on the Indian Gaming Regulatory Act makes explicit reference to Cabazon in discussing class II gaming, which has the same requirement as class III gaming that the gaming activity be "located within a state that permits such gaming for any purpose by any person, organization or entity." § 2710(b)(1)(A). The Senate committee stated that it anticipated that the federal courts would rely on the Cabazon distinction between regulatory gaming schemes and prohibitory laws, explaining with regard to the scope of allowable activities:

> The Committee wishes to make clear that, under S.555 [IGRA], application of the prohibitory/regulatory distinction is markedly different from the application of the distinction in the context of Public Law 83-280. Here, the courts will consider the distinction between a State's civil and criminal laws to determine whether a body of law is applicable, as a matter of Federal law, to either allow or prohibit certain activities.

S.Rep. No. 100-446, at 6. Under Pub.L.280, a court looks at the civil-criminal distinction to determine whether a state can go onto an Indian reservation to enforce the state's criminal gambling laws; under the Indian Gaming Regulatory Act, the court looks at the distinction between the state's civil and criminal laws to determine whether the state permits gaming activities of the type at issue.

Although the Senate committee was speaking of class II activities, its comments are equally applicable to the requirement for class III activities. See Mashantucket Pequot Tribe v. Connecticut, 913 F.2d 1024, 1030 (2d Cir. 1990), cert. denied, 499 U.S. 975, 111 S.Ct. 1620, 113 L.Ed.2d 717 (1991): "We deem this legislative history [relating to class II gaming] instructive with respect to the meaning of the identical language in § 2710(d)(1)(B), regarding class III gaming, which we must interpret." See also United States v. Nunez, 573 F.2d 769, 771 (2d Cir.), cert. denied, 436 U.S. 930, 98 S.Ct. 2828, 56 L.Ed.2d 774 (1978) (settled principle of statutory construction that same word or phrase used in more than one section of statute will be construed to have same meaning in next place if its meaning in the first place is clear).

In addition, the congressional findings set out at subsection (5) of 25 U.S.C. § 2701 support the view that Congress did not intend the term "permits such gaming" to limit the tribes to the specific types of gaming activity actually in operation in a state:

> Indian tribes have the exclusive right to regulate gaming activity on Indian lands if the gaming activity is not specifically prohibited by Federal law and is conducted within a State which does not, as a matter of criminal law and public policy, prohibit such gaming activity.

In light of the legislative history and the congressional findings, I conclude that the initial question in determining whether Wisconsin "permits" the gaming activities at issue is not whether the state has given express approval to the playing of a particular game, but whether Wisconsin's public policy toward class III gaming is prohibitory or regulatory.

The original Wisconsin Constitution provided that "[e]xcept as provided in this section, the legislature shall never authorize any lottery, or grant any divorce." For more than a century, this prohibition against "any lottery" was interpreted as prohibiting the operation or playing of any game, scheme or plan involving the elements of prize, chance and consideration. The prohibition against a "lottery" has been held to outlaw theater promotions; mercantile promotions; charitable bingo; and television games of chance. In 1965, however, the constitution was amended to allow Wisconsin citizens to participate in promotional sweepstakes (by defining "consideration" as not including listening to or watching a radio or television program or visiting a store or other place without being required to make a purchase or pay a fee). The constitution was amended again in 1973 to authorize bingo when played by charitable organizations, and in 1977 to allow raffles for charitable organizations. In 1987 the electorate approved two constitutional amendments: one authorized the state to operate a lottery, with the proceeds going to property tax relief; the second removed any prohibition on parimutuel on-track betting.

When the voters authorized a state-operated "lottery," they removed any remaining constitutional prohibition against state-operated games, schemes or plans involving prize, chance and consideration, with minor exceptions.

The amendments to the Wisconsin Constitution evidence a state policy toward gaming that is now regulatory rather than prohibitory in nature. The fact that Wisconsin continues to prohibit commercial gambling and unlicensed gaming activities does not make its policy prohibitory. See Cabazon, 480 U.S. at 211, 107 S.Ct. at 1089, rejecting a similar argument by the State of California. See also Mashantucket Pequot Tribe, 913 F.2d at 1029 (state's allowance of state-operated lottery, bingo, jai alai and other forms of parimutuel betting evidence a regulatory rather than prohibitory policy toward class III gaming although state outlawed the casino games at issue except for fund-raising purposes by nonprofit organizations under certain highly regulated circumstances).

Defendants' assertion that they are required to negotiate only the identical types of games currently offered by the lottery board misconceives the point of the Indian Gaming Regulatory Act, as well as the holding in Cabazon. It was not Congress's intent that the states would be able to impose their gaming regulatory schemes on the tribes. The Act's drafters intended to leave it to the sovereign state and tribal governments to negotiate the specific gaming activities involving prize, chance and consideration that each tribe will offer under the terms of its tribal-state compact.

Although defendants insist that their position is not that the tribes are limited to negotiating "the exact games" that the state lottery operates, they argue that Wisconsin law must give express authorization for a "gaming activity" before it can be a proper subject of negotiation. Defendants offer no authority for distinguishing between the state's current lottery games and the activities proposed for negotiation by the tribes. Instead, the state makes the bald statement that casino games "are of a wholly different character than a state lottery or on-track pari-mutuel wagering." Defendants' reply brief at 17. The state's current attorney general has rejected the imposition of artificial distinctions within the term lottery, so long as the activity involves the elements of prize, chance and consideration and is not addressed explicitly by the constitutional amendments. Op.Att'y Gen.Wis. 10-91, slip op. at 5-7. I find no reason to impose similarly artificial categories in applying the Cabazon test and in interpreting the Indian Gaming Regulatory Act.

Defendants make one final argument in support of their contention that Congress never intended to permit tribes to conduct games not in operation in the state: a large part of the reasoning behind the compacts was to utilize the regulatory mechanisms for gaming already in place in the states. Defendants' argument has some merit, but it founders on the actual language used by Congress, and the source of that language. The term is "permits," not "operates" or "is in operation." Congress has stated that "permits" is to be interpreted under the Cabazon analysis. Therefore, the fact that a state permits an activity does not mean that the state has a mechanism in place to regulate the precise activities the tribes wish to offer. A state might not prohibit a particular Class III gaming activity, but simply allow it to be conducted, without taking any steps to restrict it in any way. Or a state might allow certain Class III gaming activity to be carried out by small charitable groups on very limited occasions without having any mechanism in place to regulate the same activity carried out on a large scale basis.

I conclude that the state is required to negotiate with plaintiffs over the inclusion in a tribal-state compact of any activity that includes the elements of prize, chance and consideration and that is not prohibited expressly by the Wisconsin Constitution or state law.

To ensure that states engage in negotiations with Indian tribes, the Indian Gaming Regulatory Act requires the states to negotiate in good faith with any tribes that request negotiation, and it gives federal courts jurisdiction over cases brought by Indian tribes arising from the failure of a state to enter into negotiations or to conduct such negotiations in good faith. Pursuant to

§ 2710(d)(7)(B)(iii) and the state's concession that it has failed to negotiate over activities I have now determined must be the subjects of negotiation, the state will be required to conclude a compact with each plaintiff within sixty days.

RUMSEY INDIAN RANCHERIA OF WINTUN INDIANS v. WILSON
64 F.3d 1250 (9th Cir. 1994),
cert. denied, 521 U.S. 1118 (1997)

O'SCANNLAIN, Circuit Judge.

We decide whether certain gaming activities are permitted under California law and thus subject to tribal-state negotiation under the Indian Gaming Regulatory Act.

Numerous federally recognized Indian tribes currently engage in various gaming activities on tribal lands in California. Desiring to engage in additional activities (the "Proposed Gaming Activities"), several tribes asked the State of California (the "State") to negotiate a compact permitting the operation of certain stand-alone electronic gaming devices and live banking and percentage card games. The State refused to negotiate with the tribes, asserting that the Proposed Gaming Activities were illegal under California law.

The State and seven tribes subsequently entered into a stipulation to seek judicial determination of whether the State was obligated to negotiate with the tribes.

The district court awarded summary judgment to the Tribes, finding that, except for banking and percentage card games using traditional casino game themes, the Proposed Gaming Activities were a proper subject of negotiation. The State timely appealed, and the Tribes filed a cross-appeal.

Enacted in 1988 as means of "promoting tribal economic development, self-sufficiency, and strong tribal governments," IGRA creates a framework for Indian tribes to conduct gaming activities on tribal lands. The parties agree that the Proposed Gaming Activities are Class III games.

A tribe seeking to operate Class III gaming activities on tribal lands generally may do so only under a compact. IGRA obligates the state to negotiate in good faith with the tribe; and, if the parties reach agreement, they sign a Tribal-State compact.

If a state refuses to negotiate in good faith, the tribe can bring a civil suit, whereupon a federal district court may order the state and tribe to conclude a compact within 60 days.

In the instant case, the State opted not to negotiate over the Proposed Gaming Activities. The State asserts two reasons why it need not negotiate with the Tribes. The first reason is that the Act itself does not require negotiation. The second reason is that the Act violates the Tenth Amendment. Because the first reason persuades us, we do not reach the second.

IGRA provides that "Class III gaming activities shall be lawful on Indian lands only if such activities are . . . located in a State that permits such gaming for any purpose by any person, organization, or entity . . . ." 25 U.S.C.

§ 2710(d)(1)(B). Consequently, where a state does not "permit" gaming activities sought by a tribe, the tribe has no right to engage in these activities, and the state thus has no duty to negotiate with respect to them.

The parties disagree as to whether California "permits" the Proposed Gaming Activities. The State's argument is straightforward: the Proposed Gaming Activities are illegal. California law prohibits the operation of a banked or percentage card game as a misdemeanor offense. Cal.Penal Code § 330. In addition, according to the State, the stand-alone electronic gaming machines sought by the Tribes are electronic "slot machines." California law prohibits the operation of slot machines as a misdemeanor offense, Cal.Penal Code §§ 330a, 330b, and a California appellate court has indicated that electronic machines of the sort requested by the Tribes fall within the scope of this prohibition. Score Family Fun Center, Inc. v. County of San Diego, 225 Cal.App.3d 1217 (1990).

The Tribes offer a broader reading of IGRA, claiming that a state "permits" a specific gaming activity if it "regulates" the activity in general rather than prohibiting it entirely as a matter of public policy. Under this approach, a specific illegal gaming activity is "regulated," rather than "prohibited," if the state allows the operation of similar gaming activities. The Tribes observe that video lottery terminals, parimutuel horse racing, and nonbanked, nonpercentage card gaming are legal in California. Because the Tribes view these activities as functionally similar to the Proposed Gaming Activities, they conclude that California regulates, and thus permits, these activities.

The Tribes cite to the Supreme Court's pre-IGRA decision, California v. Cabazon Band of Mission Indians, 480 U.S. 202 (1987), in support of their view. [In that case, t]he Court found that California law permitted a large variety of gaming activities, including bingo. It concluded that the state "regulates rather than prohibits gambling in general and bingo in particular," and held that the Indian tribes thus were entitled to engage in their gaming activities.

Congress enacted IGRA in response to Cabazon. The Tribes assert that IGRA codified Cabazon's "criminal/regulatory" test. Under this approach, which was adopted by the district court in this case, a court must determine whether a gaming activity, even if illegal, violates a state's public policy. If it does, then the activity is "criminally" prohibited. If it does not, then the activity is merely "regulated" and, thus, "permitted" for the purpose of applying IGRA.

We reject this reading of IGRA. In interpreting IGRA, we use our traditional tools of statutory construction. [A]lthough statutes benefitting Native Americans generally are construed liberally in their favor, we will not rely on this factor to contradict the plain language of a statute.

Section 2710(d)(1)(b) is unambiguous. In United States v. Launder, 743 F.2d 686 (9th Cir. 1984), we adopted a dictionary definition of the term "permit" as meaning " '[t]o suffer, allow, consent, let; to give leave or license; to acquiesce, by failure to prevent, or to expressly assent or agree to the doing of an act.' " Clearly, California does not allow banked or percentage card gaming. With the possible exception of video lottery terminals, electronic gaming machines fitting the description of "slot machines" are prohibited.

The fact that California allows games that share some characteristics with banked and percentage card gaming—in the form of (1) banked and percentage games other than card games and (2) nonbanked, nonpercentage card games—is not evidence that the State permits the Proposed Gaming Activities. Nor is it significant that the state lottery, if not technically a slot machine, is functionally similar to one. In Cheyenne River Sioux Tribe v. South Dakota, 3 F.3d 273 (8th Cir. 1993), a tribe sought to operate a traditional form of keno as well as casino-type gambling. When the State of South Dakota refused to negotiate, the tribe filed suit, arguing that the video keno and charity-run casino-type gaming were legal in the state. The Eighth Circuit rejected this argument. First, it found that the state permitted charities to operate bingo and raffles, but not casino-type gambling. Second, it held that the state

> need not negotiate traditional keno if only video keno is permitted in South Dakota. The "such gaming" language of 25 U.S.C. § 2710(d)(1)(B) does not require the state to negotiate with respect to forms of gaming it does not presently permit. Because video keno and traditional keno are not the same and video keno is the only form of keno allowed under state law, it would be illegal . . . for the tribe to offer traditional keno to its patrons.

Id. at 279. The court thus concluded that South Dakota had not failed to negotiate in good faith by refusing to negotiate over traditional keno and casino-type gaming.

We agree with the approach taken by the Eighth Circuit. IGRA does not require a state to negotiate over one form of Class III gaming activity simply because it has legalized another, albeit similar form of gaming. Instead, the statute says only that, if a state allows a gaming activity "for any purpose by any person, organization, or entity," then it also must allow Indian tribes to engage in that same activity. In other words, a state need only allow Indian tribes to operate games that others can operate, but need not give tribes what others cannot have.

Because we find the plain meaning of the word "permit" to be unambiguous, we need not look to IGRA's legislative history. However, a brief examination helps to clarify why the word has different meanings with respect to Class II and Class III gaming.

The primary source of IGRA's legislative history, the Senate Report accompanying its passage, does not describe the circumstances in which a state "permits" a gaming activity in the context of Class III gaming. The only relevant passages occur in the Senate Report's discussion of Class II gaming:

> [T]he Committee anticipates that Federal courts will rely on the distinction between State criminal laws which prohibit certain activities and civil laws of a State which impose a regulatory scheme upon those activities to determine whether class II games are allowed in certain States. This distinction has been discussed by the Federal courts many times, most recently and notably by the Supreme Court in Cabazon.

S.Rep. No. 446, 100th Cong., 2d Sess., reprinted in 1988 U.S.C.C.A.N. 3071, 3076.

The Tribes point to those statements as evidence that Congress intended that Cabazon's "criminal/regulatory" test govern for the purposes of determining whether a Class II gaming activity is permitted on Indian lands. The Tribes then observe that IGRA's Class II gaming provisions contain the same language used for Class III gaming: "An Indian tribe may engage in . . . class II gaming on Indian lands . . . if . . . such Indian gaming is located within a State that permits such gaming for any purpose by any person, organization or entity . . . ." 25 U.S.C. § 2710(b)(1)(A). Relying upon the maxim that identical language in a statute should be interpreted to have the same meaning, the Tribes infer that the Senate Report establishes the applicability of the Cabazon test to Class III gaming.

However, that inference is incorrect. "Identical words appearing more than once in the same act, and even in the same section, may be construed differently if it appears they were used in different places with different intent." Vanscoter v. Sullivan, 920 F.2d 1441, 1448 (9th Cir. 1990). Such is the case for Class III gaming. The Senate Report repeatedly links the Cabazon test to Class II gaming while remaining silent as to Class III gaming—a fact that itself suggests that Class II and III provisions should be treated differently. Further, Congress envisioned different roles for Class II and Class III gaming. It intended that tribes have "maximum flexibility to utilize [Class II] games such as bingo and lotto for tribal economic development," S.Rep. No. 466, and indicated that Class II gaming would be conducted largely free of state regulatory laws. Congress was less ebullient about tribes' use of Class III gaming, however, and indicated that Class III gaming would be more subject to state regulatory schemes. Even if we found it necessary to rely upon IGRA's legislative history, it supports the plain meaning of the term "permit" with regard to IGRA's Class III provisions.

With the possible exception of slot machines in the form of video lottery terminals, California has no obligation to negotiate with the Tribes on the Proposed Gaming Activities, and the trial court judgment is reversed to that extent. We affirm the district court's judgment that the State need not negotiate over banked or percentage card games with traditional casino themes. We remand to the district court to consider the limited question of whether California permits the operation of slot machines in the form of the state lottery or otherwise.

AFFIRMED in part, REVERSED in part, and REMANDED. Each party to bear its own costs.

[The concurring opinion of Chief Judge Wallace is omitted.]

HOTEL EMPLOYEES AND RESTAURANT EMPLOYEES INTERNATIONAL UNION v. DAVIS
981 P.2d 990 (Cal. 1999)

WERDEGAR, Justice.

In 1984, the people of California amended our Constitution to state a fundamental public policy against the legalization in California of casino gambling of the sort then associated with Las Vegas and Atlantic City: "The Legislature has no power to authorize, and shall prohibit casinos of the type currently operating in Nevada and New Jersey." (Cal. Const., art. IV, § 19, subd. (e), added by initiative, Gen. Elec. (Nov. 6, 1984).)

In 1998, at the November 3 General Election, the people approved a proposed initiative statute designated on the ballot as Proposition 5—"The Tribal Government Gaming and Economic Self-Sufficiency Act of 1998"— concerning gaming on Indian lands in the State of California. The principal provisions of this statutory initiative purport to authorize various forms of gaming in tribal casinos.

On November 4, 1998, Proposition 5 became effective by operation of law. Between November 4 and 12, the Governor received a request from each of 39 Indian tribes for the state to enter into a standard "Tribal-State Gaming Compact" as set forth in the measure to cover gaming on Indian lands. Under the measure, the Governor was obligated to execute an individual compact within 30 days after receipt of a request and would be deemed to have done so if he should fail.

On November 20, 1998, the Hotel Employees and Restaurant Employees International Union filed a petition for writ of mandate in this court, with a request for a stay pendente lite. On that same day, Eric Cortez and others filed a separate, similar petition for writ of mandate in this court. [All of the petitioners will collectively be referred to as "Real Parties."]

We determined to decide the matter ourselves, instead of allowing lower courts, in accordance with our custom, to address it in the first instance, because we concluded the underlying questions were of "great public importance and must be resolved promptly."

Proposition 5 was enacted against an extensive legal background of California and federal law regarding gaming and other gambling. We briefly review the most pertinent parts of these bodies of law.

Since 1849, the California Constitution has generally prohibited all lotteries and the sale of all lottery tickets. Since 1872, § 319 et seq. of the Penal Code also has prohibited all lotteries and the sale of all lottery tickets. But since 1984, through the addition of article IV, § 19, subdivision (d), the California Constitution has provided: "Notwithstanding subdivision (a), there is authorized the establishment of a California State Lottery."

As we explained in Western Telcon, Inc. v. California State Lottery (1996) 13 Cal.4th 475, 484, a lottery is defined by three elements, namely, a prize, distribution by chance, and consideration. "Consideration" is the fee (in the form of money or anything else of value) that a participant pays the operator for entrance. "Chance" means that winning and losing depend on luck and fortune rather than, or at least more than, judgment and skill. "Prize" encompasses property that the operator offers to distribute to one or more winning participants and not to keep for himself. The property offered may exist apart from the fees the participants pay the operator or it may arise from the fees themselves, as when, in the commonly used parimutuel system, the property consists of the fees in the form of a pool that remains after the operator has taken out some amount for himself. The prize or prizes, however, must be "either fixed in advance" of the play or "determined by the total amount" of fees paid.

Commencing in 1872, the year of the Penal Code's enactment, § 330 of that code has proscribed a number of games by name; since 1885, the list has included the game "twenty-one." Also commencing in 1872, § 330 of the Penal Code has prohibited all "banking" games, that is, those games in which there is a person or entity that participates in the action as "the one against the many," "taking on all comers, paying all winners, and collecting from all losers," doing so through a fund generally called the bank.

As we expressly held in Western Telcon, a banking game is not a lottery, and a lottery is not a banking game, for the two are "mutually exclusive." In a lottery, the "operator distributes the prize or prizes to the winner or winners." The operator is not a participant and, hence, does not compete with the participants. He has "no interest in the outcome of" the lottery, "because neither the fact the prize will be disposed of, nor the value of the prize to be distributed, depends upon which, or how many," of the participants "might win it." Insofar as the operator is concerned, the result is invariable: he will give over the prize to one or more of the participants. In a banking game, by contrast, the banker "pays off all winning wagers and keeps all losing wagers." He is in fact a participant and, hence, "compete[s] with the other participants: 'he is the one against the many.'" He has an "interest in the outcome of the game, because the amount of money" he "will have to pay out," or be able to take in, "depends upon whether each of the individual bets is won or lost." The result is variable: the banker may either win or lose as to either some or all of the other participants.

Commencing in 1885, § 330 of the Penal Code has similarly prohibited all "percentage" games, that is, those games in which the operator does not participate in the action but "collects a percentage . . . computed from the amount of bets made, winnings collected, or . . . money changing hands."

Since at least 1872, all nonprohibited card games, primarily "round" games such as various forms of poker, have been permitted.

The Penal Code's broad definitions of slot machines include virtually every kind of stand-alone gaming device.

Lastly, since 1984, through the addition of § 19(e), the California Constitution has declared: "The Legislature has no power to authorize, and shall prohibit casinos of the type currently operating in Nevada and New Jersey."

We now briefly review the federal law concerning gaming on Indian lands.

[The Court here discusses Cabazon, IGRA, and Rumsey.]

While the above proceedings and those leading to this court's 1996 decision in Western Telcon, supra, 13 Cal.4th 475, were pending, a number of the tribes commenced and continued class III gaming activities without tribal/state compacts; in response, Governor Wilson refused to negotiate further until they ceased such gaming activities. Governor Wilson instead negotiated a compact with the Pala Band of Mission Indians, a tribe previously without gaming facilities, which he intended to serve as a statewide model. In part because of objections to the negotiation procedures and in part because of restrictions the Pala compact placed on the type and number of gaming devices, most of the tribes with existing casinos rejected the Pala compact.

It was to resolve such conflicts between the State of California and Indian tribes relative to class III gaming on Indian lands that Proposition 5 was drafted and circulated by petition.

A statute inconsistent with the California Constitution is, of course, void. In order to decide whether Proposition 5 is inconsistent with § 19(e), we begin by examining and interpreting each part of § 19(e).

"Casinos."

In common usage around the time that § 19(e) was added to the California Constitution in 1984, a "casino" was defined simply as "a building or room for gambling." (Webster's New Internat. Dict. (3d ed. 1961) p. 347; accord, e.g., Rose, Gambling and the Law (1986) at p. 4.) In the anticasino provision itself, it does not appear to demand any different signification.

"Of the type currently operating in Nevada and New Jersey."

"Currently" is potentially ambiguous, in that it could refer to 1984, the time of its use in § 19(e), or to the time at which prohibited casinos are purportedly authorized. We adopt the former view. To declare, "The Legislature has no power to authorize . . . casinos of the type . . . operating in Nevada and New Jersey" in 1984, addresses an evil that was knowable and, in fact, known at the time the anticasino provision was added, that is, the kind of casino then existing in those states. By contrast, to declare, "The Legislature has no power to authorize . . . casinos of the type . . . operating in Nevada and New Jersey" from time to time, addresses an evil, if evil it be, that is altogether unknown and unknowable.

The sense of the other words in this phrase within § 19(e) requires more effort to discern. What was meant by "the type" of casino "operating in Nevada and New Jersey" in 1984? Section 19(e) contains no definition of this phrase. Logic and reference to legislative history, however, allow us to see with reasonable clarity what the drafters and voters intended to prohibit in 1984.

The 1984 constitutional amenders must have had in mind a type of gambling house unique to or particularly associated with Nevada and New Jersey, since they chose to define the prohibited institution by reference to those states. On this logic, the "type" of casino referred to must be an establishment that offers gaming activities including banked table games and gaming devices, i.e., slot machines, for in 1984 that "type" of casino was legal only in Nevada and New Jersey and, hence, was particularly associated with those states. (See Rose, Gambling and the Law, supra, at p. 4 [of the states, only Nevada and New Jersey allow "[c]asinos offering the full range of gambling games"]; id. at pp. 6-7 [detailing gaming operations of the "average Atlantic City casino" in 1984]; Com. on the Review of the Nat. Policy Toward Gambling, Final Rep., Gambling in America (1976) pp. 88-89 [detailing gaming operations of Nevada casinos].)

Similarly, "the type" of casino "operating in Nevada and New Jersey" presumably refers to a gambling facility that did not legally operate in California; something other, that is, than "the type" of casino "operating" in California. The type of casino then operating in California is what has commonly been called a "card room" or "card club," a type that did not offer gaming activities including banking games and gaming devices. (See Rose, Gambling and the Law, supra, at pp. 3-4.) A California card room or card club was not permitted to offer gaming activities in the form of: (1) lotteries; (2) banking games, whether or not played with cards; (3) percentage games, whether or not played with cards; (4) slot machines; or (5) games proscribed by name, including twenty-one—all of which were prohibited at least by statute.

Thus, a casino of "the type . . . operating in Nevada and New Jersey" may be understood, with reasonable specificity, as one or more buildings, rooms, or facilities, whether separate or connected, that offer gambling activities including those statutorily prohibited in California, especially banked table games and slot machines.

Real Parties object to this approach as rendering § 19(e) merely an elevation of statutory prohibitions on certain activities to the constitutional level. But the available legislative history suggests § 19(e) was designed, precisely, to elevate statutory prohibitions on a set of gambling activities to a constitutional level.

Proposition 5, including its model tribal/state compact, authorizes what would amount to prohibited casinos. With their tribal gaming terminals and grandfathered class III card games, tribal gaming facilities authorized under the measure would constitute facilities that offer gambling activities including those statutorily prohibited to card clubs in California in 1984, especially banked table games and slot machines.

We conclude the card games in question are not lotteries, but banking games. Here, unlike in lotteries, the Indian tribe does not "distribute" to a "winner or winners" (Western Telcon, supra, 13 Cal.4th at p. 485), with "no interest in the outcome" of the play, a "prize or prizes" that are invariable because they are "either fixed in advance or determined by the total amount" of fees paid. Rather, as in other banking games, the tribe, through the prize pool, simply "pays off all winning wagers and keeps all losing wagers," which are variable "because the amount of money" it "will have to pay out," or be able to take in, "depends upon whether each of the individual bets is won or lost."

That the tribe must "pay[] all winners, and collect[] from all losers" through a fund that is styled a "players' pool" is immaterial: the players' pool is a bank in nature if not in name. It is a "fund against which everybody has a right to bet, the bank . . . taking all that is won, and paying out all that is lost." (Western Telcon, supra, 13 Cal.4th at p. 487.) Theoretically, an extraordinary run of good luck by one or more gamblers in a short period could exhaust the players' pool, thus breaking the bank, a course of events that cannot occur even theoretically in a lottery. True, the players' pool is limited in what it pays—but not in what it collects—in that the tribe is prohibited from lending the pool money "to pay prizes previously won." But, as we explained in Western Telcon, the fact that payouts on wagers must be made from a limited fund of money does not transform a banking game into a lottery. Such a banker simply finds itself "in the enviable position of a gambler who has, by law, an upper limit to his losses."

That Proposition 5 does not limit tribal casinos to card games operated as lotteries is especially clear if one focuses on the manner in which payouts are calculated under the "players' pool" system. Although this fund is the only permitted source of payouts, nothing in Proposition 5 or its model compact requires that payouts be calculated as shares of the "pool." Of course, a lottery may use fixed prizes rather than a parimutuel system. "In a fixed-prize lottery, however, the total prize amount must be fixed in advance of the draw. If fixed prizes are offered, in other words, the number of such prizes must also be determined in advance of the draw." Again, nothing in Proposition 5 or its model compact requires that the number of fixed payouts for a given game be determined in advance of the game.

Real Parties argue the games allowed under Proposition 5 are not house banked because the casino's tribal owner/operator cannot profit from surpluses in the "players' pool," which is dedicated to payment of prizes. Even if true, this limitation would not make the games lotteries rather than banking games, since a banking game, within the meaning of Penal Code § 330's prohibition, may be banked by someone other than the owner of the gambling facility. (Oliver v. County of Los Angeles (1998) 66 Cal.App.4th 1397, 1407-1409.) In any event, that the tribal operator does not profit from the prize pool's winnings is not strictly true. The tribe retains an "interest in the outcome" of play even if it "neither has nor can acquire any interest" in the players' pool itself, which is "irrevocably dedicated to the prospective award of prizes in authorized gaming activities." The more the players' pool collects from losers and the less it pays to winners, the lower the tribal operator's costs—the less likely it will be compelled to lend seed money to the players' pool in the future, the more likely it will be able to obtain repayment of seed money lent to the pool in the past. Conversely, the less the pool collects and the more it pays, the higher the operator's costs. Of necessity, moreover, the operator of a casino authorized under Proposition 5 must be concerned with maintaining ample funds in the players' pool or pools, since depletion of those funds will require lower payouts, hence worse odds on players' bets, hence less action to generate fee revenue for the operator. Even under Proposition 5's players' pool prize system, therefore, the "house" retains an interest in the outcome of play.

Real Parties point to several other respects in which tribal casinos authorized by Proposition 5 will presumably differ from the archetypical 1984 Nevada or New Jersey casino: tribal casinos will not be clustered together in an urban "strip"; tribal casinos, assertedly, may not serve free alcohol; tribal casinos will not be able to offer banked noncard games such as craps and roulette; and tribal casinos will be owned by tribes and the revenues used for tribal purposes. These asserted characteristics, however, fail meaningfully to distinguish casinos authorized under Proposition 5 from those prohibited by § 19(e). We think it highly unlikely that the 1984 constitutional amenders, who were told the measure before them would constitutionalize California's statutory prohibitions on "casino gambling," were concerned with such secondary nongambling features of casinos as their mutual proximity or service of free alcohol. As to banked noncard games, we cannot agree that a casino offering activities including banked card games and slot machines differs in fundamental type from one offering, in addition, roulette and craps. Finally, because private ownership and for-profit operation were not unique to Nevada and New Jersey gambling facilities in 1984, and, indeed, characterized permitted California facilities such as card clubs and horse racing tracks, private ownership and for-profit operation could not logically have been the characteristics to which the constitutional amenders intended to refer in prohibiting "casinos of the type currently operating in Nevada and New Jersey."

In concluding as we do, we do not overlook the finding made in Proposition 5 that "casinos of the type currently operating in Nevada and New Jersey are materially different from . . . tribal gaming facilities . . . in that the casinos in those states (1) commonly offer their patrons a broad spectrum of house-banked games, including but not limited to house-banked card games, roulette, dice games, and slot machines that dispense coins or currency, none of which games are authorized" under the measure, including its model tribal/state compact; and "(2) are owned by private companies, individuals, or others that are not restricted on how their profits may be expended, whereas tribal governments must be the primary beneficiaries of the gaming facilities . . . and are limited to using their gaming revenues for various tribal purposes, including tribal government services and programs such as those that address reservation housing, elderly care, education, economic development, health care, and other tribal programs and needs, in conformity with federal law."

To the extent the quoted findings do not consist of legislative fact, but of statutory or constitutional interpretation—interpretation of § 19(e) or of California statutory law regarding lotteries and banking games—the general rule of deference is not implicated. The "finding" to the effect that the games and devices authorized under Proposition 5 are not banked card games and slot machines, for example, is a pure statement of law that we must independently evaluate (and, having done so, have found incorrect). Most importantly, the general statement that "casinos of the type currently operating in Nevada and New Jersey are materially different from the tribal gaming facilities authorized under this chapter" is not a "finding" of "legislative fact" or indeed of any other kind of "fact." Rather, it is a construction of the anticasino provision of § 19(e). As such, it commands no deference on our part, because we construe the provisions of the California Constitution independently. "It would be idle to make the Constitution the supreme law, and then require the judges to take the oath to support it, and after all that, require the Courts to take the legislative construction as correct."

Against the conclusion that Proposition 5 is invalid as inconsistent with the anticasino provision of § 19(e), Real Parties argue that IGRA preempts the anticasino provision itself. More particularly, they argue that under IGRA states may not regulate the manner in which permitted class III games are played or, indeed, impose any regulation except to prohibit specific games, by any means other than a tribal/state compact. Because § 19(e) is not a prohibition on particular gaming activities, but on conducting them in a Nevada or New Jersey-style casino, Real Parties argue, IGRA preempts its application to tribal gaming.

Real Parties' preemption argument fails because neither of the premises upon which it rests is true. First, contrary to their representation, IGRA does not exempt gambling on Indian lands from state regulatory laws. Indeed, § 23 of IGRA provides that "for purposes of Federal law, all State laws pertaining to the licensing, regulation, or prohibition of gambling . . . shall apply in Indian country in the same manner and to the same extent as such laws apply elsewhere in the State." (18 U.S.C. § 1166(a).) Subsection (c) of the same section recognizes an exception to that rule for class III gaming conducted under a tribal/state compact but, as we further explain below, such a compact may not go into effect unless it is validly entered into under state law, which the model compact in Proposition 5 could not be, because its approval would violate § 19(e). In the absence of a valid tribal-state compact, therefore, California law regulating class III gaming activities does apply to such gaming on Indian lands, although the federal government has exclusive jurisdiction to prosecute violations of that law criminally. Second, the argument incorrectly characterizes § 19(e): that provision does, in substantial part, prohibit specific gambling activities, including slot machines, banked card games and other banking games, when conducted in a casino setting.

More generally, Real Parties' reliance on IGRA is misplaced because IGRA legalizes only gaming conducted pursuant to a compact validly entered into by both the state and the tribe. To be "entered into" by the state and the tribe means to be "entered into" validly in accordance with state (and tribal) law. (See Pueblo of Santa Ana v. Kelly (10th Cir. 1997) 104 F.3d 1546, 1555 [concluding "the 'entered into' language imposes an independent requirement and the compact must be validly entered into by a state before it can go into effect, via Secretarial approval, under IGRA"; id. at pp. 1550-1551, 1557-1559 [agreeing with New Mexico Supreme Court that compact was invalid under the law of that state because the Governor did not have authority, without legislative enactment, to bind state to compact authorizing casino gambling otherwise prohibited by state law].

With respect to a tribal/state compact, IGRA balances the interests of the state and the tribe. Its balancing is predicated on a recognition that the state and the tribe are sovereigns, albeit sovereigns subordinate to the federal union. To recognize that the state and the tribe are sovereigns entails an acknowledgment that the law of each operates in its proper sphere and, therefore, that the law of each governs the validity of its own entry into a compact. IGRA would not make lawful particular gaming activities included in a compact if the compact itself were not validly entered into under the law of both the state and the Indian tribe in question.

For the reasons stated above, we conclude that Proposition 5 is invalid because it is inconsistent with the anticasino provision of article IV, § 19, subdivision (e) of the California Constitution. We therefore discharge the orders to show cause and direct issuance of a peremptory writ of mandate compelling the Governor and the Secretary of State not to implement Proposition 5.

KENNARD, Justice, dissenting.

One of the fundamental powers reserved to the people of this state is the power to enact legislation by initiative. This court has recognized the importance of that power: "[T]he initiative power must be liberally construed to promote the democratic process." Legislature v. Eu (1991) 54 Cal.3d 492, 501.

Today, the majority rejects the will of the people by invalidating the model compact of Proposition 5. It concludes that the compact authorizes forms of gambling the state Constitution prohibits and therefore exceeds the people's power to legislate. I disagree.

First, because federal law has preempted the field of Indian gambling regulation, it is federal law, not state law, that authorizes Indian gambling. By entering into a compact with a tribe, a state may influence the conditions under which Indian gambling is conducted and the regulations to which the gambling is subject, but a state lacks the power to either forbid or authorize Indian gambling.

Second, federal law authorizes a tribe to offer any form of gaming otherwise permitted by the state in which the tribe is located. California law permits lotteries but prohibits banking games. The gaming terminals and card games regulated by Proposition 5's model compact are lotteries rather than banking games because they operate under a players' pool prize system.

The rise of Indian gambling in the past two decades has stirred deep passions and heated political debate. The voters of California sought to resolve the status of Indian gambling in our state by enacting the model Tribal-State Gaming Compact of Proposition 5. Because the model compact complies both with our state Constitution and with the federal Indian Gaming Regulatory Act, I would uphold the will of the voters and deny the petition for a writ of mandate.

AT & T CORPORATION v. COEUR D'ALENE TRIBE
295 F.3d 899 (9th Cir. 2002)

FLETCHER, Circuit Judge.

Having received conflicting determinations from tribal courts and the federal district court, the Coeur d'Alene Tribe appeals the district court's determination that AT & T Corporation need not provide toll-free telephone service for the Tribe's lottery. We find that the tribal court lacked jurisdiction to resolve the dispute, but vacate the district court's determination that the lottery itself is illegal under the Indian Gaming Regulatory Act (IGRA). We conclude that AT & T was not the proper party to challenge the legality of the lottery.

The federally recognized Coeur d'Alene Tribe ("Tribe") resides on the Coeur d'Alene Reservation in Idaho. Federal law permits tribes like the Coeur d'Alene to engage in gambling activities on Indian lands pursuant to the Indian Gaming Regulatory Act (IGRA). As IGRA requires of any tribe wishing to engage in gambling on its land, the Tribe entered into a compact with the State of Idaho. The compact permits the Tribe to offer Class III gaming, including a lottery. The Secretary of the Interior approved the compact. See 25 U.S.C. § 2710(d)(8); 58 Fed.Reg. 8478 (1993).

The Tribe created the National Indian Lottery ("Lottery"). The Lottery's administration occurs entirely on the Reservation. However, off-Reservation participants may purchase tickets by telephone from outside Idaho. In order to participate in the Lottery, an off-Reservation player establishes an account on the Reservation and funds it either by credit card or by delivering funds.

To purchase a ticket, the player authorizes a deduction from the account and either selects a sequence of numbers or requests randomly selected numbers. A player may request written confirmation of the transaction, but the lottery ticket itself remains on the Reservation. Once a week, lottery officials draw a sequence of winning numbers and distribute the prize pool to players whose tickets contain them. An off-Reservation winner receives a credit to his or her account that is redeemable in person or through the mail.

The federally approved compact itself did not specify that off-Reservation telephone purchases would be permitted. However, a management contract between the Tribe and UNISTAR Entertainment, Inc. made clear that off-Reservation players could participate telephonically. As required by 25 U.S.C. § 2710(d)(9), the Tribe submitted the management contract to the Chairman of the National Indian Gaming Commission (NIGC) for approval. The Chairman subsequently clarified in a letter—in response to an inquiry about the Lottery's legality—that:

> In the opinion of the NIGC, the Tribe's lottery proposal, which involves customers purchasing lottery tickets with a credit card both in person and by telephone from locations both inside and outside the state of Idaho, is not prohibited by the IGRA.

Following the NIGC's approval of the UNISTAR contract, the Tribe adopted a resolution and amended its Tribal Code to authorize the Lottery. Consistent with IGRA, the Tribe's resolution was deemed approved by the NIGC Chairman ninety days after its submission pursuant to 25 U.S.C. § 2710(e).

In order to attract Lottery participants, the Tribe sought to establish toll-free telephone service to its on-Reservation offices from callers in states that operate their own state-run lotteries. AT & T was among the carriers with whom the Tribe negotiated to provide such service.

Upon learning that the Tribe intended to offer toll-free "Tele-Lottery" service, several state Attorneys General sent letters to AT & T, allegedly pursuant to 18 U.S.C. § 1084(d), warning AT & T that furnishing interstate toll-free service for the Lottery would violate federal and state laws. Title 18 U.S.C. § 1084(d) provides that:

> When any common carrier, subject to the jurisdiction of the Federal Communications Commission, is notified in writing by a Federal, State, or local law enforcement agency, acting within its jurisdiction, that any facility furnished by it is being used or will be used for the purpose of transmitting or receiving gambling information in interstate or foreign commerce in violation of Federal, State or local law, it shall discontinue or refuse, the leasing, furnishing, or maintaining of such facility, after reasonable notice to the subscriber, but no damages, penalty or forfeiture, civil or criminal, shall be found against any common carrier for any act done in compliance with any notice received from a law enforcement agency. Nothing in this section shall be deemed to prejudice the right of any person affected thereby to secure an appropriate determination, as otherwise provided by law, in a Federal court or in a State or local tribunal or agency, that such facility should not be discontinued or removed, or should be restored.

Upon receiving the § 1084(d) letters, AT & T informed the Tribe that it would not provide toll-free service until the Tribe resolved its legal differences with the States.

The Tribe filed an action in the Coeur d'Alene Tribal Court seeking to enjoin AT & T from denying toll free service based on the § 1084(d) letters. The Tribe argued that the Lottery is lawful under IGRA and that AT & T is therefore legally obligated to provide the requested service pursuant to the Federal Communications Act (FCA). See 47 U.S.C. § 201(a) (requiring common carriers engaged in interstate communication to furnish service upon reasonable request). AT & T challenged the personal and subject matter jurisdiction of the Tribal Court. The Tribal Court rejected AT & T's arguments, declared the Lottery lawful under IGRA, and enjoined AT & T from refusing to provide the requested service. The Tribal Court of Appeals affirmed.

AT & T then filed suit in federal district court seeking a declaration that the Tribal Court lacked jurisdiction and that the § 1084(d) letters relieved AT & T from any obligation to provide service. The district court determined that IGRA requires a participant in a lottery to be present on Indian lands when purchasing a ticket; therefore, the district court held that the lottery was operating outside IGRA, which would otherwise preempt state law. AT & T Corp. v. Coeur d'Alene Tribe, 45 F.Supp.2d 995, 1002-1003 (D. Idaho 1998). Finding that the Tribal Court's decision was erroneous as a matter of federal law, the district court denied as moot AT & T's motion for judgment that the Tribal Court lacked jurisdiction. The court also granted declaratory relief, stating that AT & T was not required to furnish toll-free service from any State that notified AT & T that the Tribe's Lottery would violate state law. The Tribe appeals.

As a general rule, federal courts must recognize and enforce tribal court judgments under principles of comity. Two circumstances preclude recognition: when the tribal court either lacked jurisdiction or denied the losing party due process of law.

The Coeur d'Alene Tribe sued AT & T pursuant to the Federal Communications Act (FCA), 47 U.S.C. §§ 151 et seq.

Section 207 of the Act sets forth how a party may pursue remedies for claimed injuries sustained under the preceding sections. Specifically, 47 U.S.C. § 207 provides that

> [a]ny person claiming to be damaged by any common carrier subject to the provisions of this chapter may either make complaint to [the FCC] or may bring suit for the recovery of the damages for which such common carrier may be liable under the provisions of this chapter, in any district court of the United States of competent jurisdiction; but such person shall not have the right to pursue both such remedies.

By its express language, § 207 establishes concurrent jurisdiction in the FCC and federal district courts only, leaving no room for adjudication in any other forum—be it state, tribal, or otherwise.

Because exclusive jurisdiction rested in either of the two statutorily-provided federal fora, the Tribal Court lacked jurisdiction to entertain the Tribe's claim.

After engaging in lengthy statutory interpretation, the district court concluded that the IGRA unambiguously requires that a purchaser of a chance in the Lottery be physically present on the Reservation in order for the gaming activity to fall within IGRA's preemptive reach. Based on its conclusions that lottery purchases initiated off-Reservation would thus be subject to state gambling laws, the district court granted summary judgment in favor of AT & T, holding that the § 1084(d) letters required AT & T to refrain from providing toll free service for off-Reservation, out-of-state would-be Lottery participants where such service would violate state law.

In ruling as it did, the district court discounted the NIGC's approval of the Tribe's management contract with UNISTAR—a contract that made clear the Tribe's plans with respect to telephonic sales. The NIGC approval of both the management contract and the tribal resolution authorizing the Lottery were final agency decisions subject to review under the Administrative Procedures Act. 25 U.S.C. § 2714. Moreover, the district court—apparently eager to provide AT & T and the various states breathing down the corporation's neck with a definitive answer regarding the Lottery's legality—completely sidestepped two crucial considerations: (1) the effect it should accord the NIGC approval made consistent with the requirements of the detailed regulatory scheme Congress provided when it enacted the IGRA; and (2) whether AT & T, a provider of telephonic services, is an appropriate challenger.

Although AT & T has taken the lead in the instant litigation, the thirty-plus states that have briefed this court as amici—most of which operate their own lotteries—have the biggest stake in challenging the validity of the Tribe's Lottery. Since providing toll-free service for the Lottery would hand AT & T a new revenue source, the company would likely provide service to the tribe for the Lottery in the absence of § 1084(d) pressure. But faced with a stack of letters warning the carrier that it might be liable for supporting gambling in violation of many states' laws, AT & T sought some sort of definitive declaration of its responsibilities under both the FCA and § 1084(d).

In fact, AT & T's responsibilities were decided long before the parties set foot in any of the various courts that have entertained this case. The NIGC's final agency actions approving both the management contract and the Tribe's resolution indicated that the Lottery is legal until and unless the NIGC's decision is overturned.

When it enacted the IGRA, Congress created a detailed regulatory structure for the approval of Class III gaming. The Tribe was successful in its effort to obtain approval for the lottery, doing so pursuant to the IGRA's regulatory scheme. First, the Tribe and the State of Idaho entered into a compact that provides, in relevant part, that gaming will occur only on Indian lands. The compact specifies that Class III gaming must abide by the IGRA: "The Tribe may enter into management contracts for the development and management of gaming authorized by and consistent with this Compact and in accord with regulations, [IGRA], and the Gaming Code." The NIGC and the Secretary of the Interior approved the compact in 1993. See 58 Fed.Reg. 8478 (Feb. 12, 1993).

In 1995, the Tribe adopted a resolution stating:

[R]esolved, "that all Class III gaming authorized by the Compact by and between the Coeur d'Alene Tribe and the State of Idaho be conducted pursuant to tribal law. This specifically authorizes the conduct of the National Indian Lottery under the Management Agreement with Unistar Entertainment, Inc. which has been previously approved by the Chairman of the National Gaming Commission."

[F]urther resolved, "that all Class III gaming herein authorized be conducted in accordance with all provisions of 25 U.S.C. § 2710(d) and 2710(b) made applicable to Class III gaming by 2710(d)(1)(A)(ii) all of which are incorporated herein by reference."

The NIGC approved the resolution under the IGRA. Before doing so, the Commission had to determine that the resolution would comply with the Tribal-State compact, including the language requiring IGRA compliance.

Like resolutions, management contracts must meet IGRA requirements before they can win NIGC approval. The Tribe's management agreement with UNISTAR—including the "Tele-Lottery" service—won the NIGC Chairman's approval in the summer of 1996. Though the statutory framework suffices to demonstrate that the NIGC must consider the legality of Class III gaming before approving compacts, resolutions, ordinances, and management contracts, in this case documentary evidence also shows close NIGC consideration. As the district court noted, the NIGC approved the Tribe's management agreement and Lottery plan knowing that calls would be placed from other states. Although the dissent seems to entertain the view that the NIGC does not consider whether or not a particular gaming operation will comply with the IGRA, an affidavit submitted on the Tribe's behalf—and not contradicted by AT & T or the amici—tells us:

The NIGC repeatedly informed the Tribe throughout the review process for the management agreement that it would not approve the agreement unless the NIGC were satisfied about the legality of the National Indian Lottery. After an exhaustive review that took more than one year, the NIGC approved the management agreement.

The district court also quoted the letter from then-NIGC Chairman Monteau to MCI clarifying that the IGRA did not prohibit the lottery—further evidence that the Commission did, in fact, consider the Lottery's legality as IGRA requires.

Furthermore, the NIGC Chairman had an opportunity to revisit the Lottery's legality. An amendment to the Unistar Management Agreement won approval (another final agency action) from the NIGC Chairman. The amendment included notice of the use of telephone and other off-reservation means of access: " 'Tele-Lottery' means Lottery Games or other Games authorized by the Compact and conducted using any voice, data or video networks." The NIGC Chairman's approval of the amendment reads, in relevant part:

We have reviewed the Amendment and other information submitted and have determined that the standards of 25 CFR Parts 531 and 535 have been met. This letter, and my signature on the Amendment, constitute such approval.

Title 25 CFR § 531—cited by the NIGC Chairman as a regulation whose provisions must be met—requires provision that gaming will comply with IGRA.

What the district court failed to grasp was that the IGRA lays out a specific regulatory scheme whereby the NIGC's approval of a management contract is a final agency decision that may be appealed only directly and in an action initiated by a proper party in federal district court.

The NIGC is statutorily obliged to reject any lottery proposal that does not conform to IGRA. See 25 U.S.C. § 2706(b)(10) (requiring the NIGC to promulgate regulations and guidelines to implement IGRA); and 25 C.F.R. § 531.1(a) ("[A]ll gaming covered by the contract will be conducted in accordance with the Indian Gaming Regulatory Act."). In fact, the NIGC has previously refused to approve management agreements when it believed the proposed gaming activity will not be conducted "on Indian lands" for IGRA purposes. See, e.g., Miami Tribe of Oklahoma v. United States, 5 F.Supp.2d 1213, 1218 (D. Kansas, 1998).

For their part, the amici states and the United States point to the opinion of a new NIGC Chairman, who believes that the Lottery is not protected by the IGRA insofar as it involves off-Reservation ticket purchases. But even if the Chairman may undo the work of a predecessor under some circumstance, he may not do so here.

The United States and any of the amici states were free to challenge the NIGC's final agency decision directly in federal court under 25 U.S.C. § 2714. None did so. Unless and until the NIGC's decision is overturned by means of a proper challenge and appeal, the IGRA governs the Lottery.

Since IGRA applies, so too does 18 U.S.C. § 1166(d), which mandates that "[t]he United States shall have exclusive jurisdiction over criminal prosecutions of violations of State gambling laws" unless the tribe in question has consented to State criminal jurisdiction, which the Coeur d'Alene Tribe has not. Thus, where IGRA-governed Class III gaming is concerned, the federal government has the exclusive authority to prosecute any state gambling law violations applicable in Indian country. States, on the other hand, are without jurisdiction.

This brings us to the 18 U.S.C. § 1084(d) letters that ostensibly underlie the instant action. As explained, § 1084(d) permits a federal, state, or local law enforcement agency "acting within its jurisdiction" to demand that a common carrier refuse service where state gambling laws may be violated. If IGRA governs the Lottery—as it does until a proper plaintiff challenges the NIGC's approval of the management contract—then under 18 U.S.C. § 1166 the states and their various Attorneys General were not acting within their jurisdiction when they posted their § 1084(d) letters to AT & T.

For their part, the amici states are not without recourse to challenge the Lottery and to seek a determination as to what constitutes gaming activities "on Indian land" within the meaning of the IGRA. They must, however, rely on their own resources—and not AT & T's—to make their case. The states might have joined this litigation at its beginning in the district court to attack the NIGC's decision directly under 25 U.S.C. § 2714. They did not. Should they succeed at some future time in stripping the Lottery of its legitimacy under IGRA, they then will have the authority to issue § 1084(d) letters. Until such time, both the Tribe and AT & T may continue their activities—and in AT & T's case meet its legal obligations—without fear of prosecution.

REVERSED AND REMANDED.

GOULD, Circuit Judge, concurring in part and dissenting in part.

Although I concur in the majority opinion holding that the tribal court did not have subject matter jurisdiction over AT & T, I must respectfully dissent from the judgment. I would hold that the National Indian Gaming Commission ("NIGC") did not issue a final decision that the National Indian Lottery ("NIL") complies with the Indian Gaming Regulatory Act ("IGRA") and, therefore, that the district court could examine that issue in the first instance. Accordingly, I would reach the merits of the legality of the NIL and would conclude, as did the district court, that the NIL is clearly illegal under the IGRA because it involves tribe-sponsored gambling that does not occur on Indian lands. AT & T did not act improperly in refusing to provide toll-free service to the Coeur d'Alene Tribe of Idaho ("Tribe").

I see no principled basis for the majority to reverse the district court's well-reasoned decision. The majority's inexplicable decision to resolve this case solely on incorrect procedural grounds has the effect, if not the purpose, of avoiding the obvious conclusion that the NIL is illegal under the IGRA. The majority purports to exercise judicial restraint by putting off the resolution of this issue for another day. Avoiding the merits, the majority rests its decision on an incorrect procedural ground. It thereby does a disservice to AT & T, the thirty-seven states that have appeared as amici curiae, the federal government, also amicus curiae, and even to the Tribe advancing the NIL and possibly other tribes that may be contemplating similar national gambling operations. All of the governments and other entities who will be affected by this case would benefit from an efficient and correct resolution of the important issue whether an Indian nation may run a national lottery that depends on off-reservation ticket purchases. If the merits were reached and resolved against the Tribe, as I believe they must be under applicable law and consistent with Congress' intent, the Tribe could turn its attention to a proper development of its legally viable gaming options, rather than proceeding on the false hope that it will be permitted to implement the NIL.

To support its view that the NIGC decided that the NIL was authorized by the IGRA, the majority relies on an informal letter from the NIGC to MCI, which is not a party to this litigation. However, the majority's reliance on the letter is not warranted because the letter is not a final agency decision.

Not only does the majority err in relying on the NIGC letter, but it also errs in suggesting that, in approving the Tribe's management contract, the NIGC Chairman necessarily concluded that the NIL is legal under the IGRA.

The majority relies on the NIGC Chairman's August 15, 1996 letter approving the Tribe's gaming management contract as evidence that the NIGC reached a final decision that the NIL was legal under the IGRA. The problem with this argument is that the Chairman's letter does not at all indicate that he evaluated the NIL's compliance with the substantive provisions of the

IGRA as part of the approval process. Moreover, nothing in the statutory and regulatory frameworks that govern the approval process indicates that the Chairman is even authorized to evaluate the legality of the proposed gaming operations under the IGRA in deciding whether to approve the management contract. See 25 U.S.C. §§ 2711, 2712(c); 25 C.F.R. §§ 531.1, 533.4, 533.6.

As the majority indicates, the Chairman did not actively approve the Tribe's gaming resolution; rather he simply did not respond to it within the 90-day period after the Tribe submitted the resolution to him. 25 U.S.C. § 2710(e) provides that a resolution on which the Chairman failed to act within the 90-day period "shall be considered to have been approved by the Chairman, but only to the extent such ordinance or resolution is consistent with the provisions of this chapter." Thus, § 2710(e) stands for the opposite proposition to the one for which the majority cites it. It means that the Chairman did not approve the resolution by failing to act upon it: because the resolution was not consistent with the IGRA, it legally could not be approved by inaction.

I would reach the merits and conclude that the IGRA is unambiguous in its failure to authorize the NIL.

Lotteries are included under the definition of class III gaming in the regulations implementing the IGRA. 25 C.F.R. § 502.4. Class III gaming is the most stringently regulated of the three classes. Seminole Tribe of Fla. v. Fla., 517 U.S. 44, 48, 116 S.Ct. 1114, 134 L.Ed.2d 252 (1996). Class III gaming on Indian lands is permitted only if (1) "such gaming is not otherwise specifically prohibited on Indian lands by federal law," (2) the Tribe enters into a compact governing gaming with the State in which the Indian lands are located, and (3) the Secretary of the Interior approves of the Tribal-State compact. 25 U.S.C. § 2710(b)(1)(A), (d)(1) and (d)(8).

The district court correctly concluded that the term "gaming activities" plainly includes a player's ordering a ticket because, without that activity, the lottery could not operate. The NIL, beyond doubt and with any common sense assessment, involves gaming activity off Indian lands because players (1) place their bets while outside the Indian reservation, and (2) can receive the winnings off the reservation. The IGRA protects and advances on-reservation gaming; the proposed national lottery involves and encourages illegal gaming nationwide off the reservation and is not within the purview of the IGRA.

The Tribe argues that the term "gaming activities" is ambiguous, but grasps to find ambiguity where there is none in an attempt to save its lottery from being foreclosed by federal law and from running afoul of state laws prohibiting such gambling in their jurisdictions. "Gambling" is "[t]he act of risking something of value . . . for a chance to win a prize." Black's Law Dictionary 687 (7th ed. 1999). The Oxford English Dictionary defines "activity" as "the state of being active," and defines "active" as "1 [g]iven to action rather than contemplation or speculation; practical[;] 2 [o]riginating or communicating action." 1 The New Shorter Oxford English Dictionary 22 (1993). Here, the issue is whether the active aspects of gaming occurred on Indian lands.

In my view, no reasonable person could interpret the facts to conclude that gaming activities under the NIL do not occur off Indian lands. Placing the calls, selecting the numbers and receiving the winnings are indispensable elements of the operation of the NIL and all these activities occur off Indian lands. Gaming would occur off Indian lands each time and in each location a player participated in the NIL, if that person was not physically on Indian lands. See, e.g., Martin v. United States, 389 F.2d 895, 897-98 (5th Cir. 1968) (stating that telephonic transmission of wager implicates the public policies of the state from which the wager is placed), cert. denied, 391 U.S. 919, 88 S.Ct. 1808, 20 L.Ed.2d 656 (1968).

Federal law might well protect a lottery where all betting occurred by persons purchasing lottery tickets on Indian lands. That at least would serve a benign purpose to bring lottery players on to Indian lands and perhaps increase cross-cultural understanding.

Only a subterfuge and strained argument that an account is established at the reservation is offered as a justification. This is too preposterous a position and too slim a reed to support the planned national lottery to be run by the Tribe.

The IGRA clearly contemplated that each state be given the opportunity to negotiate with and reach agreement with tribes in that state for the offering of class III gaming. However, telephonic participation would undoubtedly include persons in states that have not entered into a compact, thereby circumventing the guidelines delineated in 25 U.S.C. § 2710. Here, the only state that entered into a compact with the tribe was Idaho. For these reasons, participation in the NIL occurs off Indian lands, and, with the exception of gambling activity within the State of Idaho, the NIL lacked the required predicate for class III gaming of successful negotiations between sovereigns.

The legislative history of the IGRA supports the reading that the NIL occurs off Indian lands. The IGRA's legislative history and attendant policy objectives make it clear that the IGRA authorizes tribal gaming activities exclusively on Indian lands, whereas the NIL would include activities off Indian lands. See Cabazon Band of Mission Indians v. Wilson, 37 F.3d 430, 433-35 (9th Cir. 1994) (implying that the tribe's interest in gaming activity under the IGRA derives from the fact that the activity occurs on the reservation), cert. denied, 524 U.S. 926 (1998). Congress enacted the IGRA expressly to preserve and balance mutual and competing federal, state, and tribal interests in Indian gaming on Indian lands.

The IGRA's legislative history places great emphasis on the "on Indian lands" requirement. Like the IGRA, neither the Senate Committee Report, nor other IGRA legislative history, authorizes Indian gaming activity to be played, even in part, off Indian lands. For instance, when discussing the use of modern technology to facilitate class II tribal gaming, the Senate Committee Report adheres to the historical meaning associated with, as well as the plain meaning of, the "on Indian lands" requirement. The Report states:

> In this regard [i.e., as to the use of modern technology], the Committee recognizes that tribes may wish to join with other tribes to coordinate their class II operations and thereby enhance the potential of increasing revenues. For example, linking participant players at various reservations whether in the same or different States, by means of telephone, cable, television or satellite may be a reasonable approach

for tribes to take. Simultaneous games participation between and among reservations can be made practical by use of computers and telecommunications technology . . . .

Id. at 9; see Cabazon Band of Mission Indians v. Nat'l Indian Gambling Comm'n, 14 F.3d 633, 636-37 (D.C. Cir. 1994).

Moreover, even in the context of class II gaming, which is less stringently regulated than class III gaming, Congress requires that it occur on Indian lands. If the Committee actually intended for the "on Indian lands" requirement to be applied in the manner suggested here by the Tribe, the Committee in the above referenced report would not have limited the use of "telephone, cable, television or satellite" to "between and among reservations." Instead, consistent with the plain and historical meaning of "on Indian lands," Congress recognized that technology could only be used to link reservations and players on those reservations.

It is one thing to link players at several locations, all of which are on Indian lands. It is quite another thing to link any person at any time and any place by phone or other electronic means to an Indian reservation that wants to play host to unrestricted gambling from all quarters, and thereby circumvent the clear geographical limitation of the IGRA that gaming must occur on Indian lands. The careful balance set by Congress in the IGRA, respecting rights and interests of Indian tribes, state governments, and the federal government, and their citizens, is upset by the NIL's planned disregard of geographic limitation for gaming. I see no real possibility that Congress could have intended what is here proposed, nor does Congress' language in the IGRA support the Tribe's strained construction in its rush towards national if not international and certainly unrestricted gaming.

Certainly there is authority supporting that certain statutes enacted for the benefit of Native Americans must be interpreted liberally in their favor where an ambiguity exists. However, as explained above, the IGRA is not ambiguous as to its requirement that all gambling activity be conducted on Indian lands.

The NIGC did not render a final decision as to the legality of the NIL under the IGRA. The premise of the majority's decision is in error. Moreover, the IGRA unambiguously does not authorize the NIL because the NIL contemplates Tribe-sponsored gaming activity that does not occur on Indian land. The district court was correct to grant summary judgment in favor of AT & T. I respectfully dissent from the majority's analysis to the contrary and from the judgment of the court.

Notes

1. The California Supreme Court's handiwork in *Davis* did not last long. In March 2000, voters approved Proposition 1A, which added the following paragraph to § 19 of the California state constitution:

(f) Notwithstanding subdivisions (a) and (e), and any other provision of state law, the Governor is authorized to negotiate and conclude compacts, subject to ratification by the Legislature, for the operation of slot machines and for the conduct of lottery games and banking and percentage card games by federally recognized Indian tribes on Indian lands in California in accordance with federal law. Accordingly, slot machines, lottery games, and banking and percentage card games are hereby permitted to be conducted and operated on tribal lands subject to those compacts.

Since the passage of Proposition 1A, a majority of California's 109 federally-recognized tribes have entered into compacts with the state to operate casinos. *See further* K. Alexa Koenig, Comment, *Gambling on Proposition 1A: The California Indian Self-Reliance Amendment*, 36 U.S.F. L. Rev. 1033 (2002).

2. California's experience is somewhat atypical, as most states have been willing to sign compacts allowing their tribes to engage in Class III gaming. The existence of a tribal-state compact usually eliminates disputes over the scope of permissible gaming, but can lead to other difficulties, as the *AT & T Corp.* case readily demonstrates.

3. For a further look at the process by which compacts are concluded, *see, e.g.*, John Maloney, *California's Tribal-State Gaming Compacts*, 3 Gaming L. Rev. 311 (1999); Rebecca Tsosie, *Negotiating Economic Survival: The Consent Principle and Tribal-State Compacts Under the Indian Gaming Regulatory Act*, 29 Ariz. St. L.J. 25 (1997); Kevin K. Washburn, *Recurring Problems in Indian Gaming*, 1 Wyo. L. Rev. 427 (2001); Gatsby Contrras, Note, *Exclusivity Agreements in Tribal-State Compacts: Mutual Benefit Revenue-Sharing or Illegal State Taxation?*, 5 J. Gender Race & Just. 487 (2002); Joe Laxague, Note, *Indian Gaming and Tribal-State Negotiations: Who Should Decide the Issue of Bad Faith?*, 25 J. Legis. 77 (1999); Ron M. Rosenberg, Comment, *When Sovereigns Negotiate in the Shadow of the Law: The 1998 Arizona-Pima Maricopa Gaming Compact*, 4 Harv. Negot. L. Rev. 283 (1999).

Problem 35

A state's constitution outlaws lotteries but allows pari-mutuel wagering, charity bingo, and a government lottery. The state's criminal code contains broad prohibitions on wagering, and recent legislative proposals to expand legal gaming have failed repeatedly. Can the state enter into compacts with its tribes authorizing casinos? *See State ex rel. Stephan v. Finney*, 867 P.2d 1034 (Kan. 1994).

F. AUTHORITY TO NEGOTIATE

LANGLEY v. EDWARDS
872 F. Supp. 1531 (W.D. La. 1995),
aff'd mem., 77 F.3d 479 (5th Cir. 1996)

HUNTER, Senior District Judge.

This litigation involves the effort of dissident members of the Coushatta Tribe to prevent casino gaming on lands held in trust for the tribe by the United States. On October 29, 1994, the Governor of Louisiana entered into a Tribal-State Compact with the Coushatta Tribe, a prerequisite to lawful gambling under the Indian Gaming Regulatory Act of 1988, 25 U.S.C. § 2701 et seq. ("IGRA").

The issue of the legality of the casino should be resolved prior to its opening to avoid such things as disruption of casino-vendor relationships and the casino workers' premature departure from their current jobs.

Plaintiffs would have this court enter a judgment declaring the casino site was not contiguous to the Coushatta Reservation as it existed on October 17, 1988, and have us set aside the United States Department of the Interior's action, specifically its (a) finding of contiguity; (b) the approval of the tribal state compact; and (c) the decision to take the parcels into trust for the tribe. Plaintiffs also allege that Governor Edwards did not have authority to enter into the compact with the tribe.

IGRA permits gaming to take place on "Indian lands," 25 U.S.C. § 2710(d)(1). Lands held in trust by the United States generally fall within the locations where gaming can occur. IGRA permits Class III gaming on lands acquired in trust after October 17, 1988, if "such lands are . . . contiguous to the boundaries of the reservation of the Indian tribe on October 17, 1988," 25 U.S.C. § 2719(a)(1).

The Coushatta Tribe of Louisiana is a federally-recognized Indian Tribe, with its reservation located in Allen Parish, Louisiana. See, e.g., 40 Fed.Reg. 24220 (1975). The Tribe is governed by a five member Tribal Council. In the absence of the casino project, the Coushatta Tribe and its members' economic situation was bleak.

However, the Coushatta Tribe's then existing reservation lands were not suitable for gaming activities, given their distance from any highways, current use for other tribal purposes such as housing and health facilities, and other shortcomings. The Coushatta Tribe accordingly determined that it would seek to acquire additional land, contiguous to its reservation, and transfer this land to the United States to be held in trust for the Tribe. This land would overcome all the shortcomings in the reservation lands, and would qualify for Class III gaming under 25 U.S.C. §§ 2703(4)(B) and 2719(a)(1).

The proposed acquisition consisted of a fairly narrow strip of land coming from the reservation boundary west to U.S. Highway 165, and an approximately 71 acre tract west of the Highway where the casino would be constructed.

The Department of the Interior questioned, however, whether the proposed 104 acre acquisition would be sufficiently "contiguous" to the Coushatta Tribe reservation to qualify under 25 U.S.C. § 2719(a)(1). The concern focused on the fact that the proposed gaming site was to be connected to the pre-existing reservation lands by a fairly narrow strip of land.

The Coushatta Tribe accordingly asked the Department for a determination whether, if an additional 427 acres were acquired, would the entire 531 acres tract be considered contiguous for purposes of Section 2719(a)(1). The Department of the Interior's Office of the Solicitor responded that the 531 acre parcel would qualify as contiguous, whereupon the Coushatta Tribe, by duly authorized resolution, formally requested that the 531 acre tract be taken into trust. The Secretary of Interior did so.

Federal defendants have raised the issue of whether the tribe is an indispensable party which must be joined in this suit pursuant to Fed.R.Civ.P. 19. Defendants then assert that the tribe cannot be joined because it is immune from suit, and this case should be dismissed for failure to join an indispensable party. We need not reach this issue because it is apparent that all defendants should be dismissed on other grounds.

Do these (dissident) Indian tribe members have standing to initiate an action to have [a] tribal compact entered into pursuant to IGRA declared void? The answer is "No." See Judge Barbour's opinion in Willis v. Fordice, 850 F.Supp. 523 (S.D.Miss.1994).

The Willis court held that individual tribal members have no legally protected right to be free from gaming on their tribal lands, nor do they suffer any individual or particularized injury different from that of any other tribal member. Id. at 528. Under both the Supreme Court's decision in California v. Cabazon Band of Mission Indians, 480 U.S. 202, 107 S.Ct. 1083, 94 L.Ed.2d 244 (1987), and the IGRA itself, Indians have the authority to conduct gaming on their lands, and "[b]ecause the tribes have this right, [plaintiffs] do not have any legally protected right to be free from the operation of a casino." Id.

Plaintiffs allege that they will suffer irreparable harm by the presence of a casino on the Tribe's reservation but do not state with any specificity what the alleged harm will be. They have not alleged an injury to legally-protected interests and have no individual legal right to determine what sort of business activities there should be on the Coushatta Indian Reservation. Even had plaintiffs alleged an injury to a legally-protected interest, there is no certainty any injury to plaintiffs will occur when the Tribe starts operating its casino.

[I]t is not likely that the injuries complained of by the plaintiffs would be redressed by a decision in their favor. The Tribe has not been joined in this action and cannot be joined due to the Tribe's sovereign immunity. We believe the clear line of cases compels the conclusion that plaintiffs lack standing to prosecute this action.

While the lawsuit purports to be brought against the United States Department of the Interior, two courts of appeal have held that lawsuits challenging the decision to take land into trust for Indian tribes constitute actions against the United States, and are barred by its sovereign immunity. Florida v. United States Department of the Interior, 768 F.2d 1248 (11th Cir.1985), cert. denied, 475 U.S. 1011, 106 S.Ct. 1186, 89 L.Ed.2d 302 (1986); Ducheneaux v. Secretary of Interior, 837 F.2d 340 (8th Cir.), cert. denied, 486 U.S. 1055, 108 S.Ct. 2822, 100 L.Ed.2d 923 (1988).

Like the unsuccessful litigants in Florida and Ducheneaux, plaintiffs' complaint against the federal defendants must be dismissed.

No substantive right exists to challenge the approval on the basis of alleged state law irregularities. The IGRA expresses a congressional policy of putting compacts into force quickly, by requiring the Secretary to approve or reject them within forty-five days of their submission. 25 U.S.C. § 2710(d)(8)(C). During this time, the Secretary must ensure that the compact complies with the IGRA, other federal laws, and the United States' trust obligations to the tribe. Id. § 2710(d)(8)(B).

Compact approval by the Secretary cannot be invalidated on the basis of a governor's ultra vires action, because a contrary rule would compel the Secretary to consider state law before approving any compact. That "would lead to endless delay." Since that result is contrary to the congressional intent expressed in the IGRA, it must be avoided by independent state law challenge. Kickapoo Tribe of Indians v. Babbitt, 827 F.Supp. 37 (D.D.C. 1993), appeal pending.

The Kickapoo Court ruled: 1) "Regardless of whether the governor had the authority to bind the state, the [Secretary] had an obligation to approve or disapprove of the compact within forty-five days . . . ." and 2) where the Secretary had not disapproved the compact within forty-five days, the provisions of IGRA provide that the compact is considered to be approved. Kickapoo, at 44; see Willis, 850 F.Supp. at 533.

Plaintiffs assert that the Honorable Edwin Edwards, Governor of Louisiana, had no authority under State Law to enter into the Compact with the Tribe. Because Louisiana allows such gaming as a matter of law, it may not prohibit Class III gaming by the Coushatta Indian Tribe on tribal lands. The Tribe is only bound by the Compact between it and the state, not all of the regulations contained in Louisiana gaming statutes. IGRA does not specify which branch of state government should negotiate with the Indian Tribe.

Assuming in arguendo, no indispensability, standing, or sovereign immunity hurdles, there has been no exhaustion of remedies. The tribal court action has been initiated for what is essentially a dispute among members of the Tribe. Tribal sovereignty and Supreme Court pronouncements dictate exhaustion of the tribal remedy. "When the dispute is a 'reservation affair' . . . there is no discretion not to defer." Crawford v. Genuine Parts Co., 947 F.2d 1405, 1408 (9th Cir.1991), cert. denied, 502 U.S. 1096, 112 S.Ct. 1174, 117 L.Ed.2d 419 (1992).

Plaintiffs assert that Governor Edwards has usurped a legislative function and signed a Compact on the basis of the Secretary of the Interior's illegal action in taking title in trust of the property upon which the gaming is to occur. This is simply not the case with regard to the Compact which was negotiated between the Governor and the Coushatta Tribe. The Compact does not contain provisions which are outside the contemplation of the IGRA. The Compact does not address anything other than those issues contemplated by the IGRA under 25 U.S.C. § 2710(c)(3)(A). The Tribal-State Compact entered into pursuant to the Indian Gaming Regulatory Act, between Governor Edwards and the Tribe, for regulation of casino gambling on reservation property, approved by the Secretary of Interior, was valid under state and federal law. Louisiana allowed legalized gaming as a matter of public policy. The Compact was approved by the United States Secretary of the Interior and did not address anything other than issues contemplated by IGRA.

Plaintiffs' dissatisfaction is with the Tribe's decision to permit gaming on tribal lands, and should be properly resolved within the tribal governmental and court structure.

SARATOGA COUNTY CHAMBER OF COMMERCE INC. v. PATAKI

740 N.Y.S.2d 733 (App. Div. 2002)

MERCURE, Justice.

Appeal from an order of the Supreme Court (Teresi, J.), entered April 12, 2001 in Albany County, which, inter alia, granted plaintiffs' motions for summary judgment and declared the 1993 Tribal-State gaming compact and its 1999 amendment void and unenforceable absent legislative approval.

The question on this appeal is whether, as the result of the interaction of gaming policies established by the State's Constitution and statutes and Federal law, defendant Governor had the authority to execute a Tribal-State compact and amendment with the St. Regis Mohawk Tribe (hereinafter Tribe), allowing certain class III gaming activities on the Tribe's reservation. We hold that because the basic policy decisions underlying the Governor's action have not been made by the State Legislature, the Governor did not have the authority to bind the State by executing the compact or the amendment.

The Indian Gaming Regulatory Act (25 USC § 2701 et seq.) (hereinafter IGRA) was enacted in 1988. Class III gaming, which is at issue here, is statutorily defined as "all forms of gaming that are not class I gaming or class II gaming" (25 USC § 2703) and includes pari-mutuel horse race wagering, lotteries, banking card games such as baccarat, chemin de fer, and blackjack, and electronic or electromechanical facsimiles of any game of chance or slot machines of any kind (25 USC § 2703; see Hotel Empls. & Rest. Empls. Intl. Union v Davis, 21 Cal.4th 585, 596, 981 P.2d 990, 998).

Pursuant to IGRA, Class III gaming activities will be permitted on Indian lands if "located in a State that permits such gaming for any purpose by any person, organization, or entity . . . and conducted in conformance with a Tribal-State compact entered into by the Indian tribe and the State" (25 USC § 2710; see Rumsey Indian Rancheria of Wintun Indians v Wilson, 64 F.3d 1250, 1256, amended 99 F.3d 321, cert denied 521 U.S. 1118). Further, as we held on a prior appeal in this case, we look to state law rather than IGRA to determine whether a state has validly bound itself to a compact (275 A.D.2d 145, 157).

In 1993, then-Governor Mario Cuomo entered into a Tribal-State compact with the Tribe, which allowed the Tribe to operate gambling casinos. The Tribe opened the Akwesane Mohawk Casino on its reservation near Hogansburg in Franklin County on April 10, 1999. On May 27, 1999, the Governor and the Tribe entered into an amendment to the compact to permit the operation of electronic gaming devices, and the Tribe began the operation of these devices the following day.

These actions were commenced in September 1999. The complaints allege in pertinent part that the Governor lacked authority to execute the compact or the amendment and that the types of gambling contemplated by both of them are prohibited by the N.Y. Constitution, criminal statutes, and public policy as enunciated by the Legislature. It is important to note that plaintiffs do not seek to shut down the Tribe's casino located on the Akwesane reservation insofar as it is operated in accordance with the original compact. Plaintiffs do seek to prevent any expansion of the casino operation pursuant to the amendment, including the expansion of the gambling activity onto other sites. On the prior appeal, we denied defendants' motions to dismiss the complaints for failure to join an indispensable party, lack of standing or legal capacity to sue, or as barred by the doctrine of Federal preemption, the applicable Statute of Limitations, or laches. Plaintiffs and defendants thereafter moved for summary judgment.

Fundamentally, "[t]he constitutional principle of separation of powers, implied by the separate grants of power to each of the coordinate branches of government, requires that the Legislature make the critical policy decisions, while the executive branch's responsibility is to implement those policies" (Borquin v. Cuomo, 85 N.Y.2d 781, 784). Thus, although "there need not be a specific and detailed legislative expression authorizing a particular executive act as long as 'the basic policy decisions underlying the [executive action] have been made and articulated by the Legislature'" (Borquin v. Cuomo, supra, at 785), "when the Executive acts inconsistently with the Legislature, or usurps its prerogatives . . . the doctrine of separation is violated" (Clark v. Cuomo, 66 N.Y.2d 185, 189).

The initial task, then, is to ascertain New York's legislative policy on gambling as it existed in the 1990s. Pursuant to N.Y. Constitution, article 1, § 9, the only forms of gambling authorized in New York are (1) State-operated pari-mutuel betting on horse races, (2) lotteries operated by the State, "the net proceeds of which shall be applied exclusively to or in aid or support of education", and (3) specified "games of chance" conducted only by "bona fide religious, charitable or non-profit organizations of veterans, volunteer fire [fighter] and similar non-profit organizations", and then only if authorized by a majority vote of the electors of the city, town or village in which the gambling is to take place and on the additional conditions that the entire net proceeds be exclusively devoted to the lawful purposes of the organizations and that prizes be limited to $250 for a single prize or $1,000 for a series of prizes. Notably, N.Y. Constitution, article 1, § 9(2), requires the Legislature to "pass appropriate laws to effectuate [its purposes], ensure that [the games of chance] are rigidly regulated to prevent commercialized gambling, [and] prevent participation by criminal or other undesirable elements and the diversion of funds from the [authorized purposes]."

The stated purpose of General Municipal Law article 9-A, which the Legislature enacted pursuant to that constitutional directive, is expressed in the following terms:

> It is hereby declared to be the policy of the legislature that all phases of the supervision, licensing and regulation of games of chance and of the conduct of games of chance should be closely controlled and that the laws and regulations pertaining thereto should be strictly construed and rigidly enforced; that the conduct of the game and all attendant activities should be so regulated and adequate controls so instituted as to discourage commercialization of gambling in all its forms * * * and that the mandate of [NY Constitution, article 1, § 9] should be carried out by rigid regulations to prevent commercialized gambling . . . . (General Municipal Law § 185).

Under the circumstances, we conclude that the commercialized Las Vegas style gambling authorized by the compact is the antithesis of the highly restricted and "rigidly regulated" (N.Y. Const, art 1, § 9) forms of gambling permitted by the N.Y. Constitution and statutory law and New York's established public policy disfavoring gambling (see Ramesar v. State of New York, 224 A.D.2d 757, 759, appeal denied 88 N.Y.2d 811).

Obviously recognizing that its defense to plaintiffs' separation of powers claim is seriously undermined by New York's long-standing and clearly articulated policy against precisely the type of gambling that the compact authorizes, defendants' primary approach has been to enlist IGRA as evidence of a purported New York policy favoring commercialized casino gambling. Reduced to its essence, defendants' argument is that, because the N.Y. Constitution, statutes and implementing regulations permit every form of gambling authorized by the compact, albeit under rigid controls and limitations not in existence at the Tribe's casino, the "permits such gaming for any purpose by any person, organization, or entity" criterion of 25 USC § 2710(d)(1)(B) is satisfied. That being the case, the argument continues, if the Governor had refused to enter into good-faith negotiations culminating in a Tribal-State compact, IGRA would have authorized the U.S. Secretary of the Interior to impose a compact on the State. Even accepting these two underlying premises as true, which we do only for the sake of the present argument, we conclude that defendants' argument is nonetheless fatally flawed.

First and most obvious is the fact that the Governor and Congress are not coordinate branches of government, thereby rendering defendants' separation of powers analysis inapt. Although defendants make an attempt to promote this as a "unique" separation of powers case where the challenged executive action supposedly implements existing legislative policy "established through the interplay of policies set by two policy-making bodies—the New York State Legislature and the United States Congress"—the fact is that the policy relied upon by defendants derives solely from Federal statutes and implementing regulations. The State Legislature's exclusive role in this matter was to approve highly restrictive statutes and constitutional provisions which, although generally banning gambling and at all times evidencing a strong policy against commercialized gambling, may have unwittingly opened the door to Indian casino gaming through the subsequently enacted IGRA.

Second, defendants' analysis overlooks the critical distinction between the existence of a Tribal-State compact and the provisions of such a compact. That is, even if we were to accept the premise that IGRA placed the State in a position where it had no reasonable alternative but to enter into a compact with the Tribe, the fact remains that the Governor lacked authority to define the terms of that compact. As the legislative history of IGRA makes clear, "[a] State's governmental interests with respect to class III gaming on Indian lands include the interplay of such gaming with the State's public policy, safety, law and other interests, as well as impacts on the State's regulatory system, including its economic interest in raising revenue for its citizens" (S Rep No. 446, 100th Cong, 2d Sess, reprinted in 1988 U.S.Code Cong & Admin News 3071, 3083). Here, the Governor's action deprived the Legislature of any input concerning a number of significant elements, including the location of the casino, the gaming that could be carried on there, the extent of State involvement in providing regulation and a regulatory infrastructure and the fees to be exacted for that regulation. These numerous collateral issues affecting the health and welfare of State residents implicate policy choices lying squarely within the province of the Legislature.

As a final matter, we note that defendants expressly disavow any opinion as to whether (1) under IGRA, New York must allow "all forms of Indian gaming" because some types of class III gaming are allowed, (2) IGRA preempted the question of whether the Governor's signature was sufficient to bind the State, and (3) the Legislature ratified the compact by appropriating funds for its implementation and granting the State Police access to the criminal history records of the Division of Criminal Justice Services.

ORDERED that the order is affirmed, with one bill of costs.

Notes

1. As is explained in the *Pataki* case, the St. Regis Mohawk Tribe originally entered into a compact in 1993 and then negotiated an amendment in 1999. By its own terms, the amendment expired in May 2000. In April 2001, the trial court found that the compact was void, and in May 2002 the appellate court affirmed. Nevertheless, the tribe continues to offer Class III gaming.

2. A number of other courts around the country have considered the question of whether a governor has the authority to bind a state to an Indian gaming compact. *See, e.g.*, *Willis v. Fordice*, 850 F. Supp. 523 (S.D. Miss. 1994), *aff'd mem.*, 55 F.3d 633 (5th Cir. 1995); *Kickapoo Tribe of Indians v. Babbitt*, 827 F. Supp. 37 (D.D.C. 1993), *rev'd on other grounds*, 43 F.3d 1491 (D.C. Cir. 1995); *Narragansett Indian Tribe of Rhode Island v. State*, 667 A.2d 280 (R.I. 1995); *State ex rel. Stephan v. Finney*, 836 P.2d 1169 (Kan. 1992); *McCartney v. Attorney General*, 587 N.W.2d 824 (Mich. Ct. App. 1998), *appeal denied*, 601 N.W.2d 101 (Mich. 1999).

Problem 36

After the governor signed compacts with several of the state's tribes, her opponents filed suit to have the agreements declared invalid. Because they have sovereign immunity, the tribes were not named as defendants. Should the court dismiss the action for failure to join indispensable parties? *See State ex rel. Clark v. Johnson*, 904 P.2d 11 (N.M. 1995).

G. AFTER-ACQUIRED LAND

CONFEDERATED TRIBES OF SILETZ INDIANS OF OREGON v. UNITED STATES
110 F.3d 688 (9th Cir.),
cert. denied, 522 U.S. 1027 (1997)

HUG, Chief Judge.

This appeal concerns the interpretation of a provision of the Indian Gaming Regulatory Act ("IGRA"), 25 U.S.C. § 2719. That Act precludes most gaming on land acquired in trust for an Indian tribe after 1988, unless one of several exceptions applies.

The Confederated Tribes of Siletz Indians of Oregon (the "Tribes") contest the denial of their application to have land taken in trust for their benefit for the purpose of establishing a gaming facility. The Secretary of the Interior denied the Tribes' application because, pursuant to 25 U.S.C. § 2719(b)(1)(A) of IGRA, gaming on newly acquired trust land requires the concurrence of the Governor of the state in which the trust land is located, and the Governor of the State of Oregon refused to concur. The Tribes filed in the district court an action seeking reversal of the Secretary's denial of their application and the State of Oregon intervened.

The district court found that the Governor's concurrence provision of IGRA, 25 U.S.C. § 2719(b)(1)(A), violates both the Appointments Clause and separation of powers principles because it allows a state governor to "veto" findings made by the Secretary of the Interior. The Tribes were nonetheless denied relief. The district court held that because the remaining portion of § 2719(b)(1)(A) could not function independently in a manner consistent with the intent of Congress, the entire § 2719(b)(1)(A) must be severed from IGRA.

[W]e affirm the judgment of the district court on different grounds.

The Confederated Siletz Tribes of Oregon applied to the Secretary of the Interior to have land taken in trust for the purpose of gaming. The Secretary of the Interior is authorized to take land in trust for the benefit of an Indian tribe

> (1) when the property is located within the exterior boundaries of the tribe's reservation or adjacent thereto, or within a tribal consolidation area; or, (2) when the tribe already owns an interest in the land or, (3) when the Secretary determines that the acquisition of the land is necessary to facilitate tribal self-determination, economic development, or Indian housing.

25 C.F.R. § 151.3(a) (authorized by 25 U.S.C. § 465). Gaming on Indian land, including trust land, is governed by IGRA. IGRA was the outgrowth of several years of discussions and negotiations seeking a method to allow the states to be involved in the regulation of Indian gaming in light of the Supreme Court's decision in California v. Cabazon Band of Mission Indians, 480 U.S. 202 (1987). See S.Rep. 446, 100th Cong., 2d Sess. 1-2, reprinted in 1988 U.S.C.C.A.N. 3071, 3071-72. Section 2719(a) of IGRA states:

> Except as provided in subsection (b) of this section, gaming regulated by this chapter shall not be conducted on lands acquired by the Secretary in trust for the benefit of an Indian tribe after October 17, 1988 . . . .

Section 2719(b) provides a number of exceptions to the general prohibition. The exception at issue in this case is § 2719(b)(1)(A), which reads:

> (1) Subsection (a) of this section will not apply when—(A) the Secretary, after consultation with the Indian tribe and appropriate State and local officials, including officials of other nearby Indian tribes, determines that a gaming establishment on newly acquired lands would be in the best interest of the Indian tribe and its members, and would not be detrimental to the surrounding community, but only if the Governor of the State in which the gaming activity is to be conducted concurs in the Secretary's determination . . . .

The land at issue is a 16-acre tract of land near Salem, Oregon, 50 miles from the Tribes' reservation. The Bureau of Indian Affairs requested comments on the proposal from the County and the City of Salem. [T]he Governor submitted objections to the proposal.

[T]he Secretary of the Interior found that the proposal was in the best interest of the Tribes and not detrimental to the community and sought the Governor's concurrence in his determination. The Governor refused to concur. On December 21, 1992, the Secretary denied the Tribes' application on the ground that the Governor did not concur in this determination. The Secretary invited the Tribes to reapply for acquisition of the land in trust for nongaming purposes.

The Tribes filed an action to challenge the denial of their application. The district court held that the language in § 2719(b)(1)(A), requiring the state governor's concurrence, violated the Appointments Clause and separation of powers principles. The district court also held that § 2719(b)(1)(A) must be severed in its entirety in order to be consistent with the intent of Congress to permit gaming on such newly acquired territory only with the State's concurrence. It therefore denied the Tribes' appeal of the Secretary's denial of their trust application because there was no longer an exception to § 2719(a) through which they could establish gaming on newly acquired lands.

In enacting IGRA, Congress recognized that gaming is a sensitive and controversial activity in many states. This statute attempted to accommodate the interest of the Indian tribes with the legitimate regulatory interests of the states. The provision of IGRA here at issue deals with the acquisition of land by the Secretary of the Interior to be held in trust for a tribe for gaming purposes when that land is not contiguous to its reservation. After 1987, with certain exceptions not here pertinent, an acquisition for such purposes was precluded unless the Governor of the State in which the land is located, along with the Secretary of the Interior, agrees that such acquisition would "be in the best interest of the Indian tribe and its members, and would not be detrimental to the surrounding community." 25 U.S.C. § 2719(b)(1)(A). Congress recognized the federal and state concerns and provided that both had to be satisfied by requiring action by the appropriate federal and state officials.

The separation of powers doctrine, implicit in the Constitution and well established in case law, forbids Congress from infringing upon the Executive Branch's ability to perform its traditional functions. The Tribes contend that the Governor's concurrence provision of IGRA is unconstitutional because it impermissibly reassigns the function of taking land in trust for Indians from the Executive Branch to state governors.

Although the Supreme Court has not announced a formal list of elements to be considered when determining whether a violation of the doctrine has taken place, it has consistently looked to at least two factors: (1) the governmental branch to which the function in question is traditionally assigned; and (2) the control of the function retained by the branch. In examining IGRA in light of these factors, we conclude that the provision requiring the Governor's concurrence does not violate the separation of powers doctrine.

The Property Clause of the Constitution states that "[t]he Congress shall have power to dispose of and make all needful Rules and Regulations respecting the Territory or other Property belonging to the United States." U.S. Const. art. IV, § 3, cl. 2. When land is acquired in trust for the Indians, Congress, and not the President, is constitutionally empowered to set the rules and regulations for its use.

Moreover, Congress enacted IGRA pursuant to its powers under the Indian Commerce Clause of the United States Constitution. Seminole Tribe of Florida v. Florida, 517 U.S. 44 (1996). "[T]he central function of the Indian Commerce Clause is to provide Congress with the plenary power to legislate in the field of Indian affairs." Cotton Petroleum Corp. v. New Mexico, 490 U.S. 163, 192 (1989).

Through 25 U.S.C. § 465, Congress has delegated its constitutionally derived power to acquire property for the Indians to the Secretary of the Interior. This delegation allows the Secretary to choose which land is to be taken into trust but only within the guidelines expressed by Congress. By adopting 25 U.S.C. § 2719, Congress has placed limitations on that delegation with regard to land acquired for gaming purposes without local approval. Congress has the authority to delegate limited legislative responsibilities to the Executive Branch.

The Tribes assert that the Governor's concurrence provision allows Congress to undermine the President's constitutionally assigned duty to execute the laws. By allowing a state governor to "veto" the recommendation of the Secretary of the Interior, the Tribes contend that IGRA unconstitutionally prevents the Executive Branch from interpreting and enforcing the laws of the United States. We disagree.

The Tribes' assertion that deciding when and how a law is to be applied is solely an Executive power has been considered and rejected by the Supreme Court on several occasions. Congress is constitutionally able to enact legislation which is contingent upon the approval of others. Such contingent legislation is not an invalid delegation of legislative authority and does not violate the separation of powers.

By placing a condition upon when and under what circumstances a provision of a statute goes into effect, Congress does not infringe upon the Executive's ability to execute that statute. By requiring local approval, Congress is exercising its legislative authority by providing what conditions must be met before a statutory provision goes into effect.

The district court rejected the "contingent legislation" analysis and held that the Executive's power was undermined. The court stated that with IGRA, "Congress delegate[d] to a state official the power to veto a favorable determination by an official of the Executive Branch." Confederated Tribes, 841 F. Supp. at 1488. The court held that the fact that the governor's concurrence is made after the Secretary's finding "impermissibly undermines" the executive's authority to take care that the laws are executed properly.

We conclude that the formality of which official acts first should not be determinative. The important consideration is that both officials must act. Regardless of who acts first, the effect of the provision is that the Governor must agree that gaming should occur on the newly acquired trust land before gaming can in fact take place. All parties agree that if the Secretary was prevented from considering taking land into trust for gaming purposes until the Governor approached him, there would be no constitutional problems. We see no difference between that situation and what the statute requires here.

The power delegated to the Secretary to acquire Indian trust lands for gaming purposes is a legislative power. The delegation is limited by a contingent requirement of State approval. This does not undermine an executive function, it merely places restrictions on the Executive's ability to choose which land is to be taken into trust for gaming purposes—a legislative function. We therefore hold that the governor concurrence provision of IGRA does not violate the separation of powers doctrine.

We now turn to the argument that the contested provision of IGRA violates the Appointments Clause. The Constitution provides that the President shall appoint "all . . . Officers of the United States, whose appointments are not herein otherwise provided for, and which shall be established by Law . . . ." U.S. Const. art. II, § 2, cl. 2.

The district court ruled that the Governor concurrence provision of IGRA violated the Appointments Clause by giving the Governor authority to act as an Officer of the United States without being appointed through proper channels.

We must inquire whether, under this statute, the Governor is performing duties reserved for officers of the United States. We hold that the authority vested in the state governors through IGRA does not rise to the level of that of an officer of the United States.

The district court determined that the Governor exercised significant authority under IGRA. Because the Governor was allowed to "veto" the findings of the Secretary, the district court ruled that this authority could only be exercised by a federal officer appointed by the President. We disagree.

We conclude that the authority exercised by the Governor under IGRA is also not significant enough to require appointment. Under IGRA, the Governor operates on an episodic basis concurring in or rejecting the suggestion of the Secretary for the Interior regarding gaming on lands within the Governor's state. The Governor is not given the sole authority for enforcing IGRA.

Instead, IGRA requires that the Secretary, a properly appointed Officer of the United States, determine the federal interests in the project. The Governor cannot have land taken in trust without the Secretary's approval.

No doubt, federal law provides the Governor with an opportunity to participate in the determination of whether gaming will be allowed on newly acquired trust land. But when the Governor responds to the Secretary's request for a concurrence, the Governor acts under state law, as a state executive, pursuant to state interests.

Our analysis under the "primary responsibility" aspect of our Appointments Clause analysis naturally flows from our decisions above. We hold that the Governor who exercises authority pursuant to state law does not have primary responsibility for protecting a federal interest.

IGRA does not allow a state governor to have land taken in trust by the Federal Government. Such a statute would no doubt run afoul of the Appointments Clause. Instead, IGRA is a piece of contingent legislation by which Congress conditions its consent to gaming on two events: (1) the Secretary determining that gaming on those lands would be beneficial to the tribe and not detrimental to the surrounding community; and (2) the Governor's concurring in that determination. Under this scheme, the Governor is not primarily responsible for having land taken into trust, Congress is.

It has long been the rule that Congress may delegate certain legislative functions to persons outside of the Legislative Branch of government. However, for such a delegation to be permissible, Congress must give specific guidelines to the delegee as to when the statute becomes effective. The general delegation of power to the Executive to take land into trust for the Indians is a valid delegation because Congress has decided under what circumstances land should be taken into trust and has delegated to the Secretary of the Interior the task of deciding when this power should be used. Prior to 1988, the Secretary had the sole authority to take land in trust for the purpose of gaming. The adoption of IGRA limited the delegation of congressional power by making that delegation conditional on the concurrence of state governors in certain circumstances.

Because Congress has given guidelines to the Secretary regarding when land can be taken in trust, the primary responsibility for choosing land to be taken in trust still lies with Congress. The Secretary is not empowered to act outside of the guidelines expressed by Congress. Similarly, the Governor has a limited role to play in the scheme.

The gubernatorial concurrence provision similarly meets the restrictions of the Appointments Clause. The Governor's authority under IGRA extends only to making a single determination—which is unlikely to arise often in a particular state. This narrow concurrence function does not impermissibly undermine Executive Branch authority, when exercised by the Governor as a state officer, in the performance of a state function, under an express delegation of congressional power to control Indian lands.

AFFIRMED.

MATCH-E-BE-NASH-SHE-WISH BAND OF POTTAWATOMI INDIANS v. ENGLER
304 F.3d 616 (6th Cir. 2002)

MERRITT, Circuit Judge.

This is an Indian gambling case in which the Plaintiff, Match-E-Be-Nash-She-Wish Band of Pottawatomi Indians (the "Tribe"), seeks to force the State of Michigan into negotiations for a casino pursuant to the Indian Gaming Regulatory Act (the "Act"), 25 U.S.C. § 2710(d). Because the Tribe has failed to satisfy the statutory prerequisite of owning Indian lands, see 25 U.S.C. § 2710(d)(3)(A), we hold that it is not entitled to relief under the Act. Accordingly, we AFFIRM the district court's grant of the State's motion to dismiss.

I. Statutory Framework

The Indian Gaming Regulatory Act establishes the framework by which a federally recognized tribe can require a State to enter into negotiations concerning the establishment of a casino. Under the Act, a federally recognized tribe initiates the process by making a formal request to enter into negotiations with the State. If the parties do not reach an agreement within 180 days after the request is made, or if the state fails to bargain in good faith, the tribe may invoke federal court jurisdiction to compel the State to negotiate in good faith. Under the Act, the federal court may order the state to conclude the contract within 60 days. If after that time a compact has not been concluded, the Act allows the Secretary of the Interior to authorize the operation of a casino apart from state authority. If the state asserts Eleventh Amendment immunity in the tribe's suit to compel negotiation, the tribe may go directly to the Secretary of the Interior, pursuant to 25 U.S.C. § 2710(d)(7)(B)(vii). See Seminole Tribe of Florida v. Florida, 11 F.3d 1016, 1029 (11th Cir.1994), aff'd, 517 U.S. 44, 116 S.Ct. 1114, 134 L.Ed.2d 252 (1996).

In addition, the Act defines the jurisdiction of the federal courts to hear such claims. Section 2710(d)(7)(A) of the Act limits federal court jurisdiction as follows:

> (A) The United States district courts shall have jurisdiction over—

> (i) any cause of action initiated by an Indian tribe arising from the failure of a State to enter into negotiations with the Indian tribe for the purpose of entering into a Tribal State compact under paragraph (3) [§ 2710(d)(3)(A)] or to conduct such negotiations in good faith.

The applicable part of § 2710(d)(3)(A) further provides:

> Any Indian tribe having jurisdiction over the Indian lands upon which a class III gaming activity is being conducted, or is to be conducted, shall request the State in which such lands are located to enter into negotiations for the purpose of entering into a Tribal State compact governing the conduct of gaming activities. Upon receiving such a request, the State shall negotiate with the Indian tribe in good faith to enter into such a compact.

25 U.S.C. § 2710(d)(3)(A). Lastly, "Indian lands" are defined by the Department of the Interior as:

(a) Land within the limits of an Indian reservation; or

(b) Land over which an Indian tribe exercises governmental power and that is either—

(1) Held in trust by the United States for the benefit of any Indian tribe or individual; or

(2) Held by an Indian tribe or individual subject to restriction by the United States against alienation.

25 C.F.R. § 502.12. Thus, under section 2710(d)(7)(A), which specifically refers to section 2710(d)(3)(A), federal jurisdiction seems to depend on "any Indian tribe having jurisdiction over the Indian lands upon which" a casino is to be "conducted."

II. Analysis

The Tribe is one of twelve federally recognized Indian tribes in the State of Michigan, and the only one that currently does not operate class III gaming. The Tribe owns lands in Michigan, but both parties agree that these lands are not "Indian lands" as defined by federal regulations. On September 2, 1999, the Tribe made a formal request to Michigan Governor Engler, asking that he enter into negotiations with the Tribe to open a casino. The State declined to negotiate, and after 180 days, the Tribe filed this action requesting that the district court order the State to conclude a gaming compact within 60 days, or in the alternative, dismiss the case on Eleventh Amendment state sovereign immunity grounds to allow the Tribe to go directly to the Secretary of the Interior. The State moved to dismiss on different grounds, arguing that the district court lacked jurisdiction under § 2710(d)(3)(A). Finding that the lands that the Tribe intends to use for gaming are not "Indian lands," and that ownership of Indian lands is a jurisdictional prerequisite to relief, the district court granted the State's motion.

Upon a close reading of the Act, we agree with the district court's holding. Having jurisdiction over land for the casino is a condition precedent to negotiations and federal jurisdiction. The plain language of § 2710(d)(3)(A) states that for federal courts to have jurisdiction, the tribe seeking relief must be an "Indian tribe having jurisdiction over the Indian lands upon which a Class III gaming activity is . . . to be conducted." Section (3)(A) describes not just an Indian tribe, but one that is in possession of land. As the district court found, "[t]he sentence is best read conjunctively—the party must be an Indian tribe and it must have land over which it exercises jurisdiction and it must be operating or contemplating the operation of a gaming casino." JA at 18. The Act thus establishes a jurisdictional prerequisite to federal court relief— that the tribe own "Indian lands" and that it plan to conduct the gaming on those lands.

The Tribe argues that the Court is required to address the Eleventh Amendment sovereign immunity question prior to the statutory issue because "Eleventh Amendment immunity issues are required to be addressed by the court before the merits of a case." Pet. Br. at 14. The Tribe is correct in reading this Court's prior decision in Wells v. Brown, 891 F.2d 591, 592-93 (6th Cir.1989), as requiring that jurisdictional issues be addressed prior to reaching the merits. However, in this case we are dismissing the case based on another jurisdictional issue—the issue of whether Indian tribes have standing to bring suits under the Indian Gaming Regulatory Act when they do not possess Indian lands. We are not addressing the merits of the case—whether the State of Michigan has fulfilled its obligation to negotiate in good faith and has reached an agreement within the required statutory time frame. Obviously, there may be more than one jurisdictional problem in a particular case, and that is true here.

Under § 2710(d)(3)(A), it is clear that the State does not have an obligation to negotiate with an Indian tribe until the tribe has Indian lands. The purposes of this requirement appear to be to ensure that the casino will be inside the borders of the State, to give the State notice of where it will be, and to require the tribe to have a place for the casino that has been federally approved. If the Indian tribe does not have any land in the State that can be used for a casino, why should the State waste its time negotiating about such a casino? In the absence of a location, the State would have no way to assess the environmental, safety, traffic, and other problems that such a casino could pose. The district court's holding that the State may insist that the Tribe fulfill the statutory prerequisites for negotiation before entering into negotiation is an entirely reasonable standing requirement.

As a result of the foregoing, we AFFIRM the district court's dismissal of this action.

Notes

1. The provisions in IGRA defining what is Indian land and when gaming can be conducted on newly-acquired land are complicated. Yet the general rule is simple: a tribe that had an existing reservation on October 17, 1988, can take into trust (and conduct gaming on) such land as is "within or contiguous to the boundaries of the reservation." If, however, the tribe wants to acquire non-contiguous land for gaming, the governor has the right to veto its plans.

The situation is different where a tribe has lost and then regained federal recognition and does not currently have any land. In such instances, the governor can make the state's wishes known, but the decision is up to the Secretary of the Interior. The restrictions on after-acquired land do not apply to land that is restored to a tribe, which usually happens through an act of Congress or a court order. IGRA also contains a few special provisions for certain identified tribes.

2. For a further look at when land can be used for Indian gaming, *see, e.g.,* David D. Waddell et al., *The Indian Gaming Regulatory Act's Dual Approval Process for Tribal Casinos on After-Acquired Land,* 3 Gaming L. Rev. 39 (1999); Matt Kitzi, Comment, *"Miami County Vice" & "Why Not the Wyandottes?": Two Tales of the Struggle to Bring New Indian Gaming Facilities to Kansas,* 68 UMKC L. Rev. 711 (2000); Jason D. Kolkema, Comment, *Federal Policy of Indian Gaming on Newly Acquired Lands and the Threat of State Sovereignty:*

Retaining Gubernatorial Authority Over the Federal Approval of Gaming on Off-Reservation Sites, 73 U. Det. Mercy L. Rev. 361 (1996).

Problem 37

An Indian tribe lost its federal recognition in 1954, only to have it restored in 1984. In 1998, Congress passed a statute adding certain non-contiguous lands to those listed in the 1984 law. When the tribe sought to open a casino on the 1998 lands, the governor balked, claiming that none of IGRA's exceptions were applicable. How should the court rule? *See Confederated Tribes of Coos, Lower Umpqua & Siuslaw Indians v. Babbitt*, 116 F. Supp. 2d 155 (D.D.C. 2000).

H. PROPER FORUM

GAVLE v. LITTLE SIX, INC.
555 N.W.2d 284 (Minn. 1996),
cert. denied, 524 U.S. 911 (1998)

GARDEBRING, Justice.

This case is a tort action filed by appellant Jill Gavle against Little Six, Inc. (LSI) and three of its officers. The suit alleged several tortious acts, including sexual harassment, pregnancy and racial discrimination, civil rights violations and other torts, arising from her employment with LSI.

The Shakopee Mdewakanton Sioux (Dakota) Community (the Community) is a federally recognized Indian tribe. LSI, a tribal business entity incorporated under the Community corporate ordinance in 1991, has issued one share of stock owned by all voting members of the Community. LSI is registered with the state of Minnesota as a foreign corporation transacting business within the state. LSI owns a gambling casino which is in Mdewakanton Indian Country.

LSI employed Gavle as a security guard from March 1992 to January 1993. Her job included duties at the casino (in Indian Country) and at LSI's temporary administrative offices at the Canterbury Downs complex in Shakopee, Minnesota. While Gavle's complaint details many incidents, alleged to be tortious, that occurred at the casino, it also contends that some of the allegedly tortious acts took place away from the casino, in or near Shakopee.

At the heart of this case is the issue of whether tribal business entities are subject to the application of state civil law in state court. Though it is sometimes said that state or federal courts are deprived of jurisdiction through the application of tribal sovereign immunity, the concept is more properly thought of as an affirmative defense, to be asserted by a tribe, tribal official or tribal entity as a bar to a particular lawsuit. Further, there are instances when a state or federal court may have jurisdiction over a matter involving a tribe or tribal entity, but may choose to stay its action, deferring to the concurrent jurisdiction of a tribal court. Thus, we must consider four related yet discrete issues:

a. Do Minnesota courts have jurisdiction over a tribal business entity in a civil tort matter involving actions occurring both within and outside of Indian country?

b. If Minnesota courts have such jurisdiction, must they stay their exercise of that jurisdiction in consideration of concurrent tribal court jurisdiction, under the doctrine of "infringement"?

c. If Minnesota courts have such jurisdiction and choose to exercise it, is such a suit nevertheless barred by tribal sovereign immunity?

d. If sovereign immunity would otherwise be available in this case, has it been waived by LSI's registration with Minnesota's Secretary of State as a foreign corporation?

To provide context for our discussion of these complex issues, we begin with some discussion of the historical relationship of Indian tribes to the state and federal governments. There are over 500 federally recognized tribes in the United States. Felix S. Cohen's commentary best describes the historical relationship between the United States and Indian tribes:

> Indian policy is marked by idealistic periods such as the first years of the Republic, when Congress pledged that 'the utmost good faith shall always be observed toward the Indian,' and the 1930's, when a commitment was made to revive tribal governments. Other eras were less altruistic: the period of removal, when hundreds of tribes were evicted forcibly from their ancestral lands; the allotment era, which resulted in the loss of ninety million acres of tribal lands; and the termination period, when more than one hundred tribes were stripped of the federal-tribal relationship and, in most cases, of their land.

Felix S. Cohen, Handbook of Federal Indian Law 49 (1982 ed.).

In general, the federal government has viewed the Native American more as a "political entity" than as a racial minority. Thus, until 1871 the United States recognized Indian tribes as possessed of the attributes of nationhood and, accordingly, concluded treaty agreements with them. For over one hundred years however, this country has systematically brought the various Indian tribes under the auspices of the federal government as "domestic dependent nations." Cherokee Nation v. Georgia, 30 U.S. (5 Pet.) 1, 17 (1831). In exchange for ceded land, the federal government gave Indian tribes special status that only Congress [could] remove. Indian tribes are not states; nevertheless, they possess a kind of sovereignty superior to that of states but inferior to that of the federal government. Thus, federally recognized tribes hold certain powers and privileges allowed other sovereigns; jurisdiction over certain judicial matters and sovereign immunity are two such characteristics.

In Worcester v. Georgia, 31 U.S. (6 Pet.) 515, 561 (1832), the U.S. Supreme Court held that, absent federal action, Indian tribes are not subject to the jurisdiction asserted over them by a state. Thus, absent a grant of federal authority, state courts have no jurisdiction over Indians, Indian tribes or other Indian entities.

In some states, including Minnesota, Congress has provided for state court criminal jurisdiction for matters occurring within Indian country, 18 U.S.C.

§ 1162 (1994), and for civil jurisdiction in actions to which Indians are parties. 28 U.S.C. § 1360 (1994). However, the reach of congressionally authorized state court jurisdiction provided in so-called Public Law 280 states does not extend to tribes or tribal entities.

In this matter, we find no federal prohibition on state court consideration of civil claims arising out of the acts of Indian business entities occurring outside of Indian country. Thus, we conclude that state courts have jurisdiction of Gavle's claims, including those arising within Indian country (although, of course, tribal courts may have jurisdiction as well).

As LSI notes, the governing federal principle in determining whether a court should exercise concurrent jurisdiction of the kind present here is one of deference. The doctrine at work is referred to both as "infringement" and as "preemption."

The Supreme Court views preemption as an additional means of protecting Indian sovereignty. White Mountain Apache Tribe v. Bracker, 448 U.S. 136, 143 (1980). The Court held that preemption "is not dependent on mechanical or absolute conceptions of state or tribal sovereignty, but has called for a particularized inquiry into the nature of the state . . . and tribal interests at stake . . . to determine whether . . . the exercise of state authority would violate federal law." Id. at 145.

Although the question is a close one, we conclude that the consideration by Minnesota state courts of whether LSI may assert the defense of sovereign immunity does not "undermine the authority of the tribal courts" nor "infringe on the ability of Indian tribes to govern themselves." Minnesota state courts have a strong interest in determining for our citizens the nature of the legal claims that they may assert against tribal business entities and the defenses that may be raised in response. [W]e choose to take jurisdiction only to establish Minnesota law on the issue of sovereign immunity for tribal business entities, in the hope that in so doing, we may avoid future disputes and pave the way to better understanding between the judicial systems.

It is settled law that tribes have the privilege of sovereign immunity, granted to them by Congress and existing at the sufferance of Congress. "Indian tribes enjoy immunity because they are sovereigns predating the Constitution, and because immunity is thought necessary to promote federal policies of tribal self-determination, economic development, and cultural autonomy." American Indian Agricultural Credit Consortium, Inc. v. Standing Rock Sioux Tribe, 780 F.2d 1374, 1378 (8th Cir. 1985).

[W]e conclude that the principal factors to be considered in determining whether tribal sovereign immunity extends to a tribal business entity are three: 1) whether the business entity is organized for a purpose that is governmental in nature, rather than commercial; 2) whether the tribe and the business entity are closely linked in governing structure and other characteristics; and 3) whether federal policies intended to promote Indian tribal autonomy are furthered by the extension of immunity to the business entity.

Applying these factors to the facts at hand, we conclude that, as a tribal business entity, organized for the general benefit of the Community and closely linked to the governing structure of the Community, LSI is entitled to sovereign immunity from civil action in state court.

While Gavle may argue that LSI's economic activity serves no governmental purpose, the U.S. Supreme Court, in California v. Cabazon Band of Mission Indians, 480 U.S. 202 (1987), relied upon the Bureau of Indian Affairs' view that "tribal bingo enterprises are an appropriate means by which tribes can further their economic self-sufficiency, the economic development of reservations and tribal self-determination." Id. at 217-18 n.21. This seems to recognize the unique role that Indian gaming serves in the economic life of here-to-fore impoverished Indian communities across this country.

The fact that the tribe was engaged in an enterprise private or commercial in character, rather than governmental, is not material to the availability of sovereign immunity. It is in such enterprises and transactions that the Indian tribes and the Indians need protection.

We also note that federal statutory law supports the notion that gaming activity is closely linked to the well-being of the tribe. All Indian gaming is conducted pursuant to the Indian Gaming Regulatory Act (IGRA), 25 U.S.C. §§ 2701-2721 (1994). Under the provisions of IGRA, only tribal entities can engage in Indian gaming and gaming by Indian tribes is recognized as a "means of promoting tribal economic development, self-sufficiency and strong tribal governments." 25 U.S.C. § 2702 (1994). Thus, as a matter of federal law, LSI must be a tribal entity in order to conduct gaming authorized by the statute. A mere commercial activity, incorporated by Indian individuals for the ostensible purpose of conducting gaming in Indian country, would be prohibited from doing so under federal law.

The basic tenet of Indian law [is] that tribal sovereign immunity may be waived, but such a waiver must be express and unequivocal and may not be implied. Santa Clara Pueblo v. Martinez, 436 U.S. 49, 58 (1978).

Affirmed.

KEITH, Chief Justice, dissenting in part.

I respectfully dissent. While I agree with the majority that state courts have concurrent jurisdiction with tribal courts in lawsuits of this type, I disagree with the majority's conclusion that for-profit, multi-million dollar private tribal businesses like Little Six, Inc. (LSI) may rely upon the same sovereign immunity defense to which the tribe itself is entitled. As the majority frames the issue, the question is whether LSI is a tribal entity "analogous to a governmental agency" which should benefit from the sovereign immunity defense, or whether LSI is in fact a "commercial business enterprise, instituted solely for the purpose of generating profits for its private owner." It seems to me that LSI clearly fits the latter definition. Accordingly, I would reverse the decision of the court of appeals and permit Gavle to pursue her various claims against LSI in state court.

The result of the majority's decision in this case is to grant total immunity from suit to a complex, for-profit corporate entity with hundreds of employees which transacts business both inside and outside Indian country. By extending the sovereign immunity defense to include LSI, the majority ignores the historical purpose of the sovereign immunity doctrine in this country as applied to Indian tribes, which is to grant special independent sovereign status to Indian tribes and their governmental bodies. In no way does LSI conform to the ordinary conception of a non-profit, governmental entity entrusted with promoting the welfare of its citizens: clearly, LSI is first and foremost a corporation engaged in a for-profit business venture for the purely financial benefit of its shareholders.

Non-Indians will undoubtedly think long and hard before entering into business relationships with Indian corporations that are immune from suit.

In conclusion, I believe that Gavle should be permitted to pursue her claims against LSI in state court because LSI is not an economic organization subordinate to the tribal government.

COYNE, Justice, dissenting.

That Indian tribes retain a unique sovereignty is beyond dispute. When the members of the tribe reside on the reservation and confine their commercial activities to the reservation, the State of Minnesota may not and does not subject the tribe's members to the state's tax laws. Brun v. Commissioner of Revenue, 549 N.W.2d 91 (Minn. 1996). When, however, the sovereign becomes a merchant, his license to carry on his commercial activity on foreign soil and to carry on his trade with the inhabitants of the foreign state is expressly subject to the laws of the licensor.

[I]f a commercial entity enters a commercial arena outside its own territory pursuant to a Minnesota certificate of authority to transact business as a foreign corporation, the foreign corporation is subject not merely to Minnesota's jurisdiction, but it is subject to the laws of Minnesota and the defense of sovereign immunity is, at the very least, of no more avail to the foreign corporation than it is to the state and its political subdivisions.

GAMING CORPORATION OF AMERICA v. DORSEY & WHITNEY
88 F.3d 536 (8th Cir. 1996)

MURPHY, Circuit Judge.

Gaming Corporation of America (Gaming Corp.) and Golden Nickel Casinos, Inc. (Golden Nickel) sued the Dorsey & Whitney law firm (Dorsey) in state court, alleging that Dorsey had violated state and federal law while representing a Native American tribe during a tribal casino management licensing process. Dorsey removed the case to federal district court, which remanded to the state court after dismissing several causes of action and concluding that no federal questions remained. Dorsey seeks review on the basis that federal questions remain and that the Indian Gaming Regulation Act (IGRA), 25 U.S.C. §§ 2701 et seq., completely preempts the field of Indian gaming regulation.

Gaming Corp. and Golden Nickel (the management companies) are Minnesota corporations involved in the management of gambling casinos. They have overlapping ownership and at one point agreed to merge. Dorsey is a large Minnesota law firm which actively represented Gaming Corp. for some time.

The Ho-Chunk Nation is a recognized Native American tribe in Wisconsin and was known as the Wisconsin Winnebago Tribe until 1994. The nation decided to open a casino and negotiated a tribal-state compact with the state of Wisconsin in 1992 as required by IGRA to allow it to conduct casino gaming. The nation desired to have Dorsey represent it during the process of developing the casino, and Golden Nickel hoped to receive the contract to manage it.

Dorsey had been representing Gaming Corp. but wished to begin representing the tribe. Since the management companies had overlapping ownerships, Dorsey wrote to the nation and Golden Nickel advising them of the possibility that the interests of the nation could be adverse to those of Golden Nickel and requesting their permission to represent the nation. The letter contained assurances that Dorsey would disclose no confidential information gained from its representation of Gaming Corp. In February 1992 Golden Nickel and the nation both consented to Dorsey's representation of the nation, and in July of that year Dorsey became special counsel to the nation under a contract approved by the Bureau of Indian Affairs. Dorsey states it ended its representation of Gaming Corp. in April 1993.

On October 7, 1992 Golden Nickel and the nation entered into an agreement under which Golden Nickel would manage the Ho-Chunk Casino to be constructed in Baraboo, Wisconsin. Golden Nickel was to provide financing for the construction and to maintain at all times a valid license from the Winnebago Gaming Commission, the nation's regulatory body for gaming. Golden Nickel obtained a provisional license from the tribal gaming commission in May 1993, which was valid until the end of that year. The casino was built and began operating.

In December 1993 Golden Nickel applied for a permanent license, and several months later Gaming Corp. also applied for a license. Dorsey assisted the tribal gaming commission in assessing the applications and was in charge of presenting evidence at several commission hearings held from December 1993 through May 1994.

After receiving the evidence, the tribal gaming commission denied the applications of both Gaming Corp. and Golden Nickel. The commission concluded that the individuals who owned all of Golden Nickel and much of Gaming Corp. had violated the terms of the provisional license. It found that one of the individuals had improperly attempted to influence a member of the nation's business committee to secure permanent license approval and that the testimony of the owners of the management companies was often contradictory and not credible. It also found that the management companies had failed to sever ties with certain individuals as required by the provisional license. The permanent license applications were denied in July 1994, and the management contract was terminated since Golden Nickel could not continue to operate the Ho-Chunk Casino without a license.

The management companies appealed the tribal commission's decision in the nation's courts and also brought suit against several parties in Wisconsin state court. On February 9, 1995, the management companies and the nation reached a settlement of their disputes. The nation agreed to pay the management companies $42 million in exchange for a release of all claims and for land controlled by the companies.

Meanwhile, the management companies filed this action against Dorsey in Minnesota state court on September 17, 1994. The management companies alleged numerous common law violations. The thrust of these counts was that Dorsey had made the licensing process unfair by intentionally or negligently making the management companies appear unsuitable. Dorsey allegedly used fraudulent and harassing tactics after having represented that the licensing process would be a mere formality. Several counts also alleged that Dorsey had violated a fiduciary duty owed to the management companies arising out of its representation of Gaming Corp. The management companies claimed damage in excess of $100 million.

Dorsey removed the case to federal court in October 1994. Its amended notice of removal stated that the complaint raised federal questions since many of the allegations related to gaming license proceedings governed by IGRA and since count IX arose under the Indian Civil Rights Act. Dorsey moved to dismiss the complaint in November on the basis that the management company causes of action were completely preempted by IGRA.

Complete preemption can arise when Congress intends that a federal statute preempt a field of law so completely that state law claims are considered to be converted into federal causes of action. To be completely preemptive, a statute must have "extraordinary pre-emptive power," a conclusion courts reach reluctantly. The term "complete preemption" is somewhat misleading because even when it applies, all claims are not necessarily covered.

Only those claims that fall within the preemptive scope of the particular statute, or treaty, are considered to make out federal questions, but the presence of even one federal claim gives the defendant the right to remove the entire case to federal court. Complete preemption therefore has jurisdictional consequences that distinguish it from preemption asserted only as a defense.

This apparently is the first time a federal appellate court has been asked to consider whether IGRA completely preempts state laws regulating gaming on Indian lands, but a number of federal courts have noted the strong preemptive force of IGRA. See, e.g., Tamiami Partners, Ltd. v. Miccosukee Tribe of Indians, 63 F.3d 1030 (11th Cir. 1995) ("The occupation of this field by [IGRA] is evidenced by the broad reach of the statute's regulatory and enforcement provisions and is underscored by the comprehensive regulations promulgated under the statute."); Cabazon Band of Mission Indians v. Wilson, 37 F.3d 430, 433-35 (9th Cir. 1994) (IGRA preempts state license fee based on wagers at Indian gaming facility).

Examination of the text and structure of IGRA, its legislative history, and its jurisdictional framework likewise indicates that Congress intended it completely preempt state law. There is a comprehensive treatment of issues affecting the regulation of Indian gaming. One of the stated purposes of IGRA is "the establishment of Federal standards for gaming on Indian lands." 25 U.S.C. § 2702(3). IGRA establishes a federal National Indian Gaming Commission (NIGC) to oversee regulation, licensing, background checks of key employees, and other facets of gaming. The NIGC can approve or disapprove license applications, management contracts, and tribal gaming ordinances. It can suspend gaming, impose fines, perform its own background checks of individuals, and request the aid of other federal agencies.

Short of a complete ban, states have virtually no regulatory role in class II gaming. See United States v. Sisseton-Wahpeton Sioux Tribe, 897 F.2d 358, 364 (8th Cir. 1990); see also Oneida Tribe of Indians of Wisconsin v. State of Wisconsin, 951 F.2d 757, 759 (7th Cir. 1991).

At no point does IGRA give a state the right to make particularized decisions regarding a specific class II gaming operation. States only may set the minimum licensing criteria for operators of class II facilities and impose some limitations on card parlor games. The statute itself reveals a comprehensive regulatory structure for Indian gaming. The only avenue for significant state involvement is through tribal-state compacts covering class III gaming.

The legislative history contains a strong statement about IGRA's preemptive force. The Senate committee report stated that "S. 555 [IGRA] is intended to expressly preempt the field in the governance of gaming activities on Indian lands. Consequently, Federal courts should not balance competing Federal, State, and tribal interests to determine the extent to which various gaming activities are allowed." S.Rep. No. 446, 100th Cong., 2d Sess. 6 (1988), reprinted in 1988 U.S.C.C.A.N. 3071, 3076. Although the Senate committee did not refer to the complete preemption doctrine, this statement demonstrates the intent of Congress that IGRA have extraordinary preemptive power, both because of its broad language and because it demonstrates that Congress foresaw that it would be federal courts which made determinations about gaming.

When Congress has chosen explicitly to grant jurisdiction to federal courts within a substantive statutory scheme, there may be special significance in terms of complete preemption.

Every reference to court action in IGRA specifies federal court jurisdiction. State courts are never mentioned. The broadest jurisdictional provision of IGRA specifically provides for appeal of final National Indian Gaming Commission decisions to "the appropriate Federal district court," and covers the most substantive functions of the commission, including imposing civil penalties and approving of tribal gaming ordinances and management contracts. 25 U.S.C. § 2714. Congress apparently intended that challenges to substantive decisions regarding the governance of Indian gaming would be made in federal courts.

The conclusion that IGRA completely preempts state law is reenforced when the statute is viewed in the context of Indian law. A long line of Supreme Court decisions illustrates the importance of the federal and tribal interests in Indian cases and the authority of Congress to protect those interests.

The management companies argue that their claims do not affect the nation's ability to regulate gaming because this action only involves non-Indian parties, but this overlooks the nation's relationship with Dorsey. The nation hired Dorsey to assist it in carrying out its congressionally authorized governmental responsibility to determine the suitability of the management companies.

All the claims in this case relate to Dorsey's representation of the nation during consideration by the Winnebago Gaming Commission of the management companies' permanent license applications, and all the claims must be examined individually in order to determine whether they fall into the scope of complete preemption.

The tribal licensing process is required and regulated by IGRA. Tribes must submit the results of the required background checks to the NIGC. A description of that licensing process must be included in the tribal ordinance or resolution necessary to begin class II and class III gaming. That ordinance or resolution must in turn be approved by the NIGC. 25 U.S.C. § 2710(b), (d). The question of licensing is therefore of "central concern to the federal statute," Franchise Tax Board v. Construction Laborers Vacation Trust, 463 U.S. 1, 25-26 (1983), and Congress unmistakably intended that tribes play a significant role in the regulation of gaming.

Congress struggled through several sessions to find a statutory scheme which would incorporate and balance the interests of tribes, states, and the federal government. The tribal-state compact was the device it ultimately chose. If a state, through its civil laws, were able to regulate the tribal licensing process outside the parameters of its compact with the nation, it would bypass the balance struck by Congress. Any claim which would directly affect or interfere with a tribe's ability to conduct its own licensing process should fall within the scope of complete preemption.

Dorsey argues that the management companies' causes of action are direct challenges to the outcome of the licensing process and therefore directly implicate governance of gaming. At one point the second amended complaint even refers to a "sham licensing process," and it contains numerous references to a "scheme" by Dorsey and the "members and elements" of the nation to use the licensing process to terminate the nation's relationship with the management companies.

The nation established the gaming commission as its licensing body under IGRA and prescribed the procedures to be used by the commission under the nation's gaming ordinance. The nation also has an appeals process which the management companies used in this action against the tribe. Nothing in the structure created by IGRA or in the tribal-state compact here suggests that the management companies should have the right to use state law to challenge the outcome of an internal governmental decision by the nation.

Tribes need to be able to hire agents, including counsel, to assist in the process of regulating gaming. As any government with aspects of sovereignty, a tribe must be able to expect loyalty and candor from its agents. If the tribe's relationship with its attorney, or attorney advice to it, could be explored in litigation in an unrestricted fashion, its ability to receive the candid advice essential to a thorough licensing process would be compromised. The purpose of Congress in requiring background checks could be thwarted if retained counsel were inhibited in discussing with the tribe what is learned during licensing investigations, for example. Some causes of action could have a direct effect on the tribe's efforts to conduct its licensing process even where the tribe is not a party.

Those causes of action which would interfere with the nation's ability to govern gaming should fall within the scope of IGRA's preemption of state law. In their briefs the parties concentrated their thinking on overall issues of preemption and did not explore the possibility that only some claims might fall within the preemptive scope of IGRA. In light of this, it would be unwise for us now to rule definitively on the individual claims, but some factors are likely to be of relevance to the development of the issues on remand.

The proposition that the preemptive scope of IGRA encompasses a claim is strong for claims that would intrude on the tribe's regulation of gaming or would require examination of the relationship between Dorsey and the nation. Inquiry into Dorsey's performance of its duty to the nation could threaten the tribe's legitimate interests, question the correctness of its licensing decisions, and risk influencing how counsel could serve tribes in the future. Under IGRA state law may not be applied to regulate the tribal licensing process, even if indirectly, unless a tribal-state compact so provides.

Potentially valid claims under state law are those which would not interfere with the nation's governance of gaming. To the extent a count alleges a violation of a duty owed to one of the management companies because of an attorney-client relationship or other independent duty, it may be a valid state law count. Resolution of such claims would not appear to involve attempted discovery of communications by the tribe to Dorsey or the merits of the licensing decision.

Any claims based on Dorsey's duty to the nation during the licensing process would appear to fall within the scope of IGRA's complete preemption.

Because federal questions remained, it was error to send this case back to state court. The order of the district court is reversed, and the case is remanded for further proceedings consistent with this opinion.

MASHANTUCKET PEQUOT GAMING ENTERPRISE v. RENZULLI
728 N.Y.S.2d 901 (Sup. Ct. 2001)

WHELAN, Justice.

Ordered that this unopposed motion by plaintiff for summary judgment in lieu of complaint is granted to the extent that plaintiff is awarded judgment against defendant in the sum of $5,160.00.

This matter, involving a gambling obligation incurred at the Foxwoods Resort Casino in Connecticut, appears to be a case of first impression in our Courts. The Court is asked to enforce a gambling contract. Ordinarily, such obligations are unenforceable at common law and, by statute, are void and illegal in our state. However, since these gambling debts were validly contracted in a sovereign Indian Nation, pursuant to a Tribal-State Compact governing the conduct of gaming activities, New York courts are bound to enforce the collection of such debts.

Plaintiff, Mashantucket Pequot Gaming Enterprise, doing business as Foxwoods Resort Casino, located in the State of Connecticut, is owned and operated by the Mashantucket Pequot Tribe, a sovereign Indian Nation. It is a federally recognized Indian tribe, which exercises sovereign rights pursuant to its constitution and by-laws. It operates the Foxwoods Casino in accordance with the provisions of the Indian Gaming Regulatory Act (hereinafter "IGRA"), 25 U.S.C. § 2701 et seq. and tribal law. These laws permit casino gaming, known as Class III gaming, pursuant to a Tribal-State Compact.

On or about September 16, 1994, defendant, a resident of Centereach, New York, applied for a $5,000 line of credit, which was extended to her. On or about December 13, 1995, defendant exercised her right to use the line of credit. At the time defendant applied for the line of credit, she was informed that any obligation incurred by her may be enforced in the Mashantucket Pequot Tribal Court (hereinafter "Tribal Court"). Since defendant's signature appears on the credit application, she thus consented to the Tribal Court's jurisdiction.

In exchange for receiving the line of credit, defendant signed two separate "markers" drawn on European American Bank in Centereach, New York. One "marker" was for $3,000 and the second "marker" was for $2,000. Upon presentation to the bank, the "markers" were returned to plaintiff for insufficient funds. During the next ensuing four years, plaintiff corresponded with defendant attempting to collect on defendant's obligation. Defendant did not respond.

On May 12, 2000, plaintiff filed a complaint against defendant with the Tribal Court, pursuant to the "Tribe" debt collection laws. Defendant neither appeared before the Tribal Court nor answered the complaint. On or about September 1, 2000, the Tribal Court entered a default judgment against defendant. On May 31, 2000, plaintiff commenced the instant action consisting of a single cause of action. Defendant was served pursuant to CPLR 308(2) and she neither appeared nor answered in said action. Plaintiff now seeks a default judgment against defendant pursuant to CPLR 3215 for the payment of money damages incurred as a result of the gambling debt.

Gambling in the State of New York is unlawful (see General Obligations Law § 5-401). Therefore, such a debt under New York law would be unenforceable. However, when a debt instrument is issued as the result of a gaming debt, the Courts of the State of New York will look to the laws of the jurisdiction where the debt was incurred to determine the validity and enforceability of such debt (see Aspinall's Club Ltd. v. Aryeh, 86 A.D.2d 428, 450 N.Y.S.2d 199 (1982); Intercontinental Hotels Corp. v. Golden, 15 N.Y.2d 9, 254 N.Y.S.2d 527, 203 N.E.2d 210 (1964)). A gambling debt will not be enforced in New York unless it was validly contracted in another jurisdiction and is enforceable there (see National Recovery Sys. v. Mazzei, 123 Misc.2d 780, 475 N.Y.S.2d 208 (1984)).

Title 52 of the General Statutes of Connecticut is similar to New York's General Obligation Law § 5-401 in that wagering contracts are void. Pursuant to General Statutes of Connecticut § 52-553, a contract to extend credit for gambling purposes is unenforceable.

However, in 1988 the United States Congress passed IGRA, which provides Indian Nations, i.e., plaintiff, the statutory basis to operate gaming activities on tribal land. Since Connecticut was found to be a state that regulates, rather than prohibits, gambling in general and games of chances in particular, the conducting of Class III gaming activities on the reservation is permissible under IGRA (see Mashantucket Pequot Tribe v. State of Connecticut, 737 F.Supp. 169 (D. Conn. 1990), aff'd 913 F.2d 1024 (2nd Cir.1990)).

Connecticut courts have examined the applicable Tribal-State Compact and have noted its detailed provisions covering the extension of credit and collection practices. Courts have concluded that judgments obtained in the Tribal Court are entitled to be enforced by the courts of Connecticut under the principle of comity (see Mashantucket Pequot Gaming Ent. v. DiMasi, 1999 Conn. Super Lexis 2584 (1999)), and that the Tribal-State Compact pre-empts the state law against the extension of credit for gambling (see Mashantucket Pequot Gaming Ent. v. Kennedy, 2000 Conn. Super Lexis 679 (2000)).

Here, the Tribal-State Compact provides a state sanctioned exception for an extension of credit for gaming purposes at the Foxwoods Resort Casino and General Statutes § 52-553 cannot bar enforcement of any resulting debt incurred.

Therefore, unlike the gambling obligations incurred at a casino in Aruba in National Recovery Sys. v. Zemnovitch, 250 A.D.2d 742, 672 N.Y.S.2d 911 (2nd Dept 1998), there has been a sufficient showing of enforceability of this particular gambling debt in Connecticut. The Court is cognizant of the holding in Intercontinental Hotels, supra, that "injustice would result if citizens of this State were allowed to retain the benefits of the winnings in a State where such gambling is legal, but to renege if they were losers" (id., at 15, 254 N.Y.S.2d 527, 203 N.E.2d 210).

Accordingly, the motion is granted.

Notes

1. Although the Minnesota Supreme Court chose not to go into them, the facts in *Gavle* are worth recounting. The Mystic Lake Casino, near Minneapolis-St. Paul, is one of North America's most successful tribal casinos. It is owned by the Shakopee Mdewakanton Sioux Community and operated by Little Six, Inc. ("LSI"), a corporation created by the tribe to operate the casino. Jill Gavle began working as a security guard at Mystic Lake in March 1992. In June 1992, she began having what the trial court discreetly termed "an intimate relationship" with Leonard Prescott, the Chairman and Chief Executive Officer of the casino. The affair resulted in an unplanned pregnancy. Gavle claimed that certain tribal officials were unhappy about her relationship with Prescott and purposely created a hostile working environment. She filed suit in 1994 against Prescott, LSI, and two LSI executives. Due to protracted motion practice, the case still had not gone to trial eight years after the pregnancy.

2. In *Renzulli*, the tribe was able to sue because it had entered into a compact with the state where it was located. Would the result have been different if the tribe had extended credit to the player in violation of its compact with the state? *See CBA Credit Services of North Dakota v. Azar*, 551 N.W.2d 787 (N.D. 1996).

3. The ability of tribes to use their sovereign immunity as a shield against breach of contract and tort claims has been a growing problem for non-Indian employees, gaming patrons, management companies, and even the tribes themselves (because of the reluctance of third parties to enter into contracts with them). Nevertheless, in *Kiowa Tribe of Oklahoma v. Manufacturing Technologies, Inc.*, 523 U.S. 751 (1998), the Supreme Court made it clear that only Congress can cut back on tribal immunity.

Problem 38

Following a falling out, a tribe instituted legal proceedings in tribal court against the former managers of its casino. In response, the managers sued the tribe in federal court. Must the federal action be stayed until the proceedings in tribal court are concluded? *See Basil Cook Enterprises, Inc. v. St. Regis Mohawk Tribe*, 117 F.3d 61 (2d Cir. 1997).

Chapter 9

INTERNET GAMING

A. OVERVIEW

The advent of the internet has brought gaming into every household that possesses a computer and a modem. Yet despite the web's growing popularity, many questions remain regarding the legality of internet gaming. In the absence of a comprehensive legislative solution, courts have been forced to provide answers on a case-by-case basis using pre-internet precedents.

B. PUBLIC REGULATION

PEOPLE v. WORLD INTERACTIVE GAMING CORPORATION
714 N.Y.S.2d 844 (Sup. Ct. 1999)

RAMOS, Justice.

This proceeding is brought by the Attorney General of the State of New York (the "Attorney General" or the "State of New York"), pursuant to New York's Executive Law § 63(12) and General Business Law Article 23-A, to enjoin the respondents, World Interactive Gaming Corporation ("WIGC"), Golden Chips Casino, Inc. ("GCC"), and their principals, officers, and directors from operating within or offering to residents of New York State gambling over the Internet. The State also seeks to enjoin respondents from selling unregistered securities in violation of New York State's General Business Law § 352 (also known as "The Martin Act").

The central issue here is whether the State of New York can enjoin a foreign corporation legally licensed to operate a casino offshore from offering gambling to Internet users in New York. At issue is Section 9(1) of Article 1 of the New York State Constitution which contains an express prohibition against any kind of gambling not authorized by the state legislature. The prohibition represents a deep-rooted policy of the state against unauthorized gambling (Intercontinental Hotels Corp. v. Golden, 18 A.D.2d 45, 238 N.Y.S.2d 33 [1st Dept. 1963]; rev'd on other grounds, 15 N.Y.2d 9, 254 N.Y.S.2d 527, 203 N.E.2d 210 [1964]).

WIGC is a Delaware corporation that maintains corporate offices in New York. WIGC wholly owns GCC, an Antiguan subsidiary corporation which acquired a license from the government of Antigua to operate a land-based casino. Through contracts executed by WIGC, GCC developed interactive software, and purchased computer servers which were installed in Antigua to allow users around the world to gamble from their home computers. GCC promoted its casino at its website, and advertised on the Internet and in a national gambling magazine. The promotion was targeted nationally and was viewed by New York residents.

In February 1998, the Attorney General commenced an investigation into the practices of WIGC. The investigation was prompted by an inquiry from the Texas State Securities Board which informed the Attorney General that WIGC was making unsolicited telephone calls to the public and disseminating offering materials for WIGC's securities. The petition alleges that respondents were attempting to sell what they termed a "private subscription offering," which consisted of 700,000 shares of "convertible preferred stock" at a price of $5.00 per share. The respondent's primary method of selling units of WIGC stock involved cold-calling prospective investors. The prospective investors were located throughout the United States, including New York. Respondents do not dispute that the calls originated from WIGC's headquarters in Bohemia, New York. At no time was this offering or the cold-calling registered with New York State as required by law.

During telephone solicitation, respondents claimed that investors would earn twenty percent (20%) annual dividend on their investment, twenty-five percent (25%) profit sharing and an initial public offering ("IPO") of WIGC's stock, which would likely take place within one year. Respondents also compared WIGC's projected stock price and earnings to that of land-based casinos. Respondents represented the profit margins of other Internet casinos at around eighty to eighty-five percent (80-85%). Respondents told investors that WIGC would earn an estimate of up to $100,000.00 in revenue during the first year. Respondents claimed that the investment was conservative.

Together, respondents sold approximately $1,843,665.00 worth of shares to approximately 114 investors throughout the country, including approximately $125,000.00 worth of shares to 10 New York state residents.

In June 1998, the Attorney General furthered its investigation by logging onto respondents' website, downloading the gambling software, and in July 1998, placed the first of several bets. Users who wished to gamble in the GCC Internet casino were directed to wire money to open a bank account in Antigua and download additional software from GCC's website. In opening an account, users were asked to enter their permanent address. A user which submitted a permanent address in a state that permitted land-based gambling, such as Nevada, was granted permission to gamble. Although a user which entered a state such as New York, which does not permit land-based gambling, was denied permission to gamble, because the software does not verify the user's actual location, a user initially denied access could easily circumvent the denial by changing the state entered to that of Nevada, while remaining physically in New York State. The user could then log onto the GCC casino and play virtual slots, blackjack or roulette. This raises the question if this constitutes a good faith effort not to engage in gambling in New York.

The Attorney General commenced this action pursuant to Executive Law § 63(12) and General Business Law Article 23-A. Petitioner seeks: (1) to enjoin respondents from conducting a business within the State of New York until they are properly registered with the Secretary of State to conduct business in New York; (2) to enjoin respondents from running any aspect of their Internet gambling business within the State of New York; (3) to be awarded restitution and damages to injured investors; and (4) to be awarded penalties and costs to the State of New York for violations of New York State's Martin

Act, federal and state laws prohibiting gambling, and New York State's Executive Law.

Personal Jurisdiction Over WIGC and GCC

Although at first glance Internet transactions may appear novel, "traditional jurisdictional standards have proved to be sufficient to resolve all civil Internet jurisdictional issues" (People v. Lipsitz, 174 Misc.2d 571, 578, 663 N.Y.S.2d 468 [Sup. Ct. New York County 1997]).

The Internet is a medium through which individuals may obtain and transmit text, sound, pictures, moving video images, and interactive services using various methods. The Internet also allows individuals to trade securities, execute banking transactions, purchase consumer merchandise, and engage in many other types of business and personal dealings not possible using more traditional means. What makes Internet transactions shed their novelty for jurisdictional purposes is that similar to their traditional counterparts, they are all executed by and between individuals or corporate entities which are subject to a court's jurisdiction.

Respondents in this case are clearly doing business in New York for purposes of acquiring personal jurisdiction. Although WIGC was incorporated in Delaware, WIGC operated its entire business from its corporate headquarters in Bohemia, New York. All administrative and executive decisions as well as the computer research and development of the Internet gambling website were made in New York. The cold-calls to investors to buy WIGC stock were made by WIGC agents employed and operating from this location. Thereafter, respondents sent the prospectus and other solicitation materials about Internet gambling from the Bohemia, New York location. WIGC's continuous and systematic contacts with New York established their physical presence in New York.

Moreover, even without physical presence in New York, WIGC's activities are sufficient to meet the minimum contacts requirement of International Shoe Co. v. Washington, 326 U.S. 310, 316, 66 S.Ct. 154, 90 L.Ed. 95 [1945]. The use of the Internet is more than the mere transmission of communications between an out-of-state defendant and a plaintiff within the jurisdiction.

WIGC and the other respondents are doing business in New York. They worked from New York in conjunction with another New York-based company, Imajix Studios, to design the graphics for their Internet gambling casino. From their New York corporate headquarters, they downloaded, viewed, and edited their Internet casino website. Furthermore, respondents engaged in an advertising campaign all over the country to induce people to visit their website and gamble. Knowing that these ads were reaching thousands of New Yorkers, respondents made no attempt to exclude identifiable New Yorkers from the propaganda. Phone logs from respondents' toll-free number (available to casino visitors on the GCC website) indicate that respondents had received phone calls from New Yorkers.

To establish in personam jurisdiction over GCC, the petitioner must show that GCC functioned merely as the alter ego of WIGC. The corporate form will be pierced only if one corporation is so controlled by the other as to be a mere agent, department or alter ego of the other.

The evidence indicates that GCC is a corporation completely dominated by WIGC. The use of the GCC casino website was handled from WIGC's corporate headquarters. All GCC top employees were hired by and reported to WIGC. At no time were any formalities observed to maintain a financial distinction between the two entities. Therefore, the corporate form is disregarded and GCC will be deemed an alter ego of WIGC.

Subject Matter Jurisdiction and Application of New York Law

Respondents argue that the Court lacks subject matter jurisdiction, and that Internet gambling falls outside the scope of New York state gambling prohibitions, because the gambling occurs outside of New York state. However, under New York Penal Law, if the person engaged in gambling is located in New York, then New York is the location where the gambling occurred [See, Penal Law § 225.00(2)]. It is irrelevant that Internet gambling is legal in Antigua. The act of entering the bet and transmitting the information from New York via the Internet is adequate to constitute gambling activity within the New York state.

Wide range implications would arise if this Court adopted respondents' argument that activities or transactions which may be targeted at New York residents are beyond the state's jurisdiction. Not only would such an approach severely undermine this state's deep-rooted policy against unauthorized gambling, it also would immunize from liability anyone who engages in any activity over the Internet which is otherwise illegal in this state. The respondents enticed users, including New York residents, to play in their casino.

The evidence demonstrates that respondents have violated New York Penal Law which states that "a person is guilty of promoting gambling . . . when he knowingly advances or profits from unlawful gambling activity" (Penal Law § 225.05). By having established the gambling enterprise, and advertised and solicited investors to buy its stock and to gamble through its on-line casino, respondents have "engage[d] in conduct which materially aids . . . gambling activity", in violation of New York law (Penal Law § 225.00(4) [which states "conduct includes but is not limited to conduct directed toward the creation or establishment of the particular game, contest, scheme, device . . . [or] toward the solicitation or inducement of persons to participate therein"]). Moreover, this Court rejects respondents' argument that it unknowingly accepted bets from New York residents. New York users can easily circumvent the casino software in order to play by the simple expedient of entering an out-of-state address. Respondents' violation of the Penal Law is that they persisted in continuous illegal conduct directed toward the creation, establishment, and advancement of unauthorized gambling. The violation had occurred long before a New York resident ever staked a bet.

Respondents' interstate use of the Internet to conduct their illegal gambling business violates federal law. As the legislative history behind the Wire Act indicates, the purpose of these federal controls is to aid the states in controlling gambling. Like a prohibited telephone call from a gambling facility, the Internet is accessed by using a telephone wire. When the telephone wire is connected to a modem attached to a user's computer, the user's phone line actually connects the user to the Internet server and then the user may log onto this illegal gambling website from any location in the United States. After selecting from the multitude of illegal games offered by respondent, the information is transmitted to the server in Antigua. Respondents' server then transmits betting information back to the user which is against the Wire Act. The Internet site creates a virtual casino within the user's computer terminal. By hosting this casino and exchanging betting information with the user, an illegal communication in violation of the Wire Act and the Travel Act has occurred.

Respondents attempt to circumvent federal law by asserting that none of these statutes apply to the operation of an Antiguan casino. Moreover, they allege the federal government has not explicitly ruled on Internet gambling, and therefore it is an unregulated field. Respondents disregard that the Interstate Commerce Clause gives Congress the plenary power to regulate illegal gambling conducted between a location in the United States and a foreign location. (See Champion v. Ames, 188 U.S. 321, 334, 23 S.Ct. 321, 47 L.Ed. 492 [1903].)

This Court further finds that respondents also violated the Martin Act's prohibition against the use of deception, misrepresentations, or concealment in the sale of securities (See, GBL § 352(1)).

Remedies

This Court finds the request for an injunction warranted, and directs fixing of the amount be incorporated in an order to be settled.

As for the Attorney General's request for restitution, penalties, and costs, which are available under Executive Law § 63(12) and GBL § 353(3), this Court finds the circumstances warrant awarding them in this case.

Respondents are further directed not to destroy any personal or business records relating to this matter.

UNITED STATES v. COHEN
260 F.3d 68 (2d Cir. 2001),
cert. denied, 536 U.S. 922 (2002)

KEENAN, District Judge.

BACKGROUND

In 1996, the Defendant, Jay Cohen ("Cohen") was young, bright, and enjoyed a lucrative position at Group One, a San Francisco firm that traded in options and derivatives. That was not all to last, for by 1996 the Internet revolution was in the speed lane. Inspired by the new technology and its potential, Cohen decided to pursue the dream of owning his own e-business. By year's end he had left his job at Group One, moved to the Caribbean island of Antigua, and had become a bookmaker.

Cohen, as President, and his partners, all American citizens, dubbed their new venture the World Sports Exchange ("WSE"). WSE's sole business involved bookmaking on American sports events, and was purportedly patterned after New York's Off-Track Betting Corporation. WSE targeted customers in the United States, advertising its business throughout America by radio, newspaper, and television. Its advertisements invited customers to bet with WSE either by toll-free telephone or by internet.

WSE operated an "account-wagering" system. It required that its new customers first open an account with WSE and wire at least $300 into that account in Antigua. A customer seeking to bet would then contact WSE either by telephone or internet to request a particular bet. WSE would issue an immediate, automatic acceptance and confirmation of that bet, and would maintain the bet from that customer's account.

In one fifteen-month period, WSE collected approximately $5.3 million in funds wired from customers in the United States. In addition, WSE would typically retain a "vig" or commission of 10% on each bet. Cohen boasted that in its first year of operation, WSE had already attracted nearly 1,600 customers. By November 1998, WSE had received 60,000 phone calls from customers in the United States, including over 6,100 from New York.

In the course of an FBI investigation of offshore bookmakers, FBI agents in New York contacted WSE by telephone and internet numerous times between October 1997 and March 1998 to open accounts and place bets. Cohen was arrested in March 1998 under an eight-count indictment charging him with conspiracy and substantive offenses in violation of 18 U.S.C. § 1084 ("§ 1084"). That statute reads as follows:

> (a) Whoever being engaged in the business of betting or wagering knowingly uses a wire communication facility for the transmission in interstate or foreign commerce of bets or wagers or information assisting in the placing of bets or wagers on any sporting event or contest, or for the transmission of a wire communication which entitles the recipient to receive money or credit as a result of bets or wagers, or for information assisting in the placing of bets or wagers, shall be fined under this title or imprisoned not more than two years, or both.

> (b) Nothing in this section shall be construed to prevent the transmission in interstate or foreign commerce of information for use in news reporting of sporting events or contests, or for the transmission of information assisting in the placing of bets or wagers on a sporting event or contest from a State or foreign country where betting on that sporting event or contest is legal into a State or foreign country in which such betting is legal.

In the conspiracy count Cohen was charged with violating all three prohibitive clauses of § 1084(a) ((1) transmission in interstate or foreign commerce of bets or wagers, (2) transmission of a wire communication which entitles the recipient to receive money or credit as a result of bets or wagers, (3) information assisting in the placement of bets or wagers).

Cohen was convicted on all eight counts on February 28, 2000 after a ten-day jury trial before Judge Thomas P. Griesa. The jury found in special interrogatories that Cohen had violated all three prohibitive clauses of § 1084(a). Judge Griesa sentenced Cohen on August 10, 2000 to a term of twenty-one months' imprisonment. He has remained on bail pending the outcome of this appeal.

DISCUSSION

I. Corrupt Motive

Cohen appeals his conspiracy conviction on the grounds that the district court instructed the jury to disregard his alleged good-faith belief about the legality of his conduct. He argues that People v. Powell, 63 N.Y. 88 (1875), requires proof of a corrupt motive for any conspiracy to commit an offense that is malum prohibitum, rather than malum in se. We disagree, and we hold that whatever remains of Powell does not apply to this case.

II. The Safe Harbor Provision

Cohen appeals the district court for instructing the jury to disregard the safe-harbor provision contained in § 1084(b). That subsection provides a safe harbor for transmissions that occur under both of the following two conditions: (1) betting is legal in both the place of origin and the destination of the transmission; and (2) the transmission is limited to mere information that assists in the placing of bets, as opposed to including the bets themselves.

The district court ruled as a matter of law that the safe-harbor provision did not apply because neither of the two conditions existed in the case of WSE's transmissions. Cohen disputes that ruling and argues that both conditions did, in fact, exist. He argues that betting is not only legal in Antigua, it is also "legal" in New York for the purposes of § 1084. He also argues that all of WSE's transmissions were limited to mere information assisting in the placing of bets. We agree with the district court's rulings on both issues.

A. "Legal" Betting

There can be no dispute that betting is illegal in New York. New York has expressly prohibited betting in both its Constitution, see N.Y. Const. art. I, § 9 ("no . . . bookmaking, or any other kind of gambling [with certain exceptions pertaining to lotteries and horseracing] shall hereafter be authorized or allowed within this state"), and its General Obligations Law, see N.Y. Gen. Oblig. L. § 5-401 ("[a]ll wagers, bets or stakes, made to depend on any race, or upon any gaming by lot or chance, or upon any lot, chance, casualty, or unknown or contingent event whatever, shall be unlawful"); see also Cohen v. Iuzzini, 25 A.D.2d 878, 270 N.Y.S.2d 278, 279 (1966) (ruling that the predecessor statute to N.Y. Gen. Oblig. L. § 5-401 (N.Y. Penal L. § 991) did not apply to bets executed at recognized pari-mutuel tracks). Nevertheless, Cohen argues that Congress intended for the safe-harbor provision in § 1084(b) to exclude only those transmissions sent to or from jurisdictions in which betting was a crime. Cohen concludes that because the placing of bets is not a crime in New York, it is "legal" for the purposes of § 1084(b).

By its plain terms, the safe-harbor provision requires that betting be "legal," i.e., permitted by law, in both jurisdictions. See § 1084(b); see also Black's Law Dictionary 902 (7th ed. 1999); Webster's 3d New Int'l Dictionary 1290 (1993). The plain meaning of a statute "should be conclusive, except in the rare cases in which the literal application of a statute will produce a result demonstrably at odds with the intentions of its drafters." United States v. Ron

Pair Enters., Inc., 489 U.S. 235, 242, 109 S.Ct. 1026, 103 L.Ed.2d 290 (1989) (alteration and internal quotation marks omitted). This is not the rare case.

Although, as Cohen notes, the First Circuit has stated that Congress "did not intend [for § 1084] to criminalize acts that neither the affected states nor Congress itself deemed criminal in nature," it did not do so in the context of a § 1084 prosecution. See Sterling Suffolk Racecourse Ltd. P'ship v. Burrillville Racing Ass'n, 989 F.2d 1266, 1273 (1st Cir.1993). Instead, that case involved a private bid for an injunction under RICO (18 U.S.C. § 1961 et seq.) and the Interstate Horseracing Act (15 U.S.C. §§ 3001-07) ("IHA"). It does not stand for the proposition that § 1084 permits betting that is illegal as long as it is not criminal.

In Sterling, the defendant was an OTB office in Rhode Island that accepted bets on horse races from distant tracks and broadcasted the races. The office typically obtained the various consents required under the IHA, i.e., from the host track, the host racing commission, and its own racing commission. However, it would often neglect to secure the consent of the plaintiff, a live horse-racing track located within the statutory sixty-mile radius from the OTB office. The plaintiff sought an injunction against the OTB office under RICO, alleging that it was engaged in a pattern of racketeering activity by violating § 1084 through its noncompliance with the IHA.

The Sterling court affirmed the district court's denial of the RICO injunction. It noted first that because the OTB office's business was legitimate under all applicable state laws, it fell under the safe-harbor provision in § 1084(b).

Betting is illegal in New York, and thus the safe-harbor provision in § 1084(b) cannot not apply in Cohen's case as a matter of law.

B. Transmission of a Bet, Per Se

Cohen appeals the district court's instructions to the jury regarding what constitutes a bet per se. Cohen argues that under WSE's account-wagering system, the transmissions between WSE and its customers contained only information that enabled WSE itself to place bets entirely from customer accounts located in Antigua. He argues that this fact was precluded by the district court's instructions. We find no error in those instructions.

Judge Griesa repeatedly charged the jury as follows:

> If there was a telephone call or an Internet transmission between New York and [WSE] in Antigua, and if a person in New York said or signaled that he or she wanted to place a specified bet, and if a person on an internet device or a telephone said or signaled that the bet was accepted, this was the transmission of a bet within the meaning of Section 1084. Congress clearly did not intend to have this statute be made inapplicable because the party in a foreign gambling business deemed or construed the transmission as only starting with an employee or an internet mechanism located on the premises in the foreign country.

Most of the cases that Cohen cites in support of the proposition that WSE did not transmit any bets involved problems pertaining either to proof of the acceptance of transmitted bets, see United States v. Truesdale, 152 F.3d 443 (5th Cir.1998), McQuesten v. Steinmetz, 73 N.H. 9, 58 A. 876 (1904), Lescallett v. Commonwealth, 89 Va. 878, 17 S.E. 546 (1893), or to proof of the locus of a betting business for taxation purposes, see Saratoga Harness Racing, Inc. v. City of Saratoga Springs, 55 A.D.2d 295, 390 N.Y.S.2d 240 (1976).

No such problems existed in this case. This case was never about taxation, and there can be no dispute regarding WSE's acceptance of customers' bet requests. For example, a March 18, 1998 conversation between Spencer Hanson, a WSE employee, and a New York-based undercover FBI agent occurred as follows:

> Agent: Can I place a bet right now?
>
> Hanson: You can place a bet right now.
>
> Agent: Alright, can you give me the line on the um Penn State/ Georgia Tech game, it's the NIT [T]hird Round game tonight.
>
> Hanson: Its [sic] Georgia Tech minus 7 1/2, total is 147.
>
> Agent: Georgia [T]ech minus 7 1/2, umm I wanna take Georgia Tech. Can I take 'em for 50?
>
> Hanson: Sure.

WSE could only book the bets that its customers requested and authorized it to book. By making those requests and having them accepted, WSE's customers were placing bets. So long as the customers' accounts were in good standing, WSE accepted those bets as a matter of course.

Moreover, the issue is immaterial in light of the fact that betting is illegal in New York. Section 1084(a) prohibits the transmission of information assisting in the placing of bets as well as the transmission of bets themselves. This issue, therefore, pertains only to the applicability of § 1084(b)'s safe-harbor provision. As we have noted, that safe harbor excludes not only the transmission of bets, but also the transmission of betting information to or from a jurisdiction in which betting is illegal. As a result, that provision is inapplicable here even if WSE had only ever transmitted betting information.

III. Cohen's Mens Rea

Cohen appeals the district court's instruction to the jury regarding the requisite mens rea under § 1084. Section 1084 prohibits the "knowing" transmission of bets or information assisting in the placing of bets. The district court instructed the jurors that to convict, they needed only to find that Cohen "knew that the deeds described in the statute as being prohibited were being done," and that a misinterpretation of the law, like ignorance of the law, was no excuse.

Cohen argues that he lacked the requisite mens rea because (1) he did not "knowingly" transmit bets, and (2) he did not transmit information assisting in the placing of bets or wagers to or from a jurisdiction in which he "knew" betting was illegal. He contends that in giving its jury charge, the district court improperly instructed the jury to disregard that argument.

The district court was correct; it mattered only that Cohen knowingly committed the deeds forbidden by § 1084, not that he intended to violate the statute. See Bryan v. United States, 524 U.S. 184, 193, 118 S.Ct. 1939, 141 L.Ed.2d 197 (1998). Cohen's own interpretation regarding what constituted a bet was irrelevant to the issue of his mens rea under § 1084.

In any event, Cohen is culpable under § 1084(a) by admitting that he knowingly transmitted information assisting in the placing of bets. His beliefs regarding the legality of betting in New York are immaterial.

IV. Rule of Lenity

Cohen argues that the rule of lenity, a concept grounded in due process, requires a reversal of his convictions. According to Cohen, § 1084 is too unclear to provide fair warning of what conduct it prohibits. In particular, he contends that the statute does not provide fair warning with respect to (1) whether the phrase "bet or wager" includes account wagering, (2) whether "transmission" includes the receiving of information as well as the sending of it, and (3) whether betting must be legal or merely non-criminal in a particular jurisdiction in order to be considered "legal" in that jurisdiction. None of these contentions has any merit.

The rule of lenity applies where there exists a "grievous ambiguity" in a statute, see Huddleston v. United States, 415 U.S. 814, 831, 94 S.Ct. 1262, 39 L.Ed.2d 782 (1974), such that "after seizing everything from which aid can be derived, [a court] can make no more than a guess as to what Congress intended." Reno v. Koray, 515 U.S. 50, 65, 115 S.Ct. 2021, 132 L.Ed.2d 46 (1995).

We need not guess whether the provisions of § 1084 apply to Cohen's conduct because it is clear that they do. First, account-wagering is wagering nonetheless; a customer requests a particular bet with WSE by telephone or internet and WSE accepts that bet. WSE's requirement that its customers maintain fully-funded accounts does not obscure that fact.

Second, Cohen established two forms of wire facilities, Internet and telephone, which he marketed to the public for the express purpose of transmitting bets and betting information. Cohen subsequently received such transmissions from customers, and, in turn, sent such transmissions back to those customers in various forms, including in the form of acceptances and confirmations. No matter what spin he puts on "transmission," his conduct violated the statute.

Third, it is clear to lawyer and layman alike that an act must be permitted by law in order for it to be legal. See Black's Law Dictionary 902 (7th ed. 1999); Webster's 3d New Int'l Dictionary 1290 (1993). It is also clear that betting is not permitted under New York law. See N.Y. Const. Art. I, § 9(1); N.Y. Gen. Oblig. L. § 5-401. Where a state's statute declares an act to be "unlawful," see N.Y. Gen. Oblig. L. § 5-401 ("all wagers . . . shall be unlawful"), that act is not "legal," see § 1084(b). The safe-harbor provision is unambiguous, and is not applicable in Cohen's case.

V. Aiding-and-Abetting Liability

Cohen also argues that he could not have been liable under [18 U.S.C.] § 2 for acts committed after his arrest.

Cohen could still have been liable for aiding and abetting the acts charged in Counts Seven and Eight of his indictment, even though those counts pertained to transmissions that occurred after his arrest. Cohen was a moving force behind WSE's entire operation, which continued to function after his arrest. Cohen retained his position as President of WSE while on bail after his arrest.

Although Cohen purportedly did not "deal with daily operations" at WSE after his arrest, he also made no effort to curtail those operations. In fact, he benefitted from them by receiving a salary, his travel expenses, and his legal fees from WSE. He clearly was still in a position to cause others, willfully, to commit acts that would have been crimes had he himself committed them. He could, therefore, have been found liable for aiding and abetting WSE's ongoing violation of § 1084.

VI. Deposition of a Foreign Witness

Cohen argues that the district court should have granted his motion, pursuant to Fed.R.Crim.P. 15(a), to adjourn his trial for one week so that he could depose a witness in Antigua. The witness, an Antiguan government official, was unavailable for trial due to medical reasons.

Cohen states that the witness' testimony was material to two issues at his trial: (1) whether Cohen had a corrupt motive; and (2) whether Cohen believed that he was transmitting mere information assisting in the placing of bets rather than any bets themselves. Cohen states that the witness would have testified to the advice she gave him based upon her experience as an Antiguan official and upon her alleged conversations with U.S. Government officials.

As this Court has already discussed, neither of these two issues was relevant to the question of Cohen's guilt under § 1084.

CONCLUSION

For the reasons set forth above, the judgment of the district court is AFFIRMED.

UNITED STATES v. $734,578.82 IN UNITED STATES CURRENCY
286 F.3d 641 (3d Cir. 2002)

McKEE, Circuit Judge.

American Sports Ltd. and Intercash Ltd. I.O.M appeal the district court's grant of summary judgment in favor of the government and the resulting final order of civil forfeiture of United States currency seized from bank accounts established in relation to an illegal gambling business. See 18 U.S.C. § 1955. For the reasons that follow, we will affirm.

I. FACTUAL BACKGROUND

Intercash Ltd. I.O.M. ("IOM") is a corporation operating in, and organized under the laws of, the Isle of Man. American Sports Limited ("ASL") and related companies are owned and operated by Gary Bowman. ASL and its related companies operate in the United Kingdom under valid licenses issued by that government. Intercash Financial Services, Ltd. ("IFS Canada"), is a Canadian corporation located in Toronto, Canada. Ivan and Juliana Olenych are members of the Board of Directors of IFS Canada. In the government's view, IOM and IFS Canada are the same entity. IFS (i.e., IOM and IFS Canada) was established with funds provided by Bowman and one of his companies, American Sports Betting Service. American Sports Betting Service is located in England.

Intercash Financial Services is a New Jersey corporation ("IFS-NJ") operating in South Bound Brook, New Jersey. It was incorporated in New Jersey in 1995 and its corporate records list Michael Sydor, Dennis Pokoyoway and Yar Jacobs as its district managers. IFS-NJ had three telephone numbers, but it was not listed in the New Jersey telephone books or Yellow Pages. Moreover, there are no hours of operation posted for IFS-NJ anywhere in the building where the office is located. Entry to IFS-NJ's office is controlled by an electronic buzzer inside the office. Telephone calls to the office are not answered in a manner that informs the caller that he/she has reached the offices of IFS-NJ. Rather, the phone is merely answered with a "hello."

Bowman promoted his companies on the Internet in advertisements claiming that the companies provided recreational betting services and accepted wagers on sporting events throughout the world. These advertisements detailed the wagering services that Bowman and his companies provided and explained that ASL provided a betting service and accepted wagers on most sporting events throughout the world. Most of Bowman's business was derived from North American sports such as professional and college football and basketball games.

Bowman's advertisements also explained how to remit money, set up an account and place bets. Funds were to be remitted via Western Union wire transfer for deposit in Fleet Bank, N.A., account number 2753-10-3191 to establish accounts and to place bets. ASL is the holder and beneficiary of that Fleet Bank account. Once a bettor established an account, he/she could then call Bowman's company in England via international toll-free telephone numbers to confirm the deposits and to immediately begin gambling on various sporting events around the world.

Dennis Pokoyoway was IFS-NJ's district manager, ran its daily operations, and deposited funds received from bettors into Fleet Bank accounts 2753-10-4767 and 2753-10-3191. IFS-NJ received wire transfers of funds, ranging from $20 to at least $2,000, from bettors throughout the United States. The wire transfers were typically completed through Western Union where IFS Canada/IOM maintained account number APH081580. IFS-NJ received and processed the wire transfers.

After IFS-NJ received a wire transfer, it deposited those funds into accounts maintained for the benefit of IFS Canada/IOM and ASL, including Fleet Bank account number 27523-10-4767, maintained in the name of and/or for the benefit of IFS Canada; and Fleet Bank account number 2753-10-3191, maintained in the name of and/or for the benefit of ASL.

Large sums of money were regularly transferred from Fleet Bank account number 2753-10-4767 to 2753-10-3191. For example, in October of 1996, approximately $1.2 million was transferred, and another $550,000 was transferred in November of 1996. Funds in account number 2753-10-3191 were paid out to bettors all over the United States.

IFS-NJ also tallied the funds received on an hourly basis and sent the hourly tallies to Bowman in England. Bettors were therefore able to call ASL and other Bowman betting companies using the aforementioned international telephone numbers to confirm their deposits. This allowed them to place bets soon after wiring money to IFS-NJ.

Two examples cited by the government illustrate IFS-NJ's role in Bowman's gambling operations. The first is the case of Wisconsin bettor, Brian Taff, who sent $32,000 to IFS-NJ via Western Union. Taff's telephone records revealed calls to Bowman in Manchester, England, and investigators subsequently discovered documents related to sports-betting in his garbage. The government argues that it is reasonable to conclude that Taff wired the $32,000 to IFS-NJ so that he could place bets with Bowman. These funds were included in an accounting that IFS-NJ subsequently sent to Bowman. According to the government, Taff's funds were eventually deposited into one of the accounts at Fleet Bank maintained by either ASL or IFS-NJ.

The government's second example is a confidential source that wired Western Union transfers to IFS-NJ to place sports bets of more than $25,000 during 1995. Although the confidential source was aware that the bets were forwarded to a gambling house in England, the source knew that his/her funds went through accounts handled by IFS-NJ.

On December 3, 1998, Pokoyoway (IFS-NJ's district manager), pled guilty in state court in New Jersey to charges of promoting gambling in the third degree, and conspiracy to promote gambling in the third degree. In doing so, he admitted that from August 1995 to approximately December 15, 1996, he deposited funds from Western Union wire transfers into Fleet Bank accounts owned by IFS and ASL. Pokoyoway told law enforcement agents that his duties for IFS-NJ included compiling the aforementioned hourly totals of all checks received by IFS-NJ and then informing IFS and Bowman (in England) of the amount of the deposits. According to Pokoyoway, IFS-NJ received well over $1,000 a day between August 1995 and December 15, 1996. He estimated that IFS-NJ averaged twenty to thirty Western Union wire transfers per day, for a daily total of $4,000 to $5,000. He also acknowledged that he knew that the incoming funds were derived from sports gambling.

II. DISTRICT COURT PROCEEDINGS

This litigation began when FBI agents executed a warrant authorizing the search of IFS-NJ's office, and seizure of the contents of Fleet Bank Account number 2753-10-4647, in the name of and/or for the benefit of, IOM and ASL. The warrant also authorized the seizure of all funds received by Fleet Bank for three days after service of the warrant. Thereafter, agents executed a warrant authorizing seizure of the contents of Fleet Bank account number 2753-10-3191, maintained in the name of, and/or for the benefit of, ASL. This warrant also authorized seizure of funds deposited into the account for the three days following execution of the warrant.

Pursuant to these warrants, agents seized $77,660.62 from account number 2753-10-4767 and $268,426.59 from account number 2753-10-3191. The next day, agents obtained a warrant to seize Western Union account number APH081580 in the name of, and/or for the benefit of, IOM. Agents seized an additional $243,491.61 from that account.

Approximately three years later, the government filed the instant civil in rem forfeiture action against those funds. Count I of the complaint alleged criminal violations of 18 U.S.C. § 1955, and sought civil forfeiture pursuant to 18 U.S.C. § 1955(d). Count II alleged violations of 18 U.S.C. § 1956, and sought forfeiture pursuant to 18 U.S.C. § 981. Count III alleged violations of 18 U.S.C. § 1957, and sought forfeiture pursuant to 18 U.S.C. § 981.

Following receipt of notice of the forfeiture action, IOM filed a verified claim to the property seized from Fleet Bank account number 2753-10-4647 and Western Union account number APH081580. ASL filed a verified claim for the property seized from Fleet account number 2753-10-3191. The court filed a Final Order of Forfeiture on July 24, 2000, and this appeal by IOM and ASL (hereinafter collectively referred to as "Claimants") followed.

III. DISCUSSION

A. Burden of Proof in § 1955(d) Civil Forfeiture Proceedings.

The government bears the initial burden in a forfeiture proceeding under § 1955. See United States v. On Leong Chinese Merchants' Ass'n Bldg., 918 F.2d 1289 (7th Cir.1990).

If the government satisfies its burden of proof, and the party opposing forfeiture fails to establish that the property is not subject to forfeiture, forfeiture will be ordered regardless of the culpability of the claimant. This disjuncture between criminal culpability and exposure to forfeiture arises from a legal fiction. "Traditionally, forfeiture actions have proceeded upon the fiction that inanimate objects themselves can be guilty of wrongdoing." Id. (quoting United States v. U.S. Coin and Currency, 401 U.S. 715, 719, 91 S.Ct. 1041, 28 L.Ed.2d 434 (1971)). Therefore, "the object itself is the formal defendant." Id. Thus, "forfeiture can be ordered even in the absence of any wrongdoing on the claimant's part." Id.

B. The Government's Showing of Probable Cause.

18 U.S.C. § 1955(b)(1)(i) first looks to relevant state law to determine whether a given activity constitutes gambling. Here, the alleged illegal activity occurred in New Jersey. Therefore, "[t]he relevant burden of proof requires merely that the government establish probable cause to believe that [New Jersey] gambling laws were being violated." On Leong, 918 F.2d at 1293.

The relevant New Jersey law here is set forth at N.J.S.A. 2C:37-2. That statute makes it a crime to engage in "promoting gambling," and provides that:

> [a] A person is guilty of promoting gambling when he knowingly:

> (1) Accepts or receives money or other property, pursuant to an agreement or understanding with any person whereby he participates or will participate in the proceeds of gambling activity; or

> (2) Engages in conduct, which materially aids any form of gambling activity. Such conduct includes but is not limited to conduct directed toward the creation or establishment of the particular game, contest, scheme, device or activity involved, toward the acquisition or maintenance of premises, paraphernalia, equipment or apparatus therefor, toward the solicitation or inducement of persons to participate therein, toward the actual conduct of the playing phases thereof, toward the arrangement of any of its financial or recording phases, or toward any other phase of its operation.

N.J.S.A. 2C:37-2a(1), (2). Moreover, "gambling" is defined to include "staking or risking something of value upon the outcome of a contest of chance or a future contingent event not under the actor's control or influence, upon an agreement or understanding that he will receive something of value in the event of a certain outcome." N.J.S.A. 2C:37-1b.

Given the breadth of this definition, we agree that the government clearly established probable cause to believe that IFS-NJ was "promoting gambling" in violation of New Jersey law by materially aiding Bowman's gambling enterprises. IFS-NJ was an integral component of Bowman's gambling enterprise. It received funds from bettors throughout the United States and processed those transfers so that the bettors could open accounts and place bets with ASL and other Bowman companies. It sent Bowman an hourly accounting of these funds. This allowed Bowman to monitor betting income and it also allowed bettors to call ASL and Bowman to confirm their deposits and place bets. IFS-NJ was also part of the payout mechanism that ensured that winning bettors collected on their wagers. IFS-NJ clearly "[e]ngage[d] in conduct, which materially aid[ed] . . . gambling activity." Its conduct was "directed . . . toward the arrangement of [the gambling activity's] financial or recording phases." N.J.S.A. 2C:37-2a(2).

Claimants argue that the seizure and forfeiture here "represent[] a prosecutorial excess." Their argument is largely based upon the generally accepted conflict of laws principle that a gambling transaction occurs in the country where the bet or wager is accepted. Dicey & Morris, The Conflict of Laws 1468 (1993). They insist that the gambling transactions here actually occurred in England where the bets were ultimately "accepted." Claimants insist that there was no illegal gambling activity at all in this case because gambling is legal in England, and all of the actors there were legally licensed to conduct a gambling business. According to Claimants, IFS-NJ merely "performed a facially neutral, ministerial function in the United States." They attempt to buttress this claim by reminding us that IFS-NJ "was not open to the public, listed in any telephone directory, or identified in any advertising material as a place where bets could be placed." They are also quick to point out that the company's "operations did not include fixing odds, declaring winners or losers, or accepting or relaying bets or wagers." Claimants largely rest this argument on three cases which we will discuss in turn.

The first is State v. Andreano, 117 N.J.Super. 498, 285 A.2d 229 (1971). There, the defendant was charged with bookmaking and gambling in violation of New Jersey law. His defense at trial was that he was not a bookmaker at all. Rather, he argued that he was simply acting as a messenger who took others' bets to a legal, in-state pari-mutuel race track as a favor. That court held that "when the bet is taken by a disinterested individual for placement at a lawful race meeting, such activity is not bookmaking within the statutory prohibition." Id. at 231.

Claimants contend that, under Andreano, "mere[ly] handling . . . funds, [which are] destined for a lawful location inside or outside the State, does not constitute an unlawful gaming activity." Since IFS-NJ only transferred funds to England, where the relevant parties were duly licensed and gambling is legal, Claimants insist that IFS-NJ could not have engaged in illegal gambling activity under New Jersey law.

However, Claimants' reading of Andreano is far too narrow. Andreano was charged with "bookmaking," and the government here is not claiming that IFS-NJ's operations constituted bookmaking under New Jersey law. Moreover, the statute under which Andreano was charged has since been repealed. That earlier statute did not prohibit "promoting gambling" as current law does. The government's forfeiture claim rests upon an assertion that IFS-NJ promoted gambling as currently defined in N.J.S.A. 2C:37-2, and Andreano does not assist the Claimants in that regard.

The second case Claimants rely upon is United States v. Truesdale, 152 F.3d 443 (5th Cir.1988). The gambling operation in Truesdale was strikingly similar to the operation here.

The federal government successfully prosecuted WSB's Dallas employees for illegal gambling in violation of 18 U.S.C. §§ 1955 and 1955(b)(1)(i). The government charged that the employees were guilty of "bookmaking," under Texas Penal Code § 47.01(2)(A)-(C), and that this constituted a violation of § 1955. However, the Court of Appeals for the Fifth Circuit reversed the defendants' convictions. The court's holding was based upon its conclusion that the actual bookmaking (i.e. accepting bets), actually occurred in the Dominican Republic and Jamaica where it was legal.

Truesdale does, at first blush, support Claimants' position because here, as in Truesdale, bets were actually "placed" outside of the United States in a jurisdiction where betting was legal and where the betting business was properly licensed. However, the defendants in Truesdale were charged with bookmaking, and the government's averments here are not analogous. Rather, the government alleges that IFS-NJ was "promoting gambling" under a New Jersey statute that prohibits conduct "which materially aids any form of gambling activity," N.J.S.A. 2C:37-2a(2).

Moreover, upon a closer reading, Truesdale actually undermines Claimants' position. In Truesdale, bookmaking was only one of five activities defined as "gambling promotion" under Texas law. Section 47.03(a)(3) of the Texas Penal Code made it a separate offense for an individual to "become[] a custodian of anything of value bet or offered to be bet[]" for gain. However, the indictment in Truesdale did not allege that conduct as a predicate for the federal prosecution under § 1955. Therefore, "the fact that the [defendants had] engaged in financial transactions in the State of Texas that may have run afoul of Section 47.03(a)(3) [was] irrelevant." 152 F.3d at 447.

The third case Claimants rely upon is California v. Cabazon Band of Mission Indians, 480 U.S. 202, 107 S.Ct. 1083, 94 L.Ed.2d 244 (1987). Claimants argue that Cabazon stands for the proposition that one sovereign cannot criminalize gambling activity that is legal under the laws of another sovereign. However, Cabazon is even less helpful to Claimants than Truesdale. Cabazon was concerned with whether Congress intended to allow state laws to apply on Indian reservations. This unique case involving tribal sovereignty in no way furthers our inquiry into whether IFS-NJ promoted gambling as defined under applicable New Jersey law.

Given the language of the relevant statute here, we conclude that the government established probable cause that IFS-NJ's conduct violated New Jersey's law against promoting gambling, and the government therefore satisfied its burden of proof with regard to the first element of § 1955(b)(1)(i).

The second element of § 1955(b)(1) requires that the "illegal gambling business . . . involve[] five or more persons who conduct, finance, manage, supervise, direct or own all or part of such business." 18 U.S.C. § 1955(b)(1)(ii). Claimants argue that each of the people needed to meet the second element under § 1955(1) must be present in the United States. However, they cite no authority for that proposition and we have found none. As we have discussed, the offending conduct occurred in New Jersey, and nothing in § 1955 suggests that Congress intended to require all of the persons involved in an "illegal gambling business" to be located inside of the United States so long as the other conditions of the statute are satisfied. Moreover, no such requirement arises under the Commerce Clause. See United States v. Boyd, 149 F.3d 1062, 1066 (10th Cir.1998). Accordingly, we reject Claimants' position.

C. The Claimants' Burden.

Although Claimants make several arguments in opposing forfeiture, most if not all of those arguments can be reduced to a subset of Claimants' main contention that IFS-NJ's activities in New Jersey cannot be illegal because all of the gambling occurred in England, where the relevant actors were properly licensed to engage in this activity. They maintain that the New Jersey gambling statute does not apply in England where the bets were accepted. They cite no authority for their basic proposition other than the testimony of various experts on the legislative history and intent of New Jersey's gambling statutes.

Claimants' experts testified that N.J.S.A. 2C:37-2 "was always intended to apply . . . to the promotion of 'illegal' gambling only, not gambling under a governmental license." Claimants' experts testified that the district court's interpretation of the statute would criminalize such things as legitimate interstate banking and advertising relationships. Although Claimants' argument has some appeal, it ignores the text of New Jersey's statute. That statute prohibits "conduct, which materially aids any form of gambling activity," and the scope of that language is illustrated by the New Jersey Appellate Division's analysis in State v. Fiola, 242 N.J.Super. 240, 576 A.2d 338 (1990).

The business in Fiola "involve[d] the solicitation and receipt of money in New Jersey for the purchase of lottery tickets issued by other states, the transport of money to other states to purchase lottery tickets and the return of the tickets to New Jersey for delivery to customers." Id. at 339. The New Jersey Attorney General petitioned to enjoin the defendants' business alleging that it violated the state's constitutional and statutory prohibitions against gambling. The trial court refused to grant an injunction, but the Appellate Division reversed. That court held that even though the defendants' criminal culpability was not at issue, their "transport of gambling requests and money to out-of-state gambling sites and the return of lottery tickets to New Jersey gamblers 'materially aids [a] form of gambling activity' within the intent of N.J.S.A. 2C:37-2(a)(2)." Id. at 340. The Appellate Division held that the defendants' mere "possession of lottery tickets for distribution to their customers violates N.J.S.A. 2C:37-2(a)(2)." Id.

Therefore, even if we accept Claimants' argument that the gambling occurred outside of New Jersey where it is legal, their activity inside of New Jersey was nevertheless illegal because it promoted a gambling enterprise.

Similarly, we reject Claimants' assertion that the district court applied New Jersey criminal law extraterritorially contrary to the limitations to specific provisions of the New Jersey Crimes Code. More specifically, Claimants argue that under N.J.S.A. 2C:1-3a(4) New Jersey's prohibition against promoting gambling can not be applied to IFS-NJ's conduct inside of New Jersey unless that conduct is also illegal in England.

This argument ignores the critical fact that New Jersey has not attempted to prosecute IFS-NJ for violating its promoting gambling statute. Rather, the United States government has instituted civil forfeiture proceedings based upon IFS-NJ's violation of 18 U.S.C. § 1955. We are therefore concerned with an exercise of federal, not state, authority. Moreover, as noted above, the forfeiture action is predicated solely upon conduct that occurred in New Jersey. Claimants are therefore actually arguing that the laws of England insulate them from forfeiture based upon their conduct in New Jersey. We reject that argument.

The Claimants next argue that this forfeiture proceeding is essentially being waged against an innocent, foreign citizen and his gambling companies. [A]s we noted earlier, forfeiture is not conditioned upon the culpability of the owner of the defendant property.

Claimants' also attempt to draw substance from the rule of lenity. Claimants argue that even if a "technical violation of § 1955 could have been made out," the rule of lenity nevertheless precludes forfeiture under the circumstances here.

However, the rule of lenity applies only if there is a "grievous ambiguity or uncertainty in the statute." Muscarello v. United States, 524 U.S. 125, 138, 118 S.Ct. 1911, 141 L.Ed.2d 111 (1998) (citation and internal quotations omitted). The parameters of New Jersey's prohibition against promoting gambling are not ambiguous, and they are certainly not "grievous[ly]" ambiguous.

Claimants' remaining assertion is based upon international law. They claim the seizure and subsequent forfeiture violate the Treaty Between the Government of the United States of America and the Government of the United Kingdom of Great Britain and Northern Ireland on Mutual Legal Assistance in Criminal Matters ("MLAT"). According to Claimants, under the MLAT, the United States was obligated to consult with the United Kingdom's Home

Secretary before seizing the accounts. They also claim that the United States did not exhaust certain procedures as required by the treaty. We again disagree.

The MLAT became effective on December 2, 1996. According to the treaty's Preamble, the parties entered into that treaty to "improve the effectiveness of the law enforcement authorities of both countries in the investigation, prosecution, and combating of crime through co-operation and mutual legal assistance in criminal matters." The treaty is primarily concerned with drug trafficking, and related offenses, and seizure and forfeiture of proceeds and instrumentalities related to drug trafficking. The parties to the treaty intended to allow the United States and the United Kingdom to "develop and share evidence . . . to facilitate criminal prosecutions abroad." United States v. Balsys, 524 U.S. 666, 715, 118 S.Ct. 2218, 141 L.Ed.2d 575 (1998) (Breyer, J., dissenting). However, the treaty explicitly states that it is not intended to provide a private remedy. It states in pertinent part:

> [t]his Treaty is intended solely for mutual legal assistance between the Parties. The provisions of this Treaty shall not give rise to a right on the part of any private person to obtain, suppress, or exclude any evidence, or to impede the execution of a request.

Therefore, even it if is assumed for argument's sake that the United States violated the MLAT, Claimants have no private right to enforce its terms.

Claimants' essential claim is that the district court had no jurisdiction to apply United States gambling law to a British citizen and British companies operating legal gambling businesses on English soil. To support that argument, they cite Zoelsch v. Arthur Andersen & Co., 824 F.2d 27 (D.C.Cir.1987). However, to the extent it applies, we believe Zoelsch actually supports the district court's exercise of jurisdiction. There, in affirming the district court's dismissal for lack of subject matter jurisdiction, the court of appeals stated: "[J]urisdiction is appropriate when the fraudulent statements or misrepresentations originate in the United States, are made with scienter and in connection with the purchase and sale of securities, and 'directly cause' the harm to those who claim to be defrauded, even if reliance and damages occur elsewhere." Id. at 33. The court concluded that these jurisdictional prerequisites "are only a slight recasting, if at all, of the traditional view that jurisdiction will lie in American courts only over proscribed acts done in this country." Id.

Claimants argue that Zoelsch stands for the proposition that "federal securities law does not apply to conduct in the United States that was merely preparatory to an alleged securities violation which occurred overseas." They then attempt to draw parallels to the § 1955(d) forfeiture by arguing that IFS-NJ's activities in New Jersey were merely "preparatory" to legal gambling activities in England, and they conclude that the district court therefore lacked jurisdiction under Zoelsch.

However, Zoelsch affirms that American courts have jurisdiction "over proscribed acts done in this country[]" that have the required nexus to activities elsewhere. We therefore find no merit in Claimants' jurisdictional challenge to this in rem proceeding over New Jersey property based upon conduct occurring in New Jersey. It may well be true that British citizens and British companies will be affected by this in rem action in New Jersey. This does not mean that the law of New Jersey or the law of the United States is being applied to those citizens or companies.

Claimants' international exhaustion argument arises from the fact that both the United States and England belong to the Organization of Economic Cooperation and Development ("OECD"). Claimants argue that the OECD requires "consultation and moderation by the U.S. in this context." However, Claimants never bother to explain how the government's institution of this forfeiture violated requirements of international law or, if a violation occurred, how it provides a defense from this forfeiture action.

In a related argument, Claimants insist that considerations of international comity preclude the instant forfeiture. That contention is again bottomed on the Claimants' belief that the forfeiture is an extraterritorial application of federal law against British citizens. We have already explained why there is no extraterritorial application of federal law to British citizens here.

Claimants also think it significant that § 1955 was originally aimed at organized crime, that Bowman's businesses are entirely legal in England, and that gambling no longer is regarded as the evil it once was in the United States. Indeed, argue Claimants, the fact that New Jersey itself has legalized casinos and lotteries plainly demonstrates that gambling is no longer associated with vice. Thus, the argument continues, comity required the district court to defer to Bowman's British licenses to conduct a gambling enterprise. However, the change in society's views towards gambling does not offer the district court a license to ignore a federal statute (or the state statute it incorporates) under the guise of international comity.

> Comity . . . is the recognition which one nation allows within its territory to the legislative, executive, or judicial acts of another nation, having due regard both to international duty and convenience, and to the rights of its own citizens or of other persons who are under the protections of its laws . . . .
>
> Comity cannot be the source of a disability that prevents a district court from having the power to address wrongdoing that impacts a domestic court . . . .

Republic of the Philippines v. Westinghouse Elec. Corp., 43 F.3d 65, 75 (3d Cir.1995). Congress prohibited illegal gambling businesses as defined under state law, and authorized forfeiture of related property. We have already discussed how the relevant state law defines gambling broadly to include any conduct that materially aids any form of gambling activity. These legislative enactments reflect the "strong public policies" of the United States government, and the government is not required to tolerate activity that it defines as illegal merely because it affects someone who may live in a country where the activity is legal.

IV. CONCLUSION

For all of the above reasons, we will affirm the district court's grant of summary judgment to the government and its final order of forfeiture.

Notes

1. The decision in *World Interactive* set off a minor panic in the internet gaming community: companies that designed software for on-line casinos saw the price of their stocks plummet, operators who had been taking bets from New Yorkers fretted over possible indictments, and businesses that had refused to take bets from Americans worried about being set up by undercover cops posing as foreigners. *See generally* Laura H. Bak-Boychuk, Comment, *Internet Gambling: Is Avoiding Prosecution in the United States as Easy as Moving the Business Operations Offshore?*, 6 Sw. J.L. & Trade Am. 363 (1999).

As is obvious, the opinion is grounded on a rather startling proposition: "The Internet site creates a virtual casino within the user's computer terminal." If this language is taken literally, every country in the world has criminal jurisdiction over every gaming site on the web.

Of course, it is also possible to treat the case as pure dicta. Although the operator was incorporated and licensed in Antigua and had its server in Antigua, it actually was headquartered in New York with principals and assets in New York. Moreover, the defendants were accused of selling unregistered securities to New Yorkers through a New York "boiler room" operation, and the court simply was being asked to seize a New York bank account and enjoin activities taking place in offices in New York. Looked at in this light, there is nothing very remarkable at all about the holding.

2. In *State v. Granite Gate Resorts, Inc.*, 568 N.W.2d 715 (Minn. Ct. App. 1997), *aff'd mem. by an evenly divided court*, 576 N.W.2d 747 (Minn. 1998), the court was faced with a case whose facts were similar to those in *World Interactive*. The Minnesota attorney general had filed a consumer fraud action against a Nevada company that planned to establish a gaming web site in Belize. The defendants moved to have the case dismissed for lack of personal jurisdiction, inasmuch as they had no operations or assets in Minnesota. The trial court denied the motion and the appeals court affirmed:

> Appellants, through their Internet advertising, have demonstrated a clear intent to solicit business from markets that include Minnesota and, as a result, have had multiple contacts with Minnesota residents, including at least one successful solicitation. The cause of action here arises from the same advertisements that constitute appellants' contacts with the state and implicates Minnesota's strong interest in maintaining the enforceability of its consumer protection laws. Appellants have not demonstrated that submission to personal jurisdiction in Minnesota would subject them to any undue inconvenience. For these reasons, we hold that appellants are subject to personal jurisdiction in Minnesota because, through their Internet activities, they purposefully availed themselves of the privilege of doing business in Minnesota to the extent that the maintenance of an action based on consumer protection statutes does not offend traditional notions of fair play and substantial justice.

568 N.W.2d at 721.

Like *World Interactive*, the precedential value of *Granite Gate* is questionable: the Minnesota Supreme Court affirmed the court of appeals but did not issue an opinion due to a 3-3 split among its members; the merits of the case were never reached; and because the company never got off the ground, no Minnesota resident ever lost any money.

3. Given the foregoing, it remains unclear whether individual states have the power to regulate gaming web sites. In the meantime, Nevada has passed a law specifically authorizing internet casinos. *See* Jeffrey R. Rodefer, *Internet Gambling in Nevada: Overview of Federal Law Affecting Assembly Bill 466*, 6 Gaming L. Rev. 393 (2002), and Craig Lane, Comment, *Internet Gambling: Nevada Logs In*, 22 Loy. L.A. Ent. L. Rev. 525 (2002). The United States Virgin Islands has enacted similar legislation. For a further look at whether states can regulate internet gaming, *see, e.g.*, Stevie A. Kish, Note, *Betting on the Net: An Analysis of the Government's Role in Addressing Internet Gambling*, 51 Fed. Comm. L.J. 449 (1999); Beau Thompson, Note, *Internet Gambling*, 2 N.C. J.L. & Tech. 81 (2001); Edward Yures, Note, *Gambling on the Internet: The States Risk Playing Economic Roulette as the Internet Gambling Industry Spins Onward*, 28 Rutgers Computer & Tech. L.J. 193 (2002).

4. It has been suggested by some that the federal government should step in and regulate internet gaming, and a number of bills, many authored by Senator Jon Kyl (R.-Ariz.), have been introduced to do just that. *See* I. Nelson Rose, *Gambling and the Law: The Future of Internet Gambling*, 7 Vill. Sports & Ent. L.J. 29 (2000); David Goodman, Comment, *Proposals for a Federal Prohibition of Internet Gambling: Are There Any Other Viable Solutions to this Perplexing Problem?*, 70 Miss. L.J. 375 (2000); Tom Lundin, Jr., Note, *The Internet Gambling Prohibition Act of 1999: Congress Stacks the Deck Against Online Wagering But Deals In Traditional Gaming Industry High Rollers*, 16 Ga. St. U. L. Rev. 845 (1999).

Fearing that it suddenly might be forced to prosecute thousands of cases, the United States Department of Justice has reacted warily to Congress's efforts. Indeed, the decision to have the United States Attorney for the Southern District of New York indict Jay Cohen is largely viewed as having been an attempt by the Department to demonstrate that existing federal laws are sufficient. *See further* Paul S. Hugel, *Criminal Law and the Future of Internet Gaming*, 2 Gaming L. Rev. 143 (1998). Of course, Cohen's subsequent conviction has helped to bolster the Department's argument. *See further* Bruce P. Keller, *The Game's the Same: Why Gambling in Cyberspace Violates Federal Law*, 108 Yale L.J. 1569 (1999), and Joel Michael Schwarz, *The Internet Gambling Fallacy Craps Out*, 14 Berkeley Tech. L.J. 1021 (1999).

Critics, however, point out that Cohen and the 13 individuals who were charged with him were easy targets, inasmuch as they were all American citizens who had made telephone calls and sent mail from locations inside the United States and had taken wagers only on sporting events. By walking such a fine line, the Department avoided numerous hard questions (e.g., whether existing federal laws reach foreign citizens in third countries who accept wagers on non-sporting events).

Many people believe that some sort of federal legislation is inevitable. Of course, the key question is whether the bill that finally emerges bans internet gaming outright or permits it in specific situations (and if so, which ones). For suggested approaches, *see, e.g.*, Joseph M. Kelly, *Internet Gambling Law*,

26 Wm. Mitchell L. Rev. 117 (2000); Seth Gorman & Anthony Loo, Comment, *Blackjack or Bust: Can U.S. Law Stop Internet Gambling?*, 16 Loy. L.A. Ent. L.J. 667 (1996); Michael P. Kailus, Note, *Do Not Bet on Unilateral Prohibition of Internet Gambling to Eliminate Cyber-Casinos*, 1999 U. Ill. L. Rev. 1045.

5. Even if federal internet gaming legislation is passed, its ability to reach foreign citizens outside the United States seems doubtful. *See* Adrian Gross, *Jay Cohen's Brave New World: The Liability of Offshore Operators of Licensed Internet Casinos for Breach of United States' Anti-Gambling Laws*, 7 Rich. J.L. & Tech. 32 (2001). Indeed, although parties from Canada, England, and the Isle of Man were involved in the *$734,578.82* case, the Third Circuit repeatedly stressed that the real defendant was the money, which was United States currency located in bank and wire transfer accounts in New Jersey. Moreover, the forfeiture proceeding had arisen as a result of an investigation into the betting activities of a Wisconsin resident (Brian Taff). As a result, there was no need to consider the question of whether American gaming laws reach overseas.

6. A number of commentators have suggested that what really is needed is an international treaty on internet gaming. *See, e.g.,* Harley J. Goldstein, *On-Line Gambling: Down to the Wire?*, 8 Marq. Sports L.J. 1 (1997); John Edmund Hogan, Comment, *World Wide Wager: The Feasibility of Internet Gambling Regulation*, 8 Seton Hall Const. L.J. 815 (1998); Scott M. Montpas, Comment, *Gambling On-Line: For a Hundred Dollars, I Bet You Government Regulation Will Not Stop the Newest Form of Gambling*, 22 U. Dayton L. Rev. 163 (1996). Given the divergent approaches that countries take to the issues involved in internet gaming, the chances of such an agreement actually coming to fruition appear slim. In the meantime, at least one writer has asserted that the United States can adequately police internet gaming without international cooperation. *See* Jack Goldsmith, *What Internet Gambling Legislation Teaches About Internet Regulation*, 32 Int'l Law. 1115 (1998).

7. Despite (or perhaps because of) the uncertainty surrounding the legality of internet gaming, there are now more than 1,400 such sites, and many observers believe web betting will become a $100 billion industry by 2006. *See further* Symposium, *Special Issue on Internet Gaming*, 4 Gaming L. Rev. 399 (2000). *See also* Mark Balestra, *The Complete Idiot's Guide to Online Gambling* (2000). For a further look at the some of the legal challenges posed by such gaming, *see, e.g.,* Jeffrey A. Dempsey, Comment, *Surfing for Wampum: Federal Regulation of Internet Gambling and Native American Sovereignty*, 25 Am. Indian L. Rev. 133 (2000-2001); Ryan D. Hammer, Note, *Does Internet Gambling Strengthen the U.S. Economy?: Don't Bet on It*, 54 Fed. Comm. L.J. 103 (2001); David H. Lantzer, Comment, *Internet Gaming Tax Regulation: Can Old Laws Learn New Tricks?*, 5 Chap. L. Rev. 281 (2002); Nicholas Robbins, Note, *Baby Needs a New Pair of Cybershoes: The Legality of Casino Gambling on the Internet*, 2 B.U. J. Sci. & Tech. L. 7 (1996); John J. Savilia, Note, *Cyber Games? Regulation of Internet Gambling in the United States*, 34 Suffolk U. L. Rev. 347 (2001); Mark D. Schopper, Comment, *Internet Gambling, Electronic Cash and Money Laundering: The Unintended Consequences of a Monetary Control Scheme*, 5 Chap. L. Rev. 303 (2002).

Problem 39

As counsel to a congressional sub-committee that is currently studying internet gambling, you have been asked whether a law requiring internet service providers to block access to gaming web sites would violate the First Amendment. How should you respond? *See Yahoo!, Inc. v. La Ligue Contre Le Racisme Et L'Antisemitisme*, 169 F. Supp. 2d 1181 (N.D. Cal. 2001).

C. PRIVATE REGULATION

THOMPSON v. HANDA-LOPEZ, INC.
998 F. Supp. 738 (W.D. Tex. 1998)

PRADO, District Judge.

On this date came on to be considered Defendant's Motion to Dismiss for Improper Venue and for Lack of Personal Jurisdiction, or in the Alternative, to Transfer the Action to the United States District Court for the Northern District of California for Improper Venue or for the Convenience of the Parties and Witnesses, filed August 22, 1997, and the Plaintiff's Response. After careful consideration, this Court is of the opinion that Defendant's motion should be denied.

BACKGROUND

Plaintiff Tom Thompson brought this action alleging breach of contract, fraud, and violations of the Texas Deceptive Trade Practices Act by Defendant Handa-Lopez, Inc. Defendant operates an arcade site on the Internet advertised as "Funscape's Casino Royale," the "World's Largest" Internet Casino. Individuals purchase game tokens ("Funbucks") with a credit card, which are used to play blackjack, poker, keno, slots, craps, easy lotto, and roulette. If the player wins he is entitled to receive $1.00 for each 100 Funbucks, in the form of either cash or prizes. Plaintiff alleges that on or about June 9, 1997, he was in Texas, playing games on Defendant's Internet casino when he won 19,372,840 Funbucks. He attempted to redeem them for $193,728.40 pursuant to the rules of Defendant's Internet site, but Defendant refused to pay the owed money. Plaintiff therefore brought this lawsuit.

Plaintiff is a Texas domiciliary while Defendant is a California corporation with its principal place of business in California. It maintains an Internet site on the World Wide Web, which can be accessed at "www.funscape.com" by any Internet user. The server for the Web site is located in California. The Web site is at present continually accessible to every Internet-connected computer in Texas and the world. Plaintiff entered into a contract to play the game on Defendant's Web site. Buried within the contract was an inconspicuous provision which provided that any disputes

> shall be governed by the laws of the State of California, excluding choice of law principles, and shall be resolved exclusively by final and binding arbitration in the City of San Jose, County of Santa Clara, State of California, USA under the rules of the American Arbitration Association, and, in the event of such arbitration, no punitive, special,

incidental, or consequential damages may be recovered by any party and the arbitrator shall not have the power to award any such damages . . . .

PERSONAL JURISDICTION

[T]he Texas long arm statute extends as far as constitutionally permissible . . . .

The Internet and Jurisdiction

Despite the evolution of a global Internet, the case law concerning the permissible scope of personal jurisdiction based on the Internet is very limited. In Zippo Mfg. Co. v. Zippo Dot Com, Inc., 952 F. Supp. 1119 (W.D.Pa.1997), a recent opinion from the Western District of Pennsylvania, the Court discussed the "sliding scale" that courts have used to measure jurisdiction. This sliding scale is consistent with well developed personal jurisdiction principles. At one end are situations where a defendant clearly does business over the Internet by entering into contracts with residents of other states which involve the knowing and repeated transmission of computer files over the Internet. See CompuServe, Inc. v. Patterson, 89 F.3d 1257 (6th Cir.1996). At the other end are passive Web site situations. A passive Web site that solely makes information available to interested parties is not grounds for the exercise of personal jurisdiction. See Bensusan Restaurant Corp. v. King, 937 F.Supp. 295 (S.D.N.Y.1996), aff'd, 126 F.3d 25 (2nd Cir.1997). Interactive Web sites, where a user can exchange information with the host computer, represent the middle ground. In these cases, the exercise of jurisdiction is determined by examining the level of interactivity between the parties on the Web site. See Maritz, Inc. v. Cybergold, Inc., 947 F.Supp. 1328 (E.D.Mo.1996).

Minimum Contacts

The Defendant claims that personal jurisdiction does not exist here because the Defendant does not have sufficient minimum contacts within Texas to satisfy due process. Minimum contacts are lacking, according to the Defendant, because it is a California corporation with its principal place of business in California, and its server is located in California. It does not maintain an office in Texas nor does it have a sales force or employees in the state.

The Plaintiff responds that minimum contacts comporting with due process have been satisfied because the Defendant has advertised its Casino over the Internet knowing that Texas citizens will see its advertisement. Further, it has conducted business within the state of Texas by entering into contracts with Texas citizens to play those games, which the Texas citizens played while in Texas.

The Court agrees with Plaintiff. In the present case, Defendant Handa-Lopez has directed the advertising of its Casino toward all states. It advertises itself as the "World's Largest" Internet Casino. Defendant's argument that it "did not direct any of its advertising specifically towards Texas residents" is unpersuasive. The Internet is designed to communicate with people in every state. Advertisement on the Internet can reach tens of thousands of users within Texas alone. In Inset Sys., Inc. v. Instruction Set, Inc., 937 F.Supp.

161, 163 (D.Conn.1996), the Court exercised personal jurisdiction, reasoning that, unlike newspapers, in which advertisements are often disposed of rapidly, or television and radio, in which advertisements are only broadcast at certain times, advertisements over the Internet are available continually to any Internet user.

Following the reasoning employed by these courts, jurisdiction should likewise be exercised in our case. In the present case there was more extensive interaction between the Defendant and the casino players than in Maritz and Inset. Defendant Handa-Lopez did more than advertise and maintain a toll free telephone number—it continuously interacted with the casino players, entering into contracts with them as they played the various games. Defendant Handa-Lopez did not exchange information with residents of various states hoping to use that information for commercial gain in the future. In the instant case, Defendant Handa-Lopez entered into contracts with the residents of various states knowing that it would receive commercial gain at the present time. Furthermore, in the instant case, the Texas Plaintiff played the casino games while in Texas, as if they were physically located in Texas, and if the Plaintiff won cash or prizes, the Defendant would send the winnings to the Plaintiff in Texas.

Fair Play and Substantial Justice

In the present case the Defendant argues that it would offend traditional notions of fairness to compel it to defend this lawsuit in Texas, especially since the contract at issue contained a clause which stated that any disputes "shall be governed by the laws of the State of California" and "shall be resolved exclusively by final and binding arbitration in the City of San Jose, County of Santa Clara, State of California."

Defendant claims that it has not purposefully interjected itself in the affairs of Texas because it has not directed any activity specifically and purposely toward the State. The Defendant adds that the Plaintiff unilaterally contacted and voluntarily entered Defendant's Web site and contest without any contact by Defendant toward Plaintiff, especially since the Plaintiff accepted the binding "forum selection clause" in the contract.

First, this clause is not a forum selection clause because it does not mandate that disputes arising from this contract be litigated in California; it merely states that disputes shall be governed by the laws of the State of California and shall be resolved exclusively by final and binding arbitration in California. This clause by no means requires, nor does it even suggest, that a lawsuit must be filed in California.

In addition, Texas clearly has a strong interest in protecting its citizens by adjudicating disputes involving the alleged breach of contract, fraud, and violations of the Texas Deceptive Trade Practices Act by an Internet casino on Texas residents. Furthermore, due regard must be given to the Plaintiff's choice to seek relief in Texas. Kulko v. Superior Court of Calif., 436 U.S. 84, 92, 98 S.Ct. 1690, 1696-97, 56 L.Ed.2d 132 (1978). These concerns outweigh the burden created by requiring the Defendant to defend the suit in Texas.

VENUE

Defendant also moves this Court to dismiss this case for improper venue, or to transfer this case for improper venue, pursuant to 28 U.S.C. § 1406(a), "on the basis that Texas Courts are improper venue for this case based upon a forum selection clause found in Defendant's Official Rules and Regulations."

This argument is meritless because this case was not brought in an improper venue. As previously stated, the clause at issue in the contract does not prohibit a lawsuit from being brought in Texas.

Defendant also argues that this case should be transferred to the Northern District of California pursuant to 28 U.S.C. § 1404(a), which provides that "[f]or the convenience of the parties and witnesses, in the interest of justice, a district court may transfer any civil action to any other district or division where it might have been brought." The purpose of this statute is to prevent the waste of time, energy, and money and to protect litigants, witnesses, and the public against unnecessary inconvenience and expense. To prevail, the moving party must show that the balance of convenience and justice weighs heavily in favor of the transfer. Acrotube, Inc. v. J.K. Fin. Group, Inc., 653 F.Supp. 470, 477 (N.D.Ga.1987). Therefore, when assessing the merits of a § 1404(a) motion, a court must determine if a transfer would make it substantially more convenient for the parties to litigate the case.

The criteria weighed by a court in deciding a § 1404(a) motion include:

> (1) the convenience of the parties; (2) the convenience of material witnesses; (3) the availability of process to compel the presence of unwilling witnesses; (4) the cost of obtaining the presence of witnesses; (5) the relative ease of access to sources of proof; (6) calendar congestion; (7) where the events in issue took place; and (8) the interests of justice in general.

St. Cyr v. Greyhound Lines, Inc., 486 F.Supp. 724, 727 (E.D.N.Y.1980).

In the instant case, a review of the relevant factors indicates that a transfer is not warranted. The Defendant claims that all of its witnesses and evidence are located in California. While this may be true, the same applies to the Plaintiff with regard to Texas—all of his witnesses and evidence are located in Texas. The Defendant also claims that it would be very burdensome for it to travel to Texas to defend this lawsuit. However, it would be at least as burdensome, if not more so, for the Texas Plaintiff to travel to California as it would be for the "World's Largest" Internet casino to come to Texas.

Defendant further argues that this case should be transferred to California because Plaintiff, to the extent he receives a judgment against Defendant, "would be required to enforce the judgment in California." This argument is meritless because if Plaintiff receives a judgment against Defendant, he will be able to enforce the judgment in California; California certainly gives full faith and credit to judgments received in Texas.

Finally, Defendant claims that in the interest of justice this case should be transferred since "Plaintiff agreed that the forum for any dispute regarding Defendant would be in California." As previously mentioned, this clause clearly neither compels nor suggests that a lawsuit be brought in California.

Furthermore, this clause did not give Plaintiff notice that California was a possible forum, since the clause was inconspicuously buried within the several page contract—Plaintiff did not notice it, nor would a reasonable person have noticed it. Plaintiff entered into a contract with Defendant and played on Defendant's casinos without ever contemplating that he may be compelled to fight a potential lawsuit in California.

Conclusion

Accordingly, it is hereby ORDERED that Defendant Handa-Lopez's Motion to Dismiss for Improper Venue and for Lack of Personal Jurisdiction, or in the Alternative, to Transfer the Action to the United States District Court for the Northern District of California for Improper Venue or for the Convenience of the Parties and Witnesses is DENIED.

INTERNATIONAL BANCORP, L.L.C. v. SOCIETE DES BAINS DE MER ET DU CERCLE DES ETRANGERS A MONACO
192 F. Supp. 2d 467 (E.D. Va. 2002)

ELLIS, District Judge.

This declaratory judgment trademark infringement action pits the owner of Monaco's famed gambling establishment, Casino de Monte Carlo, against an individual and five companies who have registered fifty-three ".com" and ".net" domain names that incorporate, in various ways, the name "Casino de Monte Carlo." The disposition of the parties' cross-motions for summary judgment presents substantive and jurisdictional issues.

I.

A. SBM

Defendant and counterclaim plaintiff Societe des Bains de Mer et du Cercle des Etrangers a Monaco (SBM) is a company established in the Principality of Monaco in 1863 by charter from Prince Charles III of Monaco. SBM's majority shareholder is the government of Monaco. Its business is the management of a variety of resort hotels and gambling facilities in Monaco, including four gambling casinos, one of which is the Casino de Monte Carlo. The record reflects that while SBM registered the "Casino de Monte Carlo" mark under the laws of Monaco in 1996, its application for the same trademark in this country, filed with the U.S. Patent and Trademark Office on November 7, 2001, is currently pending. The record also reflects that SBM has registered and uses various domain names, and while SBM currently provides no online gambling or gaming services, it is undisputed that SBM has such services under development.

In advertising its resort and gambling facilities, the record reflects that SBM has used the mark "Casino de Monte Carlo" in this country and throughout the world. Specifically, SBM has promoted its Casino de Monte Carlo through print media, films, and the Internet. SBM has also received substantial media coverage in this country regarding its resorts and casinos, especially the Casino de Monte Carlo.

For the past eighteen years, SBM has operated a New York office to promote North American tourism in Monaco. These New York-based promotional efforts, which include advertising SBM's Casino de Monte Carlo by using the mark "Casino de Monte Carlo," occur throughout the United States by means of trade show participation, media advertising, charity partnerships, direct mail, and telephone marketing. In each of the past ten years, SBM has spent approximately four million dollars annually on worldwide marketing efforts, with approximately twenty-five percent of this amount devoted to marketing efforts in the United States. As part of this marketing and promotional effort, SBM has annually mailed approximately 10,000 brochures that, inter alia, use the mark "Casino de Monte Carlo" to advertise this gambling facility to North American clients in the United States and Canada. A reflection of the impact of these promotional efforts is that as recently as the year 2000, approximately twenty-two percent of SBM's customers in Monaco were from North America. Undisputed evidence further reveals that the New York office was one of SBM's international sales offices from which American customers were able to book reservations.

The record reflects that SBM is aware that the geographic term "Monte Carlo" is used by other entities in connection with Internet gambling. And, while it is also true that SBM has not attempted to dispute every instance of such use, this case involves more than the use of the geographic term; rather, in this case, SBM challenges the registration and use of fifty-three domain names that allegedly incorporate in some fashion the entire mark "Casino de Monte Carlo." This use of the mark, according to SBM, creates the false impression that plaintiffs' websites are affiliated with SBM. Despite this allegedly infringing use of SBM's mark, there is no evidence of resulting financial loss to SBM.

B. The Plaintiff Companies and Levy

The declarative judgment plaintiffs are five companies: International Bancorp, L.L.C. (d/b/a I. Bancorp Europe), International Services, Inc., International Lotteries, L.L.C., Britannia Finance Corporation, and Las Vegas Sportsbook, Inc. (collectively referred to as the "plaintiff companies"). These entities are also named as counterclaim defendants in SBM's counterclaim. Also named as a counterclaim defendant is Claude Levy, a French national who resides in Belgium. Levy is the owner and operator of the five plaintiff companies, which the record reflects are all undercapitalized and have failed to observe many traditional American corporate formalities. It also appears that the plaintiff companies have (i) no officers, directors, or members other than Levy and his wife, Arja Levy, (ii) no employees, and (iii) essentially no corporate records. The record also reflects that Levy and his wife registered the disputed domain names on behalf of the five plaintiff companies, occasionally using aliases in doing so. The undisputed record also reflects that while the five plaintiff companies purport to be distinct entities, they have common leadership, common goals, and work together with a common purpose.

International Bancorp, L.L.C., a Delaware limited liability company, registered six of the disputed domain names with Verisign, located in Herndon, Virginia. Levy and his wife are the only members of International Bancorp.

The company currently has no employees, no office, and no bank account. It has no principal place of business in the United States and its members have never filed a tax return relating to the business.

International Services, Inc. is incorporated in St. Kitts, West Indies. It registered with Verisign thirty-one domain names challenged by SBM.

International Lotteries, L.L.C. is a Delaware limited liability company that registers domain names and develops websites.

Britannia Finance Corporation is a Delaware corporation that provides accounting and financial services for the other plaintiff companies. Britannia's sole directors are Levy and his wife. The record reflects that Britannia maintained no corporate minutes and has never filed a tax return in any jurisdiction. Britannia registered with Verisign four of the domain names that are now in dispute.

Las Vegas Sportsbook, Inc. is incorporated under the laws of the Republic of Panama and has registered domain names on behalf of the other plaintiff companies. Like the other plaintiff companies, Las Vegas Sportsbook has no employees, no offices, and appears to lack any source of revenue.

Levy, the five plaintiff companies, and their affiliates are in the business of developing and operating websites relating to the online gaming industry. Domain names are, of course, central to this effort. The first of the domain names at issue registered by one of the plaintiff companies was casinomonte-carlo.com, which was registered by International Lotteries in 1997.

According to the record, Levy, the five plaintiff companies and their affiliates have developed more than 150 websites devoted to online gambling. Among these websites are "Casino Monte Carlo," located at casinomontecar-lo.com and "Monte Carlo Casinos," located at montecarlocasinos.com. These two sites are central to the plaintiff companies' online gambling activities. Located at these sites are the plaintiff companies' pages describing their online gambling services and containing pictures and graphics of the interior of a casino that appears to be copied from SBM's Casino de Monte Carlo. Both sites invite visitors to download the plaintiff companies' software program entitled "Casino Monte Carlo." This program uses a greeting that reads "Welcome to Casino Monte Carlo" and contains a picture of the exterior of SBM's Casino de Monte Carlo. Levy, the record reflects, authorized the use of these pictures and graphics.

Also located at these sites are the following statements which appear in part to refer or allude to SBM:

> "This casino is owned and managed by a group of U.S. corporations, including a U.S. finance company, and an international group of companies who have been in business for more than 140 years."

> "We are the only Internet gaming company to have the double gambling license from Casino Monte Carlo and from Las Vegas Casino."

> "For your protection, your funds are held in a top European bank, established over 100 years ago, which also provides the strictest

banking secrecy in the world, something that is not available in the US."

"The best Internet gambling magazine has named Monte Carlo Casino the Best Internet Casino for 1999."

Nor are these the only allusions to SBM to be found on the plaintiff companies' websites. At gamblingmagazine.com, a site registered to Britannia and controlled by Levy, the following statements were made:

> "Monte Carlo: a town and resort forming part of the principality of Monaco, on the Riviera, with a famous casino and the destination of an annual car rally . . . ."

> "[H]ave you seen the stunning graphics of this soon-to-be famous casino? www.CasinoMonteCarlo.com."

> "[O]r would you prefer something more sublime? A location between mountain and sea, gardens, cultural events, only 29,000 residents, ideal for a romantic vacation, an independent state in the heart of Europe—the Principality of Monaco, and naturally, Monte Carlo, home of legendary casinos famous the world over. Instead of travelling [sic] there, try www.montecarlocasino.net."

Neither Levy nor any of the plaintiff companies hold any registered trademarks using the terms "Casino," "Monaco," or "Monte Carlo" (with or without a dash, joined or separated). And, as the record also makes clear, none of the plaintiff companies' websites using the disputed domain names contain any material that criticizes or parodies SBM or any of its facilities. Nor do any of theses sites specifically disclaim a commercial affiliation with SBM.

The record reflects that the plaintiff companies have on some occasions offered several of the disputed domain names for sale to the public at large by listing them for sale with online domain name brokers affiliated with the plaintiff companies. Apart from these general offers of sale, there is no record evidence that the plaintiff companies offered to sell any of the disputed domain names to SBM.

C. Procedural History

When the plaintiff companies registered each of the fifty-three disputed domain names, they were required as a condition of registration to agree to arbitrate any dispute regarding ownership of the domain names in accordance with the Uniform Policy for Domain Name Dispute Resolution ("UDRP"), adopted by the Internet Corporation for Assigned Names and Numbers ("ICANN"). On January 8, 2001, the World Intellectual Property Organization ("WIPO") issued non-binding decisions in these cases in favor of SBM, finding (i) that SBM had rights in the mark "Casino de Monte Carlo;" (ii) that the plaintiff companies' use of the term "Casino de Monte Carlo" as domain names and on web pages was identical and hence confusingly similar to SBM's mark; (iii) that the disputed domain names were registered and used in bad faith. Accordingly, the panel ordered the plaintiff companies to transfer to SBM all domain names related to "Casino de Monte Carlo," including the fifty-three domain names here at issue. To avoid having to do so, the plaintiff companies then brought this complaint, seeking a declaratory judgment pursuant to 28 U.S.C. § 2201(a) that the companies are entitled to retain ownership of the domain names in dispute. Thereafter, Verisign, having received notice of this action, deposited the certificates for the fifty-three domain names with the Clerk of this Court. SBM's response to the complaint included a counterclaim, naming as defendants the plaintiff companies and Levy. Specifically, SBM's amended counterclaim asserts the following theories of recovery against Levy and the plaintiff companies: (1) unfair competition and trademark infringement in violation of the Lanham Act, 15 U.S.C. § 1125(a); (2) trademark dilution in violation of the Federal Trademark Dilution Act ("FTDA"), 15 U.S.C. § 1125(c); (3) cybersquatting in violation of the Anticybersquatting Consumer Protection Act ("ACPA"), 15 U.S.C. § 1125(d)(1); (4) unfair competition in violation of 15 U.S.C. § 1126(h); and (5) trademark infringement under the common law of Virginia.

The relief sought by SBM in its amended counterclaim includes (i) statutory damages in the amount of $100,000 per each of the fifty-three allegedly offending domain names, pursuant to 15 U.S.C. § 1117(d); (ii) transfer of each of the fifty-three domain names, pursuant to 15 U.S.C. § 1125(d)(1)(C); and (iii) an injunction forbidding the plaintiff companies and Levy from registering domain names that contain the mark "Casino de Monte Carlo" or similar terms and from using the mark on the Internet . . . .

IV.

SBM asserts that the plaintiff companies' use in American commerce of the term "Casino de Monte Carlo" in the disputed domain names and on various websites constitutes trademark infringement in violation of the Lanham Act, 15 U.S.C. § 1125(a). To prevail on its trademark infringement cause of action, SBM must prove the following elements: (1) that SBM possesses a protectable mark; (2) that plaintiff companies used the mark; (3) that plaintiff companies' use of the mark occurred "in commerce;" (4) that plaintiff companies used the mark "in connection with the sale, offering for sale, distribution, or advertising" of goods or services; and (5) that plaintiff companies used the mark in a manner likely to confuse consumers. People for the Ethical Treatment of Animals v. Doughney, 263 F.3d 359, 364 (4th Cir.2001).

While elements two, three, and four require little discussion, the remaining two elements require more extended analysis.

As an initial matter, it is clear that SBM's "Casino de Monte Carlo" mark is used in United States commerce. 15 U.S.C. § 1127.

Use of the mark in this country, by itself, does not establish that the mark deserves Section 1125(a) protection; distinctiveness must also be established. See Sara Lee Corp. v. Kayser-Roth Corp., 81 F.3d 455, 464 (4th Cir.1996).

Descriptive marks are deemed distinctive, thus meriting protection, only if the party claiming protection can demonstrate that the mark has acquired a secondary meaning among the relevant consuming public.

The record leaves no doubt that the plaintiff companies intentionally and directly copied SBM's mark. While there is no direct evidence of intentional copying, inferring the intent of the plaintiff companies is proper, given that the putatively infringing term is identical to SBM's mark and the infringing use is in the same relevant market (gambling services). Thus, the presumption of a likelihood of confusion applies here. Of the fifty-three domain names at issue, forty-three contain the term "Casino de Monte Carlo" or its essential equivalent. Moreover, the plaintiff companies' websites contain software ready for download that features pictures of the exterior of the actual Casino de Monte Carlo. The plaintiff companies' websites also contain pictures of an interior decor strikingly similar to that of the Casino de Monte Carlo. In these circumstances, the inference of intentional copying is too compelling to deny and the secondary meaning of the mark "Casino de Monte Carlo" is properly presumed.

[I]t is clear that the "Casino de Monte Carlo" mark is considered worth plagiarizing for its commercial value in calling to minds of consumers SBM's well-known gambling facility. Finally, the uncontradicted record reflects that SBM's use of the mark is exceptionally long-standing, which suggests distinctiveness.

The final element of a Section 1125(a) trademark infringement claim is whether the record shows that the plaintiff companies' unauthorized use of the term "Casino de Monte Carlo" creates a likelihood of confusion for an "'ordinary consumer' as to the source or sponsorship of the goods," in this case, online gambling services. Anheuser-Busch, Inc. v. L & L Wings, Inc., 962 F.2d 316, 318 (4th Cir.1992).

As in distinctiveness, it is proper in this circuit to presume "a likelihood of confusion upon a showing that the defendant intentionally copied the plaintiff's trademark or trade dress." Given the circumstances, it is appropriate to infer that the plaintiff companies' copying was intentional, as was done in the discussion of distinctiveness.

[I]t has been established that SBM's "Casino de Monte Carlo" mark has secondary meaning and is, therefore, strong and distinctive. It is also clear that the plaintiff companies used the term "Casino de Monte Carlo," or a substantially similar term, in the registration and use of the forty-three domain names and on their various websites. Furthermore, both SBM and the plaintiff companies offer the same service—that is, gambling. Finally, it is evident the plaintiff companies' intended to enhance the marketability of their services by using the term "Casino de Monte Carlo" to invite consumers to believe that plaintiff companies are associated with SBM's casino. Thus, because the plaintiff companies' use of forty-three domain names creates a likelihood of confusion, they have failed to satisfy their burden of showing the contrary. Therefore, the use of the forty-three domain names infringes SBM's "Casino de Monte Carlo" trademark.

V.

SBM's claim for trademark dilution under the Federal Trademark Dilution Act, 15 U.S.C. § 1125(c), does not fare as well as its infringement claim. In this circuit, a threshold requirement for a dilution claim is a showing of actual economic harm to SBM's mark, rather than a mere threatened injury to the mark as some other circuits require. See Ringling Bros.-Barnum & Bailey Combined Shows, Inc. v. Utah Div. of Travel Development, 170 F.3d 449, 453

(4th Cir.1999). [B]ecause this record contains no evidence of actual economic harm attributable to the registration and use of the domain names at issue, SBM has failed to establish a basis for summary judgment on its dilution claims under Sections 1125(c), and, therefore, 1125(d).

VI.

Next, SBM alleges that the plaintiff companies' use of the "Casino de Monte Carlo" mark violates the in personam provisions of the Anticybersquatting Consumer Protection Act, 15 U.S.C. § 1125(d)(1). The ACPA imposes liability in a civil action on a person by the owner of a mark if, without regard to the goods or services of the parties, that person

> (i) has a bad faith intent to profit from that mark and

> (ii) registers, traffics in, or uses a domain name that—

> (I) in the case of a mark that is distinctive at the time of registration of the domain name, is identical or confusingly similar to that mark; [or]

> (II) in the case of a famous mark that is famous at the time of registration of the domain name, is identical or confusingly similar to or dilutive of that mark . . . .

15 U.S.C. § 1125(d)(1)(A).

The ACPA lists nine nonexclusive factors for courts to consider in determining whether a domain name has been registered or used in bad faith. Each factor addresses whether there is some legitimate reason for the registrant or user of a domain name to possess or make use of the disputed domain name.

The first factor is whether the plaintiff companies have any legitimate rights in the "Casino de Monte Carlo" mark. On this record, it is clear that none of the plaintiff companies own, or claim to own, any rights in any trademark or service mark that is identical or similar to the "Casino de Monte Carlo" mark. This factor, therefore, weighs in favor of a conclusion of bad faith.

The second factor is whether the term "Casino de Monte Carlo" constitutes a legal name or commonly-used name for any of the plaintiff companies. A putative cyberpirate can satisfy this factor only if its name or commonly-used nickname is the same as the domain name in dispute. It is clear that "Casino de Monte Carlo," or a similar term, is not the legal name or nickname of any of the plaintiff companies.

The third factor—whether the plaintiff companies engaged in prior, bona fide use of the "Casino de Monte Carlo" mark—also supports a bad faith finding. As the record reflects, SBM has used the "Casino de Monte Carlo" mark for over one-hundred and forty years. And, given that the SBM mark has secondary meaning, no bona fide use by the plaintiff companies of "Casino de Monte Carlo" predates SBM's use of the mark.

The fourth factor is whether the plaintiff companies engaged in any bona fide noncommercial or "fair use" of the "Casino de Monte Carlo" mark. The purpose of this factor is to protect domain name registrants and users engaged in protected activities, such as political criticism or parody. Here, the plaintiff companies' use of the domain names is purely commercial and involves none of these. Thus, this factor also supports a conclusion of bad faith.

The fifth factor is whether the plaintiff companies intended to divert consumers from SBM's online location to a site accessible under the disputed domain names that could harm the goodwill of SBM's mark, either for commercial gain or with the intent to tarnish or disparage the mark by creating a likelihood of confusion as to the source, sponsorship, affiliation, or endorsement of the website. In this regard, the wholesale inclusion of the "Casino de Monte Carlo" mark in the disputed domain names evidences the plaintiff companies' intent to divert Internet users from SBM's services. Indeed, in at least one of plaintiff companies' websites, Internet users were invited to gamble online rather than travel to Monaco. Thus, the fifth factor weighs in favor of bad faith.

The sixth factor is whether the plaintiff companies offered to transfer or sell the domain names for financial gain without having an intent to use them in the bona fide offering of any goods or services. It is clear that, whatever the motives of the plaintiff companies, selling domain names to SBM is not their sole motivation for registering domain names. Thus, this factor is neutral on the issue of bad faith.

The seventh factor is whether the plaintiff companies provided material and misleading false contact information when applying for the registration of the domain name. It is undisputed from the record that aliases were used when submitting contact information for many of the websites. While there is no evidence that these aliases were used with the intent to deceive or mislead, their use creates an atmosphere of deception. Thus, this factor marginally supports a finding of bad faith.

The eighth factor is whether the plaintiff companies registered or acquired multiple domain names that they knew were identical or confusingly similar to the distinctive marks of others. This factor is designed to address the phenomenon of "warehousing," that is, the registration of many domain names consisting of various identical or similar combinations of the marks of others. In this case, the plaintiff companies registered forty-three domain names that contain the term "Casino de Monte Carlo." This factor, then, does raise an inference of bad faith.

The ninth factor concerns the extent to which the mark incorporated in the registrant's domain name registration is or is not distinctive and famous. Given that the "Casino de Monte Carlo" mark is deemed distinctive, this factor supports a finding of bad faith.

In sum, eight of the nine statutory factors support SBM's claim that the forty-three domain names have been registered and used in bad faith. It is also apparent that the plaintiff companies fall outside the ACPA's "safe harbor," which provides that "[b]ad faith intent . . . shall not be found in any case in which the court determines that the person believed and had reasonable grounds to believe that the use of the domain name was a fair use or otherwise lawful." 15 U.S.C. § 1125(d)(1)(B)(ii).

It is clear that the plaintiff companies have not made "fair use" of SBM's "Casino de Monte Carlo" mark. Indeed, the term "Casino de Monte Carlo" is not the name of any of the plaintiff companies. And, it is clear that the plaintiff companies' services do not originate in Monte Carlo. Thus, as the plaintiff companies had no reasonable ground to think that they engaged in fair use, they may not invoke the ACPA's safe harbor provisions.

VII.

SBM also asserts a claim pursuant to 15 U.S.C. § 1126(h). This section provides protection against unfair competition and trademark infringement to the class of individuals identified in 15 U.S.C. § 1126(b), that is, any person whose country of origin is a party to a convention or treaty relating to trademark law or unfair competition to which the United States is also a party, or extends reciprocal rights to nationals of the United States by law, "to the extent necessary to give effect to any provision such as a convention, treaty, or reciprocal law." The only treaty cited by SBM, the Paris Convention for the Protection of Industrial Property, 24 U.S.T. 2140, creates no substantive rights beyond those independently provided in the Lanham Act.

VIII.

SBM also asserts a common law trademark infringement claim against the plaintiff companies, which, in the circumstances, is a claim governed by Virginia law. Because federal law adequately provides the relief SBM seeks, it is unnecessary to reach the more difficult issue on this record of infringement under Virginia law . . . .

X.

As forty-three domain names infringe SBM's mark, the plaintiff companies must be ordered to transfer each of the forty-three infringing domain names to SBM. And, the plaintiff companies must be enjoined from registering domain names containing the mark "Casino de Monte Carlo" and from using that mark on the Internet.

SBM also should receive statutory damages with respect to the forty-three infringing domain names. A review of the cases reveals that courts reserve the high-end of the $1,000 to $100,000 range for the most egregious offenders.

In this case, while SBM has proven that the plaintiff companies acted with bad faith for purposes of ACPA liability, the plaintiff companies' conduct is neither malicious nor fraudulent, as required to obtain attorneys' fees. Moreover, nothing in the record demonstrates a finding of actual economic harm. Thus, it is appropriate to award SBM statutory damages in the amount of $5,000 for the domain names casinomontecarlo.com and montecarlocasino.net, the two websites that provided the "Casino Monte Carlo" software to web surfers to download, and $1,000 for the remaining forty-one infringing domain names, thus totaling, $51,000.00.

[The remainder of the court's opinion is omitted.]

IN RE: MASTERCARD INTERNATIONAL INC. INTERNET GAMBLING LITIGATION
313 F.3d 257 (5th Cir. 2002)

DENNIS, Circuit Judge.

In this lawsuit, Larry Thompson and Lawrence Bradley ("Thompson," "Bradley," or collectively "Plaintiffs") attempt to use the Racketeer Influenced and Corrupt Organizations Act ("RICO"), 18 U.S.C. §§ 1961-1968, to avoid debts they incurred when they used their credit cards to purchase "chips" with which they gambled at on-line casinos and to recover for injuries they allegedly sustained by reason of the RICO violations of MasterCard International, Visa International, and banks that issue MasterCard and Visa credit cards (collectively "Defendants").

Thirty-three virtually identical cases were transferred to the Eastern District of Louisiana through multidistrict litigation. Of these, the two on appeal were selected as test cases and consolidated for pre-trial purposes. See In re MasterCard Int'l Inc., Internet Gambling Litigation and Visa Int'l Serv. Ass'n Internet Gambling Litigation, 132 F.Supp.2d 468, 471 n.1 (E.D.La.2001). The district court granted the Defendants' motions to dismiss pursuant to Rule 12(b)(6) of the Federal Rules of Civil Procedure. We AFFIRM.

I.

Thompson and Bradley allege that the Defendants, along with unnamed Internet casinos, created and operate a "worldwide gambling enterprise" that facilitates illegal gambling on the Internet through the use of credit cards. Internet gambling works as follows. A gambler directs his browser to a casino website. There he is informed that he will receive a gambling "credit" for each dollar he deposits and is instructed to enter his billing information. He can use a credit card to purchase the credits. His credit card is subsequently charged for his purchase of the credits. Once he has purchased the credits, he may place wagers. Losses are debited from, and winnings credited to, his account. Any net winnings a gambler might accrue are not credited to his card but are paid by alternate mechanisms, such as wire transfers.

Under this arrangement, Thompson and Bradley contend, "[t]he availability of credit and the ability to gamble are inseparable." (The Plaintiffs state that 95% of Internet gambling business involves the use of credit cards.) The credit card companies facilitate the enterprise, they say, by authorizing the casinos to accept credit cards, by making credit available to gamblers, by encouraging the use of that credit through the placement of their logos on the websites, and by processing the "gambling debts" resulting from the extension of credit. The banks that issued the gamblers' credit cards participate in the enterprise, they say, by collecting those "gambling debts."

Thompson holds a MasterCard credit card issued by Fleet Bank (Rhode Island) NA. He used his credit card to purchase $1510 in gambling credits at two Internet gambling sites. Bradley holds a Visa credit card issued by Travelers Bank USA Corporation. He used his credit card to purchase $16,445 in gambling credits at seven Internet gambling sites. Thompson and Bradley each used his credits to place wagers. Thompson lost everything, and his subsequent credit card billing statements reflected purchases of $1510 at the casinos. Bradley's winning percentage was higher, but he fared worse in the end. He states his monthly credit card billing statements included $7048 in purchases at the casinos.

Thompson and Bradley filed class action complaints against the Defendants on behalf of themselves and others similarly situated. They state that the Defendants participated in and aided and abetted conduct that violated various federal and state criminal laws applicable to Internet gambling. Through their association with the Internet casinos, the Defendants allegedly "directed, guided, conducted, or participated, directly or indirectly, in the conduct of an enterprise through a pattern of racketeering and/or the unlawful collection of unlawful debt," in violation of 18 U.S.C. § 1962(c). They seek damages under RICO's civil remedies provision, claiming that they were injured by the Defendants' RICO violations. They also seek declaratory judgment that their gambling debts are unenforceable because they are illegal.

Upon motions by the Defendants, the district court dismissed the Plaintiffs' complaints. In a thorough and careful opinion, the court determined that the Plaintiffs not only could not satisfy the necessary prerequisites to a RICO claim but also could not establish their standing to bring such a claim. The Plaintiffs now appeal.

II.

We review a district court's grant of a Rule 12(b)(6) motion de novo, applying the same standard used below. "In so doing, we accept the facts alleged in the complaint as true and construe the allegations in the light most favorable to the plaintiffs." But "conclusory allegations or legal conclusions masquerading as factual conclusions will not suffice to prevent a motion to dismiss."

III.

All RICO violations under 18 U.S.C. § 1962 entail "(1) a person who engages in (2) a pattern of racketeering activity, (3) connected to the acquisition, establishment, conduct, or control of an enterprise." As to the second element, a RICO plaintiff may show that the defendant engaged in the collection of unlawful debt as an alternative to showing the defendant engaged in a pattern or racketeering activity. A RICO claim alleging a violation of § 1962(c), as here, also requires that the defendant "participate[d] in the operation or management of the enterprise itself." Of these required elements, the district court concluded that Thompson and Bradley failed to plead facts showing a pattern of racketeering activity or the collection of unlawful debt; a RICO enterprise; or participation in the operation of management of the enterprise. We agree that the Plaintiffs' allegations do not show a pattern of racketeering activity or the collection of unlawful debt. Because this conclusion, alone, is dispositive, we need not consider whether the Plaintiffs sufficiently alleged the other elements.

"A pattern of racketeering activity requires two or more predicate acts and a demonstration that the racketeering predicates are related and amount to or pose a threat of continued criminal activity." The predicate acts can be either state or federal crimes. Thompson and Bradley allege both types of predicate acts.

On appeal, Thompson alleges that the Defendants' conduct violated a Kansas statute that criminalizes five types of commercial gambling activity. Only two sections of the statute are even remotely relevant here. Neither implicates the Defendants' conduct. Because the Defendants completed their transaction with the Plaintiffs before any gambling occurred, that transaction cannot have involved taking custody of something bet or collecting the proceeds of a gambling device. Both of those activities, which constitute commercial gambling under Kansas law, necessarily "can only take place after some form of gambling [has been] completed." Accordingly, we find that Thompson fails to identify a RICO predicate act under Kansas law.

Bradley alleges on appeal that the Defendants' conduct violated a New Hampshire gambling statute aimed at persons who operate or control places where gambling occurs. Bradley did not, however, allege a violation of the statute in his complaint. In any event, this statute is patently inapplicable to the Defendants under the facts alleged. Indeed, Bradley makes no effort in his briefs to explain its applicability. Accordingly, we find that Bradley, too, fails to identify a RICO predicate act under a state criminal law.

Thompson and Bradley both identify three substantive federal crimes as predicates—violation of the Wire Act, mail fraud, and wire fraud. 18 U.S.C. §§ 1084, 1341, 1343. The district court concluded that the Wire Act concerns gambling on sporting events or contests and that the Plaintiffs had failed to allege that they had engaged in internet sports gambling. We agree with the district court's statutory interpretation, its reading of the relevant case law, its summary of the relevant legislative history, and its conclusion. The Plaintiffs may not rely on the Wire Act as a predicate offense here.

The district court next articulated several reasons why the Plaintiffs may not rely on federal mail or wire fraud as predicates. Of these reasons, two are particularly compelling. First, Thompson and Bradley cannot show that the Defendants made a false or fraudulent misrepresentation. Because the Wire Act does not prohibit non-sports internet gambling, any debts incurred in connection with such gambling are not illegal. Hence, the Defendants could not have fraudulently represented the Plaintiffs' related debt as legal because it was, in fact, legal. We agree that "the allegations that the issuing banks represented the credit charges as legal debts is not a scheme to defraud." Second, Thompson and Bradley fail to allege that they relied upon the Defendants' representations in deciding to gamble. The district court correctly stated that although reliance is not an element of statutory mail or wire fraud, we have required its showing when mail or wire fraud is alleged as a RICO predicate. Accordingly, we conclude that Thompson and Bradley cannot rely on the federal mail or wire fraud statutes to show RICO predicate acts.

Because we find neither the Wire Act nor the mail and wire fraud statutes may serve as predicates here, we need not consider the other federal statutes identified by the Plaintiffs: § 1952 (Travel Act); § 1955 (illegal gambling businesses); and § 1957 (money laundering). As the district court correctly explained, these sections may not serve as predicates here because the Defendants did not violate any applicable federal or state law.

In the alternative, Thompson and Bradley allege that the Defendants engaged in the collection of unlawful debt. Under § 1961, a RICO plaintiff may attempt to show that the debt is unlawful because it was incurred or contracted in an illegal gambling activity or in connection with the illegal business of gambling or because it is unenforceable under usury laws or was incurred in connection with the business of lending at usurious rates. Neither Thompson nor Bradley raises the specter of usury. And, as we have already found, the Defendants' conduct did not involve any violation of a state or federal gambling law. Thus, we agree with the district court's conclusion that the Plaintiffs have not sufficiently alleged "the collection of unlawful debt."

Because Thompson and Bradley cannot prove a necessary element of a civil RICO claim, namely that the Defendants engaged in a pattern of racketeering activity or the collection of unlawful debt, we hold that dismissal is proper under Rule 12(b)(6).

Finally, we reiterate the district court's statement that "RICO, no matter how liberally construed, is not intended to provide a remedy to this class of plaintiff." Thompson and Bradley simply are not victims under the facts of these cases. Rather, as the district court wrote, "they are independent actors who made a knowing and voluntary choice to engage in a course of conduct." In engaging in this conduct, they got exactly what they bargained for— gambling "chips" with which they could place wagers. They cannot use RICO to avoid meeting obligations they voluntarily took on.

IV.

For the foregoing reasons, we AFFIRM the judgment of the district court.

Notes

1. Are you surprised that the court in *Thompson* refused to give effect to the defendant's choice of law clause? Of course, boiler plate "terms and conditions of use" language, pop-up contracts, and disclaimer clauses are common on the internet and few consumers ever bother to read them (if they notice them at all). Perhaps this is what Judge Prado had in mind when he wrote in a footnote, "Furthermore, it is very likely that this clause will be deemed unenforceable since it is not only inconspicuous but also contains an invalid limitation on claims and remedies." *See* 998 F. Supp. at 746 n.3.

Interestingly, the defendant in *Thompson* did not argue that the underlying agreement constituted an illegal (and therefore unenforceable) gambling contract. Had it done so, would the case have come out differently?

2. As the court in *International Bancorp* explains, the Casino de Monte Carlo opened in 1863. Long a favorite of statesmen, royalty, and celebrities, as well as the fictional British secret agent James Bond, the casino and its neighboring counterpart (the Hotel de Paris) are owned and operated by the SBM (the "Society of Sea Bathers") for the benefit of the government.

The casino is located in a striking building designed by the noted French architect Charles Garnier. Because of its glamour, sophistication, and hint of intrigue, it has served as the backdrop of numerous movies, most notably

Alfred Hitchcock's *To Catch a Thief* (1954), which starred Cary Grant and Grace Kelly, and John Huston's *Casino Royale* (1967), which teamed David Nivens with Peter Sellers. The casino also has appeared in various television shows, such as *Get Smart* (Episode 79, "99 Loses Control," a trivia classic because it briefly led viewers to believe that 99's real name was Susan Hilton), and *I Love Lucy* (Episode 152, "Lucy Goes to Monte Carlo," which featured a desperate Lucy trying to *lose* money in the casino).

Due to its riches, people often fantasize about (and speak of) "breaking the bank at Monte Carlo." In fact, a few lucky gamblers have actually done it, including Richard Canfield (the inventor of the game of solitaire), actress Lillie Langtry, and an Englishman named Charles Wells, who, in the summer of 1891, broke the bank repeatedly during a spectacular three-day run in which he turned 10,000 francs into one million, then lost it all when he returned the next year. (It should be noted that no one could break the casino itself. Instead, the saying refers to the fact that at one time, each roulette table was assigned a fixed reserve of money. If a player won this amount, the bank was deemed broken and the table was covered with a symbolic mourning cloth.)

Unlike the casinos in Atlantic City and Las Vegas, which are large, well-lit, noisy, and glitzy, the casino at Monte Carlo is small, dark, and subdued. As a result, visitors accustomed to American-style casinos tend to be disappointed upon their first trip to Monaco. *See further* Geoffrey Wansell, *Yes, Monte Has Had Its Chips*, London Daily Mail, Aug. 10, 2002, at 53.

3. As a practical matter, the major obstacle to any on-line gaming operation is not the legal uncertainty or even the costs of doing business—it is the difficulty of getting customers. Add to this the limited number of ".com" and ".net" names available, and it is easy to understand why lawsuits like *International Bancorp* are proliferating. For other cases of this sort, *see, e.g.*, *Rio Properties, Inc. v. Rio International Interlink*, 284 F.3d 1007 (9th Cir. 2002); *Mirage Resorts, Inc. v. Stirpe*, 152 F. Supp. 2d 1208 (D. Nev. 2000); *Alitalia-Linee Aeree Italiane S.p.A. v. Casinoalitalia.Com*, 128 F. Supp. 2d 340 (E.D. Va. 2001); *Caesars World, Inc. v. Caesars-Palace.Com*, 112 F. Supp. 2d 505 (E.D. Va. 2000). *See also* Joseph M. Kelly, *Casinos and Trademark Litigation*, 2 Gaming L. Rev. 647 (1998), and Jian Xiao, Note, *The First Wave of Cases Under the ACPA*, 17 Berkeley Tech L.J. 159 (2002).

4. Even before the *MasterCard International* litigation, the question of whether credit card companies could go after those who ran up large bills gaming on-line had become quite controversial, due primarily to a case in California.

In 1998, Cynthia H. Haines was sued in the Marin County Superior Court by Providian National Bank for $70,000 in internet gaming losses she had amassed on her credit cards. Haines responded by filing a counterclaim against Providian and twelve other financial institutions, arguing they had violated California state law by giving merchant accounts to on-line betting sites. Concerned they might lose their access to credit card customers, the sites stepped in and paid off Haines's debts. *See* Jon Patterson, Note, *Internet Gambling and the Banking Industry: An Unsure Bet*, 6 N.C. Banking Inst. 665 (2002). For a further discussion of the subject, *see, e.g.*, Michael Anastasio, *The Enforceability of Internet Gambling Debts: Laws, Policies, and Causes of*

Action, 6 Va. J.L. & Tech. 6 (2001); Paul Hugel & Joseph Kelly, *The Internet, Gaming, RICO and Credit Cards: A Legal Analysis*, 4 Gaming L. Rev. 135 (2000); David I. Gold, Note, *Internet Gambling Debt Liability: Trouble Ahead? A Consideration of Providian v. Haines*, 22 T. Jefferson L. Rev. 219 (2000); Maya Hoffman, Comment, *A Game of High Stakes Roulette: Credit Card Companies Cash in on Gamblers Bad Luck*, 32 J. Marshall L. Rev. 1197 (1999).

Problem 40

To increase traffic on her web page, a designer included links to both gaming and non-gaming sites. If one of the non-gaming businesses objects to this "forced association" with gamblers, must the designer redo her page? *See National Football League v. Miller d/b/a NFL Today*, 54 U.S.P.Q.2d 1574 (S.D.N.Y. 2000).

TABLE OF CASES

[References are to page numbers. Principal cases are italicized.]

[References are to page numbers. Principal cases are italicized.]

[References are to page numbers. Principal cases are italicized.]

[References are to page numbers. Principal cases are italicized.]

[References are to page numbers. Principal cases are italicized.]

[References are to page numbers. Principal cases are italicized.]

INDEX

[References are to page numbers.]

[References are to page numbers.]